The Venture of Islam

The Venture of Islam

Conscience and History in a World Civilization

MARSHALL G. S. HODGSON

VOLUME THREE

THE GUNPOWDER EMPIRES AND MODERN TIMES

THE UNIVERSITY OF CHICAGO PRESS
CHICAGO AND LONDON

To John U. Nef
and to the memory of
Gustave E. von Grunebaum
in admiration and gratitude

Some of the material in these volumes has been issued in a different form in *Introduction to Islamic Civilization* (volumes 1, 2, 3. Copyright © 1958, 1959 by The University of Chicago), in *A History of Islamic Civilization* (Copyright © 1958 by Marshall G. S. Hodgson), and in an earlier version of *The Venture of Islam* (volumes 1, 2. Copyright © 1961 by Marshall G. S. Hodgson).

The University of Chicago Press, Chicago 60637
The University of Chicago Press, Ltd., London
 Published 1974
Paperback edition 1977
Printed in the United States of America

ISBN-10: Vol. 1, 0-226-34683-8 (paper);
Vol. 2, 0-226-34684-6 (paper);
Vol. 3, 0-226-34685-4 (paper)
ISBN-13: Vol. 1, 978-0-226-34683-0 (paper);
Vol. 2, 978-0-226-34684-7 (paper);
Vol. 3, 978-0-226-34685-4 (paper)

LCN: 73-87243

16 15 14 13 12 11 10 09 08 07 10 11 12 13 14

∞ The paper used in this publication meets the minimum requirements of the American National Standard for Information Sciences—Permanence of Paper for Printed Library Materials, ANSI Z39.48-1992.

CONTENTS

CHARTS

VOLUME III

MAPS

VOLUME III

BOOK FIVE

Second Flowering: The Empires of Gunpowder Times

The end of everything should direct the means: now that of government being the good of the whole, nothing less should be the aim of the prince.

—*Wm. Penn*

PROLOGUE TO BOOK FIVE

The three centuries after about 1500 CE are most obviously important for us because they form the immediate background of our own age. The Islamdom that entered into Modern times was that which took shape in these centuries. Moreover, that Islamdom was not just one society among several non-Western civilizations. It was the one society that had come the closest to playing the world-dominating role which (as it turned out) the West was actually to play. If one includes the Christian and Hindu and Buddhist peoples then ruled by Muslims or enclaved by them, it is the society that lies back of the bulk of the present Islamo-Asian 'developing' sector of the world. Apart from China and its neighbours, Islam looms more or less large in the background of most of the present low-investment areas of the Eastern Hemisphere; and it is the Islamdom of just these recent centuries which, historically, has been most relevant to their present posture.

But these centuries are important also, in a less accidental way, as increasing our understanding of the potentialities and limitations of the Islamicate civilization as it had developed during the Middle Periods. The successful synthesis of the Earlier Middle Period, in which the Shar'î conscience, together with Ṣûfism, seemed to have worked out a social pattern that met the most essential conditions for an ongoing (and very expansive) social life, had led on by its very success to a triumph of the conservative spirit. Though its inner contradictions had also opened the way to diverse disruptive tendencies of the Later Middle Period, the conservative spirit was not substantially again put in question. That spirit became the setting within which Muslim individuals had to labour, and the Muslim conscience had to find expression.

Meanwhile, the pattern of society and culture that had been formed after the fall of the High Caliphal state came to some crucial impasses by the age of Mongol prestige. As earlier frameworks for cultural creativity were filled in, the conservative spirit itself seemed to be imposing limitations on any possible new creativity; in the arts and even in scholarly inquiry, one could fear that Muslims were becoming trapped in a style cycle if not in ideological stultification by the Shar'î spirit. Even more serious could appear the inability of Muslims to form enduringly legitimate governments. True legitimacy was confined to the Sharî'ah, which had come to be associated with an almost apolitical social order, to which, as well as to the Sharî'ah itself, the political heads and their garrisons were almost an alien intrusion. The problem of establishing legitimate government was presumably compounded by the basic economic problem of wastage of resources especially in the Arid Zone.

To these impasses the new age found answers without essentially breaching the conservative spirit. The answers carried their own dilemmas, but meanwhile, one of the greatest periods of human achievement blossomed out of the midst of the conservative spirit. At the start of the sixteenth century, a general realignment of political forces among all the Muslim peoples afforded an opportunity for extensive political and then cultural renewal. It had major cultural consequences almost everywhere, which largely determined the history of the two or three centuries following. Some of the most important long-run tendencies in Islamicate society were reversed. There was a brilliant renewal of political and cultural life. From the viewpoint of those who looked to absolutist government and the high culture that went with it, Islamdom could seem finally to have come into its own.

But in the light of a more specifically Islamic conscience, the renewal failed. For on a different level of consideration, the conservative spirit posed a deeper problem, not so readily solved. Governments might forge for themselves a civic legitimacy which gave them durability. The culture of the wealthy might find ways to flourish despite apparently coming to the end of the road. But the Islamic ideals did not necessarily find their fulfillment therein. It was, indeed, in part the continuing pressure of the Islamic vision that produced the new dilemmas to which the new answers were to lead. If the Islamic ideals were to be fulfilled, a more basic renewal was required. This was indeed felt passionately, if unhistorically, by the many would-be reformers as well as by those, more pessimistic, who acquiesced in the status quo.

On conscience and tradition

The beginning of the period stands out clearly for us. The realignments of gunpowder times (at the start of the sixteenth century) introduced two interdependent reversals of historic trends: one negative and one positive. In 1500, Islamdom was expanding over the hemisphere as a relatively integral cultural and political order. Despite considerable diversity of language, custom, artistic tradition, and even religious practice, the unity of the Dâr al-Islâm was a more significant fact politically than the existence of any of the states within it, which were of a local and in many cases a transient character. By 1550, a major blow had been dealt to the cosmopolitan comprehensiveness of Islam. Even on the religious level, the Muslims were divided by a newly embittered religious quarrel between Shîʿîs and Jamâʿî-Sunnîs. More important, great regional empires were going far to forge their separate cultural worlds, partitioning among themselves all of what may be called by this time the central zone of Islamdom—the whole zone from the Balkans to Bengal. Outside these regional empires, in the Southern Seas and in the Volga basin, Muslims found themselves more threatened by infidels than at any time since the Mongol conquests, and looking to the new empires of the more central zone for support.

But on the positive side, the weakening of the apolitical cosmopolitan unity was compensated by a partial solution to the problem of governmental legitimacy. The empires which, by 1550, were dividing up the greater part of Islamdom, heirs to the ideals of the military patronage state, were able to assert a considerable measure of political legitimacy within their own spheres. If it was under the primacy of the market-place culture that the international Islamicate cosmopolitanism had developed, it was largely under courtly auspices that the several regions asserted their relative cultural autonomy. The very fact that these empires were taking a major part in forming the social and cultural life of Islamdom within their domains allowed new forms of integration to be attempted within each of them. At least within their boundaries, a certain rapprochement took place between government, the representatives of the Sharîʿah law, and popular Muslim institutions. Whatever reduction in economic resources may have supervened in the mid-Arid Zone in the preceding centuries was compensated, on the level of Islamicate high-cultural life generally, by the spread of the society, of the area in which Muslim activity could be initiated and patrons found.

It was presumably on the basis of these new possibilities that spiritual renewal should have taken place. But the new order did not really answer to the old Sharʿî vision nor even to a Ṣûfî vision. Along with the establishment of the new agrarian empires, social mobility seems to have decreased, and if a certain peace and security prevailed, these hardly reflected what those who longed for the promised Mahdî would regard as justice for ordinary mankind. What is required for the vision of persons of conscience to be effective where the conservative spirit has triumphed?—that is, where the vision is maintained within a framework of mutual expectations among which truly fresh departures are not allowed for, and yet confronts new historical problems, never presupposed by its inherited forms? Perhaps a tradition of conscience that is inwardly trapped, in that it has limited the range of its vision within finite formulae, must necessarily become trapped externally also in the shifting demands of a life and history to which it has itself imparted movement.

At this point I want to reaffirm a guiding principle of my enquiries. Even under the auspices of a conservative spirit, the response of the individual sensibility, particularly as it is focused in a point of conscience, remains one of the ultimate roots of history. We may characterize three sorts of individual acts. First, some are historically accidental—the product of personal talent or self-interest or fancy—and cancel each other out (thus if one man gains by accepting a bribe, another will gain by reporting him and another by purging corruption from among all his employees). Then some are historically cumulative—because they answer to group interests, economic, aesthetic, or even spiritual, they reinforce each other (thus in some settings, the contrast between official demands and actual administrative possibilities is such that bribery becomes the only alternative to impasse, and all will connive in it). But finally, some must be called historically creative: at the interstices in the play of group interests, where pressures for two courses seem equally balanced, a personal imagination may be able to introduce new constructive alternatives which will in the end alter even the cast of group interests (thus when an administrator is baffled, he may turn to that idealistic assistant who is too honest personally to become chief, but whose imagination may suggest a way of so involving the employees in their work that the pattern of work is transformed and the need for bribes disappears).

Accidental acts may be decisive in the short-run, and indeed fill the works of some historians, but can generally be disregarded over the long run of history: sooner or later, an accident in one direction will be balanced by one in another direction. Cumulative acts (those where such cancelling out does not occur) are to be accounted for by tracing each set of interests back to its ecological context (including here the effects of past social events and the current configuration of expectations); we must indeed study the play of interests down to the last cynical observation. What I have called creative acts, those that take effect less by being reinforced by other acts in the same interest than by opening up new possibilities to which other persons respond positively, are to be set off for their long-term moral significance. They supervene on a very individual basis and are, in a sense, accidents; they must needs meet at least latent group interests or they will have no effect; yet they do not merely fit into an existent pattern of interests as it stands: they lead back not to the ecology as such but to some thrust of autonomous integration within an individual—some principle of inherent growth. Such acts are far harder to pin down, and some historians hesitate to take them seriously at all. Even in the life of Muḥammad, once indifferent chance and whim have been given their due, the temptation is to reduce the outcome to the play of cumulative historical interests, leaving no room for the impress of fresh creativity ('God', perhaps?) acting through his conscience.

Especially in the periods we are now to study, properly creative acts become hard to detect. They are disguised, and even stifled, first by the pressure of the conservative spirit, then by the overwhelming external pressures that seemed to ruin the whole civilization, and finally in more modern times by the rush of events which seem to enlist everyone in predictable stands on one side or the other. Yet even here, I am convinced, the individual creative conscience has been at work.

The most evident promise in our period for a new beginning in Islamic religion (and in the social destinies of Islamdom) was widely felt to rest in the Shî'ah. The vigorous Shî'î movements were full of millennial hopes, at the time of the great realignments as much as ever. The core of the lands of old Islam between Nile and Oxus turned to the movement enthusiastically; but the Shî'î empire that grew out of this ferment became increasingly Sharî'ah-minded in temper and, despite its spectacular splendour, left its peoples almost as ridden with poverty and injustice as it had found them.

To the west in the European-based Ottoman empire and to the east in the

Indic Timurî empire, Islam was on relatively new ground, ruling a population which in majority was not Muslim. Here Shî'ism came to play a minor part and the hope of the Islamic conscience flowed chiefly in other channels. More truly than the Shî'ah, Falsafah had its great chance: in bureaucratic agrarian empires it could see its hopes for ordered stability and prosperity partially fulfilled, and in some places in this period a Muslim Falsafah, allied with Ṣûfism, seemed about to reduce the specifically Islamic vision to playing a role in a larger Philosophic outlook and in this form make the vision successful. The greatest hopes of this kind were centred on Akbar of India and his successors, though they played some role in the other two empires; but Falsafized Islam proved unable to carry the élan of a more specifically Islamic impetus, and was rejected by most Muslims. In the Ottoman empire it was Sunnî Sharî'ah-mindedness (again not untouched by Falsafah) that had its chance: it seemed capable of achieving the political position it had failed to achieve in the time of al-Ma'mûn; and it very nearly did so—but at the expense of the central-military strength which such a position presupposed. In different ways, the limiting effects of religious communalism took their toll. In each of the two empires in newer terrain the Muslim system of rule failed to integrate crucial elements of the non-Muslim population into itself, partly just because of the form taken by the hopes of men of conscience; and drew to a moral stalemate as definite as that in the Safavî empire itself.

Strong political institutions were indeed erected in all three areas, endowed with coherence and continuity unprecedented since classical 'Abbâsî times, and for a time a considerable level of general prosperity was achieved; and collectively, Islamdom was at the peak of its political power. But finally, when the institutions of the great empires had run their course, they underwent the decline in central power every agrarianate bureaucratic state seems to have been subject to as it accumulated commitments; and they failed even to match the standard of effective durability perennially set by the ancient Sâsânian empire. By the eighteenth century, each of the empires was disintegrating, prosperity was again slipping away, and even aesthetic and intellectual expression was in noticeable decline everywhere. This was partly due to outside forces; but the society showed little resistance to them. At the end of the eighteenth century, these outside historical forces intervened to cut short this particular period; but it could already be suspected that though the period was one of great brilliance, the inherited dilemmas had not been fully solved.[1]

The end of the period was as sharply marked as its beginning, and it marked at the same time the end of any further opportunity for spiritual renewal within the agrarianate conditions which had prevailed since the time

[1] My 'The Unity of Later Islamic History', *Journal of World History*, 5 (1960), 879–914, sketches some of the points developed in this book. Unfortunately, it underestimates the achievements among Muslims of the later periods and overestimates the degree to which one can read the great technical transformations of the period as resulting from a comparative 'vigor' in the Occident.

Developments in the Oikoumene, 1500–1700

	Europe	Central Oikoumene	Far East
1492	Christians conquer Granada; Muslims and Jews emigrate to N. Africa and lands of Ottoman empire; Spanish Inquisition Columbus sails Atlantic		
1497	Vasco da Gama rounds Cape of Good Hope, enters Indian Ocean		
1502		Shâh Ismâ'îl founds Ṣafavî empire, introduces Shî'ism as state religion	
1509	Henry VIII of England (to 1547)		
1513			Portuguese traders reach South China
1517	Beginnings of Reformation Consolidation of political sovereignty by W. European monarchs Roman Inquisition	Ottomans conquer Egypt and Syria from Mamlûks	
1519–22	Magellan circumnavigates the globe		
1520		Accession of Sultan Suleymân (to 1566), expansion and definitive institutional development of Ottoman empire	
1522		Ottomans take Rhodes	
1526		Bâbur establishes Mughal empire after Battle of Pânîpat	
1529		Ottomans besiege Vienna	

1542	Portuguese establish first European commercial-colonial empire		Francis Xavier, Jesuit missionary, preaches in India, Japan, and Indonesia
1543		Ottomans subjugate Hungary	
1556		Accession of Akbar (till 1605), zenith of Mughal empire Ottoman-Portuguese naval warfare in Indian Ocean	
1566	Philip II of Spain (to 1598)		
1570		Ottomans take Cyprus	
1580s	Portuguese weakened in India; English seize Spanish and Portuguese ships		
1587		Accession of Shâh ʻAbbâs (to 1629), zenith of Ṣafavî empire, magnificent court at Iṣfahân	
1589	Henry IV of France (to 1610)		
1590s	Dutch begin to arrive in Indian trade		
1598			Unification of Japanese archipelago under the Shogun Hideyoshi, expulsion of Christian missionaries
1601	Dutch begin to seize Portuguese holdings		Jesuit missionaries in China
1603			Tokugawa shogunate founded (to 1867), Japan closed to foreign influences, seafaring forbidden, local Christian population persecuted

Developments in the Oikoumene, 1500–1700—*contd.*

	Europe	Central Oikoumene	Far East
1640	Friedrich Wilhelm of Prussia (to 1688)		
1644			Manchu conquest of China and overthrow of Ming dynasty
1656		Köprülü viziers temporarily revitalize declining Ottoman empire	
1659		Awrangzêb (to 1707), last strong Mughal emperor	
1661	Louis XIV of France (to 1715)		
1669		Ottomans take Crete from Venice	
1681		Ottomans cede Kiev to Russia	
1683		Ottomans fail in second siege of Vienna	
1688	Glorious Revolution, assertion of English parliamentarianism		
1689			Treaty of Nerchinsk, Russian-Chinese trade stabilized
1699		Treaty of Carlowicz, first major Ottoman diplomatic reversal, Hungary ceded to Austria	

of the Sumerians. Gradually in the latter part of the period new world forces had come to make themselves seriously felt. At the end of the eighteenth century, with overwhelming suddenness, the Christian European peoples made themselves the key political, economic, and cultural force in almost all parts of Islamdom. But this was not simply the ascendancy of one group of peoples over against another, of one culture over against another, such as had recurred so often during the expansion of Islamdom. Now the world was confronting—in the new sorts of investment that were introducing the Modern Technical Age—a new level of historical life, which had changed the fundamental conditions of action for all cultures and all religions, including those of the Occident itself. Any further effort at renewal would have to be on a radically different basis.

Rivalry with the Occident

In no other period does the history of Islamdom become so nearly identified with the history of the world as in this period of the great empires. Up to this point, it could be regarded as a microcosm of world history: all the major events affecting world history at large affected it, all the problems one must face in understanding world history period by period one must face in understanding the history of Islamdom in particular. And one could add that Irano-Semitic history was more than typical: it held a singularly central position. By this period, however, Islamdom had expanded so far that, though probably less than a fifth of the world's population were Muslims, yet the Muslims were so widely and strategically placed that the society associated with them did embrace in some degree the greater part of citied mankind; 'microcosm' is no longer just the word for Islamdom. World history and Islamicate history had become very hard to disentwine. (We will find Islamdom, therefore, a very revealing point of departure for understanding the advent and meaning of the Modern Technical Age in a global perspective.)

The identification of Islamicate with world history can be illustrated most graphically in the tendency of Islamdom to break up into distinct regions—India, the Nile-to-Oxus region, (eastern) Europe, and, further afield, the central Eurasian steppe, the sub-Saharan Sudan, the Far Southeast—each of which tended to develop an Islamicate life of its own, consistent with its own historic position in the Afro-Eurasian Oikoumene and with its own local traditions. It is almost as if the old articulations of the Oikoumene had reasserted themselves, only now all, or most of them, under the umbrella of Islam. This is one way of looking at the relative self-sufficiency of the new regional empires.

But, as we have noted, there were two major regions of the Oikoumene that had not come in under the umbrella; one of them, the Occident, was coming to play a specially important role in the world during this period—and to a large degree 'the world' meant Islamdom. The reaction of Islamdom to the

Islam beyond the Heartlands, 1500–1698

1503–1722	Three strong empires, Osmanlî (Ottoman), Ṣafavî, and Timurî of India (Mughal), dominate the central lands of Islam; religion, culture, and economics are moulded within these political structures; beyond them, peripheral areas assume their own distinctive Islamic life (see detailed lists for the three major empires)
1498–1538	Establishment of Portuguese domination of oceanic trade in the Indian Ocean (Vasco da Gama reaches India, 1498; Portuguese defeat Egyptian Mamlûks at Diu in Gujarât 1509; Portuguese defeat Ottoman-Gujarâtî forces, 1538)
1500–1510	Muḥammad Shaybânî, khân of a Siberian Mongol state, eliminates remains of Timurî power and establishes Özbeg rule in Transoxania, noted for Sunnî Orthodoxy and cultural quiescence
1511–1610	Five Sa'dî sharîfs establish 'Alid rule in Morocco; first defending the land against Portuguese attack, establishing a sovereign position at the expense of the Marînids (1544), and finally expanding Moroccan power over W. Africa
1500–1591	Songhai empire replaces the Mali as dominant power in Niger Sudan
1517–1801	Hausa confederation predominant east of the Niger
1507–22	Sultan 'Alî Mughayat Shâh establishes power of Acheh kingdom in N. Sumatra
1518	Fall of Hindu Majapahit kingdom in E. Java; replaced by Muslim power
1484–1526	Replacement of Bahmanids in the Deccan of India with five rival dynasties, of which Bîjâpûr becomes Shî'î
1552–56	Khânates of Kazan and Astrakhan on the Volga conquered by Russians
1565	The Muslim Deccan dynasties unite in overthrowing the Hindu kingdom of Vijayanagar in the south, last stronghold of old Hindu culture
1591–1780	Timbuctu, conquered by Morocco (till 1612) loses its prosperity and intellectual pre-eminence under Arab pashas
1609–87	'Adil-Shâhî dynasty of Bîjâpûr and Quṭb-Shâhî dynasty of Golkondâ, after fall of other Deccan kingdoms, divide S. India between them, till conquest by Mughals; rise of Urdu literature
1698	Resurgent power of (Khârijî) sultanate of Musat drives Portuguese from Zanzibar, major commercial centre of E. Africa

new role of Occidentals in the citied parts of the world was not simply one example of how the citied world reacted: it *was* the larger part of that reaction. To the Occidentals out to make their way in the world, the great threat at home was 'the Turk' and the great rivals abroad were always 'the Moors', from Morocco to the Philippines and the ports of China. Correspondingly, Muslims, who had always tended to despise Occidentals as forming one of the lesser blocs in the civilized world, and most of whom had very little awareness of the Occident at all, began in all regions (and not merely, as before, in the Mediterranean) to see Christian Europeans and especially west Europeans as a group to be reckoned with—sometimes as enemies, sometimes as producers of admirable articles of trade or even art, but in any case as one of the major human blocs.

Even in the sixteenth century, when on the whole the Europeans were not yet a major threat to the expanding power of Islamdom, the great florescence of the Occident in Renaissance times had had far-reaching effects. First, it had sent the Occidentals into all the oceans. Though in most of the new land areas they had reached they had scarcely penetrated behind the coasts (in this period, the Occidentals were almost but not quite unmatchable at sea, but had few special advantages on land), they had nevertheless found radically new sea-routes which allowed them to escape the long-standing limitations of the Oikoumenic geographical configuration which had conferred on the Nile-to-Oxus region its central role. These routes could bring them into the Southern Seas without touching either the Red Sea or the Euphrates, and could even bring them to the eastern end of the Southern Seas by sailing west and crossing or skirting a whole new landmass. Perhaps more important, from the new lands they had brought, not only to Europe but to the rest of the Afro-Eurasian Oikoumene, a series of new plants and even animals, some of which were to change the economy of many lands; more important economically than the popular tobacco was maize, a remarkably efficient fodder plant. And they had brought vast amounts of silver and gold to upset the currency structure of the whole Oikoumene. In this last point, they did not, perhaps, inject more precious metals into Oikoumenic commerce than had the Chinese a few centuries earlier, but (perhaps because the Occident was already more closely tied economically to most of the other Oikoumenic lands than ever China had been) they injected them more suddenly and directly, sometimes with ruinous consequences for such classes as had fixed incomes.

It is not to be ruled out that the new activity of the Occident may have contributed to the changes in the balance of social power within Islamdom that can be seen at the time of the rise of the new regional empires in the sixteenth century, with their more agrarian and aristocratic colouring. Slight shifts in a delicate social balance can make possible changes of large import. Yet an internal dialectic can be more readily traced or posited, which was doubtless at most supplemented by external pressures. Even in the subsequent changes visible from the end of the seventeenth century, in which the role of a transformed Occident was to be far more evident, an internal evolution with roots in Islamicate history will be found to account for much of what happened.

Muslims, indeed, were little conscious of all the channels whereby the new Occidental activity was affecting them in the sixteenth century. They took the rivalry less seriously than did the Occidentals. But at least some of them were aware that whereas before in the Chinese court no astronomers could rival the Muslim astronomers, now the upstart Occidentals could do as well and perhaps better; and some were aware that whereas before, if an artist wished exotic inspiration, it was to things Chinese he should turn, now a new Occidental style of painting charmed and troubled the tastes of the most perceptive Muslim patrons.

Thereafter, from the end of the sixteenth century on, the Occidentals gradually grew from prominent rivals into an overwhelming world force, which ended by sapping the strength of all Islamdom. We shall study what was happening to the West later. Meanwhile, we must note that if the great empires that arose in this period proved unable in the end to solve some of the basic problems of agrarianate-level society as they were posed, and failed to satisfy the Islamic conscience, it was not merely an internal impasse that they confronted: increasingly the world, and that means especially Islamdom, was confronting a radically new situation, embodied in its relation to the new West but not reducible simply to a confrontation of peoples; a situation in which no agrarianate society was any longer left to itself to solve its agrarianate dilemmas.

Two types of florescence

However inadequate was the Islamicate renewal from the aspiring viewpoint of a keen Islamic conscience or from the retrospective viewpoint of a world historian, in its own setting the age of the sixteenth and seventeenth centuries was one of the greatest in Islamdom's history. The artistic, philosophic, and social power and creativeness of the age can be symbolized in the spaciousness, purity—and overwhelming magnificence of the Tâj Maḥall at Agra. In some sense there was a great florescence.

But it was not a period when all traditions are put into question, when old traditions are fused and recast into a series of new ones, in which everything is to be discovered and built anew. Indeed, very few Islamicate traditions were drastically modified. The great figures and events invoked as authoritative by the Muslims of the sixteenth and seventeenth centuries were the same as had been invoked for generations before; in the most central aspects of the civilization they went back to the beginning of Islamic times. It was a florescence in which the conservative spirit as it had been expressed in the Later Middle Period was not explicitly called into question; it was a florescence within established lines of tradition, rather perfecting than launching them. Such a florescence shows a very different face from the sort of florescence—for instance, that of High Caliphal times or, in large measure, that of the Occidental Renaissance—where new channels of creative activity are being opened up, where the accent is rather consciously on innovation, even drastic innovation, and where, for a time, the usual conservative spirit of agrarianate-level society is damped down.

If it was a florescence, it was one oddly hard for us to appreciate. The splendour of the age is unmistakable—it would have been yet more obvious had it not been beclouded by the decline of the eighteenth century and the subsequent débâcle, which caused Muslims and Westerners alike to look with suspicion on all that seemed to lead up to that. Yet when the age is approached in detail it is more or less inaccessible, and not solely because of the subsequent clouding. The poetry of the time long was ignored by most Moderns, and the philosophy hardly less so; even the painting, while inevitably admired, has not seemed so clear as the painting of the Timurî time. The social structure, in all three empires a very complex balance of many elements, is only beginning to be appreciated. Even the military power of the Muslim states, while necessarily wondered at, has sometimes seemed some sort of miracle, perhaps to be explained by the accident of the birth of a series of geniuses, if not by some atavistic ruthlessness of ex-nomadic savages.

Perhaps we may say that this florescence was not one of *origination*, such as we have seen before, but rather one of *culmination* in a culture long already mature. Far from launching into 'new' paths, the poetry (for instance) made use of its long heritage to give it resources of complexity and subtlety which made it a delicately precise instrument in a way that a new tradition of poetry, dependent only upon its current efforts, could never be. But this makes the poetry practically unintelligible to the outsider. So, I suppose, it must have been with the whole culture of the time. Once one has learned to understand some basic premises and essential points of method, Ṭabarî or even al-Fârâbî is fairly readily accessible to any reader. Mullâ Ṣadrâ, a philosopher of this period, seems to require in his reader a mind stocked with all that has gone before, or his points will not emerge. He need not be the less important for that.

I

The Ṣafavî Empire: Triumph of the Shîʿah, 1503–1722

The military patronage states of the Later Middle Period, growing out of Mongol notions of greatness, had begun to take advantage of the political openings that appeared in a politically amorphous network of personal contracts and patron relations presided over by the Sharîʿah and by the amîrs. In contrast to China, where the Mongol notions of empire had little future, in Islamdom they found excellent soil. Such notions could fully mature and create great stable bureaucratic empires only after gunpowder weapons and their specialized technology attained a primary place in military life. This happened between about 1450 and 1550. The new empires that resulted all had some degree of Mongol tradition in their background—even the Ottomans had first appeared under Mongol overlordship—and their institutions bear considerable family resemblance.

But they were not merely the culmination of the military patronage state. To some degree, I think, they marked a resurgence in Islamdom of ideals associated with agrarian predominance: of the ideal of the great absolute monarch, in particular, and of stable class stratification, as against the universal egalitarianism embodied in the Sharîʿah and given paradoxical expression in the international political order of the amîrs. The contrast shows but a slight shift of emphasis, for even the amîrs' states had been essentially agrarian, yet it is perceptible. In the Ottoman empire in Europe and the Indo-Timurî empire in India, a strongly agrarian outlook was only natural; but even the central empire, the Ṣafavî empire, though the Sawâd no longer played a significant economic role (the Iraq was more important for its shrines from the past than for its current agricultural production), seems to have been marked by an unusually great investment in irrigation works on the Iranian plateau itself. However, this is largely conjectural. We know next to nothing of Ṣafavî economic and social history.

The change was introduced almost abruptly by a series of events which were focused, naturally enough, in the central lands of old Islam. The most spectacular event was the rise of the Ṣafavî empire itself and its imposition of Shîʿism in the centre of Islamdom. This rise, then, coincided with a series of other events, some of which were in part repercussions of the Ṣafavî movement: the expansion of the Ottoman state into a major empire, the erection of the Timurî empire in northern India, the Özbeg conquests in the

Oxus basin, and, further afield, the Russian conquests in the Volga regions, the Portuguese penetration into the Southern Seas, and the renewal of 'Alid government in Morocco and thence across the Sahara. Cumulatively these changes amounted to a far-reaching realignment of political forces.

The realignments of gunpowder times: the Portuguese

In the Later Middle Period gunpowder was used for a variety of minor purposes—including military ones—in many parts of the Eastern Hemisphere. From generation to generation its military usefulness was improved almost everywhere. From being of value chiefly for the noise it could make as a means of causing fright—perhaps its original purpose—it came to be used for the propulsion of missiles; in the fifteenth century it was gradually replacing, at least in the Muslim lands and in Christian Europe, the older siege machinery for the purpose of breaking down walls. About 1450, simultaneously among the Ottoman Turks in eastern Europe and among the western Europeans, artillery was shown to be a decisive weapon in siege warfare, and the value of the isolated fortress declined rapidly. Artillery soon became a major factor in field battles as well; meanwhile, hand guns, which an individual foot soldier could carry, were developing in western Europe to such a point that at the end of the century, there, the infantrymen armed with hand guns had become a decisive military arm. The hand-gun troops seem to have been a specially European development; they early had a central role in both Muslim and Christian Europe; they spread more gradually in other parts of Islamdom. But the command of siege and field artillery quickly came to be of fateful significance politically throughout the Dâr al-Islâm.

The military use of gunpowder, in its various forms—as is often the case with a basically new weapon—called for a variety of reorganizations in the pre-Modern armies; therewith it put in question any elements of the social pattern that had depended upon the military organization. This did not necessarily mean that old military orders must always give place to new ones; it did mean that there was a crucial struggle in many cases between old corps wishing to retain their special privileged character and new corps that might be in a position to upset this; and adaptability in the use of new weapons would often be decisive in such struggles.[1] Moreover, the implications of the changes in weapons were not restricted entirely to military organization. The relative expensiveness of artillery and the relative unten-

[1] An excellently cautious discussion of the problems that arose in the Mamlûk state of Egypt and Syria is presented by David Ayalon in *Gunpowder and Firearms in the Mamluk Kingdom: A Challenge to a Mediaeval Society* (London, 1956). Since Mamlûk rule was carried on to a large degree by an actual military oligarchy, the reigning sultans, who perceived the importance of firearms, had more difficulty in introducing them effectively than did other rulers, being forced to relegate them to secondary corps without adequate support.

ability of stone fortresses gave an increased advantage over local military garrisons to a well-organized central power which could afford artillery—not always a decisive advantage, to be sure. Perhaps at least as important was that gunpowder weapons seemed to imply, evidently from the start, a continuous development of new techniques; already in thirteenth-century China, military invention followed invention at an unprecedented pace. Those had an advantage who could afford to be abreast of the latest improvements. (This was a foretaste of characteristics of technical specialization which were later to mark off Modernity.) Such advantages for rulers with resources brought with them extensive possibilities for general political change.

Gunpowder was doubtless not the one great decisive factor in the political and social—and ultimately cultural—realignments that occurred in the three generations following 1450; but it played a distinctive role, and perhaps was the most easily identifiable single occasion for them. Probably almost as important was the secular change of balance within Islamdom as a whole between the lands of old Islam in the mid-Arid Zone and the newer lands, often more stably agrarian, which now loomed large in the total Islamicate society—and even the secular deterioration of agricultural prosperity between Nile and Oxus. Nor can we ignore such more specific events as the Portuguese interference in Indian Ocean trade and the advance of Muscovite Russian power. But techniques of gunpowder played a role in both Portuguese and Muscovite advances. The increasingly zealous growth of ṭarîqah Shîʿism among the Turkic tribes, which also played a role, was itself perhaps a reaction to the political plight of Islamdom in the Later Middle Period. We are not yet in a position to understand the full background of the realignments which took place in the Islamicate society after the advent of gunpowder as a principal weapon.

Some of their consequences are easier to trace. We have already noted some consequences of the new situation in the Maghrib and the west Sûdânic lands: consequences that can be traced largely to the new role of gunpowder in building empires. The Portuguese and Castillian advance in Spain and across onto the Maghrib coast had transformed the Maghrib's politics—henceforth it was no longer Berber-sprung dynasties from the interior that were to rule there, but representatives of the cities and their armed forces. The greater part of the Maghrib, following the interests of its ports, turned to the Ottomans. But in the far west of the Maghrib, in Morocco, where the agricultural hinterland went deeper and the chief cities were well inland, the Portuguese thrust evoked a more independent reaction. The Maghribî sharîfs (descendants of the Prophet—and more particularly of that Idrîsid family under which Morocco had first maintained its independence against the upstart ʿAbbâsids) had been coming to represent the piety of Islam as disseminated from the cities, in emulation or rivalry with the ṭarîqah piety that was also spreading among the tribes. Under the leadership of a family of sharîfs, the Moroccans rallied their forces to repel the Portuguese from their coasts—and incidentally to rebuff Ottoman attempts at rounding out their own hegemony. The new Sharîfian empire in turn, well armed and victorious at home, had found an outlet for its energies in an unprecedented expedition (1591) across the Sahara into the Sûdânic lands, where gunpowder weapons were a disastrous novelty. We have noted that this expedition led to the ruin of Timbuctu. However, the economic base of the Sharîfian empire, isolated between the Atlantic and the Sahara, was not great enough to sustain its forces and to rebuild its conquests. The Atlantic trade to Guinea, monopolized by the Portuguese, more and more rivalled that of the Sahara to the same southern regions. The Sudan was left to its own devices, saddled with a persistingly disruptive new military class; and Morocco itself relapsed into a jealous independence.

A more far-reaching consequence of the new day, and particularly of the Portuguese thrust, was the realignment of forces in the Southern Seas. The advent there of the Portuguese was spectacular, though in itself it had only limited long-term effects. During the fifteenth century, the Portuguese had not only opened trade with the Guinea coast, but pushed down considerably south of the Congo along the western African coast. In 1498 Vasco da Gama was able to sail round the south coast of Africa, so linking the Portuguese trade routes on the west coast with the Arab trade routes long established on the east coast of Africa; and so launching the Portuguese into the trade of all the Southern Seas, which was already linked with that of the east African coast. From 1501, the Portuguese Christians established the pious policy of ruining Muslim trade in the Indian Ocean. Or, to speak more realistically, they tried to cut off that part of it that led up the Red Sea to Egypt, the Mediterranean, and Venice, which Lisbon now saw as its great commercial rival; and to exact protection money from any other shipping that could be sufficiently terrorized. In the surprise of their first advent, they had some success. Seafaring in the Atlantic had led the Portuguese to develop more powerful naval equipment than prevailed in the Indian Ocean, where long runs were less necessary (only Chinese vessels were as large and strong, or even larger). This technical advantage, together with a vigorous home government, more than counterbalanced the effect of their distance from their bases in West Africa.

Conditions of the Later Middle Period had not favoured concerted Muslim political action. Trade in the Southern Seas was largely in the hands of numerous more or less independent Muslim trader cities, over which the inland powers had relatively little control in many cases. In an area like Malaysia, for instance, the chief figure in the town, the 'sultan', was likely to be essentially a merchant, who might even monopolize the trade of a given port and rule that port, and sometimes was also able to control other ports at a distance.

Into this picture the Portuguese traders fitted with ease. And without concerted Muslim action, they were in a position to put the Muslims on the

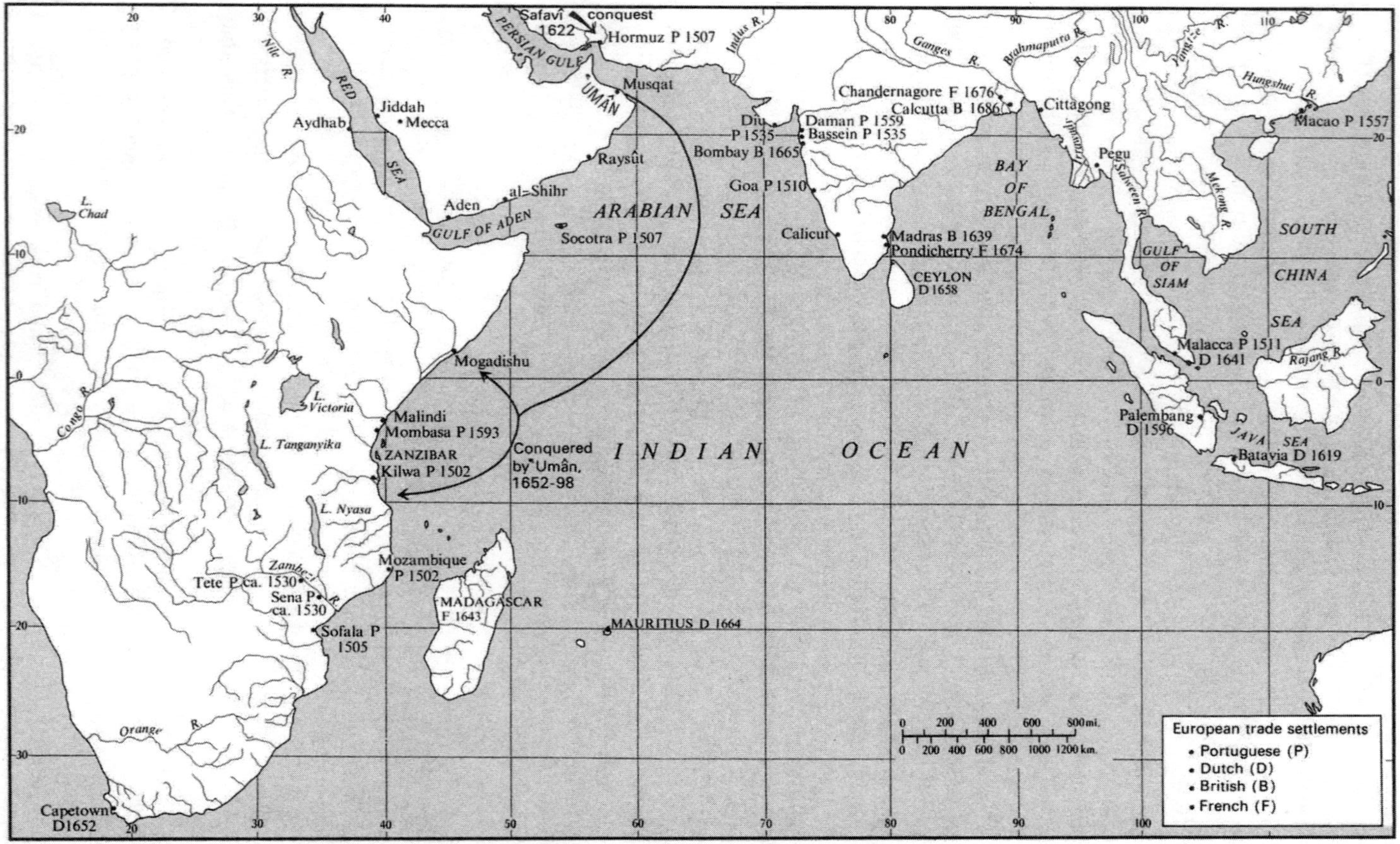

The Indian Ocean in the sixteenth and early seventeenth centuries

defensive. The relatively low cost of an all-water route without middlemen, together with the exclusive control over it the Portuguese exercised for three generations, enabled them to tap concertedly most of the growing Occidental market. Hence what was in itself a small kingdom could become the commercial outlet of what amounted to a large empire; Lisbon had commercial resources far greater than any one Muslim port. The common discipline which a corporative spirit allowed the Portuguese kingdom to exercise over its merchants—which ensured that the Portuguese continued to act as a single power even remote from home—was reinforced by a Christian fanaticism in men used to anti-Muslim crusading in the western Mediterranean, so that they felt a special solidarity in hostility to all the various nationalities of Muslim traders. Then they had incidental advantages. At first, in some cases, not only their naval equipment but also their artillery seems to have been better than that then in use in the Southern Seas, where gunpowder weapons were only then being introduced from the lands farther north. And their west African bases were as inaccessible to the stronger Muslim land empires as the inland strongholds of those empires were to the sea-based Portuguese. In sum, the Portuguese played the role of a gunpowder empire in the Southern Seas, being able to turn the technical advantages of centralization in the new military age to as good use at sea as did the other empires on land.

In consequence, the Portuguese proved stronger at sea than any one Muslim power that faced them, especially westward from Ceylon, while the several interested Muslim powers were never able to maintain an adequately lasting coalition against the intruders. In 1508, the Mamlûks and Gujarâtîs had together defeated the Portuguese; but in 1509, at Diu in Gujarât, the allied fleet was destroyed. By then the Mamlûk régime was in serious trouble at home, and this defeat was never retrieved. By 1511 the Portuguese were established with their own fortified trading posts at Hormuz (at the mouth of the Persian Gulf), Goa (on the west coast of the Deccan), and Malacca, at the straits leading into the South China Sea. In 1538 an Ottoman-Gujarâtî coalition broke up too soon to prevent another Portuguese victory, which confirmed the Portuguese position.

The Portuguese held, for the most part, only a certain number of key ports here and there; most ports continued in Muslim (or Hindu) hands, either independent or subject to inland rulers. Muslims, Hindus, and Chinese continued to maintain an important trade. But the Portuguese were powerful enough to prevent, for some time, any long-distance trade that seriously rivalled their own exports to Europe, and in particular to cut down drastically the trade up the Red Sea to Egypt. (Some of this seems to have been diverted to the Persian Gulf and overland routes; but even the Red Sea trade was restored within the century.) A severe, if chiefly temporary, blow was dealt to Muslim power in the Southern Seas and to some areas of Muslim mercantile prosperity, especially that of Egypt and certain Arabian cities.

The decisive effect on Islamicate life of the Portuguese arrival in the Southern Seas has been much exaggerated in European historical writing, as I see it, for three reasons. First, the oceanic expansions of the time had decisive impact on the western Europe of the time; and Europeans have tended to read the rest of world history as a function of European history. (Moreover, Western sources naturally tell us more about Western than about other activity.) Second, the seventeenth-century advent of Dutch, English, and French did come to have, after a time, truly momentous import; and, since the Portuguese were, in some sense, the forerunners of these later movements, the significance that Western traders had in the later sixteenth and seventeenth centuries is projected back to the beginning of the overall development. (In a purely Western perspective, it is hard to see the difference in world-historical role between a gunpowder empire such as the Portuguese, based on a development almost universal in citied life at the time, and the later Western sea empires based on radically new departures no longer shared with the rest of the world.) Finally, the effects on Muslim lands seem to have been greatest precisely in those lands nearest the West, in the eastern Mediterranean, which, for reasons that have been cited elsewhere, have tended to stand for the whole of Islamdom in the minds of many Western scholars.[2]

The realignments: the land empires (1498–1526)

Meanwhile, a decisive series of events, coming at a crucial point in military development, crystallized a new alignment of great land empires. The enthusiastic Turkic Shîʿism which had been gathering force during the fifteenth century among various ṭarîqah orders in the region around Azerbaijan and Anatolia launched a movement which at the time attracted far more attention among most Muslims than did the Portuguese coup. The leaders of the Ṣafavî ṭarîqah at Ardabîl had cultivated good relations with Shîʿî elements far and wide, especially among Turkic pastoral tribes, and led many of them in ghâzî raids against the Christian Georgians and Circassians of the Caucasus region. They had also managed to make an enemy of the most powerful family in the whole area, the chiefs of the Aḳ-ḳoyunlu ('White-sheep') tribal dynasty, sultans in Mesopotamia and western Iran. In 1500, Ismâʿîl, the sixteen-year-old heir to the Ṣafavî pîrship, was able to muster

[2] The failure of the Portuguese to fulfill their goals in Malaysia is summarily portrayed by Bernard H. M. Vlekke in *Nusantara: A History of Indonesia* (rev. ed., The Hague, 1959), chap. IV. For the continuing importance of Muslim trade through the sixteenth century, see, for instance, Hendrik Dunlop's introduction to his *Bronnen tot de geschiedenis der Oostindische compagnie in Perzië* (s' Gravenhage, 1930). It is Jacob C. van Leur, however, who effected the revision of former ideas about the sixteenth century in the Southern Seas, in *Indonesian Trade and Society* (The Hague, 1955). M. A. P. Meilink-Roelofsz, *Asian Trade and European Influence in the Indonesian Archipelago between 1500 and about 1630* (The Hague, 1962), has modified but not reversed his conclusions.

sufficient followers to set out to avenge his father's death at Aḳ-ḳoyunlu hands; by 1503 he controlled not only Azerbaijan, where he placed his capital at Tabrîz, but all western Iran and the Tigris-Euphrates basin. He was now not only pîr but *shâh*, king.

Ismâ'îl and his followers had chiliastic expectations. It is said that some of his men expected to be invulnerable in battle in virtue of his presence. Upon the populations he subjected, whether Turks, Persians, or Arabs, Shâh Ismâ'îl imposed the Shî'î creed, where necessary with vigorous persecution: the invocation in the public Friday ṣalât worship was to be said in Shî'î form, and religious notables had to curse Abû-Bakr and 'Umar as usurping the rights of 'Alî to succeed Muḥammad. He evidently expected not merely to establish Shî'î rule, but actually to wipe out Jamâ'î-Sunnism—an aspiration the Shî'îs had scarcely attempted to realize before. Moreover, he apparently hoped to do this eventually throughout Islamdom. Going beyond old Aḳ-ḳoyunlu territory accordingly, by 1510 he had attacked and killed Shaybânî Khân, who had newly united the area of the former Timurî states of Khurâsân and the Oxus basin under his Özbegs; with this blow, Ismâ'îl absorbed Khurâsân and points southeast, pushing the Özbegs north of the Oxus. (Ismâ'îl is said to have filled out Shaybânî's skull with gold and made it a drinking cup.)

In the Ottoman domains to the west, Ismâ'îl already had numerous Turkic followers, called 'Ḳizilbash', 'Red Heads', from their red sectarian headgear. These rose in his support in 1511. But here he was blocked. In 1512 the reigning Bâyezîd was deposed (as we have seen, at the will of the Ottoman leaders) by his son, Selîm, fitly called Selîm the Inexorable (or in an old rendering, 'the Grim'); he bloodily suppressed the Shî'î rising and soon led his troops against Ismâ'îl himself. Ismâ'îl planned only defensive measures for the present—indeed, he could do no more; in 1514, when the Ottomans advanced, his artillery was still engaged in the east. He was badly defeated at Chaldirân, not far from Tabrîz. Ismâ'îl had attempted to counter the Ottoman superiority in artillery and infantry with bold cavalry manoeuvres, but luck went against him. However, subsequent fighting also was mostly favourable to the Ottomans. While Selîm occupied little of Ismâ'îl's territory permanently, Ismâ'îl had to give up any hope of pushing his own campaigns further west.

In the territories that he did conquer, however, he erected a zealously Shî'î state. Jamâ'î-Sunnî ṭarîqahs were dispossessed, losing their khâniqâhs and endowments, and Sunnî 'ulamâ' were executed or exiled. Shî'î scholars (notably Arabs) were brought in from east Arabia, Syria, or wherever they could be found, to teach the new creed to the population. The work was so well done that despite serious weakness in the dynasty following Ismâ'îl's death (in 1524), his state (commonly called the 'Persian Empire') held together on a Shî'î basis for more than two centuries and left the territories he had conquered permanently Shî'î. On the other hand, in Ottoman Anatolia and in the Özbeg Syr and Oxus basins, the Shî'î minority was severely persecuted and forced underground. Islamdom was now sharply and definitively divided into Shî'î-majority and Sunnî-majority areas, each unprecedentedly intolerant of the presence of the opposite minority. The civil unity of the Dâr al-Islâm was severely crippled.

In his campaign against Ismâ'îl, the Ottoman Selîm had been opposed by the Mamlûks of Egypt. In 1516 Selîm marched into Syria against them. Here again his use of field artillery carried the day (supplemented by treachery which betrayed the cavalry manoeuvre designed to outflank it). But here, despite last-minute resistance by Mamlûks and Arabs in Cairo, the campaign resulted in a permanent occupation of Syria, Egypt, and even western Arabia.

The Mamlûk state in these areas had been losing strength for generations; the loss of revenue from shipping, because of Portuguese activities, had added to its troubles. It was now replaced by a state with far wider resources and commitments. The growing Ottoman state, in special contrast to the weakening Mamlûks, had become an increasingly strong naval power. Its fleets were seizing control of the east Mediterranean from the Italian cities. At almost the same time as the conquest of Egypt, the Ottomans received the allegiance of important naval forces in the Maghrib, where help was needed against Spanish aggression. The net result was that the Ottoman empire almost tripled its area in one generation, to stand for three centuries as the great Muslim power of the whole Mediterranean region. The empire adapted to this wider sphere the unusually solid institutions it had developed on the frontier in Anatolia and the Balkans. Though its control of the newer provinces was never so close as in the old ones, yet on the highest social levels, at least, it succeeded in moulding in an imperial pattern the social and cultural life of all its peoples. It was within the guiding lines established by the Ottoman empire that lived henceforth most Arabs, western Turks, and various neighbouring Muslim peoples.

At the same time, north Indian Islamdom received a new political establishment. The opening steps in this development were closely linked with some aspects of the rise of the Ṣafavîs. One of the late Timurid petty rulers, Bâbur, fleeing the Özbeg conquest of the Oxus basin, had sufficient repute (and support from his closest followers) to take control of the remains of Timurî power at Kâbul in the Afghan mountains; further, he had sufficient ambition and skill, using that mountain kingdom as base, to intervene in the troubled politics of the Delhi sultanate and seize power in a part of northern India. Like Ismâ'îl—with whom he was allied against the Özbegs—he typified the fragmentary and adventurous character of the political life of the Middle Periods; but he also represented the Mongol ideal of the patronage state and, like Ismâ'îl, he helped to establish a state which went far to reverse the old atomized political life. The Lôdî dynasty at Delhi seems not to have escaped the local overcommitments that had handicapped previous rulers at Delhi. In 1526, at Pânîpat, on the northwest approaches to Delhi, Bâbur defeated the Delhi armies (partly with the aid of good field artillery) and there was no rallying to the Lôdî cause. He ascended the throne of Delhi, which he reinvigorated. But by 1530 he was dead; despite some striking military successes, his sons quarrelled and were soon driven out (1540). Only in 1556 did one of them come back to seize the throne of a north Indian empire which was already developing in the centralizing direction Bâbur's line was to encourage. Bâbur (himself an accomplished Turkic author) had not, then, himself actually given form to that empire; but he contributed to it a dynastic tradition which—when its supporters later returned to power—enhanced the empire's prestige and its resources and also strengthened the active ties of Indian society with the highest cultural circles of the west and the north.

Thus major empires were carved out by three dynasties. All of them dated back into the fourteenth century, and so possessed a power base more deeply rooted than that of mere military adventurers. The Ottomans already possessed a substantial state; the Ṣafavids, authority in an extensive and militant ṭarîqah; and the Timurids of India, the prestigious heritage of Timur. To these must be added at least the Özbeg empire north of the Oxus, likewise going back to the Özbeg state in Khwârazm and its Mongol heritage. These dynasties were in a position to consolidate imperial power during the realignments of gunpowder times; and they were subsequently distinguished not only for the extent and durability of their empires but also for the effectiveness of their absolutist rule. They spread yet more widely the tendencies toward a military patronage state that I have suggested even the Ottomans were adopting at the end of the fifteenth century. At the same time, the lineaments of that sort of state—as I see it—were being renewed and modified in the new empires.

The new empires were able in large areas, by the sixteenth century, to reverse the tendency toward isolation and neutralization of the amîrs by Islamicate society. This is partly, I suppose, because the Sunnî synthesis of the Earlier Middle Period was inherently unstable—the local evolution, within the system, of so relatively stabilized a structure as that of the Mamlûks in Egypt and Syria, and the movements of ṭarîqah Shî'ism in opposition, all indicate that the delicate balance could produce both its own overextensions and its own antagonists. The military patronage state was a natural response to the possibilities of exploiting the decentralized contractualistic society, once the patterns of that society were well established.

But that major bureaucratic empires could be re-established as an outcome of these tendencies—not only in Europe and India but even (a bit later) on old Irano-Semitic territory—suggests further pressures at work. I have suggested three components in what has seemed to me the relative insecurity of agrarian power in the mid-Arid Zone: the relative sparseness of agriculture, making centralized agrarian-based power more difficult to muster; the precariousness of cultivation in marginal areas and of control over peasants; the potential rivalry with pastoralist power. The effects of these conditions were presumably partially counteracted, by the time gunpowder weapons became militarily decisive, in at least two ways: through the technical demands of gunpowder weaponry itself, and through limitations, to which gunpowder contributed, upon long-distance nomadism. Hence part of the basis for the decentralized, contractualistic, cosmopolitan Islamicate society was undermined.

I have already mentioned the advantage gunpowder might bring to rulers with special resources. By the fifteenth century, when it became a dominant force in warfare, the new constant technical innovation could determine overall governmental patterns. In any case, only central authorities were in a position financially to keep up to date. Even where gunpowder was minimally used, as in forces depending largely on cavalry, political expectations could be moulded by the ever more prevailing temper. At the same time, the increasing subjection of the ruling strata in the steppe nomadry to economic and cultural norms derived from citied society was reducing the likelihood of vast steppe empires, the most potent source of concentrated pastoral power; and possibly, before the widespread use of hand guns, the added prestige and durability artillery gave to central powers may have strengthened their hands against even local nomads. One can conjecture that such changes account for the relative effectiveness of the new absolutisms.

With the restoration of some degree of bureaucratic centralization and dynastic stabilization, the typical Islamicate contractualist norms of society generally tended to be altered in tone, if not done away with. Social mobility apparently tended to decrease, at least in some areas. In the Ottoman empire guilds probably became stronger and less flexible than Islamdom had known them before, while in India many Muslims remained organized in castes, though without the full restrictions of Hinduism. Such local continuities are not surprising. But even in the Ṣafavî empire, centred in old Irano-Semitic territory, it may be that guilds became more tightly organized; certainly dependence on the state increased.

What I have called 'military patronage states' never formed a single pattern, but at some points I think I can see common effects on such states from the special circumstances of the age. Already in the Later Middle Periods, such thrusts toward autonomy as might seem to have been budding in the cities were curbed; under the gunpowder empires, cities were under relatively close bureaucratic control. Central supervision and intervention probably reached its peak in the Ottoman empire. The development of a central bureaucracy, in principle as an arm of the monolithic and all-inclusive army, was carried so far, on the other hand, that the ruling family waned in significance. Universally the head of the family was assigned the prerogatives of caliph; but the other members of the family had little independent opportunity—and indeed might find themselves repressed as a threat to central unity. This necessarily called for a certain modification in patterns of succession.

The succession at the centre was necessarily linked to questions of succession throughout the society; hence it was bound eventually to be assimilated to the patterns of succession to lesser office prevailing among those many persons on whose support any centre depends. In at least two of the later military patronage states, when the central power was more jealously maintained than ever it was in the Middle Periods, the rule of succession by armed contest, reasonably congenial to Islamicate tradition, was formalized. Succession by designation by the predecessor (the natural alternative) was consciously ruled out—it was said that succession was in the hands of God—so that a father could not intervene on behalf of one son and exclude the equal rights of the others. All that a father could legitimately do was to give one son a position of military advantage over the others when the father's death was approaching. This was repeatedly recognized by Timurid monarchs in India; even when the Timurid Awrangzêb stated his preference that one son should succeed, he acknowledged that his other son still had an equal right to the sovereignty. The principle was embodied in an Ottoman qânûn rule. The Ṣafavid rulers recognized the applicability of the principle to their neighbours: the emperor retained at Iṣfahân a third rebellious son of Awrangzêb until his father should die, when a contest would be legally in order. (The Ṣafavîs themselves seem to have preferred a more peaceful contest in an assembly of the chief courtiers to choose which son would succeed after the monarch's death.) Though such a principle sometimes entailed anticipatory contests in the father's lifetime, yet in the absence of any formal mechanism of election like the Mongol *kuriltay* assembly, it seems to have ensured at once a direct military role in basic decisions and to have preserved, by common consent, the unity of an empire, without division among sons as had tended to happen in earlier military patronage states.

Of the many state formations that arose out of all these events of the time of realignments, the most significant culturally was that which arose in the lands of old Islam, the Fertile Crescent and the Iranian highlands. Here the central Islamicate cultural traditions received their greatest further development; here the new flowering of the culture had at once the greatest continuity with the past and the greatest brilliance of new discoveries and new departures.

The Shî'î foundations of the Ṣafavî state

It has been commonly said that the Ṣafavid dynasty re-established, after nine hundred years of foreign interruption, the old Persian empire of the Achaemenids and Sâsânids; or else, more recently, that the Ṣafavid dynasty marked the emergence of 'Persia' as a national state in the modern sense. Each notion is founded on a valid point. The Ṣafavî empire was a more adequate heir to the Sâsânian empire, in its absolutist administrative and cultural ideals, than any since the classical 'Abbâsî empire. Again, it was the Ṣafavî state that worked out the main lines along which the subsequent monarchy has continued to be defined, having its capital in the western Iranian highlands, gathering under one rule at least the western Iranian and Azerî provinces, and above all establishing an official Shî'ism. This has been the context within which the most important of the modern Iranian nationalisms grew up.

But any such notion of a specially 'national' character in the Ṣafavî state harks back chiefly, I feel sure, to two mistaken identifications, formerly in vogue: that of Islam with the Semitic 'race' (and with the Sunnism of the Mediterranean Arabs), and that of Shî'ism with a 'reaction against Islam' on the part of the 'Aryan' Persians. (Hence the 'Abbâsî empire is usually omitted, as not 'Persian', from the Achaemenid-Sâsânî-Ṣafavî sequence.) Stripped of these racialist presuppositions, the notion loses its plausibility. Just as the Ṣafavî empire can be regarded as a restoration of the Sâsânian empire only by an analogy that leaves out of account the whole inner development of Islamicate civilization, so it can be regarded as an anticipation of nationhood in the modern sense only at the cost of disregarding some of the most crucial features that go to make up the modern nation-state, and in particular the problems that yet faced those who, later, did wish to make of Persia a modern nation-state. Writers used to cite it as a paradox that Ismâ'îl, ruler of 'Persia', wrote his verse in Turkic, while his rival, Selîm, ruler of 'Turkey', wrote his verse in Persian. The paradox springs only from a misuse of the term 'Persia' for the Ṣafavî empire, which included Persians, Turks, and Arabs equally, and the term 'Turkey' for the Ottoman empire, an even more unfortunate misnomer. In itself there is nothing paradoxical in the leader of a tribal grouping writing in the popular tongue, Turkic, while the head of an established state writes in the cultivated tongue, Persian. The significance of the Ṣafavî empire lies neither in a racial restoration nor in a racial anticipation, but in the breakdown of the political decentralization of the Middle Periods not only in the more heavily agrarian regions of India and Europe but even in the heart of the Arid Zone itself.[3]

[3] The confusions that can arise through the various popular misconceptions about territory and race can become very involved. A respectable (and not untypical) historian, Laurence Lockhart in the *Fall of the Ṣafavî Dynasty* (Cambridge University Press, 1958), p. 67, can write that the 'Persians' of the Ṣafavî era had 'sadly degenerated' from Sâsânî times in having no merchant fleet, since they held the sea in horror—and yet note that the Arabs 'on both sides of the Persian Gulf' took readily to the sea—evidently not questioning whether it made sense to imply that the Persian- and Turkic-speaking landsmen of Iṣfahân had 'degenerated' from sea-loving ancestors who may once have spoken some Iranian tongue on the shores of the Gulf. All this nonsense presupposes popular stereotypes. To justify such statements, one would have to go through a chain of arguments which, once stated explicitly, looks like a parody. One must identify with a given name (however accidental) a single language, culture group, and patrilineal race—and often enough what is called vaguely a single 'country'. Because in the nineteenth century the northern shores of the Gulf were assigned (largely by European

Ismâ'îl and his followers, of course, were no more conscious of building a more absolutist state than of building a Persian nation. Theirs was a state of the military patronage type. Within the ruling establishment, one can draw no sharp lines between military and civilian: it was all the monarch's household, and the whole establishment served a military function pre-eminently, though to this end it had also to administer its lands. Men who were primarily military, 'men of the sword', usually Turks, could turn up readily in what were primarily unsoldierly administrative functions, especially on the level of high policy; for the whole state was regarded as their proper province. At the same time, 'men of the pen', normally 'Tâjîks', that is Iranians or Arabs, who were expected to be subordinated to the Turkic 'men of the sword', might turn up in military functions once they had managed to rise high enough in the establishment to meddle in policy. We find even qâḍîs following such a path. And at first, the Ṣafavî state does not seem to have pushed the pattern to any more developed phase.[4]

In particular, there was neither explicit policy nor even actual administrative practice that could assure the Ṣafavî state, in its beginnings, any different prospects from those of the states that had preceded it in the area. Despite the far-reaching shifts in the political balance of power that followed upon Shâh Ismâ'îl's career of conquest and fanaticism, the Ṣafavî state as it emerged rested on bases superficially very similar to those of the Ḳara-ḳoyunlu and the Aḳ-ḳoyunlu states. There also, as with the Ṣafavîs, the ruling power had been based on Turkic tribes from the highlands between Anatolia and Iran; it had been military in orientation; and even (in the case of the Ḳara-ḳoyunlu) Shî'î.

Yet in each of these three points, the Ṣafavî state differed crucially. The state was not merely Turkic. Though it was based on Turkic tribal powers, these were held together by a mystical allegiance which at the same time tied them to certain urban populations, notably to the devotees of the

decree) to 'Persia', then on the one hand whatever had once ever been there, from the time of the Elamites on, was implicitly 'Persian'; and on the other hand, 'Arabs' there were necessarily, by implication, recent intruders. However, 'Persia' is not only supposed to be an eternal territory; it is also imagined as an eternal state; hence if a Pahlavî-speaking government in the Iraq had made use of naval power, they were 'Persians' who were not afraid of the sea. But, of course, 'Persians' are also a patrilineal 'race'; the modern 'Persians' must be descendants of the men of the Sâsânian court *and* of their sailors (while the 'Arabs' of the Persian Gulf are not, of course); so the men of Iṣfahân have 'degenerated' in no longer loving the sea and in allowing the 'Arabs' to take over! (Cf. note 16 in Book One, chap. I.)

[4] What is valid in such an analysis I owe to Martin Dixon—what is invalid, to my own ignorance, abetted by his failure to publish. The hostility of the Ḳizilbash to a Persian, i.e., a non-military vizier, and other tendencies within the Ṣafavî administrative system at this period are analyzed by Roger M. Savory; note: 'The Principal Offices of the Ṣafavid State during the Reign of Ismā'îl I', *BSOAS*, 23 (1960), 91–105; 'The Principal Offices of the Ṣafavid State during the Reign of Ṭahmāsp I', *BSOAS*, 24 (1961); and 'The Significance of the Political Murder of Mîrzâ Salmân', *Islamic Studies* (Karachi), 3 (1964), 181–91. Note that the office of *vakîl*, personal representative, occurred also under the preceding Turkic dynasties.

Ṣafavîs at Ardabîl and elsewhere. It was not a tribal confederacy on the usual lines, but a religious fraternity which made use of tribal links but could set them aside at need in favour of a higher calling. Then the dynasty did not merely favour the Shî'ah; it seriously set about enforcing conversion to the Shî'ah upon the whole population. In doing so, it broke up or weakened major sections of the old local ruling elements by attacking their financial bases, and helped to establish new ones. Accordingly, it was not merely military. By virtue of its special appeal to the Shî'î faith, already, it implied a certain civilian commitment; this was increased when the economic pattern of urban institutions was shifted into Shî'î hands, creating a vested interest in the permanence of the dynasty which was tied to an interest in peace and prosperity.

At first, the state seemed hardly stronger than its predecessors; but with time all these points of difference made themselves felt. It survived difficulties that would have wrecked a purely tribal military régime. It survived them long enough so that eventually—later than either the Ottoman or the Indo-Timurî states, it seems—it was able to establish a full-fledged bureaucracy based on gunpowder military forces.

Though the majority of the population from Nile to Oxus seems to have been Jamâ'î-Sunnî in 1500 (in the strongly 'Alid-loyalist way of Sunnism by that time), the Twelver Shî'ah was very strong in some areas, especially since the spread of ṭarîqah Shî'ism in the Mongol period. It was especially strong in the Iraq, around the Shî'î shrines at Karbalâ' and Najaf, new cities which had arisen precisely as Shî'î pilgrimage centres and had taken the place of Kûfah; it continued dominant in such towns as Qum, which had been Shî'î from the beginning. But there were by now strong Shî'î factions in many other places. We have noted that during the fifteenth century, for instance, the great rival factions that divided Iṣfahân were no longer Ḥanafîs and Shâfi'îs, but Jamâ'î-Sunnîs and Shî'îs. And in the course of the century, the Shî'î leading families seem to have gained more and more an upper hand over their Sunnî rivals. As with the Guelph and Ghibelline parties in Italian cities, a hereditary partisanship was not always a matter of abstract ideals. Nevertheless, the Shî'î party does seem to have remained especially hospitable to hopes of general reform, and hence well-disposed to attempts at political innovation. Such hopes were expressed, for instance, by the Shî'î families who led Iṣfahân into supporting a rebel grandson against the Timurid, Shâhrukh—a rebellion then crushed in blood, but presaging the future. Ismâ'îl had, then, two sorts of Shî'î support: the Shî'ism of the tribes, not only Ṣûfî in feeling but often deviating widely from the norms of the Shar'î 'ulamâ'; and the Shî'ism of the great city families, no doubt also of a Ṣûfî cast, but relatively bourgeois and Sharî'ah-minded in many cases, though still willing to look to a new social order within these limits.

In the first decade or so of Ismâ'îl's reign, the state was founded firmly upon the position of Ismâ'îl as *murshid-e kâmil*, the 'perfect [Ṣûfî] master', assisted by his subordinate pîrs and khalîfahs, to whom were devoted the loyal Turkic tribes of murîds, the Ḳîzîlbash, who were fulfilling their spiritual discipline in following his military commands. Ismâ'îl's chief executive officer was a personal representative who expressed as much Ismâ'îl's leadership as chief of the Ṣafavî ṭarîqah as he did his administrative powers over the subjected territories. The head of the civil administration had regularly, under the preceding Turkic rulers, been a civilian (and naturally a Persian); but when, after his power was well established, Ismâ'îl chose a Persian for his personal representative, with power not only over the administration but over the relations of the murîds to their murshid-e kâmil, it was clear that he was depending less than fully on the Ḳîzîlbash tribal amîrs. When this personal representative was made commander in chief of an expedition against the Özbegs, in resentment the Ḳîzîlbash leaders deserted the commander and allowed him to be killed. Already there was clearly tension between the Ḳîzîlbash Shî'î amîrs on the one hand and the urban, largely Persian-speaking Shî'î leadership on the other.

Ismâ'îl himself, as a young man, lived very much in the atmosphere of the extremist ṭarîqah Shî'ism of the Ṣafavî-supporting tribes. His own verses proclaim him a locus of Divinity for his times, as a descendant of the Twelver imâms; and honour the imâms themselves in ways that more cautious Shî'îs could find exaggerated. There is no indication that he changed his sentiments; but toward the end of his life, especially after further westward expansion was checked at Chaldirân in 1514, he moved increasingly to break up the power of the great Ḳîzîlbash amîrs and to put civilians into positions of trust. When he died, in 1524, leaving as heir Ṭahmâsp, a boy of ten, the amîrs were still able to regain control of the state; but after a decade of their infighting, Ṭahmâsp was able to find the support he needed to take power personally and renew the enhancement of the civilian authority which his father had initiated.

Ṭahmâsp (ruled about 1533–76) was not an outstanding ruler. He seems to have been competent in his post, but to have been inactive of temperament and personally rather mean. He was highly refined in his aesthetic tastes, giving a further impulse to the patronage of the arts which became a Ṣafavî hallmark; but he perpetuated the tradition of barbarous cruelty in acts of public revenge, which since Mongol times had been intensified even beyond the common Agrarian Age usage. In his hands the Ṣafavî state was not strong enough to gain back some lands, notably the sacred cities of the Iraq, which Ismâ'îl had held but which had been lost at Chaldirân or later. The capital had been moved from Tabrîz, in Azerbaijan, to the more purely Persian Qazvîn. Yet the state did maintain its power in much of the sub-Caucasian highlands (the movement's original home) and swayed in addition the greater part of all the Persian-speaking lands, including most of Khurâsân. When the Indian Timurid ruler, Humâyûn, had to flee Delhi and come back to Kâbul, where his father, Bâbur, had founded his power, he found it useful and perhaps necessary to appeal to the protection of Ṭahmâsp, even at the cost of professing Shî'ism for the time being. The Ṣafavî empire was indisputably one of the three great Muslim powers, markedly more solidly seated than the Ḳara-ḳoyunlu and Aḳ-ḳoyunlu states had been.

The solidity of Ṣafavî power seems to have depended largely on Ṭahmâsp's success in diversifying the basis of that power. He continued, certainly, to rely on the Ḳîzîlbash tribes (but now appealing to their support more as *pâdishâh* 'emperor', than as pîr); he also could count on the newly dominant Shî'î factions in the cities, who depended on the dynasty for their position (there was a substantial body of Sunnî exiles waiting to return from just across the border, in the first generation at least). But in the course of his reign he depended more and more, in addition, on substantial numbers of new converts, either captives or free men, from the Christian Caucasian lands into which Ismâ'îl, like his ancestors, had carried raids. These new Muslims, loyal only to the dynasty, formed a substantial counterweight to the official tribal support.

In earlier Islamic times, dynasties had built special support for themselves by drawing upon socially rootless elements to support their central absolutist power against the embarrassing claims of their original supporters. This tendency had resulted, gradually, in the whole ruling stratum being more or less Turkic in the greater part of the Muslim lands, because the most obvious reservoir of socially rootless military elements was the slave supply from the central Eurasian steppe. But by now the world-historical configuration had changed. The steady expansive pressure of agrarianate society was engulfing even the steppe. With the advance of Buddhist, Muslim, and Christian cultural patterns, no part of central Eurasia was left open without some sort of established, large-scale political control; the tribal leadership was becoming an aristocracy with interests tied to those of the merchants of towns as remote from the older centres of civilization as Sibir on the Irtysh river, seat of a Muslim khânate. The steppe was no longer a free, heathen, inexhaustible source of slaves as well as of migrant tribes; it was controlled by Mongol or ex-Mongol khânates with their own interests. Since within the older Muslim lands the Turkic tribal groups had by now established for themselves an increasingly customary place, with their own local ties and interests, the conditions that had led to a universal Turkizing of the military classes were fading away. Instead ,the great Muslim empires of the sixteenth century turned to less homogeneous sources for their unattached troops. Despite a Turkic veneer, as early as the fourteenth century the Mamlûk régime in Egypt had turned for its new slave recruits largely to the Caucasian lands—especially to Circassia. The Ottoman empire looked to voluntary converts from foreign Christendom and to conscripted youths from their own subject Christian population; the Indian Timurids made use both of foreign Muslims and of local Hindus, often unconverted, to broaden their base.

The Ṣafavîs, already under Ṭahmâsp, likewise made use of elements external to the class system of their society; they used Christian converts, notably Armenians, and converted Caucasian captives, Circassians and especially Georgians. Such men not only formed troops but also rose to high positions of responsibility. But unlike the central Eurasian Turks, they did not have a homogeneous language or cultural background. A new homogeneity was given them, compounded of a Shî'î allegiance which set them off from rival imperial élites, and a Persian culture of which they could claim to rule the home ground. (In this sense, the empire became distinctively Persian.) The best of the young captives were given an excellent education, which included Persian poetry as well as archery, to put them in the full stream of the best Islamicate culture. Consistently with the new awareness of the high value of the fine arts, they were even taught painting, so as to develop their taste.

Effects of the Shî'î ascendancy

The establishment of Twelver Shî'ism as dominant allegiance in a major part of Islamdom led, within the area, to new emphases and forms in piety on the levels both of the high culture and of the folk culture; and it even erected a certain cultural barrier between the Shî'î and the Jamâ'î-Sunnî areas. This barrier showed itself politically in the chronic hostility that set the Ṣafavîs at odds with both the Ottomans and the Özbegs—though indeed, at most, Shî'ism only exacerbated conflicts such as had been taking place before. Perhaps the same barrier was not without influence upon the Ṣafavî policy of alliance with both the Portuguese in the south and then the Russians as they extended their trade into the Caspian sea; a policy that materially undermined the Ottoman struggle against those same Christian powers. Some travellers high in Sunnî circles even hesitated to take a route through Ṣafavî territory for fear of harassment. Perhaps more significant was the rise of an intellectual barrier between the 'ulamâ' of Shî'î and of Sunnî areas: thus Najaf in the Iraq, a city of madrasahs which came to be the most important Twelver Shî'î intellectual centre, had little communication with the great Azhar madrasah mosque in Cairo; and the Shî'îs of East Arabia had little with the Shâfi'îs of Ḥaḍramawt in the south. (In India, however, Shî'îs and Sunnîs still mingled fairly freely under a tolerant Sunnî régime.) Yet the barrier was never very high. The Iṣfahân school of philosophy, impregnated with Shî'ism as it was, was read everywhere among those concerned; so was the new style of poetry developed in the Ṣafavî empire. The bigoted (and Sharî'ah-minded) 'ulamâ' who stood for rigid separation between Shî'î and Sunnî almost always played a secondary role.

But within Shî'î territory, the new allegiance proved to have pervasive effects. These show some remarkable parallels to the contemporary Protestant reform in northern Europe, but did not carry so far. (What we may compare to the Shî'î movement is the early Protestantism of the sixteenth century, not, of course, later Protestantism when the Modern Technical Age had set in.) Both movements grew out of diverse traditions of protest, often chiliastic, in the preceding two centuries. Both were associated with the strengthening of royal government, and were imposed now by rulers on whole populations; and both had wide popular repercussions elsewhere as well. Both movements had an anti-aristocratic background, though when in power they were accommodated to upper-class standards; in both movements can be traced both popular and more privileged levels of ideas and practice. Both resulted in the dissolution of monastic orders and the ending of at least some traditional saint worship. However, the Shîʿî movement did not lose, like the Protestant, a whole series of secondary popular movements (perhaps because the ṭarîqah Shîʿism of the preceding century had been more vigorous in this respect already than the corresponding protesting movements among the Christians). Nor, it seems, was the Shîʿism of the time based on a concentration of fresh creative spiritual and intellectual figures as was Protestantism; it was content, for the most part, to make use of the thought, and even the organizational forms, of the preceding centuries. (The creativity that did attend it served chiefly the subsequent accommodation of other imaginative traditions to a Shîʿî allegiance.)

The similarities surely resulted in part from the tendency of movements of protest in that period, when the confessional religions had been so long established, to take on a chiliastic and/or a mystical aspect and to seek reform of the established religious order; within an Abrahamic tradition, reform movements must have some common features. The timing was surely coincidental. One can ascribe the differences to such things as the contrasts in established religious organization, and to special features such as the use of printing in Europe, which facilitated a relatively quick popular distribution of new ideas (though one must not underestimate the speed with which manuscript and oral methods could take effect!); but the presence of printing in Europe itself reflects a difference deeper and more important. In the Occident, the protest movements were associated with an increasing role of the bourgeois, associated with the florescence of Renaissance times; in Islamdom, on the contrary, if anything the culture of the bourgeois market place was losing in independence.

On the level of the high culture, the establishment of Shîʿism seriously modified the Sharîʿah-minded, the Ṣûfî mystical, and necessarily also the ʿAlid-loyalist and chiliastic sides of Islam. Where loyalty to ʿAlî and his family were the proclaimed public norm, chiliastic and esoteric hopes necessarily had to find more distinctive channels. We know next to nothing of unofficial or clandestine movements in the period, but already before Shîʿism became official, the more esoteric ʿAlid-loyalist groups had had to conceal their viewpoints as much from Shîʿî as from Sunnî ʿulamâʾ, and we know that in some cases this continued. We may surmise that protesters took refuge in one or another sort of super-ʿAlid loyalism.

What happened in other sorts of devotional life is a bit more evident. The Shî'î 'ulamâ', accustomed to independence, and sceptical of the propriety of some of the enthusiastic and even antinomian 'Alid loyalism of the Ḳîzîlbash disciples of Ismâ'îl, remained somewhat aloof from the dynasty; yet they took advantage of the change in allegiance to consolidate their own position with the people. The leading 'ulamâ', the mujtahids (unlike their Sunnî counterparts under the Ottomans), did not accept a status as part of the military régime but preferred to be ranked with the taxable subject population. From that vantage point, they maintained a stance of potential and occasionally actual criticism of the régime, which was to set them off from other bodies of 'ulamâ' as late as the twentieth century. At the same time, they maintained a solidarity of their own across the empire. There has been no study made of the difference between the Shî'î religious establishment and what had preceded it, but one can suspect that the Shî'î 'ulamâ' showed at least a specially determined independence.

The Shî'î 'ulamâ' had traditionally been hostile to Ṣûfism, always associated with the Jamâ'î-Sunnîs; and this hostility seems not to have been much weakened in the days of ṭarîqah Shî'ism. Some insistently Sunnî ṭarîqahs were broken up and their pîrs exiled, while some ṭarîqahs either had turned sufficiently Shî'î to be at ease with the new allegiance, or put on a Shî'î front, so that they continued to flourish. However, the 'ulamâ' were persistently hostile even to these, and at best the role of the ṭarîqahs was reduced. It is my impression that much of the Ṣûfî tradition, at least among the educated, was carried on a relatively personal basis, inspired by older Ṣûfî poetry; that the tradition was privately adjusted, as required, to Shî'î demands in which the 'Alid imâm played a very central role.

On the level of the folk religion, one can generalize the effects of the victory of the Shî'ah by saying that the (Shî'î) tragic drama of the world's history, with its coming finale where all would be righted, gradually replaced the (Ṣûfî) mystical quest of the soul's love for God, with its exemplification in a hierarchy of saints. Of course, such a replacement took place at most only in the public framework of the religious imagination. The Ṣûfî world image continued valid not only for those who would be personally mystics by temperament, but at least as a component in many persons' reading of the Shî'î world image. But it was no longer so universally accepted as a point of departure for non-mystics who had used the presence of Ṣûfî saints and the Ṣûfî cult for their own varied purposes. For these other purposes—moral discipline, healing, divination, group self-identification, intercession with God, and generally self-orientation in the cosmos—some sort of participation in the Shî'î drama came to be used instead. (Of course, as among the Sunnîs, however oriented to Ṣûfî ṭarîqahs, so also among the Shî'îs the basic demand for a personal moral responsibility, to be enforced by divine Judgment after death, continued to underlie all religious awareness.)

For all Twelver Shî'îs, the first ten days of the lunar month Muḥarram, and

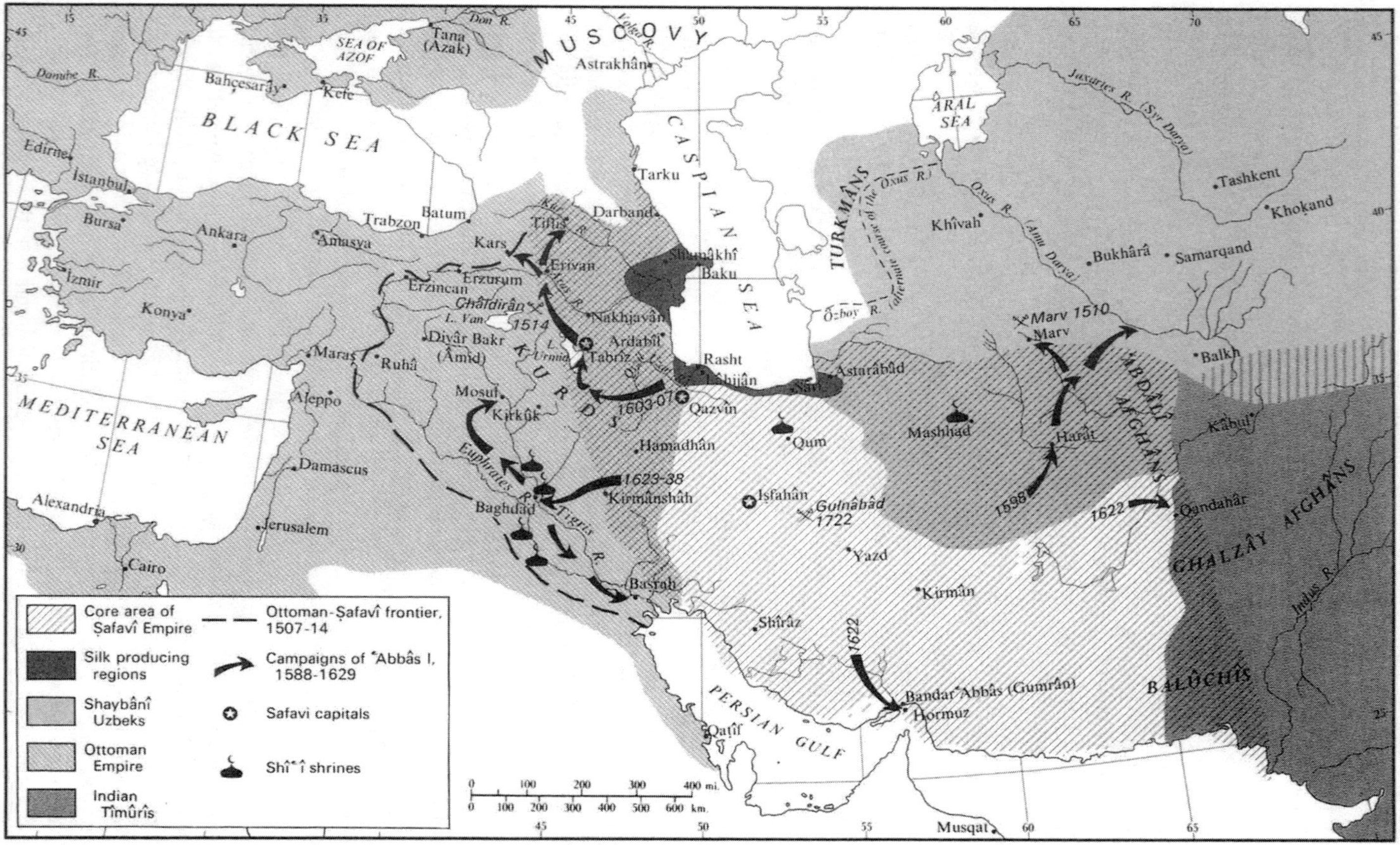

The Safavî empire, 1500–1722

especially the tenth day, were consecrated to mourning (*ta'ziyah*) for Ḥusayn, 'Alî's son killed at Karbalâ' outside Kûfah on that day. That day was 'Âshûrâ, a day already independently acknowledged by all Muslims as a day of repentant fasting; for Shî'îs it became the high point of the religious year. The tone of all public religion was set by Ḥusayn's tragedy. A sense of guilt for having abandoned Ḥusayn and left him to be killed by his enemies had given a distinctive devotional tone to the early Shî'î movement at Kûfah, deepening its political demands. Gradually the martyrdom of Ḥusayn, Muḥammad's beloved grandson, had come to be seen as a cosmic event, outshining even the murder of 'Alî himself. The death of all the imâms (all of whom, according to Shî'î legend, had been murdered by Sunnîs) was a part of God's providence; He humbled and grieved Muḥammad and his family so that out of their patient suffering He could bring forth their ultimate triumph and that of those loyal to them. But Ḥusayn's death was regarded as the most grievous and meritorious of all. In it the drama of God and man was seen as becoming fully articulate: he who shared in Ḥusayn's suffering and repented his own share of guilt for it would be forgiven all his sins by God. To this, all else was scarcely more than a prelude. Even festivals of rejoicing, such as that of Ghadîr Khumm, celebrating 'Alî's appointment as Muḥammad's successor, were shadowed by consciousness of the subsequent betrayals in which all but a handful of Muslims went over to 'Alî's (and Muḥammad's) enemies.

In every Shî'î town and village, the most exciting event of the year was the Muḥarram mourning and repentance, when men and boys scourged themselves in grief at their collective and personal unfaithfulness to 'Alî and to Ḥasan and Ḥusayn, drawing their own blood. Representations of Ḥusayn's tomb (also called *ta'ziyah*) were carried in procession to the graveyard or to the 'îd prayer grounds outside the town, to the loud sounds of lamentation. Sermons every evening recounted in graphic and poignant detail the sufferings of the little band about Ḥusayn, including his young sons, as they failed from thirst in the desert, barred by their enemies from the river, and were cut down mercilessly; and they did not omit at last to tell how Ḥusayn's severed head, on its pitiful trip to be insulted by the caliph Yazîd, performed miracles that converted the infidels and even a lion, but not the hard-hearted Sunnîs. The poetic genre *marthiyah*, elegy, was specialized to tell of Ḥusayn's griefs.

In all this, the sorrow inseparable from human life was exalted and given a transcendent meaning, and the sense of evil within one's own self was deeply confronted and exorcized. Unfortunately, this was done at the price of an intensely communal projective reaction: every moment of mourning for Ḥusayn enforced further hatred for Sunnîs. (Similarly, a perfervid contemplation of the wounds of Christ has sometimes helped inspire Christian massacres of Jews.) It is said that an infidel was sooner welcome at a Muḥarram ceremony than a Sunnî. And the tendency of all Muslims to communal exclusivism was accentuated among Shî'îs to the point that a dish used by either infidel or Sunnî might be considered forever polluted.

In late Ṣafavî times, it seems it was, dramatic representations of various incidents in the tribulations of Ḥusayn (these plays also were called *ta 'ziyah*) began to supplement the sermons and the marthiyah elegies; eventually they became the centrepiece of the Muḥarram celebrations. In this way, a popular drama attained literary status, though not entering the courtly culture—in contrast, for instance, to the popular Turkish plays in the round, which were merely alternatives to the puppet theatre and the dramatic story-tellers.

The Muḥarram mourning could displace the mawlid (anniversary) services of Ṣûfî saints, with their public dhikr; it even reduced the relative splendour of the 'greater' 'îd festival, which marked the ḥajj pilgrimage at Mecca. (The 'lesser' 'îd festival, at the end of the Ramaḍân fast, necessarily retained its appeal.) Similarly, Ṣûfî khâniqâhs as devotional centres alternative to the mosque with its formal worship were displaced in comparative importance by the *imâmbârah*, a shrine specially devoted to Ḥasan and Ḥusayn and the Muḥarram mourning. Popular village shrines, once often seen as tombs of ancient saints, tended to be replaced by, or to become, *imâmzâdahs*, tombs of a saintly descendant of an imâm. The universal intercessor now was not the Ṣûfî quṭb saint, secretly ruling the whole world, but the Hidden Imâm, the rightful ruler excluded from his rights by an evil world yet still able to help those true to him, in their necessities. The most precious apotropaic medicine was a tablet made of the clay of Karbalâ', held to be infinitely impregnated with the sacred blood of Ḥusayn; if it was put under one's pillow, one was, in effect, sleeping at Karbalâ' itself and so under Ḥusayn's protection. The pilgrimage to Karbalâ' and to other tombs of imâms tended to be seen as an adequate substitute for that to Mecca itself, and a man was called a ḥâjjî who had been on such a pilgrimage, quite as freely as if he had been to the Ka'bah; though, of course, the Meccan ḥajj was still acknowledged as necessary if it could be afforded.

All this was probably introduced quite gradually, however. Though Ṣûfîs—even those of the Ṣafavî ṭarîqah itself—were subject to persecution and even massacre from time to time, the ṭarîqahs were not fully repressed until the eighteenth century, and even then they survived fragmentarily. But soon the popular religious climate—shared *pari passu* by Twelver minorities outside the empire—came to differ sharply from that in Jamâ'î-Sunnî milieux.

The establishment of Iṣfahân

On Ṭahmâsp's death, the empire survived two disastrous reigns. Ismâ'îl II (1576–78) came to power with the support of the notables of Qazvîn, the capital. He evidently had some talent and a free-ranging religious curiosity.

He set about murdering most of his relatives as possible rivals for the throne, but had still left a few alive when he shortly killed himself with his dissolute ways. Khudâbandah (1578–87), half-blind and disinclined to assume power, allowed the Ottomans to occupy the Azerî and Kurdish highlands, restoring Jamâ'î-Sunnî groups to power there where the dynasty had its origins, and allowed the Özbegs to plunder Khurâsân, to terrorize and enslave its Shî'î families, and to destroy its shrines; meanwhile, more central provinces slipped away from the central authority, which the Ḳizilbash amîrs were again disputing among themselves. At last, in consequence of these disputes, he resigned in favour of his teen-age son 'Abbâs. 'Abbâs proved to have a strength of character like that of Ismâ'îl I and the resources of the empire responded quickly to his will. He freed himself readily of control by the amîrs; successfully risked the ignominy of a peace with the Ottomans which went so far as to offend Shî'î feeling (he agreed to halt the cursing of the first three caliphs) so as to eject the Özbegs from Khurâsân; established his authority soundly in all the provinces; and finally (1603) drove the Ottomans out of those territories Ṭahmâsp had held in the west.

'Abbâs (1587–1629) had to reconquer his empire and in doing so he established the central administrative authority more strongly than ever. He had a strong professional bureaucracy which upheld the absolute power of the throne at the expense of local autonomies. The financial administration, controlled by elaborate checks and balances, seems to have been honest and comprehensive. This bureaucracy was backed up by a military strength based increasingly on those outsiders who had already become an important element in Ṭahmâsp's time, especially converted Georgians and Armenians. 'Abbâs still made use of the military resources that Ismâ'îl had brought into play, including those of ṭarîqah Shî'ism. But even the Ḳizilbash Turkic tribes he reorganized, appealing to their devotion to himself as pâdishâh (emperor); so overriding even hereditary tribal ties.

At the peak of the empire's powers, his reign displayed the empire's splendour in all its aspects. To the gratification of all Shî'îs, his forces reconquered the Iraq from the Ottomans (it had been lost to them as early as 1534), restoring the sacred Shî'î cities to Shî'î control. Though he was unable to advance farther and seize control of Syria and of the Ḥijâz, yet an empire that included the Iraq, western Iran, and Khurâsân, where were the great majority of the cultural centres of classical Islamdom, challenged comparison with the 'Abbâsî empire to which it was the evident successor.

'Abbâs thus perfected the Ṣafavî absolutism. In some measure, this was in the tradition of the military patronage state. The division was maintained of the population into two sectors: the privileged recipients of taxes, regarded as members of the military establishment and as protégés of the pâdishâh; and the taxable subjects, at the pâdishâh's disposal. The most important industrial investments at the capital were regarded as the personal property of the pâdishâh. Yet in its very success, the strongly military character the state had had was being eroded away. 'Abbâs' reign meant, in effect, civilian supremacy in the administration.

Already by 1599, 'Abbâs moved his capital to Iṣfahân, which he proceeded to embellish, drawing on all the resources that the artistic flowering of the preceding two or three centuries had produced. Magnificent parks and palaces, great open squares where troop manoeuvres or vast polo games could proceed and, above all, impressive mosques, hospitals, schools, and caravanserais sprang up through his munificence and that of his family and his successors. The use of coloured tile to decorate buildings, especially great noble domes, was at its height; it has been complained that, typically of a 'late' art, the work was over-refined and over-resplendent: the solid lines of the structure almost disappear in the blaze of magnificent colour. This is surely a misjudgment, as we have seen. In any case, the brilliance of Iṣfahân even now does not cease to delight the imagination.

The brilliance of its art can be judged perhaps with less uncertainty in smaller individual pieces, which can be compared more directly with their rivals of other ages: notably, miniature painting and carpet weaving. In the work of Bihzâd, at the very end of Timurî times, the gem-like style of miniature painting which had developed notably in Timurî Herat reached a culmination; this, however, proved to be a new starting point. Some have claimed that later Ṣafavî painting did not reach again the tight perfection of a genre controlled with such absolute taste. Yet the painters of Qazvîn and of Iṣfahân were brilliant and delightful even when they carried on closely the traditions of Timurî times. At the same time they felt free to experiment with new genres. It seems to have been only in Ṣafavî times that the paintings, detached from any manuscript or wall to decorate, were collected for their own sake; soon even sketches were so collected. Ṣafavî artists, increasingly self-conscious in their art, produced portraits of princes with remarkable liveliness and pen-and-ink impressions of everyday scenes of a touching penetration. They expressed pathos or humour, evidently for their own sake. In his range of interest, at any rate, Riżà-i 'Abbâsî, the most outstanding painter of Iṣfahân, was practically the equal of Bihzâd himself.

But this experimental, self-conscious tendency was most impressively expressed in carpet weaving, for which court painters sometimes provided the cartoons. Making a break with the craft traditions, the carpet weavers of the royal weaving establishments now undertook to produce veritable pictures in yarn; while the technical skill was in nowise reduced, the figures produced were of unprecedented complexity and detailed charm. The experimental resources of Ṣafavî craftsmen also enabled them to discover how to make true porcelain from local materials. This was a long-standing quest: it had been attempted ever since Chinese porcelain became known. Occidentals succeeded in the quest only some time later.

If the visual arts may be called precious, the literary arts, notably poetry, especially in Muslim lands considered the highest of them, may be called so doubly. Yet the poetry of the time cannot be lightly dismissed. Among the innumerable poets who repeated the themes of previous centuries, the most outstanding (in both Iran and India) were deliberately playing games with the tradition, producing a subtle counterpoint of motifs which only the initiate could follow: in a manner called the 'Indian style'. This style was rejected as too recherché by the Persian critics of the eighteenth century (a century not noted for its own poetry), and until lately it was sometimes even said that good Persian poetry ceased with Jâmî (d. 1492). But modern poetic taste has been changing everywhere, and now the 'Indian style' is respected for its sophisticated and creative command of the rich resources of allusion and paradox which five centuries of tradition had made available. Perhaps prose literature in part balanced all this subtlety: the consciousness of creative personality was expressed not only in the visual arts but in memoirs; Shâh Ṭahmâsp himself wrote a detailed, if not very perceptive, autobiography.[5]

The prosperity which the court blazoned over the face of Iṣfahân was not restricted to the court. The great merchants were favoured by the sound administration and the peaceful internal conditions which Shah 'Abbâs had established, and they amassed great fortunes; some, at least in somewhat later decades, were in a position to maintain representatives at once in western Europe and in China to oversee their far-flung trade. The tradesmen of the great cities likewise could display considerable resources; on occasions of public rivalry, the various guilds lavished expense on their appearance. Great irrigation works were undertaken, especially around Iṣfahân. (The Mesopotamian Sawâd was not reactivated, however; the Iraq remained economically marginal, and later rulers, when they had to choose, preferred to hold the well-watered sub-Caucasian highlands even at the expense of the holy cities of the Iraq.) Even the peasants seem to have lived, in some parts, substantially above the level of sheer subsistence; their lot could be compared favourably with those of France by a French traveller. The imperial structure was sufficiently sound, after the work of 'Abbâs had been done, to endure for a hundred years with no serious risings or warfare in the inner provinces (where it ceased to be necessary to station many troops) and—except for the loss of the Iraq to the Ottomans and recurrent Özbeg incursions—with few other major disturbances even on the frontiers.

Shî'î Falsafah

Attracted to the splendour of Iṣfahân came scholars of every sort. Legists and critics and historians received imperial patronage. (But some scholars, too visibly aberrant in point of religious allegiance, were executed.) The

[5] Alessandro Bausani, in his *Storia della letteratura persiana* (Milan, 1960) and elsewhere, brings out the interest of what was happening in the 'Indian-style' poetry; he also cites some relevant Russian studies.

ornate historical school for whom Vaṣṣâf was the great model flourished, seeing great events as a frame on which to drape lyrical extravaganzas.

But there were always some historians who took the substance of their work so seriously that they made a point of not smothering in rhetoric what they had to say, preferring, as one of them said (Iskandar-beg Munshî), to be understood. (His prose is complex as compared to more simple-minded chroniclers, but quite straightforward.) Iskandar-beg, with the encouragement of Shâh 'Abbâs, wrote a voluminous history of his patron's reign, together with a substantial résumé of his dynasty before him. In addition to its judicious accuracy, its psychological perceptiveness, and the broad interest it manifests in the ramifications of the events it traces (it is a mine of social information on the time), it is notable—in contrast to some slightly earlier Ṣafavî histories—for its concern with Iran as such, apparently apart from either the dynasty or a Shî'î allegiance. Iran seems to be conceived as a land of both Turks and Persians, stretching from Mosul to Qandahâr (inclusively), and is honoured as the most important foyer of high civilization: civilization unequivocally Muslim, but not at all identified with the norms of the 'ulamâ'. Iskandar-beg's history was widely appreciated.

As to the natural science of the time, we know nothing except that it was there. But the area of most dazzling scholarly display was metaphysics.[6]

Two schools in the tradition of what we have called *Falsafah* (though they might not like that disreputable name) were especially active: the Peripatetics, holding close to Aristotle and al-Fârâbî; and the 'illuminists', *Ishrâqîs*, following Yaḥyà Suhravardî's thesis that true wisdom calls for accepting Aristotle and then going beyond him. In both schools there were both Muslims and Mazdeans, not only at Iṣfahân but in a provincial town like Shîrâz. Among the Muslims, far the best known school (yet, even so, very little studied by modern scholars) is a group of Shî'î Ishrâqîs, who built on the traditions of Falsafah and of Ṣûfism and did not claim to be introducing anything seriously new, but who also in some sense were convinced of the Shî'î mission, and glad to recast the vision of Philosophia in Shî'î terms. Shâh 'Abbâs gave his protection to more than one major thinker among them, notably Mîr Dâmâd (d. 1631). Mîr Dâmâd appeared as a theologian in the general revival of the Shî'î intellectual tradition that accompanied the party's advent to power; but he also had interests specifically in natural science; and he ultimately attached supreme value to certain ecstatic visional experiences, in which the transcendent Light in terms of which the world was created and given meaning was identified with the Light of Truth which Shî'îs found most perfectly expressed in Muḥammad and the line of imâms.

He and his school took Ibn-Sînâ as their point of departure, including his doctrine of the transcendent individual intellect and his distinctions between essence and existence, and they interpreted him as opening the way to

[6] I must thank Guiti Claffey for calling my attention to points in Iskandar-beg and other writers.

understanding religious realities. But as 'illuminists', Ishrâqîs, they refused to limit themselves to the logic that presupposes absolutely public evidence at all points—ever since Ghazâlî, that had been shown to have demonstrable limitations in metaphysics. They insisted that there could be reality that each person had to perceive privately for himself and could not demonstrate to others—such as the reality of one's own existence (the case cited by Suhravardî)—and which yet was of fundamental importance to seeing the world whole. This they saw adumbrated in such things as visional experience; hence even as metaphysicians they were concerned with what we would call the unconscious dimensions of the individual psyche, which could be expressed in visions, and with the implications of these for our understanding of the cosmos of which that psyche is an integral part. Nevertheless, they did not identify themselves directly with Ṣûfism. As good Shî'îs, they could not call themselves Ṣûfîs, for Ṣûfîs represented the helpless attempt of Jamâ'î-Sunnîs, rejecting the imâms, to reach that inner bâṭin truth in religion to which only the imâms could truly lead. But they did fully recognize the affinity of their own doctrine to the whole Ṣûfî tradition, and some of them did cultivate personally the Ṣûfî spiritual discipline.

In the Later Middle Period, with the rise of ṭarîqah Shî'ism and even outside of those movements, it had become normal for those Shî'îs who were concerned not simply with a general 'Alid loyalism or with a Shar'î viewpoint that happened to be associated therewith, but with the more esoteric and inward aspects of the Shî'î heritage, to work out a Shî'î version of what we call Ṣûfism: the true pîr was the imâm, the quṭb was the Hidden Imâm of the age, and it was through personal devotion to 'Alî and the imâms that the individual could most perfectly cultivate his own inward consciousness; for without devotion to them, he risked being trapped in self-worship. Jamâ'î-Sunnî Ṣûfism, then, was but a dangerously truncated approximation to what for Shî'îs fell harmoniously into place in their total religious scheme. All this was generally accepted by the Iṣfahân school of metaphysicians; given this insight into the mystical life, it was their task to incorporate it into a Philosophical understanding of reality so as to make that understanding more complete.

One of the most distinctive conceptions that the Iṣfahân metaphysicians tried to elucidate was the *'âlam al-mithâl*, the 'realm of images', defined by Suhravardî. This was held to be a realm of being; it was placed, metaphysically, between the ordinary material realm of sense perception and the realm of intellectual abstractions found in Aristotelianism. As the realm of true visions and true visional perception, it was not the realm simply of subjective imagination in individual consciousnesses, for true visions, as if embodying ultimate archetypes, were held to show forth ultimately valid, objective facts of life; yet it was not identifiable with the realm of Platonic Ideas, for the visions were genuinely individual and even personal, not universals—they were the stuff of which actual history was made, the biographies of individuals and the history of Islam itself. (Some said the objects in this realm were like reflections in a mirror—extended, like matter, but not material in the ordinary sense.)

By way of this realm of the symbolic imagination, one could give form to the whole range of human meaningfulness, seen to be far richer than merely a combination of sheer perception with abstract rules and structures. It served to bring to a systematic (if possibly pre-limited) clarity the sort of reality that holds on the level of personal commitment to what transcends the person; a reality, I suppose, that modern existentialists (from a quite different viewpoint) have been stressing our need to take into fuller account. The Islamic conscience had already accepted the necessity, at least in those who cannot maintain an unreflecting faith in whatever they have been told, of personal commitment based not on logical demonstration but on a more total experience. Once this fact had been accepted, this further sort of study logically proved needful for the reflective; needful for them even to fulfill (given all its unfolding implications) the elementary act of islâm. It was the advent of Shî'îsm that determined the form taken by the new studies. But some such studies were doubtless next on the agenda anyway—both metaphysically and spiritually.

The 'âlam al-mithâl was interpreted variously by different metaphysicians and each interpretation naturally carried with it a degree of reinterpretation of the whole structure of Falsafah. Later Persians called Mîr Dâmâd the 'Third Teacher', after Plato and al-Fârâbî, in recognition of the new flowering of integrative insight which found in him its most influential master.

His most important disciple was Mullâ Ṣadrâ (Ṣadruddîn of Shîrâz, d. 1640). He went back to Shîrâz to teach rather than remain in the excitement of Iṣfahân. Yet he was more outspoken than Mîr Dâmâd and his other teachers, paying less attention to Sharî'ah-minded prejudices in what he wrote; in consequence, he suffered persecution.

Mullâ Ṣadrâ, using the insights of Mîr Dâmâd and others of Mîr Dâmâd's contemporaries, built on the trans-Aristotelian logic and on the metaphysic of light which Yaḥyà Suhravardî had enunciated, in which all that exists is light in various forms; this metaphysic permitted a close identification of consciousness and reality, since light is pre-eminently the medium of awareness. The 'âlam al-mithâl was a constitutive concept in his thought (did an increasing role of dreams among later Ṣûfîs, as a key to the unconscious, predispose to this?). Hence he systematized the concept far beyond what, for instance, Ibn-al-'Arabî had done, for whom it was almost a literary device. It served him in his closely argued logical doctrine of the mutability of essences (in the course of which the existence of a thing, in the material world at least, was shown to be prior to its essence). Thus he was able to identify more closely than had Suhravardî the metaphysical 'light' with physical light: 'light' became practically what we would call 'energy', except that it was as real on the levels of intellectual abstraction and of objective meaningfulness (in the 'âlam al-mithâl) as on the level of materiality.

He was also able—what was perhaps especially important for some of his later readers—to set 'being' into historical motion. A soul could go through an indefinite progress from one state of being to another, renewing its own essence. This sort of renewal could be identified with the Shî'î sense of a historical sequence of religious dispensations, as well as with eschatological events. Thus the teaching could have not only personal but potentially social and even political implications. In fact, such implications seem not then to have been drawn, and some of his best disciples paid little attention to his more distinctive doctrines anyway; they had their effects later.

The other 'ulamâ' accused Mullâ Ṣadrâ of infidelity as too much inclined to Falsafah; but he was still genuinely continuing the dialogue that had been launched by the Qur'ânic event. We may see the history of 'Alid loyalism as a political, devotional, and finally philosophical exploration of what it can mean to be loyal to the protest that was raised when the Islamic community was first proving unfaithful to its transcendent challenge. This dialogue of 'Alid loyalism deeply moulded Ṣadrâ's thought; for him, such loyalty assured objective guidance to the inward experiences which were seminal of his thinking, preserving them from the world's corruption. That he was equally committed to an equally significant tradition of life-orientation, that of Philosophia, simply served to enrich his understanding of what was implicit in each tradition. Ṣadrâ's philosophy, like Bihzâd's art, presupposed a tremendously sophisticated heritage; but it also, again like Bihzâd's art, released the resources of that heritage for dynamic further developments. He became the master of many influential masters.[7]

Though Mullâ Ṣadrâ was accused of being too openly Philosophical—a fault for which not only the Sharî'ah-minded would blame him so long as all

[7] Henry Corbin has beautifully set forth the *devotional* meaning of the 'âlam al-mithâl in several works, and especially in *Terre céleste et corps de résurrection: de l'Iran mazdéen à l'Iran shî'ite* (Paris, 1960), in which he attempts incidentally to show such continuities as can be surmised between the old Mazdean angelology and that of Islam (flavouring his description with a romantic Iranian nationalism not really borne out by his data). Corbin's 'The Visionary Dream in Islamic Society', in *The Dream and Human Societies*, ed. G. E. von Grunebaum and Roger Caillois (University of California Press, 1960), pp. 381–408, deals with the 'âlam al-mithâl; in the same volume Fazlur Rahman's 'Dream, Imagination and 'Âlam al-mithâl', pp. 409–19, brings a welcome clarity into the subject from the viewpoint of its *metaphysics*. Corbin's magnificent perceptiveness has made us aware of the importance of both Mullâ Ṣadrâ and Mîr Dâmâd—though he has not yet replaced the inadequate works of Max Horten on Ṣadrâ, *Die Gottesbeweise bei Schirazi* (Bonn, 1912) and *Das philosophische System des Schirazi* (Strassburg, 1913).

Unfortunately, in pursuit of his romanticism Corbin can be historically inexact. Thus he sometimes translates as if the text contrasted an Oriental 'theosophy' to a Peripatetic (and implicitly Western) 'philosophy', where the text refers simply to Ishrâqîs and Peripatetics, as names of schools, without either geographical or disciplinary specification. This is an instance of his frequent overdetermination in translating technical terms: for instance, he renders *'âlam al-mithâl* as world of *archetypes*, rather than something simpler like *images*, making his texts' inclusion of mirror images seem absurd.

agreed that Philosophia could be dangerous for the uninitiated—he as well as the other masters of the Iṣfahân school were careful to write within the settled conventions, however startling their conclusions. But even apart from such considerations, these writers can seem futile to most Moderns. To the Modern reader, much of Mullâ Ṣadrâ can seem to reduce to a refinement of the perennial attempt to give metaphysical justification to the received dogmas of religion, and hence to be irrelevant to anyone who does not happen to be a Shîʿî Muslim or at least to be identified with one of the monotheistic traditions. Much of Mullâ Ṣadrâ's work is taken up, for instance, with eschatological questions—the nature of after-life and resurrection, of hell and paradise (these bulk large in the ʿâlam al-mithâl). I think the sensitive reader will find that, in any case, whenever something is said about the other life, something is being said at least by implication about this life and its moral and intellectual qualities, something that often can be seen to have its own validity apart from any eschatological belief. This, at least, a Modern may respect.

But the meaning of all this 'late' metaphysics cannot be reduced to moral tidbits snatched from among dogmatic rationalizations. Each reader must decide the meaning for him of the sort of realm that the Iṣfahân philosophers were attempting to clarify in the form of the ʿâlam al-mithâl, the realm of images, of visions. Some may reject it all as an unscientific, arbitrary construct. Some may concretize it (and possibly trivialize it) as the realm of extrasensory perceptions and interactions—whatever that realm may be, it is clear that the experiences invoked in referring to it are by definition not to be elucidated in terms of standard public statistical procedure; and just such experiences loom large in the Iṣfahân philosophers' discussions. With greater justice, it may be psychologized, any findings about it being referred to biologically given archetypal patterns which may or may not have more ultimate cosmic relevance. Whatever his attitude, the careful student will recognize that, whether in clumsy confusion or in strokes of genius, these men were trying to come to terms with genuine problems of human meaningfulness: problems lying deeper than the level of conscious formulations and yet dealing with meanings more durable than the mere subjective affectivity to which certain modern positivists used to assign all that is not 'positive'; meanings not merely 'lyrical' though they may scarcely be expressed except by way of evocative images. We have learned to be very cautious before labelling as absurd any great body of work which intelligent and sensitive human beings have agreed in finding supremely important.

The greatness of the sixteenth century: the Persianate flowering

The difficulty of assessing the intellectual achievements of the sixteenth and seventeenth centuries is symptomatic of the difficulty of assessing the period as a whole. Like its intellectual life, the period generally has been little studied by modern scholars, at least in the more central areas of Islamdom, where the achievement was evidently greatest. Even when it is better studied, there is likely to remain a divergence of viewpoint: as we have noted, if the age was a great age, its greatness lay largely in its finesse and subtlety, its culminations of refinement, rather than in feats more immediately obvious to a human being whatever his cultural background.

Nevertheless, the age could boast glories enough of a grosser kind. The sixteenth century undeniably marks the peak of Muslim political power, taken all in all. How the Muslim powers might have fared measured against China we cannot know, but one of the three empires, the Ottoman, could alone defeat any actual alliance of Christian European powers; whereas among themselves the empires treated each other as diplomatic equals and, in such clashes as they had, showed themselves to be not far from each other's equals in power. The Özbeg state in the Syr and Oxus basins, which at first often negotiated and fought on an equal basis with the three more extensive empires, was not far behind them in power; and the Sharîfian empire of Morocco was not negligible. Two or three sultanates in southern India and other Muslim powers to the south or to the north, though they sometimes had to admit the superior greatness of one of the major empires, were themselves as strong as most Occidental powers. So far as there was any genuinely 'international' law in the world in that period, it was the body of protocol and custom that governed relations among the far-flung Muslim states; and if one had to speak of an 'international' language in the world then, it would have to be not the relatively parochial French or Latin but Persian, the language of most of their correspondence.

As we have noted, Muslim power was subjected to two great threats at the start of the sixteenth century, at the time of the great realignments: the Portuguese and the Russian. In both cases, the Ottoman empire did more than any other to meet the threats (indeed, perhaps partly out of rivalry to its peers, the Ṣafavî empire sometimes collaborated with both Christian powers for the sake of developing the north-south trade through the Persian Gulf and the Caspian Sea). Ottoman military and naval men proved themselves more adventurous with their derring-do than any self-assertive Ṣafavî painter with his sketchbooks: for a time, an Ottoman captain with a handful of men occupied the whole Swahili coast of Africa, driving out the Portuguese by sheer bluff, though for want of an adequate means of transferring naval strength out of the Mediterranean into the Indian Ocean he could not hold his position. The most distant Ottoman expedition was an abortive one to help the Muslim sultanate of Acheh at the northern tip of Sumatra. (As we shall be seeing, the wide-ranging venturesomeness of the Ottomans was almost matched by a less responsible venturesomeness in distant waters by the Maghribî privateers.)

Unfortunately, the Ottomans could never long maintain Muslim solidarity with their allies. In the south, they seized and held the coasts of the Red Sea, but in the long run the Ottomans could not have given much help to the Muslims of the Southern Seas even with full trust all round. They projected digging a canal to join the Red Sea with the Mediterranean, to facilitate both mercantile and naval contact; this might have been effective in the sixteenth century (though it could not have reversed what was to happen in the seventeenth); but the project was dropped in favour of the conquest of Cyprus—which meant a rupture with their commercial ally, Venice, for whom Cyprus was a prime base. But the southern Muslims themselves proved enterprising enough to meet the Portuguese threat reasonably well. When they found themselves unable to oust the Portuguese from Malacca, they worked out an alternative trade route which enabled them to bypass the Portuguese monopoly there. The Portuguese held on to the isolated but well chosen ports they had seized (some, partly by grace of the Ṣafavîs); they were troublesome pirates and in some areas, notably on the Swahili coast and the coast of 'Umân, they exacted tribute from all the cities of the area and tyrannized them. Like other established powers in those vast seas, they could not readily be eliminated. But they could not advance either; for even their initial technical superiority was soon lost as Muslims learned the necessary tricks. By the end of the century, the volume of Muslim trade even where they had seriously attempted to suppress it was restored or even surpassed. (Early in the seventeenth century, undermined by English and Dutch competition, they lost the favour of the Ṣafavîs; by mid-century, they were driven out of the Gulf of 'Umân and by the end of the century the Arabs of 'Umân had driven them out of the Swahili coast north of Mozambique, though they continued to hold ports elsewhere.)

Based on the Muslim commercial town Harar inland in eastern Africa from the gulf of Aden, and supported by pastoral Somalis of the region, in 1527–42 Aḥmad Grañ's troops nearly succeeded in subduing Christian Abyssinia: the third highland empire—after those of Anatolia and Iran—that had loomed in the background of the politics of Muḥammad's Mecca, and one that the first Muslims had tried and failed to conquer. As if to make up for lost time, Aḥmad destroyed churches and forced conversion to Islam, but at last the highlanders' resistance won out and Christianity was restored there. For a time thereafter the Portuguese served the Abyssinians as useful allies; but of course they could not then hope to subdue Harar and the Somalis in turn.

The strength of Islamicate society in the sixteenth century can be illustrated in the Malaysian archipelago, that focal point of hemispheric cosmopolitanism. There all four major Oikoumenic cultural heritages were in direct competition: Chinese and Japanese, Hindu Indians and Buddhist Thais, Muslims of many backgrounds, and Portuguese from the Occident all had influential footholds, and all were concerned, in some measure, to bring local affairs into their own orbits. In such competition, the Muslims won: this was a century of major Islamization.

The Russian threat in the north proved more disastrous. Here again, the

Ottomans attempted to turn it in part by an appeal to sea power; they actually started work on a canal from the Don to the Volga, which would allow them to sail direct from the Black to the Caspian seas, to join forces with the Özbegs, and incidentally to attack the Ṣafavîs from the rear. But they could no more get their northern allies to agree than their southern, and the project had to be abandoned. The khân of the Crimea went off and burned Moscow on his own (1571). The northern Turks were energetic on their own account, however; in aid of their cousins in the Irtysh basin (the original Siberia), where the Muslim population was too thin to hold the land against the advancing Russian peasantry, the rulers of Khîvah and Bukhârâ sent peasant colonists from the Oxus basin. But in the course of the century, the Russians extended their power throughout the Volga basin, and by the end of it they were ruling the northern parts of it not by way of vassals but with a direct and heavy hand.

Under Russian rule, in the khânate of Kazan especially, the landed gentry, the old aristocracy, was subjected to such pressures as practically wiped out those who would not convert to Christianity; the peasants were systematically deprived of the best lands and removed into the poorer territories and the mountains to make way for transported Slavic peasants. The Muslim merchants, however, who had already been working closely with their Muscovite counterparts before the conquest, suffered little; hence while the Muslim agrarian society was sadly depressed under the conquest, and the Turkic population diluted with aliens, the Muslim mercantile element prospered as new lines of trade were opened up with the expanding Russian and north European market, demanding furs and other products from the largely Muslim hinterland to which the Volga Bulghâr merchants had ready access.[8]

But, though a certain greatness of spirit shines through the far-flung exploits of Muslim power, true greatness in the civilization must be looked for more in the quality of cultural achievement. Here we must focus frankly on the centre, where Islamicate culture had the deepest roots—that is, especially on the domains of the Ṣafavîs, including the Shî'î Arab lands whether these were at any given moment under Ṣafavî rule or not. We have already glanced at the ferment of Persianate culture that illustrated the court of Ḥusayn Bâyqarâ at Herat. The whole age from Bihzâd the painter (b. *c.* 1450) through Mullâ Ṣadrâ the philosopher (d. 1640), in which the cultural forms associated with the Persian language culminated, ranks as something of a golden age and may usefully be called the 'Persianate flowering'.

It bears several analogies with the Italian Renaissance. As in the Occident, the achievement was centred in one relatively limited area—in sixteenth-

[8] W. E. D. Allen, *Problems of Turkish Power in the Sixteenth Century* (London, 1963), contains a far-ranging and exceedingly suggestive summary of Ottoman and central Eurasian Turkic problems and ventures, which should not be neglected, though some of his data are in dispute.

century Islamdom, Iran was that—which tended to set the fashion elsewhere; but it had other foci, often major ones: thus the Özbeg court at Bukhârâ boasted painters second in fame only to the very greatest at the Ṣafavî court and is credited with creative philosophers; while, as we shall see, some of the most important initiatives in poetry and in philosophy took form in India, as well as some of the greatest works of visual art. Though in the fifteenth century they had still formed rather a 'frontier' area, in the sixteenth century the Ottomans also participated, if perhaps rather less creatively except in the field of architecture. As in Italy, the most visible expression of the new flowering was in painting, but this was only part of a larger variety of achievement characterized by individual self-expression and very often by a sense of adventure. There was even a sense of restoration of ancient pagan norms, though this played a very subdued role as compared to the Classicism of the Renaissance. The differences were more numerous than the likenesses, of course; thus the Muslims did not adopt printing (we have seen that the Shîʿî reform, unlike the Protestant, was not popularized by the printing press). Perhaps the most decisive contrast to the Italian Renaissance is that the Persianate flowering did not lead on into Modernity, a point we shall discuss later. But there are sufficient points of analogy to make a comparison suggestive.

Unlike the Renaissance, the Persianate flowering provided an age of classical institutions for those who came after. Süleymân (1520–66) in the Ottoman empire, Akbar (1556–1605) in the Timurî empire of India, and 'Abbâs (1587–1629) in the Ṣafavî empire were regarded as model emperors whose example was to be followed and then whose times were to be restored, if possible, when the empires fell increasingly into difficulties. None were founders of their dynasties; rather, they brought to culmination some of the institutions implicit in a military patronage state; they carried their states into effective bureaucratic absolutism; and, in doing so, incidentally confirmed the bureaucratic civilianization which was to undermine the central power of these states by denaturing their military organization and discipline. All three were known for their definitive establishment of the dynastic law which in a military patronage state stood alongside Sharîʿah and local custom. Süleymân was known as *Qânûnî*, the Law-Giver, for it was under him that the increased body of Qânûn or dynastic law of the Ottoman empire was brought into what was regarded as perfected form. Akbar established not only the provincial administration but the most important precedents of his dynasty, observed largely even by those successors who disapproved his religious policy. It is said that the law code of Shâh 'Abbâs is still preserved, though it has not been studied. It is perhaps not accidental that the central empire, established in the mid-Arid Zone itself, should be the last to assume the full forms of agrarian absolutism (and prove politically the weakest of the three in their time of decline).

But like many Italian princes, most of these classical Ṣafavid and Timurid rulers, in the tradition of the patronage state, were themselves artists or poets, and so were some of the Ottoman and Özbeg rulers. More important, they patronized with a highly refined taste which included recognition for the value of the creative individual. Starting with the princes themselves, literary autobiography became fashionable—not merely the scholarly self-documentation or the spiritual witness that had been common before, but general human comment on art and letters, on travel and private events.

Painting in particular was seen as great personal achievement. Ṭahmâsp, the Ṣafavid (1524–56), was a great connoisseur and patron, seeing to the training of new painters in his royal ateliers. Even so, when Humâyûn, the Timurid (1530–56), left his refuge at Ṭahmâsp's court to regain his empire in India, he had the taste and the persistence to lure away with him some of the greatest painters, to found a school of painting in India. There was considerable international trade among the Islamicate lands in works of painting and calligraphy. Most of the routine items were presumably turned out in the workshops of regular guilds, but there was also great demand, at high prices, for pieces by famous names (such as Bihzâd), both contemporary names and those from earlier generations; these were accordingly forged in large numbers, or the appropriate signature was arbitrarily added to an unknown piece, and it was a test of connoisseurship to be able to recognize an original. How far painting was expected to go as intimate self-expression is not clear. These cultivated patrons were trained at once in philosophy, in letters, and in painting; it has been suggested that both the poetry and the painting of the time often reflected the Ishrâqî philosophy in its emphasis on the personal, transmaterial realm of the 'âlam al-mithâl. There were, indeed, some symbolic landscapes intended to illustrate explicitly mystical texts in which the transmaterial symbolic land of Hûrqalyâ was described; perhaps other paintings, illustrating standard poetry, depicted that land of Hûrqalyâ more inwardly, consistently with the inner symbolic reality of the poems themselves with their Ṣûfî overtones: in some of the landscapes one can almost see the rocks as flowingly alive (as all things are in Hûrqalyâ).[9]

The art may have been surrealistically philosophical; the philosophy, in turn, was alert to sources of pre-Islamic 'pagan' wisdom which might make it more humanistically universal. It has been suggested that in their stress on the 'âlam al-mithâl, the Iṣfahân school were playing down the emanationist system of neo-Platonism, long taken almost for granted among Muslim Philosophers, in favour of an approach closer to that of Plato himself—closer to the possibilities implicit in the 'divided line' of being in the Republic.

[9] Throughout this discussion of the social place of art (as, more generally, of the military patronage state), I must own my indebtedness to oral discussions by Martin Dixon. But he is by no means to be held responsible for the use I have made of his thoughts. He would assign the Özbeg state an equal rank, for instance, with the three empires I have given the palm to; but it seems to me that neither in area nor in durability over time nor in cultural productiveness does it rank with them, though it certainly was the same sort of state as they were, developing in the same traditions.

Certainly, these Philosophers were aware of going back of Aristotle (in whose work that of Plotinus had been confounded by way of the 'Theology of Aristotle') to Plato. These Iṣfahân Platonists, incidentally, have been compared at points with their contemporaries, the Cambridge Platonists of England. But Mullâ Ṣadrâ, at least, seems to have felt that the Ishrâqî school was going back to the ancients in a more general way. He pointed out that Yaḥyà Suhravardî had drawn inspiration, for his illuminist doctrine, from the old Iranian Mazdean tradition of the opposition between light and darkness, as well as from Plato. And one of Mullâ Ṣadrâ's teachers, Findiriskî, was associated with the work going on at the Indian court of translating Sanskrit literary and philosophical works into Persian, and must have carried the awareness that the Vedanta and Ṣûfism could be seen as identical in substance—and as perhaps equally lacking in recognition of the true imâms as keys to the whole. However broadly and 'humanistically' based the new philosophy may have been, it proved very fertile. Mullâ Ṣadrâ especially had a certain influence on a number of active and even revolutionary schools of thought which were intellectually and socially important in post-Ṣafavî Iran and seem even to have had repercussions in twentieth-century India.[10]

Shî'î Sharî'ah-mindedness

The speculative metaphysics of the age naturally arouses a certain wonder in us, if not assent. But certain more prosaic intellectual currents were constructive in their own way. Alongside the enthusiasm that built on a tradition of Falsafah, in the Ṣafavî empire, came a more legal-minded zeal, which had more evident political results in late Ṣafavî times.

Shî'ism, hitherto minoritarian, had to be adapted to the requirements of large numbers of all classes and conditions, to society as a working whole. At first, the institutional religious development had been dominated by a state official, the *ṣadr*, dispenser of governmental patronage as under the Timurids; he was charged in Ismâ'îl's time with converting everyone to Shî'ism (in the sense, at least, of cursing the first three caliphs) and with purifying everyone's morals by closing all institutions of ill repute and generally insisting on the Shar'î proprieties. But this outburst of revolutionary morality soon gave way to less exacting habits. The office of ṣadr, as state functionary, steadily declined in importance; religious appointments and policies were increasingly decided by persons who served more as spokesmen of a religious establishment already created and flourishing, rather than by a person whose authority derived primarily from the militant reforming state.

[10] The state of our knowledge of sixteenth- and seventeenth-century philosophy can be illustrated with the fact that Shabbîr Aḥmad, 'The 'Addurrat ul-Thaminah' of Mulla 'Abdul-Ḥakim of Sialkot', *Journal of the Research Society of Pakistan*, I (1964), 47–78, while frankly superficial and not very critical—merely mentioning scholars and arguments without showing their development—yet does add interesting information to what is otherwise available in Western languages.

The basis of an integrative legitimation of the Ṣafavî state had been a revolutionary principle. It necessarily faded with the restoration of agrarianate normalcy. In particular, the 'ulamâ' had been integrated under the ṣadr on a basis of a chiliastic mood of dubious orthodoxy—even though the extremer teachings of ṭarîqah Shî'ism had been avoided in the cities; now they freed themselves from such uncongenial ties. From this point on, the legitimacy of the imperial government was again thrown into question, despite its acknowledged identification with the Shî'î cause.

Shî'ism, as an oppositional movement, had developed its own authorities apart from any government; Twelver Shî'îs looked in particular to men whose outstanding piety and learning qualified them to be spokesmen of the Hidden Imâm, and who were popularly thought to be directly in touch with him. These men were qualified to investigate for themselves the evidence on points of law, and were therefore called 'mujtahids'. Jamâ'î-Sunnîs recognized the same position, in theory; but the Shî'îs, in need of charismatic leadership, continued right through the Later Middle Period to grant that the most learnèd among their 'ulamâ' were still fully competent mujtahids, in contrast to the dominant Sunnîs, who had insisted on ever closer conformity, in legal matters, to what had already come to be expected. Gradually the Shî'î mujtahids asserted their independence and took over, in the face of the dynasty, the direction of the newly prosperous Shî'ism. The Ṣafavî monarch asserted his own position as spokesman of the Hidden Imâm, and at least through the seventeenth century the bulk of the régime's supporters granted him that status. But the Shî'î 'ulamâ' in the seventeenth century were no longer willing to do so. Supported by the more pious, they insisted that (ever since the last official *vakîl*, representative of the Imâm, had died in the tenth century) only a genuinely learnèd and competent mujtahid, acknowledged personally as such by the pious, could serve as spokesman.

'Abbâs, as pâdishâh and representative of the Imâm, had felt free not only to insist on the application of customary law in criminal cases to the exclusion of the Sharî'ah law of the qâḍî's court; but even to associate the ṣadr, as authority in the Sharî'ah, with the judgments of his royal customary, non-Sharî'ah courts. That is, he still represented in his person the integration of the religious aspects of society. At the end of the century, under Shâh Sulṭân-Ḥusayn, the supremacy of the mujtahids reached its peak in the labours of the great mujtahid, Muḥammad-Bâqir Majlisî, a dogmatic and bigoted scholar who achieved great power in the state. He gathered into its most comprehensive and systematic form the whole body of received Shî'î lore on the one hand and, on the other, imposed on Ṣafavî Shî'ism his own vision of Shar'î orthodoxy. He rejected as wicked all forms of Ṣûfism, even that on which the dynasty itself had been founded; and it seems that he was able to go so far as to displace even the core of explicit members of the Ṣafavî ṭarîqah (who had largely degenerated, it seems, to a corps of palace guards).

His work bore the prosaic stamp of Sharî'ah-mindedness, but it was meant to appeal to the populace and necessarily embodied much legendary, sometimes beautiful pieces. Thus he retells an old all-Muslim story: how a sequence of angels were sent to the Earth to demand of her the clay wherewith to create Adam; and each time she fended the angel off, begging to be spared the grief of having sinful mankind made from her; till finally the angel Azrael came and, insisting on obeying God at all costs, seized the clay despite her protests. So mankind was created; but Azrael the unfeeling was made the angel of death.[11]

In the flourishing independence of the Shî'î mujtahids, latent differences came readily to the fore. Two major schools of legal thought—and therefore of theological thought generally—divided the field among them. The majority seem to have stressed constant reference to the first principles, to all the sources (*uṣûl*) of the law: these were still Qur'ân; reports about the Prophet and the imâms—among Shî'îs commonly called *akhbâr* rather than *ḥadîth*; consensus, ijmâ'—in the sense of agreement within the Shî'î community, of course; and finally reasoning, among Shî'îs not necessarily restricted to qiyâs analogy (qiyâs, as such, was in fact rejected), but forthrightly denominated 'aql, reason. The proponents of this position called themselves Uṣûlîṣ (sourcemen—the name was ancient). But a vigorously protesting movement arose, reviving a position likewise dating back at least to the twelfth century, which threw doubt on the validity of 'reason' as an independent basis of law; it stressed the massive use of whatever reports (akhbâr) were available from the Prophet and the imâms. Its proponents were called *Akhbârîs*. The Akhbârîs seem to have had an orientation similar to those Jamâ'î-Sunnî groups that especially stressed ḥadîth reports; they were suspicious of the continuing tradition represented by most of the mujtahids. Though so severely Sharî'ah-minded a man as Majlisî could be an Akhbârî, many Shî'îs of mystical tendencies also preferred the Akhbârî position, presumably as allowing them at once to claim the unimpeachable authority of literalism and also to take refuge directly in the Transcendent without the intervention of tricky reasoning.

The communal bigotry that plagued the Shî'ah naturally expressed itself even in these partisan disputes. Physical contact—even indirect contact—with an infidel was regarded as polluting—as making a person ritually unclean; hence where each party regarded the other as false to Islam, the

[11] Any great man is in opposition to the currents of his time (it is for this he stands out). If one documents his times by way of his work, this can be only by discovering either what it was he was combatting, or what it was he took for granted—in neither case, the positive substance of his own work. (Unless, indeed, the times are seen explicitly as consisting only in the top moments of high-cultural dialogue—a posture requiring special precautions.) It is a measure of the immaturity of Islamics studies that till recently scholars have often taken the explicit statements of great men as directly representative of Muslims of their time, and so missed the creativity of the great as well as the actuality of their times. Majlisî is one who has been used to exemplify his times, rather than studied for himself as yet.

ban applied mutually. It is said that later, at least, some 'ulamâ' touched the volumes in a madrasah library only through a cloth, lest the volume had been touched previously by an adherent of the opposite party. However, such pettiness need not obscure the positive role the mujtahids generally were playing. The rising military patronage states had encroached on the independence of the religious establishments as of all else; I have suggested that the doctrine of the closure of the gates of ijtihâd and that of the caliphal status of sultans who enforced the Sharî'ah may have contributed to this. It is surely not coincidence that as the empire came more and more under civilian control, an independent religious establishment free of such doctrines became more and more powerful. Indeed, in all three of the great empires, the growth of civilian control (which occurred in each of them at about the same time) was accompanied in some degree by an assertion of the independent vitality of the Shar'î tradition, though in each in quite different ways.

The excesses of centralism

In the Ṣafavî case, the absolutism into which the military patronage state had grown resulted in great concentration of wealth at the centre. With an efficient system of taxation and bureaucratic control of the revenues, an absolute monarch (even apart from the expectations of patronage already implicit in the tradition) was in a position to dispose of much greater sums than any private landlord or merchant; with husbandry, these sums need not be all dissipated into immediate luxuries and benevolences, but could be used as capital. At least from the time of Shâh 'Abbâs, the monarch was the greatest investor of capital in the realm—not only in setting up industries for court consumption, such as the production of carpets and other luxuries, but in arranging and financing the production of goods for sale, notably silk for export.

This concentration of wealth went hand in hand, I gather, with an increasing 'civilianizing' of the state, theoretically founded on military patronage but more and more the expression of an essentially civilian bureaucracy. With the empire sufficiently well ordered to enjoy peace without the constant presence of troops, this central bureaucracy came to rule directly more and more provinces in the name of the monarch, rather than leaving them as resources for the troops. Thus a minimum of wealth was expended on the dynastic soldiery, and the potential resources of the central power and of those civilians who were identified with it were further multiplied. But as financial power grew more civilian, this did not necessarily contribute to its re-diffusion—rather, at least nominally, it became still more concentrated, at least sometimes to the point of inhibiting or curtailing alternative concentrations of wealth among badly placed privileged private individuals. Yet at the same time the freedom of initiative of the monarch seems to have been curtailed. Thus the empire was yielding to classical dangers of agrarian

The Ṣafavî Empire and Its Successors to 1779

1502–24	Shâh Ismâ'îl Ṣafavî carves out a Turco-Persian Shî'î empire in Iran, persecutes Sunnîs, suppresses Ṣûfî orders
1524–76	Ṭahmasp I, second Ṣafavî, strengthens Shî'î dominance; his court a center of art
1535–36	Death of Bihzâd, foremost miniature painter
1558	Death of Zaynuddîn al-'Âmilî, Shî'î theologian
1583	Death of Vahshî of Bafq, romantic and Ṣûfî poet
1587–1629	Shâh 'Abbâs I enlarges the Iranian empire, driving advancing Özbegs out of Khurâsân and the Ottomans out of Azerbaijan and Iraq; builds Iṣfahân magnificently; patron of Riżà-i'Abbâsî, most remarkable painter of Iṣfahânî school, showing some Western influence
1590s	Rise of 'Indian' (Sabkh-i Hindi) ornamental style in poetry
1620–21	Death of 'Baha'i' (Bahâuddîn Muḥ. 'Âmilî), anecdotal and entertaining Ṣûfî poet, Shî'î theologian, mathematician
1629–94	Three reigns in the Ṣafavî empire dominated by harem politics; Iraq lost to the Ottomans (but many of its population remain Shî'î); otherwise the empire retains peace and prosperity
1630	Death of Mîr Dâmâd, Shî'î theologian, in the Ishrâqî, Iṣfahânî school of metaphysics
1694–1722	Ḥusayn, the last effective Ṣafavî shâh, rules Iran with Shî'î intolerance; his rule put to an end by Afghan revolt, which takes Iṣfahân, massacres Persian nobility
1700	Death of Muḥ. Bâqir Majlisî, Shî'î scholar and theologian, vizier
1726–47	Nâḍir Shâh (ruling through puppets till 1736) briefly restores military fortunes of the Iranian Shî'î empire without reviving its cultural splendor
1750–79	Karîm Khân Zand, of Shîrâz, gives most of Iran a benevolent peace in the midst of a period of civil wars among various Turkish tribes aiming at rule
1779	Muḥammad Aga Khân founds Qâjâr dynasty, under which strong central government is re-established in Iran
1718	Peace of Passarowitz, second major Ottoman defeat to Habsburgs
1718–30	'Tulip Age' under Sultan Aḥmad III and his vizier Nevshehirli Ibrâhîm Pasha, first serious attempts at Westernizing reform, Ibrâhîm Müteferrika establishes first Ottoman printing press 1726; but reforms end with Patrona Revolt of 1730 by Janissaries and Istanbul populace
1730–54	Maḥmûd I, with peace for the Ottoman empire after victorious treaties in 1739 with Austria and Russia as a result of division among the European states
1757–73	Musṭafà III, able Ottoman sultan who despite desire for peace and sound rule becomes embroiled in war with Russia, resulting in total defeat of Ottoman armies

1774	Treaty of Kuchuk Kaynarji, Ottomans lose Crimea, tsar recognized as protector of Orthodox Christians in Ottoman lands
1789–1807	Selîm III lays groundwork for subsequent Westernizing reforms, establishes first formal Ottoman embassies in European capitals

absolutism. Whether the whole process was disadvantageous or not for the interests of masses of the population, the concentration of wealth at Iṣfahân surely reduced the flexibility of the society and the ability of its prosperity to survive any severe blow that might be dealt the central power. And though the centre was not, I gather, embarrassed, as have been so many states, by lack of funds; yet it was still vulnerable to internal paralysis.

The vulnerability was increased by a dynastic policy initiated by Shâh 'Abbâs himself—a policy based (I suppose) on personal suspiciousness, but also doubtless fostered by the civilian administrators, glad to immobilize the only natural head of the military. To avoid anticipatory rebellions among his heirs (still subject to the rule of succession by contest), 'Abbâs introduced the custom of immuring the princes royal within the female quarters of the palace. There they were effectively insulated from possible conspiracies—and from practical experience. Most of his successors were alternately bloodthirsty and ineffective. But the administration was sufficiently well-rooted so that it took its own course.

The first successor, Shâh Ṣafî (1629–42), loved to execute the great, and the net effect was to heighten the lone position of the throne. It was under him that was introduced the practice of treating the revenues of whole provinces as due directly to the royal treasury, rather than leaving them largely with the local military administration; only a minimum remained for provincial affairs. This practice was extended to all the safe, interior provinayces aw from the frontiers, and hence largely disarmed, under the next monarch, 'Abbâs II (1642–67); who, indeed, was unusually capable and personally helped sustain the prestige of the monarchy. Under Sulaymân (1667–94), the chief vizier, head of the bureaucracy, was effective ruler, at the expense of both the army and the privileged landed classes.

By the time of Shâh Sulṭân-Ḥusayn (1694–1722), the bureaucratic centralization of the state structure was weakened through incompetence, and cloven by bigotry in high places. As we have noted, the evolving establishment of Shîʿî 'ulamâ' had reached the point of full independence from the agrarianate state; but now the state, already threatened with doubts of its Shîʿî legitimacy, ceased to be independent of the 'ulamâ'. Some of them tried to retrieve the claims to legitimacy of the Shîʿî empire by way of a rigourist dominance by the 'ulamâ' themselves. Under an incompetent monarch they were allowed not only to eliminate the last traces of the dynasty's original religious support, the Ṣafavî ṭarîqah, but to accentuate antagonisms within the bureaucracy, deprived of a firm hand on the part of the monarch. For even the bureaucracy, Sharîʿah-minded or no, could no longer be long held together without effective presence of the absolute head.

Now the latent vulnerability of the system emerged. The Iraq and its holy places, indeed, had already been lost to the Ottomans in 1638 soon after ʿAbbâs I's time. Under Sultan-Ḥusayn, rebellion and invasion loomed on many frontiers; the state seemed powerless to respond to the challenge. In due time, rebellious Afghan tribal forces swept in unhindered from the east, sacked Iṣfahân (1722), and put an effective end to the dynasty in a sudden overwhelming disaster.

II

The Indian Timurî Empire: Coexistence of Muslims and Hindus, 1526–1707

Unlike the Ṣafavî, the other two great empires rose in regions still largely non-Muslim, and this fact contributed both to their strengths and to their weaknesses. But in different ways: for I think the differences in their relations to their non-Muslims account, in some small measure, for the differences in destiny between the two empires.

In Europe, though the Muslims had occupied the older creative centres, yet the larger part of the area of high culture to the north and west was beyond their grasp. European civilization continued independent of Muslim power. And Islamicate society came very nearly to ignore it after the first generations. In India, on the contrary, not only the classical creative centres in the north came under Muslim rule; almost the whole subcontinent did so as well, and the only remaining independent foci of culture of a Sanskritic type were in relatively backward pockets on the continent and in those parts of further India that Muslims did not come to dominate in turn; and those countries, in any case, did not do for the Indic culture what the Slavs and the Latins did for the European. The centres of Indic culture had to integrate the Islamic presence intimately into their views of the world. Yet the Indic heritage, like the European, persisted vital and creative even in the uncongenial circumstances. It was not only preserved, among the Hindus that submitted to Muslim rule; above all in the religious and intellectual spheres, it was further developed and perhaps even extended into some new areas. And even Muslims might foster it. Earlier Indo-Muslim rulers had already sometimes encouraged the development of the Sanskritic literary traditions in the medium of the various vernacular languages that had come to be used; this was further encouraged by the Timurî court. In any case, relations to the indigenous heritage were always a live issue.

The Islamicate culture found many Hindus (particularly of certain clerical castes) ready to participate in it even though they did not become Muslims. This of itself had consequences. Except in point of religion, Muslims and Hindus often shared the same arts and learning. Especially in northern India, many Hindus read Persian (and some Muslims read Hindi); the cultivated painting and, to a degree, architecture of Muslims and Hindus, their music, and in many polished circles their manners also gradually came to be essentially at one; and (whatever Indic elements might be included) this unity was on terms set by the Muslims and mostly in close continuity with the cultural forms of Islamdom at large. Muslim and Hindu grandee families regarded each other as substantially on a level (not without a certain explicit rivalry). Even the customs of an independent Hindu state, like the powerful empire of Vijayanagar in the south, were heavily influenced by Islamicate ways.[1] On neither side, to be sure, was the decisive difference in religion ever forgotten.

This high culture was Islamicate in that it was a development, on the whole, within Islamicate traditions; even when the Muslim Indians—and their Hindu friends of Islamicate tendencies—broke with an Islamicate past, this was precisely in response to that past; it was an intensification of the Islamicate dialogue, not the adoption of a different one. At the same time, the culture was unmistakably Indian—not so much in the sense of attaching itself to the Sanskritic tradition (the Islamicate culture made much use of elements that can be called Sanskritic, but they were structurally subordinated) as in the sense that it expressed in a new form the persistent individuality of India as a region in the Afro-Eurasian Oikoumene, with its regional predispositions, deriving not only from its cultural resources but from its natural resources and from its continuing relation to the rest of the Oikoumene. The culture of Muslim India can be seen with equal legitimacy as a chapter in Indic history and as a chapter in Islamicate history, according to the sort of questions one is asking.

This interconfessional Islamicate culture of India developed in a setting of agrarianate prosperity at its fullest phase, when a bureaucratic absolutism, with the relative peacefulness and bureaucratic prudence it produced, was at its height. In this setting, far-reaching moral questions could be posed about the meaning of the high culture and what might be achieved toward human fulfillment in it, questions that might seem almost academic in a less prosperous age, unless posed in a radically chiliastic mood; and sophisticated moral initiatives could be launched, both to maintain the prosperity and to make it more just or more fruitful. Such questions and such initiatives had to come to terms with the contrasting cultural traditions within which they took form, and most particularly with the contrasting religious traditions within which vision might be sought. Hence what should be the role of Islam itself as core of a cultural complex was freely at issue for a time.

But then the prosperity proved ephemeral—as, in societies on the agrarianate level, such prosperity always had; the very mechanisms that produced it proved its undoing. And none of the diverse moral initiatives launched in the

[1] W. H. Moreland, in *India at the Death of Akbar: An Economic Study* (London, 1920), p. 24, pointed out the Islamicate penetration of Hindu kingdoms. Details have been added by H. K. Sherwani, 'Culture and Administrative Set-up under Ibrahim Qutb-Shahi, 1550–80', *Islamic Culture*, 31 (1957), 127–41, in regard to the Andhra region.

mood of prosperity was able to halt the decline. This fact in itself, even apart from any other limitations we find in them, can serve to illuminate the strengths and weaknesses of the moral efforts of the time. In some ways, the moral challenges met with in this period may serve to complement, in retrospect, those of the Middle Periods, set in a social order in which military anarchy always threatened; in the two periods together, all the resources of the Islamic vision for the Agrarian Age in its contrary phases would seem to have been displayed.

The developments in the Timurî empire in India may have been more diverse and suggestive, intellectually and spiritually, than in the Ottoman or even, perhaps, the Ṣafavî empires, where a rather similar phase of agrarianate-level prosperity prevailed; so that the moral possibilities emerge for us most clearly in India. But these developments in the Timurî empire have been specially illuminated for us by twentieth-century events. In the debates between Hindus and Muslims, and between communalist and anti-communalist Muslims à propos of the creation of Pakistan, the Timurî period has served as testing ground for modern theories. Some scholars have insisted on the Islamicate, others on the Indian character of the political and cultural achievements of the time.

The interpretation of the fall of Muslim power has been especially fertile in controversy. It had been a thesis of earlier British historians, that Akbar, emperor at the end of the sixteenth century, had built up the empire on the basis of tolerance between the religious communities, whereas Awrangzêb, emperor at the end of the seventeenth century, had ruined it by adopting instead a communalist policy which set the religious communities at odds. The Muslim communalist historians built on this thesis, only giving it a loyalist twist: Awrangzêb became their hero (and Akbar their villain), on the ground that what mattered even more than the empire was the maintenance of the Muslim community in its separate purity, and Awrangzêb, in his communalism, had at least assured that. They found other heroes, too, in several more or less communal-minded Muslims of the period, whose influence they tended to exaggerate. The anti-communalist historians (Muslim and non-Muslim) answered by depreciating the influence of these heroes and even of Awrangzêb himself, in part by insisting on the uncontrollable economics of the decline. On both sides, Akbar was reassessed in ways as diverse as the historians who reassessed him. As a result, the inquirer finds opened up to him a considerable body of significant data, even though it is hard to find a reasonably neutral guide through the debates.

The centralizing of administration: the empire of Akbar

The most important founder of the new political forms in India was an Indian Muslim of Afghân family—one of the many Afghân families that had taken the lead as Muslim soldiers and landlords under the later Delhi sultanate as

Turks became less numerous. Sher-Shâh Sûr rose by administrative talent to the rule of Bihâr and from that position led the Indian effort to expel the Timurîs. Seizing power in 1540 on the basis of that leadership, between that year and his death in 1545 he laid the basis—in taxation and monetary policy, in organizing public works, and even in the realm of monumental art—for an imperial state which lasted (under Bâbur's Timurid line) for two centuries. Those new political forms, even in Sher-Shâh's hands, were partly based on Bâbur's example and hence on the tradition of the military patronage states; but they were initially worked out by local Muslims, especially the Afghan leadership, in co-operation with some Hindus; and were turned against the foreign Muslim domination represented by Bâbur. Despite the large element of foreign influence that eventually did come in with the establishment of Bâbur's line, they provided a framework for the flowering of a distinctive Indo-Muslim society.

The Sûr rulers, Sher-Shâh and his able son, had thirteen years between them to try to inculcate into their fellow Afghans, as dominant military element of Muslim north India, a disciplined loyalty to a common throne; and to train a corps of administrators ready to carry out the uniform and efficient organization that Sher-Shâh had tried to establish. Then, on the son's death, the Afghan grandees fell to fighting among themselves. Meanwhile, Bâbur's sons and the Timurî grandees with them were restricted, for the most part, to the remains of the Timurî domains in the Afghan mountains. Eventually, however, the ablest of them, Humâyûn, who had held the throne of Hindûstân (north India) for ten adventurous years after Bâbur's death, got control of the dynastic headquarters at Kâbul; in 1555 he led the Timurî forces down into the plains, where they routed the divided Afghans and re-established Timurî authority at Delhi and Agra.[2] Almost immediately the much-adventured Humâyûn died, leaving his newly won power to his minor

[2] The line founded by Bâbur in India, with the state it ruled, is commonly referred to as 'Mughal' (or 'Mogul' in an old spelling). This is the Indo-Persian form of the word 'Mongol'; it was applied to the Chaghatay Turkic military when they came into India, on account of their association with the Mongol traditions in the Oxus basin, distinguishing them especially from the Afghân military class which had entered India rather earlier and held power under the Lodî dynasty.

The term is awkward when the history of India is considered in a wider Islamicate context. The Chaghatay Turks, under rulers of Timur's line, were not Mongols; in the Syr-Oxus basin they were sharply distinguished from the Mongols or Mughals of 'Mughalistân', though continuing some relations with them. To use the term 'Mughal' rather than 'Timurî' is unsuitable, therefore, in describing the greater part of Bâbur's career, much of Humâyûn's, and even later activities in Kâbul or Kashmîr, where the actual Mongols, or Mughals, were involved as opponents. The correct name for the dynasty itself is 'Timurid', Timur being the recognized founder of their power. The correct term for the original body of their followers is 'Chaghatay'; but for the very mixed body of families that ultimately served them, only 'Timurî' will do—or 'Indo-Timurî', Timurî of India, wherever they must be distinguished from the Timurî nobles of an earlier period in Irân-and-Tûrân.

Subsequently, the term 'Mughal', in India, was applied to Chaghatay and other families that had served the Timurids; hence within the Indian context it has some legitimacy. Yet even there it remains unfortunate. 'Mughal' and 'Mongol' differ only in

son, Akbar (1556–1605). For four years a dependable regent maintained the Timurî Indian power more or less intact. (One of his major battles was at Pânîpat, like Bâbur's most decisive battle. At the age of seventeen, in 1560, the young Akbar took power into his own hands.

Akbar had a long reign. In the course of it he achieved the substance of what the Sûrs were aiming at, though on a different basis; and much besides. He replaced the Afghan solidarity based on inherited Indian holdings with the solidarity of families directly dependent on the Timurî court, most of the leading ones being immigrants from abroad like the Timurids themselves. On this basis he rounded out a vast and reasonably well integrated empire over all northern India (together with the eastern edge of the Iranian highlands); and this empire he subjected to an effective absolutism based on central bureaucratic control. He then tried to make of his empire a model society graced by all the accomplishments of humane civilization, with justice for the peasantry, and for the privileged all the arts in their highest forms.

For a number of years, Akbar used diplomacy almost as much as the military force of the central authority to establish his personal power in the realm; but by about 1567, he emerged undisputed master of the greater part of north India. His initial domains then included not only most of Hindûstân proper (the Ganges plain) and Panjâb, but Mâlvâ (the upper Chambal basin) south of the Ganges plain, and the overlordship of many marginal territories. It was in this area that Akbar's administrative measures were most fully applied. But throughout Akbar's life the empire continued to be extended (largely at the expense of other Muslim dynasties). By 1573, he had incorporated the powerful Muslim kingdom of Gujarât and had made vassals of most of the (Hindu) Râjpût states in Râjpûtânâ; by 1576, the remaining Afghan strongholds in Bihar and Bengal had been incorporated. (In 1592 Orissa also was conquered.) By 1585, Akbar had reasserted Timurî power in the northwestern mountains in the face of the continuing Özbeg challenge, assuming direct control of Kâbul (where for some time he had had to allow a brother independent rule) and occupying Kashmîr. By 1595, he had taken Qandahâr, the remaining possession of Bâbur's in that area, which had been occupied by the Ṣafavîs; having come round to it by way of a conquest of Sind (and eventually Baluchistan). By 1600, he had subdued even the north Deccan kingdom of Aḥmadnagar, and had made the two other Muslim kingdoms of the Deccan stand in awe of Timurî power. This was the widest empire India had seen since the height of the Delhi sultanate. It was built far more durably.

Humâyûn and Akbar inherited from the Afghan Sûr rulers, if not in full practice, at least in principle, a fairly sound pattern of taxation based on

spelling. Some unthinking writers have actually substituted 'Mongol', seeking consistency. Yet to refer to the empire of Akbar as the 'Mongol Empire' is not merely confusing, it is seriously misleading.

direct arrangement by the central authorities with the villages, and assessed chiefly by prior calculation of yield rather than shares in the crop. Even this pattern Akbar improved; in the greater part of his domains he introduced (1575–80) a standard assessment of tax obligations based on the average yield over a supposedly typical ten-year period. The tax rate was high, as in most Agrarian Age lands—commonly one-third of the produce; but while the state agreed to cushion a very bad year with remission of taxes, any extra advantages of a good year came back largely to the villages themselves; and all concerned could predict obligations and returns with relative certainty. The details of the assessment were framed to encourage more effective use of under-used lands. Akbar found skilled and devoted revenue ministers, Muslim and Hindu, in whose hands the system was sufficiently efficient to enable him, despite his far-flung conquests and his dislike of extra taxes, to amass a considerable reserve treasury.

Akbar's fiscal organization had to be accompanied by an appropriate military organization. About the same time, then, as the establishment of the standard assessment, he arranged the distribution of the revenue to the administrators and especially the military in a manner consistent with full central control. The old Mongol-Timurî way of regarding the central power as one great army at the personal behest of the sultan was retained (though even here he followed some leads of Sher-Shâh), but it became the vehicle for a very flexible system of graded rankings of office holders, *manṣabdârs*, in a bureaucracy. Each officer was assigned, as manṣabdâr, the revenue of lands which (by prior assessment) were ascertained to yield a certain amount, at which his salary was fixed. Technically, the salary amounted to what he would require for raising and equipping a certain number of men for the army—five hundred, say, or one thousand, or five thousand, though actual contingents were not expected in clearly civilian cases.

Though the salary was fixed on a cash basis, the officer was expected, in peacetime, to visit the lands whose revenue was assigned him so as to supervise its raising himself (under the regulations of the revenue bureaus); these lands were called his *jâgîr*, his holding, the Indian equivalent of iqṭâ'. Presumably this arrangement was in part a concession to a preference of the officers for direct contact with the source of their revenue, avoiding middlemen from the revenue bureaus; and in part a recognition that, in fact, in such a vast territory an extended bureaucracy would be inefficient as compared with direct collection by those to whom the revenue was due—though such of the revenue as did not go to particular officers was, of course, always collected by agents of the central revenue bureaus. (For a time, central collection of all revenues was attempted, but this did not commend itself.) Control by the central revenue bureaus (so long as major corruption in them could be avoided) was ensured by frequent changes of jâgîr land assignments among the officers, which changes were in any case made necessary by the careful regulation of their salaries: at each promotion, a larger amount of jâgîr land had to be assigned to the man promoted, and this entailed a general reshuffling of all jâgîrs.[3]

Akbar instituted many measures, then, to avoid corruption or fraud either in the bureaus or among the officers, to ensure that the revenues were used for the military purposes intended, and the peasantry not abused above the set rates; in particular, he attempted to reduce the scale of fraud at military musters (where officers were wont to pass off their troops or animals as more numerous than they actually were), and by sheer personal attentiveness he had some success. But he did not neglect the necessity for more institutional forms of control. The most important task was to extend an effective imperial bureaucracy throughout the provinces, rather than leaving everything to the governors and their own appointees. Akbar organized strong but subordinate provincial governments (which the Delhi sultanate had never had) in each of the natural areas of the empire, co-ordinating their ministries with the system of ministries at the capital. This system made possible the general exercise of direct imperial authority. It also gave sufficient substance to the state to hinder a division of it among the ruler's sons, like a personal estate, as had been customary among the Timurids till his time. Thus, as in Iran and in the Ottoman realm, a state with a background of military patronage practices was moulded into a bureaucratic absolutism.

Like the Ṣafavîs, the Indian Timurîs inherited the Timurî tradition of dynastic intervention in religious affairs through the ṣadr, the scholar appointed by the ruler to be in charge of grants of land or income made to 'ulamâ' and pîrs. With the development of the central power, the ṣadr acquired increasing authority over the more official religious personnel of the empire. An essential move on Akbar's part was to ensure his personal control over the activities of the ṣadr (which he did through a controversial dismissal of a powerful ṣadr and the reassertion of the ruler's right of dismissal as well as appointment). Even more important was the redistribution of the grants that had been given to religious figures; this involved the resumption, at least in part, of some of the larger grants, over many protests, and especially the attendance at court of the beneficiary, at least once, if he was to maintain the benefice. Considering the tradition among many pîrs of aloofness from the court of any military ruler, this measure affirmed symbolically the dependence henceforth of the religious life of the Indian Muslims (like the rest of their high culture) upon the central government and its courtly orientation. The culture of the market place could not be fully dominated by the court, of course, but it was to be secondary.

At the same time as the general reorganization of the administration, Akbar almost necessarily attended to the basis of legitimation for his power. Like the Ṣafavî ruler, Akbar tried to ground the growing central authority in

[3] Through much of this chapter, I have been greatly helped by the comments of Professor Irfan Habib, though I have had to differ from him on occasion.

explicitly Islamic principles. He asserted the prevailing Philosophical doctrine of the caliphal role of whatever ruler applied the Sharî'ah—or, more generally, justice—in his dominions, as it had been developed in the Later Middle Period, for instance by Davvânî. With his characteristic energy and conscientiousness, he went so far as to assert this symbolically by personally leading the ṣalât worship as imâm, in the manner of the early caliphs—a practice that had rarely been followed by Indian rulers. For a few years, he was very solicitous of the Shar'î 'ulamâ' scholars, giving them many grants, and even imposing the jizyah tax on non-Muslims for a short time. He also insisted on a more innovative step, which grounded his position in the system of the Sharî'ah itself by a slight reinterpretation of the Shar'î tradition: he persuaded the chief 'ulamâ' to declare (1579) that the just ruler (Akbar being declared to be so) had the authority to decide which of divergent opinions in fiqh, when mujtahids disagreed, was to be applied in his domains. If this approach had been carried through, it would have meant at least a thorough assimilation of the Sharî'ah by agrarian absolutism. But the Shar'î structure was too independent for such a reform to have been easily carried far, and in any case Akbar soon became disillusioned with the 'ulamâ' and lost much of his interest in a Shar'î legitimation. In time, as we shall see, Akbar preferred to rest his legitimation on bases derived more from Falsafah.

This shift of focus followed suppression of a rebellion of the Muslim officers in the east Ganges area, which had not been without overtones of a Sharî'ah-minded criticism of Akbar; but the shift occurred in part because the empire was coming to be based less exclusively on Muslim support, so that a more neutral legitimation might seem appropriate at least by way of supplement. Indian Muslim rulers had long been accustomed to make use of Hindus along with Muslims not only in financial administration (where as heirs to local tradition they were naturally competent) but occasionally in such posts as military command. Under Akbar, this practice was emphasized. (The neutrality of foreign Muslims as between local Muslims and Hindus probably made it easier.) The very expansion of the fiscal administrative apparatus necessarily brought into greater prominence Hindu clerks. But even in the armed forces, as the empire was consolidated on a large scale, the rise of unconverted Hindus to the highest posts was no longer exceptional.

The state continued to be unmistakably a Muslim state, and most high positions were held by Muslims. But Akbar made special use of the military talents and of the disciplined manpower of the Râjpût chieftains and their men, who held the various hill districts south of the Ganges basin, especially in Râjpûtânâ. The proudest of the Râjpût houses, that of Mewar, alone refused to submit; the gallant Rânâ (prince) of Mewar was still a fugitive, free though in the wilderness, when Akbar died; his story has become the stuff of legend. But most of these princely houses were firmly allied to the Timurid throne—in many cases by marriages (on an unprecedentedly voluntary basis) of the daughters of Râjpût rulers with the Timurid ruling family. (The later Timurids were chiefly of Râjpût ancestry save in the direct male line.) Accordingly, though Akbar's empire was Muslim in its foundation and in the ultimate locus of its power, yet Hindus and Muslims co-operated effectively in its actual management, and jointly reaped its benefits in wealth and splendour. This fact gave urgency to universalist inclinations to disregard communal lines between Muslims and others, inclinations shared by Akbar with an increasing number of thoughtful persons in India, both Muslim and Hindu.

Universalism in Indic religious life

Certainly something of the strength of the central Timurî power, as of other central powers of the time, derived from the offensive power of artillery. The Timurîs are famous for their ever more gigantic cannon, which played a large, if not fully decisive, role in the taking of the storied fortresses between the Ganges plain and the Deccan. But at least as essential was a certain cultural sophistication which lent glamour to the Islamicate centres and in particular to the central imperial court. Probably without the development of a cultural life that could appeal to both Muslims and Hindus at a very high level, even in some sense catering to their moral awareness, a vast bureaucracy based on mixed cadres, Muslim and Hindu, could not have functioned so smoothly. The brilliant Timurî cultural traditions lent themselves to this. The post-Mongol sense of the independent human worth of, say, an artistic creation allowed the religious allegiance of a painter to be overlooked even while he received social recognition. Non-Muslims could thus potentially enter into Islamicate cultural life at perhaps even more intimate a level than had been the case since classical 'Abbâsî times; in India, at least, they seem to have done so. But Akbar added important touches of his own to this interconfessional cultural sophistication. He deliberately tried to create a high interconfessional moral and even religious level through the example of the court itself and even in some measure through legislation.

Since the rise of the great confessional religions after the Axial Period, the religious history of India had been at least as complex as that of any other of the major Afro-Eurasian regions. Several major religious traditions had, of course, originated in India, especially in north India. The major Indian religious traditions (Vaishnava and Shaiva) in common recognized the priestly status of the Brahmans, hereditary carriers of the sacred Vedic literature. (Any group that accepted the Brahmaṇs in that status is called 'Hindu', whatever its particular beliefs or practices.) There were some sects that did not accept the Brahmans; of these, Buddhism as such had died out in India proper some time back, but the Jains continued to form a powerful group, especially in Gujarât and Kannada. Even among those that accepted the Brahmans, however, there were in practice almost as many religious cults as castes, for each caste had its own devotional forms and deities. Religious diversity, then, was well rooted.

There had been some attempts at religious uniformism in the period when the confessional religions had, as elsewhere, come to be associated with political power and dominate social life; there had been some persecution between Shaivites and Vaishnavites. But this had been discouraged by the Indian development of caste multiplicity; the lands of the Sanskritic tradition finally emerged unusually free of religious intolerance. Accordingly, India was religiously, as well a geographically, a natural haven for sects of all sorts, notably from the Nile-to-Oxus region. Their representatives came to India, normally, as traders, found safety from the persecutions or at least social disabilities so typical of the lands from Nile to Oxus even under the relative tolerance of Islam, and stayed to convert and flourish; forming, in effect, new (though non-Brahmanic) castes. Jacobite Christians, Jews, Zoroastrians, Ismâʻîlî Shîʻîs of more than one variety, all had their own recognized place and dignity.

Normally, this tolerant diversity was maintained through insulating the several religious communities severely from each other—through the rigidity of their caste character, which prevented close social mingling. Nevertheless it always presented the potentiality, to alert minds, for mutual confrontation and even understanding. Indic religious thought, particularly in communities of Indic origin, developed a firm tradition of universalism—the idea that all the various religious forms represent diverse paths to the one Truth, paths which are all in some degree valid. Such a universalism was, of course, not unique to India; many Ṣûfîs had admitted the abstract principle at least, in the Earlier Middle Period. In India it became a practical ground for interpreting the relations among religious communities.

In the fourteenth and fifteenth centuries, the most creative forms of Hindu spirituality were popular devotional movements stressing inward love for the One Deity beyond any precision of ritual or of social condition. Such movements lent themselves singularly well to a quite practical application of the universalist spirit. Persons of all castes were generally welcomed together into these movements, and even a few Muslims became devotees. Indeed, sometimes Muslims took the initiative. Some of the leading Ṣûfîs were willing to accept a certain number of unconverted Hindu followers (without, to be sure, ever giving up the aim of conversion, so crucial to a monotheistic outlook). At least one movement with important Muslim participation, that of Kabîr, rejected explicitly the Islamic claim to exclusive allegiance, but made a point of using both Muslim and Hindu symbolism and of insisting on the identity of the spiritual realities underlying the two traditions. Kabîr (1440–1518) of Banaras was of a Muslim family of a caste that probably retained some of its pre-Islamic religious traditions, in this case a tradition of dissident (perhaps Buddhist) religiosity stressing self-control. Kabîr moved in Ṣûfî circles, and apart from some Sanskritic terms his attitude would be undistinguishable from that of Ṣûfî circles hostile to both Ṣûfî and Shar'î establishments.[4] Kabîr's life already suggests that, in the circles where he moved, formal religious allegiance was felt to be secondary to spiritual attitude.

At the beginning of the sixteenth century was founded, in Panjâb, the most powerful of all these movements, that of the Sikhs. It was inspired in part by Kabîr and other devotional leaders, and like Kabîr insisted specially on the spiritual unity of the truths of Islam and Hinduism. The founder, Guru Nânak (b. 1469) seems to have inspired respect in members of all religious communities; he preached what has universally been acclaimed as a very pure ethic, grounded in a strict monotheism. On his death, the Sikhs turned to a succession of spiritual guides (for whom was used the Sanskritic term *guru*—while some other terms used were Persian), each of whom added something to his spiritual heritage.

But such a 'universalist' approach was naturally not satisfactory to all Hindus nor to all Muslims. Its premises were contradicted by what may be called a 'communalist' approach, though what 'communalism' meant was very different on the Hindu side from what it meant on the Muslim side. For Muslims, it was traditionally axiomatic that just as there was one God to worship, who maintained the unity of the moral realm, so there was one community that could claim human allegiance, guarding the revealed standards of moral and spiritual life, including proper doctrine. Those for whom spiritual responsibility carried with it a maintenance of the divinely imposed discipline of that community could see a universalist approach only as irresponsible sentimentalism. For them a particularist, ahistorically defined, communal loyalty was an essential defence against dissolution of religion—and of social order—into arbitrary individual whims. Accordingly, Sharî'ah-mindedness quite naturally, even apart from any particular prescriptions, carried with it a Muslim communalism, and that communalism must, for the same reasons, be either Sunnî or Shî'î.

On the Hindu side, the same defence against dissolution into individual whims was expressed by insistence on caste rules and on reverence for the dignity of Brahmans rather than by allegiance to a single community or its creed; Hindu communalists need not stress, for instance, allegiance to Vaishnavism or Shaivism. But implicitly commitment to the overall community that carried the tradition of caste rules was at stake here too, and the same term, 'communalism', may be used. But one must remember that Hindu communalism, unlike Muslim, made no requirement about the religious allegiance of the ruling class, who could believe what they pleased so long as they respected the Brahmans.

Among the Hindus, parallel to the rise of the universalist devotional move-

[4] Cf. Charlotte Vaudeville, 'Kabîr and Interior Religion', *History of Religions*, 3 (1964), 191–201; however, she defines 'Ṣûfism' too narrowly and so misjudges Kabîr's relations to it.

ments just mentioned, there had been a contrasting movement, doubtless in part in defence against the dissolving effects of Muslim egalitarianism, to tighten up the lines of social solidarity and continuity within Hindu groups. This took the form, for instance, of a stricter interpretation of caste rules, reflected in the commentaries on the sacred law written at that period. Intercaste mingling of all kinds—including mingling with Muslims—was discouraged, and in the niceties of private ritual was sought strength to maintain inherited standards in spite of the rejection of the Brahmanic intellectual and spiritual leadership by the Muslim ruling classes. On the Muslim side, there had been a persistent distrust of the more latitudinarian Ṣûfîs among the more Sharî'ah-minded. For a time in Delhi the leading pîrs were banned and they had to seek disciples only in the provincial cities. The Muslim consciousness of a social mission to rule the world on the basis of God's law persisted, if not always clearly differentiated from a conviction of the sovereign dignity of Turks as privileged fighting men, as well as of the Iranian culture they protected.

Late in the fifteenth century, under the Lôdî rulers, the demands for an Islamic social order were uncompromisingly set forth by Sayyid Muḥammad of Jaunpur, who claimed to be the promised Mahdî. (His followers were termed *Mahdavîs*.) Taking his cue from Qur'ânic passages, he taught that among the Muslims a special band should be dedicated actively to upholding the Sharî'ah law, not as ordinary amîrs, nor even as regular muftîs and qâḍîs, but as preachers—and, in the view of some of his followers, also as a sort of vigilante body, prepared to intervene wherever justice was miscarrying. To be free to fill this function, the élite should be bound to absolute poverty—trusting (like some Ṣûfîs) absolutely to God and to the current and purely spontaneous gifts of the pious for their sustenance; whatever they received above their barest needs on a given day was to be passed on to the poor. From this detached perspective they could look on the amîr and the humblest Muslim soldier or craftsman as equals, to be addressed with the same simple civility, and to be assured the same Sharî'ah-fixed rights. Property that had originated in ways illegal according to the Sharî'ah was regarded as illegitimate; family distinctions based not on piety but on worldly prestige were to be ignored; hence most current social privilege, whether in rights to income or in prestige, was condemned. By such standards, not only the received Sunnî establishment, both amîrs and 'ulamâ', must be eliminated piecemeal if not more rapidly, but even the more established Shî'î families must come under the same ban. All society must be reordered.

By sanctioning direct armed intervention by its followers, the movement in Sûr times was ready to put its principles into effect wherever its followers happened to be, without awaiting major military victories. It was perhaps the most thoroughgoing attempt, since the Khârijî movement in Marwânî times, to place Islamic social responsibility squarely on the shoulders of plain

Muslim believers and to strike down all the social distortions introduced by wealth and descent. It introduced a novel approach to implementation, which was doubtless as appropriate to the times as any so uncompromising a partisanship of justice could have found. A series of dedicated leaders patiently suffered torments and death rather than abjure their position; the movement seems to have become quite popular among townsmen and the common soldiery in the Ganges plain; within a generation it had spread south into the Deccan, and it became a major power to be reckoned with in the politics of some of the Muslim sultanates there. For its time, it reaffirmed the special historical mission of Islam as a power for truth in the world over against other, ungodly powers.

Of the two orientations, Akbar was more moved by the universalist appeal. He showed respect for the Ṣûfî pîrs, especially those of the Chishtî order, noted for its relatively universalist tendencies; and is claimed to have honoured even the Sikh gurus of his time. Even in the first years of his reign, his reforms took a direction that reflected respect for other faiths; they were less purely Sharîʿah-oriented than the typical reforms Muslim rulers commonly proclaimed in inaugurating a new reign, abolition of non-Sharîʿah trade and market taxes, for instance. He did abolish, so far as he could, such non-Sharʿî taxes in the interior of his dominions (where they were most clearly illegal); and in particular abolished those that had been imposed on certain Hindu pilgrimages, normally associated with fairs (which taxes also were questionable from a Sharʿî viewpoint); but he also forbade the unquestionable jizyah tax on ḋhimmî non-Muslims. Throughout his reign, but especially after his experiment with Sharʿî legitimation about 1580, the many reforms that he favoured and even tried to impose by law were such as expressed respect for the dignity of living beings, whether such respect was specially called for in the Sharîʿah or not.

He was opposed to enslavement. In India, where Hinduism did not bar enslavement within the confessional community, victorious Muslim armies had lapsed from the norms acknowledged (if sometimes violated in the name of Mongolism by such as Timur), in the lands of old Islam, and had enslaved war captives, in the older way, with scant regard to their status as dhimmîs or even as Muslims; to correct this was doubtless a good Muslim practice. Akbar went further, attempting (without much effect) to eliminate slave-trading generally. He made a point of distributing charities to the needy, of building hospitals and caravansarais along the highways of the empire, of maintaining surveillance against official oppression by underling officers, of trying to impose fair prices in the urban markets; such things were commonly done by the better and more powerful Muslim rulers and indeed by Agrarian Age rulers generally. But he also extended his protection to other species than the human. Gradually he gave up personally one of his favourite pastimes, hunting, and he adopted a fleshless diet during most of each year. Such a moral level could not be expected of most of his subjects (though a fleshless diet was not uncommon among Ṣûfîs), but at least he forbade the slaughter of animals on certain days (such as his own birthday) and also in certain areas held sacred by Hindus. This was a measure that would please Jains and upper-caste Hindus, among whom respect for animal life was strong. But other measures in the same basic spirit went against their prejudices.

Akbar discouraged child marriage, common in India among the Hindus and also the Muslims; he forbade the practice, prevalent among high-caste Hindus, of burning the widow along with the corpse of her husband, unless it was clearly voluntary on the part of the widow; correspondingly, he tried to allow Hindu widows to remarry. He forbade Hindu girls to convert to Islam to marry Muslim men; this extended to Hindu families the same protection Muslim families enjoyed against their daughters' marrying non-Muslims. In the social context of the time, this would be of a piece with his other efforts to remove special disabilities from any religious community. It must be noted that his moral reforms applied primarily only to city life in any case; often, in effect, only to the notables or to Delhi and Agra, the capitals. Sometimes they were simply in the nature of admonitions, e.g., his discouragement of a second marriage unless the first were barren. He was extremely patient of those who clung to traditional patterns.

Akbar maintained a respectful attitude to all religious communities, not only to both Sunnî and Shî'î Islam, but to the diverse communities to be found in India, including even the Christianity represented by the aggressive and bigoted Portuguese whom Akbar hoped to expel from those Indian ports that they had seized. He listened willingly to whatever the representatives of any religious tradition could say of spiritual life and in defence of their particular positions, and even allowed some of them to give systematic instruction to his sons. He not only disallowed persecution of any sort, even setting aside the legal death penalty for conversion away from Islam, but contributed financially to the building of temples for various faiths. In this way he put into practice a universalist orientation in religion itself, which formed an important component of the interconfessional cultural climate of the court.

So consistent a working out of a universalist moral orientation was not accomplished without a personal religious quest and even moral growth on the part of Akbar himself, who as a young man had rather liked bloodshed; in this quest some prominent courtiers were also involved. Akbar was influenced in his thinking not only by Ṣûfî pîrs but by some laymen,notably by Abûlfażl 'Allâmî, a scholar of broad views, and his father and brother. In the hope of himself understanding the competing religious positions and, if possible, of bringing their representatives into a mutual understanding which should help reconcile them, Akbar organized (from 1575 when his adminisitrative reforms were getting under way) a 'house of worship' in which at first scholars representing various Muslim viewpoints, later also scholars representing all known religious traditions, were gathered to discuss and, alas, dispute their respective faiths and claims. The Jesuit spokesmen for Christ were among the most ardent in displaying their scorn and hatred for the most cherished ideals of their fellows, but they yielded little to the several varieties of Muslims in such zeal. Akbar patiently continued the sessions for years, but eventually closed the 'house of worship'. In his personal quest, however, he continued to explore what the several religious traditions had to offer. The Hindu Râjpût princesses whom he had married in political alliance were allowed to maintain their Hindu worship in the palace, and even Akbar himself introduced ritual touches into the daily routine which seem to have been derived from several traditions, notably regarding the sun as an emblem of the divine Light.

He continued to be what we must call a Muslim, asserting a radical monotheism of the Islamic type; but he felt at last that he had come to some insights into Truth that deserved to be shared. He instituted a sort of ṭarîqah, with himself as pîr, dedicted to a universalist outlook (*tawḥîd-e ilâhî*, 'divine monotheism'),[5] to moral purity, and to personal devotion to himself as leader and ruler. He admitted a limited number of disciples, who carried his portrait on a chain around their necks and committed themselves at least to a modest minimum of moral demands, such as limiting sexual relations to such as might result in offspring. All but one of the disciples were Muslims. Some but by no means most of the higher officials became disciples; there seems to have been absolutely no preference given to disciples over others in matters of preferment.

Abûlfażl: Ṣûfism and civilization

The most consistent and certainly the grandest literary expression of the intellectual mood at Akbar's court is the *Akbar-Nâmah*, the *Book of Akbar*, by Abûlfażl 'Allâmî of Agra (1551–1602). As Ṭabarî may be called the historian for the Sharî'ah-minded, and Ibn-Khaldûn the historian for the Faylasûfs, so we may say that Abûlfażl was the historian for those who inclined to Ṣûfî metaphysics. Much as Ibn-Khaldûn attempted to apply the principles of timeless generalization of the Philosophers to the processes of historical change, Abûlfażl tried to see history and worldly civilization generally under the categories of unitive mystical thought. His attempt is probably not to be judged as so great, as a work of history at least, as those of Ṭabarî and Ibn-Khaldûn, but it was a major achievement in its own sphere.

Both Ibn-Khaldûn and Abûlfażl described at length the Islamicate culture of their time. But whereas Ibn-Khaldûn, writing in the Arid Zone and in the Middle Periods when civilization was always threatened with being

[5] The term *dîn-e ilâhî*, 'divine religion', by which the cult is now generally known, does not seem to have been used seriously in Akbar's time, as Professor Habib points out.

reduced to a minimal agrarian-urban symbiosis, stressed the social mechanisms on which civilization could be built up, Abûlfażl, writing in a well-watered region and in the time of the great gunpowder empires, stressed the material and spiritual potentialities of civilization once it was developed. Accordingly, he dealt with a most sensitive point in the struggles of the Islamic conscience, especially as that conscience faced the age of the gunpowder empires: how to reconcile the Ṣûfî stress on the inward life, to which the course of history often seemed almost irrelevant, but which had come largely to dominate sophisticated intellectual and imaginative life, with the sense of historical accomplishment embodied in the great absolute empires and their refined high culture.

We will look at Abûlfażl's work with some care. For though it expresses a highly personal vision; and though, so far as it illustrates an age, it belongs specially to Indian Islamdom; yet it draws on resources largely common at least to all Persianate Islamdom in the gunpowder-empires period, and so points up possibilities open to the whole society.

Abûlfażl had not himself proceeded far along the Ṣûfî way, but so far as his restless mind could adopt any one ultimate perspective, it was that of the Ṣûfî metaphysicians. His father, Shaykh Mubârak Nâgawrî (d. 1593), was an eccentric Ṣûfî-minded scholar of Sindhî family (ultimately, he claimed, the male line was from the Yemen), who had been persecuted on the plea that he sympathized with Muḥammad of Jaunpur, one of whose disciples he protected; but who perhaps actually raised more hostility through his general independence in matters of religion and in particular through his assertion that every religious position might have its weak point, and any position was likely to have some truth to it. Abûlfażl learned religious independence from his father, and also to expect rejection and even attack from the rest of the 'ulamâ' for his principles. But though he respected his father's guidance, he never ceased his anguished personal search for the resolution of spiritual problems. He retained (I suppose) from his father the double concern for inward cultivation and for active social justice, but he resolved the dilemma so posed in a very different way from that of the Mahdavîs.

He and his poet brother Fayżî were accepted at Akbar's court along with their father. He became one of Akbar's most trusted counsellors, and eventually rose to high position. When sent (because of his enemies' desire to separate him from Akbar) to settle affairs in the newly conquered Deccan, he proved a capable man of affairs. But his preference was always for religious disputation, and he promised himself that when he had completed his great work, the *Akbar-Nâmah,* he would retire into spiritual seclusion (the more so, that he could not hope for much favour under the next reign). This was not allowed him: in the last years of Akbar's life (and, therefore, before the history of Akbar's deeds could be brought to a conclusion) he was assassinated on the occasion of a revolt by Akbar's eldest son, Salîm (Jahângîr), who evidently held a grudge against him.

The *Akbar-Nâmah* takes the form of an encomium on Akbar. The eulogy is undisguised. Within Akbar's first day, it seems, his nurses managed to interpret some facial expression of the infant as a smile; Abûlfażl accepts the report and exaggerates it into laughter, which he then presents as a miraculous augury of Akbar's historic destiny. Probably a good deal that is in the book springs simply from the requirements of eulogy; thus he notes that a flattering comparison of Akbar's mother with the Virgin Mary was suggested to him by Akbar himself, to whom he read out the portions of the book as they were completed.

Abûlfażl was quite conscious of the implications of writing in such a genre. He notes at one point that he cannot eulogize the grandees of Akbar's empire, because it is Akbar he is praising and no lesser man; but since he does not wish to describe them straightforwardly either, since this would require mentioning their weak points as well as their strong points, he settles for not describing them at all. (This policy serves his ends in another way as well: it allows the omnipresent figure of Akbar to appear, unobscured by the interventions of lesser figures, at once on both the levels I am about to describe.) He was also explicitly aware that to eulogize meant not only to suppress some facts but even to accept some highly dubious claims at least in such relatively indifferent points as genealogy. But (like any good eulogist) he does not allow himself to praise what is wicked or petty; and if he must praise acts that might seem unlovely, he interprets them in a positive manner first, so that his praise comes to refer to whatever is indeed praiseworthy about them. As if to make up for such artificialities in his genre, he expresses frankly and at length his personal aspirations and uncertainties, so that we get a vivid sense of how he felt as he worked on the book; and he incidentally points out, of course, as it had become standard to do, that only the exceptional reader could comprehend the real intent of a serious book like his, which was necessarily written with deliberate ambiguity.

Beyond the sheer eulogy, we may distinguish two levels of intention in the work. On the first level, he is describing the ideal ruler; indeed, in a quite precise sense, the philosopher-king of the Faylasûf tradition. On the second level, he is describing the Ṣûfî 'perfect man'.

Even on the first level, he insists that true kingship is a special grace from God, representing this in terms of the ancient Iranian notion of the royal splendour which shone upon the king so long as he remained worthy of his status. And this grace belongs especially to Akbar because he is a true 'philosopher', understanding the meaning of human existence, and at the same time knows how effectively to guide the people aright on the basis of 'philosophic' principles.

The *Akbar-Nâmah* is divided into two portions: one portion sets forth the annals of Akbar's ancestors, particularly Bâbur and Humâyûn, and of Akbar himself; the second portion sets forth the institutions established by Akbar in governing his empire (this latter part is called the *Â'în-e Akbarî*, 'Akbar's institutions'). The two portions reflect Abûlfażl's goal in differing ways. In the annals, all Akbar's deeds (so far as they are recorded at all) are presented as they ought to have happened (especially as to motivation), whether they exactly happened so or not. The whole presents a vivid, detailed, and even reasonably credible 'mirror for princes', a practical image of how a king should rule; but unlike most of the works of that genre, the image is shaped philosophically—appealing to a potential ruler's highest instincts—rather than just prudentially. (We must recognize, to be sure, with Abûlfażl himself, that he had an unusually good model for his portrait.) Then in the second part, the *Â'în*, we have an image not merely of kingly rule but of civilization at large, which the ideal king is to foster.

Civilization is conceived as the fullest cultivation of all the natural possibilities offered to human beings in life. Akbar is presented more than once as inventor of new devices designed to make life function more smoothly (though as some of these devices are ascribed to other Muslims of about the same period, doubtless he was only, in most cases, patron of the invention). He encouraged the cultivation in India of those fruits of which Bâbur had complained of the absence or the poor quality. Along with the cultivation of natural possibilities went the gentling of relations among human beings summed up in the late Ṣûfî phrase *ṣulḥ-e kull*, 'universal peace' or 'conciliation'. This meant for Abûlfażl not the elimination of conflict—for it was assumed that some persons were wicked and must be suppressed—but such generosity and forgiveness to all that no occasion was left for dissension. The great error was bigotry: to reject a human achievement because its maker was of the wrong allegiance is contrary to the good sense of the civilized man, and to the first requirements of ṣulḥ-e kull. Hence Abûlfażl makes a point of citing Hindu traditions. At Akbar's court, translation into Persian (the language of polite civilization in Islamdom) was an important activity: works were translated from Turkish and Arabic and also from Indic languages, especially Sanskrit—whether of a religious colouring or not; and Abûlfażl himself is said to have translated parts of the Bible, though his history shows no knowledge of that corpus.

All this cultivation of life was seen, of course, from the viewpoint of agrarianate privilege: these refinements of life were for the benefit of those who received the revenues; the improved fruits, of which Abûlfażl boasts, were for the luxury market; though it was hoped that privileged persons would, in turn, feel responsible for the elementary welfare of the peasantry. Indeed, the cultivation of life was seen from the particular viewpoint of a military patronage state: it was not simply because the book was a eulogy of the king, but because society was so structured, that the comprehensive picture of civilization that Abûlfażl paints starts from the royal person and his household and his court, and goes out from thence in ever wider circles.

But within the limitations imposed by this privilege-minded view of life, the perspective was naturalistic, and in particular human. In this emphasis on the human it followed a Ṣûfî lead, but went further. Throughout the history, Abûlfaẓl accepts, indeed, the possibility of abnormal phenomena, which might even carry significant auguries. Adam—but then others also—may have been born without parents (into a world already inhabited); but such wonders are acceptable only so far as they leave intact a thoroughly human view of existence; that is, so far as they do not introduce a realm of events essentially alien to ordinary human experience. Abûlfażl politely demurs at the idea that before Adam there were no people—he alleges the evidence against this of ancient Chinese and Indian records—or that Enoch (Idrîs) might have ascended bodily to the heavens without dying.

He makes ready use of the perspective of the Falsafah sciences, including their symbolic ordering of all elements in the world. The topics treated at the opening of the book define its outlook: first comes praise of speech as self-expression on both levels at once, human and divine; then the explanation that the best way to praise God is to praise His greatest expression or creation, a good king—and third comes what turns out to be a study in scientific method, brought in à propos of Akbar's horoscope, which precedes the account of his ancestors. It must be recognized that natural science was not Abûlfażl's strong point; he speaks so readily in terms of the Falsafah tradition only because that had become, by his time, an integral part of general learning, and in particular of the learning of the Ṣûfî metaphysicians. But the viewpoint of the Faylasûfs is given a key role. Thus he willingly brings out the possibility of human improvement in time, whether in the stories of the patriarchs (Akbar's ancestors) who invented the various good things of life, or in the relatively recent improvements in astronomical studies as human astronomical observations accumulated with time. Though he greatly respects the pre-Islamic ancients, he sees their wisdom as only human, unlike Ghazâlî or Ibn-al-ʿArabî. Here he modifies the outlook of the Ṣûfî metaphysicians in humanistic direction: he sees that other human beings may improve upon the ancients in human ways. Religion itself can appear under the aspect of a human achievement.

In particular, the ideal king, as guardian of worldly cultivation generally, is above any particular community allegiance. Though he may be by ancestry a Muslim, he must not favour the Muslims and their contributions to human comfort and wisdom above other communities and their special contributions. (Consistently, Abûlfażl refers to Islam as 'Muḥammad's religion', as one among many; apparently the term 'islâm' is reserved for its original use, submission to God, which may be entered upon in every tradition but is rarely fully achieved in any.) The king must recognize worth, personal and cultural, wherever it is to be found. Abûlfażl makes use of the Mongol heritage to make this point plausible. The (pagan) ancestress of the Mongols conceived her sons by a pure light (in Mongol legend, the sun), which Abûlfażl traces down through the generations to Akbar quite in the manner of the primal Light of Muḥammad. Such was the respect for the Mongol heritage that a notion such as this could not well be attacked at the court directly; yet in Abûlfażl's hands it clearly made the acceptance of Islam by one of the ancestors in the Mongol line an almost supererogatory act; Islam merely added to his splendour.

Compared to this excellent debating point, the excursus on Hindu philosophy in the *Â'în* is clumsy and is not well integrated into the rest of the book. For Abûlfażl remained steeped in an Islamicate outlook (that is, as Abûlfażl makes clear, in large part an outlook traceable back to the Greeks), and he was not at home with Sanskritic notions. (He even allows himself, on occasion, to make fun of the more vulgar sort of Hindu holy men.) The excursus is intended simply to justify his assertion that the Hindus are monotheists and entitled to corresponding privileges, and indeed that there is much general civilized wisdom among them; but it is far less scholarly than al-Bîrûnî, whom he makes use of.

On the second level, Abûlfażl is describing not merely the ideal worldly ruler, but the king as type-symbol of God. This sort of thing had occurred in poetry, but now becomes systematic: here the work is deeply infused with Ṣûfî presuppositions. The second level is present throughout the work, beginning with the initial praise of speech human and divine, though it is not always so immediately evident. It is not (as Abûlfażl sees things) in contradiction with the first level, not even with its naturalism and humanism; but it gives what is human a further dimension. It is as perfect earthly lord that Akbar is the type-symbol of God, as the sun is His type-symbol in nature. Praise of Akbar is praise of God on a humanly feasible level.

In the annals, Akbar's behaviour is always laudable and always in the right, to be sure; but it is essentially unpredictable, resulting from an overflowing energy that meddles in everything that happens to come to his attention. Indeed, it often takes on an inscrutable character: in particular, his conquests, though in the end they are all for the good in establishing the universality of his empire, are justified in the instance by little save that he is the king, whose honour must not be offended. But since he is yet good, if one trusts in him all will be well in the end, however it may appear at the moment. Thus Abûlfażl tells how once Akbar jested to the son of the Rânâ (prince) of Chîtôr in Râjpûtânâ (the son being at the imperial court) that an expedition then underway was directed against the Rânâ his father, who had failed to come to court himself to offer obedience. This was meant (Abûlfażl says) partly in jest, and partly as a cover story to disguise his intentions elsewhere; but the young man took it seriously and fled, so that it would not appear that he was bringing Akbar against his own father. Abûlfażl insists that if the young man had trusted Akbar, all would have been well, both for himself and his father; but by taking fright and resisting, he brought Akbar's wrath upon both of them, so that Chîtôr was actually taken. As every stroke of fate is to be interpreted for the best, so is every act of the king; hence, perhaps, his special praise for Akbar's way of interpreting apparently unfavourable omens in a favourable manner. (One may add that on the level of the philosopher-king, such a story is more ambiguous, especially since the unfortunate young man is depicted favourably; perhaps on that level the tale contains a lesson in ideal kingship by way of a tacit rebuke to Akbar.)

Akbar, indeed, is presented as the fulfillment of divine destiny. Not only does divine providence guide individual events in his life, it prepared his perfection already in his ancestors, whose periods of obscurity are interpreted as discipline in humility, from which Akbar was to benefit. Abûlfażl even entertains the possibility that Akbar might turn out to be the renovator of mankind, perhaps the Mahdî—coming as he does seven thousand years after Adam (on the originally Shî'î calculation of a thousand years to each of the six great prophets, including Muḥammad, at the end of which six thousand-year days would come the great millennial sabbath). But more important than any such chiliastic notions is the presentation, in the *Â'în*, of Akbar as the 'perfect man', the quṭb, round whom all the world revolves now. It is not merely because he is king and chief patron of the arts and sciences that the description of civilization at large is centred upon Akbar, but because he is, above all, the spiritual guide of his time, whose care must go out to all creation spiritually even when his attention is not immediately directed to it physically. And in reverencing him, as a murîd reverences his Ṣûfî pîr, ones led to spiritual growth toward the perfection he embodies.

But these Ṣûfî ideas, in being carried over to a glorification of human civilization, are shifted in focus. In discussing a more external level of the work, we have already noticed a shift as to the human role in the cosmos. This occurs on the inward level also. Abûlfażl, as Akbar's disciple, commends an interiorizing ethic on the Ṣûfî model, in which the inner consciousness matters more than abiding by rules; but the ethic is adapted to living in society and even in a court. The ṣulḥ-e kull, universal conciliation, that Akbar brings is not only a political and social consummation at which Akbar aims as model ruler; it is also an individual moral condition to which Akbar's spiritual guidance brings his disciples: being inwardly at peace with all persons, whatever their attitude toward one (a posture which for Abûlfażl was a refuge from the press of human absurdities). The next stage beyond is the *maḥabbat-e kull*, universal love, a more positive, constructive sentiment of fostering all persons and their material welfare, whatever their blindness. (Abûlfażl felt he had also reached that stage.)

But the shift seems to affect chiefly only the more immediate range of life. It is through these more social virtues, rather than through more purely personal ascetic discipline, that one is to come to the admittedly higher and more difficult Ṣûfî stages of full acceptance of God and ultimately a unitive consciousness. These last remain the ultimate purpose of creation in all its multiplicity, and hence of civilization in all its richness. Correspondingly, Akbar's spiritual role as 'perfect man' is primarily as universally visible exemplar and fosterer of civilization; but ultimately, no doubt, he may be quṭb also in a more metaphysical sense.

It is clear that Abûlfażl's work was one vehicle for Akbar's great influence on the later rulers of his dynasty. This was due in part to his Persian style, which was frequently imitated, though (I am told) without success. He was very conscious of his style, and aware that it was a departure from previous manners. The style, in its broad lines, at least, was tailored to the message: it was unfailingly cultivated, and leisured to the point of freely using elegant epithets and pairing fine phrases, but it was not heavily weighted with merely clever similes or irrelevant verse; that is, it was decently courtly in form, but did not depend for effect on what was frivolous or superfluous—it was what we may call civilized.

Abûlfażl's ideal in style was that of his elder brother Fayżî (d. 1595), Akbar's poet-laureate. Fayżî was one of the two or three most famous Persian poets of the period, a creator of what was called the 'Indian style' of poetry (though the elements of that style had already been present in Iranian poets for a generation or so). The 'Indian style', as we have noted in discussing its role in contemporary Ṣafavî poetry, developed allusiveness to a disconcerting point of refinement; it has been suggested that the metaphors that had become stock poetic devices were now played with to take advantage of their literary history to produce new sophisticated effects: a metaphoric use of the metaphors themselves. There is no question about the aristocratic character of this poetry, appropriate only for a society where the privileged have behind them generations of taste. Fayżî and a contemporary Iranian poet, 'Urfî, who also wrote in India, have been judged to be the most important influences in Ottoman Turkic poetry during the following century or so, though their influences in Iran was more diluted.

Universalistic civilization and the Islamic Ummah

The universalist sort of cultural and moral life which Akbar fostered, and which was largely accepted as the basis for court life by Muslim and Hindu officials alike, was not in itself inconsistent with Islam. Indeed, it was cast in Islamicate terms, and attracted its most explicit support chiefly among Muslims rather than among Hindus. But it presupposed an alternative interpretation of Islam, as it bore on life and culture, which excluded the more particularist, communalistic, interpretation of the Islamic mission in the world which had always been upheld by the Sharîʿah-minded (and which had been expressed with a certain grandeur, though unacceptably to most of the Sharîʿah-minded, in the Mahdavî movement of Sayyid Muḥammad).

This limitation did not matter too much to the courtly circles themselves; by and large Akbar was able to carry the court with him in cultural and even religious policies (though not, of course, in his personal ideas), at least so far as public expression went. Within the military ruling institution, developed out of the Mongol army-government, and based neither on religion nor even on race but on service to the ruling family, the universalist sense of civilization could readily flourish; there it had a certain precedent as far back even as the time of the historian Rashîduddîn Fażlullâh and his even-handed world history. Such an outlook could figure as the refined expression of the Mongol zeal for greatness. As to Muslims (and Hindus) outside the ruling institution, even relatively privileged ones, they were little involved, for the most part, in the high culture of the court and its various moral demands. In society at large, this sort of high culture was neither in demand nor feasible. Nevertheless, the initiatives of the court were influenced by more popular trends, and in turn had some effect in ordinary society. A universalist interpretation of Islam, then, however innocuous in the court, might put in question the relations of the court to the ordinary classes of Muslims within the Timurî dominions who ultimately supported it; and, further, to the wider Muslim community beyond, whose overall vitality had made Muslim power possible.

The dominant focus of Islamicate high culture in Timurî India was unmistakably the court, and not either the market or the temple; and the court was proving sufficiently enduring to develop its own forms of legitimation, to which the rest of the society must accede. The historic special link of Islamicate culture to the mercantile classes was losing some of its basis. But if this was happening in India, it was happening elsewhere also. Islamdom had spread so far that the mid-Arid Zone now formed only a fraction of its total extent; two of the three great Muslim empires were based in relatively well-watered lands outside the Nile-to-Oxus region. But even in the heart of the mid-Arid Zone, absolutism was resurgent in the Ṣafavî state, which was restoring the agrarian stability of Sâsânian and early ʿAbbâsî times. Consequently for the time being, at least, the Islamicate society in India was able to continue to draw strength from Islamdom at large. Indeed many of the most significant cultural figures at Akbar's court came from abroad—and especially from the Ṣafavî empire.

All the Muslim powers of the time formed a single far-flung diplomatic world. The greatest powers—the Ottomans, Ṣafavîs, Özbegs, and Timurîs—maneuvered among themselves for their several ends, each attempting to keep the friendship, or win the alliance, of those with whom they were not immediately at war. Though all the ruling families were Turkic, the language of diplomacy, of course, was Persian; and the same sense of diplomatic courtesy was common to all. The Ottomans and Özbegs were commonly allied against the Ṣafavîs (and in that alliance, the greater strength of the Ottoman power was reflected in the formulas used by the Özbegs to the Ottomans being usually somewhat more flattering than those used by the Ottomans to the Özbegs). The Timurîs were relatively neutral, and were courted on occasion by each of the others; sometimes they were allied with the Ṣafavîs, sometimes with the Özbegs. When they addressed letters to the Ṣafavîs they omitted, out of courtesy, the usual blessings on the first three caliphs—unless the intent was to offend. (The Ottomans, Ṣafavîs, and Timurîs, at least, all normally addressed each other—when not at war—as equals—which meant, in effect, that each monarch was likely to call the other lord of the world, as he called himself.) But the Timurîs (ever since their early alliance with the Portuguese) tended to be cold to the Ottomans. At one point (1628) the Timurîs attempted a rapprochement, but the Ottoman reply to their formally correct letter was couched in such haughty terms as to be offensive (in addition, the Ottomans had taken to using Turkic, which offended the Timurî court as vulgar), and negotiations were broken off. Later attempts by the Ottomans to revive the possibility of an alliance (against the Ṣafavîs) were couched in more conciliatory language but came to nothing.[6]

This world was a diplomatic unity because it remained, despite the tendency of each empire to develop a distinctive regional culture centred on the court, a cultural unity. In this unity the Ṣafavî empire doubtless held the central place; but India was close behind as a focus of cultural influence. Great men came from each of the other empires to India to settle, but men rarely left India except for the holy Ḥijâz. Correspondingly, books written in India were read elsewhere, including among the Ottomans, but books written by the Ottomans were practically unknown in India. Of the four or five greatest Persian poets of the period, Fayżî, as we have seen, was of Indian family for generations back, and 'Urfî, born in Shîrâz in Fârs, did practically all his work in India. Not only poetic style, but translations from Sanskrit done in India made their mark on thinking at Iṣfahân. By the eighteenth century, at least, Shar'î work done in India was becoming influential in the Ottoman empire: a collection of fatwà decisions made for Awrangzêb was honoured there (and Awrangzêb himself was honoured with the classical caliphal title of 'commander of the faithful' by an Ottoman author). The

[6] Unfortunately, we have no studies of international law and diplomacy in this period (or, indeed, in any other period of Islamicate history—save in so far as a discussion of the foreign policy of the caliphal state may pass for such in the very earliest times, before a multiplicity of Muslim states arose). In the sixteenth and seventeenth centuries, when international relations among Muslim states were of such far-reaching importance, this is peculiarly regrettable. Aziz Ahmad, 'Moghulindien und Dâr al-Islâm', *Saeculum: Jahrbuch für Universalgeschichte*, 12 (1961), 266–90, has studied much of the diplomatic correspondence of the time, but unfortunately to little purpose, though some of his data are useful. He is so careful a writer, and so sound in some respects, that defects all too typical in the field can be exemplified respectably in him. Bemused by uncritical assumptions inherited from earlier Western writers (though he rejects without consideration some more modern Western scholarship), he fails to see the implications even of the data he himself provides, and asks few of the relevant questions. He tries to describe the relations of the Muslim great powers in terms of long-term alliances and balances of power, appropriate to the European state system of the same period but hardly to Islamdom (he even speaks of Awrangzêb as a 'usurper' in need of foreign 'recognition'). In particular, he still assumes that the Ottomans claimed the single historical caliphate in succession from the 'Abbâsids, and wastes many words trying to find a recognition of this supposed claim in the flowery verbiage of other sovereigns. Aziz Ahmad's 'Akbar, hérétique ou apostat', *Journal asiatique*, 1961, pp. 21–38, is marred by the same sorts of faults (concepts of 'sect', etc.).

Mujaddidî branch of the Naqshbandiyyah ṭarîqah order was introduced from India (by way of the Ḥijâz) to the Ottoman lands. Of Ottoman culture, in contrast, it is chiefly practical details that seem to have reached so far as India. A disciple of the great Ottoman architect Sinân is said to have taken part in building the Tâj Maḥall at Agra, and cannon workers from the Ottoman empire were valued by the Timurîs.

But though the Islamicate culture of Timurî India more than held its own in Islamdom at large, even on its universalist side (as well as in Islamic communal fields), the universalistic tendencies in it did not fail to cause a strain. The problem of the relation between a non-communal civilization and the Muslim Ummah became sharpest in India, precisely where civilization most tended to transcend communal lines. Even though a marginal shift in the basis of government could and did allow a legitimation of government and of social forms that was not tied to the Sharîʻah, yet the basis for an egalitarian, anti-aristocratic communalism persisted in a weakened form. Certainly Islamic consciences remained frequently, as ever, oppositional; the Islamic tradition readily sensitized its carriers to the folly and injustice of great courts and their luxuries. Many Muslims grumbled at Akbar's policies and those of his successors as un-Islamic, and these grumblings, while politically of little effect, left a legacy of cultural suspicion that became more serious with the centuries.

Shîʻism was something of a bugbear throughout the Timurî period in India. An accusation of Shîʻism could be damning among Jamâʻî-Sunnîs. Akbar favoured well-placed immigrants from Iran (who might, of course, be Turks) in his army; occasionally they even retained rights to land revenue within Iran after they entered the Indian service. Such men were likely to be Shîʻî, while men from the Chaghatay lands in the Oxus basin (referred to as Tûrân) were likely to be Sunnî. The political rivalry between 'Irânî' and 'Tûrânî' nobles at the court of Akbar and his descendants has sometimes been linked to rivalry between Shîʻism and Sunnism as well as between Ṣafavî and Özbeg. But that political rivalry (which did not become seriously divisive till after the time of Awrangzêb) was not so important as the tendency for universalist cultural viewpoints to be linked to Shîʻism. This tendency may have had some relation to the oppositional and chiliastic background of Shîʻism, which lent itself to religious experiment. But with Shîʻism in a majoritarian position in Iran, it now was linked with the highest aristocratic culture of the lands of old Islam; and that did indeed play a large role in the courtly culture of India. The universalist culture had more Shîʻî ties now than merely those it inherited already from the 'Alid-loyalist strands in ṭarîqah Ṣûfism. Its opponents were not slow to make the connection, even if in a crude form.

The rumours that foreigners at Akbar's court heard about his having abandoned Islam altogether reflected the popular suspicions of the time. The occasional writers who presumed to attack Akbar did so mercilessly. Some of their reports of his religious policy were grossly distorted and have affected much Muslim opinion since, including the evaluations of modern scholars. The critics (and especially the Shar'î scholar and courtier Badâonî) lumped together different sorts of acts on Akbar's part, of a more or less religious cast: the policy of maintaining some control over the religious establishment, analogous to what also happened in the Ṣafavî and Ottoman empires; policies of religious tolerance, in which much that Akbar did was in any case not unprecedented; the policy of using Hindu administrators and soldiers, and of alliance with Hindu Râjpût rulers, still less unprecedented; neutrality in intra-Muslim disputes and openmindedness to the teachers of other religions; the adoption of moral principles not required by the Sharî'ah but not contrary to Islam; and finally the expression of his own personal spiritual insights and his teaching them to his closest friends (which some modern scholars have chosen to regard as the promulgation of a new religion to replace Islam, but which did not necessarily carry such implications—as we may see from the continuation of some of Akbar's special practices by his successors, and finally from Awrangzêb's explicit assimilation of them to the practices of a Ṣûfî pîr). Akbar's critics even attacked the solar calendar which he introduced, probably because it was styled *ilâhî*, 'divine', though it had nothing directly to do with religious reform; it was a fiscal reform, typical of strong Muslim rulers, who had repeatedly to restore order in the necessarily solar fiscal reckoning, which tended to get out of adjustment because it never enjoyed the prestige of the lunar Shar'î calendar.[7]

As we have noted, the religious hostility to Akbar was sufficiently strong to lend a colour to movements of revolt against him in 1580, which received the blessing of a few of the 'ulamâ'. Some of Akbar's opponents attacked him out of a petty traditionalism—for instance, Badâonî in his history willingly distorted facts in order to blacken Akbar and his friends. But his indictment was part of a more inclusive indictment of venal 'ulamâ' generally, and not without merit. I suppose he represented that moralistic world view that has always seen in the worst possible light the luxuries, moral as well as material, of the culture-minded. And the communalist attack could be carried out on a

[7] The most important source on Akbar's reforms is Abûlfażl's *Akbar-Nâmah*, including the *A'în-e Akbarî*, which sets forth the whole network of policies of his reign, but sometimes suppresses awkward facts. Unlike many others of his line, Akbar left no memoirs, and Abûlfażl must do instead. (The translations are unsatisfactory.) Much data and a reasonably just evaluation of his (and his successors') policies are readily accessible in Sri Ram Sharma, *The Religious Policy of the Mughal Emperors* (Oxford University Press, 1940), who, however, interprets 'religious' narrowly to refer chiefly just to religious allegiance, and is specially interested in persecution of Hindus or its absence—and in the relevant chapters of Ram Prasad Tripathi, *Rise and Fall of the Mughal Empire* (Allahabad, 1956). Tripathi is 'revisionist' in discounting Awrangzêb's reversal of earlier policy, but less revisionist than some. Tripathi's *Some Aspects of Muslim Administration* (2nd rev. ed., Allahabad, 1956) is likewise judicious but not highly imaginative; it incidentally displays the sad effects that can follow from using the term 'Mughal' and unconsciously equating it with 'Mongol': sometimes he speaks almost as if Râjpûts, Mughals, and Sunnîs were three contrasting groups, and as if he expected the Indian 'Mughals' to still live by old pagan Mongol concepts.

high theoretical level. The most outstanding of Akbar's critics was Aḥmad Sirhindî, called by his followers 'Mujaddid-e Alf-e S̄ânî', the 'renovator of the second (Muslim) thousand years'.

Sirhindî, who became active in the very last years of Akbar's reign, evidently felt that most influential Muslims were aligned against the rigourist cause which he represented. He denounced Akbar's compromises with Hinduism, but he saw that the roots of Akbar's attitude lay within Islam itself, especially within Ṣûfism. But he was himself a Ṣûfî; instead of attacking Ṣûfî universalism from the standpoint purely of the Sharî'ah, rejecting all doctrines of the more inward life, as many rigourists had continued to do in the Later Middle Period, he waged his fight within the forms of Ṣûfism itself He attacked especially the monist doctrines of Ibn-al-'Arabî, adopting the alternative proposed by 'Alâuddîn Simnânî. In terms of the central experience of the mystical life, he maintained that the notion of waḥdat al-wujûd, 'oneness by existence', on the basis of which Ibn-al-'Arabî had developed his system, answered to merely one stage in the long sequence of positions in the mystical quest. He himself claimed to have passed through and far beyond this stage, ascending many ranks higher, or deeper, into mystical insight; and he proclaimed that the result of such experiences led to an affirmation of the ultimate distinction between God and His creatures—that the oneness found in mystical experience was rather a 'oneness by witness', *waḥdat al-shuhûd,* than a 'oneness by existence'.

On this basis, he tried to reconcile the very personal mystical experience, to which Ṣûfism gave a place, with an intensely social activism such as the Islam of the Sharî'ah demanded. The gulf between the most advanced believer and God was restored and the paramountcy of the outer law affirmed, over the inner motion of the Spirit. Sirhindî had joined the Naqshbandî ṭarîqah, newly introduced in India, and founded a new ('Mujaddidî') branch of it which recognized him as the 'perfect man' of his age, the quṭb or 'Qayyûm'. These Naqshbandîs persistently spread his ideas against the dominant patterns of Indian Islam under the Timurids, quarrelling with the other ṭarîqahs.

At the time, the influence of such men as Sirhindî was slight.[8] Akbar's son and successor, Jahângîr, imprisoned Sirhindî but, when he thought he had repented, showed him some honour and let him go back to his home in the Panjâb where his chief following was (who did make some trouble before long, but were suppressed). The generous moral and universalist orientation

[8] Sirhindî's followers greatly exaggerated his influence. These exaggerations have penetrated even so non-political a work as Subhan's study of Indian Ṣûfism. The chief study in English of Sirhindî's speculative thinking is Burhân Aḥmad Fârûqî, *The Mujaddid's Conception of Tawḥîd* (Lahore, 1940; 2nd ed., 1943). Unfortunately, Fârûqî's work is as exceedingly ignorant and credulous as it is bigoted. (The mood of the time in which it was written, in the agitation for Pakistan, is portrayed when he says in apparent seriousness, 'Islam was in great distress. Unbelievers could openly ridicule and condemn Islam and the Muslims.') Its historical assertions are worthless.

of culture was deeply established in the pattern of courtly life and the organization of the empire. Respected Jamâ'î-Sunnî 'ulamâ' during the seventeenth century used the right of ijtihâd to interpret the Sharî'ah favourably to Hindu rights. And the mood was taken up in out-of-the-way places: a Mazdean (of the Parsi community in India, evidently representing a distinctive sect among them) wrote in Persian (1657) a survey of religions, *Dabistân-e Mazâhib*, dedicated to the ultimate unity of all religious truth, friendly to such dissidents as the Ismâ'îlîs, yet always retaining a Mazdean colouring—but in a thoroughly Islamicate form, such that it seems only natural to see it headed with the usual Muslim formula, 'In the name of God, the merciful, the compassionate'. The work proved very popular among Muslims and even some Hindus. So long as Muslims remained indisputably the ruling element, hostility to the universalistic tendencies of the Muslim ruling classes remained chiefly a matter of internal dissent on particular policies, and did not yet call in question the destiny of Islam as such in India.

The perfecting of Indian Islamicate art

Correspondingly, the power of the Timurî empire proved able to survive Akbar's death. Jahângîr (1605–27), Akbar's only surviving son, had been a disappointment to Akbar in his old age, indulging in personal vices such as Akbar had been, or had made himself, largely free of; he had even gone so far in the last years as forcibly to resist his father in the course of an attempt to arrange for his own eventual succession, but without showing great capacity. The system established by Akbar, however, was not seriously weakened in the main lines of its operation; Jahângîr seems to have chosen his advisers not unwisely, even if he rejected some of the best. He maintained, on the whole, his father's religious and cultural policy, though with distinctly more caution in avoiding giving offence to the Sharî'ah-minded; and with a weaker hand. He even tried to maintain Akbar's ṭarîqah practices at first, giving would-be disciples his own picture to wear; but without Akbar's personality such an attempt was impracticable. Sometimes he lapsed into direct prejudice. But the orientation of the culture of the court was not seriously compromised by Jahângîr's lack of personal consequence.

Jahângîr's son Shâh Jahân (1627–58) likewise maintained the same tradition on the whole, both politically and culturally. Translation of Hindu works and patronage of Hindu poets continued at court (and even some translation from Islamicate natural science into Sanskrit!), and the share of Hindus in high office increased. But in the realm of religion he had marked leanings toward a more severe Sharî'ah-mindedness, at least in expression. Shâh Jahân encouraged conversion to Islam and stimulated certain expressions of bigotry against Hindus. He was also explicitly hostile to Shî'îs: it was in part for this reason that he pressed Akbar's policy of expansion southward at the expense of the Deccan Muslim sultanates, in which Shî'ism was strong. In any case, the military strength of the empire and its administrative effectiveness seemed to persist unaffected by changes in rulers and in superficial policies.

The greatest expressions of Timurî power, which were at the same time the greatest triumphs of the courtly civilization, came in the field of the fine arts, particularly painting and architecture. The emperors themselves and their great nobles patronized visual art of all kinds, of the most precious genius. Here supremely the Islamicate inspiration became the basis for an interconfessional cultural productivity. It is in the arts that we see most clearly the recurrent combination of foreign Islamicate inspiration, which the dynasty itself symbolized and always patronized, with a continuing formation of an autonomously Indic Islamicate culture in the region. In India, often at the hands of Hindus, the Iranian Islamicate art traditions were modified, sometimes subtly, sometimes rather drastically, to yield a distinctive complex of Indo-Islamicate arts; this complex had its origins in the pre-Timurî period, but now came to its culmination—and it came to it in part precisely under the liberating intervention of foreign models.

Under Sher-Shâh the styles in architecture that are associated with the Indo-Timurîs were already appearing; under Akbar they were fully launched. The Timurids brought with them reminiscences of their Chaghatay homeland. The plan of some noble tomb-domes of the time recalls the domes of the Timurî Oxus basin; but the work continues Indo-Islamicate traditions in detail. Perhaps more important for its catalytic effects was the spirit of the Timurid family. Akbar had inherited the Timurid love for patronizing art, and took a personal interest in the details. His personal taste had effects. His temporary capital of Fatḥpûr Sîkrî, of which he was very proud, and which has been spared to us almost intact from his time, presents an almost unique but most impressive combination of the architecture of Hindu tradition, including its flat stone beams and its low but vivid massiveness, with the arches and lightness of Islamicate art in the Nile-to-Oxus region. It was not generally imitated, but the boldness of its conception was evidently liberating.

In architecture, Akbar obviously loved to see Hindu modes imitated, though reconceived in an Islamicate spirit. In painting he remained more faithful to his ancestors. His father had brought the best available painters from Iran, and Akbar respected his example, as did his next two successors, drawing men from both Iran and the Syr-Oxus basin. However, Akbar intervened personally in the training of the Indian painters who studied under the Iranian masters, and it is possible that it was his personal perception of their possibilities that led some of those Indian disciples to strike out in their own directions, and so to produce the distinctive Indian Islamicate school of painting.

Akbar's son Jahângîr stood out as a special patron of painting. The same sorts of experiments toward an interest in art of a more genre type came to India as to Ṣafavî Iran, but (as in Iran) they did not entirely supersede the pure visuality of the Timurî painting. Even this was necessarily modified, however; for instance, Indian painters more freely stressed details of human interest. Faithful personal portraiture, likewise introduced with a certain restraint in Ṣafavî Iran, was developed heartily in Timurî India. To a significant degree, even the form was modified. A sense of space was introduced, especially into the background (while the foreground retained the conventions of the autonomy of the graphic surface)—the horizon was lowered (so that the viewer came into a more direct relation with the depicted objects), and there was even some use of perspectival effects. Some of the details in all these shifts are attributed to European example, and the luxuriant naturalism in the spirit of it all is attributed to India as such.

But whatever the sources of inspiration, much of what was new contributed to a new role the art was playing. In the agrarian monarchy of India, the Timurids had been able, as we have seen, to establish a tone of independent legitimation of their rule; and this seems to have been expressed in art, especially in portraiture. Akbar made a point of bestowing portraits of himself upon visitors as a formal gesture of majesty, and his insistence that all his courtiers sit for portraits was explicitly conceived as glorifying or even immortalizing his court. It has been pointed out that the rose became a symbol of the splendour of the Timurî dynasty and its patronage of beauty, and that when Shâh Jahân is shown contemplating a rose, this is not an aesthetic foible but a symbolic gesture. Indo-Timurî art, that is, had become in some measure a heraldic art, in which objective symbolism was regaining a place, if not for religious, yet at least for political, dynastic purposes.[9]

The art was not yet drastically modified; the greatness achieved earlier was not despised. Art served to make visible an unmistakably Indian version of the Islamicate culture, even reflecting, in this marginal way, the agrarian solidity of rich India. The Râjpût courts came to patronize schools of painting closely allied to that of the Timurî court, which indeed had its effects all over India.[10]

It is harder to be sure at what time what was happening in the more transient arts like music and the dance. We know that they were fostered with great care. Indic and Irano-Semitic music had long been closely related, with presumably much interchange (for instance, trained Indian singing girls were prized in High Caliphal Baghdad and probably already under the Sâsânians); indeed, in a broader sense, the music of the whole region from India through

[9] Alvan C. Eastman, 'Four Mughal Emperor Portraits in the City Art Museum of St Louis', *Journal of Near Eastern Studies* 15 (1956), 65–92, makes use of some of Eric Schroeder's insights from *Persian Miniatures in the Collection of the Fogg Art Museum* (Harvard University Press, 1940) and 'The Troubled Image' in *Art and Thought*, ed. G. K. Bharata (London, 1947) to show the substance of what I call heraldic art here, though he might not draw my inferences.

[10] James Ivory's beautiful film 'The Sword and the Flute' (Film Images, 1959), which vividly and skillfully makes use of Timurî and Râjpût paintings to illustrate at once the manners of the time and the ideals served by the painters, is impressionistic; but it gets at some valid points.

the Mediterranean used the same musical scale and a common family of instruments, and used modal patterns in somewhat similar ways, until Occidental music broke away with the development of polyphony. But in India the music had been elaborated in a specialized direction, each mode being assigned its own subtle emotional and symbolic tasks. In view of the common substratum, it is unclear how much may have been contributed to the north Indian musical tradition by its Muslim patrons (it was markedly different from the south Indian, patronized more by Hindus), but by the fourteenth century already in northern India, Muslims and Hindus made music in common forms. We are told that these forms continued to be improved upon from time to time under the patronage of the Muslims in the following centuries.

Of the related art of poetry, recorded in writing, we know much more. As we have seen, a refined belles-lettrist standard was maintained in Persian which attracted the study of Muslim and Hindu alike; the better Persian poets, if they failed to make a sufficient mark under Ṣafavî auspices, found warm appreciation at the Timurî court. At the same time, the vernaculars, and especially Hindi, were also lavishly patronized (and not only among the Hindus). When Ṣûfîs wrote in Hindi, they sometimes did not despise the inherited Hindi imagery with its spiritual overtones.

Shâh Jahân became the supreme patron of architecture when it was most sensitive. Early in his reign, to be sure, he caused newly built Hindu temples to be destroyed; and in conquests he liked to desecrate temples generally. But his taste in buildings of a purely Islamicate style—structured in arches and domes, even though touched with Indic vitality—must have been exceedingly chaste and large-visioned, and the builders had developed a sufficient mass of skills in the preceding reigns to meets his standards. Under Shâh Jahân we can see how very Indian and at the same time very Islamicate a style could be. For him were built a wondrous variety of buildings, from tiny mosques shining in their sculptured perfection to the incomparable Tâj Maḥall at Agra, which absorbs the eager eye for hours on end in the day-light, only to entrance still more inescapably when the magic moonlight touches its white marble. Shâh Jahân, like some others of the dynasty, was deeply attached to one woman, for whom this was the tomb; he had planned, it seems, its equal in black marble on the other side of the Jamunâ, on whose bank it stands, for himself; but before this could be built, his son, again like several Indo-Timurid sons, like Shâh Jahân himself, interfered.

Awrangzêb (1658–1707) shut up his father during his last years where he could see the wonder he had erected only by a mirror reflecting the view from a tiny window; and still greater wonders ceased to be built. Awrangzêb did not love the arts; under him the high patronage of the arts waned, and with it the detailed perfection of their best days; with them, in turn, began to wane the universalist cultural magnificence on which much of the prestige of the imperial government among the privileged classes had rested.

The wealth of India

In the minds of much of the world, including the Muslims from Nile to Oxus, India was a land of wealth. In India, according to popular tales, were to be found fabulous hoards of wealth in gold and gems. The rich rulers of India could live in unrivalled luxury. (It was assumed, of course, that the poor there might be as poor as anywhere else: wealth was a prerogative of the privileged.) The notion of Indian wealth had a basis in fact. As compared with any part of the Arid Zone, the Indic countryside was lush: agriculture flourished not just in one or another spot but continuously over vast areas; moreover—in contrast even to well-watered lands further north—there was commonly more than one harvest in a year.

India was also noted for its manufactures—precious fabrics, steel ware, all kinds of luxury goods. Trade was brisk and rewarding throughout the region: even in bulk staple goods, trade between one country and another was relatively heavy. The different countries in India varied drastically among themselves. Bengal exported foods and mood drugs, and was known as having low prices and as rarely having famines. Gujarât imported much of its food and exported cash crops—cotton, dyes, and the like; it was noted for the rich commerce of its cities—and for its especially severe famines. Mâlvâ, inland east from Gujarât, to take a still different pattern, was not famous for its role in trade at all, but it was known for never having famines: formed of a hilly river basin, it collected its waters in natural or artificial lakes and could always count on enough for its crops. The upper Ganges plain was rich in both food crops and cash crops: Agra, the most usual capital of the great Timurids (and the city of the Tâj Maḥall), was made great largely by the indigo raised around it. But collectively all the countries served to enrich the rulers in the most important centres. The great cities of northern India, such as Agra and Delhi and Lahore, were reported by travellers to be larger than any cities in either the Nile-to-Oxus or the European regions.

With all this economic activity, the variety of luxury goods that could be produced made the wares of several of the Indic countries very attractive even in more distant regions, and countries like Gujarât and Bengal and the Ganges plain exported to distant spots in the Oikoumene as well as to other countries in India; and since manufactured goods offered by distant lands often merely reproduced what was already made in India, those distant regions often had to pay in such precious raw materials as gold, always welcome anywhere. The Indic region, then, absorbed not only people, such as the dissident religious communities from between Nile and Oxus and settlers from the Iranian highlands, but the precious metals and gems that were readily transportable from the rest of the hemisphere.

When power over India came into Muslim hands, the Indian Muslim courts came to be thought of as likely to be the wealthiest in Islamdom. Certainly, especially as it extended its sway over the greater part of the Indic region, the

Timurî state had great potential economic resources, on which might be based a stable agrarian social and political order. In the seventeenth century, the court life became if anything more opulent. Yet in the reigns of both Jahângîr and Shâh Jahân, there was a steady deterioration in some of the foundations of power. By the second half of the seventeenth century, the state was in fiscal difficulties. In part, it was trying to pay out more money, proportionately, than before. In part, the economy was actually less satisfactory and there were less resources from which to pay; and this largely because of the Timurî policy itself.

The cultural life and political policies of the Timurî privileged classes both became gradually more expensive. For the sake of maintaining military moràle and even discipline, it was appropriate (though surely less essential than in the less well-established military states of the Middle Periods) that conquest continue. The Indian Timurids, unlike the Ṣafavids, remained sufficiently vigorous to maintain strong armies and to attempt to round out their empire. But such military activity became more expensive as its range increased. Especially in the attempt to maintain hegemony over the Deccan states, the army became larger and larger; the cannon, which were the mark of a great central power, became ponderous. Moreover, the administration had a harder time controlling distant areas with agrarianate means of communication: when the emperor Awrangzêb, for instance, moved his headquarters to the Deccan, there was a considerable crisis as officials made haste to put in force some of his neglected ordinances. Through all this, the army remained efficient, even if it lacked some of the rapid mobility which had characterized many of the actions of both Bâbur and Akbar. But it was not only more expensive, it was harder to keep under control; the honesty of the vast administration probably gradually declined.

At the same time, the courtly culture itself became more expensive too. The Timurid dynasty had, from the start, encouraged not only foreign scholars and artists at its court, but foreign luxury goods of all sorts. Talent that for one reason or another could find no adequate patronage in Iran or in the Syr-Oxus basin found a warm and rich welcome in wealthy India, as did traders bringing goods from China or Europe or any point between. With the establishment of a high degree of internal order and political dependability within the vast area of the empire, the luxury of the court increased, as in the Ṣafavî empire.

But this was not necessarily to the benefit of the Indian economy as a whole. The Timurî state (like the Ṣafavî) undertook the largest manufacturing enterprises in India, for purposes of courtly luxury, and to this extent increased industrial investment in India. As a predominantly agrarian power, it took little interest in commerce, which was still at least as important in that period. From the time of Humâyûn's alliance with the Portuguese against Gujarât, it put relatively little effort into controlling the seaways (after the conquest of Gujarât, the provincial authorities there had to look away from the sea), and it allowed the Portuguese to raise some prices by their monopolies. However, as in Iran, merchants could make fine fortunes. But it was the agricultural economy that was crucial.

Taxes on the land gradually rose above the basic one-third of the produce that had prevailed, at least as a norm, in the more central parts of Akbar's dominions. This rise seems to have been felt by the peasantry, whose prosperity seems to have declined during the seventeenth century. The fall in the value of money (because of American silver, presumably) accounts for most of the great money rise in tax assessments; but a real rise is also indicated. Critics of the time seem to have ascribed it to the mismanagement of their land assignments by the military officers, who (despite government rewards when they increased production in their lands) were inclined to exact maximum revenue despite effects on future yield; for the rapid rotation of assigned lands, implicit in the centralized manṣabdâr system of ranks and salaries, lessened their interest in what were temporary holdings. It would seem that overextension of the agrarianate-level administrative apparatus, necessary so as to make possible continuing centralized military discipline, could have results almost as bad as the breakdown of that discipline would have had. In any case, along with the higher exactions, some decline of production is also indicated; and there was much talk of the flight of the peasants to areas less directly under imperial control, either forested areas hard of access (where the government commonly looked on the peasants as rebels), or areas protected by lesser grandees, who had only limited lump sums to pay the Timurîs, such as petty Hindu rulers. The great emperor had difficulty finding lands sufficient for the assignments that the great ruling apparatus was demanding.[11] Awrangzêb 'Âlamgîr, soon after his accession, had to face accumulating crises, which became almost desperate in the later part of his reign.

Awrangzêb and the rebels

The Timurid family produced a number of members with something of the philosophical vision of Akbar; as we have seen, Jahângîr had tried to maintain it, though without any special flair. Jahângîr's son Khusraw may have had more breadth of mind; he died murdered as a rebel. Shâh Jahân's favoured son, Dârâ Shikoh, affiliated to the Qâdirî ṭarîqah, wrote a demonstration that the Upanishads contained revealed expression of the same truth as Ṣûfîs proclaimed; not without capacity, he lacked the toughness of mind of Akbar or Bâbur. He was set aside and killed by his brother Awrangzêb. In each of such conflicts, there were those who favoured the more Sharî'ah-

[11] Basic to studies of Indo-Timurî economic history are W. H. Moreland's *India at the Death of Akbar* (see note 1 above) and his *From Akbar to Aurangzeb: A Study in Indian Economic History* (London, 1923). On the agrarian economy these must now be supplemented by Irfan Habib, *The Agrarian System of Mughal India (1556–1707)* (London, 1963), a careful and comprehensive study covering all relevant topics.

minded of any two claimants, precisely in the name of Islam; while this did not decide any battles, the pressure within the Muslim ruling class against the universalist tradition of the dynasty was continuous, and probably continually stronger.

Awrangzêb did not immediately reverse the general policy of the preceding reigns. But he was personally of a Sharî'ah-minded and communalistic, even rather a bigoted temper. He had close relations with the Chishtî Ṣûfîs, inherited from Akbar, and was persuaded to support their use of music in the dhikr ceremonies against the decision of a muḥtasib officer; but he also seems to have been friendly to the Mujaddidî Naqshbandîs, followers of Sirhindî. He allowed experts in legal fiqh to overrule a tax, a grant of monopoly, and the like; and he was very hostile to those whom the Jamâ'î-Sunnîs condemned as heretics, executing several persons on this ground (this had been rare in Timurî India till then), and taking measures against the Shî'î celebration of the Muḥarram mourning for Ḥusayn. When choices were to be made, he tended to support Sharî'ah-mindedness and Sunnî communalism.

While Awrangzêb was still only his father's representative in the Deccan, carrying on the attempt to subdue the two remaining Deccan kingdoms (Bîjâpûr and Golkondâ), an opposition force arose that was to persist throughout his reign. The Hindu mountaineers of the Marâthâ coastlands, who had served as source of troops for the Deccan sultanates, were discontented in the new imperial context. They found a leader in Shîvâjî, a Hindu Marâthâ commander who was unable to win for himself a place proportionate to his abilities in the Timurî system, and under him they carved out an independent sphere in their own highlands; from there, they raided both the Timurî states and the Deccan sultanate of Bîjâpûr. Malcontents (including Muslims) from all over the Deccan joined them and they successfully resisted many attempts to repress them.

Awrangzêb may have felt that the answer to such threats was greater discipline within the Muslim camp, which for him would include tighter religious discipline. At any rate, he allowed his religious prejudices increasingly to affect his policies. He acted against various sorts of laxity among the Muslims, for instance, by instituting measures against wine drinking still more severe than Shâh Jahân had already attempted (but he winked at some evasions of his prohibitions, as by a colony of west European gunners who felt they could not do without). But one sort of laxity in Shar'î standards carried special significance: that which made effective co-operation with Hindus possible. In this sphere, he was relatively cautious at first: he reduced the number of Hindu festivals which (as monarch) he attended, and replaced Hindu astrologers at the court with Muslim ones; at length he forbade all Hindu festivals within the army camp. He doubled the taxes on Hindu merchants, keeping that on Muslims at the old lower rate. He retained Hindu officers, but gave them less responsibility. From 1679, however, he attempted to enforce all the disabilities upon Hindus that the Sharî'ah law called for in

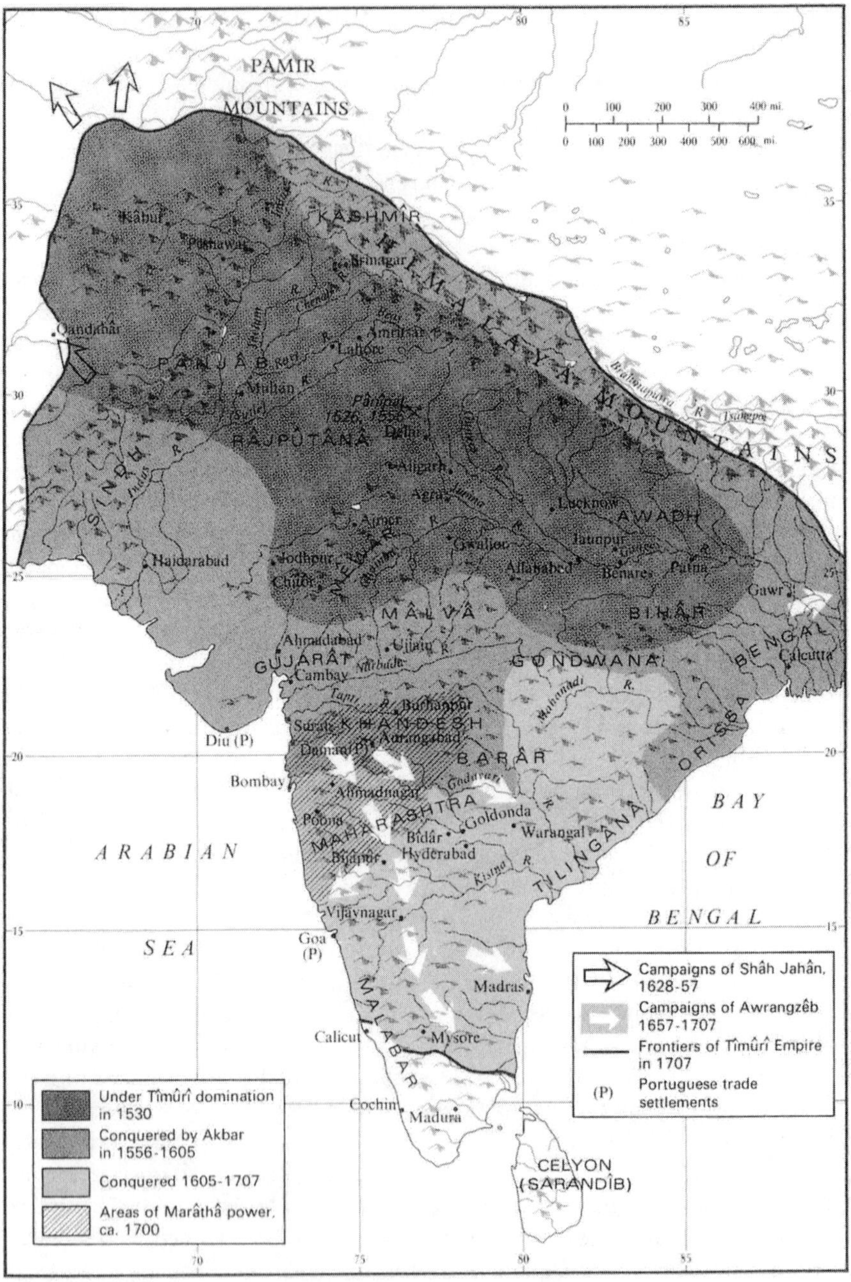

The Indian Timurî empire, 1526–1707

the case of dhimmî non-Muslims, most symbolically in the reimposition of the jizyah tax on the individual dhimmî; it was often a heavy tax, and was exacted in a humiliating manner, even from dhimmîs serving in the army. One of the most spectacular expressions of his policy was the widespread destruction of Hindu temples on various pretexts.

These religious policies complicated the gathering economic tensions. To be sure, the opposite religious policy had done nothing to relieve them, and with its encouragement of luxury it may have contributed to the peasants' woes. The genteel courtly universalism, satisfactory for allowing privileged groups of diverse traditions and persuasions to share in a common brilliant culture, seems to have done little for humane relations beyond the thin layers of the highly privileged classes. The age-old dream of universal social justice would not necessarily be served by such a culture, however amiable. Discontent seems to have increased among the less privileged classes in the provinces in the course of the later reigns. But unfortunately a Shar'î communalist bigotry did not serve to reverse the process either. Though ideally the spirit of the Sharî'ah might have called for that reduction of courtly expenses which would decisively have lightened taxation, it was not that sort of rigour to which a renewed Shar'ism actually led.

Minor peasant evasions and resistances were common enough, but major peasant revolts now appeared. It was the destruction of a popular temple that set off a major rebellion among the Hindus of the Dôâb farming lands between Ganges and Jamunâ, near Agra itself, among the widespread Jât caste. It seems to have been despair at unbearable taxation, however, that was the chief motivation. Making use of inter-village caste solidarity, peasants and lesser landlords co-operated to throw out the tax-gatherers and even take the offensive in raiding nearby towns; they maintained their independence from about 1669 to 1689. In the hillier land westward of the Jât country in the 1670s it was a religious cult, a Hindu devotional movement revering Kabîr and of the type that commonly expressed a religious universalism, that provided the ties that made possible the Satnâmî peasant rebellion. Otherwise this was of much the same pattern as that of the Jâts.

But the most firmly entrenched of these revolts proved to be that of the Sikh sect. Already during the reign of Akbar, the Sikhs under their gurus had been developing a strong social outlook in the Panjâb; they exalted crafts and trades and a tendency to disregard the claims of the military grandees. In time, they built their own town, Amritsar, and recruited the Hindu peasantry into a whole social order increasingly self-contained within the wider Indian society. Under Jahângîr they had their first clash with the court and began to work up a military discipline among their militants. Under Shâh Jahân they found themselves, for a time, at open war with the Timurî government, by which they were only partly overwhelmed. The universalism of the founder was eventually almost submerged under a very positive particular loyalty to institutions designed to create a social order in

The Indian Timurî Empire to 1763

1526–30	Bâbur, driven from his Timurî state in Farghânah, after rebuilding his power in Kâbul, seizes Islamic northern India after battle of Pânîpat and establishes Indo-Timurî (Mughal) empire; was himself the most famous Turkic writer of his time as a memoirist
1530	Death of Bâbur
1539–55	Sher-Shâh (to 1545) and his Sûr dynasty interrupts Mughal régime but continues administrative consolidation of N. India
1556–1605	Akbar, third Mughal emperor (personal rule from 1562) fosters Hindu-Muslim cultural and even religious rapprochement, completes Mughal institutional edifice, includes Gujarât and some southerly areas in the N. Indian empire; Indo-Persian school of art
1590–91	Death of Muḥ. 'Urfî, Persian poet of ornate yet obscure, metaphorical style that became Indian style, influences the Ottoman poet Naf'i and others
1595	Death of Fayżî, poet in Indian style
1602	Death of Abûlfażl 'Allâmî (brother of Fayżî), scholar, courtier, historian of Akbar, casting him as both philosopher king and 'perfect man'
1605–58	Jahângîr (1605–27) and Shâh Jahân (1628–58), builder of the Tâj Maḥall at Agra, continue Akbar's policies in Mughal empire; art, especially portraiture and architecture, reaches peak of refinement; Indian ruling class directs trade in extensive use of foreign luxuries from all parts of the hemisphere
1625	Death of Aḥmad Sirhindî, anti-Akbarist (anti-universalist) reformer, working within a classically defined Ṣûfî orientation
1658–1707	Awrangzêb, last of the major Mughal emperors; reverses policy of co-operation with Hindus, attempting to Islamize all India; after 1681 concentrates on Deccan, where he subdued remaining Muslim powers but aroused a lasting Hindu revolt of the Marâthas under Shîvâjî
c. 1700	Formalized spoken Urdu of Mughal court combines with literary popular Urdu of Islamic Deccan to form the rise of Urdu literature in the succeeding centuries
1707–12	Bahadur, Mughal emperor, despite some successes fails to reverse the weakening of the empire, which after 1720 loses its southern and eastern provinces, except for theoretical suzerainty
1739	Nâḍir Shâh sacks Delhi and puts an end to what remained of Mughal imperial power in India, which was for the rest of the century disputed between the armies of the Marâtha Hindu confederacy, the religious power of the Sikh sect of the Punjâb, and Afghan Muslim invaders
1762	Death of Shâh Valî-ullâh, Ṣûfî reformer who attempted to harmonize variant Muslim traditions on basis of Shar'ism and support from many of Sirhindî's ideas
1763	British greatly expand their control over disunited independent Indian states after defeating French in Seven Years' War

the Panjâb which was to develop egalitarian justice among at least the townsmen, and to some measure did so where the Sikh polity was able to flourish. Almost inevitably, this polity found itself poised explicitly against the ruling Muslim power, confounding anew any inclination to universal conciliation on so practical a level. Under Awrangzêb, especially from the 1690s, conflict with the empire broke out anew and on a more formidable scale; at the end of his reign, they became a major menace to Timurî power in the Panjâb.

Despite these challenges, or again because of them, from 1679 on (the time of the decree about jizyah), Awrangzêb's religious policy threatened to become his chief consideration, and led him to provoke further rebellions before he had suppressed those already in being. For a time he seemed almost to get away with such a programme. Awrangzêb's wish to Islamize wherever possible was expressed in imperious violence in a major case of Râjpût succession. He tried to turn a major Râjpût state into what some Râjpûts felt would amount to a Muslim province, destroying temples and otherwise expressing the prejudices of Sharî'ah-mindedness. Thereby he drove many of the Râjpût chiefs into insurrection. From a major military and political pillar of the empire, these became bitter opponents of his policies. There were Muslims who saw such developments as disastrous; a son of Awrangzêb rebelled, rather ineptly, in the name of restoring the Râjpût alliance; but he received little support. Increasingly in all these matters Awrangzêb appealed to Sharî'ah-minded Muslim sentiment against Hindu privileges.

As soon as the Râjpûts were repressed for the time being, Awrangzêb returned to his preoccupation with the Deccan—with the Shî'î sultanates and the Hindu Marâthâs. He began with the sultanates, whom he accused of helping the infidel Marâthâs against him. Concentrating the strength of the empire on that task, he succeeded in subduing them in 1686–87, finding new lands to assign to his officers—and driving the officers and men who had been loyal to the old dynasties into dispersion and (in some cases) into the Marâthâ forces. By about 1691 he had also managed to check the raiding, and occupy some of the mountain strongholds, of the Marâthâs, who had not found a satisfactory successor to Shîvâjî (d. 1680). Awrangzêb seemed thus to have rounded out the Timurî dominions in India and to have suppressed practically all revolts. Yet almost immediately the rebellions took on new strength. The Marâthâs began raiding more daringly than before, and the Sikhs proved not to have been crushed. By 1707, when Awrangzêb died, the resources of the empire seemed to threaten exhaustion and Timurî power was becoming shakier every year.

Had Awrangzêb's rejection of universalism been consistently carried out, I suppose, it would either have destroyed the empire, or have required a drastic reformulation of its bases (hardly feasible at so late a stage without some special genius). As it was, his policy was sufficiently put into practice to shake many loyalties very seriously. Once the monarch gave them the lead, the Sharî'ah-minded element among the Muslim grandees was strong enough to give an edge to the communalist policy; and in response the revolts, though not basically religious, took on a heroic colour of defence of religion. Any opportunity to hold together the empire on the basis of common privileged interests, despite economic difficulties, was scuttled; the economic strains were allowed to have their full effect. By the year of Awrangzêb's death, in 1707, the empire had been seriously undermined; though a communalist policy was then abandoned, the empire never fully recovered. By his own confession, Awrangzêb had neglected that side of the Sharî'ah that called for protection and justice for the peasantry. He had set as first task the preservation or establishment of Sharî'ah-minded Sunnî rule; and even here he failed.[12]

[12] On the time of Awrangzêb and after, the massive authority is Jadunath Sarkar, a writer free from partisanship, interested in economic detail, and concerned with things human. He monumentalized the judgment on Awrangzêb as a great man who yet ruined the empire. (Some of his generalizations about Islam presuppose old misjudgments.) One may mention his *Mughal Administration* (Calcutta, 1920), which is more general, and his *Studies in Aurangzîb's Reign* (Calcutta, 1933); his lengthier history is too long to supersede conveniently Beni Prasad, *History of Jahangir* (Oxford University Press, 1922), which is sound, and mostly political. For the period immediately after Awrangzêb, but with useful information about earlier times in an introduction, see Satish Chandra, *Parties and Politics at the Mughal Court 1707–40* (Aligarh Muslim University, 1959), who takes a special interest in lower-class rebellions and the economic self-contradictions of the absolutism (using a more or less mechanical Marxist viewpoint).

III

The Ottoman Empire: Sharî'ah-Military Alliance, 1517–1718

Of the great absolute monarchies that succeeded to the turmoil of the age of Mongol dominance, the Ottoman proved the most enduring and probably the strongest. Like the Ṣafavî and Indo-Timurî empires, the Ottoman associated the major civilian institutions relatively closely with the central state power. In the Ṣafavî state, this association was based on a revolutionary principle, and finally, with the setting in of normalcy, the gulf between the military-political power and the representatives of social legitimacy was re-opened. In the Indian state the association was based on a lay political, more or less universalist principle, and this proved more than the legitimizing authority of Islam could absorb. In the Ottoman state, it was based on the military aspect of the Shar'î principle itself, and might not have been expected to be subject to the same drawbacks as in the other two empires. In fact the success of the Ottoman state was, for some time, phenomenal. It also was not permanent; the dilemmas of agrarianate-level society at last displayed themselves. Here too life, as always, insistently required that even the best of the past be still transcended.

Military absolutism and the slave household

In its absolutism, the Ottoman state had a military character fundamentally similar to the others, though distinctive in its particular forms. Like others, Ottoman absolutism built upon the tradition of looking upon the central power, including all its administrative branches, as one great army; and of regarding this army as at the personal service of the monarch.[1] In the Ottoman case, some aspects of this conception were carried out with special consistency.

The original Ottoman state had been military, indeed, but far from an absolute monarchy of any kind. But the character of the military base of the state had been transformed and absolutism gradually was imposed on the ghâzî warriors' descendants. When the Ottoman military activities had

[1] Stanford Shaw, 'The Ottoman View of the Balkans', in *The Balkans in Transition*, ed. Chas. and Barbara Jelavich (University of California Press, 1963), pp. 56–80, describes this attitude with remarkable vigour as it appeared in the Ottoman empire in particular. I must thank him also for useful comments on an early draft of my Ottoman pages. Richard Chambers also kindly read those pages.

come to be channelled in major campaigns, whose distance required great central organization, the former more or less irregular ghâzî troops had tended gradually to recede into the general herding and peasant population, while their leaders became prosperous landlords, holding systematic military land grants. With their changed social position, their attitudes changed; well established themselves, they were less ready to look for a heroic chief, more ready to accept an established monarch. At the same time, their power was diluted.

The military traditions of the frontier ghâzîs persisted. The troops still regarded their destiny as the subjugation of the infidel—and perhaps, now, of the heretic Shîʿîs of the Ṣafavî empire. But their personnel had gradually ceased to be drawn from Muslim adventurers and hereditary frontiersmen. The military had come to be composed of two contrary and rival groups. The old ghâzî families, with the expansion of the empire, had come to form a landed Turkic aristocracy increasingly independent of their chief and contented with results already achieved. Under the forms of a common monarchy, they would have been glad to rule each his own domain in private.

To maintain a central government at all, Meḥmed II had leaned on the alternative sources of power which the Ottoman state had been able to build up in its sudden victories. These included partly the old families of the Balkan nobility, who had served even as Christians but in the sixteenth century were becoming Muslim. More important was the new element brought to the fore by the use of gunpowder. With the development of gunpowder weapons, the infantry became a crucial arm. From the time of Meḥmed II through that of Süleymân (1520–66), the number and variety of infantry corps, variously recruited, increased. Among them, one of the most highly trained infantry corps, the Janissaries, formed the heart of the army. As in the case of the Ṣafavîs, these and other infantrymen were outsiders (largely lower-class Christians by birth), standing apart from the powerful classes of society. Paid from the treasury, they were at the disposal of the monarch without reservation, in contrast to the holders of military land grants, with their far-ramifying connections. With a well-supported dynasty solidly established in Istanbul, then, something of the Byzantine political idea reasserted itself: the same strategic opportunities and problems were reproduced. But the political idea had been reasserted in a thoroughly Islamicate form.

Byzantium had indeed been an absolute monarchy, and not only imperial strategy but the forms of absolutism owed something to it. Meḥmed II had developed an elaborate courtly ceremonial in place of the comradely simplicity of his ancestors; relying on the diverse elements of the state other than the descendants of ghâzîs, he had not only reduced the almost independent power of the grandees of the state, but did much to organize it centrally and hierarchically. But though his models in ceremonial may often have been Byzantine, his basic political ideals were moulded by the stories of the great Muslim states: the Great Seljuḳs and the Anatolian Seljuḳs, the Mongols (who had been the immediate overlords of the ghâzî chiefs 'Osmân and Orkhan), and probably Timur himself and the Timurids.

When Selîm enlarged the empire, then, the most important segments of the central power structure were organized as a single army, with the emperor, the pâdishâh, at its head;[2] within this army, not only soldiers but many kinds of administrators held military rank and were compensated either by a military land grant or, increasingly, on the military payroll. The rewards of power were frankly conceived in military terms; the revenues of the whole empire were allotted to members of the Ottoman ruling class according to their military contributions: a conception originally appropriate to ghâzîs, indeed, but, with the dominance of the figure of the emperor, the pâdishâh, recast in military patronage form. The terminology of the ranking, however, was heterogeneous and not tied, like that of the system of manṣabdârs in India, even to suppositious contingents. The seat of government, accordingly, was wherever the pâdishâh and his army happened to be. The chief officials of the usual capital city, responsible for policing and for justice in its various quarters, and even the chief men responsible for keeping the central financial accounts, were expected to go on campaign with the pâdishâh whenever he set out with the armed forces. (They left substitutes to do their peace-time offices.)

This 'army' has been called the 'ruling institution', a term that allows for the presence within it both of bureaucrats (*ḳalemiyyeh*) and of military (*seyfiyyeh*), wielding all central power as one block. Unfortunately, probably the term cannot be further used, for it implies too sharp a contrast to the Muslim religious establishment, which however (as the *'ilmiyyeh*) was well integrated at its top into the absolutism.[3] All the servants of the absolutism formed a body apart, free, as 'army men' (*'askerî*), from taxation, and subject in theory to military discipline and to their own special qâḍîs; and the men at the top even of the bureaucracy were mostly actually associated with the military proper (seyfiyyeh). Like their counterparts in India, these imperial servants were regarded as the proper carriers of the specifically Ottoman culture.

But not only was the central power looked on as a single conquering army.

[2] The term 'sultan', used generally for an independent Muslim ruler from Seljuḳ times on, is no longer appropriate for the great empires of gunpowder times; following earlier precedents, they sometimes used the title 'sultan' for lesser figures at court. The commonest term for an emperor as such was *pâdishâh*.

[3] The phrase 'ruling institution', devised by Albert Howe Lybyer in *The Government of the Ottoman Empire in the Time of Suleiman the Magnificent* (Harvard University Press, 1913), has also been used by H. A. R. Gibb and Harold Bowen in their *Islamic Society and the West* (Oxford University Press, 1950 and 1957), rather than 'government', to indicate the organization in which central coercive power resided; this was contrasted to the several other organizations (especially the religious organizations of the several faiths, with their judicial functions—of which the Muslim was called 'religious institution' to distinguish it from a 'church' in the Christian sense) which carried on much of the process of governing.

The companion idea, that this army was at the personal service of the pâdishâh, was reinforced by an intensive elaboration of the tradition of military slavery which had developed from later 'Abbâsî times and had been prominent in the Earlier Middle Period. Apart from the still-powerful landed military families, the properly military sector of the 'army men' was, in fact, chiefly composed of personal slaves of the monarch, whether solidiers or high administrators in the bureaucracy; and the norm of personal dependence on the monarch, which they represented, came to be extended widely even to those of the army men, especially on the military side, that were not legally his slaves.

The Ottomans became quite systematic on this point. The Janissaries and certain other corps and, above all, most of the higher ranks of the central administration were almost exclusively, and with jealous care, drawn by conscription from among the adolescent sons of Christian families, chiefly in the Balkan provinces (this levy was called the *devshirme*). The importance of this conscription increased with the development of the empire. The boys were often sent for their first training to the rural households of the gentry, where they learned Ottoman Turkic and were converted to Islam (rarely was conversion refused—some families were even glad to see their sons have such an opportunity of preferment). Then they came back to Istanbul to be trained for specialized service. The bulk of them were destined to the infantry ranks, but the more promising were selected out for future officership—which included every sort of high office in the state; these were educated in all aspects of Islamicate culture and might rise to the very highest posts.

This class of 'military' imperial servant was recruited also from purchased slaves—for instance, Georgians; a certain number in these Ottoman cadres were the result of voluntary conversions by foreign Christians—occasionally highly trained men. But all alike lacked connections within established Ottoman society except through the pâdishâh himself. The trainees and soldiers and officers together formed a massive slave household, living, in principle, as part of the domestic establishment of the monarch. The trainees did such tasks as taking care of the pâdishâh's gardens. The Janissaries in service were not allowed to marry, lest they loosen their ties to the common household. (More modest subordinate households of a somewhat similar nature might be maintained by some of the older grandees themselves.)

The pâdishâh's personal role, to be sure, was diluted by the presence of the grand vizier. Such an officer had been given highest precedence under Meḥmed II, but received comprehensive authority, to be shared with no one, under Süleymân. He stood at the head of the whole apparatus: effective commander-in-chief in war and master of the fiscal and even judicial services in peace. At his side were lesser viziers, who had but little independent power. The troops were commanded by two (later three) chief generals, *beglerbegi*, one taking precedence in Rumelia and the other in Anatolia; and the qâḍîs were appointed by two 'army qâḍîs', *ḳâżi'asker*, likewise one for Rumelia and one for Anatolia. But the grand vizier loomed far above these; his status was indicated ceremonially (in the general Islamicate manner) by elaborate rites and trappings of precedence, in which he received homage short only of that received by the pâdishâh himself. His headquarters was referred to as the High Gate (in French, 'Sublime Porte'), in allusion to a prominent structure there, and foreigners referred to the Ottoman government as a whole by that term. Yet in absolutist principle, the monarch still watched and determined the fate of all his slaves, including the grand vizier; and did so in practice too, in a way, for the exalted grand vizier was sometimes summarily executed; though unfortunately (as also in other absolutisms) such an event was more likely to result from harem intrigue than from the pâdishâh's personal watchfulness.

The territorial expansion under Selîm accentuated the air of personal patronage in the absolutism. The military 'outsiders' of the slave household formed a class with considerable solidarity, rivals to the established Turkic aristocracy. The pâdishâh and his associates at the top could control the empire by playing the two groups against each other. But with the increase in the size of the empire, the newer lands, notably the Arab lands, could be most effectively handled through assignments to the rootless and movable officials rather than through an extension of the old Turkic military aristocracy. Such assignments (*iltizâms*), unlike the more purely military grants (*timars*), yielded direct income to the central treasury. The old aristocracy was tied, moreover, to the now secondary military arm, the cavalry, while the 'outsiders' were associated with the various specialized infantry corps. The latter group finally triumphed. It gave the empire its tone under Süleymân. In the seventeenth century it was almost a requirement for a high Ottoman post (apart from the Sharî'ah positions), that one be, though a Muslim indeed, yet not one of an old established family. This was legally insured by the requirement that an official be, formally, the personal slave of the pâdishâh (which legally no free-born Muslim could become)—to the point even of forfeiting his inheritance to the pâdishâh to the exclusion of his own descendants, at the pâdishâh's pleasure. The official's heirs (who did in fact commonly inherit) were supposed to enter into the Ottoman gentry, being excluded from positions of government trust. From this point on, if scions of old families wished to rise politically they must, by special dispensation. be allowed to become legally 'slaves' of the pâdishâh, as many did.

But (as in the Ṣafavî state) the same changes that enhanced the central power also diluted its military character. The ascendancy of the imperial slaves (and of the system of direct income to the imperial treasury), at the expense of the old families who held outright military land grants, gave an increasingly civilian tone to the government, despite its formally military structure. Among the 'army men' themselves, though the pure bureaucrats were never allowed a top post, it was usually (not always) those military men that had had a literary education who controlled the treasury and had precedence over the more soldierly. As in India also, the writings of Davvânî, justifying the absolute monarchy as the 'true caliphate' upholding justice, and relegating soldiers to a secondary position, were popular at court. The sense of the state as such was so strong as to be independent of the relatively transient prestige of mighty individuals and their immediate families; it supported a dynasty that lasted for centuries as the centre of a bureaucratic structure which could do its work with less and less reference to the personality of a given pâdishâh. So much was the state regarded as independent not only of the individual pâdishâh but of the particular ruling family whose service was in military theory its whole end, that it was debated, should the line of Osmân run out, what family should rightfully succeed to their position at Istanbul.[4]

Nevertheless, the central power institution continued to be informed by a military viewpoint; right through the sixteenth century and for the most part in the seventeenth century, public service was still associated with the armed forces, which formed its core. The armed forces, in turn, still depended on the booty of annexationist warfare to maintain their morale and even their accustomed level of income (in particular, to supplement the low wages of the Janissary corps itself, always ready to depose the master who did not generously give them of the empire's wealth). Moreover, the ideology that bound the absolutism to the more socially significant classes of its subjects reinforced this military outlook—and it too depended upon military success, in some measure, for its vitality. Soldiers and administrators, legally slaves of the pâdishâh, might proclaim that they served only a given ruler who in turn shared his spoils liberally with themselves. Court intellectuals might interpret the régime in terms of late Falsafah ideals of the just monarchy. For the gentry and the industrious classes, the purpose of the state was to maintain Islam and above all to spread its sway: the true monarch was still the supreme ghâzî, not now the head of frontier bands but the legally established representative of the Sharî'ah law and hence of the 'ulamâ' scholars.[5]

[4] Christian Europeans, used to a notion of fixed inheritance, sometimes took a given suggestion for a reflection of a settled law; thus arose the supposition that the Khans of Crimea were the sure alternative heirs to the Os̄mânids, whose dynastic policies made extinction always possible. A. D. Alderson, *The Structure of the Ottoman Dynasty* (Oxford, 1956), has a wealth of information, but cannot escape the usual Occidental prejudice that there *must* have been *some* rule of fixed succession, to be divined.

[5] In any study of Ottoman institutions before the eighteenth century, we start from Gibb and Bowen's invaluable *Islamic Society and the West*. Hence we must take note of its weak points. I have the impression that it started from certain conventional presuppositions which, though the points it makes serve to undermine them in the reader's mind, the book itself was not able fully to transcend. I will cite especially three, which are reflected in numerous details. (*a*) That the central cultural tradition of Islamdom can be almost identified with that of the Arabs, especially the Sunnî Arabs; and in later centuries, therefore, largely with that of Syria and Egypt. It is in part in this spirit that the authors compare Ottoman institutions with a Mamlûk 'past' rather than with the Seljuḳ-Mongol-Timurî tradition of the more central lands, for instance; though it is in part also for want of relevant studies of the more central traditions. (*b*) That the interests

The integration of Shar'î law and absolute monarchy

In all the empires, the Sharî'ah played a major role; in the Ottoman its communal claims not only served to tie together (as elsewhere) the courtly and the more popular urban life, but became the most seminal single inspiration of the higher cultural forms of the courtly life itself, playing a role comparable to that of Shî'î chiliasm in the Ṣafavî state and the tradition of Mongol ambition in the Indian. The 'ulamâ' enjoyed, in Ottoman society, a correspondingly high role.

The prevailing 'ulamâ' had always tended to accept a *modus vivendi* with the *de facto* military rulers of Islamicate society, which often amounted to an outright alliance. After the fall of the High Caliphal state, this had implied a certain legitimation, by the 'ulamâ', of the amîrs as constituted authorities within a minimal sphere; whereas the amîrs in turn were expected to leave the 'ulamâ' as a body essentially inviolate, together with their local spheres of operation. Under the states of Mongol heritage, the 'ulamâ' had found themselves somewhat more subordinated within a comprehensive military state; in the great empires that succeeded, they lost for a time yet more of their autonomy, as cultural forms of all sorts were brought into relations with the imperial institutions. The replacement of Jamâ'î Sunnî 'ulamâ' by Shî'î 'ulamâ' in the Ṣafavî empire was accompanied at first by a subordination of the latter under state authority, but this had been done in a manner inconsistent with Shar'î Shî'ism, and gradually the 'ulamâ' worked themselves free. In the end, if there was an alliance it was on the terms set by the 'ulamâ'. In India, the 'ulamâ' were brought under control by Akbar and their role was limited by the cultivation of universalist standards of culture so that the full implementation of the Sharî'ah should not undermine the Muslim-Hindu association on which the empire thrived; in the end, the more intransigent section of the 'ulamâ' was able to shift the balance sufficiently to cause the system to break down, at least in its grander political expression.

In the Ottoman empire, the alliance of 'ulamâ' and amîrs was maintained on a relatively more equal basis and indeed amounted to almost a full synthesis. The 'ulamâ' came under state control, but in doing so they brought the Sharî'ah into the centre of the state life. The earlier Jamâ'î-Sunnî

and welfare of the central absolutist government can be identified with those of Ottoman society as a whole, without question as to why or in which respects; and hence that the decline of the central power can automatically be identified with the decline of the empire itself both in military potency and in general social strength. Gibb and Bowen have shown the enormous importance of institutions other than those of the absolutism. Yet they do not entirely escape (*c*) a way of thinking reinforced by the two identifications above: that a study of conditions in the neighbourhood of the capital of the absolutism itself, plus special studies of the most prominent Sunnî Arab provinces, Syria and Egypt (this is virtually the scope of the book), can yield a reasonably adequate picture of conditions in the empire as a whole—indeed in the 'Islamic society' as a whole which was to react to 'the West' in the title. Here again, however, such selection results largely from accidents of availability of material, and is accepted only reluctantly. But the reader must be alert to discount the effects of it.

alliance with the amîrs was reaffirmed on a different level, in which the pâdishâh achieved a more extensive authority, including a fuller control of the Sharî'ah aspects of society; while the Sharî'ah and its representatives in turn were more fully recognized in the work of the military rulers. The religious establishment neither became independent, as under the Ṣafavîs, nor had to tolerate any Muslim-Christian association comparable to what happened in India. Its representatives could feel that in large measure the empire was their own.

The contrasts among the empires were deeply rooted in their histories. Like the Ottoman empire, both the Timurî state in India and even the Ṣafavî state had grown out of political structures which dated from the age of Mongol prestige and had reflected originally the various political conditions of that time: the conquering and then self-dividing military monarchy of the Timurids; the militarized ṭarîqah of the Ṣafavids, dominating the local institutions of one town as its base. In the Ottoman case, of course, the origin was in a frontier ghâzî state. The dominant formative ideals of each empire were set largely by the original heritage as modified by the course of creation of empire. The Indian empire had been inspired by the Mongol and Timurî sense of cosmopolitan grandeur, heightened in the presence of Indian courage and refinement; the Ṣafavî had been inspired by the reforming zeal of the Shî'ah in the heartlands of old Islam. The Ottoman empire had been inspired by the ghâzî sense of community mission on the borders of perennially resistant Christendom.

But whereas in the former two cases the state passed through a severe dislocation and reorganization in becoming the empire, the Ottoman state developed very gradually. Hence the institutions of the wider empire possessed not only a central inspiration but also a firm continuity going back to the institutions of the more local state. This had the incidental result that the empire, even its more closely controlled portions, was always divided into two parts: the nuclear provinces of Anatolia and Rumelia on the one hand and the later acquisitions in the southeast, chiefly the Arab lands, on the other; it was only in the nuclear provinces that the distinctive Ottoman institutions were fully developed. Perhaps a more pregnant consequence was the relative deep-rootedness of many of the traits and institutions of the society formed within the state. That is, not only were diverse heritages effectively integrated; this integration was embodied in numerous interdependent institutions locally established and hallowed by custom; and to alter any one of them without the other would require the pressure of overwhelming new interests.

In particular, a communalist sense of public spirit directly traceable (however transformed) to the ghâzîs was deeply felt and widely ramified; but only as it had been closely mingled with many other impulses and disciplined in long experience of responsibility. The relation between 'ulamâ' and state did not grow out of the sudden imposition of a new régime but out of a slow evolution in which the original indifference of the ghâzîs to the bookish 'ulamâ' and their dicta had been replaced by a profound respect for them as the mainstays of communal solidarity. But the central ideals of the ghâzîs continued to dominate the Ottoman Muslim imagination. The Shar'î 'ulamâ' were increasingly called on to define the norms of life, rather than the Ṣûfî *bâbâ* darvîshes of the militant tribesmen and frontiersmen, as the city took the place of tribe and camp as focus of Ottoman life. But it had always been the Muslim community as a whole, which the 'ulamâ' did represent, that the ghâzîs had fought for. The Ottoman cause was then still identified with the cause of militant Islam. As the generations passed, this fact impressed itself ever more fully upon the state. Accordingly, not only particular social institutions but the moral tone of the centralizing empire was already deeply set by the time that Selîm's conquests in the Arab lands (1517) gave it a first-line role in Islamdom as a whole.

The landed descendants of the ghâzîs seem to have accepted the religious lead of the urban upper classes, who followed the more Sharî'ah-minded ṭarîqahs and the Jamâ'î-Sunnî 'ulamâ'. The cause of Islam against the infidel was for them the cause of the main body of the Muslim community, essentially as it was already established. Something of the older form of the ghâzí spirit survived among the Janissary corps who, though conscripts, had something of the zeal of converts. These came to understand the Islam for which they fought partly through the eyes of the Bektashîs, a covertly Shî'î ṭarîqah set against any form of Sharî'ah-mindedness, with whom the Janissary corps seems to have been long associated unofficially. But the Janissaries themselves represented a communalist principle, in that they replaced, as Muslims, the Christian levies, that had been extensively used in earlier Ottoman times. And it was at the same time as such secondary Christian levies were replaced by Muslim troops, that the Christian holders of Ottoman land grants were gradually converted (especially after 1500); so that the landed military class came to be exclusively Muslim. The Ottoman empire, then, presented a rigidly communal Muslim front in special contrast to the Indian empire with its Hindu generals and grant-holders as well as vassals. With Selîm, this emphasis on communal Islam was carried to the logical point of internal discrimination also: not only must Ottomans be Muslims, they must be Jamâ'î-Sunnî, even Ḥanafî Muslims; and the unprecedented massacring of Shî'îs reinforced this drive for a communalist conformity. (As with the Janissaries, who never dropped their Bektashî sympathies, he was not entirely successful in such a drive.)

Selîm's successor, Süleymân 'Qânûnî' (1520–66), the 'lawgiver' (called in the Occident 'Solyman the Magnificent', for the work of organization done under him was less well known there than the dazzling splendour of his power), presided over the empire in its classical age, when its central institutions were most definitively codified in a Shar'î and communalist sense. His reign was comparable for the definitiveness of its spirit to that of

Akbar in India a generation later for the very different spirit there, except that what took place in the Ottoman state was more a development and consolidation of ways already established. Even in literary and artistic culture, Süleymân's reign marked the classical age of the Ottoman society as an embodiment of communalist Islam.

With the stress on communalism, the exaltation of the Sharî'ah, through which the community expressed outwardly its common life, naturally followed. The 'ulamâ' had great prestige and came to have great authority and even great power. Lengthy training, officially supervised and tested, was required for entry into their official ranks; as qâḍîs and muftîs they had a position of considerable impunity and were well organized. The chief muftî of the realm (called shaykh al-Islâm) was recognized as competent to authorize deposition of the pâdishâh for unfitness, and on occasion he did so (where a powerful faction enabled him).

At the same time, they were closely integrated into the state. Their organizations throughout the empire were centred at Istanbul, where their head was dismissible at will by the pâdishâh. The great central positions, and to some extent the provincial positions calling for trained 'ulamâ', were assigned according to an elaborate and undeviating cursus honorum, which included ranked levels of study and then of teaching at the great madrasahs in the area of the capital. The occupants of certain posts so distributed had power of appointment to all major Shar'î posts in the empire; to be sure, many posts supported by waqf were controlled privately at the will of the founder of the waqf. To a large degree the local bodies of 'ulamâ' retained their autonomy, but even there, the local head had power officially to exclude an individual from the body of recognized 'ulamâ'.[6]

This whole Shar'î establishment did stand apart from the main body of the absolutist régime. Unlike so much of the latter, it was staffed chiefly by Ottomans born, members of the leading families in society at large; indeed only through a career in this field did a born Ottoman have a clear chance to

[6] The legend that Selîm I inherited the title *caliph* from the last 'Abbâsid 'caliph' of Egypt, and with it a claim to ultimate lordship over all (Sunnî) Muslims, has long been refuted. The notion persists in vaguer forms, however, that the Ottomans did make such a claim. Some cite the Ottoman pâdishâhs' control of Mecca and Medina—which did give them prestige—but the Ottomans used the same title for that as had the somewhat more modest Mamlûks, 'servant of the Holy Cities'. It was the special Ottoman synthesis of state and Sharî'ah that did support the idea of a caliphate. But it did so only by the standards of the Faylasûfs and the later Falsafah-inspired legists, in the same manner as the other great monarchs of the time: all were caliphs within their own territories. The Ottomans, like all agrarianate absolutisms, bore uneasily the idea that their ruler was but one among others; they used haughty formulas and loved flattery. But before the late eighteenth or even the nineteenth century, none of all this can be construed as indicating an exclusive claim to the historical caliphate and to the supremacy that would go with it. This has been shown by Sir Thomas Walker Arnold, *The Caliphate* (Oxford, 1924), and especially by H. A. R. Gibb in his brief but packed and brilliant essay, 'Some Considerations on the Sunnî Theory of the Caliphate', *Archives d'histoire du droit oriental,* 3 (1939), 401–10, reprinted in Gibb, *Studies on the Civilization of Islam,* ed. Stanford J. Shaw and William R. Polk (Boston, 1962), pp. 141–50.

win highest position. Meanwhile, no rivalry arose between the slave household in their military-administrative careers and the Ottoman 'ulamâ' in their Shar'î careers until either reached the very top levels of the state. Possibly this segregation of personnel, which left the absolutism a free hand in central administration, was at the same time an essential ingredient in making possible the close co-operation on a level of equal dignity between state personnel and 'ulamâ'.

The Sharî'ah played a role in the state comparable to that of its representatives: that is, its authority was institutionalized at a high level and not relegated, outside the private sphere, to incidental interventions; but the initiative was yet retained for the direct authority of the absolutism. At least since Mongol times, the Shar'î term *'urf* (precedent) had been appropriated to the authority of the monarch; in Ottoman usage, then, *qânûn* (derived, in earlier Arabic, from the Greek 'canon', law) was used for an imperial administrative ordinance legitimized by 'urf. Such law was the main reliance of the administration. It was durable and impersonal, for it was expected that the qânûn directives of one pâdishâh would continue binding also on his successors. Now qânûn ordinances had to be certified in detail by regularly appointed 'ulamâ' as consistent with the Sharî'ah. Respect for the Sharî'ah was consistently maintained. For instance, the fragmenting of landownership, which would normally result from the application of Sharî'ah inheritance rules to land, was avoided not by invoking non-Shar'î custom but through a fictional state ownership so that what was to be inherited was simply an indivisible lease. (Local custom itself, 'âdah, of course, could in some cases be legitimized as such on a Shar'î basis: the way of the early community had included a degree of recognition for such customs.) Nevertheless, the qânûn ordinances of a ruler like Süleymân, though carefully shown to be not in contravention of the Sharî'ah, orginated quite independently of the Shar'î tradition.[7]

There continued to be numerous limitations on the omnicompetence of the Sharî'ah courts. Some were from below. In parts of the empire, the courts of locally prevalent non-Ḥanafî madhhabs, though not under the Shar'î hierarchy and without binding authority, were allowed recognized standing. But even including these, all Shar'î courts were limited in their scope. The various groups that composed society, not only the non-Muslim *millets* (the organized dhimmî bodies), but also Muslim villages, guilds, town quarters, etc., had their own internal means of settling disputes—often, to be sure, on a more or less Shar'î basis. In the other direction, on the governmental level, there were still courts of maẓâlim and other essentially administrative courts, not bound by full Sharî'ah procedure; these also were held in principle to

[7] Halil İnalcík, 'The Nature of Traditional Society: Turkey', in *Political Modernization in Japan and Turkey*, ed. Robert E. Ward and Dankwart A. Rustow (Princeton University Press, 1964), has, among other important things, a useful discussion of the social ideals of the classical Ottomans.

judgments in conformity with Shar'î decisions, but could be (as in the other empires) drastically abused by officials who meted out the most extreme punishments, including all sorts of torture, on an arbitrary personal impulse. (From at least the time of Meḥmed II, it was often the pâdishâh himself who gave the worst example of arbitrary cruelty, though the stronger pâdishâhs naturally tried to forbid it in others than themselves.) But the Sharî'ah remained the acknowledged and largely effective norm. Trained qâḍîs were used as local administrators in a wide variety of functions, just as two high qâḍîs and a muftî had highest rank in the counsels at Istanbul, apart from the grand vizier.

As in the Ṣafavî empire Ḥanafî and Shâfi'î law were replaced by Shî'î law, so in the Ottoman empire Ḥanafî law became the sole law applied in official courts, at the expense of Shâfi'î, Shî'î, and Mâlikî law. (In matters which did not need to be brought before an Ottoman court, to be sure, each family or guild, or more generally each region, continued to follow the ancestral law adopted locally, as interpreted by para-official 'ulamâ' of the given madhhab. In the Maghrib, Mâlikî law was too well-rooted to be ousted except in cases involving Ottomans themselves.) But whereas in the Ṣafavî state, the 'ulamâ' could not be brought to agree what proper Shî'î law was, this Ḥanafî law was well under control. It underwent some further degree of codification, to reduce the variation permissible within the Ḥanafî madhhab as well as to make legal judgment more efficient. Accordingly, along with the standardization of the imperial qânûn law went a standardization of the over-arching Sharî'ah system into which it was to fit. The result was a comprehensive and up-to-date legal system for all the diverse lands of the empire. Not only the central authority, but all the various legal institutions of the Ottoman society received a full Shar'î legitimation.

The greatest legal mind of the empire, a chief architect of the structure of rulings from which Süleymân Qânûnî takes his nickname, was Ebü-s-sü'ûd (Abû-l-Su'ûd) Khoja Chelebî (1490–1574). Himself son of a prominent scholar in Anatolia, he rose to be shaykh al-Islâm (chief muftî) in 1545 under Süleymân, and retained that position the rest of his life. He worked out the principles that justified the way the Sharî'ah was accommodated in the state: in particular, the doctrine that qâḍîs, deriving their authority only from the monarch, are bound to apply the Sharî'ah according to his directives. This was a somewhat stronger form of the same principle that Akbar asserted in India a few years later; and it was noticeably more successful in the Ottoman empire than in India, perhaps because the prestige of the Sharî'ah gained by it as much as it might have lost: a major exemplification of it was the law about landownership cited above, in which Ebü-s-sü'ûd took a big part. He also established Ottoman policy toward the various dissenting minorities that could not be allowed the status of protected dhimmî non-Muslims but could not be ignored by the centralized Jamâ'î-Sunnism of the empire; particularly the Shî'î ṭarîqahs, which were still popular. In such matters his communalism emerged: he justified killing Yazîdîs, members of an aberrant sect in Kurdistân that had usually been ignored, and also the execution of individual Ṣûfîs who had been too free in their antinomian teachings; and finally the breach of a treaty with infidels. He was called on to decide Shar'î attitudes even on the personal side, where new social conditions had developed since Mongol times. Where community discipline was not at stake, he could invoke the Islamic principle of guiding without rejecting human nature. He refused to condemn the drinking of coffee, and condoned the increasingly prominent enjoyment of puppet plays; and he legitimized various financial arrangements that purists had condemned.

In addition to his legal work, he wrote a new commentary on the Qur'ân (which others commented on in turn) and, like, his father, cultivated a certain degree of Ṣûfism. In his own time and in the following generation, his disciples held high positions in the state.

Thus the ancient ideal of the absolute monarchy, now given a monolithic military form in the spirit of the Mongol age, was granted the full support of the 'ulamâ' and incorporated the Sharî'ah and some elements of the spirit it represented. So far as this incorporation went, the agreement was probably more hearty and the synthesis more complete than in any earlier major, Muslim state. The absolutism accepted limitations on its liberty of cultural development: Meḥmed II had had a universalism of cultural interest answering to that of the Timurids, but after Selîm such tendencies were abandoned at court. The 'ulamâ' in turn accepted an institutionalization of the Sharî'ah that stood in contrast to its traditional apolitical freedom, and to its inherent demands for criticism of all in positions of responsibility. We may almost say that the latent oppositional heritage of the 'ulamâ'—even the Jamâ'î-Sunnîs had seen the victorious ascendancy of Islam in the world as validating more the community than its rulers—was provisionally overcome. Something like the integration of the political power of Islam and its public conscience, which the Marwânids had failed to maintain and the 'Abbâsids to restore, was achieved at least on a regional basis.

Ottoman prosperity

The absolutism in these circumstances was, at its height, remarkably efficient in governing the empire. The bureaucracy, in the first place, was sufficiently well elaborated to allow for a high degree of control. In the sixteenth century, provincial governors were limited not only by various centrally appointed subordinate officers, but by the division of authority even among the commanders of the several bodies of troops stationed in their territory. The powers of the governor in most provinces remained sufficient, however, so that local abuses were commonly interrupted on the basis of imperial and Shar'î norms; and any flagrant arbitrariness on the part of the governor himself, being reported to the Centre, was immediately punished.

The central bureaus concerned themselves not merely with the prevention of abuses and the fair collection of taxes, but with all aspects of the prosperity of the society of the empire. Periodic surveys were made of the population and resources of all the inhabited places in the empire, of the state of crafts, of the pressure on the land or of any want of cultivators. On the basis of such reports, for the sake sometimes of political ends (such as the Islamization of Christian Cyprus when it was annexed) but also for economic purposes, the government freely transferred settlers (not always voluntary) from one area to another; for only with maximum prosperity could the exchequer be kept full.

As the Ottoman empire spread, the territories that came under its rule normally experienced an increase in prosperity, upon which Occidental travellers were wont to remark. In the Balkan peninsula in the fifteenth century, the displacement of the old Slavic nobility (often irresponsible) in favour of direct rule of the Christian peasantry by their bishops under the careful Ottoman regulation seems to have resulted in greater productivity, in easier conditions for the peasants, and probably in an increase of population. In the sixteenth century, Syria and Egypt, under a yet more careful bureaucratic control of economic conditions, were stimulated to an increase in prosperity both for the townsmen and for the peasantry which contrasted with the noticeable decline that was felt in later Mamlûk days.[8]

The prosperity was no doubt welcomed and formed one basis for the enduring prestige of the empire. But the careful controls that helped to produce it were not always to the taste of all. Shar'î justice, on the basis of which, to a large extent, it was decided what was an abuse of privilege, was individual justice; it took no formal account of the groups—villages with their rivalries, guilds and city quarters and army corps—in terms of which individuals conceived their interests in the Agrarian Age. A certain degree of deviation from the legal norms, of what by Shar'î standards was corruption, was depended upon to make possible essential group privileges as well as to carry through the contests among rival groups which were endemic particularly in the Arab areas. Sometimes an unusually strict governor might be borne with great impatience precisely because he interfered with the natural course of local jealousies, destructive as they were and yet irrepressible.

Islamicate society in the east European region—in contrast to the Southern Seas or to the north—had started with military and landed cadres more than with commercial ones. Doubtless this fact was reinforced by the relative agricultural density of these less arid lands, and both facts served to reinforce the European character of the empire and a certain contrast

[8] Studies by Bernard Lewis and others have brought out the favourable results of Ottoman administrative efficiency. Arab nationalism still sometimes fosters the unthinking notations that the 'Turkish' conquest of Egypt in 1517 replaced 'Arab' rule, introduced misgovernment, and destroyed prosperity—notions stated with almost classic falsity at the start of a work like A. E. Crouchley's *Economic Development of Modern Egypt* (London and New York, 1938).

between its basic structures and those that had prevailed in the Irano-Semitic lands of old Islam. Whereas formerly the high-cultural élite of the ghâzî frontier state had looked to the lands of old Islam for both leadership and prestige, now with the maturing of the empire, the Arab provinces controlled by the Ottomans, at least, came sometimes to be looked down on as relatively backward and unsophisticated. But a more external fact was also at work in giving the Ottoman prosperity a pre-eminently agrarian cast.

Commercial life was indeed very active and even prosperous in the sixteenth century. Turks as well as Arabs were active as merchants and manufacturers, as well as the Greek and Armenian dhimmî subjects of the empire. But the commercial advantages in the Mediterranean basin that the Occidental cities had gained by the end of the Earlier mid-Islamic Period persisted and even increased with the growing prosperity of the northern Occidental hinterland after the Renaissance. Remarkably often, even so early as the sixteenth century, luxury goods supplied from the Occident offered difficult or even crippling competition to Muslim producers. Probably, in that century, Occidental commercial rivalry was still more serious in the Mediterranean itself than in the Southern Seas. And this despite the fact that Ottoman navies controlled the greater part of the Mediterranean, especially after the fall of Cyprus, without serious interruption until well into the seventeenth century.

The structure of conquest

The solidity of the imperial absolutism, channelling all resources into the central army of conquest, made for a constant annexationist potential as well as for the pressure to realize it. The military machine which the bureaucracy supported was run with superb efficiency, its vast camps as well ordered as, and its equipment probably better than, those of the Indian Timurîs. Occidental observers remarked with astonishment that the Ottoman army in its prime seemed to be free not only of alcoholic drinks but of gambling and even of prostitutes, generally regarded as indispensable to soldiers' morale. Süleymân inherited an empire that already was coming to dominate the politics of eastern Europe, of most of the Mediterranean coastlands, and even of the Red Sea and Persian Gulf areas. In Süleymân's time (1520–66) and then in that of his son Selîm II (1566–74) and even afterward, Ottoman power was pushed further yet in all directions. For the most part, any particular conquest was relatively small; assimilation into the empire was slow, but usually effective. Over a period of many generations, this far-flung conquest extended into a wider variety of regions and to a greater distance from the central base than had any Muslim power since the High Caliphal state, apart from Timur's for a few years.

The military machine was thought of primarily as a land army. It was on land campaigns only that the pâdishâh himself proceeded at the head of the forces as commander, his proper role. The land frontiers were the points of special prestige. Such campaigns were carried in two directions: into Europe on the Danubian frontier, against the Christian powers; and into the Nile-to-Oxus region against the Ṣafavî empire. Because of the distances involved, peace on the one frontier was normally (but not always) assured before a campaign was undertaken on the other.

It has been suggested that the monolithic military system used for conquest placed inherent geographical limits on the area of Ottoman expansion, in contrast to that of Russia, say, or even of the primitive Mongols. The Ottomans were geared to a single grand army, in which the pâdishâh must be present, as the only instrument capable of major military effort; yet at the same time they had to operate from a single capital city where the vast bureaucratic structure was necessarily centred. As a result, a major campaign could be carried only so far as a single season's marching would allow: Vienna and Mosul were as far as the army could go if it left on the accustomed day in spring and came back to winter at the capital. More distant points, even if taken, could not have been long held against really major opposition. If this were true, the consequences would be more than geographical: the army must be kept at victorious and annexationist warfare not only to keep it in practice and to keep up morale, but to provide it with the accustomed rewards. When the geographical limits were reached, therefore, and annexation could not continue, the army must fail in its discipline and the whole absolutist structure built upon it begin to decay.

It is possible that this circumstance contributed to the slow decline of the absolutism in the seventeenth century. It was, however, possible for the army to winter at Sofia or Aleppo so as to extend the range of its expeditions, even though problems both of logistics and of two-front strategy must have been increased in such cases. Again, important territory was taken, such as that around the Black Sea, with secondary armies; this contributed to the treasury and to the imperial prestige, though not necessarily to the personal prestige of the pâdishâh. In sum, the geographical limitations of monolithism can at most have been contributory to any eventual undermining of the absolutism.

Historically, conquest in the northwest was the most significant for the state, since it continued the ghâzî tradition of subjecting infidel territory to rule by the faithful and by the divine law. (However, European historians have commonly assigned it too exclusive an importance: the contest with the Ṣafavî empire, which their surveys almost ignore, commanded nearly as much attention.) The great enemy of the later fifteenth century had been Hungary, the Latin Christian kingdom of the rich plains of the middle Danube from Belgrade northward. The Balkan area never seemed secure from Hungarian intrigue and even invasion. In 1521, the Ottomans finally took the Hungarians' southern stronghold, Belgrade. In 1526 they broke up the Hungarian army at Mohacs and briefly occupied and burned Buda and

Pest, the capitals. Thereupon two factions fought for the Hungarian crown, and in 1529 the Ottomans moved to support one of them, on condition of Süleymân's being acknowledged overlord of Hungary, and they successfully installed its candidate in Buda. But the defeated faction had taken as candidate the Habsburg lord of Vienna, the Austrian capital at the head of the middle Danube plain. At Vienna, the Habsburgs were well situated to dominate the plain militarily with their highlanders. To hold Hungary would require the permanent subjugation of Vienna or else a readiness to prostrate the Austrians time and again indefinitely.

Though the Ottomans had started their initial campaign late in the spring, it was determined to push on to Vienna immediately. Unfortunately, it was an extraordinarily wet summer and the Ottoman artillery was bogged down in the mud; the largest pieces had to be abandoned. At the last minute, Vienna received German reinforcements. But the assault on its walls was so effective that the city was on the verge of capitulation when the impatience

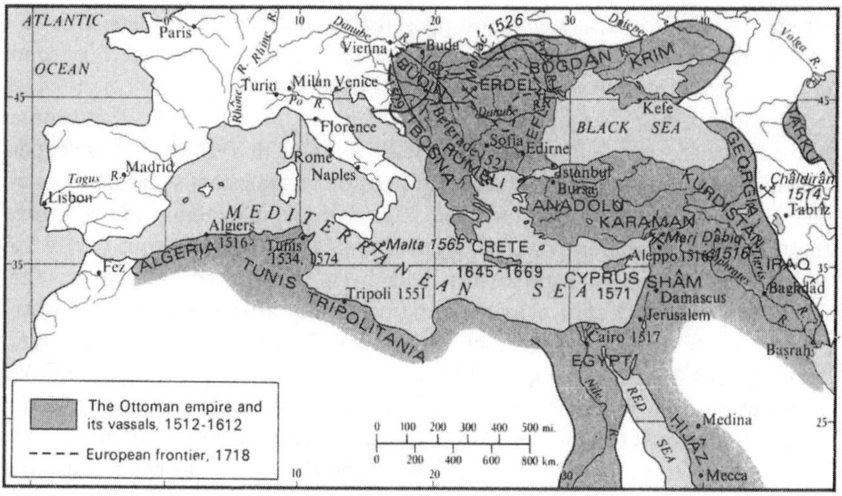

The Ottoman empire, 1512–1718

of the Janissaries to get home before winter set in forced Süleymân to retire, to the astonished relief of the Viennese. The attempt on Vienna was not repeated then. As a result, the Ottoman activities in Germany and Italy were thenceforth limited to mere raids; at the peace treaty a few years later, the Habsburgs were able to hold the northern and western fringes of Hungary. In 1541, the larger and richer part of Hungary, however, was incorporated directly into the Ottoman empire.

On the eastern front, the Iraq was conquered—as important an acquisition territorially as was Hungary. The Ottomans took advantage of Ṣafavî weakness after Ismâ'îl's death and twice occupied his old capital, Tabrîz. Though they were eventually driven out of Tabrîz, in parts of the sub-

Caucasian highland area Ottoman influence was paramount, despite active Ṣafavî rivalry there. More important, they occupied Baghdad and all the Iraq (decisively in 1534) and remained there for most of two generations. The Iraq proper south of Baghdad, however, remained Shîʿî and its cultural relations were with the Ṣafavî society; early in the seventeenth century, under ʿAbbâs, the Iraq returned to the Ṣafavî allegiance for a generation, though with interruptions.

In the sixteenth century, Ottoman advances were almost as notable in other directions than these two, however, even when the pâdishâh did not personally lead the forces; that is, across the seas, where campaigns were wholly or in part naval. At Süleymân's accession, Occidentals still retained considerable power in the eastern Mediterranean. The Ottomans were troubled in the Aegean itself by pirates protected by the Knights of St John installed on Rhodes; in 1522 they were eliminated. The Venetian republic was a more substantial opponent; not till 1540 were its last toeholds in the Aegean mainlands taken, and even then it retained not only its commercial strength—which increasingly presupposed a community of interest with the Ottomans—but also its outright control of Crete and Cyprus. But very soon Ottoman naval power was called farther afield.

We have noticed the attempt of the Ottomans to oppose the Portuguese in the Southern Seas. Despite certain ventures immediately after the occupation of Egypt, such distant efforts could not be undertaken with full seriousness till after the Ottomans controlled their own home waters, and even then they required a different sort of shipping and naval warfare from that with which the Ottoman headquarters had been acquainted. Moreover, the Ottoman power in Egypt, which at first had been fairly perfunctory, had to be set on a durable footing. This was achieved early in Süleymân's reign, when an arrangement was worked out that allowed the local Mamlûks considerable independence, as well as direct access to the Centre at Istanbul, yet ensured overall Ottoman fiscal and regulative control. Egyptian prosperity rapidly revived, at least for a time. Thereupon the Ottomans could not only garrison the Red Sea coasts, particularly the Yemen, where they forestalled the imposition of Portuguese control; but could also send out the more distant expeditions which were mentioned earlier. But in the Indian Ocean they enjoyed only transient successes. Ottoman power was essentially European, geographically, and the Ottoman sea forces did their main work in the Black and Mediterranean seas.

The Black Sea early became an Ottoman preserve. The Aegean came under Ottoman control early in Süleymân's reign; save for the presence on Crete of the Venetians, natural commercial allies of the Ottomans but their rivals in creed and for power in the eastern Mediterranean at large. But Ottoman interest had been carried as far as the Maghrib coasts in the western Mediterranean already in the first Selîm's reign. For there the Muslims were on the defensive against the Spanish monarchy in its sixteenth-century prime, newly gorged with the spoils of the Americas and the strongest military power of western Europe, where it controlled much of Italy and also the commercial Netherlands. In 1492, the small state of Granada in southern Spain, which had survived for two centuries as the last Muslim state in the peninsula, was overrun by the Christian Spanish power; in succeeding decades the Christians crossed into the Maghrib, taking a number of port towns, and threatening to complete their conquest of the extreme west Mediterranean coasts. The Spanish Christian hostility to Islam (and to Judaism) was monumental; a vast section of the population of the peninsula was driven out on refusal to convert to Christianity, including many of the most industrious classes. In the course of the following century, the Muslims and the greater number of the Jews fled for asylum to Muslim territory by the hundred thousands, many of them perishing on the way.

In the farthest west (Morocco), a new dynasty of sharîfs, claiming descent from 'Alî, led a national reaction against the Portuguese and Spanish Christians and succeeded in limiting them to a few ports in the north. In the rest of the Maghrib, those more active in resisting the Christian attacks turned to the prestige and the resources of the Ottoman empire for support. Kheyr-ud-dîn, an Ottoman-born sea captain in the service of the ruler at Tunis, thus became an Ottoman official upon the collapse of his master and led the Muslim fight against the invading Christians in the Ottoman name and with Ottoman support by sea. This support was sufficiently effective to oust the Spaniards after several turns of fortune and to assure a continued Ottoman domination of most of the Maghrib at the end of the century, when Spanish power began to decline. In the west Mediterranean there ensued a stalemate between the Muslim and Christian powers. Following the breakdown of a brief period of alliance with the French (during which the Ottomans established a naval station in the French port of Toulon), for more than a century pirates on each side, more or less officially encouraged, harassed the other side's shipping, taking captives for ransom or to be held as slaves.

Süleymân had died in 1566, after the failure (1565) of a massive naval siege of Malta, key to the western Mediterranean, which the exiled Knights of St John had fortified as their refuge; and in the midst of a successful campaign against the Habsburgs on the Hungarian frontier. Süleymân was relatively unbloodthirsty. Yet like so many monarchs under the rule of succession by contest, Süleymân had been unfortunate in his family, and in typical ways. Harem intrigues, participated in by his favourite wife, resulted first in the execution, on Süleymân's own orders, of his ablest son, the one likeliest to succeed but son of a different woman; and then in the execution of his next ablest son, over-eager to ensure himself a good vantage point for assuring his own succession. The accession of Selîm II (1566–74), then, resulted from the failure of the rule of contest; and he was best known for his drunkenness. Yet he retained his father's last vizier, Meḥmed Sököllü, and the conquests continued.

The lands north of the Black Sea had come under Ottoman administration or control partly by overland expeditions, but secondary ones; and partly by sea. Beyond the immediate Ottoman ports, the khânate of the Crimea was a hereditary and subordinate ally (from 1475). It was in the reign of Selîm that the abortive attempt was made to recapture Astrakhân, recently taken by the Russians; and to link forces with the Özbegs, the other great enemies of the Ṣafavîs (and to open better routes for traders and for pilgrims) by joining the Don to the Volga (hence the Black Sea to the Caspian) by a canal where they came closest together. These expeditions could not effectively repress the Russians, who were in the course of replacing the earlier Polish aristocracy in the east European plains with a massive absolutism that could operate on a larger scale than the Poles as the area of city-linked agriculture expanded. But the Ottomans did succeed, before the end of the century, in interfering seriously in the declining Polish state. (For a time in the following century they even controlled the Ukraine, between its adherence to Poland and its subjection to Russia.)

The Ottoman seizure of Cyprus was a minor action but typical of warfare in the Agrarian Age which we are about to leave behind. Instead of cutting the planned Red Sea canal or even of helping some petitioning refugees from Spain regain their homes, in 1570 the resources of the empire were devoted to ousting the Venetians from an island that might, had the Venetians been in a different mood, have threatened Muslim control of the east Mediterranean coastlands. Rumour had it that the reason for the decision was a grudge of one of Selîm's favourites, and Selîm's own love of Cypriote wine; the most plausible reason officially given was the need to eliminate an alleged haven for Christian pirates. When the Ottoman forces landed, some of the local population, who were supposed to serve as peasant auxiliaries for the Venetians, surrendered without a contest. (The Orthodox Greek peasants, indeed, had little love for their Catholic Venetian masters.) The Venetians, in a retaliatory night raid, slaughtered the men and led off the women and children of a village that had been too quick to give in. But very soon the capital, Nicosia, was invested and reduced. (The government at Venice did not dare send aid, lest the Ottomans attack the other Venetian territories also.) When further resistance became impossible, some of the leading local Venetians, thinking they had received assurances that they would be spared if they surrendered, had started to lay down their arms, and were then cut down without mercy. For eight days Nicosia was given over to plunder and rapine; the surviving population, that is particularly the females, were enslaved. One of the women managed to set fire to a ship on which much of the booty was loaded, and when the powder magazine exploded, thousands of new-made slaves, crowded aboard that and neighbouring ships, perished in the fire or by drowning. After the other cities were taken, one by one, the Ottomans reorganized the province. They recognized the rights of the Greek church as against the Latin; but also introduced large numbers of Muslim settlers into the island so as to bring the population up to the level of its resources, and also to ensure a loyal element among the inhabitants. Crete, however, was left in Venetian possession until 1645.

The Ottoman empire was a major sea power, but it was a sea power at all only by nature and not by choice or by design. Since the great central army was conceived in terms of operations on land, the navy suffered, especially after the sixteenth century, from a relative neglect as compared with the land forces. Fighting in the Mediterranean was still a matter of grappling among the ships, for which ordinary land soldiers might be used, and too often landlubbers were used even in positions of command. Nevertheless the Ottomans knew how to devote the needful resources to their navy. When most of the navy was destroyed, in a rare defeat at Lepanto in the Aegean (1573) at the hands of the allied Spaniards and Venetians (partly on account of the presumption of a landlubber commander), the lost ships were mostly replaced within a year, and with vessels armed in a more up-to-date manner; the Christians gained nothing from the battle but a rare boost to their morale. The Ottomans alone of the three great empires maintained an important independent power even in the Southern Seas. The vigour of Ottoman loyalty and the high stands of performance maintained among the Ottoman ruling classes were nowhere more evident than in a tradition of great sea captains, whose names were admiringly preserved even among their Occidental enemies.

Shar'ism and the cultural expression of empire

Ibn-Khaldûn, the philosophic historian, was aware that the advent of Islam had meant the initiation of a new civilization in the ancient lands of high culture, carried by new peoples with a new lettered tradition. He was also aware that this was not the first time that such a renovation had occurred: he knew that the Greek and Persian traditions of institutions and of letters which Islam had displaced had themselves displaced, long before, the traditions of the ancient Egyptians and Babylonians. Surveying the sweep of Muslim history down to the fifteenth century, he was ready to suppose that a new civilization, involving transformations equally momentous, might be already on the horizon in his time. More radically than he could have dreamed, something of the sort was indeed to come to pass in the time of the gunpowder empires; but the society that the new age first subverted and transformed was that of western Europe. The institutional and lettered tradition of Islamdom was left, for a period, more or less intact. Ibn-Khaldûn's anticipations, or apprehensions, seemed unfulfilled.

The transformed political and social circumstances of the time of the empires did bring with them much brilliant new cultural expression. But this imaginative flowering, still governed largely by the conservative spirit, was sharply limited in range; it was, by and large, a fulfillment, within the agrarianate level of culture, of possibilities opened up during the age of Mongol prestige. These limitations are nowhere more visible, at least to our hindsight, than in the Ottoman empire. Like the others, the Ottoman empire was illustrated with cultural splendour, notably in triumphs of monumental architecture. At the same time, the unitary and populist orientation of the Sharî'ah-minded most decisively showed its hand there. It set its face against such localisms as were represented in the old ghâzî cults; and while (precisely in the Ottoman empire) it co-operated to support the absolutism and the distinctive regional culture which centred on its court, it still stood for the communal unity of cosmopolitan Islamdom as a whole. Hence it defensively set its face also against anything alien to the common Islamicate tradition as that had come to be interpreted in the Later Middle Period. In the Ottoman empire, confronted first with the great florescence of the Renaissance in Italy just across the Adriatic, but especially later with the transformations of the Technical Age in the Occident generally, such a position, if not exactly fateful in fact, yet must appear for us in a singularly revealing light.

There could be little question, whatever its cultural bent, of Ottoman society entering into the overall movement of the Renaissance of the fifteenth and early sixteenth centuries (not to speak of the later wider innovations that began at the end of the sixteenth century). The Renaissance (like the later transformation also) was a development within the Occidental cultural presuppositions; its chief themes could prove meaningful to outsiders only through a special effort of the will such as is required in any crossing of major cultural barriers. In any case, as we have noted earlier, the Renaissance itself was not more notable in its contrast to contemporary culture elsewhere in the Afro-Eurasian urban zone than had been several earlier florescences; correspondingly, it imposed no greater attractive force outside the Occident than had, in the time of its first florescence, Islamicate culture outside the bounds of the caliphal state. Nevertheless, it seems to be true that the Ottomans, for all their proximity, showed no more alertness to what was happening in the Occident, and possibly even less, than the Timurîs of India. At the same time, such elements of Occidental culture of the time as were clearly significant even to outsiders did arouse some attention among the Ottomans; not, indeed, among the representatives of Sharî'ah-mindedness in the madrasahs, so much as among the circles of the absolutism itself.

The centre of Ottoman high culture was, of course, the court; and the court, the absolutist establishment with its slave household, had its own school system paralleling that of the Shar'î madrasahs. As in the corresponding schools in Iran and India, here were taught both the Shar'î disciplines and also a broad literary culture. In addition to Persian, the elaborate (and Persianized) Turkic language of the Ottoman court was carefully inculcated; for of all the states ruled by Turkic dynasties—even where much of the population was Turkic speaking—only the Ottoman state made a point of substituting Turkic for Persian as its primary language of high culture. (This process had begun by 1455, but was not fully completed till the end of the seventeenth century.) The ruling élite coming out of the palace schools was so well formed in humane letters as to suffer sometimes from the defects of a literary class. Some, at least, learned their geography from the old classics and did not keep up with the best Ottoman geographers of their time; similarly, it was a literary rather than either a scientific or a Shar'î training that led some courtiers to credit a Christian victory to good astrologers. But the schools were by no means exclusively literary, notably teaching the military arts to all the trainees.

The best Ottoman historians were probably as good as the best in Islamdom in this period. Some of them seem to have seen their task as part of the general policy of keeping administrative track of affairs, which also included the taking of censuses; in the seventeenth century, indeed, official historians were appointed to record the events of particular campaigns, and then of the empire at large. The better historians made a point of teaching posterity by illustrating the errors that had been made in the past. In order to fill in gaps, either about the ancient past of the Ottoman domains or about Ottoman foreign relations, some historians turned to Occidental sources; but modern Occidental history was scarcely considered for itself. Starting in the seventeenth century, a series of writers did attempt to analyze the reasons for the evident decay of the absolutism and its power, tracing with care the subsequent corruption of the institutions of Süleymân's time.

Even in the sixteenth century, Ottoman natural science was largely a matter of translation from Arabic and Persian into Ottoman Turkic; but not entirely. Süleymân founded medical schools, and a high level of medical learning was maintained; among these physicians, at least a bit later, were some who adopted elements of the Occidental medical innovations of the time—which, to be sure, in the sixteenth and even seventeenth centuries did not go far enough beyond the Greco-Arabic tradition to make al-Râzî and Ibn-Sînâ wholly out of date even in the Occident. In 1579 an observatory was built in which astronomers expected to improve on Ulugh-beg's observations at Samarqand. It was torn down by a superstitious vizier, but not before it had collected much data. The year following Giordano Bruno's execution in Italy, a scientist was executed for advocating a system of cosmic natural-law determinism more respectful of the tradition of Philosophia than of the tradition of the Qur'ân; but he was almost alone in such a fate, though not in retaining a Philosophic outlook.

During the sixteenth century, meanwhile, there was much quiet interchange of information between Muslims and Occidentals on points of geography. The sea captains, whose vigour we have mentioned, naturally took an interest in the oceanic discoveries of their Portuguese and Spanish rivals, and spread some knowledge of them. The scholar most alert to such new ideas was Kâtib Chelabî (called Ḥâjjî Khalîfah, 1609–57), an encyclopedist who tried to bring under control the whole range of Arabic, Persian, and Ottoman learning. At the same time, he tried to introduce wide circles to the most interesting of what had been developed latterly among the Christians, especially in geography and astronomy. He came from the court literary circles, of course, rather than from the Shar'î madrasahs. But there was a limit to what he could achieve even there. Gradually in the seventeenth century, the growing superiority of Occidental natural science became known to those few who cared; not only in cartography, but in astronomy and medicine. At the same moment, what had been a mature scientific tradition (though locally not highly creative), a tradition duly aware of the significance of experimental demonstration and the like, now rather rapidly withered.

Sharî'ah-mindedness, though in close alliance with the court, had its strongholds in the madrasahs, including especially those of the capital under state administration; and also in the khâniqâhs of the great international ṭarîqah orders. As in India, the older local orders were stimulated and in part replaced in this period by great orders like the Qâdiriyyah and the Naqshbandiyyah. The several ṭarîqah orders retained their individuality. A Malâmatî order made a stir, from the mid-fifteenth century on, by attempting a reform that would have put many convenient compromises in question. To the traditional Malâmatî position of avoiding religious pretence—normally expressed merely in not drawing attention to oneself either by noticeable piety or by apparent impiety—they added the posture of publicly espousing a radical Wujûdî position (which Ṣûfîs normally did accept, but disguised from the uninitiated); in so doing, they were making a direct assault on the whole structure of conventional religiosity of the time. After a vigorous and disciplined activity in the seventeenth century, they were forced by persecution to give up the attempt. We have noted the popular latitudinarianism of the Bektashîs among the country people—and among the Janissaries; and the poetic devotion of the Mevlevîs, cultivated largely among the privileged classes in the towns. Some of the khâniqâhs (called in Turkic *tekkes*) supplemented the madrasahs as educational institutions, forming regular schools for poets, and offering also the study of Persian (whereas the madrasahs concentrated on Arabic). Yet the orders were not allowed full independence of the state; their heads had to be confirmed by the shaykh al-Islâm.[9]

It was the great international orders, however, that set the official tone of religion. These orders had carried the accommodation of Ṣûfism and Shar'ism to the point where they stood as the chief defenders of the Sharî'ah-minded point of view in society at large (always within a Ṣûfî context, to be sure) and, as in India, Sharî'ah-mindedness carried with it Muslim communalism. The autonomous Sharî'ah-mindedness which had once attacked all

[9] F. W. Hasluck, *Christianity and Islam under the Sultans* (Oxford, 1929), tells much (though in an antiquated manner) about religion on the folk level—including the conflation of cults.

Ṣûfism and had flourished even in the Later Middle Period here and there, for instance among some Ḥanbalîs of the Fertile Crescent, seems to have become dormant. The Sharʿî ʿulamâʾ were mostly Ṣûfîs of some sort, and defended their positions in terms consistent with Ṣûfism. The positions, however, were still communalist and, by now, conservative.

Sharîʿah-minded culture was perhaps especially rich in the Ottoman empire. Within the Ottoman empire, unlike either the Ṣafavî or the Indo-Timurî, traditions of both the Persianate and the Arabic cultural zones of the Later Middle Period were represented. The Persianate was, to be sure, dominant, as it tended to be in all Turkic-ruled societies. But the two were fused, as was required in a society in which all culture tended to be centred on the capital. ʿAbd-al-Ghanî al-Nâbulusî (d. 1731), a Syrian poet and commentator on mystical writings, was a disciple at once of the Maghribî theological tradition and of the Persian-Anatolian tradition of interpretation represented by Meḥmed Birgevî, a subtle theologian who had carried on controversies with Ebü-s-süʿûd. Such writings were in Arabic. On the whole, however, the Arab lands played a marginal role in Ottoman culture, though in the Fertile Crescent there was a flourishing intellectual life, sometimes in close contact with wider circles than those of the madrasahs themselves.

After the time of Süleymân, the tradition of the central madrasahs narrowed its range. Textbooks were chosen with less Falsafah content than was found in the works of such theologians as Taftâzânî, and more in harmony with the more restrictive tradition that had been developed especially in Arabic lands. The contrast between the Sharʿî communalism of the madrasahs and the somewhat wider perspective of the palace schools became marked. Despite the Sharʿî tone even of the absolutism itself, the narrowing horizons of the representatives of the Sharîʿah did not preclude all investigation of a more liberal sort. Nevertheless, the madrasahs became the focus of a certain intolerance of experiment, which coloured the whole of Ottoman culture. The ʿulamâʾ were successful in forbidding the use of printing for Islamicate books, when this was suggested on the analogy of Christian printing, introduced into the Ottoman capital soon after it appeared in the Occident. In this way they blocked, of all the by-products of the Occidental ferment of the time of the Renaissance, what might potentially have widened horizons most. In itself, of course, printing could not have led to any fundamental transformations (any more than it did in China), but it might have reinforced the wider Ottoman culture precisely against Sharîʿah-minded restrictions.

What these restrictions amounted to in practice is not yet fully clear; it changed from time to time. But evidently such restrictions were more often effective among the Ottomans than in Iran or India. One can perceive them in the form of petty negative moralisms, but one may hope that these were the external marks of a more positive sobriety in the responsible classes: the sort of sobriety that allowed the shaykh al-Islâm to oppose with impunity even the bloody severities of Selîm the Inexorable. It is said that whereas most Muslims played chess with the usual carved figurines, many Ottomans used simple undifferentiated pieces. Skilled portrait artists were highly valued in all the empires; both Iranian and Italian painters sought their fortunes in painting the portraits of Ottoman courtiers, including the pâdishâhs. Yet whereas Jahângîr sent his best portraitist to the Ṣafavî court as a gesture of friendliness, no such frank honouring of the trade seems to be recorded of the Ottomans. In Ottoman ruling circles, portraiture could at times be a dubious indulgence. Though in some periods almost every courtier did it, a man might even find it necessary to keep secret the fact that he employed such an artist.

The art of painting generally—whatever the status of portrait painting—was nonetheless actively cultivated, though Ottoman painting is much less well known than that of Iran or of India. Some of the greatest painters came from Iran, but some were native to the empire. But it was architecture, surely, that most fully expressed the Ottoman imperial might, and it did so with a vision and a splendour—and a uniformity—worthy of the vigour and durability of the empire. And in architecture, above all it was the great mosques. In Anatolia a domed enclosed type of mosque had developed, for which the traditional courtyard was merely a forecourt. This type was further developed in Istanbul, in the presence of the great Byzantine Hagia Sophia church, to a magnificent, light-filled structure; a structure that poses a striking contrast to the Byzantine church, to which it is superficially similar. The Byzantine interior is awesome as if a whole cosmos were being enclosed; the Ottoman interior, with its windows near eye level and its spaciousness emphasized even in the chasteness of the marble décor and of the spaced columns, suggests an infinite but ordered extension rather than a monumental bulk. Outside, this type of mosque presents the graceful piles of relatively low domes, set off with high tapering minarets, that dominate the skyline of Istanbul. With little variation, this style of mosque became the emblem of the empire; thenceforth in Cairo, in Sarajevo, in Mosul, new mosques were Ottoman mosques, unmistakable in their main contours.

The greatest of the Ottoman architects, and the chief man to form this distinctive imperial style, was Ḳoja Mi'mâr Sinân (1490–1578), whose career marks him as a type of the ideal Ottoman. (He would represent the 'askerî side of the Ottoman élite as Ebü-s-sü'ûd would represent the Shar'î side.) Of Christian parentage, Sinân was a devshirme recruit from Anatolia who served with distinction as a Janissary on campaigns in his youth. He soon became known as an ingenious military engineer. His architectural talents finally received recognition when he threw a bridge across the Danube during a campaign of Sülaymân. Henceforth, he served exclusively as an architect. He built both mosques and almost every other sort of building, palaces, madrasahs, tombs, caravanserais, baths, hostels, and even little fountains, commissioned both by the pâdishâh and by private grandees, both at Istanbul and throughout the provinces, even as far as Mecca. Over three hundred buildings have been reliably ascribed to him. (Withal he found time to write a brief autobiography.) The Süleymâniyyeh mosque is considered his masterwork, and the most perfect example of the Ottoman imperial style. His numerous disciples, many of them well known, faithfully carried on his work after him.

The millets

Consistently enough, if the Islamic religious establishment was to function as expression of the conscience of those who had adopted the truth (as Muslims saw it) and as the civil expression of the pâdishâh's authority among them, good social order demanded something analogous, if more limited in scope and relevance, among the followers of falsified faiths. Corresponding to the Muslim Ummah under the 'ulamâ' were the dhimmî millets under their priests and rabbis. There was essentially one ruling pâdishâh and army; there were several religious establishments. But these were all almost as closely organized as part of the state as was the Muslim one.

Not every group that differed from the official Islam, and did not find its needs served by it, could be organized as a millet, however; all dissidents were grouped within a limited number of bodies, kept carefully under control. The Anatolian and Rumelian Shî'îs, to begin with, so far as they did not assimilate into the official structure in such a guise as that of the Bektashî ṭarîqah order, were overlooked. The Shî'î villagers carried on their own life without intellectual leadership and under the guise of an official Jamâ'î-Sunnism which they ignored as much as possible. However, in some cases Shî'î qâḍîs were given the same semi-official recognition as the Shâfi'îs or Mâlikîs. The great Shî'î centres in the Iraq, during those long periods when they were Ottoman-occupied, maintained their separate cultural life, of course, continuing in contact with the Ṣafavî territories.[10] The Greek Orthodox, Armenian, Jacobite (Syrian), and Coptic Christian, and the Jewish communities—these were given great authority over their own; but heretics in their midst were left to the mercies of the established bishops that they rejected, who were granted both ecclesiastical and civil judicial authority over them. The only legal way out of a resented jurisdiction would be conversion to Islam.

The identification of Sharî'ah-minded Islam with the state, and therefore

[10] The conventional and in some ways reasonable attitude of treating the Iraq as normally an Ottoman province which was occasionally occupied by the Ṣafavîs can lead to something less reasonable: treating such Jama'î-Sunnî life as there was in the Iraq as its primary component. On this basis, the more important intellectual life in the Iraq can be overlooked; and it can appear as merely an out-of-the-way province despite its commericial and religious importance. Cf. Gibb and Bowen's study (n. 3 above), II, pp. 155–56, which tries to ascribe the relative weakness of (Sunnî) intellectual life in the Iraq to the various calamities since the Mongol invasion, and which barely mentions Shî'ism there.

of the Muslim community as a whole with the political régime, seems to have contributed to an ever increasing segregation of the non-Muslims in all ways. Even after the elimination of Christian contingents from the armed forces, Christians and Muslims continued to share the life of the guilds side by side; but in the seventeenth century this became increasingly difficult. Following disputes between the two sections of a guild (which, after all, were governed in their civil life under two quite separate empire-wide hierarchies, no longer sharing local jurisdiction even at the top local level), it became common to separate them into two guilds, usually Christian and Muslim.

Such a tendency was encouraged by, and, in turn, reinforced the crucial tendencies among the Muslim and the Christian communities: the drive of the Muslims for a communalist Shar'ism, with ties to the other Muslim lands, but with a focus above all in the Ottoman society as a self-contained whole; and the tendency especially of Greek Christians to look to Occidental Christendom as the source of any forward-looking ideas. Increasingly, therefore, Ottoman society was divided from top to bottom in the tendencies of its civilization. In India, notable Hindu privileged sectors adopted Islamicate culture except for the intimate religious life, and throughout town life Islamicate ways penetrated even Hindus' habits to a large degree, while Muslims patronized Hindu festivals and scholarship. In Rûm, at most a minority of the cultivated Christians had any Islamicate cultural veneer at any level; save perhaps in some degree at that of the market place, where Turkic names for dishes, for instance, became widespread in all communities. And Muslims were far more chary of Christian activities or notions. Instead, the cultivated Christian élite were increasingly linking the southeast European Christian peoples into the Occidental Christian system—not to be sure in matters of religion (where the ruling hierarchy of bishops retained jealously its independence, if not its traditional superiority), but in matters of the civil life of its more wealthy strata. Even some Christians who knew Persian seem to have known Italian as well.

Such Christians, as the age grew on and as contacts with the Occident became more important, eventually turned out to be the chief channel for Ottoman contact with independent European states, while the Muslims themselves withdrew increasingly from the outside contact they had originally led the way in. The gulf between the two communities became fateful indeed by that time; for the Ottoman central power was being eroded just when the Occident was undergoing a transformation that necessarily put every other society at a disadvantage and on the defensive against it, and the Christians alone in the empire seemed to know how to profit from the situation.

The decay of the absolutism

We have noted that despite the military form retained by the absolutism as it developed, it assumed a certain civilian cast in that essentially civilian elements in the grand 'army' had dominant positions. The tendency of the 'army' to take on a civilian character, probably inherent in the bureaucratic structure of the absolutism, grew steadily from the time of Meḥmed II. In the course of the seventeenth century and above all in the early eighteenth century (when the process culminated), this gradually resulted in a serious weakening of the central armed forces. The weakening of the armed forces, in turn, undermined the absolutism itself, which had depended on its monolithic army for its strength and for its prestige.

First came the weakening of military discipline at the top. With the elimination of the old military aristocracy as rivals for governmental power and hence as a source of limitation upon the slave household as representing the absolutism, the system of slave-military rule, which for a time had enormous efficiency, came to its natural limit. The civilianizing officer class in the slave-household became almost the sole power in the state. With little delay, they allowed more and more corruption within their ranks. The sale of offices began at the very top: Süleymân himself demanded a present from his appointees at the time of appointment; and they had to pass the cost on down the line. At first, to be sure, the appointment was still made for merit and the payment was secondary; even so, it resulted in an indirect increase in the overall taxation. Yet money came to determine most issues, at least where merit was reasonably balanced. And corruption at length began to undermine competence. Even the highly developed Sharîʿah, administered for the most part by their defeated rivals, could not fully control the officers.

The slave-military discipline was blurred at all levels of the central apparatus, beginning with the very selection of the man at the top. The principle of succession to the throne by contest among the previous monarch's sons was presupposed in the suggestion of Meḥmed II that the successful son should kill his brothers lest the contest be renewed. It is natural to emphasize the personalities of the pâdishâhs in the fate of the empire; even to exaggerate the 'good luck' of the Ottomans in having ten gifted monarchs in a row, as well as to deplore the harem system that produced a sad crop later. The Ottoman state owed something to fortunate heredity (not rare in reigning families). Certainly the remarkable qualities of the first three of the line were as important as geography in establishing the Ottomans as a major power; and Murâd II, Meḥmed II, and Süleymân were also high-quality men succeeding by sheer birth, though perhaps not all up to the spectacular level of their ancestors. But the strong qualities of Meḥmed I and Selîm I were brought to the throne by contest, a contest determined by the expectations of the society of the time. And Bâyezîd I and Selîm II, for instance, though neither was a fool, surely both won their victories through the previously developed Ottoman *system* rather than through really exceptional ability. The difference in their personal prominence is surely already in part a function of the shift from a military to a civilian orientation.

In the later environment, the social structure worked for a strong vizier rather than for a strong pâdishâh, and got him for remarkably long periods at a time. Succession by contest is appropriate to a military state, but in the civilian-minded seventeenth century the principle was suppressed, if not in theory then at least in practice. Actual military contests were done away with. Finally, the potential princely contestants were not even killed but were secluded from active life; and it became customary to choose, not the son to most effectively win the soldiers, but simply the eldest man among the family, who was (in his seclusion) most likely to allow his officials free rein; this had the added advantage of avoiding a succession dispute into which the actual soldiers could actively interfere. The consequences of such a system for the character of the monarchs were comparable to the consequences of the like system in the Ṣafavî state.

Thus the monarch, the general-in-chief, was allowed to retire into impotence: and thus military discipline was corrupted at its font. Süleymân, carrying the absolutist ceremonialism of Meḥmed II along its logical path, had retired from view even at state councils. This ceremonial retirement became, under many of his successors, a general withdrawal from responsibility; for they were not chosen for their responsible character. Instead of the strong hand of the monarch, as a commanding general, the strong hand required by the bureaucracy was supplied by the grand vizier (with disastrous intervals), who now rose to his place for essentially civilian qualities, and was limited in his power by civilian considerations.

The decline of military discipline was accelerated during a series of internal troubles, the most important of them occurring around the turn of the sixteenth century. Rebellions among Kurdish tribes, among the Druze sectarians in Syria (who built up a considerable little state for a time), and even among the military landholders in Anatolia, as well as insubordination by the Janissaries at the Centre, were hampering the imperial military power in its struggles with Austrians, Poles, and Ṣafavîs. From 1632 on, under the leadership of the pâdishâh Murâd IV, the absolutism regained control; but meanwhile, it seems, the revenue system had been altered in character. Many of the urban notables had been put in charge of land and taxes in the provinces and had risen to high position there, and commonly they were expected to represent local interests at least as much as the central administration. From this time on, such notables were usually—not always—felt to be protectors of the population at large; and the central government could do little without their co-operation.

Answering to such changes in the provinces came further changes at Istanbul. The slave-household had presupposed a social isolation of its individual members save as they formed regimented corps within the whole. With corruption, the character of the slave-household changed. The dominant military section of the 'army' allowed its children to enter its ranks—and so lost the basis of such discipline as survived. (And finally bureaucrats from the ḳalemiyyeh, the non-military ranks, rivalled members of the slave-household for very top offices.) When the Janissary soldiers proved trouble-some, the civilian answer was not a more rigorous discipline, but the dilution of the ranks with untrained recruits, and finally the elimination of the conscription of 'outsiders' which had been the basis not only of the soldiery but of the whole merit system in the officer class itself; fresh recruitment on such a basis was no longer indispensable. The devshirme was abandoned. The officer-officials came to form a semi-hereditary privileged group which, however, unlike the old military aristocracy, lived from offices rather than from the older type of military land grants. Grants of land by way of tax farms were increasingly given in such a form that they amounted to sources of private income without any military implications—presumably in the hope that this would encourage the fostering of agriculture.

Finally, by the early eighteenth century, the central armed forces were themselves civilianized wholesale. Janissaries were allowed to supplement their income in civilian trades and yet remain, as 'army men', tax free and subject only to the 'army' courts. Soon whole guilds of craftsmen—commonly, I would suppose, by way of devious accommodations—were exercising these 'army' privileges. On the basis of decrees or charters sometimes well paid for, the Muslims of the capital and the other great cities were, in effect, all admitted to a variant of the 'askerî army status, which came to have a correspondingly civilian meaning (in some cases a whole town, Muslims and dhimmî non-Muslims together, became tax-exempt in this way). And such funds as were still collected to support the central armed establishment were converted into a source of income for a rentier class—for now the Janissary 'pay certificates' became negotiable investments.

The absolutism had been based on its military prestige. Its central authority was now inevitably replaced with general decentralization. The elaborate system of central appointments, based on a cursus honorum, was reduced to something of a fiction: unqualified men would be appointed on the basis of their wealth and connections (eventually by yearly rotation); they drew the titular revenues; then, commonly enough, they appointed qualified representatives to do the actual work. But these representatives, naturally, need not represent directly the central power; they were often local men, with a tacitly acknowledged permanent local position, merely confirmed by the titular central official. Bodies of local notables, largely members of the new landholding class that had arisen among urban civilians, gathered local administration into their own hands. With the disintegration of the monolithic central army, the provincial governors substituted local armies paid from the local civilian treasury. The armed core of the amorphous body of Janissaries at the capital came to be only little more than another local army.

The Shar'î spirit had had a triumph of sorts in the Ottoman empire, though this triumph was gained in a paradoxical way—in absolutism and militarism. Now the synthesis that had served as basis for this triumph was rejected in favour of decentralism and the supremacy of local group life—which had once been the great ally of the Shar'î spirit.

The less fortunate consequences of the decline of the absolutism were very visible. In some ways it was clearly deleterious for Ottoman society at large. Bureaucratic efficiency declined in direct proportion to the weakness of the absolutism of which it was the life-blood. After Süleymân, the systematic censuses were less and less often carried out; the immaculate good order of government records gave way to sloppiness, which, despite revivals under strong viziers like the Köprülüs in the later seventeenth century, became at last the norm. Appeal from local arbitrariness to the Centre finally became futile. Along with the watchfulness of the central power, the general prosperity declined. Under agrarianate circumstances it was natural for a new class of landed exploiters to arise to replace any once swept away by the Ottoman conquest; with the decline in discipline, the central army no longer had a monopoly on land; the new, uncontrolled exploitation was allowed to grow unchecked.

But the effects of civilianization and decentralization were compounded by more universal consequences of the age of gunpowder empires. Specialized gunpowder corps necessarily formed a standing army and were not able to pay themselves effectively through plunder; the more warfare among major powers relied on these, the more the central administration required steady supplies of cash. But one of the gunpowder empires of the time—the Spanish—had chanced to open up the vast silver supplies of the New World and injected them into the commercial nexus of the Afro-Eurasian Oikoumene, nowhere more massively than next door in the Ottoman empire. This sort of thing had exhilarating results where the economy was expanding or readily expandable (as in most of western Europe except for Spain, which in ousting the Muslims had just dealt itself a severe blow); but by the seventeenth century in the Arid Zone, where no great expansion was possible at that point, its results were devastating. A world-wide inflation in silver-based prices followed the flood of silver from the New World. The position of those of the more privileged classes whose investments were not in land but in other sorts of investment became precarious; and they were given no protection. This made for social disruption and further inhibited any economic expansion that might have been possible.

The strain of all these developments on the finances of the government itself must have contributed to further demoralizing military discipline as well as directly to making the Centre impotent. But the worse consequences were necessarily those on the land. Where Occidental observers had earlier commented on how fortunate were the peasants to be under Ottoman rule, they now found that the peasantry seemed oppressed, the land less well cultivated, and villages deserted, with their population poured impoverished into the cities. Yet as the land revenues declined, so must eventually the prosperity of the towns themselves.

For a long time, however, before the final stages of the process were reached, but long after rural prosperity was already suffering, the central army was kept relatively intact. And though perhaps already in the seventeenth century the empire had reached the point of no return, when state resources were so far committed that the central government could no longer (under normal conditions) muster enough of them for its own purposes to impose radical reform on those who held the rest, yet even then the absolutist tradition was still strong enough to impose a partial reform when it had good viziers; and such reform could appear very effective for a time.

Despite the two decades of ignominy at the beginning of the seventeenth century, when internal rebellions went unchastised, and a second period of ignominy toward the middle of the century, when Christian military vessels harassed even the Thracian straits, we have seen that even in the seventeenth century at least temporary territorial advances continued in the lands north of the Black Sea (and Crete was finally taken to complete control of the Aegean). This happened for the most part, but not entirely, in a brief period when the strength of the absolutism reached a secondary peak (and Ottoman territory a maximum) under the Köprülü viziers. The father, Meḥmed Köprülü (1656–61), employed bloody ferocity against the grandees of the empire to suppress the more pernicious forms of corruption; he offended even the pâdishâh's harem by laying hands on their funds and executing their favourites, and the 'ulamâ' by expropriating waqf foundations, though some of the more established breaches of military discipline he left untouched. The son, Aḥmed Köprülü (1661–76), reaped the benefits of his father's violence and ruled in a more conciliatory manner, even while maintaining his father's standards. So far recovered was the empire that even after Aḥmed's death it could proceed to a second seige of Vienna (1683) even more threatening than the first under Süleymân.

On the failure of that siege, however (Vienna having been saved by a joint effort of the Germans and the Poles), an alliance of three of the strongest Christian European powers, Austria, Venice, and Russia, proved strong enough to beat the Ottomans out of all Hungary and temporarily to seize the Morea (the southern Greek peninsula) and Azov on the Black Sea. Henceforth the Ottomans were for the most part on the defensive in Europe, despite some recapture of lost European territory (Azov, the Morea, Belgrade) early in the eighteenth century. Not only in Europe but on all its frontiers, the empire failed to expand after the mid-seventeenth century; the military forces no longer formed a concentrated engine of conquest.

The military forces were still there, however, though based on the new arrangements implicit in the imperial evolution since the start of the seventeenth century. Some remnant of a central land force was essential to maintain at least the form of a central authority. But most important, the empire's forces formed dispersed instruments of defence and of maintenance of internal privilege. In such defence, however, local reserves—decentralized

The Ottoman Empire to 1789

1514	Sultan Selîm (1512–20) repulses Ismâ'îl's western advance, defeats him at Chaldirân, seizes Azerbaijan for a time; suppresses Shî'ism in lands under Ottoman control
1517	Selîm takes over Egypt upon defeat of last Mamlûks under Sultan Ghurî, annexes to his Anatolian-Balkan domain the chief E. Arab lands
1520	Ottomans conquer Rhodes
1520–66	Süleymân Qânûnî, called the Magnificent; political-social structure of the enlarged Ottoman empire finds definitive form
1526	Battle of Mohacs, Hungary tributary to the Turks; Vienna besieged, 1529; direct Turkish rule in most of Hungary, 1541
1556	Death of Fuzûlî, mas̄navî poet in Persian dîvân style
1566–95	Selîm II (1566–74) and Murâd III (1574–95); Ottoman empire moves toward peace abroad and relaxation of institutional standards at home; following Murâd (till 1622) four insignificant sultans
1570	Conquest of Cyprus
1578	Death of Sinân Pasha, architect of Süleymâniye mosque in Istanbul and Selîmiye mosque in Edirne
1600	Death of Bâqî, master of subsequent poets, elegized Süleymân
1623–40	Murâd IV subdues the elite Janissary corps which had become autonomous, revivifies the Ottoman empire's military position; literary form in Turkish continues in sixteenth-century mould, though themes of poetry widen
1630	Kochu-bey presents sultan with memorandum detailing causes of empire's decline and suggests return to classical institutions of Süleymân's era
1635	Death of Naf'î, poet of new Indo-Persian style
1656–78	Muḥammad Köprülü and (after 1661) Aḥmad Köprülü, grand viziers, renew Murâd's attempt to restore Ottoman efficiency, after a Janissary-dominated interval of failure since 1640
1658	Death of Kâtib Chelebi (Haci Halife), encyclopedist, bookseller
1679	Death of Evliyâ Chelebi, soldier, traveller, prose writer
1682–99	Ottoman war with Austria and Poland, under less competent members of Köprülü family; first major military setbacks in Europe, including defeat at Vienna, loss of Hungary and Belgrade
1718	Peace of Passarowitz, second major Ottoman defeat to Habsburgs
1718–30	'Tulip Age' under Sultan Ahmet III and his vizier Nevshehirli Ibrâhîm Pasha, first serious attempts at Westernizing reform, Ibrâhîm Müteferrika establishes first Ottoman printing press 1726; but reforms end with Patrona Revolt of 1730 by Janissaries and Istanbul populace
1730–54	Mahmûd I, with peace for the Ottomna empire after victorious treaties in 1739 with Austria and Russia as a result of division among the European states
1757–73	Mustafa III, able Ottoman sultan who despite desire for peace and sound rule becomes embroiled in war with Russia, resulting in total defeat of Ottoman armies
1774	Treaty of Kuchuk Kaynarji, Ottomans lose Crimea, tsar recognized as protector of Orthodox Christians in Ottoman lands
1789–1807	Selîm III lays groundwork for subsequent Westernizing reforms, establishes first formal Ottoman embassies in European capitals

and in part under civilian control—proved loyal and resourceful. These continued effective well into the eighteenth century.

The decay of the absolutism is often taken for the decay of the empire and its society altogether. Such an evaluation is premature. The Ottoman society continued vigorous throughout the seventeenth century, not only militarily but intellectually; though the most creative efforts in producing an imperial style belong to the sixteenth century, naturally, at the height of the imperial absolutism. In the face of the phenomenal transformation that was overtaking the Occidental powers (and was involving also the élites of the east European Christian peoples) in the seventeenth century, any weakness in the Ottoman empire was immediately aggravated many fold in its effects. Not only were the Western powers, by the end of the eighteenth century, on a level of strength that societies still on the agrarianate level could not hope to rival; some of the same events that had served to generate the great transformations in the Occident had accentuated the problems of those lands that remained on the agrarianate level. In view of this increasing basic disparity, it is astonishing that the Ottomans were still able to control their east European territories despite the nearly unanimous enmity of the Christian peoples, and even to regain territory once conquered by them; and that they did not tempt serious molestation till the very end of the eighteenth century. In terms of the standards of the past, as against those of the future, the Ottoman empire continued very strong well into the eighteenth century even though in a different form from that of the peak of the absolutism. Much did suffer with the decay of the absolutism, but new institutions were substituted of considerable effectiveness.

Many of the Ottomans themselves felt that the greatness of the state had suffered. Some revolts associated with the older aristocracy aimed at reducing the power of the officer classes and of the Janissary troops and at restoring something of the older military ghâzî norms. The central authorities themselves hoped persistently for a restoration of the absolutism; a series of hopeful writers condemned the corruption of the old military discipline and recommended drastic reform to restore it to the condition of Süleymân's time. But the more decentralized society had a logic of its own. Under the protective and legitimizing umbrella of the imperial authority, which commonly served to assure peace among rival provincial powers, considerable autonomy came to prevail locally. The semi-autonomous governors were sometimes able to maintain a relatively high degree of order and prosperity on the basis not of the rigorously impersonal combination of Sharî'ah and bureaucracy, but of a more intimate relationship between the governing family and the local population, particularly the new class of local notables. This often pleased the population better, as their natural groupings received a fuller recognition. When at last, in the nineteenth century, the central authorities succeeded in their perennial aim of restoring the absolutism, Occidental observers could speak of it with some reason as a suppression of the liberties of the people.

IV

Before the Deluge: The Eighteenth Century

In the general history of pre-Modern civilizations, a single century is a very brief period. In the fifty some generations of Muslim history, three or four generations hardly suffice to indicate any long-term trend. Yet the depression of Islamicate social and cultural life in the late seventeenth and eighteenth centuries does stand out in retrospect. This is so chiefly in the light of what followed. With the nineteenth century came the utter collapse of the strong Muslim posture in the world: that nothing was done in the eighteenth century to forestall this smacks of inexplicable weakness or folly. But the sense that there was a depression also reflects the actualities of the Muslim lands in the eighteenth century itself.

In certain earlier centuries there was relatively little achievement of high quality, or the Islamicate social order seemed relatively less vigorous. Yet even the fourteenth century, perhaps the least promising, was the time of Ḥâfiẓ and his contemporary poets. Though the eighteenth century was not without its interesting and creative figures, it was probably the least notable of all in achievement of high-cultural excellence; the relative barrenness was practically universal in Muslim lands. The strongest Muslim governments all found themselves subject to internal political disintegration. More ominously, even the age-long expansion of the Dâr al-Islâm, though not halted, suffered unusual setbacks; the greatest Muslim powers were often on the defensive and losing ground to non-Muslim powers. Such phenomena, which suggest some degree of decline in social or cultural power, can be called 'decadence if one is careful not to assume any long-term trend without further evidence. They represented more than coincidence among diverse lines of development; in part, at least, they doubtless answered to potent common circumstances in the lands of Islam.

The presence of the West

The prosperity and power of the three great empires in the sixteenth century had represented an adjustment to the level of agricultural resources that had been reached in the Later Middle Period, particularly in the Arid Zone. In each of the empires, the eighteenth century was materially less prosperous. There seems no reason to suppose that the level of resources had declined

	Europe	Central Oikoumene	Far East
1707		Death of Awrangzêb after major Mughal defeat in protracted Deccan wars with Marâtha Confederation; empire weakened	
1715	Rise of Austrian and Prussian kingdoms		'Rites of Controversy.' Chinese emperor restricts activities of mutually antagonistic foreign missionaries
1718		Peace of Passarowitz, Ottomans defeated by Habsburgs	
1720			Shogun eases restrictions on influx of Western knowledge; rise of Western-oriented Japanese intelligentsia schooled in 'Dutch learning'
1720–30		'Tulip Age' in Ottoman empire, first attempts at Westernization, founding of first Ottoman printing press, 1726	
1722		Ṣafavî empire collapses after Afghan invasion	
1736–47		Nâḍir Shâh in Iranian lands, sacks Delhi 1739 further weakening Mughals	
1740	Enlightenment; Frederick the Great of Prussia (to 1780) and Maria Theresa of Austria (to 1780), emergence of Enlightened Despotism		
1750		Karîm Khân founds Zand dynasty in Shîrâz (to 1779), some stability reachieved in Iran	
1757		Wahhâbîs take al-Ḥasa	
1763	British expand control in India		
1774	Louis XVI of France (to 1793)	Treaty of Kuchuk Kaynarji, Ottomans lose Crimea, total defeat of Ottoman armies by Russians, tsar recognized as protector of Orthodox Christians in Ottoman lands	
1775			Beginning of major peasant uprisings in China and decline of Manchus
1779		Qâjâr dynasty rules from Tehran	
1783	Catherine the Great subjugates Crimean Tatars		
1789	French Revolution	Selîm III (to 1807), beginning of second major period of Ottoman Westernization	
1798		Napoleon invades Egypt	

much further in so short a time. Another suggestion is more promising. In the centralized empires that had resulted from the realignments of gunpowder times, at the point (after five or six generations) when the initial solutions they provided to the persistent Islamicate political problems had been worked through and proved insufficient, one might suppose there would be a tendency to social and hence cultural stalemate. Such a tendency could affect them all simultaneously. But this is not, in any case, the whole explanation.

The reason why we must be specially concerned with a single relatively sterile century is, in fact, that, whatever might have been the significance of the 'decadence' in any long-term development of Islamdom in itself, it takes on a peculiar importance in the context of world-historical development at the time. At no time had Islamicate civilization been so self-contained as to be fully intelligible apart from the wider world-historical nexus of which it was a part. For several centuries, indeed, it rather dominated Afro-Eurasian historical life, so far as any single society could do so in pre-Modern times. By the eighteenth century, Afro-Eurasian, indeed world-wide, history was taking a new turn in which the Muslims no longer had a dominant role. Whatever reality the 'decadence' had absolutely, that is, in terms of other Muslim centuries, relatively it was portentous. For it appeared just at the time when western Europe was experiencing a prolonged period of outstanding creativity which was to prove historically decisive for all the world. Relative to what was happening in Christian Europe, the Muslim decline was of no transient import; it determined the posture of Islamdom at the most fateful point in the career of the Islamicate, as of all other, societies: at the advent of Modernity.

Moreover, what we have indicated as lending significance to the 'decadence' provides also at least part of its explanation. What was happening in Christian Europe contributed to the Islamicate 'decadence' directly. What might have been a less than brilliant century anyway was sapped by external forces. This becomes clearer when we note that it was not only among Muslims that the eighteenth century was relatively sterile. It was at most a century of moderate achievement for any society apart from Christian Europe—unless one excepts Japan. To be sure, the east Christian, Hindu, and Theravada Buddhist peoples, surrounded and in some cases practically enclaved by the dominant international Islamicate society, might not be expected to be in periods of high-cultural florescence under such conditions; any wider outreach they might have, for instance, depended so largely on the mediation of Islamicate cultural forces alien to them. But even the Chinese scholars and administrators, still running a monumentally powerful and cultivated and quite independent society, were for the most part marking time.

The fact that one region was coming to take so dynamic a lead in events in the Afro-Eurasian historical complex, within which the societies had always been in some degree interdependent, must have presented cultural and historical challenges that were not easy for the other societies to resolve. Increasingly, the activities of Occidental commerce were rivalling and supplanting the commerce of other peoples. This affected Islamicate society especially: it was a fateful reversal, that Islam no longer provided the chief framework of the long-distance commerce of the citied Oikoumene. Then, increasingly, the new Occidental cultural forms were making themselves visible elsewhere. Confronted with obviously important alien cultural ways which yet were not, apparently, as a whole more potent than the inherited culture, the most active minds could neither ignore nor truly come to terms with the presence of Western commerce, military methods, or even science and art. The ineffective yet persistent imitation of Occidental illusionist techniques in the art of Iran and India illustrates the dilemma on a level where the problem of technical resources was not pertinent. Not only economically but perhaps even psychologically, the presence of the West in full course of Modernization must have accentuated the indecisiveness of the age elsewhere.

We shall deal more fully with what was happening in the West, from a world viewpoint, later on. What was decisive in Muslim lands at this time was especially one feature: the West's tremendous expansion of commercial power. In the new Occident, accumulation of capital was not just a matter of its concentration in a few hands, nor even of its increase under local conditions and in response to special external circumstances; the process of accumulation had come to be built into the economic process as such, so as to provide indefinitely renewable sources of economic power, immune in the long run to any temporary or local reverses. Such economic power put Western commerce, and eventually Western politics, on a level where no people who did not share in the process could hope to compete in the long run.

By the start of the eighteenth century, any positive effects that the transformation in the Occident might have been having in Islamdom were outweighed by the negative effects. By the latter half of the century, decay was becoming rout in the Ottoman, Ṣafavî, and Indo-Timurî domains; and where anything positive was occurring, it was the outcome of the new world forces—for instance, new sorts of economic production for the Western trade in Bengal or Java. By the end of the century, the accumulated strains in the social structure of Islamdom called for radical new adjustments, which did supervene then with the forthright establishment of Western world hegemony.

For and against the restoration of Ottoman absolutism

The 'decadence' was most visible in the centres of power, in the form of adoption of goods and fashions of Occidental origin. Such fashions might seem harmless enough; they need not appear to go seriously beyond the fashions for Chinese silks or European furs or Hindu-trained slave girls which had long prevailed at Muslim courts. Yet there were two points of difference. In the eighteenth century, the foreign luxuries were increasingly coming from one particular area, rather than from all, and the trade was increasingly in the hands of the men of that area, the Occidentals, or else of special local groups closely associated with Occidentals. Morever, the Occidental trade was playing a larger part than any interregional trade had ever played before in the luxury life of the Muslim lands (and indeed of most lands of the Oikoumene). The role of long-distance trade had long been increasing, but the increase of this new sort of long-distance trade in this one century was very pronounced, and did nothing to restore the once proud role of the wholesale and luxury merchants of the qayṣariyyah bazaars, those pillars of urban society; rather, it further undermined them.

If the total crafts production, at least before the later eighteenth century, had been at least as great under Ottoman rule as before, it seems early to have lost its upper levels, those of the best luxury trade. (People speak of a general decline in the quality of the crafts, but I take it they do not mean that all objects were less finely made, for there were always many degrees of fineness in craftswork; but rather that the finer sort of object was less often made; and we may suppose that a highly practiced skill will consequently have been wanting on that level even when a luxury market was, on occasion, available.) These upper levels of craftswork were increasingly lost to Western competition. Misgovernment, making investment insecure, has been blamed for this; but the insecurity was no worse than in the peak periods of craft artistry. Rather, the West had special internal reasons for its new dynamism. By the eighteenth century, even of the goods exported from the Ottoman empire southward and eastward, at least from Syria and Egypt, the majority were of Western manufacture.

But it was precisely the upper levels of craftswork that were, from a high-cultural and in some ways a social viewpoint, the most significant ones. (One wonders if the role of the Janissaries in the crafts guilds at Istanbul reflected the disruption of the older social leadership that must have resulted.) Whatever effect the earlier mild dampening of Islamicate commerciality may have had in helping consolidate the absolutisms in the sixteenth century, by the eighteenth century a far more serious decline was becoming decisively pernicious. Moreover, almost the whole maritime transit trade was in foreign bottoms, so that even that benefited the Ottoman society minimally. To be sure, the Ottoman empire—so early subject to the pressures of the expanding Occident in the Mediterranean—was worse hit by such developments than other Muslim regions; the through trade of Baghdad, for instance, away from the Mediterranean focus of the Ottoman empire, remained mostly in Muslim (Persian and other non-Ottoman) hands, or in the hands of dhimmîs associated with them. But then even that trade declined badly at the end of the eighteenth century.

In the Ottoman empire, the most striking display of Occidental fashions in Istanbul took place immediately following the first great series of defeats by the Occident. Since the unsuccessful campaign against Vienna in 1683 and the disastrous treaty that eventually followed in 1699, the Ottomans had been trying to recover their losses; but despite successes against the Russians and the Venetians, in 1718 the Ottomans had to sign a new and seemingly decisive treaty (at Passarowitz) with Austria, in which even Belgrade was lost. The succeeding twelve years, under the grand vizier Ibrâhîm Pasha, are called the 'Tulip Age'. It was a time of minor cultural flowering; poets were fostered who broke relatively free of the old Persian patterns, though not from the general Ottoman tradition; experiments in home décor among the wealthy (particularly the cultivation of tulips) sometimes included Occidental details, rather as a bit later the French upper classes included Ottoman or pseudo-Ottoman details in their gardens. Even architecture was rather transiently influenced by Italian post-Renaissance styles. The wealthier men at court spent their funds on Occidental manufactures. Among the scholars, who were encouraged to inquire broadly, some even took an interest in Occidental learning.

But the 'Tulip Age' was more than a display of exotic luxury. Ibrâhîm Pasha represented a court party which hoped to restore the absolutism against the defenders of the civilianized, decentralized society which had come to prevail. This court party was itself not entirely at one. The ḳalemiyyeh, civilian bureaucrats, who now were able to attain as high positions in the 'army' as their 'military' rivals from the palace service, were divided among themselves.[1] And the high 'ulamâ'—those who, by deforming the system of cursus honorum among the madrasahs leading to high Sharʿî position, had transformed themselves into a hereditary closed corps—were not consistently loyal to restoring the absolutism; for though they were an integral part of the Centre, they were dependent for their position on a drastic degree of what was being decried as corruption. But many could see the dangers of the general decentralism, if only to their own income at the Centre. Against the court party, the prevailing decentralized order was defended by two groups at the capital: the ordinary Sharʿî hierarchy—those of the 'ulamâ' that owed their position not to heredity but to training; and the Janissary troops, who now included not only the central garrison at the capital but the greater part of the artisan classes there, as well as their allies in the provinces, who enjoyed Janissary privileges. This alliance of popular elements with a learned estate, now reviving the oppositional traditions of Islam against its own superiors, was the latter-day form which the primitive

[1] Norman Itzkowitz, 'Eighteenth Century Ottoman Realities: Another Look at the Lybyer, Gibb and Bowen thesis', in *Studia Islamica* 16 (1962), 73–94, makes a number of important distinctions, reducing the monolithic appearance which even Gibb and Bowen still tend to give to the 'ruling institution'.

alliance of ghâzîs and 'ulamâ' had finally issued in.[2] In the background of the partisans of the civilianized order at the capital stood the semi-autonomous '*derebey*' powers, hereditary and well-entrenched near principalities which among them made up the greater part of the Ottoman territories in Anatolia and Rumelia; these were based on the new gentry created in the seventeenth century and were natural opponents of any absolutism. (Still more remotely in the background, and far less influential in imperial politics, were a different sort of autonomous régime, the governorates in the Arab lands—the régimes of the reviving Mamlûk corps in Egypt and of other Mamlûk slave-soldiers in the Iraq, and some nearly independent governors in Syria.)

Over against these forces, the court absolutist party, if it were to restore the absolutism, had to find a quite new basis of power. The demand for such restoration, moreover, became pressing as the empire suffered defeats at the hands of the European powers. One partial solution which Ibrâhîm Pasha envisaged was to have Christian Europeans train certain military corps where the Ottoman forces were most notably weak; but when he attempted to introduce such a measure, the opponents of the absolutism saw their position obviously menaced. Crying in the name of Islam against the infidel (and commercially competitive) luxuries of the court, they struck knowingly against the Occident-based measures which might have increased the court's power. They preferred to leave the defence of the empire to the frontier troops, backed up by the Janissaries as they stood, believing that a court that would take this task seriously could provide sufficiently for defence without enlarging its own power. Thus into what was essentially an internal quarrel was injected crucially the presence of the new Occident; at the time, that presence seemed accidental and quite secondary, from both points of view; yet in retrospect it was decisive.

Ibrâhîm Pasha was overthrown in 1730, after a defeat by Nâdir Shâh, heir to the Ṣafavî empire; both the aesthetic and the military fashions of the Occident received a setback at court under the frowns of the party opposed to the absolutism; and the attempt to restore that absolutism fell into temporary abeyance. By 1739, in renewed warfare, Belgrade had been regained from the Austrians, though not the rest of Hungary; and this could seem to vindicate the established order. But Occidental fashions of one sort or another soon reappeared on a more local basis.

With the weakness of the central absolutism in the latter part of the century, the equilibrium among local powers ceased to be maintained by the central power. Autonomous ruling families became practically independent, and what had been sporadic fights among local troops threatened to become inter-provincial wars. The de facto derebey rulers in Rumelia and Anatolia sent troops for the central government's wars only at their own good pleasure; however, they did fairly well at home. The pashas of Damascus and Aleppo

[2] Uriel Heyd, ed., *Studies in Islamic History and Civilization* (Jerusalem, 1961), includes a useful article by Heyd himself on these points.

at the end of the eighteenth century faced an impossible task: trade was declining, the Bedouin were getting out of control, taxes were pre-empted, and discipline was failing. In response, they sometimes behaved outrageously, almost ruining the local populations with extortions or with irresponsible soldiery. This made things worse. Large areas in the Fertile Crescent that had been cultivated by the peasantry were abandoned to Bedouin herdsmen. Even within the unitary province of Egypt, different military elements, including Bedouin tribes from the desert, were carving out protectorates. There the Mamlûk garrisons, which had persisted at the capital as a separate military element alongside the more specifically Ottoman troops (and had effectively counterbalanced the Ottoman commander), found violent leaders (after 1767) in 'Alî-bey and Murâd-bey, who suppressed the various more local powers and established, in effect, an almost independent Egyptian kingdom. It was in such factional activity that Western ways were invoked. In attempting to bolster their power, the Egyptian leaders too, like the Syrian pashas, became dependent on a régime of extortion; but they also took an interest in the new Occident, encouraging planting crops that the Occidental mills wanted, and introducing Occidentals as military advisers to bring the Modern techniques into their armies.

Meanwhile, the Ottoman empire as a whole had a half-century of unmolested peace with the Occident, Russia, and Iran. In such circumstances, the ignorance of the Ottoman privileged classes about things Occidental, natural under the old agrarianate conditions, was little disturbed. Yet it was inevitably fateful. Occidental statesmen knew little enough about Muslim history, or even about current conditions in Muslim lands, but they knew more than had their ancestors, and what they did not know was not crucial to them. Ottoman statesmen, for the most part, knew no more about the Occident than had their ancestors, and the ignorance was more disastrous. When Russian ships first appeared in the Mediterranean (by way of the Baltic) without having passed through the Thracian straits, the Ottoman government, resting on outdated and overly literary notions of geography, assumed they must have been transported overland with Occidental connivance.

Ignorance of Modern conditions was crucial in economic matters also. The Ottoman empire had long made a policy of arranging with the foreign Christian merchant communities (and hence with their governments) that they should govern their own internal affairs through consuls, like the religious millets within the empire; and they had accorded favourable terms of trade, at the same time, to encourage commerce. Even under pre-Modern conditions, such arrangements could be dangerous. The Byzantine government had had such with the Italian merchant republics, vigorous with the expanding northern trade, and had had to witness its own undermining and final overthrow in consequence of the uncontrollable monopoly that they acquired. On the other hand, a more strongly based government could doubtless have avoided this fate and held the merchants within due limits.

Corresponding arrangements under Modern conditions had more unpredictable results. Until 1740, the arrangements, called in the West 'capitulations', i.e., treaties arranged under *capita*, headings, had been mild enough. Then as a special favour to the Ottomans' French allies (and in the general mood of decentralization within the empire), the French were allowed more elaborate privileges, which shortly had to be extended to all the other Christian powers. The most important privilege was that of extending certificates (*berats*) of protection to non-Muslim Ottoman subjects whereby they gained the privileges of the foreign nationals themselves. This had profound consequences in view of the transformed functioning of the Modern world economy, which a Persianate literary education did not prepare the Ottomans to take cognizance of.

The beneficiaries of these arrangements were a rising class commonly called the 'Levantines', as being the most conspicuous element in the cities of the Levant—that is, the east Mediterranean coastlands from the Aegean to the Nile. These people, who often claimed to be Occidentals settled locally and used Italian (later French) as a common language among themselves, actually were derived from the most varied origins; in practice, they were neither of the Occident nor of Islamdom, or else of both. They were of Christian and Jewish religious allegiance and they looked to one or another Occidental state for their economic and political protection, but they were rooted more in the Mediterranean basin as a commercial whole than in any one country on either the Occidental or the Islamicate side. Locally, it was they, rather than the Occidentals themselves, that were the most important force in commerce. They got their start in a way very widely found among minorities without other means of rising socially: through concentrating their best men on trade and mutually supporting each other in loyal defence against the majority. Then the special conditions introduced by the new Occident gave them an unusual opportunity to become dominant, which their Muslim rivals could not match. (This was not so much because of a special Muslim social exclusiveness, as some have suggested, as because of a want of special Western contacts; Muslim traders had always been open to the world. But then doubtless sometimes this want of contacts was hardened into a deliberate defensive exclusiveness after the process was under way, and was bolstered by a sense of identification with the Muslim upper classes.)

The result of granting privileges to such a class was insidious. It put Muslims and loyal dhimmîs at a competitive disadvantage to xenophile local Christians, and soon removed almost the whole of the trading classes from the Ottoman to the privileged foreign jurisdiction. In much of the empire, Muslims were no longer the main commercial element in any case, and a further decline in this respect meant little. But the loss of power effectively to regulate or to tax the increasing commerce was to be disastrous.

When these privileges were granted, the Ottomans seem not to have been aware of any danger or disadvantage in them. But it was not only the

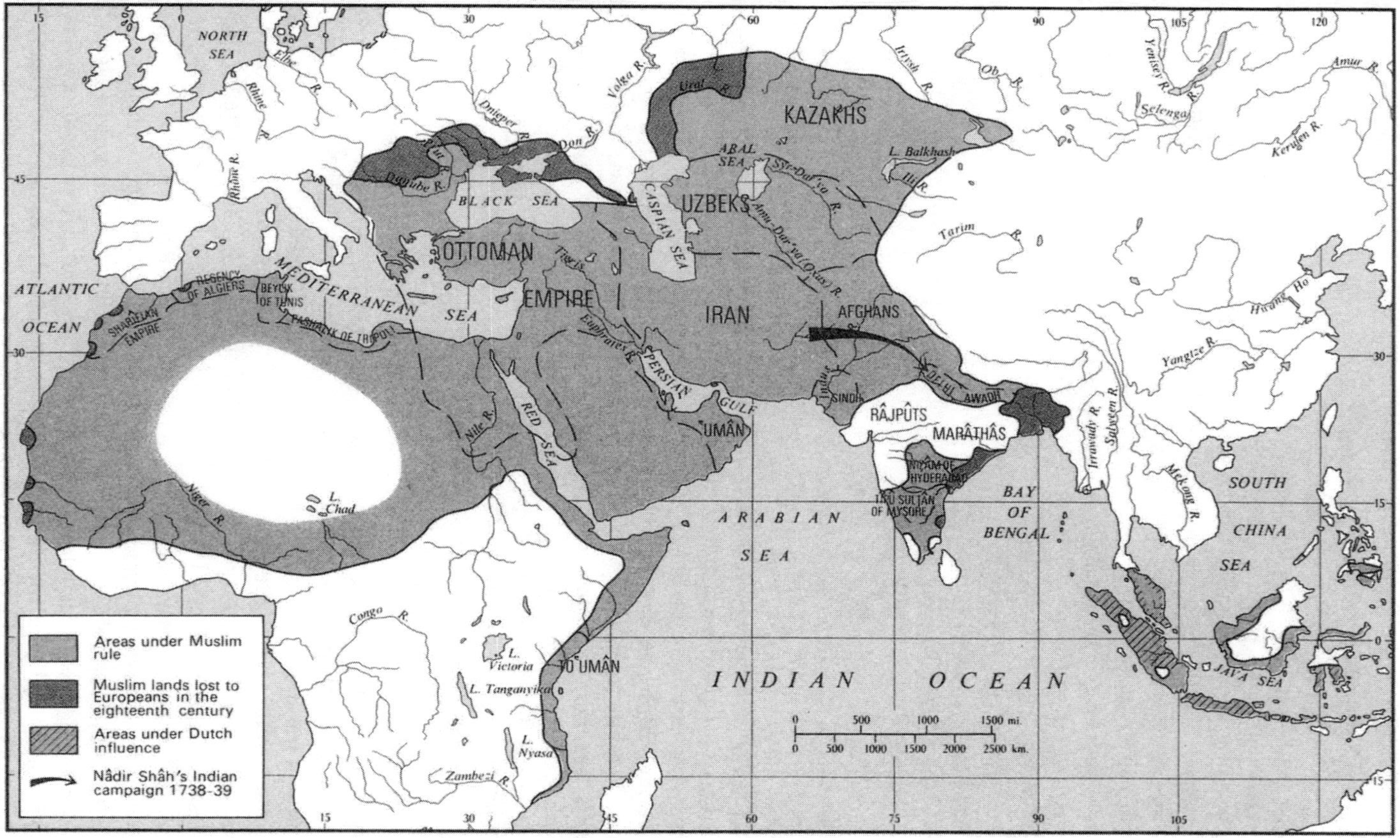

The Islamic lands before nineteenth-century European expansion

immediate disadvantages of the letter of the treaties to the Ottomans, but the clear abuses to which they were soon subject, that had such drastic results. Berats were granted indiscriminately by the European powers, and their holders tended to be protected whatever they might do. The Ottoman government very gradually realized that what had been granted as an apparently harmless favour was proving economically and at last politically dangerous; but by then the favour could no longer in practice be withdrawn, nor even the abuses checked (except sporadically), because the economic and political life of the whole empire was too fully committed—even had the Occidental powers been willing to concede a withdrawal, which later on they were not. Though the Ottoman government was far stronger than the Byzantine had been at a corresponding moment, yet the power of the new Occidental commerce, based on cheap mass production which penetrated even the minor bazaars as well as conditioning the economic role of the wealthy classes, was far more potent than had been that of any trading groups on the agrarianate level.

The struggle for succession to the Indo-Timurî empire

After the death of Awrangzêb, during a dozen years of brief and faction-torn reigns, many of the leaders of the Indian empire lost confidence in the central authority as a power capable of rising above faction. During the succeeding long, but not very vigorous, reign of Muḥammad Shâh (1719–48), increasingly this lack of confidence was expressed in a tendency for court or local notables to manage such provinces as they could control as autonomous units, generally loyal to the court but jealously guarded from interference by any opposing faction that might be in control there. The Indo-Timurî administrative patterns tended to persist wherever governors representing Delhi could maintain effective control, even though autonomously; but the all-powerful central bureaucracy soon ceased to give the patterns their efficiency.

Despite all this, at Muḥammad Shâh's court a wide range of creative men were using the remaining wealth of the imperial court and city to renew the Timurî cultural life in an atmosphere of general reconciliation of diverse cultural traditions. In arts and letters, the reign formed a curious parallel to the 'Tulip Age' of the same time among the Ottomans. Here too, there was a renewed cultivation of worldly scholarship (a certain interest in Western physicians dated from the time of Awrangzêb). Here too, poetry received a new formal influence, though its liberation from the Persian tradition was more ambiguous here than at Istanbul. The Urdu language—i.e., the local Hindu of Delhi written in the Persian alphabet and enriched with a Persian-derived vocabulary—was used by soldiers and merchants as a lingua franca all over the Timurî territories. It had already been developed as a poetic medium, particularly for religious verse, in the Deccan. Now it was taken up at court in Delhi itself, where it was the vernacular, and was disciplined in the Persian poetic tradition as a vehicle of the most cultivated poetic forms; it captured poetic primacy from Persian proper, though it did not alter the Persian poetic manner unless to emphasize its sweetness.

But the use made of Urdu suggests what was the most striking contrast to the Tulip Age. Whereas in the Ottoman domains, Christians and Muslims drifted even further apart in the eighteenth century, as east Christians became culturally assimilated more and more to the Christians of the Occident, In India, Hindus and Muslims seem to have come closer together. Though many Hindus learned Persian, the Muslim cultural tongue par excellence, Urdu was a language in which Muslims and Hindus were almost on a common footing. The Urdu developed by Muslims and the standard Hindi developed by Hindus (in the Sanskrit alphabet) were structurally the same language. It was not felt strange for Hindu writers to use Urdu and to use semi-Muslim formulas while doing so; Urdu was accessible to both communities. At the same time, Ṣûfî writers sometimes made use of Hindi and used, in doing so, a variety of literary references traditional in Hindi letters, which were based on Hindu conceptions; though the Ṣûfîs Islamized them, they retained many terms and names from the Sanskritic tradition. In secular arts, the tolerance of Hindu legends at the Muslim court was even greater. It seems to have been in this period that the Hindu temple dance, originally devoted to Kriṣṇa and other gods, was brought into the court as a form of entertainment, refined at the hands of masters of the Persian tradition, and given its classical north Indian form even while retaining many of its ancient Hindu motifs in its new secular setting.

At the Râjpût Jai Singh's royal observatory in Râjâsthân, probably the most important in Islamdom in this period, the staff composed their astronomical work in Sanskrit and in Persian (the ruler, Jai Singh, himself being a Hindu); but the main body of the equipment was modeled on the observatory of Bukhârâ and the scholarship was dependent primarily on the Islamicate tradition. However, apparently for the first time, a new tradition was introduced on the technical level: the Latin tradition of the Occident, which had meanwhile matured so as to go beyond the Arabic itself. Seventeenth-century Latin works were translated into Persian, but not the works of Kepler or Galileo—only, it seems, such works as did not presuppose major transitions from the Islamicate tradition: planetary tables, in particular. Jai Singh established an observatory also at Delhi.

The sense of a common interest in a common heritage not only persuaded the Hindu Marâthâs, later when they became powerful, to pose as servants and protectors of the Timurî emperor, but eventually brought even so remote a Hindu ruler as the Râjâ of Travancore, in remote southern Kerala where Muslim rule had never penetrated, freely to petition Delhi for a mandate as subordinate ruler.

Nevertheless, in contrast to the Ottoman empire, the decline of central power in India was not replaced by a stable decentralism; it soon provoked an explicit struggle for succession to the Timurî power, which filled the politics of later eighteenth-century India. The presence of the new Occident, always marginal, yet always a persistent factor to be taken into account, was felt everywhere; though the form of its presence varied with the local circumstances. In many of the Indic lands, in contrast to the Ottoman, the Europeans had occasion to interfere directly on the political level.

The Marâthâ Hindu soldiery and its highland chieftains, who had raised the first major persisting resistance within the Indo-Timurî domains and had undermined Awrangzêb's power in his later years, meddled in factional strife at the Timurî court after his death to such advantage that by 1720 their polity was accorded virtually official recognition. Gradually they established so systematic an authority throughout the central Indic lands that they rivalled in power the Timurîs themselves in mid-eighteenth century. But as the power at Delhi was undermined, and especially after the Iranian ruler Nâdir Shâh had sacked Delhi and looted the imperial treasury in 1739, the position of the Marâthâs as alternative all-Indic power was contested by several further rival powers either in northern or in southern India. In the south, the Indo-Timurî administration was maintained by the governor Niẓâmulmulk on a provincial basis in the Deccan from Haidarabad as capital, whence a sharp limit was put to Marâthâ claims. Further south yet, a potent Hindu state based on Mysore, with a Muslim commander-in-chief, likewise resisted them with success; later the Muslim commanders became its rulers.

In the north, the Marâthâs were arrayed against not only a number of local Muslim powers more or less rising out of the fragments of the empire, but also against three active new powers with wider ambitions. Two of these had local antecedents. The Sikhs, the reforming body from Akbar's time in the Panjâb who had become militant against Muslim rule by Awrangzêb's day, saw in the troubles of the empire a chance to establish their own dominion at least in the Panjâb. They established a confederation which finally controlled most of the Panjâb against all comers.

Beyond them in the mountains to the northwest, the Afghan tribes had won a certain political solidarity and independence of action from the time when they rebelled and tore down the Ṣafavî state in 1722; their independence was reinforced by Iranian confusion after Nâdir Shâh's death. They now sent their leading fighters into the north Indian plains to establish a new Muslim empire. In 1761, the Marâthâ power was at its height: under the headship of the leader in the west Mahârâshtrâ mountains, its generals had occupied outright Mahârâshtrâ, Gujarât, Mâlvâ and most of the nearby lands; including Delhi, where the Timurî monarch was under their protection. In most other Indic lands, they collected a fixed tribute. The Marâthâs claimed the intention of restoring the Timurî empire under their own protection. The local Muslim powers in the north joined with the Afghan king of Kâbul, Abdâlî. He temporarily suppressed the Sikhs in the Panjâb and met the Marâthâs at Pânîpat, defeating them; but the Afghans withdrew under political complications, the Sikhs revived, and the local Muslim powers fell to quarrelling. Nonetheless, the Marâthâ power too was checked and its generals ceased to co-operate among themselves. Thenceforth, each held his own area on his own, and India fell into an uneasy political stalemate.

One may conjecture that the power of Aghäns, Marâthâs, and other groups in the eighteenth century may have been due in part to a further development in the technology of gunpowder weapons which temporarily favoured more mobile small units over the Centre: the widespread availability of relatively effective handguns, muskets, which could outmanoeuvre the heavy field artillery that the central powers had learned to depend on.

In such political circumstances, Muslim dissatisfaction with the role of Islam in India took a radical turn. The Islamicate tradition had always been linked with the Irano-Semitic tradition of the region from Nile to Oxus; even in the sixteenth and seventeenth centuries, Iranian culture had retained much prestige. But Muslims in more distant regions had generally felt themselves fully at home in their own countries. In the eighteenth century, however, we find the beginnings of a mood in India that was later to be very consequential: Muslims began to feel uneasy about their very presence in India, to feel that India as such might be a threat to their Islam.

This uneasiness reflected a series of contingencies. First, nowhere was Islamdom more readily alienated from its international ties. Unlike most regions into which the Islamic allegiance was brought, India was the heartland of major high-cultural traditions which could effectively rival the Irano-Semitic. In this respect the Indic case was paralleled only by the European; but it can be contrasted to the European case in several ways. The Indic heartland was conquered entirely, and those lands of Indic culture that did not fall under Muslim hegemony were few (chiefly in the Indochinese valleys) and not ready to take the sort of cultural lead that was being taken by the Occident in Europe. The representatives of the Sanskritic tradition did not turn elsewhere, as the more adventurous east Europeans did, but accepted the Muslim leadership and invited its co-operation.

This might not have been felt as a danger, however, if the Muslim community had not had unusually ambivalent roots in the region. The conquest had brought with it relatively little immigration from other Muslim lands, in contrast especially to Anatolia where the population gradient acted to bring in a large population with no pre-Islamic loyalties. And, in contrast to the Balkans, there was no general conversion of an indigenous landed class with its inherited pride in its own land. Hence the Muslim population in the more central parts of north India tended to be polarized into social extremes: at the top, highly honoured and dominating both politics and culture, were families that had more or less recently immigrated from Îrân-and-Tûrân, and kept alive the memory of that fact. The rest of the Muslims were mostly converts from locally disadvantaged elements, often from castes that the Hindus despised; they too were made to remember this. Even a native Indian Muslim of foreign ancestry was on occasion compared to a native Indian horse, generally regarded as inferior to any imported horse. With the advent of rule by non-Muslims, then, the tenuous Muslim superiority could seem to be disappearing altogether.

In consequence, in the very success of Islam, when the representatives of the Sanskritic traditions made it easy for the Indo-Islamicate culture and its Ṣûfî-minded carriers to assimilate indigenous Sanskritic elements, many Muslims found a threat to their identity as Muslims. Those Muslims whose background as Hindus was unpalatable could be very insistent on the distinctiveness of Islam: their conversion had been, in a sense, an escape from India. Those Muslims who cherished their foreign ancestry could be alarmed to see Islam becoming just one more Indic caste, in which their foreign links would be irrelevant. There were many for whom identification with the general Irano-Semitic cultural heritage, as the proper Islamic heritage, could become as important as adherence to the central religious affirmations of Islam. When they saw Islam losing even the distinction of identification with power, their latent fears could emerge vividly. India itself could become the enemy that Indian Muslims must guard against; at all costs, India must be subdued—and some would add, even at the cost of rule by cruder peoples from the Iranian highlands.

The most important representative of such a response to Muslim political collapse was Shâh Valî-ullâh, a Ṣûfî intellectual who lived for some time outside the courtly sphere even though at Delhi, but who attracted the respect of all. He was suspicious of the cultural universalism of the court, and upheld actively the integrity of Shar'î Islam; to this purpose, he revived the tradition of Aḥmad Sirhindî's opposition to Akbar's religious universalism. But Sirhindî's quarrel with most other Muslims he did not adopt; it was essential now that Muslims unite. Hence he tried to show the potential harmony of all the main strains of the Islamic tradition—in particular, maintaining that Sirhindî's mystical system, jealously asserting the transcendence of God against the speculative followers of Ibn-al-'Arabî as well as against the universalistic tendency to tone down the Sharî'ah, was in fact in harmony with a true understanding of Ibn-al-'Arabî and his tradition. I gather that, building on Ibn-al-'Arabî's conceptions of the potential in each human being to respond to some aspect of divine love, he tied this cosmic potential to a person's positive work as a Muslim in the world; and hence to the Shar'î community.

The foundation of Valî-ullâh's work was perhaps a keen sense of religious psychology, which was expressed in a systematic attempt to show the rational function of the various prescriptions of the Sharî'ah. (He instigated extensive ḥadîth study also.) But this was oriented to making the Sharî'ah more practicable in India in his time, as a basis for resistance to 'Hinduization'. His sense of the social purpose of the Sharî'ah led him to condemn the licentiousness of the upper classes and their exploitation of the poor as leading the Muslim power along the ruinous road that the Roman and Sâsânian empires had followed; and he recommended fiscal recentralization as a partial remedy. He meddled in politics: in contrast to most Muslims, he was at least complaisant toward the disastrous Afghan attempt to subdue northern India. So far as Indian Muslims produced an eighteenth-century response to the disruption of Islamicate society comparable to that of the memorialists of the Ottoman empire, Shâh Valî-ullâh was its leader. His followers, including some notable descendants of his, played the leading part in north Indian Islam (west of Bengal), often as reformers, for the century and a half that followed his death.[3]

Meanwhile had appeared the third expanding new power in northern India, which aroused less notice among the Muslims at the time, perhaps because at first it did not look like an independent power at all. Already after 1748, when Niẓâmulmulk died in Haidarabad, the British trading company had begun to interfere in the warring in the Deccan, offering the wealth and forces of their fortified trading posts in return for local privileges; they supported the opposite side to that which their competitors among the French traders were already supporting. The result was that the European enmity, between French and British, reproduced in their trading companies, was almost as decisive in determining the course of the rivalries among the powers of southern India as was the position of the Indian powers themselves. Shortly, all the east coastal districts were handed over to the trading companies—chiefly to the victorious British—as tax collectors and general administrators; from this technically subordinate and transitory authority, before long they gained complete control.

The British maintained their position only with the aid of alliances with other Indian rulers, at best; and they were by no means uniformly successful in particular wars. The brilliant Muslim general-turned-ruler of Mysore (in the southwestern Deccan), Haydar 'Alî (d. 1782), defeated them in the field and maintained his position against them in two wars. But the British power outlasted all reverses and, when Indian powers were weak for a time, could always take advantage of this to increase its local base.

The British gained their greatest power further north, in Bengal. There they were allied financially with the local Hindu merchants who, like most of the foreign merchants also, had centred their trade in the fortified and privileged British port station, Calcutta. Civilian and mercantile elements, including Hindus, had risen to increasing power at the Bengal court with the general civilianizing and decentralizing of the Timurî empire in the eight-

[3] Shâh Valî-ullâh has been discussed at length by Indian Muslims recently; perhaps the most suggestive brief summary of his thought is that by Fazlur-Rahman, 'The Thinker of the Crisis, Shâh Waliy-Ullâh', *Pakistan Quarterly*, vol. 6 (1956), which is unfortunately too brief to be more than tantalizing.

eenth century. By 1756, some of these elements were so deeply committed to the British that their court intrigues could use the British presence as a prime resource; while the British, in turn, felt confident in anticipating the success at court of a party favourable to their interests; and no interference from the now weakened central authority was to be feared. A show of independence by the British in 1756 led to their expulsion from Calcutta (an event marked by exaggerated tales of Indian cruelty), but sealed the doom of the too zealous Bengal governor who expelled them. In 1757 the British returned. This they did with the aid of their private troops, but they could not have succeeded without the active aid of a Bengali party that may be called pro-British, though it was no creation of the British. This party (including both Muslims and Hindus) held high posts in the Bengal court and freely betrayed the incumbent governor, who belatedly invoked countervailing French support to no avail. The treachery of the 'pro-British' party then gave the British a victory over the governor in a skirmish (at the village of Plassey); and this event afforded that party the excuse to install a new governor of their own at court, who enlarged the British privileges—and hence those of the Indian merchants allied with them.

But the British turned out to be no mere tools of one party against another. The new governor soon found himself little better than a puppet in British hands; a Bengali effort to restore independence in 1764 failed; and thereafter the Muslim governor was a mere figurehead. The British trading company found themselves in a position to force the emperor himself, at last, to grant them the right to collect taxes and to govern directly, on the emperor's behalf, the land of Bengal together with the dependent lands of Orissa and Bihâr. For a time the emperor, frightened out of Delhi by the wars of Afghans and Marâthâs, even established his court in Bihâr, under the protection of and with subsidy from the British traders. From this time forth, the British company formed a power on an equal footing with the other Indian powers; like them it owned nominal allegiance to the Timurid emperor.

For local purposes, its official language was Persian, that of the court, and it enforced the Sharîʿah among Muslims. But it was unlike the other powers in having a permanent political base in the British kingdom across the seas; and in being founded not on simple military strength, or even on a religious allegiance, but on that commercial strength which had first caused the economic centre of gravity of Bengal to shift to the little new town of Calcutta: the new and continuous economic expansion of the Occident. The institutionalized pattern of capital increase was giving even overseas merchants of the West a source of ever-renewable economic strength, ultimately inaccessible to the rivalry of any local Indic power. The Western merchants became like Antaeus to the Indian Hercules, with the sea playing the role of Mother Earth.

As in the Ottoman empire, this situation led to consequences that seemed marginal at the time, but were decisive on a plane where pre-Modern men had not been accustomed to look for serious historical events. The Europeans seemed merely a new source of mercenaries, to be paid off, like some others, with lands. The fact that they were more than that was betrayed by the eagerness of a number of Indic courts, both Hindu and Muslim, to bring in Europeans (usually French, as opposed to the more dangerously victorious British) to train their troops in the newest methods of Europe. When lands were given to these mercenaries as tax-collectors, the newcomers treated their lands not simply as a domain from which to draw the land revenues, but as a part of a new political-commercial system; a local base for that wider system which at the same time was beginning to undermine the luxury trades of the whole area. When a local court, such as that of Muslim Lucknow, encouraged certain local crafts with its aristocratic patronage, this was no longer to be taken for granted, but was a notable pressure against the trend. Occidental physicians were able to gain great, if transient, prestige. So powerful was the trend that even in the domain of courtly art, where Occidental works were not yet imported, local artists experimented with Occidental techniques of perspective painting. The results were not happy: they confused the older tradition without achieving any great creativity in the new.

After the British obtained untrammeled control in Bengal in the latter part of the century, however, the results were quite visibly disastrous. Those decades are referred to as 'the plundering of Bengal'. The British felt no local responsibilities, and experienced no external restraints on their superior power. But unlike earlier conquerors, they were not interested just in eliminating a rival gentry and receiving the land revenues for themselves: they made their gains in exploiting trade and industry. The first result was an irresponsible rush on the part of the individual traders to seize everything —a rush in which they had the full co-operation of Hindu traders, notably those called 'Mârwârîs', almost equally alien to Bengal by origin. The British obtained rights of toll-free trade which effectively excluded all competitors; then they forced agreements on the local craftsmen so onerous that the craftsmen were ruined. Shifts were being made, meanwhile, even in the kind of crops grown in the countryside. The destruction of the old order was completed when, with the end of proper reserves even on the land, general famine supervened, carrying off vast numbers notably in 1770. The disaster was so great that any further trade was threatened, and reform had to be undertaken. Warren Hastings, as head of the British company in Bengal (1772–85), took the most essential measures to insist on honesty in administration and on elementary protection of the remaining peasantry, arousing indignation among the hitherto unchecked individual traders. His work, precipitated by unusually early disaster, was an early anticipation of controls that were to be required everywhere else sooner or later.

The loss of Muslim political initiative internationally

In the Ottoman and Indo-Timurî empires the presence of the new Occident was adding, to the growing decentralization, an insistent disruption and dislocation. In other parts of Islamdom, the effects of the new Occident were sometimes greater, more often rather less (at least in any direct form) than in those two empires; but almost everywhere the new world-historical situation was in some sense decisive. Everywhere there was less opportunity, even if a certain local strength was displayed, for building solid and creative institutions; the resources that would have been necessary were dwindling. In increasing numbers of areas, Muslims and Muslim powers were on the defensive against non-Muslim powers; they were unable to continue that political initiative which had been characteristic of the expanding margins of Islamdom for so long, and in which Muslims from all over Islamdom had been wont to participate. Most tellingly, in many lands Muslim (and former dhimmî) populations were falling under the rule of infidels: in India, under that of Hindus and of Christians; in the Tarim basin, under that of Chinese; in various parts of eastern Europe, under Christians, as also in the Southern Seas. And the Muslims were rarely evacuated from such territories (a notable exception is the Ottoman empire in withdrawing from Hungary). To the opportunities produced by the age of gunpowder empires, opportunities largely, after all, of their own making, the Muslims had responded very creatively; but to the new age that had supervened—this time not of the Muslims' making at all—they found no such response. It is hard to estimate what subtle effects such facts may have had on the more sensitive and potentially more creative Muslims. The Muslims' awareness of who they were in the world was never entirely parochial, always at least subliminally responsive to a sense of the mission of Islam in the world as a whole. At the ḥajj pilgrimage in Mecca news would be exchanged from the farthest corners and it would be discussed on a level free of local political preoccupations. But even apart from such interchanges, concerned Muslims found the tone of the age unpromising.

Even in the central region, where the Ṣafavî empire had flourished, political disorder and economic depression were severe. Throughout the post-Axial ages, the great arteries of intercultural contacts had converged in Iran and the Fertile Crescent; this interregional pattern had still nourished early Ṣafavî grandeur. Now this pattern was yielding to a very different world configuration. The most central Muslim areas were rapidly becoming a backwater.

Despite what appeared, at first, a brilliant assertion of military and political might, the Ṣafavî dominions, like the Indo-Timurî and the Ottoman, suffered a dispersal of power during the eighteenth century. The Afghans that had occupied Iṣfahân in 1722 with such sudden destructiveness failed to establish a dynasty there (though they did effectively assert their independence at home, which endured thereafter despite a brief interruption). A vigorous general, Nâdir Khân, reorganized the Ṣafavî armed forces, making good use of the new advantages of musketry, and soon expelled the Afghans from western Iran. He tolerated nominal Ṣafavid rulers till 1736; then Nâdir proclaimed himself ruler as Nâdir Shâh and carried the arms of the state for a moment into greater sway than they had ever had. It was his armies that defeated the Ottomans of Aḥmed III in 1730, reannexed the Caucasian area, and brought an end to the Tulip Age; it was his armies that invaded India in 1739 (after a Timurî failure to co-operate in their province of Kâbul against the Afghans of Qandahâr), and rather by accident sacked Delhi, ruining the city of Muḥammad Shâh; to the north, his armies occupied the chief Özbeg capitals along Zarafshân and Oxus, where no earlier Ṣafavî ruler had been able to march; to the south they occupied 'Umân, centre of the reviving Arab mercantile power in the Indian Ocean.

Nâdir Shâh sometimes showed a cruelty and pettiness that have seemed incompatible with greatness. He reverted to building towers of skulls, which doubtless were intended to recall illustrious precedents as well as to serve an immediate policy of terror. But he was miserly with money, a trait that especially shocked those around him, for it was generally expected that not only many individual adventurers but much cultural life would thrive on royal largesse. But he had a measure of larger vision. Being of a Turkic tribe, he was brought up a good Shî'î, of course; but he seems to have been given to religious experimentation in more than one way. His most important religious venture could have had far-reaching consequences if it had been successful. He seems to have lost any specially Shî'î attachments (he is commonly called a Sunnî, but doubtless was no more attached to the one allegiance than the other), and conceived the hope that the Shî'î and Jamâ'î-Sunnî communities would be reconciled. He hoped to persuade the Shî'î 'ulamâ' scholars to accept the idea that the Shî'î community formed merely another madhhab school of law alongside the Ḥanafî or Shâfi'î, and that they need not condemn the Sunnî madhhabs (by publicly cursing their heroes as the Shî'îs did)—as if it were only on points of fiqh law that the difference lay. Then he hoped to see the new madhhab be accorded equal rights at Mecca with the four Jamâ'î-Sunnî madhhabs already recognized there. On an expedition into the Iraq (which he failed to occupy permanently because of uprisings in his rear), he persuaded the Shî'î 'ulamâ' of Najaf to accept his proposal, in some sense; but he could not persuade the Shî'î 'ulamâ' generally. Nor did he persuade the Ottomans, overlords at Mecca, though he signed a friendly treaty with them after his victories. (In this he used the term 'caliph' of the Ottoman emperor in a complimentary way but not, of course, in any technical form such as might have been taken for an acknowledgement that the Ottoman had any superior status).

The more zealous Shî'îs looked on Nâdir Shâh as an interloper, at least after he deposed the last of his Ṣafavid wards, and doubtless his religious policy did help undermine his position; but his ferocity did so perhaps as much. He had to face almost continuous rebellions at the end of his reign, and only multiplied his atrocities in response. When at last he was killed in 1748 his family held power only a matter of months.

But a Ṣafavid restoration, under the protection of the beloved general of Shîrâz, Karîm Khân Zand, was unsuccessful. In Iṣfahân itself it was challenged; while in many parts of the Iranian plateau, and not only at Qandahâr and Kâbul, where the Afghans rose again, but even at Ṭihrân (near the old Rayy) in the heart of western Iran, military tribal leaders established their independent power. Karîm Khân Zand abolished the Ṣafavid pretence in 1753 and ruled such of the empire as he could salvage in his own name till 1779. His descendants were then soon set aside by the Qâjâr tribal power, centred at Ṭihrân; it was led by a man who had been made a eunuch when captive as a boy at the Zand court, and who wreaked his bitterness in new ferocities such as mass blinding of the men of Kirmân and, of course, a tower of skulls. By 1794, he had established a west Iranian state which succeeded to such prestige and authority as could be retained from the Ṣafavî tradition. He then devastated the Caucasus and annexed a part of Khurâsân, but failed to take either Herat or Baghdad before he died in 1797, leaving the Qâjâr state what turned out to be permanent limits.

There are indications that by the end of the eighteenth century the population of the great Iranian cities had declined drastically.[4] Notably Iṣfahân, the great metropolis, was reduced by half or more to perhaps 200,000 people; the next largest city was Herat, with about 100,000. As in many other parts of the world then, the scourge of pestilence seems not to have been to blame in the eighteenth century: that relative immunity which has contributed to modern population growth around the world was affecting Iran also. It is warfare that effected so much destruction and, doubtless, famine in the vicinity of the campaigns; around the cities could be seen desolate empty villages. But on a reduced scale trade was still active in all directions; merchants repaired the roads themselves at need. The industries of Iṣfahân and Yazd and lesser crafts centres were active and their products were even exported, especially westward (whereas more was imported from India than was exported thither).

By the time of the rise of the Qâjârs, however, the European presence was coming to be of great importance. Occidental and Russian goods were playing an increasing role. More subtly, the Western cultural presence overshadowed men's minds. A European physician was looked to necessarily

[4] Gavin Hambly, 'An Introduction to the Economic Organization of Early Qâjâr Iran', *Iran, Journal of the British Institute of Persian Studies*, 2 (1964), 69–81, says but little about economic organization but does offer some useful and sober estimates on population and mercantile patterns (unfortunately following a too usual pattern, he defines 'foreign trade' as if he were dealing with a modern state unit—so that trade between the Tehran-ruled and the Kâbul-ruled parts of Khurâsân is deemed international—so obscuring any estimate of actual long-distance trade).

as a sage; and the European embassies—already in the Napoleonic time, representing the British-French rivalry—were at the centre of foreign policy, and of the sense of status that was bound up in that for an Iranian monarch. When the Qâjârs tried to re-establish a centralized absolutism, the story belonged to the nineteenth century as did the corresponding efforts in the Ottoman empire.

In the midst of this turmoil, Shî'î thinking was not unmoved. The most outstanding figure among the Twelver Shî'îs in the late eighteenth century was Shaykh Aḥmad al-Aḥsâ'î (d. 1826), from east Arabia. In the holy cities of the Iraq he preached new hope for the future of mankind. He seems to have come from an Akhbârî legal background, circles that rejected the Uṣûlî system of elaborate legal reasoning which, they felt, usurped the direct authority of the imâms. But, responding to the philosophy of Mullâ Ṣadrâ, which was highly formative for him, he seems to have spiritualized this reverence for the imâms' Shar'î role. The Iṣfahân school had stressed the metaphysical position of the Imâmate; it was now explored more thoroughly as a means of human access to Truth. The result was a renewal of Shî'î chiliasm (a 'sub-Shî'ism' within the now majoritarian Shî'î establishment) but in a highly civilized form.

According to al-Aḥsâ'î's chief disciple, Sayyid Kâẓim Rashtî (1759–1843), the prophets and imâms and the imâm's representatives were the perfect mirrors of the divine will, norms which were drawing all mankind gradually into perfection (a conception not unlike Shâh Valî-ullâh's); the work of the Hidden Imâm was to foster human moral improvement (through his representatives) to the point where the outward Sharî'ah would be entirely internalized among people, its externalized legalism being superseded by way of the spontaneous spirit, following God's will directly rather than following merely a formulated record of it. The largest body of Shaykh al-Aḥsâ'î's followers were called 'Shaykhîs' and formed a school of fiqh (especially strong in Azerbaijan) independent of those of the Uṣûlîs and Akhbârîs. This was a kerygmatic Shar'ism yet more speculative than that of Shâh Valî-ullâh of Delhi, but equally reformist; however, as befitted the central lands of Islam, perhaps, it seems rather more optimistic, despite the difficult political fate of the Shî'î populations.

In all this period, the Özbeg principalities in the Syr and Oxus basins were incapable of seriously intruding into the confused affairs of Iran, for they too were in a period of political weakness. Khîvah, capital of Khwârazm; Bukhârâ, whose khân ruled the Zarafshân valley; Khoḳand, up eastward in the mountains, all were independent Muslim powers. But their continental trade was becoming insignificant as the sea routes became ever more efficient and reduced the land routes to local dimensions. The Russians were an ever more dominant commercial power throughout central and northern Eurasia. But they concentrated on the northern forests. Such trade as persisted further south lost its cosmopolitan quality and became specialized locally.

Despite their great centres of Jamâ'î-Sunnî learning at Bukhârâ, the people of the Syr and Oxus basins were increasingly isolated from the wider Islamicate and world currents. They came to look abroad more to sources of Shî'î or Christian (Russian) slaves than to a fertilizing trade (rather like their contemporary powers of the Maghrib). The Muslim powers not yet destroyed by the Russians took little initiative. By the mid-1700s even the Chinese empire was able to occupy the Muslim states of Kâshgharia, in the upper Tarim basin; henceforth, the more northerly Muslims were divided between the Russian and the Chinese empires, not without occasional local resistance. Only at the end of the century—as we shall see—did an economic revival among the Muslims of the Volga basin, hitherto submerged by Russian oppression, lead to a new vitality in the more northern parts of Islamdom; but this revival was oriented not to Islamdom at large but to the new West.

In the Southern Seas, Muslims had a greater part in the increasingly lively interregional trade; in the seventeenth century, the Ibâḍî Khârijîs of 'Umân, building up their own commercial network, were able to expel the Portuguese not only from the Persian Gulf but from a good portion of the coastal lands of east Africa, the Swahili coast, where they established their own power. But the internationally most important routes no longer made much of the Swahili coast. Other Muslims had continued to build their power, side-by-side with that of the Dutch, in the Malaysian islands, increasingly dominating the commercially less important interior. In the eighteenth century, these powers continued to maintain themselves, but by and large with little initiative; the 'Umânî power in the Swahili coast, for instance, broke up into autonomous city-states, unable to push the Portuguese out of the Mozambique coast further south. In the interior of the 'Horn' of East Africa, Islam was advancing among the Gallas and through them into the Abyssinian highlands, but without the spectacular effects Aḥmad Grâñ had produced in the sixteenth century there.

The Dutch and British powers, which had replaced the Portuguese, gradually became stronger in the eighteenth century than the Portuguese had been even in the sixteenth. The Dutch in Malaysia had early begun altering the whole economic pattern of the areas where they traded, encouraging new crops oriented to Occidental commerce; at first, they doubtless stimulated increased prosperity, but their increasing power gradually caused disruption. Now they came to be felt as serious threats for the first time by major Muslim kingdoms. In the seventeenth century, for instance, the Dutch establishment at Batavia was woven into Javanese historical symbolism on friendly terms; in the eighteenth century, such court historical writings were no longer willing to accord it such recognition.

The Maghrib had already long since been a special stronghold of the conservative spirit and was not much affected by Persianate culture anyway; moreover, it probably suffered, already in the sixteenth century, more insidiously from the Portuguese sea trade (that with the Guinea coast) than any other major Muslim area. But the Muslims there had shown for a time, at the same moment when Islamicate energies were so expansive elsewhere, an unprecedented spurt of perverse energy. In the course of the fifteenth and sixteenth centuries, their trade with western Europe had decreased in importance, especially as compared with the greatly increasing total volume of western European trade; the Maghrib 'island', off the European coast, was being left out of an economic life in which once it had played a premier role and which by geography would seem essential to its commercial ports, which formed the main part of Maghribî citied life. In the sixteenth century, Muslims and Christians in the Mediterranean found themselves most of the time at war, and privateering against enemy shipping was taken for granted on both sides. Muslim captives were held as slaves by the Christians and Christian captives by the Muslims, except as each side managed to redeem some of its own by ransom. But in time, most Christian shipping had found more profit in legitimate commerce, and slavery (though lingering in Italy into the nineteenth century) did not pay well on the continent of Europe. In contrast, the commercial resources of the Maghribî ports had not increased and probably had decreased. By the seventeenth century, privateering had become a primary economic activity, and the use of slaves, black and white, became a style of life among the better classes.

This privateering had led to daring exploits. The Muslim privateers—or pirates, as they must be styled, in the increasing intervals between declared warfare—were based both in Morocco and in the more or less autonomous Ottoman provinces of the Maghrib; they terrorized Christian shipping and even Christian ports in the whole western part of the Mediterranean; and, knowing where the greater trade was coming to be by then, they also ventured up the Atlantic coasts, raiding as far north as England. The whole movement, in fact, was an early reaction, in an area most closely concerned, to the new economic and social order which was developing especially in northwest Europe—and which was already casting the whole Mediterranean economy into new forms. Many of the Muslim pirates were actually converted Christians, Englishmen and others, expressing so their own alienation. These Muslim 'Barbary corsairs' were romantic in their daring, but they could not reverse a steady trend; they were sterile economically and, in the end, socially, even for the Maghrib itself. By the eighteenth century, even the pirate raids were losing their élan. They were limited to the nearby Mediterranean.

In the Sûdânic lands alone, the new Western presence was not a serious factor directly. Here we find the opposite extreme from the Volga Muslims' direct participation in the new industrialization: in the Sûdân, there was practically no contact with the West at all. Here, Islam had continued a substantial expansion, its more concerned representatives concentrating on Islamizing an ever wider sector of the population. Even so, in the eighteenth century in the Niger Sûdân, the Muslims were on the defensive against revivals of pagan power. But it was a time of patient scholarship, intent on spelling out for the rulers and the city population what was meant by justice and proper living, in the Islamic sense, in Sûdânic conditions. The most prominent scholar of the time was writing long-cherished studies in which he taught not only the details of the law, but the broader principles of fair dealing in commerce, in government, and in courts of justice. In the Sûdânic lands generally, Islam, representing the international urban society over against diverse tribal parochialisms, was still carrying out, in a series of states relatively peaceful (except for the continuing slave trade victimizing the heathen to the south), its secular task of civilization.

Reformers in the back country: primitive Wahhâbism and the new ṭarîqahs

To eighteenth-century Europeans, the inefficiency and corruption in many Muslim lands was monumentally obvious: everyone in a public position seemed to be for sale except as he might be checked by brute fear of an unscrupulous tyrant; and even when something was agreed on, a task might be delayed endlessly and then accomplished indifferently. To be sure, such judgments in their extreme forms must be discounted: there was much of both integrity and competence, even by later, nineteenth-century, standards, at least in some fields. Nevertheless, such judgments were founded on realities that contrasted to ways becoming common in the new West. Within these realities, a distinction must be made. On the one hand, there was inefficiency and corruption peculiar to eighteenth-century conditions in Muslim lands; on the other hand, much that seemed to go under the same heading was in fact hardly separable from agrarianate conditions of life in all periods except under special circumstances.

A certain amount of venality and of disregard for practical 'business-like' conveniences was normal in pre-Modern times; if all venality disappeared for a time, it was that disappearance which required an explanation. For instance, the servants of a great man normally required tips for their part in facilitating access to him, whether the cause pursued was that of justice or some more personal suit. In part, this represented the highly personal tone of such relationships before the days of filing cabinets and punch cards; in part, it represented the tribute due from the rich, who alone normally had affairs on a level worthy of the great man's time, to the poor upon whose labour they lived—or to those of the poor that were lucky enough to have escaped the village and wangled a chance to enter the fringes of privilege. In either case, the situation recurred naturally wherever it was not repressed by special arrangements implying abnormal pressures. An especially strong government might sometimes insist on such repression, at least in its higher ranks; this seems to have been the case, to a considerable degree, in the peak period of the prevalence of military discipline in the Ottoman administration. Such a government might also exact an unusually high standard of practical efficiency in some spheres. But in a pre-Technical society, precision soon brought diminishing returns: there was a limit to the degree of efficiency that would be profitable in any one sector of a life and economy where in most other sectors the degree of precision open to calculation or prediction remained very limited.

In the eighteenth century, the great central governments were mostly no longer in a position to exact any extraordinary virtue even in limited sectors; the normal casualness of pre-Modern times prevailed. But in addition, in the areas of all three great empires, the decline or collapse of the central power had left a gap between formal procedure and actual practice which accentuated the normal gap between ideal and reality. Where there was a pretence of maintaining the institutions once upheld by the central power, though that power was no longer effective, the way was opened for an unusual number of abuses; some of them were as fictive as the forms they abused, but others were real enough. Serious Muslims in the Ottoman lands or in India were impressed especially by this gap between form and practice, which troubled them where much that would disturb a Modern did not disturb them. By the end of the eighteenth century, the number of earnest reform movements being launched surely exceeded the average. We have noticed something of their mood at the centres of power: the chiliastic Shîʿîs in the Ṣafavî realm, the revivers of Sirhindî's Sharîʿah-minded Ṣûfism in India, even the memorialists in the Ottoman empire.

At that time, just as the Occidental presence was contained within limits which appeared to make no fundamental breach, so the reformers themselves remained within traditional reform patterns. They denounced the political powers in age-old terms; they found much to criticize besides the political situation, but it was nothing radically new. As always, at their best they championed a moralistic social equality against claims to social privilege and against respect for the cultural excellence that commonly goes with it. Now this was directed especially against the established Ṣûfism. The Ṣûfî ṭarîqahs, with the centuries, had everywhere grown more burdened with the weight of endowed property and popular superstition. Many of the more established orders had notoriously compromised their principles, either for wealth or for popularity; too many of those who took the Ṣûfî name were mere charlatans. The reform of Ṣûfism, in one degree or another, had long become a concern and now became an important target of the reform movements because of the intimate place of Ṣûfî organizational forms in most Muslim societies. But reform movements that remained close to the centres of power were limited by the weight of the institutional patterns they wished to reform. It was in more outlying areas that relatively innovative attempts could be carried out.

The most spectacular of the reform movements, as it later developed, was sown in independent Arabia, on the edge of the Ottoman domain. It grew out of the Ḥanbalî movement and was not satisfied merely to reform some Ṣûfî ṭarîqah but was frankly hostile to Ṣûfism. The Ḥanbalî madhhab was ranked in later Jamâ'î-Sunnî theory, by the wishful thinking of Ḥanafîs and Shâfi'îs, with the other three Sunnî schools of fiqh law as one of four equally and mutually tolerant schools; but Ḥanbalism had never really been primarily a school of fiqh at all. It remained a comprehensive and essentially radical movement, which had elaborated its own fiqh in accordance with its own principles, but whose leaders were often unwilling to acknowledge the same kind of taqlîd as provided the institutional security of the other schools, and rejected the ijmâ' tradition of the living community on principle. Ijtihâd inquiry remained alive among the Ḥanbalîs; each major teacher felt free to start afresh, according to the needs of his own time for reform in a puritan direction.

Since Ibn-Taymiyyah (d. 1328), there had been few figures, even among the Ḥanbalîs, to stand out with great intensity against the casting of all religious life into the mould of Ṣûfî ṭarîqahs. Most reformers had accepted this pattern even when attacking the Ṣûfî spirit. Ḥanbalism as such had declined to a dwindling minority even in its old strongholds, Damascus and Baghdad, where it formed the most ardent counterweight to the Shî'ism that flourished nearby from Aleppo to Baṣrah. In the mid-eighteenth century, however, it was sufficiently alive to inspire a young seeker, Muḥammad b. 'Abd-al-Wahhâb (d. 1791), who came forth from the Najd in the heart of Arabia to try all lines of Muslim development offered to him (always within the Jamâ'î-Sunnî pale) and, after a period as a teacher of Ṣûfism, ardently adopted Ḥanbalism and set out to imitate Ibn-Taymiyyah. He returned to the Najd, and, succeeding where his exemplar had failed, converted a local ruler, Ibn-Sa'ûd, who set about establishing a state on these principles. Within a few years, the whole of the Najd had submitted, acknowledging the Ḥanbalî doctrine, in the form given it by Ibn-'Abd-al-Wahhâb, and quaking with a noble determination to allow no corner of public or private life to escape the rigorous if benign sway of the divine law.

The result was as drastic as if a revived Khârijî zeal had suddenly taken power. Ibn-'Abd-al-Wahhâb, to be sure, enforced the Sharî'ah in all its correctitude against the tribal custom which had survived with relatively little social erosion in the heart of Arabia among the Bedouin ever since the time of the Riddah wars. But above all he hated everything that smacked of Ṣûfî devotion—its theory and the popular aspects of its practice, which he felt made gods of the Ṣûfî saints. Those that paid reverence at the tomb-shrines of saints were, he was sure, quite as much idolaters as if they worshipped still the old gods which (in fact) those tombs had often replaced. He was out to rid Islam of the corruption of the presence of these tombs and their worshippers, as well as of Shî'îs and others who put any man—not only 'Alî but even Muḥammad—in the unique place where God ought to be. For, consistently enough, he opposed the reverence for Muḥammad's tomb as much as any other. This, in effect, relegated the overwhelming majority of Muslims to the status of idolaters subject to the death penalty for abandoning Islam, and it condemned many of the favourite ceremonies at Mecca and Medina at the time of the ḥajj pilgrimage as mere idolatry to be destroyed.

Ibn-'Abd-al-Wahhâb was not the first to denounce most other Muslims as infidels to be killed, but the 'Wahhâbî' state built up by the Sa'ûd family proved effectively powerful and, not long after the death of the first generation, the movement was still strong enough, under Ibn-Sa'ûd's grandson, to conquer the Ḥijâz and occupy Mecca and Medina. To the horror of the Muslim world, they proceeded to destroy all the sacred tombs, including the tomb of Muḥammad, to massacre the Muslims of the holy cities, and to impose their own standards on future pilgrims. It was a number of years before the Ottoman empire was able to overcome them and put down the movement, at least as an independent political force, for the time being; but this was done (1818), even in the heart of the Najd, and the danger was seemingly averted.

The suppression was carried out—and gained much of its force, including its ability to penetrate the heart of the Arabian peninsula—under new and unexpected circumstances, as we shall see: the Ottoman lieutenant who did it was wielding a new sort of army, one based on the equipment and the discipline that had been evolved in western Europe in the course of the preceding century. Without this, he surely would not have been so readily successful in putting down the Wahhâbîs. But the date at which Wahhâbism appeared affected its destiny not only in the manner of its suppression, but in the nature of its successes. Not unexpectedly, it inspired a number of other movements in other areas. Numerous pilgrims who came to Arabia during its ascendancy learned of its principles and were enthused by its militancy. Hopes to purify Islam and to fulfill its godly promise—particularly as against the prevailing Ṣûfism, which a Sharî'ah-minded purist could not but distrust, and which now no longer provided much exciting novelty for a young idealist—were encouraged by so striking an example.

In the latter part of the eighteenth century a number of reformers preached, if less intolerantly, yet with great insistence, against the evil condition of Islamdom: the most important source of inspiration was the Muḥammadiyyah movement, also born in Arabia. Such movements, to be sure, took the form, as before, of ṭarîqahs. Their founders had scarcely been aware of the Occident. But they, too, were to interact with the new impulses of Modernity. In consequence, they were to play a role in Islamdom other, and perhaps more radical, than what might have been anticipated for them: in contrast to many earlier reform movements, their impulse broadened into a general climate of opinion in nineteenth-century Islamdom, which finally reversed the ages-old Ṣûfî trend in a manner determined by the challenge of the Modern Occident.

BOOK SIX

The Islamic Heritage in the Modern World

Bliss was it in that dawn to be alive,
but to be young was very heaven.
—*Wordsworth*

PROLOGUE TO BOOK SIX

The revolution of our times

Everyone is nowadays made aware that we are living in the midst of a world-wide 'revolution'. But the revolution is interpreted variously. Some have seen it as a political drive, since the War of 1939–45, of formerly dependent peoples trying to achieve and consolidate independence. Some see this drive itself as but a moment in a wider movement, dating further back in this century, of 'underdeveloped' peoples toward economic as well as political equality with the West—the 'revolution of rising expectations'—said to result from the 'awakening' of non-Western lands from a supposed 'traditional' torpor. Some see these new expectations, in turn, as merely one phase of an all-inclusive twentieth-century world turmoil. They see a struggle, which engulfs both the West and the rest of the world, to replace a decadent, self-destroying nineteenth-century bourgeois social order, outdated by new technology and science, with a social order more vital in all spheres, one that will answer to the most recent economic and intellectual requirements. In the West this struggle has expressed itself in such diverse forms as dadaism, surrealism, Freudianism, existentialism or Christian neo-Orthodoxy, nationalist totalitarianism, or socialism, as well as in more recent movements. This general Western rejection of its own nineteenth century, and the attendant uncertainty and political confusion, naturally result, in 'underdeveloped' areas which had been held in awe of Western prestige, in a widespread rejection of the West itself. This rejection likewise has taken many forms: imported existentialism or nativistic religious revival, anti-colonial nationalism, communism, or a drive for a xenophobic industrial independence. Thus the movements in the technically less advanced areas are to be understood only against a background of rooted discontent and disruption within the technically most advanced part of the world, to which they react and which they largely echo in their own ways.

So comprehensive an analysis of the upheavals of our century is still not adequate for our purposes. It recognizes the fact that these many twentieth-century movements are all related to one another; but it is not easy to see all the relations of the various movements to each other if one is limited in scope to this century alone. Most of these movements visibly reach back deep into the nineteenth century, as do the conditions to which they are responses. Indeed, the present revolutionary situation, if it is to be taken as a totality in all its aspects, must be seen as going back at least to the generation of 1789 (though it has gone through more than one phase since then)—and this not only in the West but also in the majority of non-Western areas, particularly in the Muslim lands. It was then that an old order was everywhere destroyed or irremediably undermined and has not yet been dependably replaced. The main elements that have combined to produce the present world-wide 'revolutionary' situation, in fact go back within the Occident still earlier by at least two centuries. That is, if one is to understand the present 'revolution'—even as it affects Muslim lands—in terms of the full range of social and cultural transformation and struggle now interrelatedly in progress, one must start not with the status quo at the end of the nineteenth century, but with that at the end of the eighteenth century or even of the sixteenth. Such a time-span need not frighten us. It is a very brief period as human history goes.

Against this background we can then distinguish between the results in the West and those in Muslim lands of what can be seen as a single world-wide historical process, the advent of the Modern Technical Age. The presently 'awakened' Muslim lands were not asleep but, at most, briefly stunned by the effects of the Modern transformation itself; and their latter-day activity is only secondarily a product of corresponding movements within the West. Fundamentally, it grows out of two centuries of the developing Modern experience in Islamdom itself, and is a direct response to the same total historical situation that is troubling the West.

On past heritage and present community

The Muslim peoples have been caught up, like all others, in this vast historical event that has been taking place now for several generations. Their story has become a part of that wider story. This fact raises difficulties. In this final part of the book we are in a position almost as ambiguous as in the very first part, where we studied the genesis of the Islamicate society. There we studied a number of situations and events that formed the background for and helped to produce a new society; but in that period the new society, properly speaking, was not yet in being. Likewise it could be maintained that, in most historically significant senses, in this sixth period the Islamicate society is ceasing to exist. From this point of view, what we are to read about is not the evolution, as before, of a single civilization, but rather a number of situations and events that have resulted from the former existence of such civilization: chiefly the separate responses of the several Muslim peoples to a new modern world society of which they are all coming to form a part, and in which religion does not make a decisive difference.

These various peoples possess, it could be said, a more or less common cultural and religious background, but otherwise do not respond to the conditions of the new world, normally, as a common Islamicate body; they respond simply as diverse peoples, no closer to one another (as regards the major motive forces of current events) than they are to any other of the 'less developed' peoples in their part of the world. By and large, the interaction is less intensive among Muslim peoples than it is between each Muslim people and certain non-Muslim peoples; and even such interaction as there is among Muslim peoples is often unrelated to any Islamicate tradition. The common basis of the lettered culture—to take the most crucial point for the definition of a 'civilization'—is now for the most part, on the scientific, on the journalistic, and even on the imaginative levels, one which they share with non-Muslim peoples—in which, in fact, non-Muslim peoples have taken the lead, and in which Islam plays no decisive formative role. From this point of view, this sixth period forms something of an epilogue to our story in the same sense that the first period formed a prologue to it.

The social unit, in a sense comparable to that in which the great civilizations could formerly be called social units, is now a much larger part of the world and probably the whole of it. Social and even cultural interrelations are now closer and more immediate in the world as a whole—especially on some of the most crucial levels—than they were within the Islamicate society two centuries ago (a fact that has itself forced into new prominence the many sorts of divergences among nations and even within them). Whatever common fortunes may come to the Muslim lands as a result of common presuppositions and a degree of exchange of experience and even of conscious solidarity, they no longer form a single society, an independent primary overall social context, in the old manner; nor, therefore, a relatively autonomous field of overall culture-historical study. (The same can be said now, in an important sense, of the Occidental lands also.) To the extent that the Muslim lands can still be studied as an active cultural grouping, it is not as an Islamicate *society* but as sharing the Islamicate *heritage*. It is this legacy of past experience, specially treasured and still of special authority among Muslims, which is now relevant; and it forms only one component—more or less important according to the particular instance—in a wider world-cultural nexus.

If we can no longer speak of the Islamicate society, however, it is premature to judge that the Islamicate heritage is ceasing or has ceased to exist except in a secondary way as a matter of local background. The heritage does remain an active cultural force, even as a single whole. In the first place, the Islamicate background has been decisive in determining the spiritual and cultural posture of all the Muslim peoples in modern times, and to some degree they have actively shared their problems and their hopes in regard to it. Moreover, there is still a very active interchange among the Muslim peoples on many levels and in many fields—not merely in what could most strictly be called religion—even though in many crucial matters the determining influences in the interchange have nothing to do with the boundaries of the Dâr al-Islâm. This interchange often does reflect a common Muslim consciousness; it might come to have increasing importance under some circumstances. In any case, the whole Islamicate heritage is at work in the persisting conscience of the concerned as they face modern problems from an Islamic spiritual viewpoint. Such conscientious men may not be prominent, but they may often prove creative in moments of crisis, and hence disproportionately influential.

At any rate, in this sixth period we must treat of Islamicate life in a quite different way from previously. What we will be above all concerned with, will be precisely the Islamicate heritage and how it has fared in modern circumstances. We will not be primarily concerned with economic progress in all Muslim lands (though we must say something of this if we are to understand what has happened to the heritage), nor with the whole of modern politics nor even of modern culture in the more restricted sense. The complexity of our story in this period will thus be kept more in proportion to the theme of the book as a whole.

Even so, our story will be structured with special considerations. In the first place, the wider historical setting will have a far more intimate place in the story than could previously be the case. We must begin our story with the modern transformations of western Europe as they were to bear on the rest of the world in our period. Then when we come to the particular Muslim peoples, much that we shall have to go into would also apply with fairly little change to other areas of the world. These chapters must take the form of chapters in world history, with global preconditions and implications present at all points. More than ever, in this one respect, Islamdom can be seen now as a microcosm of world history. On the other hand, though the interconnection on the world level is close, there will be rather less in the way of specifically Islamicate interconnection among the developments in the various Muslim peoples. The development of each people will illustrate, with variations in emphasis, a more or less common story in a world setting; but the separate developments have had less effect one on the other than has the common world situation on each of them.

Accordingly, what I shall do is to point up different cases of a common process affecting all Islamdom. First I will present a chronological sequence from about 1790 to about 1870, and more summarily to about 1905. Then I will illustrate, in the case of several major Muslim peoples separately from about 1870 to about 1940, primarily whichever aspect of the general process shines clearest in each case; so that the whole picture will emerge only as it appears in the end from the combined stories of the several lands. And last, I will close with a renewed chronological sequence from about 1905 dealing particularly with the years after 1940.

The Islamic Heritage in the Modern World, 1800–1950

THE OTTOMAN EMPIRE AND TURKEY

1789–1807	Sultan Selîm III, tries to establish new military and bureaucratic structures alongside traditional institutions, but is overthrown by Janissary, derebey, and a'yân resistance
1808–39	Sultan Maḥmûd II, centralizes political control through modernized military and administration, destroys Janissaries, suppresses derebeys and a'yâns, subordinates 'ulamâ'

1815–17	Serbian revolt
1821–30	Greek war of independence
1832–48	Wars with Meḥmed-'Alî who penetrates deeply into Anatolia; European powers save sultan and force Egyptian retreat, European merchants granted broad commercial concessions in Ottoman empire
1839–61	Sultan 'Abdülmejîd, with Reshîd, 'Alî, and Fuad Pasha, inaugurates overtly Westernizing reform era of Tanẓîmât in Hatt-i Sherif (1839) and Hatt-i Humayun (1856) to allay big-power concern with 'the sick man of Europe'
1854–56	Crimean War resulting from European rivalry over protection of Christian minorities in the empire
1861–76	Sultan 'Abdül'aziz, continues Tanẓîmât reforms, leads empire to bankruptcy with huge loans from Europe, resulting in establishment of Ottoman National Public Debt Administration, in which European governments and bankers control Ottoman finances
1865	Foundation of Young Ottoman Society led by Namık Kemal, Ziya Pasha, and 'Alî Suavi; rise of literary intelligentsia using simplified vernacular and journalism to popularize ideas of Ottoman patriotism, constitutionalism, and Islamic modernism
1876	Sultan deposed by palace revolution, new sultan, Murâd V, soon deposed because of insanity in favour of 'Abdülḥamid II whom Midhat Pasha persuades to promulgate first Ottoman constitution
1876–1909	Sultan 'Abdülḥamid suspends constitution, forces political opposition underground, rules despotically through spy network; major reforms in education, transportation, and communications; nationalist sentiment spreads among Christian minorities
1889	Military students in Istanbul found first 'Young Turk' revolutionary organization, Society of Union and Progress
1894	Armenian revolutionaries brutally suppressed with use of Kurdish irregulars, 10,000–20,000 Armenians massacred, revival of traditional European anti-Turkish prejudices
1896–97	Cretan revolt, Turco-Greek War
1903	Union and Progress splits between Ahmet Riza's Turkist centralizers and Prince Sebahettin's minority-oriented decentralists
1908	Young Turk revolution forces sultan to restore constitution and reconvene Parliament; era of political freedom and great intellectual activity in which conflicting ideologies of Turkism, Islamism, and Westernism are openly debated; Ziya Gök-Alp articulates basic concepts of Turkish nationalism
1909	Counterrevolution in Istanbul demanding return to Sharî'ah crushed by forces from Salonika, 'Abdülḥamid deposed in favour of Muḥammad V (to 1918)
1910	Albanian revolt

1911–13	Tripoli lost in war with Italy; Balkan War
1913	Young Turks seize direct rule through coup d'état; pro-German triumvirate of Enver, Talat, and Cemal leads empire into World War I and defeat
1919–22	Turkish War of Independence; Nationalist forces based in Ankara under Muṣṭafà Kemal (Atatürk) rally to defeat Greek invaders and resist European dismemberment of Anatolia
1922	Sultanate abolished
1923	Treaty of Lausanne insures Turkey's territorial integrity, abolishes capitulations; Republic of Turkey proclaimed; Republican People's Party established
1924	Caliphate abolished; civil courts replace Sharî'ah courts
1925	Ṭarîqahs closed; fez abolished; Kurdish revolt suppressed; Kemal eliminates major political rivals
1928	Islam disestablished; Latin alphabet introduced
1932	People's Houses organized; Turkey joins League of Nations
1936	Montreux Convention restores control of Straits to Turkey
1938	Death of Atatürk, Ismet Inönü succeeds as president
1939	Annexation of Alexandretta (Hatay) from Syria
1945	After remaining neutral during war, Turkey declares war on Germany to join United Nations
1947	Transition to multiparty regime as political opposition is allowed to organize; Truman Doctrine and U.S. resistance to Soviet territorial demands against Turkey
1950	Democrat Party of Bayar and Menderes opposing étatism and religious restrictions badly defeats RPP in free elections and ends three decades of one-party rule

EGYPT

1789–1801	Napoleon occupies Egypt; French savants create Egyptian interest in European culture
1801–5	French withdrawal followed by struggle for power among Ottoman governor, Mamlûks, and Meḥmed-'Alî's Albanian brigade
1805–48	Meḥmed-'Alî attempts to build Egypt as a modern industrial and military power independent of Ottoman control; massacre of Mamlûks (1811); industrial monopolies and confiscation of landed property and waqfs (1816); educational missions to Europe; suppression of Wahhâbîs, conquest of Sudan (1822) and Syria (1831); advance into Anatolia against Ottomans (1832)
1841	European powers intervene to save sultan, forcing Egyptian withdrawal from Syria and dismantling of industrial-military complex
1848–54	Khedîv 'Abbâs I; Modernization interrupted by anti-European reaction

1854–63	Khedîv Sa'îd; grant of Suez Canal concession; contract of first foreign loans
1863–79	Khedîv Ismâ'îl, attempts to transform Egypt into part of Europe; cotton boom during American Civil War, opening of Suez Canal (1869); bankruptcy due to excessive European loans; sale of Canal to British (1875); establishment of European control over Egyptian finances (1876)
1871–79	Influx of Syrian intellectuals fleeing Ottoman censorship; rise of Egyptian journalism and constitutionalist opposition to khedîv and increasing foreign dominance; al-Afghânî in Egypt
1879	Ismâ'îl deposed; Tawfîq becomes khedîv
1881–82	Native Egyptian officers under 'Urâbî mutiny protesting Turkish-Circassian privilege, join forces with Constitutionalists and al-Afghânî's followers to temporarily impose their government on khedîv, but popular uprising leads to British occupation
1882–1907	Lord Cromer British proconsul; economic expansion and stabilization; improved irrigation; increased market production of cotton; rapid population growth; abolition of corvée
1849–1905	Muḥammad 'Abduh, abandons al-Afghânî's revolutionism for collaboration with British and gradualism; attempts educational and legal reforms as rector of al-Azhar and grand muftî; articulates Islamic Modernism
1906–07	Dinshawî incident crystallizes growing politicization and nationalism through formation of Muṣṭafà Kâmil's Nation Party and Luṭfî al-Sayyid's Umma Party
1914	Egypt formally declared British Protectorate after outbreak of World War I
1919	Sa'd Zaghlûl leads delegation (wafd) demanding independence; his deportation touches off 'nationalist revolution', Milner Commission
1922	Egypt granted formal independence, but Britain retains control over defence and foreign policy and Sudan
1865–1935	Rashîd Riḍà, leads *salafiyya* movement to revive and reinterpret orthodox Islam
1923–30	Wafd led by Zaghlûl and Nahhâs wins three large electoral victories under liberal constitution, but each government forced to resign under pressure of British or king
1931–33	Sidqî Pasha abrogates constitution and attempts to crush wafd
1936	Wafd returns to power, but compromises nationalist demands in Anglo-Egyptian treaty recognizing Britain's right of occupation; death of King Fu'âd; accession of Farûq
1942	British force king to replace pro-Axis prime minister with Nahhâs
1940s	Political and economic failures of liberal governments compounded by hardship of war and humiliation of Palestine defeat (1948) lead to increase of popularity and terrorism of Ḥasan al-Banna's fundamentalist Muslim Brotherhood

1945	Formation of the Arab League
1951	Nahhâs unilaterally abrogates Anglo-Egyptian treaty, guerrilla warfare against British in Canal Zone
1952	Battle of Ismâ'îlya, 'Black Saturday' riot in Cairo. Coup of the Free Officers and deposition of Farûq

IRAN

1797–1834	Fatḥ 'Alî Shâh; rise of European influence and rivalries in Persia
1814	Treaty of Gulistan, Caucasian territory ceded to Russia
1828	Russians advance around Caspian Sea and into central Asia, receive capitulatory concessions
1835–48	Muḥammad Shâh
1848–96	Nâṣiruddîn Shâh, travels widely in Europe
1844–52	The Bâb leads townsmen's protest against Qâjâr landlord rule; attempted assassination of shâh triggers mass persecution, which won European sympathy for the Bâbîs' successors, the Bahâ'îs
1857	Persians take Herat, but British force their withdrawal and recognition of Afghan independence; British granted concessions
1872	Baron de Reuters granted railroad, mining, and banking concessions; intensification of British-Russian commercial rivalry
1878	Russians train Cossack regiment in shâh's army
1892	Shâh forced to cancel tobacco concession by agitation of mujtahids and bâzârîs
1896	Shâh assassinated by follower of al-Afghânî, succeeded by Muẓaffaruddîn Shâh (to 1907)
1901	Oil discovered; concession granted to D'Arcy
1905–6	Bâzârîs lead revolutionary movement forcing shâh to proclaim constitution and establish Majles
1907	Anglo-Russian agreement divides Iran into spheres of influence and undercuts Constitutionalists
1908–11	Civil war; Russians intervene and support counterrevolutionary coup of Muḥammad-'Alî Shâh, who is then overthrown by Azerî and Bakhtiârî forces
1914–17	Iran occupied by British and Russian troops; government's effective control limited to Tehran
1921	Coup d'état of Reżà Khân and Cossack brigade
1921–25	Suppression of tribal rebellions and consolidation of military control; centralized political foundation laid for Iran's first attempt at national integration
1926	Reżà considers proclaiming Turkish-style secular republic, but instead assumes title of Shâh and founds Pahlavî dynasty

1925–41	Oil royalties and heavy direct taxation used to finance railroad, communications, and industrial development; Westernizing cultural reforms in law, dress, and religion
1941	British and Russian troops invade Iran and depose Reżà Shâh, accession of young Muḥammad Reżà Shâh
1945–46	Proclamation of autonomous Republics of Azerbaijan and Kurdistan with Soviet backing; Soviets withdraw troops after grant of oil concession and separatist movements collapse, after which concession is rescinded and given to British
1949	Tudeh Party outlawed because of alleged implication in assassination attempt on shâh
1951–53	Muṣaddeq and National Front nationalize foreign oil holdings; European powers impose boycott and Iranian economy is prostrated
1953	General Zahedi leads coup against Muṣaddeq, Shâh returns to power, new agreements negotiated with European oil firms

INDIA

1798–1818	British hegemony established over all India, except Indus basin, either by outright conquest or by treaty
1830s	Sayyid Aḥmad of Rase Bareli popularizes Wahhâbism in India, opposing Ṣûfism of Shâh Walîullâh and Hindu inroads into Islam, declares jihâd against British and Sikhs
1843–49	British occupy Indus basin
1857–58	Indian Mutiny, anti-British uprising in N. India of those still loyal to last Mughal emperor, whom British later formally depose
1817–98	Sir Sayyid Aḥmad Khân, in post-Mutiny wave of anti-Muslim discrimination by British, argues for collaboration, adoption of British culture, and conformity of Islam to natural law; establishes Aligarh College (1875); attacked by anti-imperialist al-Afghânî and by orthodox 'ulamâ' who found rival school at Deoband
1889	Aḥmadî sect mixes messianic heritages of the Mahdî, Krishna, and Jesus
1891	Amîr 'Alî, launches defensive Muslim apologetic, claiming that original Islam is source of all European progress
1914	Deaths of Ḥâlî, poet and major reviver of Urdu literary culture, and of Shiblî Nu'mânî, reinterpreter of classical kalâm having contacts with Egyptian *salafiyya* movement
1905–11	Partition of Bengal, seen as British attempt to divide Hindus and Muslims, crystallizes nationalist movements and encourages communalism; Muslim League founded (1906); separate Muslim and Hindu provincial electorates (1909)
1919–24	Khilâfat movement, pan-Islamic support for Ottomans during war and campaign to preserve the caliphate in Turkey
1920–22,	Gândhî leads two civil disobedience campaigns mobilizing mass

1930–32,	support for Congress' campaign for Swarâj, which complements Nehru's organization of the middle class and intelligentsia
1936	Muḥammad-'Alî Jinnâh assumes leadership of Muslim League and radicalizes it as a virulently communalistic organization in an attempt to break Congress support from the majority of Muslims
1876–1938	Muḥammad Iqbâl, nationalist and Islamic poet, combines Sûfism and Western philosophy of vitalism and evolution; first theoretician of Pakistan
1940–47	Muslim League adopts idea of separate Islamic state and leads agitation resulting in polarization and widespread communal rioting (1946), creation of Pakistan from Muslim-majority areas opposing secular India with a large Muslim minority (1947)
1947–56	Conflict over definition and proper constitution of an 'Islamic state', especially between groups of 'ulamâ', Modernist politicians, and Maudûdî's Jamâ'at-e Islâmî
1953	Anti-Aḥmadiya riots; religious fanaticism fanned by conflict over definition of being a Muslim
1954	Munir Commission Report investigates causes of riots and criticizes the 'lack of bold and clear thinking' in the constitutional debate
1956	Ratification of first constitution of Pakistan

THE FERTILE CRESCENT AND THE ARABIAN PENINSULA

1803–13	Wahhâbîs occupy Ḥijâz (Mecca, 1806)
1811–18	Wahhâbî power in Arabia crushed by Ibrâhîm Pasha; Egypt controls Ḥijâz
1820	British pacts with Persian Gulf shaykhs
1830	Maḥmûd II reconquers Baghdad, ending Mamlûk rule
1831–40	Egyptian occupation of Syria; opening of Levant to Western commerce and beginnings of reorientation of Druze landlord–Maronite village relations
1839	British occupy Aden
1860–61	Druze revolt and massacre of Christians in Lebanon; French intervene militarily to protect Maronites and demand Lebanon be made an autonomous sanjaq with a Christian governor
1866	Foundation of American University of Beirut by Protestant missionaries, fosters Arabic literary revival among Syrian Christians led by Butros Bustani and Nasif al-Yaziji (d. 1871)
1881–82	Secret societies briefly agitate for Syrian independence
1891	Musqat and 'Umân under British protection
1896	Theodor Herzl publishes *Der Judenstaat*, first Zionist Congress (1897)
1908–22	Early Rise and Failure of Arab Nationalism:
1909–14	Revolutionary organizations arise among Syrian and Iraqî officers in reaction to increasingly Turkish nationalist orientation of Young Turk governments

1913	Conference of Arab intellectuals in Paris calls for Arab independence
1916–18	Arab Revolt against Ottoman empire led by Hussein, sherîf of Mecca, in alliance with British
1917–21	Balfour Declaration, publication of Sykes-Picot agreements; San Remo Conference; French occupy Damascus and overthrow Faysal government; Faysal established as ruler in Iraq and Abd-Allâh in Transjordan
1924	Ibn-Sa'ud conquers Ḥijâz, expels Hussein, establishes neo-Wahhâbî kingdom
1926	Sanjaq of Lebanon enlarged and detached from Syria as a separate republic
1932	Iraq granted independence and admitted to League of Nations
1936	Increased Jewish immigration provokes widespread Arab-Jewish fighting in Palestine; Bakr Sidki leads first of several military coups in Iraq
1930s	Sati' al-Husri emerges as chief ideologue of Arab Nationalism, attempts to create Arab consciousness among Egyptians
1943	Bishara al-Khoury and Riad Sulh negotiate National Pact as basis of Christian-Muslim accommodation in Lebanon; beginning of Zionist terrorist campaign in Palestine
1945	Arab League founded under Egyptian General Secretariat
1946	Jordan, Lebanon, and Syria recognized as independent; withdrawal of British and French troops
1948	British end Palestine mandate and United Nations approves partition and creation of state of Israel; Arab armies routed in war with Israelis
1949	Militarization of Syrian politics; three successive coups in one year

I

The Impact of the Great Western Transmutation: The Generation of 1789

Hitherto I have been stressing the relative evenness of historical development among all the societies of the Afro-Eurasian Oikoumene. I have brought out such facts as that the lunar theory we know as Copernican was developed just a century or so earlier among Muslims; or that the efficacy of the big guns against fortresses was demonstrated by the Ottomans at Constantinople (by land) and Rhodes (by sea), and then only slightly later by Occidentals in France and the west Mediterranean. My point has been less that one or another group had priority in a discovery, than that the societies of the Agrarian Age did maintain this rough parity among themselves. For the same reason, I emphasized that the Portuguese intrusion was effectively contained in the Indian Ocean in the sixteenth century, and more generally that the flowering of the Occidental Renaissance was of the same order of creativity as those of the High Caliphate or of T'ang-Sung China. But now we come to changes that are qualitatively different from those we have studied hitherto. Henceforth the gap in development between one part of the world and all the rest becomes decisive, and we must understand its character in order to understand anything else.

The Western Transmutation as a world event

Between the late sixteenth century and the late eighteenth century a general cultural transformation took place in western Europe. (It is conventional to see Modernity as beginning a century earlier, between 1450 and 1500; but such a dating, as I see it, obscures crucial distinctions.) This transformation culminated in two more or less simultaneous events: the Industrial Revolution, when specialized technical development decisively transformed the presuppositions of human production, and the French Revolution, when a kindred spirit established likewise unprecedented norms in human social relations. But these events did not constitute the broad transformation I am speaking of; they were its most obvious early consequences.

This broad transformation had far-reaching effects not only among

Europeans but—almost as soon—in the world at large. Its long-run implications for us all have not yet become entirely manifest. Some of them will be taken up later. From the point of view of the world at large, however, and particularly of the Muslim peoples, there was a more immediate consequence which will concern us here. This was that by about 1800 the Occidental peoples (together with the Russians) found themselves in a position to dominate overwhelmingly most of the rest of the world—and, in particular, to dominate the lands of Islamdom. The same generation that saw the Industrial and French Revolutions saw a third and almost equally unprecedented event: the establishment of European world hegemony.[1]

It was not merely, or perhaps even primarily, that the Europeans and their overseas settlers found themselves in a position to defeat militarily any powers they came in contact with. Their merchants were able to out-produce, out-travel, and out-sell anyone, their physicians were able to heal better than others, their scientists were able to put all others to shame. Only a limited part of the world's surface was actually occupied by European troops, at least at first. European hegemony did not mean direct European world rule. What mattered was that both occupied ('colonial' or 'settled') areas and unoccupied ('independent') areas were fairly rapidly caught up in a worldwide political and commercial system, the rules of which were made by, and for the advantage of, the Europeans and their overseas settlers. Even 'independent' areas could retain their local autonomy only to the extent that they provided European merchants, European missionaries, even European tourists, with a certain minimum of that type of international 'law and order' to which they had become accustomed in Europe, so that the Europeans remained free to vaunt a privileged position and to display among all peoples the unexampled new physical and intellectual luxuries of Europe. (For otherwise, the European powers would feel forced to intervene; and wherever one of them concentrated its efforts it would almost infallibly succeed.) Thus all peoples had to adjust their governments to a modern European international political order; but also to adjust their economies—a harder task—to the competition of technically industrialized Europe; and finally to adjust their mental outlook to the challenge of modern science as studied in Europe. The mere presence of the Europeans was enough for their new power to be felt.

We may summarize this by saying that the Europeans (including, of course, their overseas descendants) had by 1800 reached a decisively higher

[1] I choose the term 'hegemony' as less strong than 'paramountcy', and as suggesting the *leading* role of Europeans: they did not immediately dominate all lands in the world, but they immediately dominated all interstate relations—political or commercial or even intellectual: thus the Europeans were the leading foreign merchants in the ports of all the world, however resistant for a time these areas were to European interference; and the European consular representatives were everywhere the leading foreign political figures to be reckoned with. In this sense, the Europeans exercised full *world* hegemony even before they had imposed their conditions effectively within all regions.

level of *social power* than was to be found elsewhere. (The exceptional position of Europeans in the eighteenth century, with their institutionalized capital accumulation, already reflected an advanced stage of this process.) Individual Europeans might still be less intelligent, less courageous, less loyal than individuals elsewhere; but, when educated and organized in society, the Europeans were able to think and to act far more effectively, as members of a group, than could members of any other societies. European enterprises, such as firms or churches or, of course, governments, could muster a degree of power, intellectual, economic and social, which was of a different order from what could be mustered among even the most wealthy or vigorous peoples in the rest of the world. It is perhaps premature to refer to what had happened in Europe simply under the heading of 'progress'. This word implies a moral judgment: 'progress', as against regress or mere digression, implies movement toward a goal, or at least in a good direction. It can be disputed what aspects of our modern life have meant change for the better and what have meant change for the worse. What concerns us here is not any general 'progress' that may have occurred, but the immediately decisive rise in the level of social power, whether for better or for worse. We will find this point important when we come to try to understand the responses of the Muslim peoples to what had happened in the West.[2]

At least till very recently, there was a tendency among Europeans (including, of course, Americans) to take this remarkable fact for granted. (In the same way many Muslims, before the Western Transmutation interrupted, assumed a natural superiority in Islamicate institutions which would make them prevail over all infidels sooner or later.) Such Europeans have wondered why in recent years, after many centuries (so they suppose) of static quiescence, the various 'backward' peoples are now stirring. They have overlooked the wonder of how it could be that, for what was in fact a rather brief period of little more than one century, Europeans could have held so unique a position in the world.[3] The real question, from the standpoint of the world at large, is simply, What gave the Europeans such overwhelming power for a time?

I have styled the cultural changes in Europe between 1600 and 1800 which led to this increase in social power, a 'transmutation'. I intend no close biological analogy. Yet the changes, in so far as they led to this rise of social power, formed a markedly interrelated unity, which can, with proper caution, be discussed as a single, though vast and complex, event. This event

[2] For my usage of the terms 'West', 'Occident', and 'Europe', see the Introduction in volume 1, section on usage in world-historical studies.

[3] The notion of the 'millennial torpor' of 'the East' remains so widespread partly because of touristic misimpressions but also because it has been subsumed in the approach of two sorts of scholars: the Westernists, who downgrade all alien societies, and the area-students, who suppose all pre-Moderns were overwhelmed by tradition. Compare 'On determinacy in traditions,' in the section on historical method in the Introduction, volume 1.

was relatively sudden, compared with other human history. Moreover, the essential changes were constitutive: they altered not merely particular social and cultural traits but some of the most elementary presuppositions of any subsequent human social and cultural development. Henceforth, historical events all over the world took place, in certain respects, in a radically new way.

What happened can be compared with the first advent several thousand years BC of that combination, among the dominant elements of certain societies, of urban living, literacy, and generally complex social and cultural organization, which we call 'civilization'. The 'civilized', that is, citied agrarianate, communities—starting probably with Sumer—found themselves on a much higher level of social power than the other agricultural groupings, to say nothing of food-gathering tribes; it was not long before an urban type of life came to have a decisive role in wider and wider circles, both politically and, in the end, culturally. What had happened in Sumer soon (as ancient time-spans go) determined the fate of much of the Eastern Hemisphere. Among these societies on the agrarianate level, the very character of historical change was so altered that what had come before we sometimes call 'pre-history': for instance, its pace was immensely speeded up, so that a degree of change that before consumed thousands of years now consumed merely centuries. Similarly, after the Western Transmutation the kind of changes that earlier, in agrarianate times, had required hundreds of years now required, at most, decades; once again, a new sort of historical process was loosed upon the world.

A. THE TRANSMUTATION IN THE WEST

At this point, then, we must consider just what had happened in the Occident itself. For though these events have been analyzed innumerable times, the analysis has not normally been made from a genuinely world-historical viewpoint, but virtually always from the standpoint of the local Occidental past. Hence I cannot count on my reader's being able to sort out for himself what it is that is relevant on that world-historical plane where we must be studying Islamdom.

Technicalism and society: the decisive institutional traits of the Transmutation

The Western Transmutation can be described, for our world-historical purposes, as consisting (in its internal aspect) primarily of transformations of culture in three main fields: the economic, the intellectual, and the social. In economic life, there took place that great increase in productivity—due to a sequence of new techniques, and carried out through a concentrated control of production based on capital accumulation and mass markets—which led up to and culminated in the 'Industrial Revolution' and the accompanying

'Agricultural Revolution'. In intellectual life came the new sort of experimental science which started with Kepler and Galileo and opened indefinitely the horizons of accessible time and space leading more generally to the philosophical exploratory independence made widely popular in the Enlightenment. In social life came the breakdown of old landed privileges and supremacies and their replacement with a bourgeois financial power which ushered in the American and French revolutions, with their repercussions throughout Europe.

In all these fields, those changes that in retrospect can be seen as decisive, from the viewpoint of the Occident's level of social power in the world as a whole, can be dated to a period of not much more than two centuries. In the sixteenth century on the whole, as we have seen, the parity of the citied societies of the Oikoumene still prevailed. Despite the general Occidental florescence associated with the Renaissance, the west Europeans were, politically, receding even before the Ottoman empire, while commercially the Muslims were still at least their equals in most parts of the Oikoumene. Culturally too, the Muslims were in one of their most brilliant periods. This occurrence in world history reflects European history in that the Renaissance florescence did not yet, in itself, transcend the limitations of agrarianate-level society. But the crucial changes were clearly under way by the end of the sixteenth century. And, by the end of the eighteenth century, they were all of them completed, at least as regards some particular field in some particular place, for example as regards astronomical physics throughout the Occident, or cotton-cloth production in England. Correspondingly, Islamicate society was already rooted in a land like Bengal.

Just as to include the Renaissance within the actual transition to Modernity, rather than among its prior conditions, is to falsify the picture from a world-historical viewpoint, so also to extend the critical period beyond the eighteenth century is to confuse arbitrarily one or more phases of the unfolding consequences of the decisive event with the world-historical event itself. Subsequent changes have been of enormous importance; for instance, the later introduction of electricity as a basic form of industrial energy, or the theory of relativity in physics. But as regards the nature of the historical change involved, they merely carried further the Modern pattern of development already established *in nucleo* by about the year 1800. In any case, it was the transformations of the seventeenth and eighteenth centuries that served to set off decisively the Westerners from the rest of mankind.

What was the relation among all these changes, that they should all happen at once; what was it that made for such a relatively sudden and comprehensive transformation of the society, with such far-reaching effects? It is clear that the changes were closely interrelated and, indeed, interdependent. However, this was not always in the sense that particular changes in one field depended on particular changes in another (thus scientific and industrial developments long went parallel, with only relatively superficial contacts); rather, all the changes presupposed common social resources and even common psychological patterns of expectation.[4]

Hence many have seen the Transmutation as the expression in many fields of a single overall basic change: a change from what is called a 'traditional' to what some call a 'rational' society. In a 'rational' society, they say, choices can be determined less by the dictates of ancestral custom and more by practical calculation of immediate advantage. Persons, then, will be granted status and authority less on the basis of their birth and family connections, and more on the basis of their effective competence as individuals. Efficient, predictable organization will prevail over familial, patriarchal arrangements and social relations will be determined less by private personal commitments and more by impersonal legal status. Immediate efficiency will be valued more highly than continuity with the past, and people will therefore be less hesitant about change lest it prove degeneration; instead continuous practical improvement, even at the expense of what has been valued before, will not only be welcomed as 'progress', but expected as a natural social condition. Once 'rationality' was established and innovation was accepted as normal, all the economic, social, and intellectual improvements followed naturally. This was, in effect, the emancipation of mankind from a long and mostly irrational dark past.

Some such shift did occur in the Transmutation. But this change was by no means so basic or so definitive in its human implications as some suggest. For in fact the standard picture of a custom-bound 'traditional' society is rather

[4] From the time of Burckhardt, we have had many perceptive attempts to analyze just what 'modern man', that is a European of the Technical Age, really 'is'. However, apart from some distorted information on what is called 'Oriental', these attempts have usually made use only of data from within west European and ancient Greek history; hence they have blurred the difference between local stages within the Occidental evolution, and changes more universally relevant. Area-studies men, on the other hand, rarely know anything about *any* part of the world before the nineteenth century. Hence I have had to develop my own analysis.

For historical purposes, one ought to analyze the Great Transmutation as a historical *event* or process, not merely as the presence of a new *state* or age of human culture; but such attempts have been infrequent. Schumpeter, however, successfully transforms what even for the Marxists is a relatively static capitalist 'stage' of society into a complex and long-term event, with a decisive onset, a course of development which never reaches real equilibrium, and a foreseeable end. In such a perspective, the analyses of the capitalist market by the conventional bourgeois economists, as if it were a condition essentially based on an approximated equilibrium, take on an unreal air: at most, they are analyzing short-term equilibriums in a process which itself is creating and modifying the market which they presuppose.

In this perspective my own study is doubly lacking. I have treated the Transmutation primarily as a shift from one state to another; and as being completed with the generation of 1789, when it was achieved *in nucleo* in certain fields in certain places. In the long run, it must probably be treated as a completed process only from the perspective of the day when all relevant fields of social life and all parts of the world will have been technicalized, if such a day comes. From such a vantage point, the seventeenth and eighteenth centuries will seem merely preliminary, though they will still retain their special status. At present, however, I cannot venture to assume such a perspective.

a fiction. As we have seen in discussing the nature of a cultural tradition, even in a very 'primitive' society cultural traditions must be in constant development to remain viable, for they must always effectively meet some current need or no amount of ancestral prestige can save them. Moreover the 'rationality' referred to, that is, the impersonal and innovative private calculation called 'rationalization' in industry, is a relative matter. Most agrarianate-level societies could even be evaluated as quite 'rational' in comparison to even the merely relative 'traditionality' of most pre-literate societies. In respect simply of 'rationalization', the sort of shift that occurred in the Transmutation was one that had occurred, on one level or another, time and again in history—not only at the advent of cities, but in every great cultural florescence and even, on a lesser scale, whenever a new religious or political tradition was being initiated. At all such times, independent, innovative calculation (but not necessarily human rationality as such) has been more emphasized, and authoritative custom less. Morever, some residue of such attitudes has commonly been institutionalized in subsequent social life, especially in the more cosmopolitan societies.

Thus Islamdom, being more cosmopolitan in the Mid-Islamic periods than was the Occident, embodied more provision for independent calculation and personal initiative in its institutions. Indeed, much of the shift from social custom to private calculation which in Europe was a part of the Transmutation's 'Modernization' has the air of bringing the Occident closer to what was already well established in the Islamicate tradition. (This is especially true of those 'Modern' developments that were beginning already in the Renaissance and are often cited to show that 'Modernity' had already begun then.) The depreciation of aristocratic birth in favour of greater social mobility did not go so far in the Occident as it had in Islamdom; the inclination to allow a primary role to freely made individual contracts as against the authority of guilds and estates was in accord with the principles of Sharîʿah law.

The shift therefore from reliance on custom and continuity, to reliance on calculation and innovation, although it occurred only in a limited measure, was not in itself what was specific to the Modern Western Transmutation. It was not this that set the Westerners apart from both their ancestors and the rest of the world. It merely accompanied and facilitated a change in the patterns of investment of time and money. This, as we shall see, occurred only in a special form, one that I shall call *technicalistic*, so that *specialized technical considerations tended to take precedence* over all others. Indeed, in that special form—rather than in other forms—the shift went to unprecedented lengths, so that the results set new conditions for all historical life. It was not that the human mind as such was suddenly emancipated, as if by some mutation, and could therefore begin freely to explore all calculable possibilities where, before, new paths could be opened only by chance and despite the weight of customary bias. Rather, concrete new sorts of opportunity for social investment, hitherto impractical even for the most emancipated mind, became practicable, attracting even minds that still, by and large, resisted any deviation from intellectual habit. And then the resistance was gradually reduced.

To begin with, we must identify what was distinctive in the new forms of investments, as such. The calculative innovation in the Renaissance still presented a degree of initiative and creativity 'normal' for great florescences in the Agrarian Age. But in time such a florescence would normally taper off. Usually, such activities had found sooner or later a point at which further cultural complexity was so subject to interruptions by historical accidents that it did not repay the risks it incurred. This was especially true in any field that required large-scale social investment of time or money since this in turn required freedom from such disorganization or arbitrary intervention as would disrupt the peace and social orderliness which such investment presupposed. This was a far more pressing danger than the oppressiveness of too grand an internal balance which might trap men's minds in some form of style cycle. But by the end of the sixteenth century, just those kinds of calculative, innovative investment that were most dependent on freedom from social disruption were reaching levels rarely reached before: that is, improvements in technical methods of achieving concrete, material ends by way of multiple, interdependent specialization. And, despite such disasters as the Thirty Years War and the English Civil War, nothing happened to stop the process as a whole, especially in northwest Europe. A very similar process had been stopped in later Sung China under the nomad dynasties. The Occidental florescence did not taper off.

Rather, innovative investment had persisted till a critical point of social development was reached by about 1600: by then, certain types of investment (material and mental) which all through the Agrarian Age had been sporadic and precarious, even during florescences (and during the Renaissance), were now occurring on a sufficiently large scale so that they could be institutionalized, built on further, and finally be made socially irreversible. This new situation offered a new set of opportunities to human enterprise, new occasions for cultural creativity of many sorts. The new opportunities were swiftly taken up; on the basis of the new creativity, new and rapidly developing 'technicalistic' traditions proliferated, and the new patterns were established as rapidly as the process of evolution in cultural traditions could carry them. When the inner dialogue in a tradition is unhampered and its field of action is as yet unexploited, this can be very fast. And the historical conditions that allowed this at all, allowed it in many fields of endeavour at once. As a result, the previous precariousness of any cultural complexity beyond the agrarianate base-level of the urban-rural symbiosis was at last overcome; a new, higher base-level was presumably established.

These new impulses carried everything with them, including old institutions. Existing institutions had, to be sure, proved sufficiently open to make such an advance possible. (Probably any set of mature institutions can provide a great deal more flexibility than is at first apparent.) But such institutions were hardly well adapted to it, surely no more so than, say, the Islamicate institutions Yet they were pressed into serving the new possibilities, or were superseded. A good deal of institutional rigidity was implicit in the Occidental corporative expectations, and some of this rigidity acted as an obstacle to the new impulses. (For instance, the church Inquisition was more oppressive to the ordinary thinking citizen than anything to be found in Islamdom.) Nonetheless, this very corporative structure—when the occasion was ripe—did act to protect individual innovation at least as effectively as might the social mobility and the Shar'î autonomy of Islamdom.

At the core of the new innovation was the pattern of multiple technical specialization. Such technical specialization was not altogether new: since the introduction of gunpowder weapons, that aspect of military practice had represented a microcosm of the innovative technical specialization which was to be the hallmark of the Transmutation. But now it reached a breadth of scale, a 'critical mass', which allowed much more extensive institutionalizing of such innovation than before, an institutionalizing which was to embrace and finally dominate all the key sectors of the whole society. Economically, this could be seen in certain forms of industrial and commercial investment in northwest Europe during the seventeenth century: capital was systematically re-invested and multiplied on the basis of continuing technical innovation and of anticipated expansion in market patterns. (We have seen the effects of this in India.) Intellectually, it could be seen in the work of such associations as the Royal Society: in many cultures there had been associations for cultivating existing scholarly learning, which might welcome the occasional piece of new information; but in the seventeenth century the Royal Society aimed explicitly at gathering and disseminating that new knowledge which would replace the old, and did so largely in expectation of the continual new inventions of the by then professionalized scientific instrument-makers, and of the new observations they would make possible.

One must suppose that the intellectual side of the movement was dependent on the economic side; but not in the sense that natural science benefited directly from the inventiveness of industry. Rather, the expansion of industrial investment released more resources to the whole economy; and these were then made use of, among scholars, in a manner consonant with the expansive mood of which the pace was surely set by the exhilaration associated with the new mercantile and industrial ventures. But the intellectual development was apparently quite autonomous. After a certain point is reached in the development of natural science, at any rate, it cannot advance further without a disproportionate amount of human investment on all fronts at once: i.e., increasing specialization in many different fields. Whether or not we suppose that a lull in scientific work in the Occident after 1300 resulted from the difficulty of proceeding further with the then available level of specialized human resources, it nevertheless seems that science had reached the point where the sudden increase of such resources could have great liberating effects—and precisely in those aspects of knowledge that were most dependent on multiple specialization.[5] To the extent that industrial experience entered into scientific advance, it was mostly by way of the increasing skills and technical resources of the instrument-makers, whose specialized innovations surely confirmed the technicalistic tendency in science.

In both scientific and economic life, the sheer scale of the increasing technical specialization brought with it qualitative changes. Perhaps most obviously, it reached a level on which it paid to invest the requisite time, funds, and concern into institutions that embodied and further confirmed the technical specialization. These very institutions, then, helped to hasten the process. Gradually, in the seventeenth and eighteenth centuries, such investment became so well-rooted and widely ramified in Occidental society that no social process or historical event originating outside the process could reverse it or seriously slow it down. But this institutionalization presupposed further a close interrelation among specializations. There was no mere conglomeration of individual technical advances; as isolated technical specialization, the techniques of mechanized cotton spinning, for instance, could be reckoned equivalent to the highly specialized and relatively efficient ancient techniques of the Coptic land surveyors in Egypt. But now within the main fields in which the process occurred, everything depended on the growth of an increasingly inclusive and interdependent nexus of technical specialism, such that the technical efficiency of any particular activity was increased by its use of the fruits of other specialties, and it in turn served to increase their efficiency. For such a process to be carried far, a major part of all the activities of a society must become involved. Once this process was well-established, new discoveries and inventions, along with the human and financial investment needed to realize them, grew at a geometric rate of progression; for each new round of inventions, once exploited, cleared the way for yet another.[6]

It will be readily seen that such a technicalistic process left behind the most basic presuppositions of all agrarianate society. Even those agrarianate-level societies that were not themselves immediately agrarian—being, say, pastoralist or mercantile—had depended for their existence on the social relations prevailing in their agrarian hinterland, in which the agrarian surplus provided the chief income on which the carriers of the high culture,

[5] [Author's added note: Among historians of science, Derek Price has focused on the crucial need for an increasing number of diverse specialists inspiring one another if science is to get past a given level.—R.S.]

[6] The term 'take-off', which W. W. Rostow, in *The Stages of Economic Growth* (Cambridge University Press, 1963), has used for a later stage and more specialized aspect of this whole development, is applicable at this initial overall level also; indeed, unless this basic level is studied—and the differences in its characteristics in the original Occidental case and in derivative cases—serious error can result in any such analysis.

the chief market of the mercantile cities, depended. The growth of interdependent technical specializations freed the income structure of the privileged classes in large areas from primary dependence on agrarian exploitation of the agriculturists.

It did so, of course, not because industrial production could take the place of agricultural in providing the common necessities of life, such as food; rather, what the non-agricultural sectors of the economy could support now was the special income of the privileged, the carriers of the high culture; and this not only in a few immediate urban situations, as before, but in the overall economic nexus. Even with no increase in the agricultural surplus, that is, with no increase in the number of non-agricultural labourers that could be fed, technical specialization could vastly increase productivity, and hence total production, till so much of it was non-agricultural that a correspondingly large proportion of income in the society need not be determined by agrarian relationships. But of course if the technicalistic process was to progress far (and if the proportion of the privileged in the society was ultimately to expand), not only greater productivity per labourer was required but, also more labourers (and also more agricultural raw materials). Hence even the limitations on agricultural production, imposed by localized manual and animal methods, must be escaped by extending the new social process to agriculture itself (though a partial alternative could be to import agricultural products from distant lands not yet undergoing the technicalistic process—which could mean, of course, exporting manufactures thither, displacing the local craftsmen, and turning those lands more solidly to agriculture than before). All phases of the new role of agriculture and agrarian relations were to become significant in the future of Islamdom.

This overall process, and then the condition of society in which it has resulted, I call *technicalization*, which I will define as *a condition of calculative (and hence innovative) technical specialization, in which the several specialties are interdependent on a large enough scale to determine patterns of expectation in the key sectors of a society.*[7] I choose the word 'technicalization' in contradistinction to 'industrialization', for industrialization is only one aspect of the whole process, though sometimes it is seen as its essence. The Industrial Revolution at the end of the eighteenth century was constituted by the joining of specialized machines, adapted to an expanding 'mass' market, to the indefinitely expandable resources of steam power. 'Industrialization' has meant the prevalence of such power-mechanized industry in a country's economy. (When steam power is replaced by electric power or by atomic power, or when the efficiency of any source of power is multiplied by the use of assembly lines or of automation, the human consequences may be important but the basic equation established at the end of the eighteenth century,

[7] For justification and closer definition of the term 'technicalistic' in comparison to various alternatives, see the section on usage in world-historical studies in the Introduction in volume I.

marking the contrast to the role of industry in agrarianate-level society, remains essentially unchanged.) This was certainly the culmination of the seventeenth- and eighteenth-century economic transformations; and in recent times the preponderance, in a country's economy, of power-mechanized industry has been taken as the essential token of Modernity: for a country to be Modern has meant for it to be industrialized. But this is as yet only a token.

For our purposes we need a far broader conception. 'Industrialization' may not exclude a highly Modern (and certainly technicalized) land like Denmark, for, though Denmark is primarily agricultural, the prevalence of power-mechanization in agriculture itself, and especially in the processing subsidiary to agriculture, may be included by extension under 'industrialization'. But the whole process of technicalization is far more inclusive even so. Even in actual economic production, there could be, historically, a high degree of technicalization without power-mechanization—at a time before power-mechanization had imposed itself (as it did once it became available at all) thenceforth on any would-be competitors participating in industrial technicalization; thus several industries in France in the eighteenth century, before power-mechanization, already displayed many of the traits of technicalization in their internal evolution and in their consequences in world trade. But most important, the process of technicalistic specialization in the sciences and in social organization and even in other aspects of society was equally decisive with that in economic production. A term like 'technicalization' will neutrally cover all aspects of the process, without assigning primacy to any given aspect.

Moral dimensions of technicalism

Now we must look to the indispensable psychological side of such investment patterns. Reliance on multiple technical specialization was correlated with a pattern of what we may call technicalistic expectations. Some such expectations in a certain sector of the population had been necessary to get technicalization launched, but then the process itself evoked them in others and intensified them.

Central to the technicalistic spirit was the expectation of impersonal efficiency through technical precision. There had in all times been concern with efficiency, especially military efficiency, in limited ways. There had also been a certain amount of technical specialization and precision, for instance in fine craft work. Even technical inventiveness had held a respected place within a more rounded economic pattern. But now in western Europe technical efficiency was increasingly given a primary role, such that all other considerations of a less universally or obviously objective sort—aesthetic, traditional, interpersonal—were increasingly made to yield to this, and it was relied on as the most important basis for excelling in constructive activities.

On this psychological level, to say that all aspects of social organization were being technicalized means that they were organized primarily in terms of specialized procedures calculated to yield maximum efficiency for the limited ends immediately in objective view. It is in this form that technicalization meant institutionalizing a major shift from authoritative custom toward independent calculation.

It is on the psychological level, then, that we come to the contrast that has been expressed by the words 'traditional-rational'. Despite a general awareness among us that much in Modern life is less than humanly rational, the current literature of economic and social development gives evidence that there is still need to warn the reader against identifying the technicalistic spirit with human rationality as such. The exercise of human reason cannot be identified with the calculative pursuit of any given sort of goals alone. Sometimes even a narrowly practical innovation, however shrewd, may be so risky (in its disregard of immemorial experience) as to be positively irrational. But in any case, to subordinate all considerations of ethics or beauty or human commitments to maximizing technical efficiency, however successfully, is quite likely to prove an irrational nightmare.

It may be said that 'rational' and 'traditional', as differentiating Modern from pre-Modern, bear technical meanings: 'rational' means 'calculative with regard to specialized technical aims', and 'traditional' means 'authoritative by way of custom'. But the terms have in fact been understood, both by readers and by the writers themselves, in a more general way. It is quite natural, if a bit arrogant, for a modern Westerner to see his own technicalistic ways as rational and to condemn the ways of agrarianate societies as the effects of blind tradition set in contrast to rationality. The scholarly use of the terms, however well-intentioned, merely reinforces this bias. All too often it is necessary to demonstrate what should have been obvious: that the 'Modern', i.e., technicalistic, sector of an economy often proves less than rational in the ordinary human sense so long as other than technical considerations are ignored, or that 'traditional' institutions may be undeniably rational in the ordinary human sense, and even contribute to technicalistic development. It will be wise to reserve the terms *rational* and *traditional* for their more normal usage. In this usage, every society is traditional in that it operates through cultural traditions—however rapidly those traditions may evolve in some cases, notably under technicalism. And every society is rational in that its institutions will long survive only as they are pragmatically functional. This, because the personal decisions of its more intelligent members reflect rational calculations so far as serious alternatives are envisageable and actually practicable—however narrow the range of practicable alternatives may be in some cases. It can be argued, indeed, that the greatest advantage of the highly technicalized lands has been the continuity and effectiveness of their *traditions*, which have served to channel individual rationality; while the greatest problem of less technicalized lands has been ungoverned opportunistic *rationality* among them, which has been loosed by the severe breaches in high-cultural tradition they have suffered.

In economic production, the technicalistic spirit emerged in an increased dependence on such things as even more clever inventions, and statistical analysis of output and market. These and other expressions of a demand for technical efficiency increased throughout the two centuries till there resulted new presuppositions for any economic activity: instead of considerations of craft family continuity, of personal status, of mercantile solidarity, the weight shifted more to considerations of productively reinvesting returns on capital, of external economies in location, of keeping ahead in technique. The family trade secret was replaced with the public patent office.

In scientific work a similar technicalistic spirit appeared. Even in astronomy (like military practice, a field where an element of 'technicalization' had already prevailed) the new spirit took noticeable effect. Starting with Brahe and Kepler (in contrast to Copernicus), infinitesimal precision of measurement, with the aid of highly specialized technical instruments, was the keynote of the new type of investigation. I doubt that Kepler would have conceded priority to the ellipse over the geometrically 'purer' circle, despite his metaphysical justifications of it, if he were not, unawares, coming to assign priority to technical precision and manipulation over philosophical elegance. The result was to place in jeopardy any sense of a cosmic whole. The natural-science traditions had maintained also in the Occident that degree of intellectual autonomy they had early won from commitment to the intellectual predispositions of overall life-orientational traditions; this autonomy had made itself apparent on occasion among both Muslims and Christians in a relative empiricism, bound to but not overwhelmed by philosophic notions of the teleological and hierarchical nature of entities. But now, with intensive specialization, the autonomy of the natural-science traditions was pushed much further, and the accompanying empiricism became almost routine. Every major scientist found himself forced to try to work out for himself (if he cared) his own sense of the cosmic whole; and alert laymen were left with 'all coherence gone'. By 1800 the technicalistic spirit had spread from astronomy and physics to chemistry, geology, and biology. From Descrates to its culmination in Kant, the new epistemological philosophy was inspired by the new technicalistic science and by its very disengagement from ultimate questions.

Finally, in social life, administration came to reflect a like technicalistic tendency, though at first with traits less unprecedented from a world point of view. The new absolute and 'enlightened' monarchies (inspired in part by older Chinese precedents) were still at first bringing Occidental administration up to an effectiveness already achieved in some parts, some time earlier, for instance in the Ottoman empire. But by the time of the French Revolution, the increase in the efficiency of legally operated social control, the technical precision of its files and its reports, and (more important) the implementing of the whole conception of government as a public service to be judged by its usefulness, had gone beyond even Sung China and had made obsolete every earlier governmental tradition in Europe; so that in the following decades they all found it necessary to reconstitute themselves, or be reconstituted, on a new basis.

Necessarily, as the interdependent range of technical specialties widened, the new standards of efficiency came to hold not only for a small circle of learnèd men or experts, but for a large section of the west European population. It was only because British clerks and factory hands had gradually grown accustomed to working on the new basis that it was possible for those who introduced power machinery at the end of the eighteenth century to find workers to make the delicately adjusted machines and workers to run them without catastrophe. (It was only later, after the power-machinery was well-established, that relatively raw recruits could be trained in large numbers.) Increasingly large proportions of the population were involved in even the intellectual innovations, as the use of printed books spread amongst Protestant and also Catholic townsmen. Almost any major undertaking came to depend on the fairly immediate contributions of a great variety of specializations, each increasingly technical and difficult for an outsider to penetrate without disproportionate training. In some degree, practically the whole population, and certainly all the more ambitious elements in it, came under pressure to cultivate a technicalistic viewpoint and technicalistic expectations.

Indeed, from the viewpoint of the moral qualities involved, it may be said that technicalization has proceeded far enough to characterize social organization generally at the point when technical specialization is sufficiently diverse and intricate so that it has become the socially determinative situation that a given worker or scholar is no longer able to follow in detail the whole of the process of which his own work forms a fragment. Goethe, the greatest writer of the generation in which the Transmutation culminated, has suitably been called the 'last of the universal men'; yet even he cannot have hoped to follow minutely all the technical processes in which the tools were cast which made the machines to service his theatrical innovations. Either Ibn-Khaldûn or Leonardo could still have done the equivalent in their time.

There was, thus, something of a dehumanizing implication in technicalism. At the same time, the Transmutation also saw important moral changes of a creatively human kind. A distinctive ideal human image (or, rather, a complex of such human images), new equally to the Occident and to the rest of the world, was becoming increasing attractive in wide circles. Closely related to the growth of technicalism was the spread of the image of the man who would undertake new and imaginative efforts with resourcefulness and dedication—no longer merely as a private adventurer, but as representative of hopes for new patterns of life in a wider public. This 'projector', satirized from the time of Ben Jonson and immortalized by Swift in *Gulliver's Travels* (and given more level-headed advice in Kipling's *If*), became increasingly a recognizably effective type among the proliferating business classes as investment increased—active not only in business affairs but in science, administration, and even religion. Seemingly in contrast to the image of the 'projector', but not unrelated to it, was the image of the man of humane 'civilization'. Indeed, the time of the Transmutation saw new moral standards of an explicitly humane bent which had little to do directly with the technicalistic spirit. Notable was what may be called a 'gentling of manners', based on the active expectation that much of what had always been acknowledged as an ideal might be realized in practice. The manners of the better classes were being softened and 'civilized'; and consistently with the new gentler tastes, heretics were being left alone and even torture was being dispensed with, both as punishment and as means of extorting information. The idea was arising that with more 'philosophical' or else 'natural' education, and freer laws, human minds and spirits generally might be enlightened and 'perfected'.

Much in the newer human images recalls earlier similar images: for instance, the glorification of individual effort found in different forms in the Iranian heroic tradition of Firdawsî or Rûmî, and in still different forms in the chivalric tradition of the Occident satirized by Cervantes. But the tone now was the reverse of aristocratic; indeed some strands, conservatives found disquietingly vulgar. It was surely one of the contributions of the Renaissance (though it might have come from some other florescences almost as readily) to glorify a human image of boundless individual initiative on a quite mundane and pragmatic level. Such an image is crucial in defining the possibilities open to a society, and, in this way, in keeping them open.

It was doubtless the optimistic spirit, as well as the economic expansiveness, produced by the progress of technicalization in its proper spheres that made such idealism suddenly appear practical. Yet the idealism does seem to have helped mitigate the arbitrariness of state officials and especially the destructiveness of warfare, which after 1648 became increasingly limited in aims and disciplined in conduct. It is quite possible that without such mitigation, governments might (as had happened before) have killed the goose that laid the golden egg: they might have allowed the work of scientists and investors to be disrupted, thus showing that further technical specialization would not, in fact, pay.[8] By the generation of 1789, the new moral outlook burst out in the most diverse directions and contributed importantly to the psychological gap between the West and the other societies. But by then, as we shall note, it was carrying a considerable element of the expressly technicalistic mood.

The 'gentling of manners' initially, at least, largely took the form of a

[8] John U. Nef, the same man who has brought to our attention the basic role of the 'earlier industrial revolution' in England, has brought out this point also in several works and notably in *Cultural Foundations of Industrial Civilization* (Cambridge University Press, 1958).

religious and aesthetic development, by no means so epoch-making (especially as compared with what had happened in some other florescences in agrarianate times) as the scientific and economic developments, yet not to be overlooked. Particularly in religion, partly under the impact of the new philosophy, the evolution marked by several figures from Pascal to Schleiermacher was laying the groundwork for a religious consciousness grounded in direct human spiritual experience and not requiring an élite mysticism to free it—or cut it loose—from communal dogma; so that dogma itself had therefore, in the end, to be rethought on a more universal basis. (The advent of Protestantism as such, of course, marked no step outside the religious presuppositions prevalent in agrarianate times—some of its key traits can be found equally in agrarianate Islam, for instance—though it may have facilitated the subsequent religious development.)

Nevertheless, there seems to have been some degree of narrowing in the range of reality that Occidentals were prepared to invest greatly in exploring. Even other technical ends than those to which an investment in interdependent specializations could contribute, at least under the circumstances of the time, were not taken up or much cultivated (as if the keenest minds were too busy exploiting the new specializations opened up). Notable especially are areas that can mean much to an individual person. In the field of health, personal human regimen in its various aspects received little more attention—perhaps sometimes less—than physicians had given it for millennia, while technical means of curing ills (once they had been allowed to happen) multiplied. The intense muscular training for dance or fight, which developed (sometimes fairly late) in several high-cultural traditions, received no real Western equivalent. Perhaps most notably, Westerners did not much explore some areas that could not be formulated in concrete, material terms. For instance, the sort of specialized mystical techniques represented in certain forms of Yoga and also of Ṣûfism were almost ignored, despite promising beginnings earlier even in Christian Europe; or they were severely curbed within communal religious assumptions; though elsewhere they often have carried pragmatic rational calculation and personal initiative to an extreme, and have called for, or seemed to call for, a ceaseless attempt to improve on predecessors, often by discovering new techniques.

To a large degree, then, the main changes in patterns of expectation which accompanied the process of technicalization did reflect not merely a generalized mood of rational optimism but a selective and recognizably technicalistic spirit, which both Westerners and Muslims were to call 'materialistic'.

The accompaniments of technicalism

The primacy of technical efficiency implied several correlative tendencies, which can be included within the technicalistic spirit. Like the emphasis on rationalized technique, they can be subsumed under a shift from authoritative custom towards independent calculation. They were, however, orientated to the needs of multiple technical specialization, not to rationality of every possible sort, and were, moreover, cultivated on such a scale as to institutionalize not merely occasional expressions of the shift but its most basic traits directly. A rationalizing calculativeness, crucial to technical specialization, depended, especially at first, on an *expectation of continuous innovation:* on encouraging an attitude of willingness to experiment, taking as little as possible for granted what had already been thought and done, rejecting established authority of every sort, and running the inherent risks of error that such rejection entails. At the beginning of the period, even though the full sway of the conservative spirit was to some extent subsiding during the Renaissance, the dominant institutions, in the Occident as elsewhere, represented agrarianate conservation: the maximum retention of established patterns holding out for order against the chaos which the natural flux of life's instability must tend towards. (Indeed, the very definition of culture is still the transmission of ways of doing from one generation to the next, so that each individual need not start out from scratch.) By the end of the eighteenth century, however, some of the most important institutions in the Occident had come to embody frankly and zealously the very principle of change, of innovation. Scientific journals, like the scientific societies, existed not primarily to preserve old knowledge but to seek out new. Legal protection of rights to inventions by patent recognized what had become a commonplace in industry: success went to whoever innovated most effectively most quickly. In the new social organization, innovation was institutionalized.

At last, government itself embodied this principle. The very institution of a legislature—an assembly whose explicit task it was not simply to grant taxes, nor even just to appoint administrators and decide on current policy in wars and crises, but to meet regularly to *change* the *laws*—reflected the degree to which conscious innovation lay at the heart of the new social order. Thinkers since the Axial Age—of whatever civilization—had granted that administrators must change and even current policies must change with circumstances; but the laws, if nothing else, ought so far as possible to be eternal. The laws were in fact sometimes changed in all societies at all times; some level provision was generally made for this, for instance (in the Ottoman case) in the regularizing of qânûn law decrees; but the whole purpose of social institutions was to obviate or at least minimize such change. Yet the very name of 'legislature' suggested an opposite conception.

It was inevitable in such an atmosphere that the notion of 'progress' became for the first time the dominant theme of serious thinking about historical change. Not merely perpetual variation but constant improvement of all kinds became a routine expectation. The normal 'old man's' assumption that the younger generation was going to the dogs was at least counterbalanced by the youthful hope that every new generation could build bigger and better.

Somewhat slower to appear, but perhaps eventually even more essential a corollary to technicalism, was the *mass participant society:* one in which as many as possible are drawn into the nexus of multiple technical specialism in all its aspects. The new economic order depended on a large and mobile supply of skilled labour, and particularly on a mass market of persons living above subsistence levels to absorb the steadily increasing product of what was becoming mass production. With mass production and mass consumption, the lower classes, even the peasantry, had to share in the refinements associated with urban living at levels previously reserved to an élite: eventually it became clear that mass literacy was required if a technicalized society were to function well. Inevitably such masses became a political force. (In the end it proved that even those technicalized societies in which power was in fact most systematically reserved for a few, were not merely to tolerate a political role for the masses; they were even to require the active loyalty and participation of the masses in a 'totalitarian' political process, so that the pervasive machinery of the state would be able to run more smoothly.)

In fact, the enormously extended role of the state, which entered every home in unprecedented detail and with inescapable efficiency, was as characteristic of technicalized society as was the notion of progress. Intervening groups based on personal contacts, such as had stood between the individual and the ultimate government in most agrarianate-level societies, were reduced to relative impotence or replaced by functional groupings based on specialized roles in the new technicalism, and not humanly integral. The state dealt, to a degree unprecedented in large territorial societies, directly with the individual. Only the impersonal power of the state, to which everyone was compelled equally to submit, seemed adequate to controlling so vast an interlocking network of technical specialties as emerged in the mass society.

Finally, technicalization carried with it an important moral discipline of its own, which merged with and reinforced the gentling of manners we have noted. It presupposed not only a mass society but, as its complement, an *individual at once privately isolated and yet highly cultivated and co-operative.* Only an independent, self-reliant individual, not tied to guild rules or tribal loyalties or communal religious conventions, could innovate with the freedom required, or even cultivate second-hand the ever-new specializations demanded for technical efficiency. This made for an increasingly high valuation of individual freedom from controls by other individuals. It also meant ultimately a tendency toward anonymity and impersonalization as all intermediaries between the individual and the mass were attenuated (till finally the individuality was to seem distilled into a filing card number). Yet as important as independence and private isolation were private integrity and personal growth and cultivation, which were to develop in conjunction with the spirit of teamwork and willing co-operation. Hence, at the same time, technicalism meant an expectation of high personal moral standards and respect for the individual's special gifts.

Accompanying the British Industrial Revolution itself was, in fact, a specific moral revolution in which 'bourgeois morality' asserted the primacy of its own norms. By the next generation it had gone far towards doing away with not only the grosser forms of dissipation and display in personal life, but even with graft and bribery in politics. More than ever, more even than in Islamdom, equality of rights was required.

The specialist, by technicalistic standards, was respected not for any arbitrary status he might have by ancestry or other connections but for his individual achievement as it contributed to the common development. The only ascriptive status still accorded unquestioned recognition was that of a human being; to this human status was transferred the personal inviolability which hitherto had been the preserve of various personally-linked in-groups protected by their power or their sanctity. This fact contributed to the great achievement of the eighteenth-century Enlightenment in mitigating public cruelty. Hand in hand with respect for innovation and for technical efficiency went an increase in opportunities—for ordinary persons to find a career suited to their talents; for the exceptional, sometimes, to express their unique visions.

All these changes, especially for those who made their way to the centres of social control, made for an enormous increase in physical power available, and hence in material wealth; an enormous increase in positive knowledge, and hence in imaginative possibilities; a great multiplication of channels of opportunity for accomplishment, and hence of the basis for constructive personal freedom. Wealth, knowledge, and freedom further reinforced the direct effects of technicalized organization in making for a high and constantly increasing level of social power: power to produce goods, to discover facts, to organize human life to whatever ends presented themselves.

For Muslims all this had a special moral significance. At least in some measure, the Occidentals had managed to solve the moral dilemmas of citied society as they had confronted the human conscience since the beginning of civilization, and especially as they had been articulated in the Irano-Semitic spiritual tradition, in which, indeed, the Occidentals shared. They had developed institutions which seemed to assure at least personal legal security and a sustained high level of social order and prosperity in which even the least advantaged increasingly began to share. Moreover, even on the level of personal purity they had established standards of individual honesty, industry, loyalty, and modesty, and a capacity to rise above personal competitiveness, which, while far from assuring moral perfection in Europe, yet were increasingly visible in the more responsible classes.

For an unbiased devotee of Shar'î Islam there was much to admire. Taking its cue from Muḥammad himself, the Sharî'ah had posited egalitarian justice and had presupposed a degree of social mobility, stressing individual responsibility and the nuclear family; more than any other great religious tradition it had catered to bourgeois and mercantile values. It had struggled persistently against any merely customary authority and usage in the name of universal law and the dignity of the individual, and had borne, sometimes vocally and sometimes more silently, a witness to the crucial place jointly of good government and of personal morality in human prosperity, which it acknowledged as a divinely sanctioned good which it was a human responsibility to guard. In all these matters, the Christian European peoples following the Great Transmutation went far in translating ideal into reality. From fairly early in the nineteenth century, in fact, there were to be alert and respected Muslims to declare that the Europeans were leading a better life by Islamic standards than were the Muslim societies themselves.

In fact, to be sure, the basic moral problems of society were not yet fully solved; such progress as had been made had been by way of altering the very terms in which such problems had been posed since Sumer, and this had been done at a cost which no one could yet be prepared to evaluate. Some Muslims were sceptical, from the start, of the value of the power and prosperity of the new Europe, and eventually many were to be disillusioned when the solutions proved imperfect.

Why only the Occident?

It is perhaps not to be expected that we can find any absolute standard for judging the excellence of a society and of its achievements in any given period. We have learned to beware measuring even prosperity and decline simply by the power a society can exert and the resources it can command at a particular moment. We are quick to look for signs of inner decay, and this is what some scholars think they find in Islamdom as a basis for contemning its apparent greatness in the later periods. It seems safer to measure a society's progress by its development in technology and especially in natural science, regarded as indicative at once of its rationality and of its inner freedom. But science and technology are not the only possible indicators of truth and freedom; rather, they afford an almost expressly technicalistic criterion, well-tailored to justify the superiority of the Modern West. In our day, we are increasingly aware that (as it has been put), though our natural science can claim to be *useful*, it is more doubtful that it is *good*, and in the ultimate sense it cannot claim to be *valid* and true. Indeed, generally we have reason to doubt most of the criteria that have made us proud of the Modern Western achievements.

Nevertheless, even if we can no longer ascribe absolute or exclusive value to the sort of 'progress' the West has represented in the last three hundred years, it remains true that technicalization and all that accompanied it was a tremendous human achievement in its own way. It was an immense triumph, to the credit (whaever its ultimate outcome) of the Occidental peoples and of the strength of their local institutions, the vigour of their spiritual and intellectual life, the prosperity of a large part of their population. The Transmutation grew largely out of the remarkable cultural florescence of the Occidental Renaissance, which had already carried the Occident in some ways beyond the cultural equality with Islamdom which it had achieved in the High Medieval period. In effect, the Transmutation resulted from the zeal and intelligence that succeeded in making permanent certain aspects of the innovative vigour of the Renaissance. The question then arises, what was so special about the Occident that it, and not other societies, achieved this?

First, we must recall that, in any case, it had to happen, if at all, in some one place rather than in others. Just as civilization on the agrarianate level had appeared in one or, at most, a very few spots and spread from there to the greater part of the globe, so the new technicalistic type of life could not appear everywhere among all citied peoples at the same moment; it too appeared first in one restricted area, western Europe, from which it has spread everywhere else.

It was not that the new ways resulted from conditions that were limited entirely to one area. Just as the first urban, literate life would have been impossible without the accumulation among a great many peoples of innumerable social habits and inventions, major and minor, so the great modern cultural Transmutation presupposed numerous inventions and discoveries originating in all the several citied peoples of the Eastern Hemisphere, discoveries of which many of the earlier basic ones were not made in Europe. In particular, most of the more immediately formative elements that led to the Transmutation, both material and moral, had come to the Occident, earlier or later, from other regions. Some of the crucial inventions (notably the famous early trio: gunpowder, the compass, and printing) which had prepared the way for the subsequent Occidental development had come ultimately from China, as did, apparently, the idea of a civil service examination system, introduced in the eighteenth century. In such ways the Occident seems to have been the unconscious heir of the abortive industrial revolution of Sung China. More pervasive, if less specifically spectacular, had been, of course, the elements coming from the other Mediterranean societies, particularly the Islamicate, with its incalculable impulse to science and philosophy in the Occident as early as the High Medieval period.

And perhaps at least as important was the very existence of the vast world market, constituted by the Afro-Eurasian commercial network, which had cumulatively come into being, largely under Muslim auspices, by the middle of the second millennium. The vigorous internal evolution of the Occident was completed by its access to the large areas of relatively dense, urban-dominated populations that formed the world market, in all its rich variety. There European fortunes could be made and European imaginations exercised. In particular it was the mercantile expansion which followed the Iberian oceanic ventures of the fifteenth and sixteenth centuries, that initiated the financial growth which became the immediate occasion of the earlier period of major capital accumulation. Without the cumulative history of the whole Afro-Eurasian Oikoumene, of which the Occident had been an integral part, the Western Transmutation would be almost unthinkable.

Nevertheless, it could not actually happen in the whole Oikoumene at once. All cultural developments, in any part of the Oikoumene, had begun in terms of a local cultural context and had been borrowed only slowly elsewhere. The same was true of the changes that made up the Great Transmutation. When the time was ripe for it, the actual cultural transformations could take place only within a given culture and in terms of the background of that culture—as it happened, the Occident.

It is not yet established what determined that the Transmutation should occur just there and then. Of course, in a general way it could hardly have happened before the second millennium CE; only then, presumably, would the expansion and intensification of the hemispheric commercial nexus, and in particular the accumulation of inventions, have reached an adequate level from which to begin. Then it would be a matter of which area would first combine a sufficient number of favourable local conditions. Presumably several different combinations might have been effective in producing some such transmutation; one cannot simply look at the combination that happened to occur in western Europe and assert that only this could have led to any sort of major acceleration of productivity and innovation such as occurred.

We may suppose, however, that a social tradition and economic resources favouring specifically industrial investment will have been essential: we have seen that the role of such investment had increased among both the Chinese and the Occidentals and apparently contributed to giving them an increasing interregional role already in the Mid-Islamic periods. But surely other conditions would have been required, if only to reinforce the effects of a shift toward such investment, and to prevent its disruption. We may conjecture what some of those that happened to be effective in the Occident were.[9] For the Occidentals did have special advantages. First was the relative

[9] [Author's added note: Often single cultural traits have been stressed as explaining how institutionalizing of such investment became possible just in the Occident and just at that time. Explanations range from the effects of the combination of alphabetic script with printing technique (a theory that underestimates the viability of the Chinese script) to invocations of Christian doctrines of the creation of a world with *positivistic* values matured and liberated only after centuries; or of Greek notions of rational organization of the city and of science, fecundated by Christian compassion or positivity, or else by 'northern' concern with material equipment for the hard winters. Such theories, as usually stated, underestimate the positivity, rationality, compassion, or industry of the rest of mankind. All these elements may have played some role, but even

virginity and extensiveness of their own soil: the largest continuous well-watered region that still lay adjacent to the old citied regions, not having proved amenable to earlier forms of exploitation because of its northern cold. Once they had learned to farm it well, it offered much room for expansion and hence for the patterns of an expanding economy; all this at a juncture in world history when much was to prove possible that would surely have been impossible much earlier, had the north European forests been cleared much earlier. (The stimulus provided by new agricultural methods in south China, which strengthened the Sung Chinese economy, affected a far smaller area than the vast north European plain, and was presumably far more vulnerable to local setbacks.) No doubt almost equally important were subtler things, such as the stimulus to the imagination provided both by ready access to other citied societies (Europe was barred by no Himalayas) and by the crossing of the Atlantic (which would have occurred by way of the northern islands or of Brazil, surely, even if Columbus had not ventured on the long middle route; whereas no Chinese venture into the Pacific could have had such success). We must add, perhaps (but this is less clear), a relative freedom from universal massive destruction and especially from alien conquest (notably at the hands of the Mongols) for a relatively long time.

Perhaps, given time (that is, some interruption of the Occidental development), we might have found similar transmutations taking place independently in other agrarianate-level societies, some sooner and some later, each with its own forms in terms of its own background. It cannot be ruled out that the Chinese might later have repeated more successfully their achievements of the Sung period, with its enormous and sudden expansion of iron and steel production, its proliferation of new technical advances, and its general cultural effervescence; for though this was cut short and China re-agrarianized under the Mongol conquest, cultural patterns cannot be fixed forever by such events, as organisms may be. One can also imagine conditons that could eventually have given great impetus to an Islamicate India. But once one such transmutation had been completed in one place, there was no time to wait for the like to happen elsewhere. In its very nature, such a cultural change, once completed, soon involved the whole globe, and the fact of its occurrence in one particular place, foreclosed the possibility of its happening so anywhere else.

To understand this consequence, we must recur to the parity that had been maintained among the agrarianate societies. Within the Afro-Eurasian historical complex, the overall rise in the level of social power that had everywhere taken place was cumulatively very marked. In the sixteenth century, the Spanish, the Ottoman, the Indian, or the Chinese empires could, any of them, have easily crushed the ancient Sumerians at their strongest—as one

when taken cumulatively they still require supplementation by considerations of the world historical moment in itself.—R.S.]

of them did crush the Aztecs, who were on a comparable level. But the rise was very gradual. In any given era, each society within the Oikoumene had to reckon with the others essentially as equals, whatever temporary superiority one of them might gain. For instance, the superiority of the Arabs over the Portuguese in the eighth and ninth centuries and the briefer superiority of the Portuguese over the Arabs in the sixteenth century were both based on relatively superficial local advantages, neither people going beyond the limitations implicit in agrarianate-level society. In each case, the superiority was soon reversed, not by a radical transformation of the hard bested people but by a general shift of circumstances. In various periods Greeks, Indians, and Muslims each had their days of splendour, but in the long run all remained roughly at parity. This was because over the millennia any really basic new developments had been gradually adopted everywhere within the space of four or five centuries—or even more rapidly in such a case as gunpowder weapons.

But it was part of the transmutational character of the new transformation that it broke down the very historical presuppositions in terms of which such gradual diffusions had maintained parity among Afro-Eurasian citied societies. In the new pace of historical change, when decades sufficed to produce what centuries had produced before, a lag of four or five centuries was no longer safe. The old gradual diffusion and adjustment was no longer possible. Very shortly—at the latest by the end of the seventeenth century—all non-Western peoples were faced with the problem of coping as outsiders with the new order of civilized life as it was emerging in the Occident. Unless, by the oddest of chances, they happened to have started a comparable transmutation of their own at precisely the same moment as the Occident, there was no time for them to follow their own independent developments, however promising. Yet, still moving, culturally at an agrarianate pace, they could also not simply adopt the Western development for themselves year by year as it proceeded (as would have been required for such adoption to be effective). Those untransmutated agrarianate-level societies that did not share the Western cultural presuppositions had perforce to continue developing in their own traditions at their own pace, adopting from alien traditions only what could be assimilated on that basis. Hence the Western Transmutation, once it got well under way, could neither be paralleled independently nor be borrowed wholesale. Yet it could not, in most cases, be escaped. The millennial parity of social power broke down, with results that were disastrous almost everywhere.

B. THE TRANSMUTATION IN ISLAMDOM

Everything about the Transmutation made it impossible to isolate. It had not been isolated even in its origins, since it presupposed the wider historical complex of which the Occident formed a part; and the growth of technicalism in turn accentuated its dependence on the world at large. Soon the fortunes of the Occident were tied up with the course of events all over the globe. In its nature, an expanding technicalism could recognize no artificial limits: if a potential market was hard to exploit, that was another reason for achieving its exploitation. A culture where innovation and discovery were at so high a premium and where no limits were set to the search for technically efficient activity, and especially a culture in which the unbounded resources of machine energy had been unleashed, could recognize no geographical limits upon the activity of its individuals. Indeed, its spirit of innovative rivalry forced them to seek ever new frontiers, ever new markets and resources and objects of study. Soon what happened in Rangoon, in Zanzibar, and in Patagonia became of direct relevance to people in London.

The advent of the Modern Technical Age

Thus was ushered in a new period of the world's history, in which the bulk of mankind were no longer articulated into a number of relatively isolated civilizations each with its autonomously evolving lettered tradition, but rather came to form a global society of closely interacting nations. For when Zanzibar came to matter intimately to London, London made itself important to Zanzibar too; before long all parts of the world found themselves involved in what happened in the Occident. I am speaking, of course, of changes in the preconditions of *historical* life, not of immediate changes in daily ways. Yet, since in the citied societies of the Oikoumene, daily life has come to depend on precarious balances of historical pressures, changes in the historical level must be seen as decisive.

There have been many names for the new age, which has most commonly been identified simply as 'modern'; but since 'modern' is properly a relative term, and even as a period name has a way of getting stretched or shrunk according to various parochial European standards, it will be convenient here to use a term more precise from a world-historical viewpoint. To refer to the period since the advent of the European world hegemony, which put an end to the form in which world-historical evolution had been articulated since Sumer, we may use the term 'Technical Age', because of the central role in its advent of technicalism and the associated social forms.

The Technical Age as a world-historical period is characterized by the presence within it of fully-fledged technicalization in at least some portion of mankind, and by the decisive effects of that presence upon the rest of mankind. It is a temptation to characterize it only by the institutional traits of technicalism in the evolutionary development which formed its nucleus. But even within the most advanced countries, technicalism had also an *irruptive* force which—in less industrialized districts—produced effects often the reverse of those associated with its *nuclear* institutional traits. In the world at large, such irruptive effects were at least as significant as the nuclear traits.

All historical events now took place in an unprecedentedly close-drawn global context. Moreover, at least in the first centuries, the pace of such events did not merely increase; it was constantly accelerating. In the technicalized centres, naturally, the more innovation, the more new basic inventions, the faster the way was opened for still more discoveries, inventions, and basic changes. Presumably there is ultimately some sort of biological limit to this process, if an end is not imposed by design or by catastrophe; but meanwhile it has been of drastic significance for all. For the technicalized centres set the pace and determined the relevance of activity everywhere.

Basic changes in those centres exacted altered responses everywhere else even when no tangible changes followed. For a long time many lifeways did seem to continue with little material change. But this was illusory. Often there was in fact a degeneration in their effectiveness, which outside observers were incompetent to observe, though it could have decisive consequences. Yet even part from this, the vital meaning of a single cultural trait—a primitive form of transport say—was in fact highly diverse in the age of the fast stagecoach, in that of the railway, and in that of the automobile. Likewise, a particular form of words, a statement of belief, say, is one thing when it is still simply traditional in that it is the normal notion that 'everyone' has, but is quite another thing when it is in fact traditionalistic, held despite significant persons' having rejected it, and in explicit loyalty to a now idealized past. For peoples whose overall fate was being determined in a technicalistic context, it is the meaning of their ways within that context that is historically relevant, and not the continuity of the external form. At the same time, the rate of change in the technicalized areas had also very tangible effects elsewhere. Even the overt evolution of political and economic practices and of human thought was in fact very rapid in the non-technicalized parts of the world.

But even more than the acceleration of historical events in their global context, what set off historical action in the Technical Age was a change in the social basis of civilized creativity. In the technicalized areas, with the development of the mass society, the old distinction between a lettered urban élite and the peasant mass ceased to be fundamental; its place being taken, perhaps, by functional specialization. Gradually, as technicalism spread over the world, the same was to take place everywhere. But meanwhile, in the non-technicalized areas what was significant and creative in cultural activity was keyed not to the problems of an urban élite in an agrarian society but to those of non-technicalized élites in a technicalistic world.

For the dominant fact of world history (*qua* world history) in the Technical Age has been the great contrast in social power between the technicalized societies and those not technicalized, or less so. This has created a power gap or, to speak more hopefully, a development gap who has, from the beginning, divided the world into two sets of peoples who have been inescapably bound up with each other, yet have found it bafflingly hard to comprehend each other. It is this bafflement that is expressed in Kipling's 'East is East and West is West and never the twain shall meet'. The line marking the development gap has been sharp, as such lines go. The crucial point has been whether a given national society, as a whole, was in a position to take up the new patterns more or less *pari passu* with their development in the most advanced Occidental countries. Those that could, despite 'backward' districts within their own boundaries, were able on the whole to maintain a position of power parity, or at least an appearance of maintaining such a position; those that could not, and yet found themselves gripped in the same world market and political complex, long found their relative power position getting steadily worse; the same forces that built up the economies and cultures in the advanced lands broke down theirs, and they became the 'underdeveloped' lands, those with relatively low investment levels.[10]

The development gap has brought a new meaning to some ethnocentric terms. The term 'Western' has been rather loosely applied to the technicalized lands, at least so far as they have a European connection; in this sense it has included, therefore, the Christian lands of eastern Europe as well as the Occident proper. The term 'Eastern' has been the even looser complement to 'Western', at least so far as the 'underdeveloped' lands had possessed a citied culture and shared in the Oikoumenic historical complex: it has been applied to all the Islamo-Asian parts of the world, from Morocco west of Europe to the Sino-Japanese Far East. The two terms are strictly speaking legitimate, if at all, only with reference to the Technical Age, the peculiar

[10] The best theoretical statement, in brief form, of at least the economic side of the consequences of the Western Transmutation on the non-Western parts of the world is to be found in Gunner Myrdal's *Rich Lands and Poor: The Road to World Prosperity* (New York, 1957), English title: *Economic Theory and Underdeveloped Regions* (1957). He points out that the unhampered operation of the market tends to exaggerate any initial inequalities through the cumulative effects of even slight differences, and that in particular it intensifies differences between regions, rewarding any advantages one region may acquire and correspondingly penalizing the other regions that are in a common market structure with it. He notes that economic development in one place thus tends always to have 'backwash' effects that depress the economy in other places, places that must compete with the more developed area on increasingly less favourable terms; the 'spread effects', which economic development also carries with it, which might stimulate development in neighbouring areas, are normally much weaker than the backwash effects. The world market in the nineteenth century illustrated this principle excellently, and Myrdal brings this out effectively. Unfortunately, many other theorists of economic development fail to take this into account; too often they assume that every people starts 'at scratch' or, if late-comers, even with preponderant advantages provided by the technical skills available from the developed countries. [Author's added note: In those non-Western lands long urbanized, highly cultivated and most closely integrated into what was becoming already a world-wide complex (as contrasted with non-citied and remoter areas), one of the backwash effects was that the population explosion came before industrialization, and so made the creation of an agricultural excess for the transition period into industrialization internally very difficult.—R.S.]

historical configuration of which (especially in the nineteenth century) they clumsily express.

I hope it has become clear that the problems of the Muslim peoples in the nineteenth century and since, are not the result of their having 'fallen behind' some otherwise normal standard of steady progress, and cannot be attributed to inherent defects in Islamicate culture, whether religious obscurantism or political incapacity, as is so often assumed. Still less can we speak of the collapse of Islamicate power as exemplifying some biological law that any civilization must, as if it were an organism, flourish and then age and decay. At the very most, we may say (using economic rather than biological terms) that a society may encourage investment in one sort of opportunity so heavily that it cannot quickly marshal its resources in other directions when new circumstances make other sorts of investment more profitable; that to some degree, the very excellence with which Islamicate culture had met the needs of the Agrarian Age may have impeded its advance beyond it, even though it had helped lay the groundwork for such an advance. Yet even such a judgment is of doubtful validity. We have no real grounds for supposing that, if the Transmutation had not occurred where and when it did, it could not have occurred later in an Islamicate setting.

The view I have presented runs radically counter to the usual Westernistic image of world history, which not only pure Westernists but most Western Christians and Jews have accepted to some degree. That image—in direct continuity with Medieval Occidental notions—divides the world into three parts: the Primitives, who were supposed to have no history; the Orient, which produced great cultures at a certain point, but, for want of a sense of due proportion, stagnated thereafter and regressed; and lastly the West (composed, by arbitrary fiat, of Classical Greece plus the Latin Occident), where due proportion was introduced by the Greek genius, which in turn produced Truth and Liberty and hence a Progress which, if at first less spectacular than the Orient, at last necessarily led to Modernity and to world dominion. In accord with this image, Islamicate culture, as a late manifestation of the 'Orient', ought to be at most a latter-day reworking of earlier cultural achievements, and must certainly have soon degenerated into the normal 'Oriental' stagnation. So it has been interpreted almost unanimously by modern Western scholars. On the other hand, Modernity would be but the latest stages of age-long progress as exemplified most normally in the West. In accordance with this image, many speak of the 'impact of the West'—not of technicalism—on Islamdom, as if it were two societies, not two ages, that met; as if it were that Western progress had finally reached the point where Muslims could no longer escape it, rather than that something new had happened to Western culture which thereby was happening to Islamdom and the whole world as well. It is symptomatic of this attitude when the new age is dated from 1500, from the first larger contacts between the West and the other civilizations, rather than a century later, when actual technicalism supervened; as if what was decisive were not the *new level* of social process in the *world*, which happened to have emerged in the West, but rather the *new outreach* of the *West*, which happened soon to be going on to new levels.

We have met this sort of thinking in Islamicate history before. I have tried throughout this work to show how various ingrained misperceptions, leading to a false posing of questions and a misreading of evidence, have distorted Islamics studies. As I have indicated already in the summary chart at the Prologue to Book Four, a great many of these misperceptions are integral to the Westernistic world image. But perhaps nowhere else in the conventional history of Islamdom does the influence of the Westernistic world image intervene more directly than in our conceptions of the relation of Modernity to Muslim history.[11]

The generation of 1789

The men and women active from about 1776 to about 1815 formed one generation, *sensu largo*, whose high point must be put in 1789. This astonishing generation of 1789, which saw not only the great French Revolution but also the establishment of the new American republics and the wave of Napoleonic convulsions throughout the Continent, has been well compared to an earthquake in which a pressure that has arisen within the rocks is adjusted. Through the period of the Transmutation, the actual balance among the social and economic forces had become increasingly poorly expressed in the forms of social and political life, which responded to the new impulses more slowly. In the culminating generation, there was a

[11] See also the section on the history of Islamics studies (vol. 1, p. 39), for the particular ways in which the Westernistic bias has evolved. The Westernistic world image came to its first major expression in Hegel's philosophy of history; it can still be traced in the most recent attempts at world-historical synthesis. It regularly makes for difficulties in handling Islam and Islamicate culture. Since the Middle Ages, Islam has been seen as the skewed imitation and doomed rival of the West; that it should loom so great at so late a date may befit old notions of Antichrist, but is a stumbling-block to the Enlightenment's notion of Progress. After the Ottoman threat finally receded, it could be comfortably ignored, and often has been, if with an uneasy conscience, not only in historical works but in philosophy and even in studies of religion. Islam caused difficulties even for Spengler and Toynbee, who superficially departed drastically from the Westernistic historical image (though for both, the Westernistic conception of the fall of Rome remained paradigmatic); for both, the history of Islamdom was strangely anomalous. Even in the remarkable work of William McNeill, *The Rise of the West*—by some tests, the first genuine world history ever written—the Westernistic image still prevails in the evaluation of Islam, despite his Toynbeean awareness of the importance of non-Western cultures and the influence of an anthropological diffusionism in forming his work (and despite his kind citation of an earlier version of this present work as formative for his views). What troubles me in his work more than his condescending attitude toward Islam, or even than his conception of it as stagnant after the High Caliphal Period, is his persistent exaggeration of the high seminal traits of 'the West'—of which his attitude to Islam is but a corollary.

WOW

sudden yielding to the resultant tension and, like rock slipping along a fault, the received patterns of society were readjusted, one way or another, to the new technicalistic realities. This phase of sudden readjustment does not account directly for all the remarkable transformations of that generation. Some of them, such as the advent of wide use of steam machinery production in the same generation (1785), primarily mark the culmination of steadily cumulative processes. But even these were hastened or even forced by the cataclysmic events of the time. The events of that generation became epochal through the intensification of an already cumulative process in the open and fluid circumstances of the moment when an increasingly untenable social situation was readjusted.

The same is true of the establishment of European world hegemony in the same generation. That hegemony became an inescapable political fact in all the citied parts of the Eastern Hemisphere by the end of the Napoleonic period; there was no delay between the *Umsturz* at home and abroad. In the eighteenth century, European power in the Islamo-Asian regions had been growing but was not yet decisive nor sufficiently regular to be reckoned with systematically at home or abroad. The papal division of the world between Spain and Portugal had been a mere gesture; the world was not at the pope's disposal. Even the later struggles between French, British, and Dutch, in the citied part of the world, had been primarily over trading stations and only marginally, in favourable cases, for influence with various courts in the Southern Seas area. (It is an illegitimate anticipation when some historians want to call the Anglo-French wars of the eighteenth century 'world wars'.) The Chinese had still been able, for instance, late in the eighteenth century, to drive back the Russians from territory about equidistant between the two capitals. But during the Napoleonic wars the European powers developed their military and economic potentialities to the maximum and became incidentally, in the process, more deeply involved in internal affairs in many Muslim lands.

By the time of the Congress of Vienna, the germ of the Concert of Europe, the European powers were in fact in a position to issue in earnest such a decree as the pope had once issued by way of anticipation; and throughout the nineteenth century, affairs of remote parts of the world were, in fact, settled among the Powers. All the remaining citied lands of the hemisphere were by then politically at the mercy of the Europeans, though in some cases neither Europeans nor the local people fully realized the fact at first, even yet. In the Far East of China and Japan, the world political transformation was for a time disguised though the Napoleonic years were subtly decisive even there (an indicator is the opium trade, which had its decisive growth then). It was, however, another generation before the overwhelming power of the West was recognized. Especially the chief parts of the Islamicate zone, far the largest sector of the Eastern Hemisphere, were overpowered right away by Europeans, either in outright conquest or through subtler interventions; and here there was generally no mistaking the reality. In Egypt for a time, in India and Malaysia permanently, the Muslim populations of the hinterland were subdued by modern Occidental arms. Elsewhere, notably in the main part of the Ottoman empire, the generation of 1789 produced irreversible acknowledgements of Occidental superiority in power. Almost everywhere in the Islamicate part of the world and in its Christian, Hindu and Buddhist enclaves, this generation learned that the chief datum to be dealt with by any statesman, any merchant, and even such thinkers as were truly adventurous, was the Europe of the Technical Age. The generation of 1789 was almost as fateful elsewhere as it was in Europe itself.

What had happened was not purely a by-product of the sudden development within Europe, but was partly parallel in its internal mechanism to the European events themselves. To some degree the establishment of effective European world hegemony was (like the English Industrial Revolution) the intensification, under pressure from the eruptive situation within Europe, of a tendency which had been at least latent for some time: in the face of new problems within Europe, Europeans discovered powers which they had hardly been aware of earlier, and developed them further. But the establishment of effective hegemony also answered, in certain cases at least, to a process of readjustment (no doubt likewise hastened by European events) within those of the Muslim lands where the eighteenth-century Occidental presence had been most serious. Almost unobserved, the activities of the newly powerful Occidentals had altered the internal balance of forces in the Muslim countries, till in some places the tension between form and reality made the existent patterns untenable. As in Europe, readjustments were made. But the discrepancies had been of a different sort and the readjustments were correspondingly different from those in the West.

Whereas in the West the readjustments were in the direction of making explicit in formal institutions the technicalization of society which had been developing in diverse aspects of life, in the Islamo-Asian regions, or in such of them as experienced a major readjustment at this time, what was required was to make explicit and to bring under some sort of order the power relationships which had emerged across the development gap. Where local luxury industries and commerce had been most undermined by Western competition, the whole internal balance of the society now proved to be upset.[12] With the élite of the old trades weakened, an element which had been especially significant in the Islamicate societies, with their anti-agrarian bias, proved missing; when, in addition, ever more policy decisions had to be focused on the new West, old ruling elements proved incompetent—and

[12] [Author's added note: Muslim rulers of the generation of 1789 were in fact attempting to meet a situation that had been developing throughout the eighteenth century, including the disappearance of the Muslim luxury crafts and the consequent undermining of the basis of urban prosperity independent of an agrarian base. Such a situation had been especially destructive in the relatively highly urbanized Muslim lands.—R.S.]

their incompetence was aggravated locally by the indigenously developed weaknesses of the major empires in the eighteenth century. Moreover, at the same time that the old foundations of order and prosperity were undermined, the new economic relationship with the West opened up new possibilities of buying—and selling—which had taken on unwonted importance.

The readjustment, then, took the form of establishing what has been called a 'colonial' order: a régime in polity and economy of complementary dependence on one or more Western lands. Generally speaking, the dependent land turned to producing export items—normally raw materials—which were fed into the industrial processes being established in the West; in return it received the cheap finished goods produced by Western industries. Correspondingly, the dependent land established a polity such as could guarantee the kind of order necessary to carry out such a trade and prevent local attempts at deviation from the pattern: normally some sort of absolutism in which the various alternative loci of power typical of pre-Technical times were eliminated. In the hardest-hit areas the new order of complementary dependence was established immediately, with revolutionary impact. Elsewhere it was established somewhat more gradually during the course of the century. In neither case did it make a decisive difference in this respect whether there was actual Western rule or not.

Three of the most striking instances will illustrate the diverse forms the advent of the Technical Age could take in Islamicate societies. Bengal, occupied outright in the decades before the French Revolution, was the base for the British conquest of all India in the decades that followed it; here a dependent régime was established by Westerners. In Egypt, though French troops briefly occupied it, the *Umsturz* was the work of local men responding to the new challenge autonomously; and the same was true of the Ottoman empire generally. Finally, among the Volga Tatars we find a Muslim community taking part in the Western Transmutation in large measure from within—and subsequently playing a major role in establishing a dependent order in other Muslim lands.

The new order in Bengal and India

The British conquest of India presents the classic case of outright European occupation and rule of a major area of Islamic culture. Incidentally, it illustrates usefully the transformation which came over the Europeans themselves between the eighteenth and the nineteenth centuries, which in turn brings out the meaning of the Transmutation and hence of its impact. It could be said that the overt conquest was simply the outward expression of a change in relationship between the British and the Indian population, a change which was equally important in all aspects of British rule.

In the eighteenth century, though, as we have seen, European power and prestige were growing in India, the British trading community in Bengal and the Andhra coast, and Madras and Bombay cities, still lived on a basis not very different from that of two centuries before. The plundering of Bengal represented, indeed, the new power of the Europeans; but it was a power expressed within the presuppositions of a recent time when they were less powerful. Hence its unparalleled irresponsibility. The British lived essentially as equals with the local trading population, with whom they shared the exploitation of Bengal and Bihar. Britishers were known to establish harems in the local fashion and—as became official agents of the Timurid emperor—they naturally continued the use of Persian in the administration. The ruining of Bengal through a perpetuation of the old attitudes showed clearly enough that the new power of the Europeans needed to be controlled if trade were to continue profitable—and by whom if not by the Europeans? The reforms of Warren Hastings, who established direct British rule in Bengal (1772–85), were obviously required in the mercantile interest itself. Yet they were almost ahead of their time. They met with such intense resistance among the local British that his colleagues had him brought to trial, an extended trial (1788–95) during which the British at home took a long shocked look for the first time at the whole situation among the British in India. Hastings was then acquitted but public opinion condemned his company. The British public was aroused to what proved more than a century of high responsibilities in India, for the trial proceeded in the midst of the French Revolution.

What the public found so shocking in British ways in India, but which was so ingrained in those ways that even their reformer, Hastings, found himself accused of a measure of it, would certainly have shocked no one in the time of Drake. What made the difference was the rise of standards in government responsibility: the expectation that government must be organized efficiently and predictably as a pure instrument of civil order, not of power and glory in themselves. Hastings was attacked, for instance, for having assisted his ally the (Muslim) ruler of Awadh in the Gangetic plain to overwhelm his neighbours, the (Muslim) Ruhelas, praised in London for being a 'free people' who ruled their lands well. Britishers now must respect, even abroad, law and order above all. A major count against Hastings was that he had encouraged the ruler of Awadh to fleece his female relatives (to pay his British debts) after the British had earlier given the ladies a special guarantee against this, an intrusion of personal wilfulness into what must operate as an unimpeachable, impersonal, technical administration.

The high moral tone of the indignation at the trial echoed the classical Romans. Burke attacked Hastings with Cicero's oration against Verres in the back of his mind. This rigorous moral tone was itself a significant element in the British conquest of India. But in practice it led to quite different results from its equivalent in Rome, and in numerous other peoples. Hastings' tentative reforms were successfully followed up by his successor, Cornwallis, with a reorganization far more fundamental than the jury reform which

Cicero was supporting. Both Hastings and Cornwallis were, in effect, charged by the trading company with setting up a state machinery that would be apart from and supreme over the private interests of the merchants. In part this meant simply restoring essential order to the plundered country. But it also meant doing so on the basis of integration into a technicalistic world order. In 1786 a reasonably workable system of taxation was finally worked out, probably almost as effective as had existed under the Timurîs. But Cornwallis was impatient to go beyond this. Even at the price of renewed agrarian disruption, he put taxation on a predictable, budgetable basis so that the government could devote its attention to the services for its subjects which were now to be its major concern. In 1790 the highest court of Bengal—hitherto presided over by a Muslim—was put under an Englishman with Muslim and Hindu advisers, while the judicial system was all reorganized on modern English lines, embodying among other things the principle of the regular jurisdiction of the courts over a corporate 'government' as well as over individuals of every degree. By 1793 he had worked out an overall code which proved satisfactory, in its main lines, for supporting the whole subsequent proliferation of Indian administration.

Cornwallis and his successors had the advantage of attracting a better class of men than the adventurers who had swarmed over Bengal with Clive, and against whom Hastings had had to contend. As the effects of the Transmutation had become more visible, Europeans had gradually come to feel that their own culture formed a world of its own, demonstrably superior to that of the Southern Seas. Now they conceived the mission of bringing the fruits of it to the benighted heathen. The Protestant missionaries that arrived in Madras and Bengal in 1793 came explicitly in this spirit. Not very distant was the spirit that now animated many of the better administrators and judges sent out to rule Bengal in the name of law and order. These new men brought their wives along with them and determined to live a pure Western life so far as the tropics would allow it. Social equality with the 'natives' was therefore frowned on, and still more so intermarriage. At the same time—indeed, in the same spirit—they felt a great responsibility to improve the natives' lot. The missionaries in particular set up printing presses and soon were publishing both the Bible and works on modern science in the vernacular Bengali, works which soon had a far larger market than the Persian and Sanskrit books which the 'orientalizing' savants of the old school had lately been publishing too. Some of the nuclear aspects of the great Transmutation, not merely its military and commercial by-products, were now re-echoed in Bengal and shortly throughout India.

But no integral technicalistic evolution took place. Instead there was a general rearrangement of the social order suitable to a dependent role which was not an extension of, but complementary to, technicalized society. In this dependent society such things as modern technology and science entered only so far as to reinforce the materially and morally incontestable supremacy of the West. More basically, Bengal felt, rather than the nuclear institutional traits, the irruptive effects of the Transmutation in their fullest development. These effects may be summed up with respect to the economy, the social structure, and the intellectual élite.

The sounder ordering of the Bengal government failed to overcome one crucial problem which a Cornwallis could not hope to solve. The plundering of Bengal by Mârwârîs and Britishers had had temporary effects in ruining the Bengal craftsmen, particularly the cotton weavers. The vagaries of the British trade policy, which now controlled the Bengal production, caused a further slump when, from 1779, the European market to which the British traders were tied, was barred by war. But most serious was the competition, from at least 1790, with English machine-produced cotton goods. From this, Bengali industry could not recover; it could hardly occur to a British administration to take special measures against British trade to help it to do so; this would scarcely have been really possible without an isolation in the Japanese manner, which was anyway out of the question in Bengal. Agriculture therefore became henceforth for a long time the sole stay of Bengal's economy. It was not, however, the same agriculture. In the course of the nineteenth century, it became increasingly turned not to local food production but to raw materials for the industrialized sector in the world market, notably jute and indigo. Thus Bengal entered economically into a typical dependent phase of Technical Age society.

Both the manner of managing such production and the involvement in the vagaries of the world market imposed on the Bengal villager an economic régime of which the ultimate determination lay with the technicalized world order. For cultivating technicalistic traits himself, with their dependence on parsimony and saving, on satisfactions through individual achievement rather than through group expression, the peasant would have needed a certain amount of accumulation of capital as a basis; since, paradoxically, an expansive wedding as a group delight can be much less expensive than long-term investment for individual enterprise. But the mechanism of the market militated against the villager's accumulation of capital at least until certain technicalistic traits should be already developed. He was in a vicious circle. For so far as the villager's own cultural ways did not, in fact, develop in a technicalistic direction, he was doomed to material and moral alienation from the larger order of which he was a part.

The expansive weddings took on a sinister meaning: they came to imply more a spiralling individual debt in a context of impersonally pitiless law, than a re-affirmation of a now basically compromised social integration. Each new generation must still have its weddings, however costly: the alternative was a dreary withdrawal into unrewarding private isolation. But the financial effects of the weddings were no longer cushioned by village solidarity and internal autonomy. In the uncorrupt law courts, money-lenders could exact the last penalty for improvidence. The villagers fell into an impersonal servitude to the money-lenders; with the suppression of local violence, the villagers were steadily degraded by law rather than occasionally wiped out by lawlessness.

The sound government of Bengal did, indeed, succeed in suppressing pestilence, famine, and warfare, the three great scourges of earlier citied societies. The population, whatever its economic level, now could grow if it had only a bare subsistence; and it did. In the course of the century, the population increased unprecedentedly, but unlike that of the industrialized countries, it had all to stay on the land. As the land became increasingly crowded, the villager was pinned within whatever his village already possessed. The mobility into opener lands which had allowed enterprising groups—even whole castes—to raise their status, was steadily more restricted. The social order became more rigid. The rigidity was capped by a new sort of ruling class at the top. It was neither agrarian, to be grown into; nor military, to be overthrown by new adventurers; it was technicalistic, and could only be approached if the nuclear institutional traits of technicalized society, not merely its irruptive effects, were assimilated. Even with Islam, a Hindu could always enter the charmed circle by conversion, chiefly a matter of realigning one's loyalties; but one could not be converted to Englishness except, at best, through a thoroughgoing redesigning of one's personality in a complete educational experience.

The British ruling class, then, held sway in splendid, unquestionable, isolation. In rank just below it, it protected a landed gentry which was conceived in the new legalistic terms and so tied to the British interest. The whole structure was expected to be a 'permanent settlement', from the peasantry up to the governor-general. An overly hasty attempt at this produced in Bengal a 'permanent' revenue settlement which, as it worked out, displacing the men *in situ* and overriding traditional peasant rights, added to the social dislocation. Its poor working in the Ganges area led to setting up a system somewhat more favourable to the peasants in other areas; but the spirit of the various policies had the same tendency to rigidity everywhere. Benevolent as the new absolutism might be, its great tendency was to ease and perpetuate the new order of complementary dependence on Britain.

In such conditions, the more ambitious did naturally try to become Anglicized, even at the risk of sacrificing their own inherited cultural identity. Already within the generation of 1789, there were individuals who advocated some sort of Europeanization. The Persian and Sanskrit traditions suddenly looked outworn and heavy with age. These traditions were challenged from within on the basis of new premises inspired by the new masters. Even more important, the new English learning attracted the brightest, or the most ambitious, students. The Sanskrit and Persian traditions began to pale; their disease was an onset of gradual social starvation.

The internal transformation of British rule in Bengal was quickly followed by the definitive occupation of India as a whole. Hastings had already begun to assert the latent British superiority when, in sending an expedition straight across the subcontinent from Calcutta to Bombay in 1782 and defeating an alliance among the chief Hindu and Muslim powers, he proved the British to be an all-India power. But in 1784 the government in London tried to prevent any further adventures of the kind, barring any aggressive war or interference in the affairs of the Indian states.

It was the situation in the wider world during the following generation, as much as that in India itself, which utterly reversed this cautious policy. To assure the position of British traders generally, and in particular to forestall the rise of any great empire (out of the fluid condition of Indian politics) which might be hostile to British interests, the British found themselves in a position to make supportive alliances with various Indian powers and did so. From 1765 to 1792, the British held Bengal and Bihar, as well as the Andhra coast, a district around Madras, and the small island of Bombay. They had considerable influence in Awadh, up the Ganges, and in Tamilnad (the 'Carnatic'), both still Muslim-ruled. The other major powers, occupying most of the subcontinent, were Mysore in Kannada, and Haidarabad in the heart of the Deccan, both Muslim-ruled; the Marâtha confederacy (Hindu) across all the central parts of India, whose primary ruler was at Poona in Mahârâshtrâ, and which controlled the titular Timurid emperor at Delhi; and a number of Râjpût and Sikh states in the northwest, under the shadow of the threatening Afghan power. Already by 1792, to prevent the aggrandizement of Mysore, the British, in alliance with Haidarabad, annexed considerable territory in the far south. But by 1798, when Wellesley became governor-general, it was clear the British must advance further or recede. The ruler of Mysore was in alliance with the French, who hoped to displace the British from India; and Haidarabad and other states were using Frenchmen to train their armies in modern methods. In 1798–99 Wellesley subdued Mysore and made its remnant a British protectorate. Between 1803 and 1805 he broke the power of the Marâthas and ensured the military pre-eminence of British power throughout India. He developed the system of administering directly only selected areas in each part of India, leaving the remainder under Hindu and Muslim rulers in 'native Indian states', which, however, had to accept British controls. After a period of renewed caution in London, a subsequent governor-general completed the process between 1813 and 1818, in the years of Napoleon's defeat, making dependent allies of the remaining Râjpût and Marâtha rulers and establishing the unquestioned political paramountcy of Britain from the Thar desert in the west to the Bay of Bengal.

The new patterns introduced into Bengal quickly spread, with local adaptations, through the rest of India, particularly those parts which the British administered directly (an ever-increasing proportion). In the next generation, their internal logical consequences were being quickly unfolded. In 1829 came the first major official measure of social reform, the abolition of suttee among Hindu women. Already in 1827 the supremacy of Islamic culture in India had been symbolically ended when the British ceased to offer even a token allegiance to the puppet Timurid emperor at Delhi for their lands. Yet it was not till 1835 that an English education (and hence an English cultural background) was offered as the normal preparation for government service, finally replacing Persian as prime requisite for any Indian youth who wished to gain a good position.

The British conquest of India may profitably be compared with the Muslim conquest. Superficially, they each introduced a new culture which was then gradually assimilated in many respects, setting apart religion, by the subjected Hindus. In fact, however, the two conquests were remarkably different in their implications. It is not merely the much greater rapidity in the British case. It is true that the Muslims commonly evinced a greater social power than the older Hindu culture, before it adopted many Islamicate elements, seemed to possess. But the difference was one of relatively minor degree. Hindu states were soon able to attempt come-backs, and such Islamization as they had undergone was of secondary importance in those come-backs. What the modern British introduced was a radical difference of kind. The assimilation of the new culture meant a basic structural transformation of both Hindu and Muslim life, which in comparison with the modern standards seemed much on a level. Not only were new standards set up in law, in administration, in medicine, in science, even in the very nature of religion itself. Whole new social classes have eventually been created, the relation between country and city has been changed, the character of civilization itself and of all civilized traditions has been put in question.

The new order in Egypt and the Ottoman empire

The Ottoman empire, in the years of the British conquest of India, remained politically independent. Instead of Occidental conquest, it saw the launching by Muslim rulers, of measures aimed at adopting just so much of the new Western methods as would lead to renewed Muslim military power without compromising Muslim independence. In their degree of success and its consequences, as well as in their areas of failure, they illustrate the ambiguous alternative to a conquest such as occurred in India. For in fact the measures taken amounted to establishing polities and economies of complementary dependence to the West as a whole, 'colonial'-type régimes analogous to those established in India.

As we have seen, after defeating Austria and Russia in 1739, the Ottomans retained till 1770 an imperial sway nearly as extensive as it had been at its height in the sixteenth century, except for the important loss of Hungary; though Ottoman central power and its control in outlying territories, especially the Maghrib, was far weaker. By 1774, however, the Ottomans, in war with Russia, had lost their control of the Black Sea and in 1783 Russia annexed the large territory around the Sea of Azov. A potential conquest seemed at hand. Like some of the Indian rulers, the Ottoman rulers tried to meet these defeats by subjecting at least parts of the armed forces to European training. In this they were slower and less successful than the Indian rulers at first; perhaps because after the breakdown of the Timurî empire the Indian rulers were mostly new men, with fewer traditions to bind them, they faced less entrenched resistance than did the Ottoman rulers. But the relative strength of the Ottoman state, and especially the mutual deterrence of the European powers, allowed the Ottomans more time than any Indian state was given. The Russian advance was stopped and neither Austrians nor Frenchmen were allowed to take its place. In the Napoleonic period, at any rate, the Ottoman lands were not conquered outright.

The reforms at Istanbul itself seemed at first to be abortive and their full accomplishment took another generation.[13] Selîm III came to the throne in the midst of further war with Austria and Russia, in which the Turks barely managed to get by with only minor losses. In 1792, with a respite of peace imposed by European considerations (the explosion of the French), he undertook a far-reaching military and political reform of the empire, which he named the *Niẓâm-e Jadîd*, the New Order. This partly involved restoring the older centralism—which, from the absolutists' viewpoint meant pruning away abuses—just as in Bengal the British had in part simply to restore the good order of Timuri times. Thus the curbing of the unruly Janissary troops had been a concern of absolutistic Ottoman sultans for generations, and Selîm now turned to it as a primary task. But partly it involved a progressive recasting of the social patterns of the capital so as to support a policy of orderly and profitable economic and cultural dependence on the West. The administrative practices must fit in with Occidental expectations and the whole empire must be opened up to rationalized exploitation. It had long been impossible to restore the old institutions, and now even the superficial adoption of details from the Occidental technical store, such as the absolutists in the eighteenth century had attempted, was no longer sufficient. The intestine wars in Europe afforded only a respite from a common European power much greater than before and determined on having a world order satisfactory to itself. Still disunion within Europe could delay its force. But even among the Ottomans the new commercial relations, for which the new 'law and order' were required, were becoming indirectly a greater concern than older trades and agrarian interests. The undermining of the luxury crafts had presumably contributed to Janissary control of the guild system that remained, and anyway had eaten away the better leadership of the guilds element, so sapping the alliance between the 'ulamâ' and the townsmen. For a time, that alliance still had a veto power, but it could act at most only

[13] [Author's added note: The reforms of Selîm (and also those of Meḥmed - 'Alî a few years later) should be seen as still based on an acceptance of traditional norms; see H. Inalcik,'Traditional Society', in D. Ward and D. Rustow, *Political Modernization in Japan and Turkey* (Princeton University Press, 1967).

negatively. For positive results a more thoroughgoing new orientation must be found, not based on the expiring local industry and trades.

Selîm, with some of his court, was interested in the ideas of the French Revolution, though in the character of enlightened monarch rather than of radical democrat. For help in reorganizing his state he turned at first to the fount of modernity who was modernizing Europe itself—Napoleon. In 1806, however, the conservative 'ulamâ' and the Janissaries were able to stir up Istanbul against him and by 1807 he, his fellow-reformers and, outwardly, his reforms were dead. But the die was cast. His friend and successor, Maḥmûd, was able to learn from his mistakes and to profit from how he had opened men's minds. Patiently, step by step in the next two or three decades, he produced in more practical form those changes Selîm had envisaged, and more. When the Janissaries next showed their incompetence in the war (after 1821) against the revolting peninsular Greeks, there proved to be a sufficient 'public opinion' concerned for stability and dependability in the governmental power to allow Maḥmûd to destroy the Janissaries and initiate a new type of absolutism, using new Western technical methods and devoted to maintaining the type of order the Europeans wanted—and to win their support at last.

Meanwhile, however, one of Selîm's lieutenants was having a more immediate and spectacular success in his province of Egypt. Perhaps more than anywhere else in the empire, economically centralized Egypt had seen its luxury trades replaced by Occidental competition; higher grades of cloth, for instance, came almost entirely from France, chiefly through Levantine hands. The social order was correspondingly undermined. Yet the Occidental presence had remained overtly more strictly commercial than in more variegated parts of the empire. In 1798 Napoleon landed in Egypt, ostensibly to protect French merchants there from local misrule, but more especially as a base of operations against the British in India. The Egyptian Mamlûk troops were helpless against him, having maintained still less than other Ottoman troops an awareness of modern military developments. The population generally was likewise relatively parochial in outlook. The French set up as much as they could of the apparatus of the Enlightenment on Egyptian soil: modern hospitals, impersonal administration, scientific laboratories (they set about, among other things, recording in scientific detail the non-technicalized ways still prevailing, which were presumed about to vanish before modern French civilization); they invited the astonished local savants to inspect the show and acknowledge the moral superiority of the Revolution—claimed to be true Islam. What is more, they carefully worked out plans for turning Egypt into an orderly and prosperous economy which would complement the French economy to everyone's common benefit.

By 1801, when the French had to evacuate as a result of British interference, Egyptians were aware that the world had changed since the last Frenchmen, as undisciplined medieval knights, had vainly attempted to invade an Egypt too civilized for them. In the chaos which ensued, by 1805 there rose to mastery of the country one of the Ottoman commanders who had been sent against Napoleon: an Albanian, Meḥmed-'Alî, a selfish, illiterate genius (1769–1848).

Meḥmed-'Alî, supported by Muslim Albanian troops, first restored the Egyptian government to something of its former effectiveness. In 1807 he was able to resist a passing British attempt to intervene; by 1811 he had broken the power of the Mamlûk troops and slaughtered their chiefs (success at a point where, in the corresponding case of the Janissaries, Selîm had failed); and by 1813 he had established Egyptian rule (under Ottoman suzerainty) in the Ḥijâz, where the reforming Wahhâbîs of Najd had overthrown Ottoman rule in 1803–4. But Meḥmed-'Alî was not satisfied with this sort of power. He was alive to the vast possibilities open in the new age, and aware that unless he took advantage of them he could not long enjoy even the power he had, for a minor success against the British was no long-run assurance of independence.

From the beginning, Meḥmed-'Alî set about centring control of all the lands of Egypt in his own hands, soon (by 1812) withdrawing all land assignments and introducing a direct interference by the central state into the land relationships within the village, which had formed the heart of the traditional social structure. Over the less formal council of village shaykhs he instituted an *'umdah* (headman) responsible to the state.[14] The landed endowments of the pious foundations were confiscated along with the other lands and the schools and other institutions which depended upon them were made directly dependent on the state.

With the old social order ripped open and all power for the moment centred in the ruler (not an entirely unprecedented event), he went on to more fundamental changes which prevented the situation from ever reverting. To begin with, he retained French advisers; indeed, in time most of the plans which the French occupiers had worked out were put into effect. He set up, on modern presuppositions, an administration which proved a very effective instrument for his further plans. He soon established a marketing monopoly over all commercial industries and crops, putting himself in a position to manipulate the whole economy. By 1820, he had launched several projects which, as they were pursued, transformed the Egyptian society into one linked complementarily with the European. He began to restore the old canal system, parts of which had fallen into disuse even long before the eighteenth century, when it was further damaged. But he restored it in the perspective, if not always by the methods, of his modern engineers; the restoration proved the first step in a total reconstruction of the Egyptian irrigation system which eventually dispensed with the ancient annual flooding altogether. His single

[14] The increasing importance of the village headman in this period has been studied by Gabriel Baer, 'The Village Sheikh in Modern Egypt (1800–1950)', *Studies in Islamic History and Civilization*, Scripta Hierosolymitana, vol. 9 (1960), pp. 121–33.

most momentous move was to introduce, on the lands which came under state control, an improved variety of cotton for export to the British textile mills, now mechanized and ready to absorb an indefinitely expanding quantity.

From here on increasingly, the economy of Egypt was tied to the international market. When Lancashire suffered a panic henceforth, the Egyptian peasant cultivators were made to feel its effects directly. The commercialization of Egyptian agriculture, which steadily followed, bore only superficial resemblance to the days when Egyptian tribute-wheat formed the mainstay of Byzantium or of Medina. The old staple wheat was replaced with a non-edible and market-fluctuating crop, and eventually Egypt had to import much of its food on terms dictated by the modern international price system. The rapid increase in Egyptian production was soon paralleled by a rapid increase in the population; for modern medicine also was introduced, to check epidemic disease, though it could as yet do little to help the daily health of the individual peasant. All this was administered with a relative efficiency which left few channels of escape.

The net result (not unlike what happened in Bengal) was great wealth and power and even legalistic security in the ruling circles, in a close, if dependent, relationship with European interests. Even the peasants benefited after a time from a (temporary) wave of rural prosperity, but they had lost many of the traditional social compensations which a loose administration and a multiplicity of local centres of authority had afforded. Cultural institutions sometimes suffered severely. Its endowment rationed out by the state, the Az'har was forced to stop trying to teach philosophy and astronomy and music and restrict itself to law and theology, leaving wider subjects to the new European learning—such as it was. Its narrowness, already marked by modern standards, was intensified. The most hated expression of the new tyranny was military conscription, as efficient as, if less patriotic than, that of the French Revolution. Conscription, however, turned the Arab peasant into a soldier, allowed Meḥmed-'Alî to dispense with his Albanian troops, and made Egypt the centre of an external empire not only in Arabia but also in the Nile Sudan and finally (when Meḥmed-'Alî turned against his Ottoman suzerain in 1831) in Syria. It also provided the students for the schools of medicine, of engineering, and of modern languages which Meḥmed-'Alî later created in the hope of freeing himself from dependence on his European specialists. It was in this way ultimately the instrument of making ordinary Egyptians to some degree into active and not merely passive participants in affairs.

Meḥmed-'Alî succeeded in overcoming the deadening effects of the eighteenth-century Occidental competition and in making the most of the new Western world order. In this sense, he geared Egypt into the modern technicalistic order; and he did it, both economically and politically, without direct subjugation to Europeans. He failed dismally, however, in an attempt to make of Egypt a modern state on a technical level with those of western Europe. The human material he had to work with had not been prepared by the two or three centuries of gradual transformation which the Occident had known; indeed, it had been affected negatively. The finer craftsmen Egypt had once known had lately disappeared. When he tried to introduce modern factories at a single blow, his manpower proved inept and the supporting technical resources were wanting. He was reduced to depending on animal power to run machines, with expectedly poor results. The pupils recruited for his schools—even when the problem of language was somehow solved—had no idea of how to learn a science based on its everyday procedures directly on indvidual, experimental, innovative inquiry. They were drawn inevitably from the Az'har madrasah, where they had learned to memorize the ancient books and dispute loquaciously with their masters on literary details. But memorizing an engineering textbook could not make an engineer, and instead of disputation there must be manual practice, which was regarded as socially degrading. In all aspects of Meḥmed-ʻAlî's more technicalistically-minded work, despite occasional brilliance, there was this sort of hollowness.

In 1833 and again in 1840 he found that his empire still rested on the sufferance of the European powers, which could thwart his moves at will, if they were agreed on a policy. He was even forced to give up his marketing monopolies, as inconsistent with the individually based commercialization which European trade presupposed and which now supervened also within Egypt. After 1840, he abandoned further concern with his ambitious schools and acknowledged that for the time being, though independent in form, Egypt must content itself with a dependent position in the civilized order as a whole.

The Volga Tatars and Turkistan

The Great Transmutation had taken place among the west Christian peoples of Latin heritage in the western part of the European peninsula. All these lands had more or less common institutions at the core; hence in all these lands the Transmutation was at home, in the sense that any innovations it required could build on much the same foundation. All had possessed feudal political institutions; all had developed at least the elements of post-feudal nation-state structures. All were familiar with the same literary and religious heritage in its Latin form and had participated in the High Medieval and Renaissance developments of that heritage. There were close social and economic ties among all these peoples; innovations in one place were readily known and not uncommonly paralleled everywhere else, for similar circumstances and problems tended to prevail, at least in the corresponding sectors of each people.[15]

[15] Specific effects of late eighteenth- and early nineteenth-century changes in a

As a result, the changes were everywhere a matter of piecemeal modification in established institutions, never of wholesale replacement of them. When various monarchs in the eighteenth century determined to reform and improve their governments and societies, none of them felt this to be a matter of imitating some more advanced country even though they might in fact borrow a certain number of points from France, say, or England. These 'enlightened monarchs' and their courts felt the movement of reform to be simply 'enlightenment'. It was regarded, that is, not as adopting alien ways but as making natural improvements in their own ways. In the most backward and the most advanced countries, much the same attitude prevailed, and rightly; for in each country the 'enlightenment' grew out of local thought and initiative responding to the local forms of what were at all stages common problems and common aspirations.

The peoples of eastern Europe, with a Greek and Orthodox Christian heritage, did not move within the same institutions and social presuppositions as those of the Latin-using Occident proper; but they shared the same ultimate traditions, and at all periods there had been much commercial and cultural and even political interchange between the Greek and the Latin halves of Christian Europe. Until the High Middle Ages, the Christian Occident had continued culturally and economically tributary to Byzantium, at least as regards the more refined levels of its life; even politically, the most advanced parts of Italy owed allegiance to Byzantium for a long time. In the course of the Earlier Mid-Islamic Period, the direction of dependence was gradually reversed. By the Late Mid-Islamic Period, parts of Orthodox Christendom were under Occidental political rule, both in the east Mediterranean and in the heart of Orthodox Slavic territory; this political rule answered to a measure of economic domination by German and Italian merchants. Much as the Orthodox Christians continued to look down on their Occidental brethren, there was an increasing cultural interchange also; Christian Europe continued to have a largely common life, even though eastern Europe did not enter intimately into most of the evolution through which the western European lands were all passing.

Accordingly, by the end of the eighteenth century, under Peter the Great, the Russians were sufficiently close to the Occidentals, and their more active elements sufficiently alert to what was happening among them, so that they could be brought to an active assimilation of the results, up to that point, of the Transmutation; they entered into the process of the Enlightenment, its scientific, industrial, and even in some measure its social advances, at a sufficiently early stage so that (though always consciously apart from the Occident, which invariably seemed to be a few steps ahead), on the whole their level of social power did not lag sufficiently to put them on the wrong side of the development gap. Though it required the sheer mass as well as the

Lebanese mountain village may be examined in W. R. Polk, *The Opening of South Lebanon, 1788–1840* (Harvard University Press, 1963).

still imperfect technical development of the Russian nation to make this possible, yet in the eighteenth century Russia became one of the great European powers.

In this way there came into being a single 'Europe', basically west Christian or Occidental, but including on a more or less equal footing the east European peoples, at least such as possessed independent states. This new Europe, including Russia (and joined to some degree by the extra-European settlements overseas and in Siberia), came to represent the active forces of the Great Transmutation as it impinged on the rest of the world. (It is this new European grouping that can be called henceforth 'Europe' in the exact sense.)

Of this new Europe, the Muslims of the Volga region, Turkic-speaking descendants of the old Bulghâr nation, formed a part: an increasingly active part. After their conquest by the Russians in the fifteenth century and the subsequent shattering of their landed leadership in the Russian drive for conversion, their territory came to be shared with Russian settlers, so that they gradually ceased to form even a majority in their own lands. But they retained their mercantile élite intact. The tsarina Catherine of the Enlightenment, in the latter half of the eighteenth century, determined to integrate the Muslims, or 'Tatars', into her empire on an equal basis; and in certain respects she succeeded. The Volga 'Tatars' were relieved of most of their remaining civil disabilities; above all, of restrictions on residence in cities, and of harassments intended to force conversion to Christianity. They entered forthwith on a course of economic expansion in which they entered actively into the new world of commerce and even of industry.

In the generation of 1789, Tatar enterprise took two forms. Protected by Russian law against foreign Muslim commerce within the Russian territory, and strengthened by the increasing Siberian trade, the Tatars were able to seize leadership in the central Eurasian trade from the merchants of the now impoverished Zarafshân cities; it was merchants from Kazan who could trade freely at once in Bukhârâ as fellow-believers and in Moscow as fellow-subjects. Like the Russians with whom they sometimes formed partnerships, the Tatars then turned to investing in relatively large-scale industry at home, where Kazan became a manufacturing centre; and while their new industry was not on a level with the most modern west European factories, being still semi-artisan in type, it was sufficiently advanced to hold its own in the more backward Russian scene. The madrasahs of Bukhârâ kept their premier position for some time, and even increased their hold on the Volga Muslims, as regards social and literary practices, yet economically and even socially at last, the leadership fell to the Volga Tatars. For their colonies, which gradually multiplied in all the Russian conquered Muslim lands, were like those of Russians in representing the new technicalistic tendencies (within limits), yet maintained their close links as Muslims with the local populations.

Yet the Volga Tatars remained insistently Islamicate, not only in cult and creed, but in the whole imaginative dimension of culture; and their Islamicate culture was, for some time, modern only in its technical mechanics—in using the printing press, for instance—not in its substance. Kazan in the north, their cultural capital (to which Astrakhân on the Caspian, in the new age, became distinctly secondary as to culture, though not as to commerce) was a major centre of Muslim printing, but this printing was long in Chaghatay Turkish, Persian and Arabic; and it was mostly a matter of re-editing old books, or of new books written in the manner of the eighteenth and even earlier centuries. The Tatars not only kept up their social contacts with their fellow-believers in the Syr and Oxus basins and the neighbouring mountains—in what may be called Turkistan; they even assimilated their dress and social habits closer to those of people who were their chief customers, though these latter were little touched by the nuclear tendencies of the Technical Age.

It was thus under Tatar auspices that the Syr and Oxus basins early in the nineteenth century turned to raising cotton for export to the burgeoning Russian market. Without a Napoleonic expedition or a Meḥmed-ʻAlî, and oriented to the technically less developed Russian factories, the quality of the Turkistani cotton was not seriously improved until later in the century. There were no local experiments, thus early, in modernized administration nor even (despite an interest in Western arms) in a seriously modernized military, not to mention modern schools or newspapers. The Tatars retained a willingness, for some decades yet, to do business on something like the old basis. Yet even in Turkistan, in Muslim territory more inaccessible to the new avenues of the world commerce of the Technical Age than any other save the inner Sûdânic lands, the basic economy entered upon the path of modern commercialization, forming what very soon proved to be a complementary dependent relation to the modern Russian economy—and with it particularly to that of the modernizing Muslim Tatars.

Yet these Tatars themselves, though they went beyond any other Muslim peoples, not only adapting their mercantile traditions to the new age but actually entering into, and even locally taking a lead in, manufacturing enterprise, carefully cut themselves off from the intellectual aspects of the new life. Later in the nineteenth century, as modernization was intensified among the Russians, they found their enterprises seriously hampered by this limitation.[16]

[16] See A. Bennigsen and C. Lemercier-Quelquejay, *The Evolution of the Muslim Nationalities of the U.S.S.R. and Their Linguistic Problems* (Oxford University Press, 1961).

II

European World Hegemony: The Nineteenth Century

The generation of 1789 had seen Europe come to exercise an ultimate hegemony over the Islamic peoples. Whether a European power ruled directly or whether there was merely a generalized dependent relation to the European social order as a whole, it was in the power of the Europeans, if they were agreed on a policy, to enforce their will in most Muslim lands. In any case, no independent general Islamic leadership was to be tolerated. Indeed, the only major outright conquests at the time were those of the British in India and those of the Dutch (with some British intervention) in the Malaysian archipelago. During the eighteenth century the Dutch had extended their hold over the independent Muslim coastal ports in the archipelago, and in the Napoleonic decades they extended their power inland over the Muslim agricultural kingdoms in Java and Sumatra. Henceforth they exercised paramountcy in most of the archipelago except for northerly parts, including Malaya, where the British remained. In the Maghrib, where the mutual raiding between the north and south shores of the Mediterranean had been a way of life for so long, the eighteenth century had already seen a curbing of Muslim 'piracy' by Christians grown newly responsible themselves; but only after the turn of the century were the Maghribî corsairs finally suppressed, a process in which even the new North American republic took a hand.

But even in a land so relatively off the main European lines of interest as the Qâjâr realm in Iran, the pressure was determinant. Beginning in 1800, when the Russian tsar was proclaimed king of Christian Georgia (then in revolt against the Qâjârs), the Qâjârs found that their new-won monarchy was facing Russian aggression in its all-important Caucasian region. Whereas two generations before, the temporary Russian advances after the fall of the Ṣafavîs had been on a level with the Ottoman advances (and as easily beaten back by Nâdir Shâh) now, there was no displacing the Russians once they had moved in. Before long, the Russians had occupied much further Caucasian territory and a good part of the key province Azerbaijan, and the Qâjâr ruling element had become fully aware that only a counter-alliance with another European power—on commercial and political terms dictated by that power—could save them. They made such alliances alternately with the British and with the French, each power moving in its general advisers and its military officers and insisting on the ouster of representatives of the other as the price of its good will. At last the most which such intervention (only half-hearted after the end of the Napoleonic wars) could achieve was to reduce the Russian presence from a leisurely conquest to a mild protectorate.

International law and the rationale of world rule

It had always been a function of government to legitimize and stabilize the rights which the stronger were to have on the basis of one or another status, and so to exclude alternative impositions by them. This continued as the primary function of government in the technicalized lands. But with the primacy of individual technical achievement came the rise to power of the class of moneyed enterprisers who, in its early forms, pre-eminently represented such individual achievement. From their viewpoint, all ascriptive statuses, such as those inherent in a person simply by descent, tended to be subordinated to the one status of proprietor: it was in their common interest to allow the legitimations only of the market, in which ownership and legal right practically coincide. Such became the principle of the European hegemony.

The security of property rights against arbitrary interference or suspension, either from a government itself or from more local powers which a government ought to be controlling, became, then, not merely one ideal but the supreme obligation of a sovereign government in the Western state system of the Technical Age. If in a given society the existing government was able to assure the Europeans of this, the Europeans commonly agreed to respect it as sovereign and admit it to a place in the recognized international order analogous to what the European states accorded one another. It was then expected to obey the various rules which the Europeans had evolved to govern inter-state relationships, called 'international law'. Any pre-existing bodies of custom, such as those holding among Muslim states, were given at most a secondary and local recognition so far as they could be fitted into the European principles.

If, however, a government failed to assure 'law and order'—that is, the security of property interests, particularly those of Europeans but by extension those of local merchants on whose activity the Europeans might depend—or if, in particular, it violated the rules of inter-state intercourse established by the Europeans, then it forfeited its rights of sovereignty. In that case, it was held legitimate for one or more European powers to intervene to protect its subjects' interests and those of the other Europeans. Depending on the jealousy of other European powers and the degree to which local resistance might prove inconvenient, the intervention might lead to any degree of control, from having officials changed, to complete occupation and administration. (In principle, it was not recognized that a European power could be permanently defeated by local resistance; it was a bitter scandal when the Italians later met such a defeat in Abyssinia.) Even apart from any control of dependent governments, however, it early became customary to insist that Europeans and their foreign protégés be under the jurisdiction of their own consular officials (stationed now all around the world) who would try them by their own European legal standards in any case of accusation, rather than entrust them to local courts. This special jurisdiction, called extra-territoriality, was generalized from the case of Islamicate dhimmî courts, run by a man's co-religionists; but under European hegemony it was extended so that the foreign jurisdiction claimed superiority to any local one. Thus Europeans would not be at the mercy of a lesser power even in those states recognized as sovereign.

On one basis or another, the chief imperial European powers—France, Britain, and Russia—continued to expand their direct control in the Islamo-Asian regions during the century. From 1830 the French occupied the central part of the Maghrib, the Ottoman territory of Algiers, and though a remarkably able and devoted leader arose, 'Abd-al-Qâdir, to champion Muslim independence in the part of the country that was not occupied at first, and though he made a point of honourably abiding by all agreements with Europeans, he was finally hounded down like a rebel. The fate of the more closely held Ottoman provinces, however, was a concern of all the main European powers, and by and large they were subjected to no more than a joint protectorate. The largest expanse of Muslim lands remaining relatively open to any interested European power was that lying between the Ottoman empire in the east Mediterranean and the British empire in India, and northward. Here the British and the Russians were rivals. The Indus plain had formed part of the Indo-Timurî empire. Ruled by petty Sikh and Muslim powers, it was sufficiently unstable politically to invite British intervention lest one of the local powers grow strong enough to trouble the related territories already under British paramountcy; by 1849 it had been subdued. But most of the territory, either Iranian or Turkic-speaking, was relatively inaccessible from the centres of European power.

By the end of the eighteenth century, the lands which had been dominated by the Ṣafavî and Özbeg monarchies were divided into a number of relatively small town-centred states, which controlled only loosely the pastoral tribes of mountain and steppe. In the course of centuries, the range of the Iranian-speaking population that had been predominant over much of the area had receded; the Turkish of the steppe tribes had come to prevail among peasantry and townsmen in most of the lower-lying lands north of the Iranian plateau itself, so that the old Persian towns Marv and Balkh (Mazâr-e Sharîf) were now Turkish-speaking. Even in the mountains of Azerbaijan west of the Caspian, and at the headwaters of the Syr Darya, north of the Pamirs, the population was mostly Turkish. Within the Iranian-speaking area, some more aberrant local languages had been disappearing, however, and from the Pamirs to the mountains of Fârs some dialect of Persian proper was spoken; in the mountains of the farthest west, however, the Iranian language was Kurdish; in those of the farthest east it was Pashtô (language of the Afghans).

The most important state in the region was the monarchy established by the Qâjâr Turkic tribe, heir to some of the central Ṣafavî traditions, with a capital at Tehran, near the earlier Rayy. It ruled over much of the Caucasus region, especially Turkish-speaking Azerbaijan on the one hand, and over the Persian-speaking plateau of western Iran on the other. It exercised more or less suzerainty over much of Kurdistân, over the Arabic-speaking plain of the lower Dujayl, and over the western parts of Persian-speaking Khurâsân. Its official language was Persian, as was that of the other Turkish (and Afghan) courts in Iran and Turkistan. Though only a little more than half the Persian-speaking population was within its borders, it was called 'Persia' by Westerners. The great majority of its population, Turkish and Persian, was Shî'î.

In the further eastern parts of the Iranian-speaking area there were several states, much the most important being the sultanate of Kâbul, ruled by an Afghan dynasty and controlling many of the Afghan-inhabited mountain valleys as well as a large Persian-speaking area. This state came to be called abroad, and eventually at home also, 'Afghanistan'. The majority of its population, both Afghan and Persian, was Jamâ'î-Sunnî.

In the Syr-Oxus basin to the north, the great Özbeg monarchy had long since broken up into several smaller khânates, notably those centered on Khîveh, Bukhârâ, and Khoḳand. To the east of the Altai passes, the Muslims were under Chinese rule. The whole vast Turkish-speaking area, including the Tarim basin under Chinese rule, was called 'Turkistan' and the several states in it were named after their capital cities. They were almost entirely Sunnî, as were the pastoral tribes of the great Kazakh steppe to the north, loosely grouped under independent Khâns.

Since Shâh Ismâ'îl's revolution, zealously adopted in much of the Iranian and Caucasian highlands and as zealously attacked in the Syr-Oxus basin, Shî'î Iran had been at odds with Sunnî Turkistan. By geography the two areas were painfully bound to one another: many Shî'î captives, regarded as unbelievers, were taken as slaves to suffer in Turkistan; the legendary rivalry of Îrân-and-Tûrân was applied anew to the two regions. But the most important bond, by the nineteenth century, was the common shadow of the Russian power. By 1813 the Russians had occupied many Caucasian areas, including large parts of that Azerbaijan which was the military mainstay of Qâjâr rule. In 1828 they imposed a treaty on the Qâjârs which gave them control of the Caspian and rights of interference in 'Persia', including extra-territorial rights like those embodied in the Ottoman Capitulations. At the next succession, the Russians, in concert with the British, escorted their candidate to Tehran. The loss of much Turkish-speaking territory accentuated the Persian character of the Qâjâr kingdom, though the bulk of its armed forces continued to be recruited in what remained of Azerbaijan.

Towards the middle of the century, and after a long period of increasing commercial exploitation through the Volga Tatars, Russia began to absorb outright most of Turkistan, west of the Altai passes, and at last even some of the independent Persian-speaking highlands in the upper Oxus region (called Tâjîkistân). It left the Özbeg khânates of Khîveh at the mouth of the Oxus, and Bukhârâ along the Zarafshân, autonomous but surrounded by Russian territory. (The Russians strongly garrisoned Samarqand, which they had occupied in 1868.) The Afghan and the Qâjâr Persian kingdoms were independent to the south, but the Türkmen tribes of the Kara-Kum deserts, whom the Qâjârs tried in vain to control, were subdued by a Russian railway which also put the Russians in a position to interfere in Khurâsân. The British, mistrusting a Russian advance toward India, counteracted the Russian influence effectively in Afghanistan, but were not able to match the increasing Russian influence at Tehran. They retained commercial supremacy in the Arabic-speaking areas of the Persian Gulf and eventually established protectorates there, in both the formally Ottoman and the formally Qâjâr zones. But in most of 'Persia', Russian manufactures had become the commonest imports in the Persian markets and the Russian presence the most important single external political factor. The most the British could do was to freeze the frontier beween Tehran and Kâbul midway, in Khurâsân. It happened to be in Khurâsân at the start of the century.

This was indeed the net result, in one respect, of much of the imperial activity of the European powers: to freeze boundaries, to freeze dynasties. The Europeans made a great point of inventing boundaries where they did not exist and defining them in permanent settlements where they did exist, at whatever point they seemed to have reached at the moment when the Europeans came to take an interest. This was but one aspect of a general imposition of a legitimistic international order: with the boundaries defined, it was clear which government was to be held responsible for any given stretch of territory and no further disrupting quarrels were to be allowed. But even more serious was the imposition of dynastic legitimism. The Europeans insisted that in each of the states so defined, there must be a sovereign monarch whose succession must be fixed, after the European manner (though not necessarily by primogeniture), so that the nuisance of succession disputes should be eliminated. But with the suppression of free military competition, still another regulative force was blocked; as with the weakening of the higher trade guilds, this blocking made it all the harder to rise to the European challenge. In the course of the century, several protected dynasties of India, guaranteed against revolt by the British, degenerated in despotic irresponsibility, sometimes to such an extent that even with the help of British advisers they could not maintain the required law and order and had to be replaced by direct British administration. The same process was begun in the Iranian-Turkic regions when the Russians made sure that the Qâjâr scion whom they regarded as the 'legitimate heir' succeeded to the throne in 1834, though he was a youth of no special competence. The British interfered more than once in the succession at Kâbul to assure themselves a 'friendly' ruler there, without as full success as they would have liked: politics in the Afghan mountains proved harder to freeze.

The phase of initial resistance

Naturally, the first response to the imposition of European world hegemony was resistance. In still 'independent' areas, the rulers led the resistance. But the more far-seeing rulers saw in the threat of continued and increasing Western encroachments a compulsion to modernize their armies—that is, to make them as much as possible like Western armies—and, to introduce enough other changes in administration, and sometimes even education, to support the new armies. Such changes themselves evoked bitter resistance. Still more so did the corresponding changes being introduced under direct Western rule. Such resistance remained at this time essentially a conservative one, itself almost untouched by the new social ways, though evoked by them. But sometimes it did already imply some renovation within the older cultural forces themselves.

During this early nineteenth-century generation Meḥmed-'Alî continued (till about 1841) to push his innovations within Egypt and Syria. He won the favourable smiles of Western public opinion, but the increasing hatred of his subjects. The Syrians, who had at first welcomed his armies as ridding them of corrupt Ottoman oppression, soon hated him for the efficiency with which he levied the few but heavy legal taxes he retained, disarmed the people to end their feuds, and finally conscripted them for state service. With European help they were shortly rid of him: the Egyptians loved him little more, and his whole dynasty inherited some of his taint, though resistance then was effectively stifled.

In the northern parts of the Ottoman empire, Maḥmûd (1808–39) was struggling to do much what Meḥmed-'Alî was doing, and was rousing a resistance at once less deep and more effective, in proportion to his efforts, which, as well as his successes, were less drastic. Maḥmûd faced a bitter situation. Not only was the empire suffering the economic dislocation already mentioned. The various Balkan Christian nationalities of the empire, having already in the eighteenth century associated closely with western Europe, were soon aflame with a nationalistic feeling (well before it had developed among the Muslims). Increasingly they were wishing to carry out their own Westernization as independent states. As a result, their rebellions seemed ready to dismember the stricken empire.

Their success was restricted by the limited amount of European support they won, but this was overmuch for the Turks. In the course of Maḥmûd's reign, Russian interference in the north cost the empire many remaining Black Sea territories and the autonomy of small states in Rumania and

Serbia, while joint European interference in the south permitted a small independent Greek kingdom to be established, to which henceforth the important Greek element throughout the empire would be bound to have a certain inclination. In the southeast, Egypt itself, of course, also became in effect independent, and for the time being even Syria (and the Ḥijâz) were lost. Indeed, as his reign closed, European intervention was required to save from Meḥmed-'Alî's arms the half of the empire which remained.

Yet in the reduced territories which he still controlled, he and his ministers were able to establish a fisc and police sufficiently centralized and up-to-date to permit the state subsequently to carry out such modern measures as all elements could agree on. Skilfully they played off the autonomous gentry against the 'ulamâ' and Janissaries of Istanbul till the government was able to bargain itself into a basis for real power, including central conscription. Only in the last years of the reign was it possible for outright 'Westernizers', trained in the diplomatic service or in the reformed administration rather than in the court tradition, to 'Westernize' the forms of governmental procedures. Schools for teaching the modern knowledge were set up. The wearing of the fez, a truncated cone-shaped felt hat, was introduced to identify Ottoman subjects without regard to their faith, replacing (at first among government employees) the miscellaneous headgear setting off 'ulamâ' from darvîshes, merchants from princes, Christians from Muslims. In all such measures, the small band of Westernizers were resented not only by the lower 'ulamâ' but by most of the Turks generally. Maḥmûd dared destroy the Janissaries only after they had helped him reduce the greatest of the autonomous gentry and at a moment when their obvious military incompetence had lost them respect even among the city conservatives. Opposition to the fez particularly became a symbol of the popular dislike.

The same generation saw the great early reforms in India and the launching of English education there. Criminal law and education were both made to conform in essentials to modern British standards under the leadership of the historian Thomas Babington Macaulay. In the midst of this, some private Hindus in Bengal early began to press for Westernization of Hindu life, although very few of the Muslims, who felt themselves socially displaced, did so.

A great many leading Muslims acquiesced passively in the new order, in so far as it assured them their wealth; but those who did not—for instance, those who lost their privileges and gained nothing in return—could be all the more embittered, as the changes were occurring under infidel rule and not under Muslims, as in the Ottoman domains. Some of these found a new application for the tradition of Islamic reform that had been growing in the eighteenth century. With Wahhâbî doctrine established in Mecca, pilgrims were readily inspired with purist ideas. The consequences in India were not unparalleled in some other areas; though few, if any, Indians became actual Wahhâbîs, the vigour associated with Wahhâbism might have helped inspire many of them to a militant defence of Islam against the lax relations with infidels that had been prevailing. A number of internal reforming movements became popular among the lower classes in northern India. In Bengal the most extreme insisted that Muslims had no right to exist complacently in lands where Islam no longer ruled: Muslims must either rise and overthrow the infidel government as contrary to God's good order, or else leave and resettle in genuinely Islamic territory. This doctrine served to justify violent action by Muslim peasants against the new landlords, Muslim and Hindu, which the British 'permanent settlement' of the revenues had established. While most of the 'ulamâ' of the school of Shâh Walîullâh, dominant in the Ganges plain, remained loyal to the modus vivendi established between the Timurî court and the British, some, more active, gave the resistance movement intellectual leadership and a certain political validity, especially in the Panjâb, beyond what could be carried by peasant guerilla forces.

The next generation saw a final effort in India at a restoration of the pre-British order. In what the British called the 'Sepoy Mutiny' but what some Indian historians have dignified as a national rebellion, the 'Sepoys', Muslim and Hindu troops maintained by the British, revolted throughout most of northern India in 1857–58, gained the support of much of the landed nobility and some rulers of 'native states', and tried to re-establish the rule of the Timurid emperor at Delhi and of his former Muslim and Marâtha vassals. The rebellion failed, however, to produce any new political principle and was put down piecemeal as soon as the British gathered their forces. The Muslims were burdened with the chief blame for the rebellion, from which they might have had the most to gain.

The phase of upper-class accommodation

In the beginning of the century, in India as everywhere, some of the remaining rulers had acquiesced more gladly than others. In any case, changes had been pushed from above; from below had come chiefly resistance. But as it came to be generally realized that the Islamic societies were to be indefinitely at the mercy of the West, so did the more ambitious strata in the population themselves begin Westernizing projects. Following the revolt of 1858, a great many Indian Muslims, including some rulers of states, began to realize the importance of Muslims' entering into Modern life and culture at least sufficiently to receive their share of government positions under the new régime. By 1875, under the leadership of Sayyid Aḥmad Khân, a Muslim college was founded at Aligarh (a bit south of Delhi), which taught on the one hand the Muslim religion and on the other hand the modern European arts and sciences, the latter in English. Thereafter the Muslim youth had no need to risk going to Christian or secular schools to learn the new knowledge. Aligarh college rapidly became a centre for all the more vigorous Muslim life in India.

Thus came to Muslim India a period of eager co-operation on the part of the top stratum of Muslims with the cultural forces of the Modern West. Such a period had come in some other Muslim lands even earlier. Among the Ottomans, after Maḥmûd's death his reforms from above were now accepted and justified by a new generation of the upper and upper middle classes. The reforms which Maḥmûd had introduced were given occasion above all by military needs. Whatever men felt about Islamicate and Western civilization, the military strength of Europe must be met, so that Ottoman independence could be retained, even if one's whole purpose was to remain in every sense Islamic. Those who desired a more general change, together with the more perceptive of at least those absolutists who did not, could agree on the need for military reform. Indeed, from the beginning, Muslims had almost never ceased to adopt new military methods wherever they were to be found, and for some centuries many Muslim governments had been glad to adopt Occidental methods in those military points where the Occidentals had latterly been proving superior. But effective military reform required more and more a general Westernization of the armed forces and even, as became increasingly evident, of the civilian governmental régime (to support the military) and of the social habits of important strata of the population as a whole (to support the civilian government). With the new reign of 'Abdülmejîd (1839–61) was officially launched an overall reform programme under the heading simply of 'regulations': 'Tanẓîmât'.

The official purpose of the Tanẓîmât was to put into force the current European standards of law and administration, with civil equality and standard liberties for all. Some of the purposes could in principle have been fulfilled by restoring the vigour of the earlier Ottoman government: thus corruption and inefficiency were no part of the ancient Turkish heritage, and bureaucratic responsibility for general good order had been an Ottoman strong point. But other intentions of the Tanẓîmât implied the direct adoption of (Modern) European principles. There was some hope on the part of the reforming ministers to limit the sultan's power of arbitrary interference in government, in favour of the predictable impersonality of the apparatus. Persons of all confessions were to have identical legal standing—an innovation resented by Muslims and of doubtful benefit to non-Muslims, who were accustomed to a wide sphere of autonomy within their own communities and did not necessarily welcome direct governmental jurisdiction. A public, secular university on European lines was to be established, in defiance of the 'ulamâ' and in the face of the nation's almost universal sense of the religious function of learning. The great minister of the Tanẓîmât, Reshid Pasha, at first attempted even such liberal measures as ending *corvée* (forced labour by peasants on public works in lieu of taxes) and establishing the right of peasants to move away from their village, at least in the Balkan provinces. Not only did the gentry resist their application but the Muslim peasants seem to have been indifferent, while the expectation of such liberties gave the Christian peasants a further motive for rebellion when the Muslim gentry blocked them.

The reforms seemed to fail woefully in their official purposes. Europeans ridiculed the parodies of European ways which often resulted: officials in European garb who neglected to fasten their buttons at the most essential places; persisting corruption behind absurd red tape. The decrees did not restore the old Ottoman efficiency, nor could they transform an Islamicate heritage into a heritage of Christendom. Such projects as that of a university tended to stay chiefly on paper. When (on the principle of equality) the special taxes levied on non-Muslims were abolished and non-Muslims were supposed to be inducted, like Muslims, into the army, in fact the army remained Muslim, while non-Muslims paid instead a commutation tax to avoid military service. Little seemed to have changed except the names of things.

Nevertheless, the reforms on paper formed the fraction of the iceberg above the surface of the water; they reflected a far more basic re-alignment of social forces in the course of the century. The centralization carried out by Maḥmûd did mostly persist and was gradually strengthened. This was no doubt crucial, but still more basic was a change of spirit. This was reflected above all in the proliferation of modern Western-type private schools of many varieties, many sponsored by Christian (and Jewish) missionary groups and patronized by the moneyed classes. The sons of the privileged classes learned French and sometimes got to know Victorian European notions better than anything from their families' own past. The spirit of modernization and co-operation with the West went far in introducing the physical apparatus of nineteenth-century life over the face of the cities.

The international position of the Ottoman empire illustrates how far it had accepted an integral role in the new international order. Tripolitania, at the eastern end of the Maghrib coast, had been as autonomous as any other Ottoman province; but in 1835 the central government found itself able to land troops and re-establish direct Ottoman rule there. The Ottoman régime may be compared with that which the French were establishing at the same time in Algeria. The Ottomans did not do the job nearly so well, but they attempted the same sort of things: they reorganized the police to ensure a complete network of legal control and organized a centralized local administration; they then encouraged firstly olive planting, and secondly integration, as a complementary economic dependency into the international market. In 1853–56 the Ottomans found themselves, in the 'Crimean War', allies with the French and British, whose troops fought alongside the Turkish troops in a war from Turkish bases against Russia. At the victorious end of the struggle, they accepted explicit membership in the otherwise 'Christian' diplomatic system of the Concert of Europe: full-fledged membership in Europe itself, a logical culmination of the Tanẓîmât.

In short, in the main areas of Islamdom, the middle generation of the nineteenth century was one in which governments, and at least the moneyed classes of the people, were both pushing assimilation to modern Western life. Resistance of any kind was for a time at a minimum; acceptance of Western leadership and control, and even outright trust of Western good intentions, were at a maximum. Muslims so learned to see themselves through European eyes that they accepted identification as 'Eastern', allowing themselves to be lumped miscellaneously with Hindus and Chinese, their international status determined by their relation to the Great Western Transmutation rather than by their own civilizational past. They gradually even learned a certain solidarity with the other groups which were likewise 'Eastern' in European eyes.

It was in this period that the Qâjâr Shâh, Nâṣiruddîn (1848–96), began to find his greatest pleasure in royal tours of Europe and was highly flattered by being honoured with a European chivalric order. He assured his European acquaintances that he despised his own subjects and was eager not only for the personal financial rewards but for the national improvement of his realm. As he saw it, this could result from selling concessions to European entrepreneurs to build railways and telegraph lines and manage any other enterprises that promised profitability through efficient exploitation (although, when some of his own subjects published a journal in which they appealed to Europeans to contribute advice on the national problems which the journal would expound, Nâṣiruddîn suppressed it directly). Nâṣiruddîn, however, found no great product wanted by Europeans to which to turn his country, and Persia remained a backwater, internationally speaking.

The sultanate of Zanzibar was more typical of those countries which did discover a special niche in the world market. In 1832, Sayyid Sa'îd, lord of Musqat in Arabian 'Umân (1804–56), settled on Zanzibar the better to control and extend his dominions along the Swahili African coast. His government at Musqat had already bound itself to special relations with Britain in the Napoleonic period and these relations continued; in particular, he had to sign a treaty with Britain putting serious limits on the slave trade, a staple source of income to the traders along those coasts. But he knew how to use the new order profitably and made up for losses in some sorts of commerce, by turning much of Zanzibar island into a clove plantation for export. He also put much effort into opening up the hinterland of his Swahili coast ports, establishing trading posts inland which also became centres of local military control owning his supremacy. In such areas, where Europeans were not yet ready to go, the Arab traders penetrated and brought ivory and hides to be taken round the world by the Europeans. On his death, however, the British navy intervened (on a plea of preserving legitimate succession) to separate Zanzibar as a sovereign state independent from Musqat, so weakening both.

Sayyid Sa'îd had lived in patriarchal simplicity, but his son and second successor, Barghâsh (1870–88), made a point of Westernizing the style of

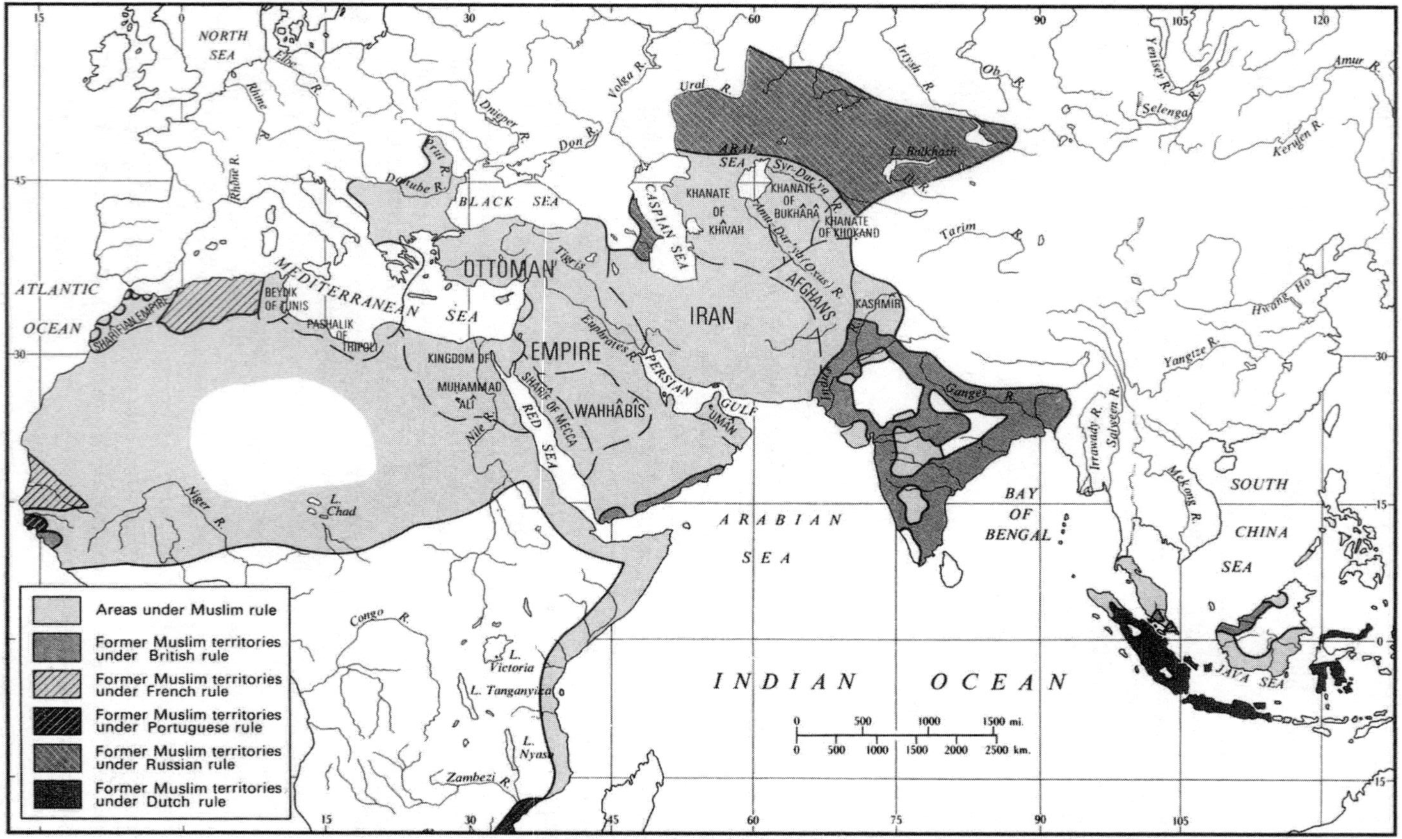

The central Mediterranean through India, mid-nineteenth century

his court and the appointments of his capital. In his time, however, European powers divided his inland dominions between themselves on the plea that his control there was not effective. With the loss of that income, the borrowed splendour of Zanzibar was reduced. Meanwhile, the British had insisted that the slave trade be banned altogether. Barghâsh could do nothing. Like his contemporaries 'Abdülʿazîz in Istanbul and Ismâʿîl in Cairo, Barghâsh had over-extended himself, planning his Westernizing expenditures without a sound financial base; so that by two years after his death, the British felt obliged to step in and take over the administration, though the sultanate was officially maintained in the islands.

During this period, despite an often unmistakable use of power for profit, some of the best features of Western leadership were showing themselves. We have seen how many-sided was Western domination, taking more often indirect forms than direct, and showing itself in its cultural and intellectual presence as well as in political and economic controls. While many irruptive effects of the advent of technical times could take place without any particular contact with the nuclear side of the modern ways of life, the development of an effective role of complementary dependence in the technicalized world order carried with it a significant amount of such contact. The police and the military establishment had to be technically developed to maintain the kind of order Europeans required. The financial and commercial, and to some degree even the productive, side of the economy, where the cash crop or mineral was concerned, likewise required technical adaptation to the world market. Finally neither military nor economic technicalism could work well without a certain amount of local intellectual awareness of modern norms. Whether there was any direct rule or not, all of these technicalistic features were to be absorbed only by direct or indirect tutelage to the West.

This whole complex of influence, often very subtle, is what gradually came to be called 'imperialism', a term which covered far more than outright conquest. Subsequently almost every aspect of this domination came in for a harsh judgment, being seen in the context of the whole. Sometimes, however, more conciliatory persons could approve many aspects, such as the teaching of modern science, the practice of modern medicine, the assertion of the rule of an impersonal law. One of the chief vehicles of these things was the missionary movement, which had been built up especially since the start of the century and was now a major element of the Western impact. In this mid-century period of relative good feeling, the missionaries were often welcomed.

Technically the purpose of Catholic and Protestant missionaries was to convert non-Christians to Christianity, but at least in Islamic lands (even within the Russian empire, in net effects) their actual function tended to be rather different. It early became apparent that few Muslims were likely to be converted; partly because of social pressure, including the death penalty against apostasy which many Muslim communities were willing unofficially to apply, but perhaps more because the Muslims generally felt their own way of worshipping God to be at least as universal and at least as pure as that of the Christians. In some areas, such as Russia and Indonesia, conversion was of some importance among local minorities which had not yet turned Muslim. But in the central areas, Catholics had long since turned to working among the local Christian groups, and when Protestants arrived they did the same thing. This led to sad schisms within the various eastern Christian communities. Perhaps more important, it also led to a relatively rapid adoption of Modern standards among many of these groups. The Christian part of the population acquired the new scientific and cultural skills in the missionary schools, and soon the Muslims themselves began to attend the same schools, and use the same hospitals, not to be converted, which they usually were not (except, on what proved to be a temporary basis, in Russia), but to absorb the Modern way of life in its secular aspects. In this role, the western Jews were not far behind the western Christians in sending out missionaries to their co-religionists.

Thus the Catholic, Protestant, and Jewish missionaries, as it turned out, went far toward bringing into the midst of the Muslim peoples much of the more inward spirit of Modern times which merchants and soldiers were not in a position to convey. Even where, later, the bulk of the new educational institutions were established by local governments, they were largely inspired by the missionary schools.

The self-perpetuation of the development gap

Nevertheless, the introduction of nuclear traits of the Technical Age into non-Western lands did not necessarily imply a gradual transition through a condition of complementary dependence into increasingly technicalized social patterns, such that the power gap would be erased and all lands would become developed technicalistically on a level with the Occident. In fact, the dependent position of the non-Western lands proved self-perpetuating: under world market conditions, the development gap seemed ready to yawn ever greater and more decisive.

One might have expected that the Islamic societies would have had special advantages in assimilating technicalistic social patterns. The Islamicate commercial and cultural network had played a central role in Afro-Eurasian history in the agrarianate period: its relatively urban character and high social mobility, with its geographically focal position, gave it an expansive flexibility. Yet now these traits were being eroded away rather than reinforced. The overall configuration of Islamicate society was disrupted even geographically. The primacy of the old-Islamic area from Nile to Oxus, which had been formative even for the empires that had grown in the European and Indic regions; the cultural interdependence of the central Eurasian commercial region on all sides of the steppes; the interrelations of the different coastlands of the Southern Seas—such lines of contact and development of the Islamicate society were weakened or even disrupted and replaced by such common ties as those which arose through being dominated by a single European power. New centres of influence arose. On the one hand were centres of European influence, such as Kazan, displacing Bukhârâ; and Calcutta or even Bombay, as publishing centres, rivalling Delhi and Lucknow. Counterbalancing these in some measure was a new importance gained by some out-of-the-way areas as foci of resistance: Najd in Arabia as the Wahhâbî centre, or inner Cyrenaica as home of the Sanûsiyyah ṭarîqah.

A most striking shift was the decline of Iran, its tradition as a cultural arbiter and the rise of the eastern Mediterranean lands. Istanbul, as seat of the strongest remaining 'independent' power, drew increasing respect, so that its ruler was able, toward the end of the century, to claim the caliphate as successor to the all-Islamic rulers of early days; and its Turkish language gained a somewhat less wide recognition as the official language of Islamdom. Cairo, as the most active centre of the Jamâ'î-Sunnî eastern Arabs, finally attracted into its orbit in greater or less degree the Maghrib and West Africa and most of the Southern Seas region, while Arabic and its literary tradition were given renewed attention everywhere, partly through the stimulus of Western Islamicistic interest. Young people commonly wanted to reject the immediate past, which Europeans condemned, in favour of a half-fancied remoter time which even European historians could be seen to admire. In this spirit, in many Muslim minds by the turn of the century, Ṣûfism, Persianate ways and cultural degeneracy were associated one with the other, and contraposed to Shar'ism, Arabism, and ancient Islamic glory.

In fact, the Persian tradition had ceased to be a vehicle of international understanding and mobility and had become a practically irrelevant classicalism cultivated by literary élites. The Ṣûfî organizations, undermined since early in the century by the failing of the guilds and by the centralizing of the governments, who often took over the waqfs, had likewise ceased to be a vehicle of urban stability and cosmopolitanism and had been left stranded as depositories, too often, of superstition and conservatism. The detailed Sharî'ah itself, it must be added, from being a means of universal mobility had become an obstacle to accepting the new, European, international standards. Though historically the rejection of a later, Persianized, Islamicate culture in favour of an ideal pre-Ṣûfî, pre-Persian purity might be fallacious, yet it reflected a reality: the apparent advantages which the Islamicate international society might have had as a basis for a modernization of its own had been largely destroyed, and the remnants of what might have been advantageous traits appeared as hindrances. This phenomenon represented the most general cultural aspect of what was repeated in many details: the very existence of the development gap tended to undermine whatever might have made it easier to bridge it, and even to reinforce whatever could serve to widen it.

As we have noted, the question is not why the Muslim lands lagged behind in technicalistic development, but why they did not 'catch up' (whether this was ultimately desirable or not). Here one is dealing not with what might be called a strictly 'economic' problem, but with a total cultural problem, of which economic activity was but one aspect. The old institutions that might have been built upon were being broken down; but even the new, more or less technicalistic institutions which might have been expected to be the nucleus of a more general development suffered intrinsic weaknesses. Alien in origin, they created a gulf within the Muslim societies themselves, answering to the development gulf in the world at large. Often enough, those who carried on the new commerce, the financial systems, the new scientific and intellectual skills were alien to the main body of the Muslims: Levantines in the east Mediterranean, but almost equally foreign elsewhere sometimes: Indians in 'Umân, Arabs on the Swahili coast, Tatars in Turkistan. But even when they were not, the scions of the old families became alienated from their cultural environment to the extent that they became adapted to technicalistic society. The Muslims who had been to the new schools, coming from home backgrounds where the new skills and attitudes were little prepared for, were often but ill-trained in the new ways; yet they became dissatisfied with and alien to the old. They might well be mistrusted, and mistrust themselves, as having gone over, in practice, to the enemy without even the reward of being able to beat him at his own game.

This inner psychological gulf created by the fact that technicalistic traits had to be borrowed abroad, in forms developed for an alien culture, was perpetuated by the economic consequences of initial inequality. This latter produced cumulative changes to reinforce the inequality, more often than countervailing reactions to reduce it. The less highly developed the resources of a given area, the less likely it was that the presence of a few technicalistic installations—railroads, oil fields, even rationalistically planned commercial crops—would serve as a stimulus to other, more balanced developments within the economy. Outside the specialized islands of 'colonial', or dependent, economy, attempts at technical development would be nipped in the bud by advanced Western competition, as surely as the old crafts had been withered in their bloom by it. Return on capital was bound to be higher where development was more extensive and, in normal circumstances, such local capital as there was tended to be exported. Accordingly, when the population, universally rising under cover of the elimination of the great scourges, passed the limits of expansion provided by the relatively rigid dependent economies, further increase in population served only to dilute any secondary positive effects of dependent development that there might be.

Later, theorists in the dependent societies were to complain of the tendency of the long-run terms of trade to deteriorate as between an agricultural country and an industrial one. Certainly the market of the one-product dependent economies was both unpredictable and inclined to be inelastic in demand, as compared with the markets of more balanced and industrial economies. But the deterioration of the terms of trade was but a symptom of a wider fact of nineteenth-century international life: to those who had was being given, and from those who had not was being taken away even that which they possessed.

The phase of rising nationalism

Under the impact of such circumstances, what had been a living civilization, an autonomous social context for the unfolding of the creative possibilities of a lettered tradition, was being transformed into a bloc of nations sharing a common lettered heritage, to be sure, but no longer forming an independent civilization, creative in its own terms. Amid the debris of what had been a spiritually vital world civilization, frustrated by the indignities and even the insoluble dilemmas of a nationally dependent condition, a younger generation was impelled to try to carve out new channels of aspiration, of spiritual creativity. By the end of the nineteenth century almost everywhere Muslim societies were entering the phase of rising nationalism. Even in societies where involvement in the new world order had got under way relatively slowly, the phases succeeded each other that much more rapidly. The phase of initial resistance had soon passed into that of upper-class accommodation. Now, under the pressure of the increasing tempo of world events and in response to the deepening frustration of Islamic civilizational consciousness, the phase of rising nationalism came with even more nearly a chronological simultaneity: beginning in the east Mediterranean in the 1860s, it was very widespread by the 1880s in one form or another.

Whereas the very top layers of society might remain satisfied with the modus vivendi worked out with the West, more ambitious members of that class or less satisfied members of classes slightly lower on the social scale wanted to change the terms of the bargain. In this phase, much of such goodwill as existed toward things Western was breaking down. Zeal for modernization continued strong and pervaded still larger circles in the major countries, but it increasingly led to a breach between people and rulers of an opposite kind to that which had occurred at the start of the century. The more advanced and younger elements—the products of the new schools—opposed their local rulers in the name of more fundamental reform, and in so doing also opposed the power of the West as a whole. In the end, the whole complex of Western domination was to be opposed as 'imperialism' in the name of the overall cause of reform and modernization which was formulated as 'nationalism'.

In Egypt the new nationalism made its most dramatic early bid for power and met its first decisive defeat at the hands of the West itself. The independent Turkic rulers of Egypt in the nineteenth century had made of it a showcase of modernization in its more external features. In few other lands had the breakdown of the pre-technical economic and social patterns gone so far as in the land of Meḥmed-ʿAlî, and probably in no others had there been so marked an increase in commercial prosperity and even political power under a régime of complementary dependence. The Egyptian peasants, for the first time in millennia, had formed great victorious armies, and Egyptian cotton was bringing high prices to those who controlled the land; and gradually this came to include a rising number of Arab Muslims. The citizenry of Cairo, Levantine or not, were as assimilated to European norms as in any Muslim city. The prosperity served to make Egypt, particularly Cairo and Alexandria, the centre for a long time of eastern Arab cultural activity—even many Syrians came to work there. But the very prosperity, power, and modern awareness which appeared in Egypt served to accentuate the sense of frustration of its Muslim Arab population, highlighting how small a relative share they had in it.

The Khedîv Ismâʿîl (1863–79) was an ambitious ruler, whose stated goal was to make Egypt a part of Europe. His predecessor, Saʿîd, had begun this tendency, but Ismâʿîl was a model of accommodation to the European world order. The dependent order which Meḥmed-ʿAlî had founded in the hope of building something else, Ismâʿîl perfected with remarkable consistency. Co-operating with Western capital interests, he introduced in Cairo (and Alexandria) all the modern conveniences of a European capital, waterworks, gasworks, even a grand opera house in which Italian troupes sang. His Europeanization was not purely a luxury veneer: under Ismâʿîl, after a cautious period following Meḥmed-ʿAlî's experiments, the government opened great numbers of modern schools and encouraged French culture among the well-to-do classes generally. At all points, his policies served to hasten and improve on the dependent participation in the European economic and financial nexus which Meḥmed-ʿAlî had assumed. He had factories built for processing sugar; but his greatest interest was cotton. During the American Civil War, with cotton prices high, he and other large landholders turned to raising cotton more massively than ever. He invested in improved irrigation works and abandoned even the Egyptian shares in the Canal company for the sake of raising more cotton.

His greatest public triumph was, in fact, the opening of the Suez Canal in 1869 in the presence of European royalty. This had been launched by Saʿîd and might seem a mere renewal of the several Red Sea canals which had served at various times to link the Mediterranean with the Southern Seas through Egypt, and to give Egypt a master position in the interregional economy. But under the conditions of the Technical Age, it did not strengthen Egypt politically, but rather swept it even politically into the tug of European rivalries. (It was this latter consideration which had helped dissuade earlier rulers, less trustful of Europe, from approving the project.) At the same time, he carried through an ambitious military policy:

he persuaded the Ottoman suzerain to allow him military autonomy, and sent his multiplying armies to occupy more of the Nile Sudan and the Abyssinian highlands (in which latter area, however, they were beaten out by the Ethiopian forces). Again the ambition recalled earlier Egyptian feats; but this time he hoped to increase the European trade in which Egypt would serve as intermediary; true to this goal, he tried to replace the slave trade, dear to Meḥmed-'Alî but abhorrent to European consciences, with an exchange between raw materials and the products of the new factories. But such ambitious projects cost money, which he confidently raised from European sources; and with the uncertainties of the cotton market and the mistrust of the better European financial circles, finally he found himself inextricably in debt to world finance.

Through all this, Ismâ'îl saw no reason for popular institutions—which might oppose modernization and which were not generally encouraged by the Europeans in dependent lands. Ismâ'îl retained a close grip on personal power (despite an experiment with a representative chamber of notables); and he executed that power (as had all his dynasty) largely through Turks and other non-Arab elements. But the more fortunate part of the local Arab population were gaining wealth as village headmen and self-confidence as soldiers. As they became more conscious of their potentialities as landowners, educated officials, and army officers, they resented Ismâ'îl's policies. By 1878, Ismâ'îl's financial over-extension had led not only to threat of bankruptcy but to direct European intervention: the Powers insisted on a system whereby they controlled the finances through a foreign Christian-run national council; they even had the Khedîv replaced by his more pliant heir.

At this point, Arab officers in the army, already resentful, and perhaps also fearing a forced reduction in military expenditure, led a move to demand a constitution to restrict the monarch and to replace the European intervention. They were encouraged and supported by many civilians of the lesser ranks, especially the more active among the growing Arab gentry and the young 'ulamâ'. The Khedîv was forced to make Aḥmad 'Urâbî, as leader of the Arab officers, minister of war; but when 'Urâbî tried to eliminate the European control, the British (the only European power ready to act at the time) bombarded Alexandria and then in 1882 occupied the land in the name of the Khedîv, suppressing 'Urâbî's resistance and exiling the leading malcontents. They restored the absolute monarchy under their own tutelage.

Under British occupation, the British consul-general served as resident, empowered to intervene wherever he saw fit. The most important of the British residents, Evelyn Baring Lord Cromer (1883–1907), a highly cultured, observant, and dedicated man, represented a classic Modern Western attitude to those peoples who had not participated from within in the Modern Transmutation; to their place in the world, and to their nationalism. He found them (in this case, the Egyptians) a backward race, needing to be protected and guided by Europeans for their own good as well as for the safety of the Europeans. Cromer had opposed the decisions which, by exacerbating relations with 'Urâbî, he felt had made necessary the British occupation; he had hoped that a minimal measure of European control would be sufficient to ensure European interests. This was not, however, because of concern for the Egyptians (for them, British rule was the best possible fate), but because of the burden on Britain. He did not rule out the possibility that these junior partners in the human race might eventually share in European progress enough to learn to rule themselves in a European-led world. But he could not see their becoming fully civilized unless it were by being fully Europeanized—a dubious prospect. At best, 'Orientals' would require institutions consonant with their own not wholly rational spirit. Islam, in particular, he felt, was in its nature opposed to progress. In response to the idea that the Islam he was acquainted with might be changed for the better, he asserted that no part of the Islamic system could be changed without undermining the whole, that 'reformed Islam is Islam no longer'.[1]

Cromer's attitude presupposed the general ignorance of world history at the time, which allowed Europeans to imagine that they had been in the forefront of human progress for two or three thousand years and might be expected to remain there. But it was founded also on hard experience. He saw in Ismâ'îl's financial troubles, correctly, something more than sheer personal ineptitude, and though his historical and psychological analysis of the pattern in question was very naïve, he did pinpoint matters which the nationalists had to contend with if they were to succeed.

In expounding on 'the abuses which spring up under Eastern governments wheresoever they may be situated', he hesitated to relate the more horrifying incidents that could be told of some members of the Egyptian dynasty, for want of sure confirmation in some cases; but the milder stories he did tell were sufficiently illustrative of what he thought of as 'the want of mental symmetry and precision, which is the chief distinguishing feature between the illogical and picturesque East and the logical West . . .'.[2] The steamer of Ismâ'îl's predecessor, Sa'îd, once got stuck in the mud when the Nile was low, and he ordered the steersman to receive a hundred lashes.

[1] Earl of Cromer (Evelyn Baring), *Modern Egypt* (New York: 1908), vol. 2, p. 229.

[2] Cromer, *Modern Egypt*, vol. 1, pp. 5 and 7. (The following story appears on p. 20.) The parts of Cromer's book which deal with his views on the Egyptians and with British policy in Egypt provide an impressive documentation of the European imperialist viewpoint at its best. Cromer, who had come from the Indian Civil Service, was an intelligent and cultivated gentleman, who felt himself to be deeply concerned for the Egyptians and devoted to their welfare. He admits his own inability to make sense of 'Orientals' (he knew some Turkish, the aristocratic language of Egypt, but no Arabic, though had he known Arabic it would have made little difference); this incapacity explains why his book leaves out of consideration whole aspects of Egyptian life. Nevertheless, he presents cogently aspects of what happened, during the period of fullest British rule, which a post-imperial age may forget.

When it got stuck again, he roared out, 'Give him two hundred', whereupon the steersman jumped overboard; carried back, he explained that he feared further flogging more than drowning. Said Sa'îd, 'Fool, when I said two hundred, I did not mean lashes but gold coins' and the steersman was given a bag of money. Cromer added, correctly, that many 'Orientals' would be far more struck with the generosity of the gift than with the injustice of the flogging. But from the viewpoint of technicalistic social standards, we must make a distinction. Murders, extortions, and exquisite tortures of the most degrading sort were frequent enough at Muslim ruling courts to shock and disgust the Modern Western observer, but they were duly chronicled as evil and unjust by serious Muslims themselves. What was perhaps too commonplace to have shocked the traditional Muslim, except from the idealized perspective of the Sharî'ah, was the want of an impersonal, predictable, legally guaranteed context for individual decision and initiative and, more especially, the want of even minimum assurance of a level of personal inviolability as between man and man, whatever their relative ranks.

The cited incident suggested to Cromer a further 'Oriental' trait: the inconsequence in Sa'îd's behaviour, which to Cromer exemplified a general mental inconsequence and want of symmetry. Here, again, we must make distinctions between what belonged to pre-technical life patterns and what was merely misunderstood. The mental inconsequence of which Cromer complained dissolves, upon analysis, into a number of components no one of which proves so radical as he supposed. He gave a number of lamentably typical examples of inaccuracy of thought and word. Such inaccuracy sometimes simply expressed a sense of decent good form such as could be practiced in a more intimate and leisurely age. But it could also answer to rational calculation under pre-technical conditions: it might spring from reasonable fears (such as those of a peasant who concealed his substance before men who might prove tax-gatherers' agents) or from a sober sense of proportion in a pre-technical age (for instance, casualness in calculating time, where saving a few minutes could cause inconvenience without materially enlarging the possible scope of a man's achievement). Most of such forms of inaccuracy could have been well attested in the pre-Modern Occident. With these genuine imprecisions of thought, Cromer confounded all those culturally conditioned differences of expectation that baffle any close intercourse between cultures unless the stranger is of an exceptionally sympathetic and long-suffering turn of mind. He could not understand why a man would awkwardly twist round his right hand to point out something on his left side; for he overlooked the common practice, salutary under some circumstances, of restricting the left hand to the less clean operations.

Finally, he linked to the 'illogic' of the 'Oriental mind' all the morally defective social patterns which the anecdote of the steersman can suggest; and which indeed came to light under agrarianate conditions everywhere at whatever point the protective cloak of group affiliations was rent by catastrophes, such as warfare, or the presence of an absolute monarch. But of the moral equivalent of this, in technicalized society, a later generation has become more painfully aware than Cromer's generation generally could be.

However mistaken Cromer was in his historical evaluation of the 'Oriental mind', his way of perceiving it was almost inevitable for most Occidentals and determined the attitudes of many of the best of them toward the populations and institutions of Muslim lands. At the same time, the realities that gave rise to these perceptions did have to be dealt with. They formed a cogent occasion for European intervention on behalf of European public standards anywhere that Europeans were attempting to work or live; and they formed a major obstacle to surmount in any attempt by Muslim populations to assimilate technicalistic ways for whatever purpose.

The British were occupying Egypt to protect the rights of their own and other European subjects; rights, that is, as interpreted by 'civilized' standards, or in other words, Modern Western ones. Accordingly, payment of the foreign debts naturally had financial priority. Ismâ'îl's over-confidence had been such that these debts consumed a major part of the state revenues. After the debt had been taken care of, however, Cromer and the British were eager to improve the lot of the common Egyptian. Their first reforming moves were against the personal indignities which degraded the peasants: notably the free use of the lash by anyone in authority (especially in exacting the payment of taxes), and *corvée* in which peasants were forced to contribute unpaid personal labour to state purposes in addition to their taxes. As a contribution to a predictable context of individual initiative, they insisted on minute registration of landownership within villages—so reducing all the complexities of customary law to a single legal standard. They also abolished some of the more vexatious petty taxes, such as reforming Muslim rulers had always tried in vain to abolish. However, with a modernized system of accounting introduced at the same time (to the disgust of the traditional Coptic account keepers, who lost their monopoly) and with a Modern system of police and of courts, these reforms were made to stick. At last, they undertook works of technicalistic public utility, notably the first Aswan dam, which completed the control of the Nile waters which the Cairo barrage of Sa'îd's time had begun: with additional canals, irrigation came to be year-round almost everywhere and the old natural flooding was done with.

As we shall see, most of these reforms had a negative aspect: for instance, the elimination of customary law was sometimes calamitous for the poor, and the new courts often made so little sense to them that their net effect was to introduce a new form of injustice. But nationalist Egyptians at the time paid more attention to other shortcomings. The privileged financial and commercial position of the foreigners in the land could not be done away with by an authority whose *raison d'être* was to protect the legal position of those foreigners; even the modifications Cromer wished to introduce were vetoed by the European Powers. The mass of the Egyptians continued to face this initial disadvantage in any enterprise. Still more important, there were no financial resources available, under Cromer's internationally sound management, to encourage education as it had been encouraged under Ismâ'îl, despite Cromer's belief in its value. But most important, the Egyptians found themselves culturally homeless. The older civilization was gone as a framework for creativity. But under the British, even more obviously than under Ismâ'îl, they were dependents, in all ultimate historical decisions, upon an alien world; and they were further than ever from entering that world on an equal footing as a modern nation.

The same situation was increasingly felt elsewhere. In Tunisia in 1881, the French took over in a move parallel to that of the British in Egypt, despite eager efforts by a local élite at indigenous modernization. In the Ottoman empire, with better preparation than in Egypt, but following a rather similar period of bankruptcy through foreign debt, the reformers tried in 1876 to introduce a constitution. The West, however, which held ultimate power, stood complacently by as the sultan 'Abdülḥamid abrogated it and used all modern facilities to establish a repressive despotism, receptive of Western investment and Western financial controls, but deadlier than Cromer to any liberal reform.

It was after such easy defeats of the first attempts at reform in some degree from below, that nationalism began in earnest as a mustering of all available social power to form a nation able to stand independently on a level with the European nations in the modern world. Nationalism in the Occident, in its most developed form, had arisen from the French Revolution, when the French learned to act as 'a nation in arms', no longer as Normans or Gascons or Burgundians, nor as first or second or third estate, but as equal citizens of a common fatherland from whose weal all would gain and from whose woe all would lose in all that mattered. It was through some form or other of such a nationalism that the various European states were able not only to throw off an incipient French imperial sway but to build the modern technicalized institutions on which the French power in Napoleon's day was founded, and on which the other states proceeded to build a like power. It gradually became clear to the would-be reformers in Muslim lands that individual public-spirited patriotism was not enough; what must be built was nations with a truly national spirit. Only then could the impersonally efficient institutions of a mass society cut through the maze of personal and parochial loyalties which divided the population and made unworkable any general schemes for reform. Men must learn to think of themselves first of all as Egyptians committed to a common Egyptian destiny, or as Ottomans, Iranians, or Indians and any lesser social identifications must be functional and related to the nation as a whole.

Egyptians, Ottomans, Indians? Men must identify themselves in some such workable units, to be sure, but what ones? Was not an Egyptian also an Ottoman? Could a Christian be an Ottoman? Or could a Muslim be anything but a Muslim; were not the Copts the only true Egyptians? What was India, what did it mean to be an Indian?—an entity imposed rather by a conquering British government than by anything in nature. What was Iran?—the accidentally annexed domains of the Qâjârs: was an Azerî Turk an Iranian, and what of a Persian of Herat, ruled from Kâbul? For the first time we are dealing not just with ethnic groups but with nations, not with ethnic feeling but with national feeling; and first the nations themselves had to be defined or invented. A nation, to serve as carrier for the modern institutions, might in principle be based on almost any common circumstance central enough to people's lives to make plausibly for a common fate: a common dynasty (the Ottoman?), a common faith (the Shî'î?), a common language (the Arabic dialects?), or even a common conqueror (the British?). But these overlapped: there were Shî'îs not only in Qâjâr Iran but living under the Ottoman ruler and speaking Arabic dialects, for instance. The historical accident of inclusion within a single sovereignty, independent or under some European jurisdiction, might form the readiest starting-point for national self-definition; but such an accident did not easily inspire the heartfelt sentiments required unless they came to be forged in the imposed necessity of a common struggle. But even the common struggle would be hard to rouse without some sense of what the nation was. The search for an effective basis of national self-definition was to preoccupy the most active minds in the coming decades, as the struggle for modernization in the nuclear sense unfolded: that is, for developing in the whole social fabric the traits of technicalized society and, as this struggle more and more clearly presupposed, national identifications.

Modernization in this fuller sense required three sorts of developments. It required most obviously Westernization: the new traits had to be adopted in the form impressed on them by the local heritage of the Occident, to some extent; not merely for want of time to invent anew, but because so far as a technicalized society was inescapably a world society, some things had arbitrarily to be done in the same way everywhere. But every Western community was founded on an intense sense of the nation; so that Westernization presupposed nationalism. Yet Modernization could not be merely Westernization, not merely copying; for at the heart of the Modern spirit was the sense of innovation, of enterprise, of spontaneity, without which the copier must always be several crucial steps behind. The new nations must find resources to be building on that were their own, although this, too, in effect demanded a revival of something that could be called national, upon which to build. Finally, Modernization demanded some sort of revolution, of displacement from power of those ruling elements in society which profited from the existing relation of dependence to the West and which inevitably resisted whatever changes might endanger it; and revolution above all called for national solidarity if it were to succeed.

The completion of the European world conquest

Nationalism in the last decades of the century was a growing force in the main Muslim centres, and after 1905 was to dominate political development there. At first, however, it had little strength compared to the ongoing career of imperialism. After 1880 there was a renewed impulse of Europeans to include within their spheres of influence even the more out-of-the-way areas, including those that had had little or no part in the inter-regional market of pre-technical times. In particular, the bulk of the sub-Saharan African interior, Muslim and non-Muslim, had remained relatively untouched and now was rapidly divided up.

Here the Europeans themselves came into contact with the reforming movements which had got underway at the end of the eighteenth century and had developed their special genius in the nineteenth. Hitherto, the reformers' quarrel had normally been with Muslims; the Wahhâbîs' struggle with Meḥmed-'Alî set the tone. Such puritanical movements had been trying to maintain an egalitarian Shar'î vigour against the Islamic ruling classes, which seemed to have been tempted away by new-fangled and disruptive luxuries. Without necessarily understanding the cultural and economic processes involved, they rejected violently the upper-class accommodation with the imperial West as a betrayal of Islam. By virtue of a centralized control and a rigorous discipline, the new ṭarîqahs were enabled to hold their own in extensive parts of the more remote territories and operate as effective governments in some areas.

The advance of Ismâ'îl in the Nile Sudan had brought on, in reaction, a Mahdist movement, aimed not only at restoring the primitive purity of Islamic organization and faith, but at reforming the whole Dâr al-Islâm and ultimately Islamizing the world as a Mahdî should. The Mahdî himself and his successor (khalîfah) swept the Egyptians and their European mentors out of the Nile Sudan and set about reforming the morals of the population; but they quickly set about expanding their power further, notably in the direction of Egypt. The Mahdî's programme, published at the pilgrimage in Mecca, aroused great interest among Muslims everywhere, some relatively conservative Muslims looking forward to his victory as a possible resuscitation of Islam in the world. It was the time when attention was being focused on Istanbul, with the collapse of other Muslim powers, where claims were being made for a pan-Islamic caliphate. For a time, the Sudanese Mahdî and his caliph appeared as a possible alternative to the Ottoman sultan as leader of a world Islamdom waiting to be united. Even some modernistic Muslims of a nationalist type were interested in making arrangements with the new movement. But the more established reform movements, in their strongholds, such as the Sanûsiyyah in the deserts west of Egypt, remained aloof.

By the end of the century, the British had reversed the Egyptian defeat and suppressed the Mahdists. Under pressure from the Mahdists, the Egyptians, who had occupied the Abyssinian and Somali coasts, withdrew and their place there was taken by the British, Italians, and French, who ultimately shared the whole Abyssinian and Somali territory between themselves and a revived Amḥaric Christian power (Ethiopia) of the Abyssinian highlands. The rebellion of another Mahdî (miscalled the Mad Mulla) in northern Somaliland, whose movement stemmed from one of the reforming ṭarîqahs, was repressed. In the same period, the British and Germans shared between them the mainland dominions of the sultan of Zanzibar, inland from the Swahili coast, though he had not been forced to withdraw by any rebellion. In the Chad and Niger Sudans and on the far west coast, the Muslim territories were occupied within a space of three decades by German, British, and especially French forces, who drew arbitrary boundaries with reference to paths of European trade rather than to local ethnic considerations. By 1905, after agreement had been arrived at between the French and British as to their respective spheres, the whole sub-Saharan territory was partitioned out.

III

Modernism in Turkey: Westernization

The Turks of the Ottoman empire (the western Turks) were the most successful among the major Muslim peoples in maintaining a measure of genuine political independence right through the nineteenth century and into the twentieth, when even the Iranian lands were succumbing to British and Russian intervention. They were also the most successful in discovering a viable basis for national self-definition. In the end, this self-definition was crystallized in a Westernizing form: they defined themselves as a European nation; nowhere else in Islamdom was an explicit Westernization adopted so wholeheartedly. The possibilities and limitations of Westernization as a means of Modernization come out more clearly through the Turkish example than through any other.

The western Turks in, but not of, Europe

The Ottoman and other Muslim powers which advanced in eastern Europe in the Later Middle Period carried with them a cultural orientation away from western Europe. Commercially, the west Europeans continued to play a great role in the lands under Ottoman rule, and political relations were lively. Some west Europeans themselves fell under Ottoman rule, notably in Hungary. Culturally, however, the Ottoman ruling classes, governed by the Islamicate legal and religious and literary traditions, had little in common with Christian Europeans east or west. Their social order was evolving out of problems posed as much by the general Islamicate (and in particular the Mongol-Turkic) heritage of social expectations as by the European setting in which they found themselves. Meanwhile (in contrast to the independent Hindu lands, where Islamicate ways proved very attractive) in western Europe, by the Later Mid-Islamic Period, the Islamicate culture and society were no longer a serious formative force, as they had been in the preceding period. In the fifteenth century, the Occident was in a period of vital florescence to which the now relatively conventional life of Islamdom seemed to have little to offer. Both Christians and Muslims turned away from each other. Hence on the level of the ruling classes there was an unprecedented breach between the life of western Europe and such parts of eastern Europe as were under Muslim rule.

Among the Christians of eastern Europe, however, including those under Muslim rule, there was no such breach. In contrast, again, to what happened in India under the Timurî dynasty, the Christians of the Ottoman empire were not absorbed into the higher political and cultural life of the empire save as converts who learned Turkish and largely cut their ties with their own peoples. The more alert east Christians of the empire, accordingly, like those of independent Russia, readily looked to western Europe, whose prestige increased as the Ottoman empire declined. They did not, to be sure, participate in the 'Enlightenment' so directly as the west Europeans themselves. In large measure it came to them from outside; it was at once a process of 'enlightenment' and of assimilation to the standards of hitherto alien western Europe. Yet even in the eighteenth century this process proceeded a considerable distance among the east European Christian peoples, not only among the Russians but among the subjects of the Ottoman Turks.

In contrast to the Volga Tatars, the Ottoman Turks maintained their agrarian aristocracy and their political power intact and lost instead their commercial and industrial lead. The Ottoman Turks, therefore, when by the generation of 1789 the Great Western Transmutation had displayed its full implications, found themselves in a peculiarly exposed situation. In Europe yet not of it, they were being out-distanced by their own subject peoples as well as by the independent Russians in coming to terms with the momentous forces of Modernity.

There were, then, both strong examples and also a peculiar shame in the idea of Modernization. It was natural that Turks should think of Modernization not as a process of rivalling Europe but simply as joining it. Once the necessity of fully sharing in Modernity was accepted, this was, indeed, the form in which it was accepted: the Turks must become Europeans. But the same situation put serious obstacles in the way of this process. It was not just that adopting Occidental ways seemed to imply lowering oneself to the level of one's subjects. The very monopoly of those subjects on careers and contacts which might be most conducive to Westernization, reinforced the isolation of the Muslim Turks. Hence, in part, the possibility for Turkish policy to be at one point severely Muslim and backward looking, and at another to swing, most radically of all independent Muslim peoples, into Westernization.

The liberalism of the Young Ottomans

Maḥmûd's successful attempt to restore the absolutism had already carried with it the adoption of many ways from the Modern Occident not only in military technique (and in the amenities of luxury) but in the structure of the government and in the educational and legal patterns of society. The period of the Tanẓîmât generalized these adoptions; the trappings of a Modern state, even explicitly European social patterns, became standard practice. Still (so far as the public at large was concerned) the aims of the leadership were centred on improving the power and efficiency of the state, and maintaining the essentials of internationally acceptable order. Increasing numbers of Turks of the better classes, however, became interested in the ways of Modern Europe from the viewpoint of their general human value, apart from the strength or weakness of the central power of the state, except as such power might further such human values. They wanted to live as the Westerners did because the Westerners lived better. In the latter part of the nineteenth century, the initiative in 'Westernizing' began to pass from the heads of state to the lower ranks of the privileged classes, who were looking for a better form of society. This new sort of Modernists can be called 'Liberals', in that they looked to an increase of personal liberties among all mankind, though especially among the educated, among persons sufficiently well off to be able to explore new ideas and new ways of living; hence they tended to sympathize with the various humanitarian and libertarian causes of their time in Europe. They found themselves soon enough at odds with the 'Westernizing' governments and coming to trust less and less the powerful European friends of those governments. Finally they rejected outright the modus vivendi which had been reached with the West.

The new spirit was first expressed, among the Turks, in literature. At the start of the century, the flow of Turkish poetic inspiration (as in some other Islamic lands also) seemed to have dribbled to a stop. If there were potential poets, they could no longer produce good work in the old manner and not yet anything in the new. But by the middle of the century the old tradition had been exorcised. However refined it was, it was decisively unsatisfying to serious minds, who were glad to read even crude writing if it had a Modern message. By now the classical standards, that is, were a thing of the past; naïve, unpracticed, tentative efforts in new directions were no longer compared with the old perfections by those who mattered; they were gladly appreciated for whatever they offered. And in fact a number of writers of good quality did arise to create a new Turkish literature, imitative no longer of Persian but of French, in a language no longer of courtly complexity but of relatively colloquial simplicity.

Through the new mediums, a writer like Shinasi, imbued with values like freedom and progress, could present human life in such a way that his readers were inspired with a respect for the same hopes and concerns as himself. He brought into the Ottoman tongue, and into the Ottoman social context, the points of view of the Western romanticist writers. In this guise, they could produce a more effective personal awareness in his readers than they could through works in French or English or German, or even translations of such works. Shinasi became the revered guide of the more forward-looking youth.

In the 1860s, disgusted with the superficial extravagance of the reign of Sultan 'Abdül'aziz, with the impotence in which the government yielded to

Occidental dictation, and generally with the backwardness and lack of scope for living in cities like Salonika or Istanbul as compared with the great cities of western Europe, a number of young men launched demands for liberal reforms along Occidental constitutional lines. They can be called, as some called themselves, the 'Young Ottomans'. They had not all had a Western-type training, though some had, but they were all more or less aware of the liberal idealism of the West in one or another aspect, including, in particular, liberal nationalism such as had been cultivated in Italy. They were convinced that peoples, to be free, proud and creative like the Western peoples, must cast off the shackles of despotism; and that if the Ottomans were inspired by liberal ideals, put limits on the sovereign, adopted and lived by a constitution, and swept away what they saw as the superstitions of the past, they too would be a great nation as they rightfully should be. The most prominent of these was a writer, Namık Kemal, who dramatized for the educated Turks the new conception of national patriotism.

The Young Ottomans were mostly convinced Muslims, though they felt that Islam could be purified of some of the rigidity imposed by the 'ulamâ'. In their eyes, Islam, if properly understood, contained the essential principles of Western liberalism: the exaltation of freedom and of justice, the condemnation of superstition, even the love of country—for which they cited a ḥadîth report which became famous, to the effect that love of one's native place is a part of faith. Without any very deep study of isnâd-criticism or of theological niceties, they convinced themselves that Qur'ân and ḥadîth could be read, by those willing, in full accordance with the Modern liberal viewpoint. Moreover, they felt that Islam, so understood, was the purest religion on earth—far more rational, for instance, than Christianity with its trinity—and hence specially appropriate for a Modern people. Some even considered the desirability of a partriotic union of all Muslim peoples.

The Young Ottomans tried to publish their ideas to reach at least the educated sector of the population, but since to make their points they had to criticize the administration in being, their publications were quickly suppressed. As they mostly lived by government jobs, they found themselves posted to out-of-the-way places where they could not cause trouble. The leaders fled to Paris, where they carried on their campaign in exile, getting their papers smuggled into Turkey.

Meanwhile, within the administration itself there were those who were coming to a like conclusion. The aim of the absolutists was gradually getting out of date. To be efficient, the government must be Modern; but to be Modern, it must enlist the active co-operation of the leading sector of the population. Without this, corruption and indifference were ruining the best-laid plans of the heads of the bureaucracy. But to gain the support of the subjects meant to govern in their interest. This had, indeed, always been the absolutist theory; but now it must mean Modernization and liberalization.

One of this mind, Midhat Pasha, found it possible to so reform the administration of the district along the Danube of which he was in charge, that it became a model of prosperity and efficiency, free of corruption and the other vices which Westerners were commonly criticizing in the empire. He was able, above all, to evoke some local co-operation in schemes which had tended to be regarded as serving only the absolutism, but which could now be shown to be of positive local benefit. Sent to Baghdad, he was able even in that remoter provincial town to do much the same. When, despite jealousies, he came to the top at Istanbul, he was ready to introduce a liberal constitution for the whole empire, embodying the non-communal ideals of the Tanẓîmât and their guarantees of individual liberties, and a permanent check on irresponsible frivolity or extravagance at the court.

Despotism in Modern style: 'Abdülḥamîd and pan-Islamism

Midhat's rise led to the deposition of the irresponsible 'Abdül'aziz but, unfortunately, the next sultan, to whom the liberals had looked for support, was declared deranged shortly after his accession; his brother, 'Abdülḥamid II, was installed in his place. 'Abdülḥamid had quietly developed his own conception of progress, solidly within the absolutist tradition. He arrested Midhat, suspended the constitution, and proceeded to show what despotism could do equipped with Modern methods. An end was put to further implementing the non-communal and liberal features of the Tanẓîmât, to say nothing of the new liberalism. All independent voices criticizing corruption, inefficiency, and entrenched iniquities, as well as, above all, the representatives of the Christian nationalism, were silenced.

This silencing was accomplished, on the one hand, through the use of Modern police methods: the centralized and Modernly trained gendarmes, who had replaced the old military detachments and local guards, were able to perform their duties much more subtly than could any minor army; moreover, they operated nearly as well in the provinces as in the capital. The railroad and, above all, the telegraph allowed 'Abdülḥamid to reach his arm into every city with equal speed.

But 'Abdülḥamid needed more than Modern technical apparatus to enforce his despotism. He needed what we would now call an ideology. This he achieved through rallying conservative Muslim opinion generally, and particularly through encouraging a sentiment for world-wide Muslim political solidarity, a sentiment labelled 'pan-Islamism'. He gave honour to the 'ulamâ' such as had been threatening to slip from them under the Tanẓîmât, where the emphasis was on Western training. But he did not seriously move toward reviving the Sharî'ah in any spheres where it was ignored. Instead, he fostered a new doctrine (incompatible with the old Shar'î opinion): he insisted that he was a caliph with spiritual authority over all Muslims everywhere, an authority more important, perhaps, than his immediate political power. In this way he took over some of the enthusiasm struck up by the Young Ottomans, so far as they looked to pan-Islamic hopes, but turned it his own way.

This he did by virtue of a combination of historical circumstances. At the end of the eighteenth century it had proved convenient to the sultans to take advantage of Christian confusion about the caliphate in diplomatic negotiations; on ceding territory to Russia, the sultan retained a toehold by insisting that though he was no longer the secular ruler there, he remained the one universal Muslim caliph and as such had the right to a sort of religious overlordship of the mosques. Since the Ottoman sultans, like other great Muslim rulers, were using the caliphal title in its later sense as Shar'î ruler, while the Europeans conceived it in its earlier sense as Commander of All Muslim Faithful and then thought it parallel to the Papacy, the Europeans were readily persuaded to accept a claim which meant something quite different to the Muslims, answering rather to the autonomy conceded Christian millets under Islam. But now, with the decline in Muslim learning and the rise of a class of educated Muslims of chiefly Western education, 'Abdülḥamid found it possible to take the notion seriously in the universal sense given it by the West. In India, particularly, his ambition coincided with a malaise which had been felt since the Timurî emperor had been deposed by the British in 1858, spurred on by the challenge of the Wahhâbî-type reformers. How could true Muslims be content to continue their merely private lives under bare-faced and unmitigated infidel rule, allowing the Sharî'ah, which should order the world aright, to be reduced to a mere personal code? The answer was that if even one substantial Muslim territorial power remained, this would be sufficient to form a base for Muslim society and Muslims in other lands could look to that power as fulfilling the essential requirements of the Muslim conscience. This was to give the caliphate a new meaning, which 'Abdülḥamid was glad to assume as head of the Muslim state with the most prestige, and that which controlled the holy cities. The great symbolic gesture of the new caliphate was the building of a railway in the Ḥijâz, from Damascus to Medina, for the ḥajj pilgrims; Muslims contributed to the caliph's project from all over the world.

'Abdülḥamid's reign began with some crushing losses. Even before he came to the throne, risings in the Bulgarian lands south of the Danube in favour of a separatist nationalism had led to ferocious retaliations on the part of the jittery Turks, who destroyed and massacred savagely. Russia used the occasion to invade, in hopes at last of compassing its long-standing aim of controlling the Thracian straits. The French and British did not intervene militarily this time and the Russians proved the quality of their Westernization. Under Western threat, however, they stopped just short of Istanbul. A treaty which would have eliminated Ottoman power from practically all the Balkan peninsula was revised by the European powers. Still, in 1878, the empire lost all its Balkan provinces except for a strip of land running from Albania through Macedonia to Thrace, into which many Muslims now migrated from further north to join the large number of Muslims already there. Henceforth no province was without large numbers of Muslims and, moreover, the less advanced but majority Turkish Anatolia played a larger part in Ottoman destinies. 'Abdülḥamid had used the military defeat to justify his suspension of the constitution. His subsequent pan-Islamic policy was doubtless eased by the loss of so many Christian provinces.

The defeat, however, by no means solved the empire's problems. It had gone into debt to European bankers in the Crimean war and still more so under 'Abdül'aziz, and it became necessary for 'Abdülḥamid to accept a large measure of European control of the Ottoman finances so as to ensure the payment of the debt (this was the alternative to outright European occupation). In return, the European powers gave their indirect but potent support to his despotism. When, even within the strip of Balkan territory remaining to the empire, rival bands of Christians began fighting each other in view of eventual annexation by the rival Christian states around and the Turks could not assure order, the European powers undertook to take over even the provincial government.

Meanwhile, Modernization went on, in all but such realms as constitutional liberty, and despite the relative inefficiency of a régime which flouted the sentiments of the increasingly Westernizing urban classes and was founded on a programme of maintaining old privileges against change. 'Abdülḥamid's new despotism depended, itself, not only on the technique which only the presence of men trained in Modern ways could provide, but on more subtle institutional changes. It presupposed the breakdown of the old autonomous, locally rooted solidarities, like guilds or local mosque schools, replaced by more anonymous, impersonal institutions such as the new army whose officers might be drawn from anywhere, and the national professional schools little touched by family ties, and more readily controlled by a career-determining and relatively impersonal government.

Even 'Abdülḥamid's new universal caliphate and his new pan-Islamic ideology depended on Modern forms of communication around the world. The Ḥijâz railway was matched by the Baghdad railway, built by the Germans for commercial purposes, extending the west European rail systems (which had been carried to Istanbul) into Anatolia and on to Baghdad. 'Abdülḥamid seems to have been quite aware of his dependence on Modernity and he sought out men who could incorporate it within his ideological limitations. He brought in a prominent reforming administrator from Tunis; he lured to Istanbul (and then kept him carefully under control there) the most famous intellectual reformer of Islam of the time, Jamâlud-dîn Afghânî, who combined an ardent pan-Islamic vision with scorn for the doctrines of the conventional 'ulamâ' and zeal for the spread of the European sciences. Modern schools multiplied under this reign. Despite a certain reactionary preciousness in much of the literature, letters flourished and, above all, translations from Western fiction, carrying its own human vision. At last, despite the total censorship, liberal sentiments made such headway among the educated Turks that in the latter part of his reign 'Abdülḥamid seems to have increasingly distrusted any highly placed Turk, preferring to use men from peoples whose élites were somewhat less advanced, Albanians and Arabs.

Ottomanism and Turkism: the Young Turk revolution

'Abdülḥamid's peculiar version of Modernity could not, in fact, be permanent. A secret league of army officers planned to restore the constitution, and, though the sultan learned of it from spies more or less piecemeal, he could not take drastic measures of suppression without, in effect, wrecking his army altogether, since it was shot through with discontent; and he was too clever to do that. In 1908, then, he had to yield to a mutiny in Salonika and restore the constitution. All the urban Ottoman subjects met the occasion with joy, Muslims and Christians fraternizing in the streets. In the parliament that followed, the Party of Union and Progress, which had been formed by the successful officers, rose to power. And now the enlightened 'Young Turks', as they were called, were faced with making the big decisions as to what was to become of Turkey.

Now came to light all the ideas for reform which had been suppressed in 'Abdülḥamid's long term of power, and at the same time all the contradictions between hopes and actuality which were to frustrate those ideas. A constitution, to be workable, presupposed a nation of the Occidental type. What sort of nation was the Ottoman constitution to represent? The problem had long presented itself with a special insistence apropos of the subject Christian peoples. The Ottomans were intensely aware of the drive for independence on the part of their increasingly Westernized subject Christian peoples. These peoples, regarding themselves as Europeans in the fullest sense, felt superior to their backward rulers. Yet (especially under the Capitulations) they were the merchants, and often even the artisans; they formed the economic arteries of the empire; they could not be disregarded. Their co-operation (and the respect of the European powers generally, whose support the subject peoples would require in order to rebel) must be won by reform of the society as a whole as well as of the military. Already in the time of the Tanẓîmât, a major concern had been to create the idea of a trans-communal Ottoman nationality, which should hold the allegiance and satisfy the interests of Christians integrally with Muslims. For the body of the Balkan peoples, this had not worked. There were, however, sufficient Christian minorities left, in Macedonia or Armenia, to keep the idea alive. It was now expanded to carry further implications. For, to the differences between Christians and Muslims were being added differences between

Albanians, Turks, and Arabs, who had Islam as an increasingly tenuous bond between them.

After 'Abdülḥamid, the Ottoman Turks confronted with special intensity the problem of their total relation to what was happening in the Modern Occident. Who were they to be? Were they to be first of all Muslims, or first of all Europeans, or could they be both at once? Their Christian subjects had decided for themselves that they were above all Europeans—Europeans even above being Christians; for as Christians they must look on the Occidentals as heretics, but as Europeans they formed one society with them. For the Ottoman Turks, adoption of Modernity seemed to imply accepting the same path as their Christian subjects and as the Russians—becoming Europeans, becoming Occidentals. To Modernize was to Westernize, to enter Europe. And this meant in turn to subordinate their religious difference, as had the Orthodox, to a common European life. It seemed to mean shifting from the Islamic civilization of the past into the new European civilization: they must exchange their old heritage for a new one.

Many traditional-minded Turks drew this full conclusion and balked. However mighty, the new civilization was not necessarily beautiful in its Victorian age, nor (especially as seen from without) morally or spiritually sound. At first, the situation had not presented itself so starkly as that to most reform-minded Turks. To become European did not mean dropping Islam itself, just as for the Greeks it had not required dropping Orthodox Christianity. As for the rest, most Turks could hope that as little need be changed as possible. Now such a half-way position was becoming increasingly untenable.

Excluding pan-Islamism, there seemed to be two possibilities. The nation might be Ottoman, disregarding either religious or linguistic lines, modelled after the dynastic state of Austria-Hungary which likewise combined many peoples under a single sovereignty. Or it might be primarily Turkish—which to many meant 'Turanian', in the hope that with the Ottoman Turks might be joined the Turkish-speaking populations of the Russian empire (lately hit by defeat and mass revolt), from the Crimea to the Chinese frontier (and past it), in a vast new national unity of great potential strength. Officially, the Young Turks tried to continue the pattern of an Ottoman state—naturally enough. But they interpreted 'Ottoman' pretty much to mean Turkish, to the increasing annoyance of the more alert, not only of Greeks and Armenians and Macedonians but of Albanians and Arabs, who noticed that the Parliament, for instance, seemed to give a noticeably higher proportion of representation to the Turkish-speaking provinces.

Their policy proved no more tenable than that of 'Abdülḥamid. Their policies seemed to require an increasingly tight central power and a homogeneity in the Ottoman nation which naturally carried with it control by Turks and pressure on all others to accept Turkish language and culture as the common medium of the empire. This was resisted now as it would not have been before, and the resistance was repressed with censorship and violence.

Under 'Abdülḥamid, Christian peasants had often enough been brutally treated. Since 1905, there had been massacres of Armenians in particular (who were accused of taking their new liberties under the Constitution too seriously), often by their Kurdish enemies. But within the Muslim and especially the upper urban classes, 'Abdülḥamid's most serious weapons had usually been imprisonment or exile. The Young Turks were eager to assure security to all, in the abstract, and were shocked at the massacres of Armenians (which recurred in a brief uprising against the Young Turks' Modernism); but they introduced political violence within the ruling group, condemning political opponents to death. This tendency was only strengthened when, from 1911 on, Turkey found itself almost continuously at war to defend what remained of its territories.

In fact, the retirement of 'Abdülḥamid had provoked an international assault on the empire—perhaps on the expectation that this might be the last chance; the Young Turks were too hard pressed to show what they might have been capable of in peace. Austria-Hungary annexed the fragment of Balkan territory it had been administering. Worse, Italy, in 1911, undertook to conquer the remaining Ottoman territories on the coast west of Egypt. The Turks were quickly driven out, and the unyielding Muslim resistance had to be carried on locally by the Sanûsî ṭarîqah, ensconced in its deserts. Finally, the Balkan states combined to drive the Turks out of their peninsula, leaving them by 1913 only a short stretch of land back of Istanbul (the Albanians having seized the opportunity to proclaim independence). Then in 1914 the Young Turks allowed the Germans, with whom they were increasingly allied for commercial and developmental purposes, to drag them into the war with Russia—and hence with Britain and France. There was little leisure or surplus of resources for reforms.

But in the midst of this turmoil there had been much public consideration of future possibilities. One of the best known of the writers on policy was Ziya Gök-Alp, who rejected the idea of an Ottoman nation as in its nature unsound. He had been deeply influenced by the French sociologists and evolved, on their bases, his own interpretation of the Turkish situation. Humanity is articulated into nations, apart from which human beings are scarcely human. Each nation has its own folk culture: its own common memories and customs, its own aspirations expressed in folk stories and in popular songs. These are intimately connected with its language, and therefore the speakers of a given language (normally in a given area) can be expected to form a nation. Any such nation, then, may be associated with other nations in a wider civilization on the level of technique and the various specialized arts: on the level of courtly literature, of political forms, of legal and large-scale institutional structures. But such civilizations are incidental to the nation itself: it can adopt them at one time, cast them off or change them at another. The Turkish nation had adopted the Perso-Arabic or Islamic civilization long ago, when that was the most advanced in the world; now it could turn and adopt the Occidental civilization instead without changing the basic character of its nationhood. Indeed, that national life could be fully expressed only through the most advanced civilization possible; and it would not be possible to adopt Western civilization except as a nation with its own distinctive folk culture.

Ziya Gök-Alp was much concerned for religion, and like other liberals he came to feel that Islam, truly interpreted, was not necessarily bound up with the old Perso-Arabic tradition but could be carried by the Turks into their new civilization as another faith alongside Catholicism or Protestantism in western Europe. In line with the revival of literature at the end of the nineteenth century, he tried to write poetry expressive of the national sentiments, which should be in sufficiently popular form and language to win people's hearts and form their spirit.

Ziya Gök-Alp best formulated and popularized, then, against Ottomanist or pan-Islamic ideas, the idea of a strictly Turkish and Westernizing nationalism, which indeed he tended to conceive in terms not of all the Turkish peoples but of those of Anatolia and Thrace, as having a closer common folk heritage. But his ideas remained somewhat academic. Among the Muslim folk to whom he wanted to appeal, pan-Islamism had the greatest appeal, so far as any programme for a Modern national basis appealed to them at all. Among the official classes, Ottomanism seemed the only practical approach. Unlike the Greeks or Armenians, the ruling Turks did not consider themselves a nation, an ethnic group apart, but simply the leading class among Ottoman Muslims generally. The educated Turks did not identify themselves with the Turkish peasants or herdsmen, on whom they looked down as uncouth (the very word Turk, reserved for these latter, was rather an insult term). That a Turkist nationalism, such as that preached by Gök-Alp emerged sharply as the exclusive ideal of the leading Turks, was due to circumstances which unfolded in and after the First World War.

Forging the western Turkish nation

In the First World War, the Russians were kept busy on the German and Austro-Hungarian fronts, and as Bulgaria was allied with Austria-Hungary and the Ottomans, there was no renewal of the land threat to Istanbul as in 1878. Except for a time on the northeast frontier, the serious enemy was Britain, with its navy and its base in Egypt. The Young Turks hoped to liberate Egypt across Sinai while Britain was preoccupied in the west, but their resources were inadequate, despite active help from the Germans. The British navy was then charged with landing in the Thracian straits—in the Dardanelles—so as to move directly on Istanbul itself. The officer charged with the land defence, co-operating with German naval units, was Muṣṭafà

Kemal, later known as Atatürk. Muṣṭafà Kemal became a national hero by successfully forcing the British to withdraw. Jealous, the leader of the Young Turks (Enver Pasha) sent Kemal to the less prominent northeastern front, where he held off the Russians. (In 1917, when the Russian revolution broke out, it was, as it happened, on this frontier, that the Turks found it possible to re-occupy territory which had been taken by the Russians long before.) Elsewhere the Turks more or less held their own, till finally, in 1918, the British in their turn crossed Sinai, aided by revolting Arabs, and drove the Turkish armies back north through Syria. The defeat was threatening to become a rout when Kemal was put in charge of the beaten armies. He kept them intact and helped ensure that when a truce was signed the Turks still had an active army in being. By the end of the war the Ottoman Turks had a renewed sense of common experience, in which the Anatolian peasant soldiers received a share of recognition. They also had a common hero.

Nevertheless, at the end of 1918, when Ottoman resistance ceased, the capital was occupied by French and British troops, while the territories of the empire were being divided among the French, British, Greeks, Armenians, Kurds, Italians, and the revolting Arabs. Only parts of northern Anatolia and Istanbul—which revolutionary Russia was in no position to claim—were left to the sultan. The chief Young Turks were either taken or they fled (Enver Pasha fled ultimately to the Turkic lands of Russia in a fruitless attempt to raise a pan-Turanian state).

From the Greek viewpoint, this was the time to restore to Greek rule all the Aegean basin and its hinterland, which had not only been Greek historically but which still had a numerous Greek population: including Macedonia and Thrace to the north, and the western part of Anatolia. As the Greek forces proceeded from Izmir to occupy western Anatolia, raising the local Greek population to a mastery which often resulted in massacres of local Turks, many established Turks looked to a British or an American protectorate to save them from a worse submersion under the Christian minorities; but many of those having less to lose went into guerilla action. As this point, Muṣṭafa Kemal defied the submissive sultan and assumed command in the heart of Anatolia of all those Turks willing to resist the victorious Allies. He called a Grand National Assembly to replace the parliament in Istanbul. The Assembly spoke effectively for the established classes of the nation, and he was able to control it by his incisive determination.

The sultan declared Kemal a rebel and (heedless of the Greek threat) sent such troops as he still had, supplemented by bands of Muslims loyal to him as caliph, against the resisters. Meanwhile with Allied help, the Armenians were trying to make good their own state in the formerly Russian and Turkish territories in the eastern highlands; the French were occupying their sphere north and northeast of Syria. The Kurdish republic, however, was still-born; Kemal expressed his gratification at the secession of the Arabs; the Italians had not yet landed in their allotted sphere in the southwest; and

Kemal did not yet attack the British, who were either at a distance in the Iraq and Palestine, or established at the capital itself. Even so, he was pressing four wars at once. The 'armies of the caliphate', despite initial successes, were routed by the new patriotic spirit in the countryside; the Armenians (who had been further decimated by massacres during the war of 1914) were pushed back to the former Russian frontier, behind which they retained a miniature republic; the French were convinced, after meeting desperate resistance, that Arab northern Syria was the most they should annex. Against the enemy best supported and most determined, the Greeks, there was a long holding action. Supplies and ammunition were collected or made in whatever manner came to hand, peasant women carried ammunition on their heads over the mountains, even the aristocrats at Istanbul proved their solidarity by winking at thefts from the Allied depots. At last, Kemal's lieutenant, İnönü, launched a massive assault. By the end of 1922 the Greeks had been driven back to Izmir (amid massacres, in turn, of Greeks by Turks) and into the sea. As the victorious Turkish troops approached the Straits, the British yielded and the sultan went into exile. Kemal reclaimed eastern Thrace, but made no major attempt to reverse the settlement of 1913 in the Balkans. A new peace treaty not only cleared the remaining territory of foreign troops but did away with all the apparatus of Occidental privilege, intervention, and control which had grown up in the nineteenth century.

For his successes, the Grand National Assembly accorded Kemal the title 'ghâzî', warrior for Islam. This Kemal accepted, at least for a time. But he insisted whenever possible that the victory was to be interpreted in a national rather than a communal religious sense. On his return to Ankara from the first great successes against the Greeks, religious leaders of the town urged him to come with them and offer thanks for victory at the tomb of the local saint. This would have been a matter of course for earlier Ottoman captains, and moreover the nationalist cause needed the support of the religious class against the claims of the sultan at Istanbul. But he refused them with insults, telling them it was the soldiers that had won the victory, and not their saint, whose cult should in no way profit.

Partly by the prestige he had gained in the War of 1914, but chiefly by his success against the Christian Greeks, when he had replaced the sultan in leading so spectacular a recovery after defeat, Kemal was undisputed master of the new nation he had helped call into being. In the wars of resistance, Turks had learned to feel themselves first of all Turks. Kemal now adopted uncompromisingly the Turkist ideal of which Ziya Gök-Alp was the most articulate spokesman. His success had been based largely on a deliberate abandonment of the Arab provinces; what he chose to reconquer was only that part of the empire in which Turks formed at least the best-placed part of the population, and preferably the majority of it. He had succeeded by relying on the sense of a common west Turkish fate that was shared among the Turkish-speaking common people: that is, precisely the (west) Turkish folk of which Gök-Alp spoke. Kemal made peace with the Allies on the basis of a west Turkish nationality, though indeed he tried to include as much Kurdish territory as possible (in a Turkish environment, Kurdish families on the rise tended to be Turkified); the new boundary lines were drawn, in principle, on the basis of language, to which religious allegiance was assimilated. In particular, the two peoples, Greeks and Turks, which had been intermingled on both sides of the Aegean and had both claimed the whole area, partitioned the area between them so as to establish territorial national states. This arrangement was confirmed with a massive exchange of population: Greeks (that is, Christians owning the Greek church, who usually—but not always—spoke Greek) living in what was to be Turkey (except in Istanbul) were to be sent to what was to be Greece, while Turks (that is, Muslims, usually Turkish-speaking) living in what was to be Greece (except in western Thrace) were to be sent to what was to be Turkey. Kemal's own home town, Salonika, was left to Greece; but Izmir, which had been chiefly Greek-speaking, became a purely Turkish city.

The Kemalist republic: secularism and Westernism

Having established an independent Turkish nationality in a limited area, Kemal proceeded to take that nationality into the Occidental civilization. The Grand National Assembly was as much a product of the struggle as was the Turkish national consciousness; Kemal pointed out that in proclaiming it sovereign a republic had been proclaimed, the fact was accepted, and no sultan was installed. For a time the pan-Islamic fiction of a caliphate separate from the abolished sultanate was retained, but in 1924 this too was eliminated. Gradually, Islam was disestablished and made a private matter (though the state still held some of the purse strings). All the ṭarîqah orders were abolished and their properties seized—many khânagâhs were turned into museums, as were a few mosques (though most mosques were allowed to remain open and attracted large numbers); madrasah colleges were closed, and the state-supported training of 'ulamâ' scholars ceased; the government-controlled system of waqf endowments became a secular matter. Above all, all traces of Sharî'ah law were officially eliminated by the wholesale adoption of European law codes, in particular the Swiss personal law with only slight modifications.

Islam, to be sure, remained, but chiefly as woven into the character of the Turkish folk. On this level, even Kemal, unbeliever as he was, was loyal to the Muslim community as such. Kemal would not let a Muslim-born girl be married to an infidel. Especially in the early years (as was illustrated in the transfer of populations with Greece) being a Turk was still defined more by religion than by language: Greek-speaking Muslims were Turks (and indeed they wrote their Greek with the Turkish letters) and Turkish-speaking Christians were Greeks (they wrote their Turkish with Greek letters).

Though language was the ultimate criterion of the community, the folk-religion was so important that it might outweigh even language in determining basic cultural allegiance, within a local context.

Muṣṭafa Kemal set about, so far as law could carry, example could prevail, and the choice of economic investments could undergird it, to make Turkey a Western nation. Kemal's primary instrument in his work was the Republican People's Party, which he founded, whose membership rolls he controlled, and which alone could make effective nominations for the Grand National Assembly. It was more than an electoral device; it was a society for propagating the reforms. One of its most effective labours was to establish 'people's houses' (*halk evleri*) throughout the land, which served as community centres, libraries, and adult education schools, popularizing the new ways.

The party's principles, ultimately embodied in the constitution of the Republic, were summed up in six words. Republicanism, the principle of an elective, constitutional government; nationalism, basing that government on cultivation of a specifically national culture and loyalty; populism, recognition of the dignity and needs of the common people as its first concern; *étatism,* the responsibility of the state to establish and maintain economic prosperity; laicism, rejection of any communal religious privilege; and finally revolutionism (or reformism), the continuing adoption of the new and better at the expense of the merely traditional.

Populism implied not only universal adult suffrage; but equal rights, political and economic, for women; and mass education, pushed steadily and with cumulative (if not immediately fully successful) effect in widespread village schools. It implied at the same time a special care for the peasant. One of the most drastic reforms was the abolition of the old land tax on the crops, which had inevitably been exacted in a way that bore heavily on the peasants, even though it had been reduced already in the nineteenth century. (Since it was given a Shar'î form, it was necessary for Kemal to reassure the peasants that its abolition would not excite God's wrath; when this was assured, it was acknowledged as a blessing which doubtless compensated largely for the unpopularity of Kemal's other reforms.) The state's revenues were derived instead from state monopolies and indirect taxes, which weighed far less on the poorer peasants. The concentration of much land in relatively few wealthy hands, however, was only slowly attacked by the party, whose original support in Anatolia had been largely from the gentry. As to the working class in the cities, it was small and given few privileges by Kemal.

Étatism was adopted somewhat later than the other principles, though it followed naturally enough from the Turkish actualities, where such capital as had been present in the country had been controlled by non-Muslims, many of whom had left and the rest of whom were little trusted. Already the Young Turks had succeeded in multiplying the number of Turkish-owned factories, and despite their hostility to Istanbul as a half-foreign city, the

Kemalists succeeded in greatly multiplying that new number in turn. But the larger investments had to come from the state, which had reason to want to keep the pattern of investment under its control.

In the planning of education, including adult education, in the establishment and application of law, the same for all faiths, in the encouragement of the mechanization of agriculture, in the establishment of industries, the Kemalists tried to make Turkey Modern; and the Modernity they sought was clearly to be based on the traditions of what Kemal called 'the whole civilized world', whose good opinion alone he cared for, the West. The Turkish nation was to drop the Perso-Arabic and adopt the Occidental civilization. At two points this became especially clear.

It was in 1925, immediately after the Kemalists had suppressed a revolt of Kurds in the eastern provinces which had been staged in the name of Islam (in suppressing the revolt Kemal had taken the occasion to have executed a number of leaders among those Turks who opposed his policies), that he introduced some of his most drastic reforms, including the suppression of the ṭarîqahs. However, that which roused the greatest outcry and the largest number of riots was the introduction of the Occidental brimmed hat. Men were forbidden by law to wear either the fez of Maḥmûd or any other brimless headdress. Since in performing the ṣalât men kept their headdresses on, a common feature of all Islamic headdresses was that they had no brim which would keep the forehead from touching the ground in the ṣalât. Accordingly, the hat law outlawed at once all the various turbans, caps, and other headcoverings which had continued to distinguish many of the different groupings in the Ottoman empire, notably the 'ulamâ' and the adherents of the diverse ṭarîqahs; for the fez had been adopted only by certain urban classes, apart from the officials.

The act served, then, several functions at once. It symbolized the rejection of the Perso-Arabic and the adoption of the Western heritage (in itself the brimmed hat was not particularly Modern—for instance, it was not particularly efficient—but it was very explicitly Occidental). More substantively, it carried Maḥmûd's reform further, abolishing for the whole population the old distinctions of status which headdress had marked and which were incompatible with the interchangeable homogeneity which a Modern nation-state presupposes; and it particularly reduced the visibility of those religious classes whose prestige and influence Kemal had to eliminate if the secular Republic were to survive. Finally, it served as a psychological *coup*. Even in language, 'the hatted man' had meant a European, and 'to put on a hat' had, as a phrase, meant 'to Europeanize'—that is, 'to desert Islam, or the state' (which came to the same). Kemal was demanding, in effect, that every Turkish man own himself a traitor to all that the Ottoman state had stood for. It was one of those blows which forces people to come to an inner decision: either they must resist now, or acknowledge defeat and henceforth hold their peace. Those most so minded did resist and were crushed; the rest now had overtly to admit Kemal's authority, if not his wisdom, and found themselves implicitly committed to whatever more might be implied in Westernization.

Accordingly, when in 1928 a still more substantial symbolic gesture was made, overt resistance was minimal. It was decreed that henceforth the Occidental letters should be used for writing Turkish, and printing in the old letters was forbidden. The new alphabet was, indeed, phonetically clear and much more appropriate to Turkish than was the Perso-Arabic alphabet as then used. The writing system of Turkish had become chaotic and a real handicap to quick mass education. Yet the Perso-Arabic letters were, in principle, readily adaptable to any Modern needs: a few changes in type font could have made them as clear and efficient as the Modern Occidental letters. The Ottoman spelling was confusing but no worse than the English, and a reform in orthography (such as several Occidental lands were undertaking) could have done, in principle, all the simplifying that the new alphabet did. What the new alphabet did achieve was twofold: it ensured that the reform should be psychologically complete and irreversible; and that the younger generation should be abruptly cut off from all the printed books then in the libraries—from the Ottoman literary heritage.

Other moves toward language reform supplemented these effects. By the end of the nineteenth century, liberal Turkish authors had been simplifying the courtly Ottoman language, to write in a less Persianized Turkish, more like that spoken by ordinary people. This tendency now was implemented systematically. Not Ottoman but Turkish was to be the language of the new Turkish Republic: Turkish, the speech of the enduring folk, so far as possible restored to what it was before ever the Turkish nation adopted the Perso-Arabic civilization. Superfluous Persianisms—which were more numerous and more alienly handled than ever Latinisms in English—could be swept away simply by inspiring a spirit of straightforward simplicity. But the Turks wanted to eliminate the Perso-Arabic technical terms also, especially when they were little understood by the less literate, and launched a campaign for genuinely Turkish terms analogous to that of the Germans for Germanizing their words. They searched out available expressions, and roots on which new terms could be constructed, surveying all Turkish dialects past and present. Here the reformers were not fully successful although they did materially alter the vocabulary.

So far as possible, indeed, even the technical terms of civilization, which were relevant to the specialized callings of an international society rather than to the culture of a folk, were rendered through Turkish roots, which in many cases, at least, made them easier for ordinary people to learn when they needed them. But in this realm it was only natural, by the standards established by Ziya Gök-Alp, that the languages of the new civilized heritage be drawn on as had been formerly those of the old. Hence often French and Gallicized Latin were drawn on to replace Persian and Persianized Arabic.

The net effect, of course, was to assure permanence to the temporary effect of the change of alphabet. Younger Turks can no longer readily follow the vocabulary of the old literature even if it is transcribed into the new letters.

Especially following the world-wide depression of 1929, Kemal did his best to industrialize the country, partly so as to make it somewhat less dependent on imports from abroad, perhaps as much so as to create in Turkey the same institutions as prevailed in Occidental lands: which meant (whether this was recognized or not) the same economic classes and therefore interests, points of view, and habits of life, such as industrialization was bound to bring. He succeeded at least in ensuring the Modern industrial complex a position in Turkish life. The increase in industrial production in Turkey in his time was small absolutely, but relatively it came third after that in Russia and Japan, which led the world in rate of increase. But another institution of the Modern Occident was more crucial to introduce and still more difficult: the guarantees for individual freedom and for public criticism of official policy which can be afforded by a recognized, independent, but responsible political opposition. More than once, Kemal tolerated or even encouraged a party in opposition to his Republicans; each time he soon had to suppress it. The popular pressure to restore the old Ottoman-Islamic ways proved still too overwhelming and too violent: an opposition party was seized on by the masses as a means to undo the Republic itself.

By the time Kemal Atatürk died in 1938, however, his principles, 'Kemalism', were well established among the great majority of the educated youth, the only people capable of carrying on the Modern institutions in terms of which Turkey was actually functioning, and necessarily the carriers of whatever high cultural heritage Turkey was to have. Under his leadership, Turkey had resolutely answered the question, what does it mean to come to terms with Modernity, in a form which completely identified Modernization and Westernization: to become Modern was to join the West as one nation among other Western nations, sharing unreservedly in whatever was Western, for better or for worse. It was characteristic that a Turkish youth, writing as a member of an organization of young Europeans looking to greater European unity, could question whether the insular British were entitled to be included within the European fellowship. When, after the Second World War, the Turks showed themselves so eager to join the several new European organizations, such as NATO, it was perhaps as much to assure themselves that their cherished new identity was recognized as to gain economic and military advantages.

The survival of Islam

The religious conscience as such took little part in the drive for Modernization. The official stance of the Atatürk Modernizers was that religion should be Westernized like everything else. The state should be a 'lay' institution, of course, and religion a private matter of the individual conscience. This much was achieved by the disestablishment of Islam. But it was hoped further that modern citizens would take a 'Western' attitude to Islam; that is, that Islamic piety would take on the social and emotional features of modern Catholic and perhaps especially Protestant or Reform Jewish piety. To some degree the state intervened in this sense. The state continued to appoint imâms and muezzins to the mosques, as before; hence it was in a position to require that the call to ṣalât worship be made in Turkish rather than in Arabic. This meant at once a declaration of national independence from 'foreign' religious traditions, and an assertion of 'modern' rationality; for it meant an explicit breach with the Sharî'ah even in the realm of worship, in favour of direct intelligibility of the words to the public. At least in the immediate presence of official bodies, this was done; but very few Muslims seem to have accepted the Turkish substitute phrases as the true equivalent of the Arabic. (Much later, when permission was given to revert to the Arabic, the Turkish words disappeared.) There were individuals who suggested an extensive reform of the surface of religious life, in the hope that a different pattern of surface behaviour would contribute to a new inner point of view more in harmony with the new Western status of Turkey: mosques should have pews installed, where a congregation would listen to good Islamic preaching rather than focusing on the out-of-date bodily exercises of the ṣalât worship; but such notions were never taken seriously. Islam found its own way essentially in separation from anything that was happening on the level of the state: not only did it not directly contribute to the Westernization; it was not seriously Westernized itself.

It was Islam that was to become the test case, then, of what was to happen to the whole traditional heritage under Westernization. There was a Westernizing class, which carried the reforms and imposed them on the surface of public life. There was also a Modernized sector of life everywhere, represented in the schools. The public schools presented a rigorous Modernism, strictly nationalist in outlook, and admitting a minimal recognition of Islam as an element in the Turkish heritage. The public school teacher became the chief representative, among the lower-class and rural parts of the population, of the new standards. He and the Modern physician and the party bureaucrats, with their links to the big cities and the government, were not to be ignored. But they commonly felt themselves isolated. Even decades after the reforms, at least in a small village, the public school teacher could find himself in a losing rivalry with the local preacher or imâm, and carried on something of a contest to see whether the village children would, consistently with the law, follow his courses and accept his training in modern life, or whether they would in fact pay greater attention and respect to the Qur'ân school and its implicitly anti-modern, anti-state viewpoint.

Islam was markedly changed by the process of Modernization, but not necessarily in the manner that the modernizers anticipated. The public activities of the ṭarîqah orders had been banned and identification with them prohibited, whereas the official worship at the mosque continued essentially as before under state patronage. With seeming reason, it was the relatively rational, sober Shar'î cult that was favoured (with its long tradition of accommodation to the state), while the more unpredictable and personal aspects of Islam, never wholly at ease with any official propriety, were distrusted: the imâm of the mosque could be assimilated to, say, a Lutheran preacher, while the wandering darvîsh, in an age when even the members of Catholic mendicant orders no longer actually wandered about the countryside, was obviously 'medieval' and 'oriental', a scandal to Turkey's Modernity. But even Sharî'ah-minded Islam could not be trusted by men who wanted to make over the nation's legal and social pattern on a Western secular basis; hence the suppression of the madrasah colleges seemed necessary in the hope that as the present generation died out there would prove no further need for Shar'î training as the younger generation was emancipated from such norms. A good preacher need not know obsolete fiqh jurisprudence nor even antiquated kalâm disputation. But in fact the prestige of the imâm had rested not merely on his governmental position and his ability to threaten the masses with the pains of hell; it had rested very largely on his 'ilm knowledge, on his long and difficult intellectual training, which only a madrasah college could effectively provide. As no new trained men appeared to take over the leadership of Sharî'ah-minded Islam in the mosques the authority of what was regarded as the relatively sober and dependable aspect of Islam declined. Meanwhile a mere suppression of outward forms was much less effective against the Ṣûfî ṭarîqahs. Outward displays could be eliminated, or even any formal organization into ṭarîqah orders. But there was no way to prevent a pîr from conversing with his friends and their children in the privacy of his home; and this was all that was needed to carry on the mystical tradition. There was little reason for the authority of the Ṣûfî aspect of Islam to decline among those who took religion at all seriously.

In fact, it seems that a great part of the population did not see Atatürk and his reforms as hostile to Islam as such. The suppression of the madrasah colleges did not affect most people directly, but chiefly only a hitherto privileged element most of whom preferred to turn to modernizing schools anyway. The suppression of the ṭarîqah orders could be felt as a blow not against Ṣûfism but against the corrupt pretenders to Ṣûfism who made such public display of their piety. For, as in many societies, even people who were very pious and expressed their piety by turning to all the established claimants to pious status still were inclined to be sceptical of any given holy man, of any given darvîsh or pîr; they might feel that a general suppression of all ṭarîqahs was rather drastic, but would have to admit it was not without cause in these 'latter degenerate days', and might regard it as a gesture toward purifying Islam, though in a different sense from Atatürk. Atatürk himself continued to be accorded very generally the title of ghâzî—of victor in the jihâd holy war for Islam against the infidel Greeks. Such religious people might be ill disposed toward Atatürk's reforms generally, but they would not see them as any direct threat to religion (unless, possibly, in such an immediately effective detail as the wearing of a brimmed hat in which the ṣalât worship could not be performed); they would be inclined to resist the trend privately, waiting till times changed again.

In this atmosphere, though Sharî'ah-minded Islam withered, Ṣûfî Islam could be reaffirmed and perhaps even strengthened spiritually. One member of the radical Bektâshî ṭarîqah wrote a well-known book to claim that the revolution was fulfilling the egalitarian and freethinking aims which the Bektâshîs had had all along, so that there was now no longer any need for a separate Bektâshî organization; but most Bektâshîs will hardly have agreed. The Mevlevîs, always largely upper-class in appeal and so on relatively easy terms with the Modernizers, and little concerned for the Sharî'ah law anyway, were little troubled by the authorities. Their chief religious centre, the tomb of Jalâluddîn Rûmî and of his chief successors at Ḳonya, was turned into a museum where tourists could gaze at the relics of darvîsh piety under state auspices. But the Mevlevîs continued their technically illegal ceremonies in private, including the distinctive dance, and trained up their youth even though in reduced numbers (so that years after Atatürk's death, when it was desired to reproduce the Mevlevî ceremony at the museum as an attraction to the growingly important tourist trade, the difficult dance was performed perfectly by numerous young men). Indeed, the museum at Ḳonya still functioned as a shrine to the surrounding population, to pilgrims who visited it, and even to the museum guards themselves, whose republican emblems did not prevent them from worshipful enthusiasm if those in attendance seemed at all sympathetic. Ṭarîqahs like the Qâdiriyyah and the Naqshbandiyyah, more closely associated with Shar'î rigour and a sense of social propriety in the old Islamicate sense, were less tolerantly treated, but their traditions remained fully alive. When, after the War of 1939–45, greater freedom for religious expression was allowed, the vitality of Islam seemed to lie chiefly on the Ṣûfî side; the old ṭarîqahs proved very attractive, at least in the form of personal cultivation, even among many of the class which in other ways had wholeheartedly accepted Atatürk's reforms, and new ṭarîqahs arose and became very popular even though still illegal.

But Islam was not simply disciplined by secluded pîrs instead of by public madrasahs. As the formally trained 'ulamâ' scholars died out, popular Islam tended to lose any consistent discipline at all. It could become difficult to distinguish religious superstition from serious religious concern. Ordinary people displayed their respect for the Arabic letters by hanging sacred formulas written in Arabic as charms or talismans on buses or taxis. Though a civil ceremony in the state courts was recognized as essential to a marriage (except in the far eastern part of the republic, where the mountaineers largely ignored this requirement), the real wedding, indispensable to a proper married state, was felt to be that arranged by the imâm, however ignorant he might be even of Shar'î rules. After the War of 1939 even the devotees of Atatürk saw that it was necessary to reopen formal Shar'î training so as to bring the power of religion under more rational control.

The great public question, after the war, turned out increasingly to be what should be done with Islam. A ṭarîqah order which in the Maghrib, where it originated, had been conservative, even pro-French, became, on arrival in Turkey, a spearhead for a religious drive to undo the work of Atatürk. Such a religious drive was less strong than some feared, yet it was tacitly, and even sometimes overtly, the most emotionally laden issue between political parties even though all parties agreed in theory to maintain Atatürk's secularism. In any case, secularism, despite the distance it set between the state and the religious establishments, had in no way introduced the Modern Western conception of religious liberty, in which any form of religious faith could be tolerated without fear. So soon as the Sharî'ah-minded were allowed to establish formal religious training again and regain a recognized voice, it became clear that they took it for granted that the religious forms that they might expect to be tolerated should be just those that were tolerated under the Ottoman régime. If a ṭarîqah order paid respect to the Sharî'ah, its suppression was simply a question of state policy. But some, at least, took it for granted that the many Shî'îs of the republic, most of whom were sufficiently Bâṭinî in orientation not to respect any Sharî'ah, Shî'î or Sunnî, could never be granted religious toleration, not because they were dangerous to the state, but because their doctrines on the point of Sharî'ah were incorrect. Eventually one of the most active points of debate became just the question of religious liberty, which neither Atatürk's state nor the Ṣûfî leadership had made familiar to the bulk of the population, though religious liberty might prove essential to any real spiritual growth which would accommodate the practical culture of the modernizing classes to the spiritual demands recognized even by a large section of the Modernized classes and felt as fundamental by a large part of the population.

The operation of shifting from one heritage to another was not so complete or so unequivocal as it might appear. Even in nationalist consciousness, the Occidental agrarianistic past, for instance, had not really supplanted the Islamicate agrarianistic past, which remained (for one thing) the field in which past Turkish greatness stands out. Nor was it easy to divorce the Muslim religion, as a private spiritual exercise, from the great civilization which had formed around it. The masterpieces of Muslim spirituality are at the same time the masterpieces of the Perso-Arabic literary heritage. It was often found that those persons who took most seriously a personal spiritual cultivation might also cultivate a conscious and considered rejection at least of the cultural aspects of Kemalism. Many Kemalist Turks have hoped that a truly vital Turkish 'Reformation' of Islam might come, which would free it from the more extraneous elements of the older heritage and make Islam not only a Modern but a fully Western religion. Such questions touched the point in the heart of human beings where any cultural life must face its most critical test.

At times, Atatürk's solution might have seemed tentative or superficial, at best. Many Kemalist Turks were horrified to see occasional crude expressions of a popular reaction against Westernization: as when an approving mob in 1930 watched its leader first shoot and behead an officer who tried to interfere with an anti-government demonstration, and then display the severed head in the streets. But the Kemalists themselves indulged in a display of communal bigotry during the war, when Nazi German power was at its height: a capital levy was decreed, the chief provisions of which applied explicitly to non-Muslim businessmen (including foreigners, however, only if they were Jewish subjects of Germany or its allies). It was administered with no provision for appeals or review, in such a manner as to ruin them and often imprison them at hard labour, as an added penalty for their Christian or Jewish status. As German power receded, the prisoners were released.

IV

Egypt and East Arab Lands: Revival of the Heritage

More than any other major Islamicate people, the Arabs had been culturally depressed just at the time when the Great Transmutation was taking place in western Europe. Though few Arabs had much participated in the Persianate culture, yet in the most important of the Arab lands, especially Syria and Egypt, political power and social preference went to men who could be at home in the Ottoman Turkish culture with its Persianate background. There was a tendency for those who had a purely Arabic education to be limited to the more strictly religious sides of culture as 'ulamâ' or as Ṣûfî pîrs. During the Gunpowder Empire Period, the Arab lands had seen relatively little creative activity. Even the Arabic language, which had never been replaced for serious work by the vernacular dialects, had languished except for narrower theological purposes. It was treated as a dead language almost as much as it was in the rest of the Muslim lands, where the vernaculars were unrelated to it and the population made no pretence at using it as their primary cultural vehicle. Any manuscript tradition is subject to erosion over time; but during the Later Middle Period the great bulk of the scholarly and literary production of the classical Arabic time (that of the High Caliphal Period) had become inaccessible and, presumably, permanently lost, like that of classical Greece. Much that was left was more likely to be found in Istanbul than in Cairo or Baghdad.

At the same time, commercial life during the eighteenth century was increasingly dominated by east Mediterranean Christians just as in the Turkish parts of the Ottoman empire, and the Christians, both Arab and non-Arab, were increasingly in touch with the rising Occidental culture. But the Muslim Arabs were not even the rulers over those Christians, as the Turks were: the privileged position of the foreigners (and of the Arab Christians and Jews) was unmitigated. Hence the Muslim Arabs were backward at once in terms of the Islamicate heritage and of the rising tide of Modernity. The need to develop or revive local cultural strength, if they were to face up to the European challenge, was, then, at the same time more urgent and more difficult than among the Turks, or indeed than among any other Muslim people.

Despite this, the leading eastern Arab centres (but not most of either Arabia or the Maghrib) had been assimilated more than most other Muslim centres into the international European system. Under Ismâ'îl, Cairo had taken on the outward appearance of a European city and the revolt of 'Urâbî had already been infused with Western idealism. The Egypt of Cromer was in fact far advanced not only as a colonial economy but, with Syria, as a focus of attempted Modernization in manner and in spirit. In contrast to its past, and without much positive support from it, Egypt was to move toward becoming a major leader among Modern Muslim peoples. Nowhere else was the need for finding a base in the older heritage for a Modern sense of nationality at once so problematic, so urgently pressing, and so passionately and fatefully dealt with as in Egypt and Syria.

Reviving the Muslim-Arab heritage: Muḥammad 'Abduh

The Egyptian Arabs were turned more painfully against Occidental political power than were the Turks: they were under direct occupation by an Occidental power; smarting from the British sense of superiority, not always so subtly or so gently expressed as by Lord Cromer, and in any case daily present at least among the educated classes; and already feeling threatened by a relatively subordinate historical position even among Islamicate peoples. At the same time, alert Egyptians were as aware as were any Turks of the necessity of coming to terms with Western culture. One of the fruits of British concern for the personal immunities was that Arabs in Egypt were relatively free to work through their dilemma in print unlike either Arabs or Turks under 'Abdülḥamid. The journalistic press multiplied in the later nineteenth century in Egypt, as in Turkey, but it expressed more freely and at large the problems facing Muslims in Modernization.

In these circumstances, a wide variety of possibilities were suggested; but the most popular involved one or another sort of stress on the specifically Arab heritage. Especially in Syria, more particularly in Mount Lebanon where, in conjunction with the thriving port of Beirut, there was a large Christian peasant population, many Christian Arabs had been educated at mission schools. There they had become interested in the wealth of their Arabic language and the historic splendour of the Arab past.

Despite the association of that heritage with Islam, in its language and in its remoteness, both, it was at least dissociated from the then ruling Turkish exponents of Islam. The language was revered in all Muslim lands and respected by Western scholars; the Christians, taking an economic lead among the Arabs, were glad to appropriate the rest of the Arab heritage at the same time. In the latter part of the century, a few of them had attempted, without perfect success, to reproduce, in Arabic, works of a strictly Western style. But others were taking more successfully to a conscious revival of the style of the classical 'Abbâsî period; for instance, Nâsîf al-Yâzijî, who wrote Maqâmât in the purest manner, directly following Ḥarîrî. He became a master of most later writers, as to sheer style. In this way, the small Syrian district of Lebanon turned out to be a focus of Arab cultural revival.

For want of local Egyptian Arabs with the necessary preparation, it was Christian Syrians, often imbued with zeal to revive Arabic literature in the name of Arab glory, who took the lead in establishing Arabic journalism in Egypt. In this way, the sense of Arab identity received a strongly literary and classical turn, being expressed in an attempt to revive the ancient Arab glories, specifically those of the classical 'Abbâsî period, over against the prevailing Perso-Turkish environment. Such an orientation proved very welcome to the Muslim Arabs of Egypt.

Among the Muslims, however, the revival tended to include not only the literary but the religious greatness of the Arab past—the earlier past of Islam. Nowhere did demands for a purification and fortification of Islam as a vital faith find a more zealous support than in the eastern Arab lands. Even the form of language taken by the literary revival eventually depended largely on the enormous importance which was attached to maintaining the purity and supremacy of Islam. Already the Arab lands had been the scene of the Wahhâbî movement itself, in Arabia, and of some of the other movements designed to purify Islam of later accretions. In this atmosphere, in the days leading up to the 'Urâbî revolt, a brief visit by Afghânî, a fiery Persian preacher of the revival of Islamdom, launched a vigorous ferment intellectually and even politically. Afghânî's most influential Arab disciple was the Egyptian scholar Muḥammad 'Abduh (1849–1905), who had collaborated with him on the journal *Al-'urwah al-wuthqà*. Afghânî had taught a revival of each Muslim nation internally as part of a general pan-Islamic movement in which the reviving nations were to co-operate. But this emphasis tended to be international. Shaykh 'Abduh, when he was forgiven his involvement with 'Urâbî and allowed to resume activity in Egypt, was equally zealous; but he concentrated his efforts on Egypt itself, and stressed immediate moral reforms, enlightened education, and careful reinterpretation of religious doctrine.

Muḥammad 'Abduh worked above all against taqlîd in the extended sense that notion was popularly taking on in the nineteenth century. This amounted (in effect) to even more than the closing of the gate of ijtihâd in Shar'î matters, which had been agreed on in the Later Middle Period. With the increasing challenge from alien ways in the eighteenth and nineteenth centuries, taqlîd finally came (as an attitude of mind, if not theologically) to include a conscious rejection of all the new and culturally alien ways of the Occident. The old ways, however legally dubious, tended to be lumped together as sanctified by ancestral custom. 'Abduh rejected this whole point of view. Some Egyptians who rejected it were trying to become, in effect, replicas of Modern Frenchmen. Their superficial efforts aroused the scorn of observers like Cromer. Muḥammad 'Abduh himself liked to visit Europe to restore his faith in mankind. But he accepted nothing from the West unless it passed his own rigorous standards. When he rejected taqlîd and tradition, he rejected them not in favour of Westernization *ad libitum*, but of Muslim ijtihâd—again taken in a correspondingly broad sense: the free exploration, within the originally established rules of legal inquiry and the moral norms of Islam, of what was best here and now. He was influenced by many Modern European thinkers and by none more than by Comte, whose positivism had exalted scientific objectivism even in the analysis of human culture, yet who called for a new religious system to meet a persisting human need, provided it be consistent with science. But 'Abduh was convinced it was Islam which could provide that religious system.

His influence was in part a personally moral one: he fought all superstition and corruption in the name of self-reliant honesty and efficiency. His vigilance was able, for instance, to restore, in certain departments of which he had charge, a high level of expectation of personal integrity and honesty. He helped renew the tradition of institutional charity, disrupted with the government seizure of the waqfs, through Modern voluntary associations. But even in such efforts he sometimes made a point of reforming in his own Muslim way rather than the British way. He reintroduced the principles of ijtihâd into Muslim law, notably invoking maṣlaḥah (consideration of public welfare) as a criterion in applying qiyâs as it had been developed, for instance, by Ibn-Taymiyyah. But this was not simply an excuse to adopt European standards, but a living application of Islam; even in courts applying Western law, he was inclined to use the same sort of principle, insisting on his right to ijtihâd and to the use of the criterion of maṣlaḥah, despite technical precedents. Thus he Islamized even the Western law in spirit. His most comprehensive influence lay in making the classical Muslim-Arab heritage, in its most distinctive aspects, respectable among Arabs with European interests as a legitimate alternative foundation for a Modern society.

In the first instance, he was bent on showing to Modernly trained men the validity and relevance of Islam as a faith. Perhaps influenced by his Persian master, Afghânî, he appreciated the Faylasûfs' attitude to politics—as represented especially in Ibn-Khaldûn—but he took the Islamic faith as such more seriously. He chose to follow Ghazâlî in his attitude to revelation and to the Muslim community, deprecating not only legal taqlîd but the old kalâm, and relying on the continuing and more open witness of spiritually sensitive individuals. He followed him also, accordingly, in his reception of modern science (assimilates to Falsafah)—though 'Abduh was naturally more strongly positive in urging its reception, and went further than Ghazâlî in acknowledging the ability of reason to demonstrate basic truths; he took a Mu'tazilî view of the ability of reason to show *a priori* what must be the good, which was therefore incumbent on God. 'Abduh's commentary on the Qur'ân demonstrated the possibility of a cautious but firm reinterpretation of the sacred text in line with Modern needs. He used the old technique of *bi-lâ kayf*, of recognition that anthropomorphic and other dubious expressions must be received without attempt to envisage what they can really mean. He recognized, as had al-Shâfi'î, that in any case the meaning of the textual words was a function of the Arab culture of the time. Though he was sometimes a bit daring, as in suggesting that the jinn might in fact be microbes, he found it unnecessary to introduce any radically new principles, such as a general principle of historical cultural relativity which would put in question all the imagery of the texts. Thus, within the lines set down in the classical period of Arabic creativity he was able to allow as much as necessary for reception of Modern science and technique. At last made chief muftî of Egypt, ultimate expositor of the Sharî'ah there, he worked carefully within the context of the historical tradition, finding it sufficient to encourage all tendencies to restore the adaptability and moral concern that had characterized the law in its formative period.

His return to the classical period of Arab Islam in matters of faith was at one with his return to the same period in literary culture. Like the Syrian Christians, he was eager to revive the old books, long neglected, and the old Arabic, which was their medium. One of his greatest concerns was to reform instruction at the Az'har mosque-university where the chief eastern Arab 'ulamâ' were formed. He did not succeed very far, but he introduced many of the students there to wider currents of thought. These included—perhaps most importantly—the study of secular classical Arabic literature, as well as a certain amount of Modern Western subject matter. He fostered a high-level Modern jouralism, but insisted that it be carried out in a pure classical Arabic—himself setting the example of a simple Arabic prose which yet conformed to the ancient grammatical and lexical forms.

Egyptian nationalism and Arab nationalism

Muḥammad 'Abduh felt (as had earlier Egyptian reformers before him) a warm attachment to Egypt as such. His attachment to the classical Arab heritage was largely an expression of this attachment to Arab Egypt, as was perhaps in part even his continuing interest in the Dâr al-Islâm at large, which he retained from the days of Afghânî's inspiration. But in terms of practical nation-building, these several loyalties need not be automatically in harmony. The dilemmas implicit in loyalty at once to Egypt, to Arabism, and to Islam were eventually forced into the open. Some of them came out already in the first two decades of the twentieth century, as the complacent world hegemony of Europe, expressed in the outlook of Cromer, was abruptly cast in doubt.

Less cautious than Muḥammad 'Abduh, who was willing to see some temporary virtue in the British reformers, a group of men around Muṣṭafà Kâmil were insisting that the aims of 'Urâbî must after all be fulfilled, the British must be expelled and constitutional government established in Egypt on the basis of co-operation of both Muslim and Christian Arabs. After the defeat of Russia by Japan in 1905 (regarded as a victory of

'Orientals' over 'Europeans') nationalism in many Muslim lands took heart. Then in 1906 occurred an incident which gave occasion to Muṣṭafà Kâmil's group to rally all Egypt behind them. Some British officers out shooting pigeons got into a scuffle with some villagers among whom they had trespassed, an officer and a villager being killed; the government hanged some villagers and flogged others in punishment. The Egyptians were shocked to see the British behave like any 'Oriental' despot and those who were persuaded that Egyptians were capable of carrying out their own reforms without British supervision established a formal nationalist party to that end. At the same time, a crisis in the international market, including the cotton market, highlighted the limitations of the new prosperity. By 1913, the Egyptian consultative chamber had evolved into a political theatre in which parties could debate and a political solution in terms of mass campaigns had become credible.

In the War of 1914, Britain in its Egyptian bastion was aligned against the Ottoman empire. The Egyptians tended to sympathize with the Muslim empire to which they were nominally attached rather than with the Christian empire which controlled them. On the other hand, many Arabs in the Ottoman provinces had become dubious of their future in a Turkist state such as the Young Turks were making of the Ottoman empire since the revolution of 1908. The literary revival which had started among the Syrian Christians had already been finding echoes among the educated Muslims, especially in Syria, who were developing something of the same sense of Arab greatness, associated with the classical 'Abbâsî period, as had appeared in Egypt. The educated classes remained predominantly made up of families who traditionally furnished 'ulamâ', and would probably have preferred to remain loyal to the Ottoman sultanate. They would have welcomed some sort of decentralization in the empire which would have allowed them an equal position for Arabic with Turkish as languages of education and administration, perhaps in an Arab-Turkish federation like the Austro-Hungarian dual monarchy. But in the face of Young Turk repression of any such discussion, activists had formed secret societies, within the army as well as outside it, aimed at Arab independence. The war gave them an opportunity: in 1916 they persuaded the sharîf of Mecca, head of an Arab family who ruled the Holy Cities as agents of the sultan but had their own independent following there, to ally himself with the British, upon a British promise of Arab independence, and to proclaim an Arab revolt against the Ottomans in the Ḥijâz.

Wartime conditions proved hard everywhere. In Egypt, the concentration on cotton production for the British market resulted in near famine with the curtailing of sources of food supply. In Syria, also, the war's disruption produced famine, aggravated by savage repression of Arab discontent by the Young Turks. The revolting Arabs of the Ḥijâz gave important help to the British thrust into Syria in 1917–18 and were allowed to occupy

Damascus, where the sharîf's son Fayṣal was subsequently proclaimed king, to the great delight of the Syrians. Everywhere the end of the war-time sacrifices and restrictions was felt as the dawn of a new era of liberation. In western Europe, the mood carried great expectations of democracy and liberty, and something of the mood carried over to many Arabs. But meanwhile the British government had more conservative plans. Upon the break-up of the Concert of Europe, when the European powers fell to fighting, had followed the break-up of the system of joint European controls which had been especially highly developed in the Ottoman area. But the victors in the war did not anticipate the end of European hegemony, only its rearrangement in their own favour; they assumed that any important 'backward' area would, at least indirectly, be under the control of one or another of the victor states, and divided conquered areas accordingly into spheres of influence. If there were to be Arab states, they would be expected to fit into this scheme.

In the east Arab area, the victors assumed the British would be retaining Egypt and the Nile Sudan; for Egypt, with its Suez Canal, was regarded as essential to British lines of communication with India. The French were granted central and northern Syria where they had special interests growing out of the Catholic missionary work, especially in the Lebanon, that work having been under French protection in the Ottoman time. The British took the Iraq because of the importance of the Persian Gulf area for the defence of India and because of British oil interests there; the French and British divided the Jazîrah between them. The British, already controlling the eastern and southern coastal city-states of Arabia, and having led in the negotiations with the sharîf of Mecca, regarded all Arabia as in their sphere except for the Red Sea coast of the Yemen, where the Italians claimed special interests. It had been intended that southern Syria (Palestine) was to be under international control, but during the war the Russians had been knocked out by revolution and the British had promised the Zionists, a Jewish movement, that they would be allowed to make there a national home for Jewish immigrants who wanted to escape minority status in Christian Europe by establishing a Jewish state in the land of the Bible. Hence the British were to have Palestine too for this purpose.

The revelation of the plans for dividing up the loot, which had been kept diplomatically secret, shocked not only the Arabs but also the Americans, who had been persuaded to enter the war on the Anglo-French side under the impression that their victory would mean a triumph for democracy and that enduring peace would be established on the basis of the self-determination of peoples. The Americans were satisfied, however, when at the peace conference at Paris the Concert of Europe was replaced, as a means of ordering international affairs, with the League of Nations, which any supposedly independent non-European government could join on the same basis as the European governments; and when the spheres of influence in conquered lands were proclaimed to be temporary means of tutelage, under mandate from the League of Nations, in which the French and British would guide the backward peoples to independence. (Many Americans supposed that mankind could be sorted out into so many 'nations' which, if not yet ready to govern themselves, need only be given a period of benevolent tutelage under some 'advanced' power till they could enter into the Western international system as equal members without further ado.) The Americans then withdrew from what they assumed had been a temporary venture into international affairs.

Many Arabs had hoped for American support. Fayṣal of Syria had gone to Paris to appeal before the world to the principle of self-determination, against French occupation; the Syrian population, particularly that of Palestine, had made clear to an American mission of inquiry that they cared neither for British nor for French rule and especially that they did not care to have any part of Syria turned into a Jewish state in which the Arab population would find themselves foreigners. But the British and French troops persisted in occupying their respective portions of the Fertile Crescent, though the French had to crush active Arab resistance in taking Damascus, and the British soon faced an open revolt in Iraq which they put down only with difficulty. In Egypt, Muṣṭafà Kâmil had died before the war and his party had dwindled, but in the course of the war the followers of Muḥammad 'Abduh, who had tended to stay aside from his party, had become convinced nationalists; at war's end they took the lead in demanding independence for Egypt too. The official Egyptian government was powerless, but Sa'd Zaghlûl, a close disciple of Muḥammad 'Abduh and of Afghânî himself, who had made a name for himself as a leading reformer in the administration, formed an unofficial Egyptian delegation intended to represent Egypt at the Paris peace conference, called the Wafd ('delegation'). In 1919 the British imprisoned the would-be delegates, which act provoked such general disturbances and boycotts throughout the towns and villages of Egypt that for a time the British were isolated in Cairo: the Egyptians were in open rebellion. For the sake of restoring order, the delegates were released and allowed to go to Paris where, however, they, too, could accomplish nothing.

There followed a period of settlement in which the British and French attempted to establish a semblance of Arab independence or at least participation in self-government. Fayṣal, ousted from Syria, was made king in Iraq in 1921 by the British but tied by provisions which left the British in control; even so the Iraqîs were restless; finally in 1932 Iraq was given formal independence with an end to the mandate and made a member of the League of Nations—at the price of being bound by a treaty which gave Britain certain rights of military garrisoning and a vague but perceptible ultimate power. In Egypt, in the face of Wafd demands that the British leave both Egypt and the Nile Sudan, which was to be Egyptian, the British refused to turn over the Sudanese to their former Egyptian conquerors and tried to settle the matter in 1922 by unilaterally granting Egypt limited sovereignty as a kingdom under Meḥmed-'Alî's line, with a continued British occupation. But the Egyptian populace remained loyal to the Wafd, who won overwhelming majorities in every election except those not based on general suffrage, though British intervention and especially royal intrigue usually prevented them from forming a parliamentary government; only in 1936 was a treaty finally signed, similar to that with Iraq, allowing for continuing British occupation of the Suez Canal and joint sovereignty over the Nile Sudan, and making Egypt, too, a member of the League of Nations. The French eventually tried to accomplish something similar in their part of Syria, after first dividing it into still tinier states set off against each other and having to put down, nonetheless, several bloody revolts. They carved out a greatly enlarged Lebanon (gerrymandered so as to yield a bare Christian majority which it was hoped would keep it loyal to France) from the rest of northern Syria, and in 1936 they too drew up treaties with their new states, which were not, however, to come into effect till 1939. By this time a new war had started. Only after the war did the British finally force the French to get out of an independent 'greater' Lebanon and a truncated 'Syrian' state. Palestine, except the land east of the Jordan (which became a protected amîrate), remained under direct British administration, despite Arab pleas.

In the Arabian peninsula, the British retained their control over the coastal city states, but abandoned the sharîf of Mecca when he refused to accept the peace settlement on their terms; another British protégé, 'Abd-al-'Azîz Ibn-Sa'ûd, who was reviving the Wahhâbî state of his Sa'ûdî ancestors in central Arabia, was allowed to occupy the Holy Cities and establish a new Sa'ûdî state over the greater part of the peninsula. The renewed Wahhâbî power, while still ferocious for a time in its persecution of the Shî'îs of east Arabia, proved far milder than a century before in the Ḥijâz and was soon accepted as a legitimate and even honourable Muslim power by Sunnî Muslims everywhere. In the Yemen, the long-standing Zaydi Shî'î sect, in chronic revolt against the Ottomans, established a secluded mountain state of their own under an imâm.

The moral consequences of the various local struggles were twofold. On the one hand, the Fertile Crescent was divided into artificial political units by the Europeans; the Arab portions of the Ottoman empire were broken into seven portions, not counting Egypt, most of which had quite artificial boundaries, though outside of the four Syrian fragments there was at least some natural basis for the units. On the other hand, people of all areas had learned under stress to value highly their common quality as Arabs, Christians and Muslims together, and to distrust and even hate the British and French rulers. In Iraq and especially in Egypt the heightened Arab patriotism attached itself to the new kingdoms (though not necessarily to their ruling families); but in many areas, including Iraq, and especially in the Syrian states—apart from the Christian population of Lebanon—it also attached itself vaguely to a wider body of Arabic-speaking populations, for want of a genuine national identity within any political unit, especially any of the fragments resulting from the Anglo-French partition of Syria. In any case, with the complete breach with Turkey and the solidarity of diverse sects against the foreigners, a wider Islamic sentiment had become inappropriate, even embarrassing so far as it did, in fact, persist among the Muslim people.

The transformation of agriculture

Political life between the wars seemed unrewarding and, save for outbursts of violence, stalemated. It was chiefly in the hands of the landed classes and, even apart from a general feeling that ultimate decisions in the French and British spheres were outside Arab control, differences among parties (or, more often, factions) revolved less around basic issues than around personalities. In an atmosphere of frustration, most men in politics became corrupt. This happened in Egypt, in the Wafd itself, soon after the early death of Zaghlûl. By 1928, his successor as leader of the Wafd was already involved in a scandal over favours at court; and while the Wafd kept its peasant support till the treaty was signed in 1936, at the next election thereafter it lost heavily. But its rival politicians were often scarcely freer from corruption. In Iraq the steadily rising figure of Nûrî Sa'îd, rebel against the Turks, friend of Britain, and apostle of reform from the top down, was personally incorruptible and outlasted other transiently more powerful men. His personal ascendancy, which lasted beyond the Second World War till 1958, may have limited corruption somewhat, but his favouring of the privileged classes made him equally distrusted among the more concerned nationalists. Politics did not offer great immediate promise, passionate though interest in it was everywhere.

But many of the Arab reformers had been aware that a Modern economic life was an essential part of the European power and (like the Young Turks and Atatürk) in particular were eager to see the rise of a modern factory industry. In the inter-war period in Syria and especially in Egypt, there was some development of such industry—especially in textiles and in secondary processing of various kinds. In Egypt, the new industry, along with new Egyptian-owned banking facilities, was developed chiefly by the disciples of Muḥammad 'Abduh with the conscious intention of aiding in national revival. The new industries accounted for an increasing proportion of the national product by value, partly making up, statistically, for the loss of industrial crafts in the nineteenth century. Yet the number of families directly involved was very small; the increase in the industrial labour force was commonly less, proportionately, than the increase in total population.

The increasing population forced into the cities took up unskilled jobs or service trades, such as menial labour or retail street selling, or remained (especially after the world financial crisis of 1930) more or less unemployed, dependent on relatives or occasional labour.

It was, therefore, the rural population, cultivators of the land and those who carried on auxiliary trades in the villages, that still formed the bulk of the masses; even many of those who came to the cities kept their roots and their hearts in their villages, whither they returned for holidays or for old age. This was especially true of Egypt, where the line between city and village had been especially persistent. In contrast to the cosmopolitan, Levantine character of the Egyptian cities, half Greek and Italian and Turkish, the village population retained a relative homogeneity and continuity and even when villagers came to the cities to live they did not feel at home. The effect of Modernity on Egypt was ultimately the effect of Modernity on the villages; only if the villages could be moulded into a Modern nation could Egypt be. Reformers, therefore, also turned haltingly to the life of the village: what did a Modern nation require there?

Nowhere did village life change under the Modern impact earlier and more fatefully than in Egypt. In several ways, the Egyptian case is extreme. Yet it represents forces at work throughout the Islamic lands, and can be studied in some detail. Moreover, because of the pivotal role of Egypt among the Arabs, its peasant life takes on a special importance.

Even before the nineteenth century, Egyptian peasant life had not been unchanging: new crops, like maize; new amenities, like coffee; above all new religious patterns, not only Islam itself but the proliferation of Ṣûfî ṭarîqahs with their popular dhikrs and the centring of popular reverence for authority on the Shar'î experts of the Az'har, had altered the pattern of village life physically and morally.[1] But from the beginning of the nineteenth century, the changes had begun to affect the basis of the peasant's relation to the land. The arbitrariness and violence of Meḥmed-'Alî's inter-

[1] We know very little of the earlier history of Egyptian village life. Henry Habib Ayrout, *The Egyptian Peasant* (translated from French [1938] by John A. Williams with revisions by the author [Boston, 1963]), stresses the identity of twentieth-century Egyptian peasant life with that of Pharaonic times, citing the similarity of some tools as well as some other details and certain general social circumstances. The book is perhaps the most sensitive short introduction available in English to the physical life of the villages (it is not strong on the religious or spiritual life), but it is psychologically and sociologically naïve, nowhere more so in its stress on the changelessness of the *fallâḥ*, the Egyptian peasant. Such changelessness as he describes is that of many other peasant masses; but the bulk of the descriptions in the book could apply only since the time of Meḥmed-'Alî or at most since the general conversion to Islam. What he does highlight is the relative uniformity of Egyptian villages as compared, for instance, to Syria. On the evolution of the Egyptian village in the nineteenth century, see Gabriel Baer, 'The Dissolution of the Egyptian Village Community', *Welt des Islams*, n.s. 6 (1959–61), 56–70. In the twentieth century, see Jacques Berque, *Histoire sociale d'un village égyptien au xxᵉ siècle* (Paris and The Hague, 1957), one of the author's several perceptive studies on the subject, dealing particularly with observations in one large village, on which the following pages are chiefly based.

ferences on the land had been more noticed at the time than the more fundamental changes he launched: the commercialization of agriculture and the interference with the flood system of irrigation. These had begun a process of individualizing agricultural initiative and breaking down village autonomy, which confirmed his establishment of direct relations between the fisc and the village, despite tendencies already beginning in Meḥmed-'Alî's time to revert to an iqṭâ'-type system; and which went on to make possible, by the time of Sa'îd, the legal entrenchment of individual proprietorship in land.[2]

By Ismâ'îl's time, cotton became the major crop and its price in Europe largely determined Egyptian prosperity. The shift from flood toward perennial irrigation was well advanced. Finally, the land was becoming full: the old fear of a shortage of manpower disappeared with a great increase in population, and the untilled land was occupied. Under Westernizing rulers, these changes had led to private ownership; that is, possession of land had become a matter of individual legal process in the civil courts rather than an internal matter within each village. From 1858 on, in those courts, land was treated exactly like any other private posesssion. The village lost its collective responsibilities (except for *corvée,* which ceased to be collective only under the British) and each peasant was responsible directly before the government for his land and his taxes. Under these circumstances had already begun to grow, by Ismâ'îl's time, a class of large absentee proprietors living in the cities, whose lands resulted not (as before) from state grants but from foreclosures or purchases from other proprietors; and, perhaps more important, a new class of intermediate proprietors, of rural well-to-do families, differentiated from the other peasants only in degree of wealth, but furnishing the 'umdahs, government-appointed village headmen, and sending their sons, often, to seek city careers. Even so, the impact of Modernity on the cities had been far more rapid; the traditional cultural gap between village and city had been only accentuated.

From Ismâ'îl's time on, new pressures were building up. Once, the scarcity had been in manpower and the authorities had tried to tie the peasants to the land; now the population continued to increase headlong, and the scarcity became more and more one of land, which it became the peasant's dearest objective to hold on to. For a time, the pressure was held at bay as the engineering works of Sa'îd's time were perfected and supplemented; perennial irrigation, almost doubling or even tripling the production from a

[2] The inappropriateness comes out strongly here, of a term like 'feudal', which has been commonly used in a vaguely Marxist sense (i.e., to cover anything pre-capitalist) in most Islamic lands whenever large landholdings are in question. Neither the iqṭâ' nor the large private estate was a 'fief' in anything like the developed Medieval Occidental sense of a military vassel sub-state. But if the word has to be used at all, it can certainly be applied only to one or the other but not to both types of land arrangements, if such transitions as this are to be brought out; unless, indeed, the term is used in a careful and explicit Marxist manner, which is not usually the case.

single plot of land, became nearly universal by the turn of the century. But the fruits of perennial irrigation could not be doubled again, and with an end to famine and plague the population continued to multiply. Meanwhile perennial irrigation, less free in its distribution of the life-giving silt of the Nile, and not leaving enough time for the soil to dry out and aerate, threatened to diminish the fertility of the rich Egyptian soil. The peasants used animal dung to meet this threat, but could do less about the parasitical diseases which now sapped the strength especially of the males, who worked in the ever-present water. The relative prosperity of the countryside, which had resulted from the new agriculture and had been especially marked under the British, was being undermined.

In the twentieth century, the pressure on the land increased desperately; the ancient poverty returned in a new and harsher form. Concomitantly, the same forces which had upset the balance within the village were finally beginning to close the gap between village and city life, likewise in a new form. Even the pressure on the land tended to contribute to broadening the villager's perspective beyond the village. At least two acres were needed to sustain a nuclear family. With the concentration of land in large holdings, a large proportion of peasants became landless labourers on the estates, often established in 'company towns' apart from the ties and social security of any recognized village, or else working sporadically for smaller owners. Many of those who did have land had too small a plot to live on. But even apart from concentration of ownership, in the inter-war period the population expanded past the point where all those who wanted to live from the land could do so. Not really needed in the family fields, where they used up food without contributing a proportionate increase in production, many peasants went into the cities, especially the men, to work as unskilled labourers. Sometimes they returned to the village; always they kept in touch.

Those who led in introducing new technical patterns to the village, which further tended to break down the homogeneity within the village and its isolation from the city were sometimes poor lads who had made good in the city, but more often the wealthier peasants of the 'umdah class, who had got hold of more land. Already before the War of 1914, the complete transfer to perennial irrigation had broken down the old collective patterns of water use. Each family group tried to establish its pumps on the canal, which no longer overflowed of itself; the wealthier families could also grab more favoured positions here. In the inter-war period, the type of pump was improved and became more expensive; hence trade in water helped to differentiate further the rich from the poor. At the same time, the co-operative milling of flour, in which the families of the several family groups had joined in neighbourly equality, gave way to the patronizing of relatively mechanized private bakeries, which could manage more cheaply and simultaneously gave further openings to the rising rural business class.

Village community life put in question

In the course of such changes, the cultural forms which had expressed a common village life began to give way to patterns derived from city life, patterns in which an individual nuclear family was more on its own and the solidarities of village life counted for less. New sorts of vegetables had been introduced into the village menu already in the nineteenth century. Such vegetables (potatoes and tomatoes) became commoner, more wheat and rice were used, and more meat by those who could afford it, while some older rural recipes were practically forgotten, at least in the larger villages. Clothing, even when retaining the same basic cut, became a bit more elegant. By the fifties, at least, the man more often wore underwear, the woman's dress clung slightly closer to her form, shoes of some sort became far commoner (in protection against disease). The homes of the well-to-do were better built, often with second stories, and furniture was becoming generally more important—even to the point of reducing the role of jewellery in the woman's trousseau and on her person.

Though most of the villagers continued loyal to Islam, and for that matter to the bulk of village superstitions, there was a change in the religious emphasis. Interest in the Ṣûfî ṭarîqahs declined. The cult of the local saints' tombs retained its full vigour (though not always the cult of regional saints at other villages), but the living brotherhoods and their dhikr services were relatively neglected. This change reflected not only the rise of some new religious fraternities with a puritan attitude, but the mood of the Azhar itself, which remained the unimpeachable centre of intellectual prestige recognized in the village. Since the nineteenth century it had increasingly played down the ṭarîqahs and stressed the more Shar'î side of Islam. As earlier in the cities, so now even in the villages all the less strictly Shar'î side of village cultural life tended to be toned down, for instance extravagant mourning at funerals. In effect, this meant toning down all the more emotional and much of the more collective side of religion; and as the emotions were withdrawn from the cult, they were invested in politics. From the time of Muṣṭafà Kâmil's nationalist movement, peasants had been becoming aware of the possibility that political action among the city leaders might be directed to their own peasant needs. In 1919, the villages had taken an active part in the resistance to the British; support of the Wafd was general in the twenties and after 1936, with the discrediting of the Wafd, even lesser parties had their chance. It was as if the national political parties, partly identified with local inter-family rivalries, were absorbing the intenser passions of the ever-frustrated villagers even as the 'ulamâ' were repudiating them.

Indeed, perhaps the most serious consequence of the advancing commercialization of village life was the reduction in all that gave the villager the personal sense of being part of a larger common life. The expansion of population had chiefly taken the form of expansion in size of the old villages rather than their multiplication, so that a single village often became impersonally large (villages often reached 15,000 or more in population while retaining their essentially agricultural make-up). Moreover, even within the village, the old pattern of closed quarters, with many dead-ends and little direct communication from one neighbourhood to the next, was giving way before the cutting of through streets, at least in the larger villages, unsealing the neighbourhoods from each other. At the same time, the peripheral open spaces were disappearing under the pressure for land. The all-village ceremonies which had used the open spaces in common now had to make do with the various village streets. The close-knit neighbourhood family groups likewise had less in common: the same city-inspired law which had insisted on opening up streets for access was likewise suppressing the intra-village feuds, and the prominent old families (often ruined in the financial uncertainties of the twenties) no longer had their fighting bravi. The men of a group of families used to eat many joint meals in the common hospices; but the hospices were becoming fewer and men more often ate at home in the nuclear family, among (if possible) the newly favoured home furnishings. For the more ambitious, the Az'har, with its close ties to old village families, was being supplemented as a career opening by the multiplying secular professions and successes were likely to be felt at least somewhat as personal rather than as family triumphs. Even the village poet, who had sung (often very giftedly) community events like marriages, deaths, and feuds, was being replaced by the offerings of the radio, impersonal, universal, and often political.

In the inter-war period, the consumption of strongly brewed tea had increased drastically as compared with the older, less potent coffee. Experts complained that among the poorest, where a disproportionate amount of a family's resources went to tea, the habit was having serious nutritional consequences; and tales were told of peasants who lost their little remaining land through the indulgence. At the same time, the debilitating hashish, which had long been used in the cities but had been restricted to limited circles, became common in the villages despite government attempts at suppression; it became a normal accompaniment to a social evening among well-to-do males.

By the time of the War of 1939, many of the more alert in the cities had become aware of the possibility of improving the patterns of life in the village by methods more basic than had yet been tried. In the nineteenth century, the reformers had imposed a French-style legal order, in part so as to assure the individual's status, but it proved incomprehensible to the villagers and often actually resulted in injustice. True improvement must be more perceptive of village realities. Again, new crops and table foods had been promoted; they were accepted, but they changed nothing basic. Improvement must be more comprehensive. It must be more knowingly planned than was, usually, even the provision of elementary schools, where too many villagers learned their letters only to forget them in a life where they were not called for. A comprehensive programme was required, combining schooling adapted to village needs, health clinics and preventive measures such as the provision of pure water, training in agricultural methods so as to improve the yield and even centres for adult education and community activity to transform the overall outlook of the sceptical and unenterprising peasant. Inevitably, villages resisted trying anything new on a slim margin for risk, or indeed trying anything sponsored by government, which they had learned over the ages to regard as a prime enemy, urging increase of production only to take it for itself. If an effectively comprehensive programme were to succeed, it called for young men with sufficient city education to understand the broader needs and sufficient personal dedication to melt village prejudices. Men of such dedication were already proving rare: judges, teachers, physicians sent by the government into the villages too often, on meeting the sullen resistance of the peasants, abandoned any idealism they might have had and settled for getting through their assignment as painlessly and as profitably as possible.[3] The result was very general frustration among those who hoped to improve the increasingly desperate peasant life.

Reform and national culture

Such problems called for the devotion the Christian missionaries had been showing or, more recently, the communist cadres: it called for a sense of mission, grounded in clear ideas of what the national life might become. It called for some sort of ideology, and that implied coming to terms in some way, positively or negatively, with the cultural heritage of the past and its ideals. Such a cultural orientation was needed equally for the young educated men who were to work in the villages, and for the villagers themselves, whose local bases of integrating their lives were being undermined. Under the circumstances of the time, it must centre on an ideal of nationalism of some sort, giving that nationalism substantial cultural content.

The solution of Atatürk in the Turkish republic was, in a sense, the obvious one. To live effectively in the Modern world, the Turks suggested, a people must adopt wholesale the ways of those peoples who had created Modernity and exemplified it most fully at its best. A people must Westernize in the sense of joining with the West. But it was not yet clear whether that solution would prove adequate even in Turkey. The Turkish population had been poor; but without the intense population pressure of Egypt, as yet,

[3] A novel illustrating the frustration of a sensitive city man assigned to work in a rural setting is Tawfîq al-Ḥakîm's *The Maze of Justice*, Anglicized by A. S. Eban (London, 1947). (A corresponding report on problems of reform in a Turkish village—at a much later date, to be sure—is Mahmut Makal's *A Village in Anatolia* [1950], translated by Wyndham Deedes [London, 1954].)

and with a relative homogeneity of population by the time of the republic, they were under far fewer stresses. In the involved tensions of Egypt, the difficulties of a purely Westernizing solution stood out more quickly. Yet, even in the villages, there could be no question of simply building upon the cultural life of the past as it stood. Even in the villages, the past patterns had been undermined and their satisfactions were disappearing.

In Muḥammad 'Abduh's day, the intellectual classes had been divided into two parts. The wearers of the turban, the traditional 'ulamâ' typified by the Azhar shaykhs, represented continuity with the past. The wearers of the fez, which symbolized since the day of Maḥmûd II the Modernizing élite, journalists and graduates of the Modern-type schools, represented Westernization. The followers of Muḥammad 'Abduh were typically from among the latter class; but they were concerned not merely to Westernize, but to build on the values of the past: they agreed on the importance of a reform in Muslim-Arab life which should hark back to the classical 'Abbâsî age. Yet even among them, the solutions were radically diverse.

Some of his followers led a movement which eventually spread throughout the Arab lands and even to Malaysia: the 'Salafiyyah' movement among those 'ulamâ' who sought to reassert a Sharî'ah-minded Islamic orthodoxy free of traditional Ṣûfism and still more of local superstitution. They hoped to use Modern methods: the press, and lay organizations for propaganda and service works. For many of the Salafiyyah movement, the effective unit of social allegiance should be Islamdom as a whole, but they tended to exalt the Arabs as the special heirs and guarantors of Muḥammad's mission, as Muslims par excellence. Hence, their potential pan-Islamism, calling for a federation in which Arabic would be the universal language, tended to amount to a demand only for a pan-Arab nationalism on a Muslim basis. However, this movement was shy of any radical social changes. Eventually it found itself in close sympathy with the Wahhâbî movement in Arabia in its more conciliatory twentieth-century form, dedicated to a restoration of a pure Shar'î life adjusted to Modern technology but with a minimum of concessions to Modern ideas of human relations. Under the political needs of an inter-faith Arabism in the inter-war period, and under the increasing social stress in Egypt, such an outlook lost popularity.

On the other hand, many of Muḥammad 'Abduh's followers and associates were so concerned with social reform in a Modern Western sense that their concern with the old Arab culture and even with Islam was reduced to a minimum. Among the many causes which they took up, Qâsim Amîn led an assault on the segregation and restriction of upper-class women, demanding that women be allowed to play an equal role in society with men; when his first, mild, pious criticism of the traditional attitude of male supremacy was violently attacked as heresy, he reacted with a far more radical book maintaining that a culture varied directly in excellence according to the cultural level of its women, teachers of the children and humanizers of the men. Here he went so far as to depreciate even the classical Arabic culture as less advanced than the Modern Western, in part for this reason. Opposition to his ideas was very vocal. Nonetheless, in the inter-war period, when feminism was rampant in western Europe itself, a number of Egyptian ladies, home from a feminist conference in Europe, boldly threw aside the veil. Soon upper-class women were entering the hitherto all-male professions and taking an active part in society.

In the villages, where there was no veil anyway, the relevance was indirect. It was a question of what should be the inspiration of the cultural norms on which Egypt, that is, village Egypt, was to be rebuilt. This must ultimately depend on the choice of the articulate cities. Under conditions of political stalemate, it was largely in literature that the issues were fought out. The issues were mirrored, in fact, in the development of the literature itself, torn between old forms inadequate to Modern concerns and new forms for which both writers and readers were unprepared. If it was through a reform and revival of an older heritage that an adequate image of the future were to be achieved, it must be achieved in terms of a common literary medium. In fact, if the whole Arab community was to re-assert its consciousness without division among sects and between Muslims and non-Muslims, revival of literature, taken in a rather open sense, might be even more important than revival of religion: for in literature, Christian and Jewish Arabs could and did participate along with Muslims. Yet revival of the classical Arabic literature as a basis for Modern cultural life seemed to involve a contradiction on the very level of language, before one could even get on to the more substantive level of genre and literary form.

Modernizing the Fuṣḥà Arabic

Even in the nineteenth-century West, once mass participation in higher urban-type culture had become a requirement of the new industrial life, language was being consciously simplified and purified of alien complexities (such as overmuch Latinism in English). For each nationality that now insisted on an independent life required a standardized literary language which should reflect as closely as possible the spoken local dialects of its ordinary people; it dared no longer indulge the Agrarian Age luxury of a literary language which required years for even a privileged minority to acquire. Literature must be written in the vernacular, the spoken tongue of the people. Not only did the major languages, long used for general purposes, oust Latin even from scholarship; even what had been thought of as local dialects were endowed with a developed literary style by patriotic local authors.

Yet language had long been developing with the times in the West and presented no fundamental problems. But in most of the non-Western civilized lands the standardized literary languages existing in 1800 had been crystallized for centuries and no longer answered very closely to any living dialects, even when they were related to the dialects spoken by those who used them for literary purposes. Moreover, the whole vocabulary of Modern life was in any case missing, as well as any received literary pattern for expressing its moods. As in Turkey, where the answer was a drastic rejection of the old standardized form of the language, one of the tasks of Modernization everywhere was to work out an appropriate literary style for the new mass-based culture.

Among the Arabs—that is, those peoples whose spoken vernaculars were derived from the ancient Arabic and still sufficiently close to it so that to learn it was decisively easier for them than for others—the task of forming a literary style was even more complicated than among other Muslim peoples. In some respects, they might even seem to be in the position of the many Muslim peoples whose vernaculars were not developed literarily at all; of the Somalis, say, who had no literary language save the Arabic of their 'ulamâ', which bore little relation to their own home tongue. For the Arabs also, unlike the Turks or Persians, the standard Arabic of the 'ulamâ' was all they had on a high literary level. And the standard Arabic was distinctly further from the spoken Arabic-derived vernaculars than was literary Persian from spoken Persian or even than was the basic core of literary Turkish from spoken Turkish. The standard literary Arabic, preserved among all Muslims as a learnèd tongue (called Muḍarî or Fusḥà) was based upon Arabian dialects spoken in the sixth century. All the vernacular Arabic-derived dialects (called 'Âmmiyyah) had long since deviated from it very markedly, to a degree which corresponded to the deviation of the late Medieval Italian and Spanish dialects from literary Late Latin, that of the Vulgate. For instance, the noun, which had been declined in classical Fusḥà Arabic (as in Latin) had ceased (as in Romance) to be so; correspondingly, the use of fixed word order and other such devices for grammatical precision had become more decisive. The vocabulary, of course, was modified still more than the grammar, both in pronunciation and by substitution of new words for old. Something of the difference could be disguised in writing by the incomplete character of the usual Arabic script, which could write 'kilma' and 'kalimatun' identically. But even for an insensitive ear the spirit of the 'Âmmiyyah vernaculars and that of the older Fusḥà language were incompatible. Even in the Later Middle Period some popular tales had been set down in a form approaching the 'Âmmiyyah, but no Dante arose to formalize the 'Âmmiyyah literarily.

An attempt was made in the nineteenth century in Egypt to develop a written 'Âmmiyyah language to replace the Fusḥà, so that ordinary persons could read it without the training of 'ulamâ'. This attempt differed in kind from the parallel effort at reform of Turkish, for it required not merely pruning archaisms and literary excesses but coming to terms with a new linguistic structure. It was as much like putting a new language into writing as like reforming an old one. As in any development of a new literary medium, it involved, implicitly, standardizing some one dialect (perhaps that of Cairo) and working out a whole range of stylistic nicety which would give it that flexibility in an involved or precise context which is essential for serious literature, though scarcely needed for conversation. It could be questioned whether a literary 'Âmmiyyah was worth such effort when the 'Âmmiyyah dialects were so close to the Fusḥà, already well established. Why not have all Arabs learn that?

In fact, the efforts toward a literary 'Âmmiyyah were contemporaneous with the revival of the literary style of the classical period—which meant a restoration of the Fusḥà to active and versatile use. All those who were concerned more with reviving the classical heritage than with immediate mass appeal—Lebanese Christians establishing their place as Arabs, as well as Muslims concerned to purify Islam—joined in reviving the Fusḥà. They were adapting it to Modern needs, modifying the semantics of its vocabulary in accordance with the concepts used in Modern French and English and inventing new terms for wholly new objects and conceptions. While poets and essayists showed that this adapted Fushà could be used for most Modern literary purposes, journalists created a simplified version of it. This journalistic Fusḥà made some crucial concessions to the non-desinential grammar of the 'Âmmiyyah, but without accepting any of its more distinctive devices. If, in consequence, it was not very subtle, yet it was not too hard for a common individual to learn and was practically intertranslatable with Modern French journalese. This revived Fusḥà offered to fill the role that might have been assigned to a literary 'Âmmiyyah and, in fact, serious experimentation which might have developed the 'Âmmiyyah was abandoned.

Apart from the association of the Fusḥà with the classical Arab heritage, there were several other practical reasons for using the Fusḥà. Perhaps more important than its convenience to writers educated in the old manner was its universality. The 'Âmmiyyah was not constant from place to place; its development threatened to break up the Arab peoples into several small nations. This was a cultural threat from the beginning, being inconsistent with revival of a common Arab life. Eventually it became a political threat, too, which the Arabs, seeking strength through wider union, could not ignore. To be sure, unity might conceivably have been built with the 'Âmmiyyah. The Arabic dialects differed among each other roughly as much as the various Italian and Spanish dialects, being all more alike than they were like the Fusḥà. A standardized dialect of Cairo, for instance, might eventually be understood as well at Damascus and Baghdad as Florentine at Naples, enough to form a suitable common literary medium. But there was no early prospect of agreement on any one dialect; the Fusḥà alone was geographically universal among all who could be claimed as Arabs.

But it was finally the cultural associations which tipped the victory to the

Fusḥà for serious work. As in Greece, where conservatives have insisted on using classical Greek rather than the vernacular, the Fusḥà carried with it suggestions of cultural glory and religious sanctity which could not be sacrificed. The very literature which might give a national dignity and a shared sense of pride to a people very much in need of these could become an alien antiquity, reserved for the scholar, if the 'Âmmiyyah became the medium of education. Perhaps still more important, the Fusḥà was almost by definition the language of the Qur'ân. So strong was the identification of Fusḥà Arabic with Islam that Christians in many places were debarred by custom from teaching the Arabic language in the schools, whatever their qualifications, on the ground that they were not exposed in youth to its irreplaceable model, the Qur'ân. Muslim Arabs were glad to persuade themselves that they, unlike other Muslims, themselves spoke the sacred language (though 'corruptly' as they acknowledged) and were therefore especially competent to interpret its texts. Accordingly, the dynamic of the Arab drive for self-assertion made for Modernizing the Fusḥà rather than developing the 'Âmmiyyah.

Many writers found it difficult to be fluent and natural in the Fusḥà and by the mid-twentieth century some of the younger left-wing writers were again in revolt against it, one way or another. Above all, it proved unsuitable for the casual writing that elsewhere would be colloquial in style. Just as there was no literary style in the 'Âmmiyyah, so there was no colloquial style in the Fusḥà. (Indeed, the very possibility was not envisaged; the same words were used for 'colloquial' and 'vernacular' on the one hand and for 'literary' and 'classical' on the other.[4] Literate Arabs could converse in the

[4] Western Islamists have inexecusably perpetuated this confusion. Most, with their classical bent, frankly take sides against the 'Âmmiyyah. It is natural that they are not worried by the confusion which assimilates the difference between the Fusḥà and 'Âmmiyyah speech forms to a mere difference of style such as is found in Western languages, which they themselves do not always distinguish from deviations from standard dialect such as are found in the European provincial dialects. If Arabs can persuade their dissidents that the case in Arabic is in principle no different from that in German or French, which also have many spoken dialects not used for literature, they can strengthen the case for the Fusḥà. But they can do this only by ignoring the fact that standard English and German and French are spoken at home among the educated classes, albeit in a colloquial *style,* whereas there is no Fusḥà spoken in Arab homes, colloquial or otherwise. Specialists in teaching reading skills are not the only ones to have noticed the problem presented by the Fusḥà in elementary education, where the child is taught the Fusḥà *as if* it were his mother tongue—and in consequence receives the false impression, widespread among Arabs, that Arabic is an uncommonly difficult language (or at least *grammatical* Arabic: for Arabs are led to suppose by their very terminology that only Fusḥà is grammatical and that the 'Âmmiyyah has no grammar!). But it is less noticed that the down-grading of the 'Âmmiyyah insures that cultivated conversation can have no proper norms, or at least that these cannot be subject to formal discipline, for no regular distinctions are made among sheer slang, a proper colloquial style, and pedanticism: all alike are regarded as mere corruptions, in different degrees, of the only correct language, the Fusḥà. The confusion of terminology, in which the word 'colloquial' is used when 'vernacular' is meant, merely reinforces this misapprehension. It is another of the tendentious mis-usages which scholarly Islamicists should abandon.

Fusḥà when they were forced to, having been educated in it; but one could not crack a joke in it. Nonetheless, the disadvantages of the 'Âmmiyyah outweighed those of the Fusḥà.

Arab heritage and modern literature

All the reasons that favoured using the Fusḥà as literary language favoured also, in a more general way, basing other aspects of the Modern Arab culture on the classical heritage generally, rather than trying—in language or in culture—to start from scratch, presumably in outright Westernization as among the Turks. The Fusḥà in particular, and the classical heritage in general, were relatively familiar in their resources, which were rich and deep. Both teemed with glorious historical and religious associations to counteract a fear of inferiority over against the West. Both could be common to the peoples of a large and potentially wealthy group of lands, solidarity among which promised greater strength for all; indeed, the very question of how inclusive a group could be claimed as Arabs was not easily settled on the most inclusive basis, a broad linguistic one, save on the basis of tacitly subsuming the Arabic-derived dialects under the Fusḥà, which carried with it the older associations of the term 'Arab': first, the idea of ethnic descent from the Bedouins, and then use of the language of the Qur'ân—both notions being in themselves less inclusive, within the potentially 'Arab' sphere, than a broadly linguistic one.

At the same time, both the Fusḥà in particular and the classical Arab heritage in general suffered disabilities. In tying oneself to a pre-Modern cultural tradition generally, as in attempting to use a literary medium no longer actually spoken, the individual could feel constricted, bound to standards which, once all had agreed on them, were hard to make free with under the impulses of living experience. Above all, it was questionable how much such cultural norms, like the Fusḥà language itself, could serve to knit the increasingly restless masses into the positive idealism required for building nationhood.

Ṭâhâ Ḥusayn, the essayist whose memoirs form perhaps the most memorable piece of inter-war prose and who became minister of education at last, wrote in 1938 an analysis of the Egyptian educational system in which the cultural viewpoint of the school of Muḥammad 'Abduh received a practical latter-day embodiment. Education is the point at which considerations of cultural orientation must become most explicit—and might be most crucial. Education formed the individual's sense of self-identification, beyond the village level, and the frame of discourse which he would share with his fellows in his attempts at common understanding and action. Hence, amid suggestions for more democratic and more flexible methods, Ṭâhâ Ḥusayn presented also a theoretical position. He insisted that Egypt not only is but always has been a part of Europe, in broad cultural terms—a part of the Western as against (as alternative) the Indic cultural zone; and (conventionally) blamed the failure of Egypt to participate in the Modern west European evolution upon the Ottoman rulers.

This is an ideological position which could allow for as drastic a Westernism as Atatürk's. But Ṭâhâ Ḥusayn presupposed a different notion of culture generally, not making Gök-Alp's distinction between culture and civilization; he could think of the classical Arabic civilization at once as specifically Arabic and also as one of the high points of an ongoing Western civilization, and as being therefore still as valid as ever for Arabs. Hence in his educational proposals he stressed careful training in Fuṣḥà Arabic and its classical literature and also religious education. In religious education for Egyptians he included, to be sure, Christian education for the Copts; but his special interest was in Muslim education. Convinced that a people can find its sense of purpose only through the symbolic realm of religion, he turned his talents in his later years to rewriting the story of early Islam—in beautiful Fuṣḥà prose—as a sequence of inspiring historical images. He tried to be true to modern scholarship in doing so, but he aimed above all at presenting the moral archetypes which the image of the first generation of Muslims could afford. In such memories the new Egypt could be built.

At once the importance and the difficulty of revival of the classical heritage appeared nowhere, apart from religion, more immediately than in literature. Indeed, in some respects literature was performing some functions which religion had performed; the opening of new dimensions of moral awareness. Modern literature in the West reflected both the outward consequences of Modern innovative mass society and its inner spirit of inquiry and individuality. The outward impact of Modernity made for the use of media of popular communication such as the essay, the short story and the novel, which presupposed not only the printing press with its large, ephemeral market, but a diverse and anonymous audience. The external conventions of these media were keyed to such an audience: for instance, the fluency of their language, which dispensed with elaborate form or recondite allusion and was self-contained within each piece. Any audience, including Islamic ones, confronted with the fluidity of Modern conditions and needing to cope with them in artistic terms, could appreciate such flexible media. But the more fundamental formative traits of the novel, for instance, reached deeper than such conventions, into the inward spirit of Modernity. They reflected the new sense of human personality, above all; an awareness which could also be expressed through reconceiving an older literary form, tragedy. In fact, the fiction of the Modern West played a fundamental role in bringing to self-consciousness the Modern attitudes to human life and in giving moral discipline to those attitudes. It can be suggested, for instance, that without the Modern novelists' prior exploration of the nuances of individual personality, the work of Freud could hardly have been done. In most non-Western lands, fiction could serve to alert the audience to some of the more evident levels of Modern moral concern—for instance, to the social condition of women; but it could not so easily enter into the more intimate moral functions of Modern Western literature for an audience very differently situated.

In the realm of poetry, the revival of the classical inspiration was probably most effective. The old forms purified, the old themes, perhaps seen from a European-type viewpoint, reappeared. The poet Shawqî wrote an effective dramatic poem based on the tale of Majnûn and his beloved Laylâ which brought out symbolically (and romantically) the highest qualities of the ancient Arabs: using the Fuṣḥà forms and the old ideals to underpin Modern life. Even here, the vernacular verse of the villages (whose best exponents might be Az'harîs) went its own way little affected.

Dramatic presentation, in the widest sense, was at once a medium reaching the most popular, even illiterate, audiences and likewise singularly sensitive to the conditions of Modernity, which more readily left the ivory tower alone than the street. Among the Arabs, it naturally came to reflect most inescapably the problem of language, as well as all other literary problems, which it can serve to exemplify.

From at least the Later Middle Period on, satirical shadow-puppet plays and dramatic recitals of heroic legends formed the best public entertainment of the street. First in the Egyptian cities, then elsewhere, these were gradually replaced, in the nineteenth century, by troupes of players, evidently in imitation of the Italian players who toured the Levantine communities, but using the Arabic vernacular (as had the shadow plays and legend recitals). The players' themes were of the same sort as those of the shadow plays and the reciters: often stories from *The Thousand and One Nights* or satire on common human types, often farce or burlesque. Men took the female roles to avoid scandal. Singing was an essential part of the acting. These plays were patronized at once by rich and poor, though scorned by the Modernly trained élite. To this point, what was essentially a continuing tradition was being renewed, under changed conditions, in new forms, without any basic cultural cleavage, if also without special excellence.

In the later nineteenth century, the players became more ambitious, sometimes adapting French or Italian plays, especially farce or melodrama. After the War of 1914, with a certain amount of government encouragement, both in Egypt and elsewhere, the troupes were differentiated. Some continued to specialize in musical farce and burlesque and came to be patronized only by the lower classes and then the villages. Others turned anew to the Occidental inspiration, now accepting it more fully: despite the 'ulamâ', feminine roles were played by women, and serious translations of European plays were used, not mere adaptations, as well, occasionally, as original plays in the European style. These were patronized by the upper classes. At the same time, in fiction for the private reader, the short story and the novel were being adopted; here, too, the Modern Western genres were more appropriate than classical Arabic ones to the day of journalism. But whether in drama or in simple fiction, those Western themes that were easiest to absorb were themes of anecdote and moralizing tale, of melodrama and especially of historical romance—themes not too different from those of the Maqâmât or of the heroic legends of the street reciters. Novels and plays dealing with the complex growth of personality, the most intimate level of Modernity in the West, were slow to develop. There was no tragedy.

The writers of stories and novels adopted the Fusḥà of the Syrian journalists in writing for an educated audience; with the increasing sophistication, more and more serious playwrights likewise used the Fusḥà rather than the 'Âmmiyyah. This was relatively appropriate to historical plays or to symbolical ones which made no attempt at a naturalistic effect. It was evidently inappropriate to the elucidation of intimate character, where the spontaneous language of daily life alone could carry the overtones required. The linguistic problem simply reinforced the tendency to avoid such themes, for which the audience was not yet ready. The most sophisticated classical Arabic genres were out of vogue, while the most sophisticated Modern genres were not yet able to replace them.

On the other hand, the field of dramatic presentation as a whole, in which for a time the troupes of players had been gaining an exclusive position in the cities, was being broadened again for the popular audience first by films and then by radio. Here, except for special highbrow programmes, the medium was the 'Âmmiyyah; but here there was little attempt at serious dramatic presentation. It was not in popular films that the more intimate development of personality could be looked for. The films continued the older traditions of the musical farce or the musical melodrama, drawing on *The Thousand and One Nights* or historical legend like the earlier players. On a serious level it became a test of Arab cultural loyalty to use the Fusḥà; meanwhile, popular culture was typified by the 'Âmmiyyah.

Modern Arab life threatened to be split between two sets of cultural norms; the more cultivated ideal doing little to discipline the mass popular culture, just as the norms of the Fusḥà could do little to discipline ordinary conversation. The gap between the more cultivated norms, informed by some contact with the great accomplishments of the past, and the more popular cultural life was indeed a common one under Modern conditions. Among the Arabs, the attempt to revive a classical heritage helped to accentuate the problem. By a path designed to avoid the dilemma of the Turks, whose new culture was divorced from the roots of popular cultural feelings, the Arabs were arriving at a like dilemma. Even on the higher educated level, it was editions and translations, together, that formed perhaps the most valuable part of the reading material offered the early twentieth-century Arabs. The most inspiring of the old literature was revived by re-editions, the most inspiring of the new was introduced by translations. But neither expressed the life of the here and now, neither could offer a vision of what a Modern

Arab nation was and could be. This had to be striven for more painfully from historical film to historical film, from tentative novel to less tentative novel. As in the case of language itself, to attempt to create a new vehicle from nothing might require sacrifices which would deprive the new of its greatest potential advantages; but to attempt to build the new directly on the old threatened to stultify the new and limit its potential range. It required a creative spirit to break through the dilemma.

Most of the more secular of Muḥammad 'Abduh's followers, such as Ṭâhâ Ḥusayn, when taking the lead in working for Arab cultural revival, thought primarily in terms of Egypt. The unit for the Modern institutions was to be the Nile valley, and it was for the people of the Nile that the new inspiration must be brought. But the classical Arabic heritage was common to all Arab peoples, and the natural field for its revival necessarily included the Fertile Crescent with Baghdad, the 'Abbâsî capital. Other Arabs with a similar viewpoint soon included all Arabs as their solidarity group. For a time, the Egyptians could feel culturally self-sufficient and even look on the *'Arab*, the Bedouin, as essentially foreigners. Yet Egypt, and especially Cairo, was becoming in the inter-war period, even more than before, the centre of east Arab cultural life. The Azhar at Cairo had long been the premier madrasah of east Arab lands; but in the twentieth century, Cairo was also becoming the film centre of all Arabic-speaking lands, not to mention its major role in the press and even radio. If Cairo could feel aloof from the provinces, the other east Arab lands were often jealously aware that Cairo was an essential part of the Arab people. The Arabs of the Fertile Crescent and, increasingly, of the Arabian peninsula itself were eager to work out their new social and educational, as well as economic and political, patterns on an all-Arab scale. For this, Egyptian co-operation was indispensable. The Egyptians had to come to terms with this demand one way or another. The circumstance which finally forced a positive response from the Egyptians was a political one: the presence of the Zionists on the Egyptian doorstep, just across the canal.

The test case: Zionism

The uplift of the peasants was bound to be slow. The struggle for independence from the great European powers had to be carried on against a built-in handicap which it was the very purpose of the struggle to overcome. But however inadequately, as yet, the Arabs had solved those problems, they could feel proud, by the time of the War of 1939, of having renewed their cultural life. Not only in literature, but in urban social and financial patterns, in religious thinking, and in the arts and sciences generally, educated Arabs had effectively assimilated the methods of the West and were as active and creative as the people of any Muslim lands; in fact, more so than most. Most educated Arabs little trusted the various governments, which were often corrupt, and in any case were limited by foreign influence and internally controlled by the privileged classes; yet they had some confidence in the Jordanian and Iraqi and especially the Egyptian armies and air forces, which were reasonably well equipped with the weapons of the inter-war period. But in the midst of the east Arab countries, in Palestine, was a standing challenge to their self-assertion.

Zionist nationalism had grown up parallel to Arab nationalism and as a result of the same overall world conditions in the nineteenth century. The various east European peoples of that century were all trying to establish themselves as nationalities and free themselves of the dominant empires in the area so as to enter Modern Western life on an equal basis; but the Ashkenazi Jewish population of northeastern Europe, professing a different faith and even speaking a different language (Yiddish, a Germanic dialect) from the main body of those peoples, were excluded from such movements. Indeed, the new nationalism of the peasants and the landed classes turned violently against a group which in Poland or Russia represented an urban, middle-man element possessing a social ambivalence (though not a power) equivalent to that of the Levantines in the Ottoman empire. Yet there was no single concentrated area in eastern Europe where the Ashkenazi Jews formed a sufficient majority to hope to establish their own state. At the same time, the west European Jews found that Modernity, with its stress on the individual and the state, though it toned down religious or ethnic differences, had only imperfectly erased the long-standing Christian hostility to Jews. On occasion that hostility even received renewed force through the new nationalism as it was interpreted in some classes. If they were not massacred, as in eastern Europe, their position remained insecure. Hence when Ashkenazis of east Europe worked out what seemed a solution to their problem, migration to Palestine, they received the support of a large section of west European Jews. The proposed solution was, in fact, in line with accustomed Western thinking.

Europeans, convinced that it was the deep-rooted and enduring superiority, of their own peoples, and no transient accidental circumstances, which had led them to develop Modern life and to establish their dominant position in the world at large, often looked on the rest of the world as being more or less at their disposal, within limitations imposed only by their own sense of justice and generosity. Regarding other peoples as culturally static and capable of advancement at most only through Occidental benevolence, they looked at their current nineteenth-century condition and made little allowance for any negative effects Modernity had already had on them or even for a possible future internal development. In some areas, such as North America, the multiplying and land-hungry Europeans met only weakly organized primitive agriculturists or hunters and simply removed or liquidated them, taking over their lands in the name of a superior civilization. In more civilized regions, such as the Muslim lands, this was not so simply done.

In Algeria, for instance, the French encouraged French agricultural settlement from 1830 on, but they did not attempt to wipe out the Muslim population. In fact (as it did almost everywhere else) that population proceeded to increase enormously. The French attempted to settle only in what they could call legally their own: on lands seized from 'rebellious' landlords, for instance, or reclaimed by themselves from waste territory. Sometimes, indeed, they mistakenly assumed land to be 'waste' because it was not being used for intensive cultivation, though it was an essential part of the local land-use pattern. Sometimes the peasants suffered for their landlords' stubbornness. But even apart from such lapses, what the French failed to see as an injustice was that an alien community was being introduced into the society, an alien community which, as part of the Modern Western society, was possessed of both economic and political power to mould the life of the land without regard to the wishes or interests of the established population. The French believed that they were 'developing' Algeria: with modern farming methods, modern transportation and administration and commercial methods, from which the Muslims did receive some benefit, they were not only profiting themselves but bringing progress and prosperity to the Muslims. If the French retained the lion's share of the advantages for themselves, this was only just, as it was they who had created them. Otherwise (they believed), the Muslims would have continued to languish in their immemorial, unchanging cultural torpor, in despotically ruled poverty and misery. The French invited the Muslims to share in the French privileges, in fact, if only they would share in the French responsibilities by taking on the legal position of French citizens, which meant giving up their legal status as Muslims under the Sharî'ah. To the French, this seemed a slight sacrifice of an outworn creed, which only blind prejudice could balk at. The Muslims, however, even those highly educated in French schools, rarely chose to become Frenchmen, however French their culture usually was; and even though, till the War of 1939, they saw little hope of ending French rule. The European settlers (elsewhere sometimes called 'White Settlers') in Algeria remained a caste apart, privileged and wealthy amidst an increasingly dissatisfied population of whom they knew little.

In the nineteenth century, the idea of introducing European settlers into lands considered 'empty' or at least undeveloped, and appropriate for a European type of life, was as yet almost unchallenged even among idealistic circles. Some idealists in Ashkenazi Jewish circles found it only natural to combine this idea with the age-old aspiration of all Jews to return to the Holy Land and re-establish the Jewish nation in spiritual perfection. Instead of waiting for the Messiah to lead them, they should return at once with the aid of their European capital and of the new economic resources which Modernity had brought them as Europeans. By European standards, at least, all Syria seemed an 'empty' and certainly an undeveloped land, with plenty of appropriate space for European settlers. If the Jews could not have their homeland in Europe this was because they were divinely destined to have it only in their own land—in Palestine. Jews should return now to Zion.

Zionism soon caught on as an idea and even as a personal act. In the later nineteenth century, numbers of Jews did immigrate and began using the long unspoken Hebrew language even in their home life, raising children whose mother tongue was Hebrew and who knew no other homeland than Palestine itself. They were received sceptically by Arabic-speaking and by other Yiddish-speaking Jews, who could doubt whether Hebrew, as a sacred language, should be debased to everyday use, or whether it was human initiative that could set up a nation of spiritual perfection. Nevertheless, the vision was strong enough to create an increasingly well-rooted Hebrew-speaking community under easy-going Ottoman auspices. They bought up lands from absentee landlords and set about reclaiming many acres that had been swamp and derelict, and generally introduced a progressive European element into the economy.

It was this community which served as foundation for turning Palestine into a Jewish homeland under the British mandate. Though immigration from Europe increased little in the twenties, the Zionists received official recognition; Hebrew was made one of the official languages of Palestine. But meanwhile, the Arab national consciousness was being intensified through the struggle with the British and French. As the possibility became ever more realistic of a residual European settler rule in southern Syria, in the midst of the Arab lands, even if the British could be expelled, Arab national feeling focused on the threat of Zionism. The European Jewish settlers were seen as a present excuse for and support of British rule in Syria and as a future bastion of Europe, designed to control the Suez Canal immediately and in the long run to divide Egypt from the Fertile Crescent and to keep the Arabs under a permanent threat of military intervention.

The local Arabs at first tended to look to British fair play, hoping that when the British realized that the land was not 'empty' they might limit Jewish immigration sufficiently so that the danger of alien rule over the Palestine Arabs would be minimized. However, under the pressure of the world commercial depression of the thirties, anti-Semitism in Europe turned much more virulent. The Nazi government of Germany, from 1933 on, transformed a latent anti-Jewish feeling into a systematically brutal murderousness hitherto found only in eastern Europe, and there only sporadically. Jewish immigration from Germany, and then from all Europe during the War of 1939 as the German government expanded its control, became a flood. The local Arabs of Palestine finally turned to violence, which alone the British seemed to respect, and won promises that immigration would be restricted. But the pressure from Europe only increased at the end of the war, when those Jews who had survived the Germans' mass murders (seconded too by many Poles, Frenchmen, and others) longed only to escape from a Christian Europe which they could not trust. The independent countries, with relatively open spaces, such as the United States, where they might have been absorbed with relative ease, barred their doors; anti-Jewish prejudice was not unknown there either. Only in Palestine did they find a local community, already at odds with the British government, eager to receive them and to use smuggling and even terrorism to help them. To Palestine they pressed in tragic shiploads, won over in desperation to a Zionist zeal, and eager to establish a national Jewish state, at whatever cost, which they could call their own. Indeed, they scarcely were allowed by the Christians any real alternative.

By this time, all the politically conscious eastern Arabs were vitally concerned both for the immediate fate of the Palestinian Arabs and for the long-term implications of an alien state entrenched in Syria. There seemed hardly space enough in the small strip of mandated Palestine for the enormous wave of people that was looming, in addition to the crowded population (nearing two million) it already contained: someone would have to give. Already in the late thirties, Arab farmers in Palestine, sometimes displaced by immigrant Zionists, were suffering severe land hunger; this was hardly counter-balanced by the special efforts made by the British in their one area of direct rule, which had resulted in the best educated Arab population outside Lebanon. With further immigration, the Arabs would find themselves, at best, a foreign minority in their own homeland; at worst, lacking the capital and the technicalistic skills of the immigrants, they would become a pauperized rabble or even be forced to leave altogether to make space for the newcomers. Nor were the Muslim and Christian Arabs themselves lacking in anti-Jewish feelings; especially for Muslims, the prospect of Jewish rule seemed the ultimate point of the degradation they had been forced to acknowledge in the face of the Christian West. Jerusalem was a holy city for both Christians and Muslims as well as for Jews. The Arabs of Palestine prepared to fight and called on the relatively independent Arabs around them for help in expelling the invaders; Iraqis, Syrians (of all three states), and even Egyptians and Sa'ûdî Arabians were glad to respond.

The Arab armies and their peoples, proud of their advances, felt confident of victory. Already at the end of the war, in 1945, the Arab governments had formed a League to co-ordinate their efforts in common causes, leading among which was that of Palestine. In the Palestine issue, Muslims and Christians, Arabs of the Fertile Crescent and Arabs of Egypt, all felt threatened in common. On this issue, at least, the Egyptians were willing to acknowledge a nationalism which would be neither purely Egyptian nor broadly pan-Islamic, but all-Arab in a secular sense (whatever its Muslim undertones). Here the validity of a common harkening back to their Arab heritage would be proved.

By 1948, Western overseas rule was everywhere in full retreat and the British had no mind to continue administering so thorny a problem as Palestine, where fighting between Arabs and Zionists had already begun. They got the United Nations (successor as world authority to the League of

Nations and the Concert of Europe) to take over responsibility for Palestine, where it proclaimed a partition between Zionists and Arabs; then the British withdrew. Though the Zionists at first held out for the whole of mandated Palestine, partition was in fact still a victory for them, as it gave them a state, though small in territory. As for the Arabs, who were all along protesting against any partition of Syria, acceptance of partition on a slightly smaller scale would still have been defeat; the Arab states launched an attack as soon as the British left. But with an initial advantage in airplane fighting, they soon began bickering over the future of reclaimed Palestine. Amid mutual charges of betrayal and under a cloud of corruption and ineffectiveness within each of the governments, the Arab forces were defeated. The Zionists not only held the area allotted them in the partition but added a good deal to it, and the circumstances, of the war allowed them to be rid of the bulk of the Arab population as well, several hundred thousand of whom were driven or fled as refugees into the neighbouring Arab-held areas. The Zionists proclaimed their state of Israel and the Arabs universally felt radically shamed: the existence of Israel seemed standing proof that they were not yet able to hold their own in the Modern world, after all.

V

Iran and the Russian Empire: The Dream of Revolution

Faced with the overwhelming power of aggressive Western nations, and aware that that power arose from the very cultural fibre of the Western societies, many Ottoman Turks drew a reasonably obvious consequence: national salvation in Modern times depended upon dropping the weaker social heritage of the Islamicate past and adopting the stronger heritage of the European present. The solution was to Westernize; the genuinely Westernized state could then hold its own among other Western states. The location of Turkey within eastern Europe and its close involvement with the Christian east European peoples helped the Turks to come to this conclusion, but it was a natural point of view, which had its exponents everywhere. The dominant line of Ottoman and Republican Turkish reform was, or at least was conceived as, Modernization through Westernization, through Europeanization: a course eased by the already fashionable Westernism of many of the more wealthy. Such a course appealed to most Muslim peoples; but even among the Turks it was not quite enough, simply to adopt Western ways; some kind of settlement had to be come to with the local cultural past. Partly this could be revived and built on, partly it could be swept away in revolution; the Turks did something of each.

Among the Modernizing Arabs, particularly, many felt that a revival of the older heritage was the main key to modernization. They distrusted too radical a response to the challenge. Rather than switching heritages, they wanted to revive their own older heritage, to purify it of what were conceived as accretions of an intervening time of decadence, and face the West with a strength newly derived from their own deepest roots. They wanted to Modernize on the basis of revival and reinterpretation of the Islamicate past. In practice, the difference in intention did not make a very obvious difference in outcome, but the way in which the leading classes conceived what they were doing, especially in the inter-war period, left its mark in many fields of activity.

The west Iranian kingdom also went through an intense Westernization, especially of the public facets of society, during the inter-war period. There, too, a naked Westernization was not sufficient. There was an ostentatious harking back to an ancient heritage; but the most dramatic component in the west Iranian Modernization was the sense of revolution; the hope for it and even the presence of it. The Qâjâr state was probably the only Muslim state in which the dynamism of a great street revolution, classic in Europe since 1879, unfolded to any extended degree. Parts of the Iranian and Caucasian lands were also involved, permanently or temporarily, in the Russian revolution of 1917. Modernization in this whole region has been coloured deeply by the dream of revolution.

Revolution in the first instance meant the overthrow of a relatively small layer of the most privileged, including royalty (who were often allied with the Western powers), in favour of allowing a Modernizing urban middle class greater scope. But once made central to people's hopes and carried to its logical conclusion, the dream of revolution could brook no compromise with existing imperfections. In the twentieth century it came to mean, in some minds, rebuilding society from scratch: wiping away the Sharî'ah certainly, but not adopting European codes, even if improved on; rather, creating a new order of the future better than that of either old Islamdom or present Europe. A people might displace not only the men in top positions of power but all the most privileged classes, carriers of the existent high-cultural traditions, whether native or imported. Then it could be free to reconstruct its life on a novel pattern altogether, which might draw on, but would not be an extension of, any other form of society, local or foreign. It would, like the republican Turks, drop the Islamicate heritage; yet without assimilating to the West as such; rather, it would distil a pure Modernity which should stand on its own, being neither Islamic nor Western, but superior to both. But such a dream emerged only slowly.

The social protest of the Bâbîs

The Iranian and neighbouring lands in the Iraq and the Caucasus, long so central to Islamicate culture, were relatively isolated from the earlier impact of the new Europe. European trade, indeed, had been vigorous in Ṣafavî times (there had even been Catholic missions), but its importance had been reduced in the eighteenth century, with the internal political disruption; by the end of that century, European interests were represented largely indirectly—by way of the more central parts of the Ottoman empire, or of India, or of the Volga region. At the same time, the cultural tradition of the area, heartland of the Persianate literary tradition and given to Shî'î loyalties, was relatively independent of that in the areas most immediately affected by the new Europe. The Iraq and Iran maintained well into the nineteenth century a high level of philosophical and religious creativity almost unparalleled in other Muslim areas. Even early in the nineteenth century, though the position of the commercial classes was being undermined, the 'ulamâ' were making serious developments in jurisprudence, and the Persians honoured a major new philosopher (Mullâ Hâdî, 1797/8–1878) in the school of Mullâ Ṣadrâ. It is only after the 1830s that, by subsequent Shî'î reckoning, the writers must be relegated to the position of epigones.

We have taken note of one of the philosophical minds of the late eighteenth century, also influenced by Mullâ Ṣadrâ; that of Shaykh Ahṣâ'i. He developed a Shar'ism that differed strikingly from that of the Wahhâbîs and Sanûsîs, his contemporaries, in that it was not only deeply 'Alid-loyalist but also highly philosophical, looking to a long-term spiritual improvement of mankind. But like theirs, it was reformist, and opposed to the Ṣûfî ṭarîqahs. Indeed, it was explicitly chiliastic, and, like theirs, it took on great subsequent significance under the impact of the Western Transmutation. It was in an atmosphere still relatively uncorrupted by the Western presence, yet keenly aware of it as restricting the power of the Islamic community and presenting new and unexamined possibilities of living, that many Shî'îs of the Shaykhî school in the 1830s were expecting, more insistently than ever, the renewed presence of the Bâb, the special spokesman of the Hidden Imâm, who would order society aright again. A young man of great theological and spiritual gifts, 'Alî-Moḥammad of Shîrâz (1819–50), won considerable following among them and in the tradesmen classes of the town population generally. 'Alî-Moḥammad, as Bâb, proclaimed (beginning in 1844) a new and quite liberal Sharî'ah, a new set of symbolisms to replace those of Shî'î Islam, and the expectation of a new prophetic dispensation of social justice soon to be realized among his followers.

The Bâbîs, as his followers were called, were impatient to see the new justice realized. They preached vigorously and soon came into open conflict with the Shî'î 'ulamâ' and then with the Qâjâr government. 'Alî-Moḥammad was arrested but in prison he continued to be the inspiration of a devoted band of idealists. There were riots and finally extensive revolt; 'Alî-Moḥammad was executed; the movement was suppressed with much bloodshed in 1852.

After 'Ali-Moḥammad's death, the majority of his followers gradually accepted the lead of another young man, Bahâ'ullâh (1817–92), who then, in 1863, proclaimed himself the new prophet predicted by 'Alî-Moḥammad; those Bâbîs who accepted him were henceforth known as Bahâ'îs (the others, as Azalî Bâbîs). The Bahâ'îs retained the social mission of the Bâbîs, which had favoured the town merchant and artisan classes and allowed women a much freer role than had traditional Islam. (A Bâbî heroine publicly tore off her veil in 1848.) But they abandoned the idea of immediate revolt within Iran, looking rather to a more general conversion of the world by the disciples of the new order. Bahâ'ullâh already had a cosmopolitan outlook; on his exile from the Qâjâr realm, the Ottoman government detained him, as potentially subversive, settling him finally at Acre in Syria; there he attracted converts from beyond Iran itself, though the largest concentration of followers of the new faith were always to be found in Iran. He was succeeded (in the Shî'î manner) by his son, who won many converts from among Europeans (especially in the United States), whose tastes he pleased with a universalist liberalism in religion (he discouraged killing, either of humans for political reasons, as in war, or of animals for food). He in turn was succeeded by his grandson, trained at Oxford, who organized the faith on a world-wide basis with institutions designed to expand, with persistent missionary effort, into a world political order founded on faith.

The Shaykhî religious vision continued to be the starting-point for that of the Bahâ'îs, whose demand for a universalist moral outlook and a liberal social order reflects a Ṣûfî-type emphasis on the imponderables of the spiritual life as combined, by such movements as the Shaykhî, with the 'Alid-loyalist concern for a spiritual organization of just social order. But by the later part of the century the movement had become deeply tinged with the liberalism of nineteenth-century Europe and came to form, in some measure, an instrument for introducing the moral sides of technicalistic Modernity into western Iran. Eventually Bahâ'î schools, partly staffed with American converts, shared with those of the Western missionaries (and of Zoroastrians, staffed from India) the education of a new liberal generation, attracting many non-Bahâ'î students.

Jamâluddîn Afghânî and the concessions to Europeans

For the period in which insurrectionary Bâbism was being superseded by education-minded Bahâ'ism was that in which accommodation with the West was becoming fashionable even in the Qâjâr realm. In 1848, Nâṣiruddîn, the new shâh (1848–96), launched an effort at ministerial responsibility and generally tried to Europeanize the forms of his régime. In 1852 was founded what was intended to be a government institute of higher education on Western lines; from 1840 on, the various Western-sponsored schools began to multiply, and, from 1858, local students were sent to Europe in far greater numbers than in the Napoleonic period. Already after 1823, printing had become widespread and after 1851 there were rudimentary newspapers; by and large, the Westernization of the surface of urban life proceeded in Ṭehran rather as in Istanbul or Cairo, if somewhat less intensely. The shâh himself made extensive tours through Europe and wrote with amusement, respect, and a certain amount of admiration of what he had seen, using a simple literary style which the reading of French was commending to fashionable circles.

Yet not only had the Islamicate cultural tradition retained greater vitality in the Qâjâr state than elsewhere. Those Persians and Azerîs who were not under direct Russian rule did, even late in the century, remain more nearly untouched by the new international forces than either the inhabitants of the Ottoman empire or those of India. Meanwhile, older forms of land tenure remained more nearly in the condition they had reached after the end of Ṣafavî times; the guilds were much less seriously affected by international trade, and to the end of the nineteenth century continued to be the strongest form of organization in the cities. The attempts at governmental modernizations, such as they were, did not produce an efficient despotism, though the old tacit understanding was effectively broken down, whereby the bulk of the population had been immune to direct interference from the centre. Perhaps it was with the development of a more centralized perspective among the wealthier families, it became customary to recognize (by informal consensus) a single mujtahid as the most authoritative, even though he was not the Bâb of the Imâm. His fatwàs were binding on all Shî'îs, and the wealthy from all over the kingdom and beyond sent to him, rather than to local mujtahids, their offerings to the imâm (the *khums*). This development helped to keep alive the independence of the mujtahids under the new conditions, especially when the so recognized chief mujtahid resided in the Iraq, out of reach of the shâh. It is symptomatic that while in the Russian-ruled Muslim lands, the European language which was learned by the tiny *avant-garde* group interested in things Western, was Russian; in the Qâjâr state it remained French for the most part rather than either English or Russian, the languages of the peoples most commercially and politically prominent there. The more positive response to Western Modernity, that is, remained largely a theoretical matter among the élite, who chose that Western language which had most prestige in the West, rather than most practical relevance in Iran.

But the shâh's interest in the West did not remain academic: it was not limited to expensive luxury tours. To pay for the tours, among other things, he proposed to grant concessions to European businessmen in his dominions, ranging from railway building and oil prospecting to a state lottery; the shâh was to share in the profits. He seems to have felt relatively secure that these ventures, which brought European interests into the kingdom in a more intimate way than did sheer foreign trade, would not in fact limit his own independence, such as it was. He was aware of Russian power; indeed, (rather than undertake the expensive and doubtful task of Modernizing local forces) he brought in a special 'Cossack' brigade as a support to his throne, trained and officered by Russians who were still under the control of the Russian army command of the Caucasus. But he also cultivated relations with the British and could hope that neither power would allow the other to take over entirely. At this point, in 1889, the shâh invited Jamâluddîn Afghânî to Tehran, the glowing-eyed preacher who was stirring Muslims all round the world to a vision of a common Muslim front against the West, whom we have already met as the master of the young Muḥammad 'Abduh in Egypt. His influence was already feared by the British empire, and acknowledged in Russia where he then lived. If the shâh thought he could tame this ascetic zealot by keeping him in a gilded cage, he overestimated himself.

Originally a Persian from near Hamadân in the Qâjâr kingdom, Afghânî is said to have studied at Najaf, the great Shîʿî intellectual centre near old Kûfah. He gained his early political experience in Afghanistan. Exiled thence in 1868, when he happened to be on the losing side, he became acquainted with Muslim reform movements in India, where he seems to have been disgusted at the willingness of Muslims to accept Western domination and merely to try to carve for themselves a more comfortable niche within it. From that point on he travelled about persistently, in Egypt, in India, in the west Iranian kingdom, in Russia and in the Ottoman empire, always trying to arouse Muslims to unite to reassert Islamic might. He urged them to go back of latter-day tradition, to the simpler and sterner elements of the Early Muslim Period precisely in order to free the Muslims to use modern science and technology in this cause.

Afghânî does not seem to have originated many new ideas, but he saw what point or plea at a given moment would serve his cause and could effectively crystallize developing sentiment. In this way he became a vigorous and sometimes violent advocate of all kinds of reform: political, religious, and social. Intellectually, his roots seem to have been in the tradition of Falsafah, for which revealed religion was, above all, a political force. Free of any of the political caution which too individualistic a Sharîʿah-mindedness might have inspired, and ready for any sort of intellectual venturesomeness, he looked to a combination of modern science on the intellectual level and Islamic ʿaṣabiyyah, group solidarity, on the political. He denounced the Ṣûfî tradition for its quietism and the conventional ʿulamâʾ for their obscurantism, calling for a 'Muslim Luther'. Yet with his admiration for the technical and intellectual vigour of the Occident, he condemned it vituperatively (at least on the level of the unphilosophical public for whom he wrote) for its godless materialism. Enduring strength, he said, would be found only in Islam. He taught that each Muslim people should bestir itself and strengthen itself to co-operate with other reviving Muslim peoples in a 'pan-Islamic' movement of political solidarity against the West. Though he took up the pan-Islamic notion after the Ottomans had begun to push it, and was willing to consider the Ottoman sultanate as one candidate for leadership in the hoped-for Muslim unity, his notion of pan-Islamic solidarity had ultimately little to do with that of ʿAbdülḥamîd.

It was in Egypt in the 1870s that Afghânî first evoked an active response, winning some of the best Egyptian youth to a militant anti-Western Muslim Modernism. After the suppression of the ʿUrâbî movement, he published the most influential of the Arabic journals of the time in exile at Paris: *Al-ʿurwah al-wuthqâ*, in 1884. (Muḥammad ʿAbduh collaborated with him on this.) Violently anti-British, it was prevented by the British in Egypt and India from reaching a sufficient paying audience to keep it going; yet it was eagerly read wherever copies could be smuggled. But Afghânî had by far his most spectacular impact in the Qâjâr kingdom. There the populace was already widely restive at the shâh's new despotism and especially at his involvements with foreigners. Many young Shî'î intellectuals were captivated with the idea that what was called in the West 'democracy', identified with the 'rule of law' as against the rule of despots, could in fact be seen as most perfectly embodied in the principles of Islam and its insistence on the rule of the Sharî'ah—as represented by independent mujtahids. In the name of 'Islamic democracy', they gave Afghânî zealous support. He soon broke with the shâh, who had no intention of reforming under his guidance.

Afghânî was able, with his wide perspective, to point out that the apparent immunity of the Qâjâr territories to further Western interference was not dependable: that foreign concessions could lead to further foreign domination by giving some Europeans the kind of legal foothold which other Europeans would respect as an excuse for intervention. Consequently, when, in 1890, the shâh proposed a concession to a British company of a tobacco monopoly, which would have power to control all the trade, internal and in export, of that weed universally used among Persians, and the people proved inclined to resist, Afghânî seized on this as a singular illustration of the shâh's disregard of the Muslims' welfare in his pursuit of foreign money. The growers would be put at the mercy of a monopsony, the many small dealers would be displaced, and the consumers would be receiving their smokes at the hands of infidels whom strict Shî'îs tended to regard as impure.

Afghânî agitated this issue, among others, from his asylum at the Shî'î sanctuary near Tehran, Shâh 'Abdul'aẓîm (the ancient Rayy); he roused much popular sentiment; not only the nationalist intellectuals, some of them devoted to Afghânî's every word, but the tradesmen of the *bâzârs* felt the force of the danger. But a still more important group responded also. In contrast to the Jamâ'î-Sunnî lands of the Ottoman empire, where Afghânî was but ill received by 'ulamâ', who were in close traditional alliance with the rulers and desired no basic change, he was able to evoke a considerable response among the Shî'î 'ulamâ' in their jealous independence of the dynasty. The Westernizing shâh aroused their particular suspicion; what most aroused them was any threat of foreign infidel intervention. When Afghânî was expelled to the Iraq in 1891, he wrote to the recognized chief mujtahid, who resided there, urging him to act against the tobacco monopoly. This the mujtahid did: he decreed it contrary to religion to smoke tobacco till the monopoly was withdrawn in 1892. The decree was obeyed throughout the Qâjâr dominions: tobacco disappeared even from the palace, where in such a matter the mujtahid was better obeyed than the shâh himself. The self-control of the people was so great that mere promises to abolish the concession did not beguile them into relaxing their discipline. Only when the concession establishment was clearly being dismantled did the mujtahid decree tobacco again legal, and Persians smoked again.

Thus Afghânî helped to forge an alliance among the Shî'î 'ulamâ', the tradesmen of the bâzârs, and the Westernizing intellectuals. The first results were ambivalent. To get out of the tobacco concession without destroying his credit in the European capital market, the shâh had to pay compensation to the tobacco monopoly. To this end he felt it necessary to take out a British loan secured on the southern customs—an expedient less evidently obnoxious, but in fact perhaps even more dangerous, as the Egyptians had discovered in the time of Khedîv Ismâ'îl. But the alliance endured, of the 'ulamâ' with the new intellectuals; the shâh's continued policy of mortgaging the realm became increasingly unendurable. Afghânî had been invited to Istanbul and there found himself almost silenced as an involuntary guest of 'Abdülḥamid. But a close disciple of Afghânî, after a trip to Istanbul where he consulted with the master, assassinated the shâh in 1896 and, after some initial shock, was acclaimed as a tyrannicide by the Bâzâr, whose viewpoint the 'ulamâ' did not discourage. The Qâjâr government requested extradition from the Ottomans of certain others of Afghânî's followers, who happened to be (Azalî) Bâbîs (though Afghânî was presumably hostile to the Bâbî faith as such, as disrupting Islam); they were executed. Afghânî himself was not yielded up, but died the next year in circumstances which led the Iranians to believe Sultan 'Abdülḥamîd had had him done away with.

Afghânî's way of improvising political doctrine according to the occasion could be justified on the basis of the old philosophy, which did not expect the masses to act rationally on the basis of consistent ideals. But Ibn-Rushd and Ibn-Khaldûn, who had made this point, did not attempt to be revolutionaries. Afghânî presumably saw that the times were different and called for a more radical immediate policy. But he could not achieve a new philosophical basis for his new politics. Overtly espousing 'Abdülḥamîd's programme was philosophically politic; encouraging elements that could only be hostile to that programme was politically sound; but when he did both at once, he was caught by 'Abdülḥamîd, who played that sort of game better. Afghânî's dilemma echoed that of many other Iranian intellectuals of sensitive conscience, who looked to reform by way of an élite such as the Faylasûfs had always counted on but hoped to support the élite by an appeal to the 'ulamâ' and to popular sentiment. This sort of approach maintained maximum continuity with the Islamicate past not only in society at large but even in the minds of the radicals. It helped to make possible rather spectacular results for a time. But eventually it surely contributed to relative inability of the Iranians, and most especially those of the west Iranian kingdom where this approach was developed, to achieve satisfactory Modernization; hence it contributed to the demand for a yet more drastic revolution. For the moment, however, its positive effects predominated.

The new shâh, Muẓaffaruddîn, was a relatively weak man and those whom Afghânî had helped bring together soon began to demand of him that he reverse his father's policies. Muẓaffaruddîn was not so inclined; he, too, wanted to travel in Europe and needed money to do so in regal style. For a time, he made some gestures at domestic reform, but soon turned to foreigners: Belgian personnel, sympathetic to Russian commerce, were put in charge of the customs of the realm and, in 1900, a Russian loan negotiated, secured on the northern customs. In the following years (with Britain distracted by a war in South Africa), Russian influence continued to mount rapidly, to which the tradesmen of the cities reacted with what sometimes came to riots, and many 'ulamâ' reacted with explicit warnings to the shâh that his power had no sanction if he did not stay within the Sharî'ah. But in 1904 Russia was engaged in war with Japan, which soon proved disastrous for the Russians. By 1905, upon the defeat of Russian arms, the Russian people were everywhere in revolt against tsarist absolutism; and by the end of 1905 the leading men of Tehran had launched their own revolt against its Qâjâr minion.

The previous shâh's ventures in Modernization now proved to have set aside the old order sufficiently to arouse resentment against the new injustices but not sufficiently to prevent the resentment from becoming effective in a general popular movement. At the same time, the Modernized elements, with their theoretical bent, proved sufficiently aware to make very liberal plans and to set about them responsibly; but not sufficiently backed by Modern institutions, even on the level of complementary dependence, to carry their plans through.

The revolutions of 1905–17

Japan had seemed as subject as any other land to Western pressure; when it defeated a major European power, the world took hope that Europe was not invincible. This fact helped embolden Ottoman Turks and Arabs against their West-allied rulers in the immediately following years, in the Young Turk revolution and Muṣṭafà Kâmil's nationalism in Egypt, and likewise launched hopes of home-rule in India. The Persians and Azerîs, among the most immediately affected, acted soonest and most decisively of all. They were inspired by events in Russia, but took their immediate cue from some high-handed actions of the government against merchants, who were traditionally relatively immune from despotic arbitrariness. At the end of 1905 a number of 'ulamâ' and others at Tehran took refuge, *bast*, at the shrine of Shâh 'Abdul'aẓîm, where the shâh dared not touch them; so great was their popular support that the shâh promised to concede their demands: to dismiss his chief minister and to establish a chamber of justice with the right to correct abuses.

But when they left their refuge, the shâh failed to fulfill his promise; upon further agitation, the 'ulamâ' of the capital were soon exiled to Qum. In July 1906, a more serious bast occurred. In the first days 5000 persons took refuge, and eventually around 13,000 persons found themselves camping out—this time on the grounds of the British embassy (a refuge more secure against royal perfidy than any shrine, so long as the British officials accepted the refugees and regarded their honour as at stake in protecting them, by the new European international law). The guild organizations, relatively intact compared to other Muslim lands, and new political clubs provided the leadership which maintained not only good order but cleanliness and adequate distribution of the food supplies which the citizens brought. The movement at Tehran was watched closely in the main provincial cities, the substantial classes in each of which had their own occasions for resenting the oppression of the Qâjâr family—some of whom were appointed as peculiarly rapacious governors (contrary to the cautious practice of the days before Europeans guaranteed the succession). In Tabrîz, in Azerbaijan; in Rasht, the Caspian emporium; in Iṣfahân and Ṣhîrâz, sympathetic basts took place; some were at the British consulates, for the British generally showed themselves sympathetic to oppressed peoples seeking redress, and in particular were the most evident counterweight to the ascendant Russian power. The demand now was not only for dismissal of ministers but for a constitution and a national assembly to set limits on the royal finances and administration, and for a code of laws and regular courts to administer them in that sphere which in the past had been left to the shâh and his governors.

The bast amounted to a general strike; the bâzârs were all closed. The bastîs being largely merchants and guildsmen (the 'ulamâ' being at Qum), the government threatened to have rough soldiers break open the shops and plunder them. But the bastîs formed a commission to assure common action. Modernly educated men on that commission, aware of European constitutionalism, persuaded them to hold fast till an actual constitution should be granted. As in Russia, a representative assembly was deemed the essential reform, from which all others would follow. Some of the 'ulamâ' issued a declaration reminding the shâh that he ruled only on sufferance, the true lord being the Hidden Imâm. The Modernizers drew up a constitution, which the vacillating shâh finally proclaimed. It was largely copied from that of Belgium (regarded as a model one by Europeans). Its most significant provision called for a national assembly (Majles), elected on a limited franchise which, however, included all elements of any means. Elections began immediately, and by express provision the Majles began sitting as soon as elections at Tehran had provided a nucleus, not waiting for the often delayed elections in the provinces, where royal governors sometimes prevented them.

The arrival of the delegation to the Majles from Tabrîz and Azerbaijan set the Majles on a firm course. Nowhere was there greater pressure for Modernization and liberalization than in Azerbaijan. Tabrîz was the seat of the heir-apparent, a singularly self-seeking and arbitrary governor; but, in addition, the Azerî Turks were in contact with their countrymen across the Russian border. There, at Baku, oil had been found and a relatively cosmopolitan atmosphere reigned in the city (though not in its hinterland).

Azerî Muslims under tsarism had developed an awareness of Modern possibilities second only to the Volga Tatars. They read the Ottoman press and many were sympathetic to the ideas of the Young Turks. They were actively involved in the Russian revolution of 1905, even though less radical than many Christians. Later, when reaction set in in Russia and the more ardent revolutionaries were being repressed, several leaders from Russian Azerbaijan crossed the border to take an active part in the continuing struggle in the Qâjâr realm.

The first concern of the new Majles in 1907 was to do away with the necessity for foreign loans by limiting the shâh's spending to a civil list (as in Europe), by reserving for the treasury a larger share of the taxes nominally raised for the government, and by establishing a national bank to make loans from within the country to cover the immediate financial difficulties the shâh had already brought on. Many people of relatively small means made great sacrifices to build up the capital for a national bank, but in the end not enough was raised to make it a success against the active opposition of the foreign banks already established. It was easier, however, to limit the shâh's spending. But precisely this control the new shâh was most determined to do away with.

For at the beginning of 1907, Muẓaffaruddîn Shâh had been succeeded by his son, the notorious governor of Tabrîz, Muḥammad-'Alî Shâh, who had indeed signed the constitution but with little intention of abiding by it. Throughout 1907 there were uprisings and other actions in the main cities against local acts of oppression, encouraged by the shâh, and in precaution against royal shipments of arms. The more democratic element in the Majles, led by the deputies from Tabrîz and especially by Sayyid Ḥasan Taqî-zâdeh, a learnèd young 'âlim (25 years old), pressed for more extensive reforms. Municipal councils, modelled on those for some time established in Russia, were authorized. The democrats urged that all subjects be given equal legal status. This idea the 'ulamâ', who led a more moderate, yet still reforming, tendency in the Majles, opposed; the democrats answered that Islam was essentially democratic. Throughout the land, democratic political clubs sprang up, supporting the more liberal party in the Majles and publishing often excellent papers. To oppose them and support the shâh against the Majles, counter-revolutionary royalist clubs sprang up also, encouraged by some of the 'ulamâ'.

At the end of August 1907, the shâh's new minister seemed on the verge of persuading the Majles to accept a Russian loan after all, for a planned German loan (preferred as less dangerous politically) had been blocked. At this point, the minister was assassinated. The event stunned most of the royalists and stiffened the resolve of the constitutionalists. The democratic ascendancy thus gained was confirmed when the British signed (on the same day) an agreement with the Russians, in which they acknowledged special Russian interests in the whole of the northern Qâjâr territories, including Tehran and Tabrîz. This was part of a wider deal in which the Russians and British were forging an alliance against the Germans; but from an Iranian viewpoint, the British, in effect, abandoned the Qâjâr subjects to facing Russian pressures alone without the possibility of interference from the alternative European power (unless perhaps the formal independence of the state were threatened), or even the possibility of competitive bargaining. Meanwhile, the political clubs set up night schools and other philanthropic projects in the cities, while the Majles developed detailed plans for a financial reform which would be as just to the existent beneficiaries, case by case, as would be compatible with governmental solvency, and for a national army which would allow the Majles to enforce its decisions.

In December, the shâh attempted a *coup* in Tehran, but the political clubs came armed to the successful defence of the Majles. On the other hand, nothing positive could be done against the shâh for fear of giving a pretext for Russian intervention which the British would be bound to accept. By June 1908, the shâh's plans were better developed. Under cover of a joint Russian-British ultimatum against resistance, the shâh's Russian-officered 'Cossack' brigade attacked the Majles. The Tehranîs were eager to resist again, but the leadership persuaded them to accept the proffered negotiations with the shâh. One volunteer shot himself on the spot, saying he could not face his wife if he went home without fighting. The Russian commander then arrested or scattered the leading constitutionalists, and put the city under martial law. But if the Majles had no national standing army, neither had the shâh, whose unreformed administration could hardly have produced one. The obverse of the relative intactness of the guilds was the relative weakness of the despotism as compared with the Ottoman or the Egyptian. The Cossack brigade could hold Tehran, but against the rest of the country the shâh had only tribal levies, which plundered and destroyed but could not long hold down the country. Tabrîz held out for months heroically and by the time it was knocked out of the fight by a Russian occupation, other key cities had risen and civil war was general.

Meanwhile, refugees were doing their best to rouse European opinion in favour of the revolution. The revolutionaries managed to prevent any violence to foreigners throughout the fighting, counting on the good faith of the Europeans and especially of the British, that if no pretext were given for intervention none would be invented; and in fact full-scale Russian interference at this time seems to have been prevented by an anti-interventionist party within the Russian government itself, though numerous Russian troops were introduced here and there allegedly to protect foreigners just in case. Finally, in 1909, tribesmen from the south and constitutionalists from Rasht joined forces against the royalists, occupied Tehran, and deposed the shâh (who was allowed to flee to Russia).

A number of outstanding royalists were now killed, including one leading mujtahid who had agitated against the constitution in opposition to his fellow mujtahids. But by and large the old ruling circles were retained, so far as they would co-operate with the Majles. This was partly from respect for European (and Russian) opinion, but partly for want of a sufficient class of new men with the necessary practical training, such as 'Abdülḥamid's army and bureaucracy helped to provide for the Young Turks. Though the newest shâh was a minor under a regent of the Majles' choosing, the court remained an essentially autonomous force controlling the administration. The new men whom the revolution did bring forward were not always trusted even by the majority of the Majles. At any rate, they did not venture to displace the old administrative families. The Majles restricted itself to making choice of the 'liberal' among them and tried to change their ways. It was in this sense that the constitutionalists understood the doctrine of 'separation of powers' which their European friends urged on them: the court and its cabinet were to share power with, but not be displaced by, the legislative branch.

Even so, the manner of administration changed somewhat. The officials appointed under the constitution responded to the efforts at Modernization by building bureaucracy and breaking down the old patterns of local responsibility on the part of the landholders, as had happened earlier elsewhere. This sometimes had immediately unfortunate results; but the grosser tyrannies of the arbitrary governors were ended. In an effort to build up a central power, Swedes were brought in to train a new *gendarmerie* (especially in the south away from the Russians), which proved consistently loyal to the democrats. Americans were brought in to reform the finances and given extensive powers, including that of recruiting their own fiscal *gendarmerie*.

It was the efforts of the Americans which promised to prove too successful for Russian patience. By 1911, Russian tsarism had its internal revolutionary movement under close control and was ready to deal with that in Persia. First it sponsored an invasion by the ex-shâh, which was defeated. Then it issued an ultimatum that the Americans be dismissed. The Americans had earned the dislike of the European colony by following protocol appropriate to employees of the Iranian government rather than to Western diplomats, so breaking the Western solidarity; and they had offended the court families and the cabinet by refusing to allow privileged exemptions from their reforms. When the Russians followed up their ultimatum with full-scale invasion, the Europeans were apathetic and the cabinet was quite willing to sacrifice the American financial experts; only the Majles and the people were for them. The Majles held firm (at one point a patriotic women's society trooped into the Majles and suddenly brandished guns in a demonstration of constitutionalist fervour which their menfolk could not ignore). It was necessary to disperse the Majles and run the country thenceforth through a cabinet with scant legality but supported by Russian guns.

During the First World War, the belligerent Europeans regarded the

Qâjâr realm as a passageway elsewhere. The Germans (and Ottomans) hoped to raise a revolt in India in the name of pan-Islamic sentiment for the Ottoman caliph if they could get a sufficient supportive force through to Afghanistan. The British and Russians saw control of Iran as essential to blocking such a move and as a base for their own moves against the Ottomans; they frankly divided the country, north and south, between them. Meanwhile, many of the more democratic constitutionalists, or nationalists as they were now called, had fled to Istanbul to the protection of the Young Turks, as had revolutionists from Russian-held Azerbaijan. Before long, the realm was again in civil war, this time both chaotic and destructive. The nationalists established a government at Kermânshâh under the protection of the Germans and Ottomans and controlled much of the south, where the tribes as well as the Swedish-officered *gendarmerie* supported them against the British- and Russian-sponsored 'moderate' authorities at Tehran and the royalists. But the Ottomans were preoccupied, the Germans were distant, the tribes unruly, and the *gendarmerie* ill-maintained with scanty tax resources. By 1917, the British and Russians had nearly gained control. When the great Russian revolution began, the new (moderate socialist) Russian government found it necessary to liquidate its commitments in the Caucasus and Iran. With Russian pressure lifted, a nationalist cabinet took power for a time in Tehran and even in the south the British were besieged in their encampments in an upsurge of nationalist hope. But after a winter of famine, in the course of 1918 the British found it possible to regain their hold and even to take the Russians' place in the north; where, indeed, they passed forward across the tsarist borders to intervene in the Russian revolution itself.

The Tatar Jadîdîs and Russian revolutionism

With the war's end, there was great pressure at home for the British also to liquidate their commitments in the Caucasus and Iran. During 1919 they tried to arrange for favourable local régimes. With the Tehran government, in particular, they drew up a treaty which would leave the more 'moderate' constitutionalists in power there, as against the nationalists, and would give the British an effective protectorate without the necessity for extensive military occupation. But despite all its failures, the spirit of the Persian revolution would not brook a European protectorate; and now the Russian revolution was taking a course which made resistance to the British demands more feasible.

The Tatars, as the dominant Muslim people in the Russian empire, meanwhile had been pursuing a course which contrasted markedly with that of the independent Persians. The Persians' politics and their revolution had taken place under the sign of dependence to Russia and the West. But the Tatars found it appropriate to participate in the general Russian political life; and to a limited but fateful extent they carried the other Muslim peoples in the empire along with them.

The Russians, with their ambivalent position within the Western sphere, forever striving to catch up, had long been intensely conscious of the difference between the society that is, and the society that might be. Nowhere was the possibility of revolution more tantalizingly dangled before the vision of the youth. A whole spectrum of idealistic outlooks was offered: some clung to a relatively conservative faith in the world mission of the Slavs as carriers of east Christian Orthodoxy, as a heritage on which to found a future more spiritual than might be provided by the more typical nineteenth-century liberalism of western Europe. From this the outlooks ranged to the hopes of the most ardent Westernizers and futuristic revolutionaries. But since the revolution of 1905, which had come to very little after reaction set in, Russians had shown little expectation of much positive from the tsarist régime and some sort of revolution loomed tacitly as the only real future hope.

Young Russian intellectuals tended to take revolutionary ideas especially, in the later nineteenth century, more passionately than their opposite numbers in western Europe. Eastern Europe, being in its own way in Europe but not fully of it, faced special dilemmas in assimilating technicalistic Modernity. The Russian autocracy, even while making use of modern techniques in its army and administration, catered strongly to established privileged classes, especially to a large landed nobility. The educated youth were fully exposed to the intellectual and social forms of the new Western life, but they found relatively less Modern business and especially political outlets for their energies, while a peasantry sadly poverty-stricken by most west European standards aroused their sympathies. Moreover, the modern ideas were not linked to the evolution of centuries, but appeared as a powerful new system of truth challenging all old concepts. The need for a drastic overthrow of the existing order, so as to take advantage of the vast potentialities of modern ideals and capacities, appealed to the conscience of almost any concerned young man.

By the end of the century, revolutionism was a major political reality, already threatening to overthrow the tsarist government. After the revolution of 1905, its alignments were crystallized. In its most cautious form, it called for a constitutional democracy in the manner of west European bourgeois liberalism. More socially minded revolutionaries wanted a more thoroughgoing disruption of economic class privileges, in which the peasants would be the greatest beneficiaries. Some even looked to a radical anarchism which would substitute voluntary co-operation for all forms of politically sanctioned compulsions.

Young Volga Tatars (and the Turks of the Crimea to a lesser extent) could not escape the challenge of all this ferment about them. Already in the later nineteenth century, the Westernizers and revolutionists, full of ideas of universal human liberty and equality and of the need for radical social reform, made a great appeal to young Muslims who were finding there was a world beyond the narrow confines of the old-line 'ulamâ'. Those who would revive Slavic Orthodoxy, who tended to see truth as the special province of the Slavic peoples, could not make the same direct appeal. But the Muslims, finding themselves in like circumstances, developed their own version of such an outlook, in which it was Islam that should be revived, and in particular Turkic Islam, the Turkic peoples being the chosen bearers of the Islamic world mission. But both the revolutionism and the Turkism were coloured by a sense of grievance against a dominating Russian social and economic order which all Muslims needed to be freed from first of all. For the Volga Tatars, technically advanced though they had been, still found themselves politically and psychologically aligned against Europe and identified with the other, less developed, Muslim peoples of the empire; and even with the Ottoman Turks outside it.

In the earlier part of the nineteenth century, the Volga Tatars had moulded their social customs and even their revived and flourishing educational and intellectual life on the traditional models represented at Bukhârâ and Samarqand. They had introduced the veiling of women and persecuted those who would explore Western thought, even while commercially and even industrially they were riding the wave of Western expansion. Such a cultural policy answered in part to the immediate commercial advantage of assimilation to their most important markets, but it answered also to the difference in the inherited lettered tradition and the ideals and norms it carried: Muslims could not so readily adopt the literature and philosophy of the Occident as could the Christian Russians, and on the contrary were under great pressure, by their very identity as Muslims, to maintain the cultural solidarity of their own divinely grounded community. But once the policy was carried through, it had decisive consequences. The relatively modern segment of Tatar society was quite thin: in contrast to the merchants, the peasants, forced by the government into the less productive lands in favour of immigrating Christians, were even poorer and perhaps less enlightened (though rather more literate) than the Russian peasants; those who eventually migrated to the towns for industrial labour kept themselves apart from the Christian workers and were given the least skilled jobs and no training. Toward the end of the century, even the merchants were officially discriminated against as non-Christians, and found their advantageous headstart in Turkistan legislated away from them, serious investment there being forbidden them. Especially after 1880, the much more rapid modernization of the intellectually more Westernized Russian industrialists was putting the Tatars even in the Volga region at a disadvantage they were quick to feel. Without the full stimulus of a technicalistic outlook, their industry was stagnating in outdated methods and being closed down by competition.

Beginning in the latter part of the nineteenth century, efforts toward Modernization became increasingly popular—and, by the end of the century, predominant in Tatar urban circles. They centred on methods of educational instruction. A popular method which became the hallmark of those who resisted the old-line way of teaching the Qur'ân was called the new, *jadîd*, method; its advocates, and hence the Modernists generally, were called Jadîdîs. The Jadîdîs were 'new' not only in the way they taught the Qur'ân but in their whole approach to literature, science, social life, and economic activity. From imitating the Turkistanîs, they shifted over to almost complete assimilation to Russian patterns, only within Muslim cultic limitations and in a Tatar linguistic form. It is among the Jadîdîs that it was disputed what sort of Turkic ought to be used in newspapers and literature, an all-Turkic standard or a vernacular for each people; the vernacular won out under the impress of Russian models, more attractive than the Ottoman models. It was also among the Jadîdîs that new attitudes to politics arose, some sort of revolutionism being mooted even as early as 1885.

The Volga Tatars were increasingly scattered, as peasants seeking freedom for their faith, as businessmen, and latterly as labourers, among the larger Russian population. But they could not simply fade into the Russian scene, however 'developed' their leading strata became. If they could themselves have broken their solidarity with the Islamic community, they yet would not have been permitted to forget their initial handicaps as a group in competition with the dominant Russians. The Tatars, therefore, found themselves sharing one destiny with the other Muslim peoples of the empire, and cast for leadership among them. Tatar Jadîdism was adopted almost whole by the Modernizing element in these peoples. But whereas among the vocal classes of the Tatars it was the dominant viewpoint, elsewhere it was represented only by an alert minority. And before long it became clear that the interests of peoples which formed complementarily dependent, 'colonial'-type, societies over against the Russians diverged seriously from the interests of the Tatars, who, for all their difficulties, remained on the European side of the economic divide.

This was specially evident in Turkistan and in the steppes of Kazakhstan to the north of it. The economic transformation of Turkistan was increasingly complete: under Russian occupation, technicalistic elements such as railroads had been far more extensively introduced than in the independent Iranian states, though the railroads were run by Russian workers. Especially in the upper Syr valley, in Farghânah, but also in the Oxus valley, within and without the boundaries of the autonomous Khânate, and even along the railroad in Turkmenistan at the foot of the plateau, cotton became ever more dominant. By the end of the century, the amount of import and export trade from Turkistan was relatively greater than from Russia proper. Kazakhstan was being transformed almost as radically: from a pastoral economy it was being turned into agricultural territory by Russian immigrants. And whereas in Turkistan there was sufficient resentment at the introduction, as a privileged caste, of a relatively small number of Russian settlers to manage the more technical operations of the new economy, in Kazakhstan (and also in the Qirghiz mountains) the coming of the Russians meant mass starvation for the herdsmen, who were restricted brutally to the poorest areas, where in a bad year their herds perished. When they revolted, as they sometimes did, massacre or the attrition of exile took the place of famine. For these areas, the great problem was the competitive presence of technically advanced Russian settlers. And far from sympathizing fully with this problem, the Tatars often contributed to it themselves. The little Tatar colonies in Turkistan stood apart from the local Muslims almost as did the Russians, with Russian protection. In some parts of the empire, it was often Tatar peasants who were the relatively advanced settlers, from whom the other Muslims had to fear displacement.

Despite the intellectual bustle of Kazan, Bukhârâ remained throughout the nineteenth century a world centre of Sunnî orthodoxy, drawing students from India and China and the Volga itself. Its learnèd and Sharî'ah-conscious 'ulamâ' disregarded the Russians as infidels, but counselled political accommodation to them; they paid scant attention to the new tendencies among the Tatars. Especially within the Bukhârân state, left autonomous, the 'ulamâ' developed unusual power. Only after 1905, and the greater awareness of political possibilities which it brought, did more than a very few of the Turkistanî intellectuals join the ranks of the Tatar Jadîdîs in their search for more efficient education and a broader outlook. Such Muslim intellectual stirrings as were to be found there depended largely on the Tatar colonies, and seemed correspondingly alien.

After 1905, the leading Tatar Jadîdîs joined the constitutional democrats among their Christian fellow-subjects in demanding political liberalization in the Russian empire. They added to the general demands only the requirement of an autonomous Muslim cultural régime for all Russian territories, in which the Tatar merchant class would naturally take the lead. For a time, they carried the other Jadîdîs with them. But soon differences appeared. On the one hand, Jadîdîs in other Muslim peoples, which still retained their compact territorial majorities, looked to local autonomy or even independence from Russia nation by nation rather than to a non-territorial autonomy of Muslims throughout the Russian empire. To this basic difference of approach was added the challenging presence of other parties which finally pushed the constitutional democrats into the background.

Already at the start of the twentieth century, a Marxist socialist movement, inspired by the Marxist labour movements of western Europe, was rivalling all the older revolutionary movements, however radical they were. The Marxists taught that in what we have called technicalized society the class relations which marked all the societies of the more agrarian pre-technical citied times would necessarily be superseded by a common relation of all persons, as job-holders, to the Modern machines (the control of which was the material source of all Modern social power); and that these machines and all means of production in society would then be controlled not by a few privileged persons, skilled or fortunate in financial manipulations, but by the common body of the people who worked the machines. With the displacement of all the old classes which had carried the high culture of the past would come a new culture of the future, not a class culture but a human culture building all anew.

The rapidly growing body of ex-peasant wage-workers in the new technicalized industries found themselves without the residual social guarantees of their old village life yet without many of the lower-level urban institutions which could intervene between them and the powerful employers. Union organization was violently discouraged, yet without it they had only the bargaining power of desperation, for they could not go back to the village. The contrast with the past was even more sudden and more total than it had been in the early years of industrialization in Britain. More markedly than in the case of any other class, the circumstances of the modern industrial workers were divorced from any earlier evolution of social relations. Thus it was that their practical exigencies fit in especially well with the theoretical breach with the past which was felt by the educated revolutionaries in their wholesale reception of new Western ideas. The wage-workers soon received talented and well-informed theoretical guidance from a growing number of Marxists. For the Marxist thesis proved widely convincing among the educated youth. And it proved to have touched a peculiarly dynamic historical potentiality in teaching that since it was precisely the industrial workers who at once controlled the machines dominating any modern economy; and who at the same time had no stake in the old order, and so had nothing to lose from a revolutionary reorganization of it; therefore it must be the industrial workers who will create the new just order in which all—like the industrial workers themselves before their machines—would be equal in rights and privileges.

The communist triumph

It was in Azerbaijan that the Tatar lead and the constitutional democratic policies were both first challenged among the Modernizers, the Jadîdîs, themselves. Already in December 1904, the Marxist party had led a general strike to wrest better conditions from the profiting company in the Baku oil fields, in which the Azerî workers participated along with the Russian and Armenian workers who were also numerous there. At the time there seem to have been almost no Azerî Marxists as yet. But after the revolution of 1905 had aroused general political interest, local Azerî parties developed with a Marxist socialist tendency. An Azerî Marxist party, with the usual programme for collective social control of such economic institutions as factories and oil fields, became the most popular among the Azerî wage-workers at Baku. Among Russian-ruled Azerîs at large, the strongest party came to be the Müsâvât, Equality party, founded by men who had been in the Marxist party and now added to a mild socialism a programme for federative union among all Muslim states, in sympathy with the Ottoman Young Turks.

In 1917, Muslims from all the Russian empire came together to present common demands in the new revolutionary era which had dawned with the overthrow of the tsar. But the Tatars fought doggedly against the demands of the other nationalities for local territorial autonomy, insisting on their purely cultural, non-territorial all-Muslim régime in which politically the Muslim Turks and the Christian Russians would merge in one great and presumably bourgeois republic. In consequence, the Tatar leadership was rejected by the others and Muslim unity of action was renounced in fact; for the Azerîs, the only alternative source of leadership, were not strong enough to take the Tatars' place. In the rapidly disintegrating empire, each Muslim people now sought its own destiny. But the Tatar leadership had taught all the Jadîdîs, even so, to seek their destiny in terms of Russian ideologies and parties, even if not exclusively the constitutional democrats. This fact facilitated what more fundamental developments were meanwhile making likely: the ultimate retention of all the Muslim peoples of the empire within the domain of the new (and not bourgeois) Russian republic.

By 1917, the Marxists had split into two parties. One, more cautious, looked indeed to an ultimate workers' socialism but expected this to be built gradually as the working classes learned to undertake the necessary responsibility. When it came to power with the revolution, it was willing to continue the war against the German powers in the name of common Russian interests. Soon the Volga Tatar leadership had shifted its alliance to these moderate socialists, as the constitutional democrats receded from the scene. But the other Marxist party, eventually calling itself 'communist', rejected all compromise and (in a revolutionary situation where all conventional cautious assumptions had proven false and anything seemed possible) soon captured the loyalty of the bulk of the Russian soldiers and wage-workers and even many peasants for a drastic reconstruction of society immediately. They called for an end to the war at any cost, and for immediately wiping away landlordism and so were able to seize power at the end of 1917 on the basis of *ad hoc* local councils (soviets) set up in army units and factories and villages, which by-passed entirely the authority of officers and managers and landlords. And consistently with the grass-roots spirit of such a policy, if not with its cosmopolitan theory, they promised all the nationalities of the empire the right to set up their own régimes and even to secede entirely from the new republic formed by these Russian soviets.

By early 1918, the various Muslim nationalities accepted the invitation and their Jadîdîs arranged, in uneasy co-operation with the 'ulamâ', for a show of autonomy or independence. But in all these areas there was a substantial Russian population of mill workers and railroad workers and oil workers and even peasant settlers. The governors and officers and mill-owners found themselves impotent (except as the remains of the tsarist Russian army, occasionally held together under vigorous counter-revolutionary leadership, here and there maintained them by bloodshed); but the new Russian soviets were unwilling to let themselves be submerged in independent Muslim-ruled societies. Early in 1918 there were *coups*, by soviets, in principle led by the communists, almost everywhere where Russians were numerous. Everywhere, the technical facilities for both economic and political operation were in fact in the hands of the Russians, who were therefore at an advantage even where they were a small minority; and often the 'ulamâ' preferred to trust any Russian régime—all Russians seeming alike—rather than the alien-minded Jadîdîs, the only Muslims apparently capable of handling the Modern apparatus. Soon most of the Muslim republics were absorbed in the communist system of soviets.

Azerbaijan at first seemed to have a different destiny. Along with the other areas south of the Caucasus, for a time it was controlled by some of the few remaining tsarist armies, holding the front against the Ottomans. But in March 1918 there was a communist-soviet *coup* at Baku (during which Russian workers, allied with the Armenians for the moment, massacred Azerî workers in an outburst of old hostilities). The communists at Baku then aided the more radical nationalists at Anzalî, the main Persian port on the Caspian Sea, who proclaimed a socialist ideal for Persia as the last tsarist Russian troops withdrew. With the disappearance of the tsarist armies, however, in the rest of formerly Russian Azerbaijan the Müsâvât party proclaimed an Azerî republic; at the end of the summer the Ottoman troops established its power even in Baku. At this point the British had moved far enough north in Persia to suppress the Anzalî nationalists and carry their campaign on to Baku, where in turn they eliminated the Ottomans. But with the general withdrawal of British troops from the area in 1919, the Müsâvât-dominated Azerî government was left in control. This control it was not able to maintain. The Müsâvât party was torn between its original Jadîdî, socialist-minded founders and a landlord element which it had been necessary to admit to govern the rural parts, where the Muslim peasants had been little inclined to seize the lands for themselves. It got no support from Atatürk's Turkey, too busy for adventures outside the old Ottoman boundaries and, later, allied with the Russian communists, who were able to send it arms. The 'ulamâ', mostly Shî'îs, intensely distrusted the secularistic and Turkist-nationalist notions of the Müsâvât Jadîdîs, which had almost led to submergence in the Sunnî Ottoman state. When, then, the Russian and Armenian wage-workers at Baku, entrenched in the key technical positions, showed themselves eager to renew a soviet régime, the government was forced to open negotiations with the Russian communists and finally in 1920, to the relief of many, Azerbaijan was made a soviet republic federated with the Russian Soviet Republic and assured internal order by it.

From Baku, the Communists sent help to the nationalists at Anzalî and to nearby Rasht in Persia. But here there were almost no Russian settlers and, in fact, relatively less technical apparatus and relatively fewer wage-workers of any background. There could be no local soviet rule of the sort found north of the tsarist boundary. Here, too, the democratic government at Tehran, as the British began to evacuate, undertook negotiations with the communists. But the 'ulamâ', far from having learned to accept Russian domination, were themselves identified with the local revolutionary movement. There was little question of accepting communist control.

In fact, at this point the communists were in the midst of attempting to implement on an ever-wider basis their ideal of allowing autonomy and independence to the subject nationalities not only of the tsar but of all the European empires. The world-wide revolution, which it was hoped the west European working classes would soon join, must find its expression also in the dependencies of the Europeans. But there it must be accepted that it would take a different form and doubtless develop more slowly, since the technicalistic life, which was to be the social and economic foundation of socialism, was less developed. On orders from Moscow, accordingly, the local communist parties had been opened to the Muslim Jadîdîs in Muslim areas, whether or not they were very clearly wage-workers and peasants. The parties were even allowed to be dominated by them and by their Turkist nationalist ideas for a time. In the name of communism, notably in Turkistan, there was a revival of a nationalism which proclaimed general socialist ideals (especially as against Russian property owners) but was above all interested in social Modernization and Turkic independence, regardless of class lines and in fact chiefly to the advantage of the educated, mercantile classes. To launch a yet wider movement, the communists held a great conference at Baku to which they invited delegates from all the lands which found themselves in one measure or another suffering under European imperialism. To it came representatives of the new Muslim-dominated communist parties within Russia and of many relatively radical nationalist movements in the dependent lands beyond. There was great enthusiasm for the coming new order.

In this spirit, the communists offered a treaty to the Persian government which abandoned almost all tsarist Russian claims and offered a secure northern frontier at the old boundary, on the understanding that thus the Persians would be able to free themselves from imperial domination by Europeans and incidentally form a buffer against Western capitalist attempts to attack the new Russia again from the south (as had in fact happened at the end of the war). The Iranian Majles, finally summoned to meet again in 1921, duly ratified the Russian treaty and rejected the British protectorate, and the British could only withdraw. At this juncture, a commander of the troops which had been built up by the Russians during the war, Reżà, joined forces with some democratic reformers, seized power in Tehran (apparently with British approval), and, left free of foreign interference, proved capable of maintaining it and fulfilling at least some of the ideals of the Persian revolution in the next decades.

The communist solution

By now there was a small but significant number of activists in the Qâjâr state who were identifying themselves with the communist policies and looked forward more or less vaguely to recasting society through collective control of the economy by councils of wage-workers and peasants, on the model and with the support of the Russian soviets. They were probably almost as numerous as those with like ideals in the former tsarist territories of primarily Muslim population. But whereas for the Muslims north of the border, society henceforth was moulded by communist power, and the 'revolution' came to be felt as a thing of the past and present, for those south of the border their revolution went much less far: for all its reforms, it preserved the basic class structure intact, and radicals could feel it had only begun. Increasingly, the meaning they could assign to the hope of revolution, if it were to go beyond what was to be offered by commander Reżà, was determined by the presence of the communist revolution across the border. What happened there proved a warning to some against allowing revolution to take its course, while to others, in increasing numbers, it exemplified the solution to all the problems of Modernization in a technicalized world: it seemed a dream come to reality.

Marx had hazarded no blueprint of what sort of society the wage-workers should build when they finally took power and eliminated any separate class of profiting owners. It was assumed that the wage-workers, having been brought into a common economic relationship to the machines of modern life, would not split up into new economic classes. Since it was also assumed that economic interests were the only serious social interests which could actually produce basic conflicts of policy (differences of cultural heritage, including religious heritage, being regarded as in themselves essentially impotent as social forces), this common economic interest of all would mean that there would be no further social conflict. But otherwise the only goal set was a very general one, a society 'in which the free development of each is the condition for the free development of all'. But certain norms seemed implicit in the very process of bringing all members of society into a common wage-labour relation to the means of production, the process which the revolution was to complete. For this was to accept the technicalistic society as ultimate and to push certain of its implications to the extreme. If, as was in fact the universal tendency in technicalized society (though not in original Marxist theory), everyone was to function economically as a maximally efficient job-holder, his preparation and activity being differentiated functionally by specialization rather than according to extrinsic status expectations, then all those differentiations which were functionally irrelevant were dispensable or even vicious.

Economically the technicalistic pressure was immediate. Not merely was the small-scale enterprise, the one-man shop or farm, technically less efficient than larger-scale enterprises, up to a point; it was culturally less conducive to that indefinitely proliferating specialization on which technicalized society was founded. In the capitalist societies, and most typically in North America where tradition offered fewest trammels, there was an overwhelming tendency for one-man undertakings (even in some sectors of agriculture) to be absorbed into larger-scale enterprises or else to become economically subsidiary to such. In the communist society this tendency was deliberately encouraged and even enforced by state management as a means of more rapid Modernization, as well as of assuring more dependable homogeneity to the universal wage-working class. Especially the 'idiocy of rural life', of peasant life in which the individual was confined to an inherited ancestral routine which he could not escape, was to be dissipated as, with modern machines and financing, the land was assimilated to the city.

In the same spirit, differentiations by ethnic background and nationality were felt to be superfluous accidents inherited from an earlier social stage and to be outgrown as each person came to have status only in terms of his individual skills and economic function. The 'free development of each' was to presuppose a radical social equality of all, in which cultural heritage, no more than family inheritance, should not set off some at birth as differently endowed from others. If at first the communists conceded demands for separate national expression in the formerly subject peoples, this was to overcome the habit of national privilege expected even by the wage-workers among the Russians, and to assure a subjective sense of self-determination among the others. But in the long run, wage-workers could be expected *ex hypothesi* to feel no group interests other than those common interests determined by their common relation, as job-holders, to the machines of the Technical Age.

In fact, after a relatively brief period of some protest within the Communist Party itself (on the ground that the true liberation of the masses of the world must include liberation from the West, even from the privileged Western and Russian working classes), the Volga Tatars seem to have become almost indistinguishable, on the surface, from the Russian majorities among whom they lived, though they retained their own language and a distinct literary tradition. In the Muslim-majority republics, the development seems to have been less simple. The distinction between European on the one hand and Muslim on the other remained a major social distinction, coinciding to a large degree with the distinctions in social class which inevitably persisted.

Very early, Communist Party leadership of the soviets had been turned to outright control on the ground that only the party could ascertain the true common interests of the workers. There followed an increasing centralizing of power and of doctrine within the party. Soon after the Baku conference, a more properly Marxian ideology began to be restored in the parties of the Muslim republics, which were restored to a central, and hence a modified Russian domination from 1921 on. The Muslim revolts which followed this tightening of control were suppressed; though not without a decade of fighting, especially in Turkistan where a guerilla movement called the Basmachis was at one point given leadership by the Young Turk leader, Enver Pasha. The 'ulamâ', during the crucial twenties, continued to prefer rule from a Russian Moscow to their own local Jadîdîs. For some time (except for the dispossession of the gentry by land distribution to the peasants) it was above all the Russian (and Tatar) sector of society which was most deeply affected by communist measures.

Even so, Muslim life was shaken at some sensitive points. There was a continued overall Modernization of city life, Muslims being invited to share in the veneer of Europeanization. Literacy and feminist freedom were pushed and religion, Muslim as well as Christian, was attacked officially as a trick of the exploiters. But (after some early attempts to suppress the veil had provoked fierce resistance) even so primary an anachronism as the veil, symbol of feminine subjection as well as of old upper-class vanity, was not forbidden outright. Though the position of the 'ulamâ' was being undermined (and their quality lowered by the elimination of madrasahs), the effect was sporadic in the bulk of the population and those who still listened to them could practice their faith, on a purely tolerated basis, as before. The Jadîdîs, on the other hand, were conciliated with the official fostering of an active cultural life in the several Turkic (and Persian) tongues. The new literature was strictly in the modern vernaculars (both the old Chaghatay and Ottoman Turkish being eliminated) and, by 1928, in the Latin script; the latter in forms carefully differing from that used in the Turkish republic so as to minimize not only continuity with the heritage but any specifically Modern Turkist tendencies in a national sense. Yet even so, the great men of Islamic times were accorded locally heroic status and at least in academic circles the Turkic and Persian heritages were accorded a certain revival.

Only when the specifically Muslim revolts had largely subsided did the Muslim population get greatly involved, in the republics. From 1928, in an effort to introduce the standards of city life into the countryside, began the drive for collectivization of the farming, bringing the small peasant plots together for large-scale mechanized operation. The immediate effect in Turkistan was to reactivate the two greatest complaints that had been felt against tsarism. With collectivization came attempts to settle the pastoral tribes; the campaign served as a means of almost destroying—again by starvation and emigration—what was left of them and of their herds. Correspondingly it helped to introduce still more European settlement. With such leadership as it had had broken or divided by the revolution, the local population was yet more defenceless to resist than in tsarist times. At the same time as collectivization came the drive for industrialization of the thirties, which meant forced social savings: that is, a maximum of the annual product, including most of any increased production resulting from growing technicalization, went not to people's consumption but to state-decreed capital investment.

In this period, under the pressure for rapid technical development, it became obvious that the revolution had as yet failed to overcome the tendency for nationality and class lines to coincide in the republics. As before, most Muslims (except those corresponding to what the French called in Algeria the *évolués*, the assimilated Muslims who had accepted French culture) lived in separate quarters of town and held different, less skilled, and less remunerative sorts of jobs. The ruthlessness of the period of forced industrialization engulfed the Muslims, however, as it did the Russians. In the course of the thirties, purges of the party—often going beyond mere power shifts to physical punishment of those on the wrong side—eliminated most of the nationally-minded Muslim leadership and established the system whereby alongside a Muslim head of state or of party normally stood a Russian second-in-command representing Moscow; and whereas the offices in closest touch with the population were filled by Muslims, the less visible but more sensitive posts went to local Russians. By the end of the thirties a renewed Russification set in under orders from the Centre: from 1938, the Muslim alphabets were gradually shifted from Latin letters (opening access to Occidental literatures) to Cyrillic letters in line with the Russian; this tendency culminated in the post-war doctrine of permanent and retroactive Russian cultural primacy in the area of the Soviet Union, in terms of which much of the heritage from Islamic times had to be re-evaluated negatively.

Eventually, the forced pace of Modernization and industrialization made for a rising level of consumption. Muslim peasant homes were equipped with electricity and sewing machines. The average level of prosperity in the majority-Muslim areas was not far behind that in Russia proper: still very low by Occidental standards, but markedly higher than a generation before and particularly than in the Persian kindgom south of the border. And what prosperity there was tended to be shared relatively equally. Despite high salary differentials between management and labour, there was no longer an idle profiting class to drain off whatever extra the peasant or the worker managed to produce: the landlord, the moneylender, and the bourgeois rentier were gone. And old prejudices of status were severely limited: the countryside did learn much of the sophistication of the city. By the post-war period, a young peasant woman could be not only a member of the Communist Party, directive society of the land; she could be elected head of her village council. And at that council—to cite an instance—she could combine the newer sophistication of communist doctrine with the older (and then *passé*) city sophistication of wearing the veil.

For the ambitious, willing to be assimilated to (communist) Russian ways, there was substantial equality of opportunity: literacy was general among the youth, by the thirties. (And, with the ambitious, any potential non-communist leadership was skimmed off from the remaining populace.) Granted that what matters, for the good life, is not anything that can be derived from any of the older heritages, but a personal unfolding of talent or skill, in the context of technicalistic society, for its own sake; that it is not the fulfilling of cultural values evolved in the past, but the meeting of social goals set by the present for the future; then those who were talented and willing had won a range of personal choice, a freedom to enter a career that fitted them and to rise as far as they were competent, dazzling in its possibilities compared to the limitations of pre-revolutionary days.

Despite all the arguments about national culture and a sincere interest in certain sorts of pre-revolutionary literature, in fact the older heritages—Islamicate and also pre-Modern European—were consigned to honoured places in the museums. The old philosophic dialogues—Islamicate or Occidental—were regarded as of only antiquarian interest, filled as they were in fact with the conceptions of their patrons, the landlords and the rentiers. They were superseded by the modern dialectical thought of Marxism which reflected the positivism and dynamicism of the Technical Age; the old artistic traditions, likewise, were to yield to the every-day modern light of 'socialist realism'; and the traditions of religious faith, including the whole venture of Islam, were also consigned to the museums. The wisdom that was respected as dependable was positive, scientific knowledge: and this was reformulated year by year in the unceasing Modernization of the Technical Age. Under such conditions, the traditions to which one people or another might be uniquely loyal—over against a universal up-to-date factual equipment equally meaningful to anyone whatever without regard to any personal spiritual or aesthetic commitment—became mere local colour (for instance, distinctive folk dances or basket-weaving patterns). They were threatened with reduction to the level of tourist-bait if not of superstition. It could be noticed that the elements of Islamic religious ideas most visibly kept alive in the Muslim republics were the petty lore of the old women: charms against the jinn, or the invocation of saints on behalf of a happy marriage. The mosques and their learnèd tradition, reduced to the merest ritual and theology, attracted almost none of the youth.

But with the loss of the heritage as a living force went one more foundation for dissent and difference on points of taste and of ultimate purpose: with the narrowing of the opportunity for seriously different cultural groups was lost one social basis for controversy and compromise, within which an individual might have elbow room for developing his own opinions. It became relatively easy for the supposedly correct view on almost any basic question to be decreed from the Centre; and in fact, it came to be so. In an excess of zeal, the Modernizers endeavoured to control opinion so firmly in the cause of progress that the elementary facts came to be difficult of access: statistics were turned to a political tool, to support which, travel and free observation of actuality became weirdly curtailed. (And massive official brutality too often found a cover of secrecy.) It could be hoped that in a technicalized society such a situation was anomalous and transient; but the pressure for conformity in basic matters was in any case overwhelming for a people of job-holders, who must learn to be what in North America are called 'good organization men'. At the same time that a man was freer to follow an ever-vaster range of worldly careers, the option was increasingly ruled out, in practice, of his exploring freely and deeply into his unique and ultimate selfhood and its unpredictable and uncensorable place in the universe.

Reżà Shâh and the intellectuals

South of the border, where commander Reżà was making himself all-powerful in the Qâjâr realms, the revolution had been founded on no major shifts in the potential relative power of various classes and had issued in no comprehensive realignments of social power; it had not even developed a comprehensive ideology of its own apart from the vague general principles of nationalism and modernity. What Reżà did was build his power upon the army. In his first years, he figured primarily as head of the army and bent all his efforts toward building it up on the popular plea of securing national independence against future foreign intervention. When his idealistic allies of the 1921 *coup* proved inconvenient, he cast them aside and co-operated with the landlords (who had by now learned to entrench themselves in the Majles) till the army was strong enough to crush any internal source of opposition. He even occupied that part of the Mesopotamian plain which had been assigned to the Qâjâr state. The local Arabs looked in vain to their British protectors, who made an arrangement with the new government about the oil. By 1924, he was ready to toy with the idea of a republic along the line of Atatürk but shied away when too many people proved frightened by the explicit hostility to Islam that seemed to go along with republicanism in Turkey. At last, in 1925, he had the last Qâjâr deposed and had himself proclaimed shâh and founder of a new (Pahlavî) dynasty. In principle, nothing seemed to have changed save that the Iranian kingdom was once again free of entangling foreign loans and commitments and (supposedly) in a position to defend itself for the future.

Nevertheless, the Persian revolution as it came to fruit under Reżà Shâh issued in a complex of Modernizing patterns. Imitated largely from Atatürk's reforms, like Atatürk's they were in some points strikingly parallel to those issuing from the Russian revolution as it came to fruit under the communists. Even the overall cultural posture was partly analogous. Reżà too, like the communists, seems to have looked to a cultural future which would transcend the Islamic heritage and yet not simply adopt current Western culture instead. But whereas the new cultural inspiration among the communists did indeed develop a certain independence of spirit, under Reżà Shâh it remained largely on the level of appearances. Pre-Islamic Iranian traditions were to have provided the new inspiration. But such an inspiration showed itself most notably in the façades of new government buildings. In fact, under his rule the 'ulamâ', as representatives of Islam, were steadily undercut economically (above all in eliminating them from their remaining strongholds in the educational system) and in point of prestige (for instance, in a ban on some of the more emotional displays in the Shîʿî Muḥarram festival and, above all, in the partial replacement of religious holidays by a new system of national secular holidays in a solar calendar). But the practical inspiration for the institutions which were restricting the public role of Islam was, in fact, the modern Occident. The contrast to Atatürk's frank Westernism lay chiefly in what was excluded, not in something positive: Reżà encouraged an intense official anti-Western xenophobia, claiming to be interested in Western knowledge only in the barest technical sense. Accordingly, the new solar calendar was not in the Western Gregorian but a new national Iranian one.

As in the Soviet Union, the Persian government compaigned against illiteracy and (with less success) for feminism. Reżà even went so far as to ban the wearing of the veil, in contrast to the Soviet Union, and there was considerable training of women for professions like nursing, already given over to women in the West; but young women did not become presiding heads of villages. Reżà was eager to build modern machine industry and established many factories by state investment, as well as such technical aids as a railway across western Persia; but the new factories tended to remain isolated in the economy and operated at a loss, despite tariff protection. Apart from building an army perhaps even stronger than necessary for suppressing internal dissent, Reżà's greatest success lay in breaking the independence of the pastoral tribes—his ruthless measures to settle the tribes in fixed homesteads being only less disastrous (and to that extent less final) than the corresponding measures of the communists with their tribes. As under the communists, an official ideology was enforced through suppressing any information or public discussion unpleasing to the government, and it moved toward a forced Persification of the non-Persian peoples of the Qâjâr realm, notably the Azerî Turks, who showed an interest in building a Turkic culture; a Persification more explicit than the Russification in the Soviet Union.

By the end of the 1930s, for all its inadequacies, Reżà's state was solvent and able to maintain strict discipline within its boundaries. The kingdom was decorated with modern-looking cities cut by wide boulevards and lit electrically; the people had a sense of forming a nation, wore something approaching a Western cut of clothes (enforced even in villages if they were relatively accessible to Reżà's zealous *gendarmerie*) and, moreover, were kept elementarily aware by press and radio of the events of the world. Most important, a growing body of educated youth had been trained in the various branches of the technical life of the Modern West and had learned to see life from a technicalistic point of view. The villagers, the bulk of the population, however (though spared the trials of collectivization), were still brutalized in the old misery of exploitation by landlord and moneylender, while the wealthier families in their idle luxury seldom felt any incentive to invest their funds in the doubtful cause of industrialization in the cities or technical improvement on the land. Except in the field of poetry (commonly in opposition or even written in exile) the dominant families did not even show much creative cultural zeal under Reżà's censorship, but were content with French novels in translation. The option of the continuing dialogue in the heritage was kept open, but relatively few were much interested. But Reżà had brought national self-respect and most people of all classes seem to have supported his régime, except the tribes—and except, at length, the newly educated intellectuals of the cities, whose growing interest in communism was, however, rigorously suppressed.

With the Second World War came the end to some illusions. When Germany attacked the Soviet Union in 1941, the Soviet government mobilized all resources; some Muslim peoples were exiled *en masse* from the more westerly territories of the Union to less sensitive areas where their potential disaffection could present no danger, but where they found it very difficult to rebuild any satisfactory life, individually or nationally; and on the steppes a new flood of European settlers completed the process of turning the Muslims into minorities in their own lands. The west Iranian state became important to the Soviet Union as a rare channel of communications with its Western allies, especially for importing *matériel* from Britain (and America), still far ahead in technical development. The British and Russians demanded free transit and military assurances; Reżà (for whom Persian independence was his life) refused; the army availed nothing and the land was occupied, the north by the Russians, the south by the British; whereupon Reżà abdicated an impotent throne.

VI

Muslim India: Communalism and Universalism

Indian Muslims were forced to take a position toward Modernity on peculiarly severe terms. Among no other Muslim people was the problem of the meaning of their cultural and spiritual heritage posed so searchingly. As we have seen, some sort of nationalism has regularly served as the framework for solving the day-to-day problems of so reorganizing social life that the disadvantages of Modernity can be most effectively overcome and its advantages benefited from. But what sort of nationalism was open to the Muslims of India, who had no territory of their own? In fact, several conflicting types of nationalism were open, on none of which all could agree. But the experience was significant for Muslims of all the world. For Islam forms in principle a single world-wide society. And in the world as a whole the Muslims are, as in the more local case of India, distributed among a non-Muslim majority. The problem of the Muslims of India was in the end the problem of the Muslims in the world.

Indo-Muslims under British occupation

By 1818, the British had become the paramount power in most of India, ruling directly in Bengal and the Ganges plain where Islam was very strong. Within a few decades the British had also absorbed the lands of the Indus basin, almost solidly Muslim. In some cases, the advent of British rule meant a transfer from one sort of infidel rule (in part of the Panjâb, that of the Sikhs) to another, perhaps less obnoxious sort of Infidel rule. For some time, since the British perpetuated the administrative patterns of the Timurî empire, including the use of Persian as official tongue, the fact that a handful of Christians were at the top made relatively little difference in day-to-day routine. But when the British decided to eliminate Persian in favour of English it became evident that British rule—which for Hindus was mostly merely a change of masters—for Muslims meant a deposition from the position of ruling class and, rather more pervasively, the undermining of the basis for their traditional cultural life, which had presupposed the prestige and wealth that came with power. Under these circumstances, members of the privileged Muslim classes, brought up in families for whom the dignity of life lay in sharing in the privileges and responsibilities of rule, tended to see little compensation for their families' eclipse in studying English and learning to serve the British Company. Thereupon, it was largely the Hindus (even in half-Muslim Bengal, for instance) who took the training necessary for positions of responsibility, commercial or governmental, while the Muslims had the added pain of seeing their former subjects taking the lead over them. Such a spectacle tended to drive them to withdraw further into their disgust, living as well as they could from their landed revenues.

As late as 1857, a great many Hindus shared the prevailing Muslim sentiment which would have liked to see the Timurid dynasty restored to genuine power and the Hindu-Muslim co-operation under Islamic auspices, for which it stood, re-established. Hindus and Muslims of the lower urban classes remained more or less loyal to the ruling elements which had stemmed from the empire and sceptical of the representatives of British culture, British or Indian. When rumours spread that (for instance) pig fat, abhorrent to Muslims, and cow fat, which no Hindu should dishonour, had been used in greasing the cartridge cases the Indian soldiers were to open with their teeth, a joint mutiny ensued against the British officers. With large bodies of the local soldiery of the company mutinous, many of the local rulers launched a general revolt against the British, in which both Muslims and Hindus joined. The pensioned Timurid emperor, powerless at Delhi, was persuaded to lend his name and a fierce war raged for restoration of conditions of more than a century before.

The princely states did not co-ordinate their efforts. The British Moderns proved eminently efficient and resourceful even though taken by surprise far from their home base and with few reserves immediately present; a sufficient number of Indians either were genuinely loyal to the new order or estimated its strength high enough to hold by the British. After deeds of outstanding valour and outstanding atrocity on each side—the mood of each was desperate—the British won decisively. They were inclined to blame chiefly the Muslims (whether loyal or not), as their natural rivals in India, and for a time British policy added itself to the Muslim sentiment to eliminate the Muslim families from public life.

At this point, the more alert Muslims saw that a direct restoration of the past was out of the question. One of the most active of them in northern India, Sayyid Aḥmad Khân (later knighted as Sir Sayyid), proposed an overall programme of Muslim revival on the basis of full co-operation with the British. For him personally, his programme was justified through an interpretation of Islam which accorded with the Liberal nineteenth-century world view most prominently presented in British culture: the world view according to which the primary source of truth was natural-scientific inquiry, the trend of human life was by nature an ever-expanding awareness of such scientific truth and hence actualization of human potentialities for good; and the good life meant, above all, human prosperity and individual freedom. Aḥmad Khân taught that Islam was essentially the spirit of the Qur'ân, without later accretions. In the spirit of the Qur'ân he found an appeal to recognition of the natural world, an earthy sense of human well-being, and a strong activism which (particularly as compared with most forms of Ṣûfism) could well be interpreted into a doctrine of the supremacy of the Lord of nature calling us to fulfill our own best nature. He called his doctrine by an Arabized English term, *nêchariyyah,* 'naturalism', and offered it as a reform within Islam.

British Liberalism, which joined with its appeal to progress doctrines of political laissez-faire and moral overtones exalting savings and profitable investment over personal liberalities and the erection of pious foundations, appealed as a world view to business entrepreneurs in an age of expanding productivity, willing to give a certain margin to the 'worthy poor' but impatient of social restrictions on business; it gave them noble justification for their present preoccupations and, in its conception of material and moral progress, an eternal dimension as well in justifying their labours as being for the welfare of future ages. The doctrine was no more consistent with Christianity than with Islam, but its inconsistency with traditional Islam shone more obviously, partly because the doctrines of the 'ulamâ' and the courtly traditions (buffeted though they were by events) had not yet experienced the wide variety of reformulations and dilutions which Christianity had known for two centuries; partly because few Indian Muslims were in an expanding economic and social position comparable to that of the British businessmen. The 'ulamâ' effectively tore Aḥmad Khân's specific arguments apart and his new theology was not widely received.

But the practical implications which, for Aḥmad Khân, were justified by the new ideas were more closely related to Indian circumstances. These were, not to live as the British themselves lived, but to carve a place for themselves within the British establishment. To do this, it was not necessary to adopt British Liberalism, but only to accept some of its values as at least a second-best substitute for the vanished Mughal glories. This, perhaps, some aspects of Aḥmad Khân's thinking helped Muslims to do: apart from actual theology, his stress on the practical reasonableness of Islam was in fact acceptable generally among the well-to-do Muslims. With this to go on, they supported his foundation of a Muslim college at Aligarh, which was to teach Modern subjects in English and provide at the same time straight Muslim theology taught more or less in the traditional way, and whose graduates should be qualified to serve in British business firms or in the British governmental apparatus, while remaining good Muslims. They accepted his political lead, which was to try to forge a special alliance between the British and the Muslim upper classes, founded on implicit loyalty to the British régime as the bringer of Modern good order and enlightenment to India. So, a common Muslim awareness could be retained, and the personal interests of individuals satisfied simultaneously.

Some of his disciples worked out a less radical justification for such a policy, interpreting Islam, to be sure, as basically Liberal; but seeing in the

Islam of the classical 'Abbâsî caliphate, with its cultural openness and its fostering of science, a sufficient model for their present departure. Borrowing the theme of certain Western Islamists, they declared that science and progress had come to the Occident from Islam to begin with; that in the ages of Ṣûfism, Islam had declined from its pristine progressiveness; and that what they must now do was recapture, as apprentices to the West, what Islam had meantime lost. Thus consciousness of the Islamic historical heritage was kept alive, and young Muslims encouraged to work out their destiny as Muslims rather than just as Indians.

Bourgeois Islam and Urdu

The Islam of the villages was vivid enough, but did not form a separate total culture strongly marked over against village Hinduism. Whole villages, even whole areas (as in Sindh or east Bengal) were Muslim, and Hindus appeared there only as representatives of an outside class—landlords or moneylenders. Where a village was mixed Muslim and Hindu, the Muslims formed, in effect, distinct castes like the several distinct Hindu castes. For the villages, then, a contrast of Hindu and Muslim meant different things according to the local circumstances, but was always a matter of economic class: sometimes, for instance, the landlords were Muslim and the peasants Hindu, sometimes the reverse. Hindu-Muslim conflict could be severe, but was localized in its implications and sharply focused as class conflict within what remained on the whole a common cultural context.

In the towns, Islam formed a broader cultural entity. There were Hindu shopkeepers and Muslim shopkeepers side by side; most of their folkways and social outlook tended to be similar; but the difference of religion occasioned a pervasive difference in other matters also. They had different festivals, read or listened to different books, lauded different historic heroes, dressed differently (every caste, in fact, tended to have its own costume) and even tended to eat slightly different sorts of food—the Muslims delighting in animal flesh while the Hindus tended toward a fleshless diet. Here mistrust was sometimes a matter of conflict of group economic interests, but more often reflected the division of the same economic class into two groups differentiated according to culture. The two groups did not inter-marry nor (usually) go to the same schools and despite individual friendships tended, therefore, to form separate social circles. The separate circles were not bound together by the ramified interrelationships by which marriage and other common memberships knit together even those personally unknown to each other. Hence arose differences of economic interest which were not so much conflicts of class as rivalries within a single class position.

In the towns, then, an assertion of specifically Muslim cultural life was at the same time an assertion of loyalty to the Muslim community at the very basis of that community's existence. Any emphasis on ultimate ideals must be suspect if it undermined the concrete actuality of cultural ties. There was severe pressure to maintain the intimate ways of cultural life as they had been.

This pressure was reinforced by the danger, which appeared in the later nineteenth century, of outbreaks of communal violence between Muslims and Hindus. In the villages, class violence naturally took on a confessional, a communal colouring. In the towns jealousies, not always discouraged by the British, ready to divide and rule, were exacerbated by the diverse forces with which Modern conditions threatened every group. As Hindus attempted to revive their heritage as a base for their own self-identity in the face of the Modern challenge, they were inclined to look behind the period of Muslim domination to the older Sanskritic culture of Hindu greatness. They tended to try to eliminate the many more or less Islamic strains interwoven into their life. For instance, in the upper Ganges plain the common tongue was written in two forms: with the Persian alphabet (in which form it was known as Urdu) and with the Sanskrit alphabet (in which form it was known as Hindi). Many Hindus deliberately turned away from Urdu, filled with Persian words and associated with Islam, to Hindi, in which the Persian words were often replaced by Sanskritic equivalents and the literary associations were Hindu. When Hindus founded an association intended to replace the prevailing Urdu with Hindi, Muslims (not without support from non-communally minded Hindus) founded a counter-association for the defence and propagation of Urdu. When such rivalries were picked up by the uneducated, they were sometimes expressed in deliberate provocations: Hindus would plan noisy processions by a mosque at the time of Muslim ṣalât and Muslims would make a point of publicly slaughtering cows to eat. By the middle of the twentieth century, such communal tension had become endemic in important parts of India, leading to periodic riots.

To the end, Persian had remained the official language of the Mughal empire, as the language of international Islam from which that empire never felt itself severed. The flowering of Urdu in the eighteenth century, reflecting in part the loss of the power of attracting talented Muslim foreigners to India, had remained unofficial. In the nineteenth century, with Persian no longer of official significance in any case and with the need to rally the Muslim population as intimately as possible, Urdu, as the ordinary Muslim language of diverse areas and in particular of the home provinces of the Mughal empire in the Ganges basin, became the primary language of Indo-Muslim culture.

From an early time, Urdu served at once two functions. It was the prevailing urban tongue of Delhi, Lucknow, and Lahore, the centres of the Mughal tradition; as such, though in many areas it was at most a bâzâr language, and (in Bengal, for instance) often not even that, it served as vehicle for those who identified their fortunes with the Indo-Muslim Mughal tradition. Arabic remained, no doubt, the language of Muslim theological scholarship; Persian was still avidly studied in the nineteenth century, by both Muslims and Hindus, as an incomparable repository of cosmopolitan grace; but Urdu had become the instrument of a specifically Mughal-Indian historical consciousness binding the Indian Muslims in a common community. Yet for the upper Ganges plain at least and, to some degree, in cities elsewhere, Urdu was also the current vernacular, used in ordinary family life. As such, it was the inevitable vehicle of a Modern literature of verse and fiction following the English lead in interpreting the dilemmas and the moral meaning of daily life.

In the midst of the Modern consciousness, Indian Muslims retained many of the forms of the older Indian culture. Nowhere had purda, the veiling and segregation of women, been more rigorously observed than in India, where the very point of being a Muslim was to be upper-class and aristocratic manners were given special emphasis. Hindus likewise had naturally followed the custom. The unveiling of women was correspondingly slower than in the main centres of the Ottoman empire; while the men of the family learned to go out and work in offices, wearing Western garb and using English, the women were kept as nearly as possible in a style befitting the days of Timurî supremacy. Literature itself kept vivid the old tradition. Even while novelists were coming to present the homey themes of nineteenth-century Western fiction, Urdu poetry was producing some of its greatest triumphs precisely in the genres sanctified by the Persian tradition (though not without Modern modifications). Even to the middle of the twentieth century, in contrast especially to Turks or Arabs, Indo-Muslim youth delighted in public (male) poetic contests in which poets chanted their verse within established forms, capable of being judged and ranked by the audience then and there, with public acclamation to the winner. With persistent vitality, the contests were adapted to the railroad age, to radio and to the fast pace of change, so that at last they become integral with the most inward aspects of Modern life.

The age of Gândhî

With the end of the First World War came, throughout the world, new hopes of a new fulfillment of the promise of social abundance and personal dignity which the industrial and liberal revolutions had seemed to promise. Europeans especially had seen what prodigies could be accomplished toward destruction; they felt that the old order which led to the war could surely never be restored; that now like prodigies must instead arise for peace and prosperity. Each side blamed the horrors of war on the wickedness of the other and so discounted any sombre reflections they might raise about themselves. At most what seemed to be needed was to check the irresponsibility of the governing classes. Throughout Europe there was a wave of revolution and popular reform: old privileges were to be swept away and new liberties and dignities for everyman inaugurated. The Marxist revolts were but a part of general dreams of a new age which were also expressed in the proliferation of permissivist children's schools, often enough pacifist and vegetarian; the rapid spread of co-operative economic projects, together with extensive governmental action to ensure that all sections of the population should share in the security and the opportunities hitherto reserved to privileged classes; and an experimentalism in painting and literature which recklessly dispensed with the disciplines of centuries to pour out a desperate need for radical fulfillment.

From a concert of monarchies, Europe became a congeries of republics united for peace in a 'League of Nations'. Instead of the Liberalism of the nineteenth century, the watchword now was 'democracy' and the dignity of the commonest man. In the general fervour for realizations of what had been the dreams of the *avant-garde* of the nineteenth century, it was chiefly the most sophisticated intellectuals only who were dominated by misgivings about the abyss in mankind of malice and destructiveness which the war had revealed.

It was naturally western Europe that was the centre at once of the greatest hopes and of the profoundest forebodings. Other parts of the world reflected the mood, usually indeed the optimism rather than the pessimism, according to their relation to the ongoing process of Modernity. In India the British had leaned heavily on Indian support for their war effort. Indian soldiers had seen service far overseas; substantial new war industries had been established at home. The slow pace toward greater Indian participation in governmental authority had seemed inadequate to most Indian leaders, especially among the Hindus; to encourage fuller commitment, liberal British had persuaded the government to promise home rule for India when the war was won. The large segment of urban Indians that had been assimilated into the Modern nexus of affairs and had espoused nationalism was jubilant with anticipation.

It was not long after the end of the war that the impracticality of granting so great a measure of independence to the most substantial portion of their empire was impressed on those British whose wartime fervour had led them to accept more liberal ideas for the time being. It was again pointed out that India was no nation nor even a group of homogeneous nations, but a congeries of disparate peoples. 'Self rule' would mean, at best, rule by the dominant class of one or more of the local peoples over all the others, if not anarchy followed by a different and less enlightened foreign, perhaps Russian rule. To maintain good order, the British felt they must assure their own position at all costs. Serious reforms were postponed. A crowded demonstration was bloodily suppressed by jittery officers. Soon the British government showed its intention of continuing imperial rule as before with only modest modifications. The Indian public, accustomed to British legality and honour, was scandalized and mutinous, yet apparently helpless.

At this point the leadership passed from budding Indian industrialists and white-collar politicians to an eccentric Hindu lawyer and journalist, Mohandas Gândhî. Gândhî had studied law in Britain, and was doing very well. But his heart was won by the new radical humanist ideals which he met with there and subsequently in English literature: the ideals, for instance, of Thoreau, Ruskin, and Tolstoy, looking to a co-operative society of non-violent, creative individualists. He was impressed with the ideals of democracy and of socialism, if not with some of their practical expressions; he was won by the *avant-garde* mood of religious universalism, pacifism, and vegetarianism. He honoured the tremendous human achievements of the Modern West, especially as these were reflected in legal assurances of individual dignity and opportunity, though he did not despise the material welfare of common persons, especially in matters of hygiene and education. But he listened carefully to the critics of Modern society, who pointed out the inhumanity of over-mechanization, particularly of assembly-line factory labour; the hollowness of the life of many of the well-to-do, divorced from the soil and from the immediate human need which gives labour its savour; the falseness and perverse ugliness of public commercialism and political demagoguery and chauvinism which were to find a natural expression in the Great War. Inspired by what was most idealist in the Modern Christian tradition, he learned to appreciate anew some of the strengths latent in Hinduism. He recognized that simple political democracy and even industrial socialism, while having their good points if won through free agreement, would not be enough. India must be Modern, but he did not want India simply to follow the current ways of the West, even if it could. India must find a new path for itself, better than that of the West, one which, indeed, the rest of the world might then follow.

Gândhî had confronted Western racial pride and injustice in South Africa, where he led the Indian community (partly Muslim, partly Hindu) in a successful struggle against certain race discrimination policies in the years before 1914. In South Africa he developed his own approach to the problems of Modernity and indeed of life generally. His immediate concern was with the personal moral life; he established an idealistic colony where the members shared together in brotherhood. In this work his companions were Christians, Muslims, and Hindus, Europeans and Indians. But personal morality could not be divorced from public life: if the customs of the land were degrading, personal dignity required that they be combated and overcome. To this end, the members of his colony were trained as soldiers of what he called *Satyagrâha*, 'Truth-force'. He taught that sheer truth was the most powerful force for good in human life: first of all, as he had learned as a lawyer, the truth of sheer fact; but ultimately the moral truth to which all human beings are heirs however they may have tried to shield themselves from it in their weakness. With the handful of members of the colony as a nucleus, he created whole truth-force armies out of the day-labourers in the South African coal mines and even their women. With a non-violent demonstration of their convictions and their human dignity through strikes and through refusal to obey unjust laws, taking all resultant suffering upon themselves without any retaliation, they won their campaigns, reversed discriminatory laws, and, above all, proved to themselves their own manhood.

Returning at last to India, Gândhî dreamed of a nationalism which should reinforce the face-to-face local relations rather than destroy them, but should broaden their outlook, enlarge their economic foundations, and ennoble their goals. He was concerned to save economically and renew morally the Indian village rather than to mechanize the Indian city. Typical of his outlook was his offer of a prize for the invention of machines which should combine high productive efficiency with such simplicity of operation and repair that they could remain under the informed control of a small group of people, such as those of a village using and depending on them. Modern inventiveness should serve human efficiency as well as sheer economic efficiency. Consistently with his ultimate goals, he did not try to win power at the top and inaugurate reforms from there. He believed men should win their welfare through their own efforts, winning each reform through a personal demonstration of its true human validity; otherwise they would not be fit to use their winnings to higher spiritual ends.

Gândhî began his public life in India (where he was well known for his South African work) with the immediate cause of winning home rule from the British. But he conceived this cause not so much in terms of strategies of interest and privilege as in terms of the personal responsibility of each Indian to put an end to a system in which his honour as an Indian was compromised. He hoped that Indians would rule with a greater sense of Indian welfare than had the British, but he respected British rule. His concern was that, for better or worse, Indians should have full dignity in their own land. To his mind it must be all Indians, not just the educated élite, who should learn the self-respect that was his chief aim; accordingly his first suggestion was to involve the masses, even the illiterates, in the nationalist movement. In the crisis of nationalist hopes, his leadership was accepted on that basis.

From the caliphate campaign to village self-reform

A first concern of Gândhî was to establish the nationalist movement as transcending all confessional lines. Under the continuing influence of Aḥmad Khân's principle of loyalty to British rule, most of the Muslim community had been holding aloof from the general Indian sentiment for home rule, which would in any case no longer mean Muslim rule. Hence national unity meant bringing the Muslims, a quarter of the Indian population, into the movement along with the Hindus, Sikhs, Parsis, and Christians. Gândhî's solution was to adopt a popular Muslim cause along with the more general cause of *Swarâj*, 'self-rule'. Since the time of Jamâluddîn Afghânî, Muslims had focused increasingly their sense of integrity as a world community on the continued independence and prestige of the Ottoman state; since the propaganda of 'Abdülhamîd, they had even accepted the Ottoman sultan as caliph and had come to look on him as guaranteeing the juridical and moral status of Islam everywhere despite the local facts of infidel rule. It had been bitter to Indian Muslims that their British government had been at war with Ottoman Turkey (the majority of Indian troops sent to fight the Turks had been Muslim and the experience had brought them personal shame). At the end of the war, they were eager to see a generous peace granted to the Turks so that the caliph should continue sufficiently strong to maintain a crucial nucleus of free Muslim rule, preferably including the Holy Cities of the Ḥijâz. This was a cause of honour, which inevitably appealed to Gândhî however little he shared its particular premises; moreover, ardent Muslims were ready to carry the cause to the people at large. The brothers Muḥammad 'Alî and Shaukat 'Alî had organized a vital popular movement supported by the 'ulamâ', which by-passed the Muslim League, organ of those more privileged Muslims who still wished to co-operate with the British. Men's dignity as Muslims was at stake in the treatment of the defeated Turks, and even villagers were moved by the appeal, without necessarily understanding its technical demands (they had never heard of Turkey, of course).

Accordingly, in 1920 the Indian National Congress joined the two demands: that the British grant self-rule to India and allow an honourable peace to Ottoman Turkey. Broadening massively the scope of the experiments he had undertaken with success in South Africa, Gândhî and his lieutenants organized an India-wide campaign of non-co-operation with the British authority for so long as it refused to honour the just demands that had been formulated. The campaign for self-rule included such measures as refusal to pay taxes, boycott of imported British goods in favour of Indian-produced goods (preferably, because of Gândhî's concern with the village economy, village homespun) and refusal to obey the regulations made to suppress the movement. It was impossible to launch such direct action in the campaign for the caliphate (in Persian, *khilâfat*), but most lower-class Muslims, made desperate by the added privations which the war had superimposed on their poverty, were glad to join heartily in the general Congress campaign for home rule.

The excitement was almost universal save among the wealthiest families. Men like Muḥammad 'Alî and Gândhî found ways of reaching not only townsmen but peasants and giving them a large measure of at least temporary discipline, willingness to be beaten and jailed without either giving in or unleashing destructive (and in the circumstances futile) violence. The enthusiasm was contagious. Many Muslim peasants in northwest India came to the conclusion that if they should not co-operate with infidel unjust rule, the honourable course was to go all the way (as indeed many Muslim legists had maintained through the centuries) and emigrate from infidel-held land to where they could practice Islam in full under a Muslim government. The nearest such territory was Afghanistan. The Afghan government naturally turned them back when they reached the borders and they perished by the thousands. Other Muslim peasants in the southwest coastlands, Keralam, called Mopillahs—an unusually impoverished and resentful community—decided to set up a true Muslim caliphate right where they were and drive out the Hindu landlords. The threat to vested interests was drowned in blood by the British army. The main body of the movement for self-rule remained under non-violent discipline, with increasing hopes of success, till early 1922. Then violence broke out even within the Congress-sponsored activity. The incidents were isolated, but Gândhî believed they showed that Indians were not yet ready to rule themselves in restraint and justice. More years of discipline and preparation were still needed. Without waiting for violence to spread and for the British army consequently to gain the initiative, he called off the movement, to the consternation of all, who nonetheless obeyed.

The struggle for the caliphate, unrealistic from the beginning, necessarily ended about the same time as that for home rule. When the Turks deposed their own sultan, little remained that the Indians could even demand. But now opened a less spectacular and perhaps more fundamental phase of the work. Gândhî and his followers set to training Indians for true liberty by leading them in rectifying the abuses in their ways of life which depended not on the British but on themselves.

Among the Hindus, the centre of attention was elimination of untouchability, that rigid segregation of certain castes (such as tanners or sweepers) which were forced to lead an insulted and degraded existence in the midst of their fellows. The techniques of truth-force were used by the untouchables, with heroic patience and perseverance, to force upper-caste Hindus to face the unlovely truth of their unfair behaviour, and finally to change their ways. But Gândhî's interests were more general: he tirelessly moved from village to village, garbed as simply as the villagers themselves, preaching a new way of life. He had early won the confidence of the Indian common people as a saint. Now he taught them the value of cleanliness: he complained immediately if a village allowed carelessness in disposal of garbage or other unsightliness (as most villages did). He encouraged them to use the under-employed leisure time to produce their own cloth, and helped them to relearn processes which had sometimes declined since the advent of mechanized production from the West, and to raise their own vegetables to supplement their diet. The Gândhists gradually, in the succeeding decades, developed innumerable programmes of this sort; concentrating eventually especially on finding a practical sort of 'basic' education, based partly on the teachings of Dewey but thoroughly adapted to the needs of the Indian village. It was found that conventional teaching of literacy was often futile—without occasion to use letters, literacy was totally lost again in a matter of years. The Gândhists proposed to teach young villagers total self-reliance, teaching them to raise their own food, spin their own school-grown thread, weave their own clothes, even build their own schoolhouse, so that they could, at a pinch, feel fully independent if left to their own resources; and above all bring back what they had learned to their elders in the rest of the village.

The full development of the Gândhist programme was a slow matter, interrupted with renewed campaigns for political independence and constantly exploring new paths of action as the endlessly knotty problems of Indian life revealed themselves. In it Gândhî's Muslim followers took a large part. On the intellectual level, the Muslim 'âlim, Abûlkalâm Âzâd, proved one of the most important leaders. Often the head of the National Congress, he formulated especially for Muslims the theory of independence and co-operation among Muslims and Hindus to build a free and just India. For him the message of the Qur'ân was universal righteousness; the mission of Muslims must be, not necessarily to rule others outright, but to act as a consistent force in any social situation for justice and human dignity; hence Muslims should be in the vanguard of whatever movement promised best to bring freedom and justice to themselves and all their fellow-Indians. On a more practical level, Muḥammad 'Alî (on the collapse of the caliphate movement) devoted himself to a new school founded not far from Delhi, which had split off from the conservative Aligarh College: the Jâmi'ah Milliyyah, 'Nationalist College' where a nationalist Muslim leadership along more or less Gândhist lines was to be trained.

The fullest practical expression of Gândhism anywhere in India appeared among the Afghan tribes along the northwest frontier of the Indian empire, under the leadership of 'Abdulghaffâr Khân. Noted for their feuding and raiding, these tribesmen (mostly among the villages rather than in the towns) were won to an active and almost universal programme of social self-reform. Feuding was stopped, discipline was imposed under 'Abdulghaffâr Khân in the name of Service of God (*Khudâî-khidmat* in Persian), and such innovations as schooling were encouraged. When nationalist campaigns for independence were launched, the Khudâî-khidmatgârs, as these Afghans were called, gave effective and faithful support. At all times they remained disciplinedly nonviolent; Qur'ânic encouragement of forgiveness as better than revenge became the foundation of a highly Muslim interpretation of Gândhî's ideas. But such Hindus as were to be found in the area were admitted to participation if they undertook the same discipline, even though they did not profess Islam. A relative lack of strong class differentiation helped make the movement acceptable to all, as (in contrast to most of India) fairly full implementation would ruin relatively few vested interests; hence a major barrier which Gândhists encountered elsewhere was removed, and the more positive attractions of Modernity were allowed to act with less interference. After decades, the concrete results were notable throughout the area in the form of increased prosperity, social discipline, and readiness for responsible self-rule.

Communalism

Not all Muslims, of course, were content to accept a nationalism of so universalist a type. A certain number of idealists—no longer, however, the aristocratic heirs of the Mughal supremacy, now firmly pro-British—cherished again the hope of Muslim rule in India. Apparently agreeing with the British that the Indian masses needed a master-people to rule them, Mashriqî seems to have believed that that people should be formed of revitalized Muslims. He organized large numbers of petty bourgeois into troops, called Khâksârs, devoted to para-military training and to service in social emergencies; like a Modern Mahdî, he insisted that only his followers were really true Muslims, basing their Islam neither on common traditional ways (which he regarded as corrupted) nor on the teachings of the 'ulamâ' (whom he assailed) but on the social-political mission of the Qur'ân and the early conquering caliphate. His gospel was puritanical and called, like the Gândhists, for efficiency and discipline. He too accepted an occasional non-Muslim as follower if he were a monotheist, but his Khâksârs (pledged blindly to follow his orders) were clearly to stand ready to form a task-force to re-establish order on an Islamic basis when the British were driven out of India in whatever way that might happen. When the Khâksârs began to be sent, as an exercise, to interfere in tense situations, the British found it necessary to suppress them.

Nationalism for Indian Muslims could be on an all-India territorial basis, then, either in co-operation with other confessions on the basis of the Islamic demand for universal justice, or in potential rivalry with other confessions for dominance on the basis of the Muslim claim to carry the essentials of a superior social order in their faith itself. The first alternative was long the most popular among the masses, who followed the National Congress and revered, though they did not usually accept the demands of Gândhî and the Gândhists. The second alternative had a very limited appeal. But increasingly the early enthusiasm of the immediate postwar years, revived in a renewed civil disobedience campaign at the start of the 1930s, wore off. A second failure of the Gândhî-led nationalist movement to win independence discouraged many. In the great Depression of the 1930s India too suffered, and general hopes gave way to immediately pressing grievances. Gândhî was concerned, above all, with the moral purification of India, to which the struggle for independence was simply one means; he stressed non-violence, village cottage industry, elimination of caste barriers; for many, especially when that purification was expressed in Hindu terms, this seemed too long-term a goal. Urban Muslims began to turn to a third sort of nationalism, a nationalism at once oriented to India as a unit and yet limited to a non-territorial segment of it. They began to feel themselves as primarily Muslims and to seek special status and privileges for Muslims as such within a wider Indian framework, whether that framework were still under British rule or independent. This tendency to think in terms of the confessional community within a particular territory rather than of the territorial nation as a whole was called 'communalism'.

Communalism took various forms. Most mildly, it took the form of separate Muslim organizations working side-by-side with the National Congress for the same or nearly the same ends. The Aḥrâr, or Freemen, a middle-class party of the Panjâb, advocated an independent, democratic, socialist India for which they worked in co-operation with the Congress (and without having to compromise so many diverse views as the Congress did), but always as Muslims and on the basis of Qur'ânic injunctions. But most such Muslim groups tended to be more strongly interested in causes restricted to the interests of Muslims as such. They encouraged Muslims to think of themselves just as Muslims rather than as Indians or as Panjâbîs or Bengalîs, or even as workers or shopkeepers or peasants with common interests with other workers or shopkeepers or peasants. The most persistent communalist Muslim organization was the Muslim League. Representing the well-to-do and landed classes, it remained lukewarm to any Indian independence but, whatever happened, insisted on Muslims as such being given special guarantees.

This communalism did not look to the whole Muslim community, which was world-wide; it drew its limits at the boundaries of India. The common sentiment it rested on was essentially the sense of a common Timurî-Indian heritage. Its more extreme leaders exalted the days of the Timurî empire and regarded Urdu as the peculiar vehicle of their culture (even though the majority of Indian Muslims did not speak Urdu) because it represented that culture in its latest form. But instead of attempting outright to restore Islamic rule as in Timurî times, communalism tried to separate off the Indian Muslims as a nation of their own. They spoke of India as containing two nations in the same space: the Hindu nation (in which they tended to include Sikhs, Parsîs, and Christians) and the Muslim nation, each of which, they claimed, had its own culture and social structure. They demanded in effect that there must be two parallel political structures, so far as possible, to express the two social structures.

Such an orientation went against one of the chief purposes of any nationalism: to eliminate special differentiations and privileges within a territory so as to permit new and Modern institutions to be built up on a wider, more impersonal basis. Yet it expressed, in a situation where Muslims formed a minority but could not be the ruling minority, the persistent demand that Islam form a total society in itself. (It was popular primarily in the Gangetic plain where Muslims were in the minority but had their main Urdu cultural centres; in Muslim majority areas it had less appeal.) As such it had enormous potential appeal, the more Muslims became conscious of themselves as a community. It seemed to provide a way of retaining the historic Muslim vision intact in a day of territorial nationalism, without just merging (as 'vanguard' or not!) into a general national movement which inevitably, whether so intended or not, took on a Hindu colouring.

At the hands of the Muslim League, communalism remained for long, however, essentially a technique of slowing down dangerous change. Above all, the Muslim League demanded a communal electoral policy: Muslims and

Hindus should vote for separate lists of candidates rather than voting on common lists; that is, Muslim candidates should appeal only to Muslim voters, Hindus only to Hindu voters. This was a policy perfectly designed to force candidates to support whatever might seem to bind Muslims together as Muslims, that is, whatever divided them from Hindus, whereas election on a common list would force them to try to please both Muslim and Hindu voters at once and so to find what would bring them together. Communal voting could please only communalists who feared social change in any case and were chiefly concerned to maintain various group privileges: the Hindu Mahâsabhâ (the strongest party of communalist Hinduism) on the one hand and its opposite number, the Muslim League, on the other. The Indian National Congress, which relied on Hindu-Muslim unity and looked to extensive progress which must presuppose that unity, could not accept it without undermining its own future together with that of Indian harmony generally. Till the end of the 1930s, the Muslim League continued to represent a minority of Muslims, as did the Hindu Mahâsabhâ a minority of Hindus.

The dreams of Iqbâl

Muḥammad Iqbâl (1876–1938), of a good Muslim family of Lahore, was exposed as a youth to traditional Islam and with it, of course, to the speculations and the poetry of Ṣûfism, which he deeply loved. He early became known as a gifted Urdu poet. He was also, on the principles of Aḥmad Khân, exposed to English learning. In 1905 he went to England, where he earned a Ph.D. in philosophy. In 1908 he published an important study of certain Muslim, especially Ṣûfi philosophers; it is clear that their thought was still very important for him. In particular, he was taken with the system of Bahâ'ullâh, the disciple of the Bâb, a system which had built in turn on Mullâ Ṣadrâ. His description of Bahâ'ullâh's thought reads like an anticipation of his own later exposition. But his philosophic mind was formed at least as much by the latest in European fashion, late romantics and post-romantics: Bergson, Nietzsche, Whitehead, the English Idealists and those who debated with them. It was in terms of these moderns that he described the older Muslim philosophers.

Returning to India, he practiced law and taught philosophy for a time. But he found himself so disgusted with the prevailing hypocrisy, pusillanimity and incompetence in Indian Islam that he gave up his official post and even, for a time, scarcely wrote any poetry. Meanwhile he was formulating his own response to the degradation of his people partly through philosophical analysis, partly through poetic inspiration.

Iqbâl was preoccupied with moral philosophy. What sort of life is worth living? To answer such a question, he had to adopt some conclusion as to what life was: an ontology. Here he presupposed, as must most Moderns, the overwhelming importance of the fact of evolution. Life at a later time has unpredictably new features which it lacked at an earlier time. At the same time, again with most Moderns, he recognized the incalculable value of indefinitely varied individual personalities. Accordingly, life could not be reduced to a closed system, fixed in its natural categories, such as Medieval philosophers had elaborated. The rightful human position in the cosmos could not be exhaustively analyzed as of any given moment of time or any given set of values. Yet Iqbâl was unwilling to admit in consequence a simple relativism: to say that the cosmos was simply a congeries of events, any observable order in which had only the practical meaning of allowing us to manipulate events to meet any current wishes we might have; and to say that our wishes, in turn, could be judged by no standard outside the purposes which any of us happened, by training or by interest, to have formulated and recognized. He was convinced that some purposes were inherently sounder than others; that Muslim decadence in India was bad not just because it was inconvenient or aesthetically offensive but because it violated enduring cosmic requirements.

Iqbâl was persuaded that precisely in the infinite potentialities of total individuality lay the solution. It was not any given value that counted, but the uniqueness of individuality itself. The whole cosmos presented, in its totality, an absolute uniqueness: it expressed the individuality of the Absolutely Unique Individual, to be identified with what Islam knew as God. The destiny to which each finite individual, each human being, was called was to be more and more like God: more and more uniquely individual, and therefore more and more creative. Time, evolution, was not a mechanical sequence of disappearing points but the unfolding of individual creativities; time was merely a tool, an expression of the individual, which transcended it; hence novelty and contrast were not occasions for seeing the old as meaningless but for seeing the cosmic potentialities realized. History, and even historic progress, therefore, as the field of individual creativity (and a key part of cosmic evolution) must be the centre of moral attention and even provide the test of moral validity.

Islam, as the most intensely historical of all faiths, seemed to fill the need for a historical foundation for moral life. But the Islam which could do this must be the Islam of social order and political action, the Islam of the Sharî'ah and of the great ghâzîs. In this Islam he thought he saw action at once dynamic and responsible, creative yet never divorced from an overriding cosmic perspective and authority. He rebelled violently, therefore, against the un-Islamic passivity and self-effacement which he saw in what he called 'Persian' Sûfism (in accordance with the nineteenth-century rejection of Ṣûfî religion and Persian culture as decadent). But his own outlook made use of ways of understanding Islam which the Ṣûfîs had made acceptable. He was more concerned with the inner spirit of Muḥammad's revelation than with its outer detail; moreover, he looked to exceptional individuals to embody this spirit in their own lives on behalf of the community at large.

When he cited justificatory parallels to his thought within the Islamic tradition, it was preponderantly from Ṣûfî writers.

He saw Islam as fulfilling at once two social needs. On the one hand, it provided for continuity in social life through the enduring Sharîʿah and the vast network of popularly engrained lifeways which it guaranteed, not subject to any arbitrary alteration by single persons or even wilful groups. This continuity would provide inescapable long-term standards by which any individual could always measure himself, and a dependable context in which individuals could unfold. At the same time, Islam embodied a principle of development. Though stable, the Sharîʿah was not, in principle, static; built into it were devices which should allow it to respond to new needs as individuals proved creative and society evolved. Iqbâl insisted (with good precedent) that ijtihâd must always remain open and that the Qur'ân demanded searching individual inquiry and experiment. He tried to show, in fact, that it was precisely in Islam that originated the spirit and method of the empirical attitude and inductive inquiry, which he regarded as the key to conscious systematic progress.

He saw Islam as placed at the centre of world history. In pre-Islamic times human society and human thought had progressed steadily, if somewhat haphazardly; but from the time of primitive tribal cult and magic right up to the time of the rise of the historic confessional religions like Hinduism and Christianity, men's minds were dependent upon intervention by the special and not fully rational process of revelation—of the prophetic genius of men who knew more than they understood, who proclaimed truths higher than what they could demonstrate. The greatest achievement of the intellectual efforts of that time, the classical Greek philosophy, still reflected the limitations of minds not fully freed from primitive shackles. Classical Greek thought, he felt, remained essentially deductive, tied to abstractions that were, in fact, simply highly rationalized myths; it was not set free, in full consciousness of its own powers, to investigate empirical actuality.

Muḥammad's revelation was the final and most perfect revelation precisely in that it brought to mankind the principles which made further revelation superfluous. With its absolute monotheism and vital pragmatism, it brought liberation from all myth and directed men to unprejudiced empirical inquiry henceforth. In the primitive human condition, such liberating insight could be achieved only on a prophetic basis; but once achieved, further supra-rational insight was not needed, for empirical, inductive science would suffice to carry men further. Iqbâl tried to show the presence of this intellectual achievement in the simple directness of Qur'ânic teaching and then in the various essays at experimental science and at non-Aristotelian metaphysics which appeared tentatively in various Medieval Muslim thinkers. Accepting a Western judgment that it was from the Muslims that western Christendom had learned experimental as against speculative science, he attributed the vast and rapid efflorescence of Renaissance and Modern Western science as resulting from application of this Islamic principle. But the West had taken this liberating principle, which was a principle of change and evolution, without balancing it with the equally important principle of continuity which Islam also carried. As a result, the Western development was rapid, but unbalanced and morally unsound and would eventually end in collapse.

Islam, meanwhile, had clung to the whole of Muḥammad's revelation: tentatively and slowly it had begun to adopt the liberating principle of development (which led so far in the West) but it had also maintained the continuity of the community founded on Muḥammad's own social perceptiveness, which kept liberty from becoming license. In the West, individualism had been idolized and pursued without regard to its dependence on the Absolute Individual, God; hence it was falsified. In Islam, if Muslims would awaken to their heritage, a truer individualism, free without license, would arise. Even now, the Muslims had a crucial mission as the sole witnesses to the uncompromising unity of God with all its ultimate implications both for freedom of human thought and for moral direction to individual genius. In its materialism, Europe was bound to destroy itself. Then Islam would stand ready to lead chastened humanity more soberly and more securely on the path of progress toward full individuation.

Such an historical role presupposed, as had Ṣûfism, a special, creative role for a spiritual élite. It was the exceptional individual who, indeed, was the chief beneficiary of the principle of development and of freedom in Islam; it was through such individuals that history moved, greater individuality and variety was expressed, and the fullness of God's potentialities approached. Such individuals were on the way to becoming what Nietzsche called the Superman, and what Iqbâl described in classical Ṣûfî terms as the Perfect Man, the end of creation and even its reason for existence. As had been the case with Ṣûfism, though such an individual might see beyond the current form of the Sharî'ah to possible future, better social forms, he was bound to uphold the Sharî'ah as it stood meanwhile for the sake of social solidarity; for the masses could not be expected to understand truths on such a level. Eventually, all mankind should approach nearer and nearer to perfect individual uniqueness and so to God; meanwhile the purpose of God's creativity was being fulfilled in those who most nearly approximated to this. As for the Ṣûfîs, so for Iqbâl, Muḥammad was the prototype, in his universality and rationality, of the ultimate perfect man.

This system, presented in vigorous prose as well as more ambiguous verse, won its impact in part at the expense of intellectual caution. In his legal analysis of the flexibility of the Sharî'ah, he assigned (for instance) to ijmâ' the role of embodying conscious and deliberate accommodation to new conditions and views, a role quite inconsistent with its original use in the system of al-Shâfi'î. While thus gaining a point for the principle of development, he failed to show how the principle of continuity was to be maintained if al-Shâfi'î's analysis were abandoned. His interpretation of Medieval Muslim thinkers was often strained to his purpose and his view of the evolution of Modern Europe was shallow and one-sided. He was assured that Islam contrasted both to a system like Hinduism, which possessed only the principle of continuity, and to a system like that of the Modern West which, because of crucial weaknesses in a Christianity which had rejected the Law, now possessed only the principle of development. But he never gave serious evidence to show that other Medieval systems, such as the Hindu, could not likewise show possession of a principle of development; or that Islam would be better able than Christianity to survive Modernity without endangering its principle of continuity, which his writings take almost for granted. Nevertheless, Iqbâl's system presented a more sophisticated vindication of Islam than the condemnations of Islam and the vindications of Christianity which Muslims were accustomed to finding in Western writings; indeed, his distortions of history were no more flagrant than those presupposed by any of the popular Western attempts to make history revolve around Christianity.

The natural consequence of Iqbâl's combination of militancy with caution, his sense of the high ultimate destiny of Islam together with his tenderness for its current institutional embodiment, however inadequate, was to justify Muslim communalism. Iqbâl did not believe, to be sure, that Muslims should limit their social or political outlook within any one territory. The Islamic community with which he was concerned was world-wide and he worried about the position of Muslims in Palestine as well as about their position in Delhi. It was indicative that he wrote in the international Persian, not in the local Indian Urdu, the most important of the poetry in which he presented his message to Muslims. He opposed any overly absolute territorial nationalism as divisive of world Islam (though he sympathized with a certain degree of local national emphasis in areas where Muslims were a majority, if this seemed necessary to social renovation). But in practice an emphasis on the social and cultural independence of Muslims apart from any particular territorial nation they happened to be in served the cause of Muslim cultural conservatism in India as against the wider outlook of Indian nationalism. However presently inadequate, the independent organic evolution of Islam must be safeguarded. In fact he co-operated with the Muslim League.

Gândhî was an activist; he found degradation but trusted in an underlying nobility and, in fact, in the course of his action he brought out the noble in almost all those he dealt with. He had read relatively little, though he had read that well. But he longed for, and preached, a contemplative life: he always regretted not having time for the higher activity which was yoga. Iqbâl, in contrast, was himself a contemplative, supremely a poet. He found a like degradation about him and, despairing of his own generation, longed for, and preached in gripping verse, a life of high-minded action which a new generation was to take up after him. Meanwhile, he looked more to defending whatever could be salvaged from the present wreck rather than to building anew right away. Gândhî was highly practical in current constructive activities, never failing to sense the right man or the right moment. But he had never inquired far into philosophical questions and, at least as fatefully, his larger historical perspective was naïve (as he himself partly realized at last). Iqbâl had a far stronger sense of the movement of history and the vitality of a continuing tradition; hence he was more 'realistic' in sensing the political requirements of the cultural institutions of his own generation. As interest in Gândhî waned among Muslims, as communal pressures increased and historical Islam became more actively important for them, the younger educated Muslims looked to Iqbâl for inspiration.

Pakistan

The Second World War precipitated events rapidly. Hardships and even outright famine were much greater than they had been in the First World War. It became rapidly evident that India was finally to become independent even if the British came out victorious, and that following independence there would probably be a new order in many ways. All politically alert elements feverishly jockeyed for such power as they might hope to win in determining how the new order should be structured. Only Gândhî and the Gândhists persisted in thinking primarily not of who should hold power but of the moral level of the society within which the power would be exercised; their measures appeared fatuous to the more impatient, and Gândhî's leadership rapidly lost ground. With the (possibly unconscious) help of the manœuvres of some of the British (still hoping to avoid independence at all), communalism became dangerously inflamed. The masses of Muslims were more and more polarized into a minority who still supported the Indian National Congress and a large majority, especially in the Ganges plain, which supported (directly or indirectly) the ever more extreme communalist demands of the Muslim League.

The leader of the Muslim League had been for some years Muḥammad-'Alî Jinnâḥ, an astute politician who won an almost fanatical devotion among the politically-minded educated young Muslims, who called him the Great Leader, the Qâ'id-e A'ẓam. In the later 1930s Jinnâḥ was able to make of the Muslim League a more broadly popular movement. The war, in which of course he supported the British, only strengthened his hand. Thereupon he carried the doctrine of 'two nations' to a logical, if somewhat grotesque conclusion. In negotiating over questions of home rule or independence, he claimed that the British should negotiate not with groups representing all interests concerned but with the nation or nations as such, represented by the strongest single organization in that nation. He asserted that the National Congress represented Hindu India and that his Muslim League represented Muslim India. The British seem to have accepted this notion and refused to deal with other Muslim groups, however well they had shown at the polls, for fear of alienating Jinnâḥ. Other Muslim groups were ignored and seemed destined (in the swift-moving course of events) to have no voice at all unless they joined the Muslim League bandwagon, which they tended to do. The Congress was forced into negotiating only on behalf of Hindus (and tacitly of non-communalist Muslims) with the League claiming to speak on behalf of all Muslims.

The thought had been held for some years that in case of Indian independence at least those provinces which were predominantly Muslim ought to have autonomy or preferably full independence so as to be free to pursue Islamic policies unhindered by the Hindu majority in India as a whole. In approximately 1937, this idea was crystallized into the notion of 'Pakistan', to be an independent Muslim state in the Indus basin. In 1940 the slogan of Pakistan was adopted by the Muslim League.

Perhaps some thought of it chiefly as a bargaining point against the Indian nationalists, for if realized it would, of course, be as disastrous for communalist hopes of Muslims in the rest of India (that is, where the League had its largest support) as it would be successful in fulfilling the communalist hopes in the Muslim provinces (where the League was less strong). But the idea caught fire as rapidly and as emotionally as had the earlier and somewhat similar idea of supporting the Ottoman caliphate. Muslims all over India felt it more important that somewhere, at least, Islam should rule in independence than that they themselves should have any special guarantees or privileges against discrimination by Hindus in the greater part of the land that was left outside Pakistan. The 'ulamâ' generally and officially opposed the notion, but almost all classes ignored them. For the peasants, it was a case of religious revivalism: the true justice of Islamic rule was to be restored, at least somewhere and perhaps eventually for them as well. The 'ulamâ' had been against reforms before and on the side of the landlords and naturally would be now again. For the educated townsmen the ideal was cast in more secular terms. They felt that Urdu culture throughout India would be stimulated and vivified if at least some sections of it were allowed the vitality of political authority. Yet for the townsmen likewise there was a touch of millennialism in the cause. Their Islam, diluted by some generations of liberalism, had come to be more a matter of communal allegiance than of cosmic awe. Yet Islam, however debased, remained all the religion they had; to restore at least a nucleus of the Mughal-Islamic culture of full political power became a sacred cause.

Evidently sensing a popular mystique, Jinnâḥ proceeded to make the demand for Pakistan the exclusive and uncompromisable demand of communalist Islam, not insisting on communalist terms in the rest of India at all. He kept the idea deliberately vague, finally formulating it only after years as demanding not only northwest India but northeast India as well. The combined areas demanded would have a bare majority of Muslims and would obviously not elect any Muslim communalist group to power if non-Muslims were given an equal vote with Muslims. The patent unrealism of the demand itself and of the imprecise ways in which he always presented it seemed calculated to delay any agreement through such negotiation as the British were willing to arrange; and to delay, with agreement, independence itself. But independence could not be further staved off. Meanwhile, the whole discussion, beginning with the effective encouragement given by communal voting to communalist politics and exaggerated by the unbearable tensions of the war years, had resulted in extreme tension between Muslims and Hindus, virulent mistrust of each other, always on the edge of open violence. Muslim imaginations were centred on the demand for Pakistan and if it had been denied there would certainly have been civil war. Whatever their original intentions, the situation had now gone so far that the British had to partition India on leaving it, whether they wished or not.

They compromised, including in the new Pakistan much less than had been demanded—not six great provinces, but only those administrative districts which had actual Muslim majorities. Thus the new state had about seventy per cent Muslims, a comfortable majority, though it included only about three-fifths of the Muslims in India. The new boundary lines, splitting the peoples of Bengal and the Panjâb down the middle, were hastily drawn and power handed over to the new Indian and Pakistanî states in August 1947. Thereupon, to the astonishment of almost everyone, the pent-up passions, the accumulated fears and distrust on both sides poured out in the greatest non-military massacres of history.

There was great violence elsewhere, but in the Panjâb the ethnic character of the country was permanently changed. The whole of the Panjâb had a mixed population of Muslims on the one hand and Hindus and Sikhs on the other; the western part, allotted to Pakistan, had a distinct majority of Muslims, as had the eastern part of Sikhs and Hindus; in the central areas, divided between India and Pakistan, the proportions were fairly evenly divided. When the partition decree was announced and as transfer of sovereignty approached, all India but especially Panjâb was full of rumours. The Muslims, aware that caste-conscious and revivalist Hindus regarded them as unholy outsiders, had been taught by the League to believe that the Hindus were only awaiting independence to subject them to the grossest tyranny. Even when Pakistan had been conceded, some feared that the much larger India would attempt to recover the lost provinces once the British were gone. The Hindus and Sikhs had interpreted the resulting Muslim behaviour to mean that the Muslims intended to suppress any non-Muslims within the area of Pakistan and then to use Pakistan as a base for reconquering the rest of north India and restoring Muslim rule (the majority of men in the Indian army were Muslim). How far the tyranny and the suppression might go was left vague by communalists on both sides. Many on each side were prepared to hear the worst of the other side.

The worst soon seemed to have happened. Old grudges, new suspicions touched off riots even days before the actual transfer. With the disruption of authority and communications at the transfer, all Panjâb was filled with rumours of villages wiped out, of massacres in towns. On each side of the line, retaliation on the minority community was immediate. As violence mounted, fears of invasion from the other side spread and men seemed to feel that extermination of the minority could alone prevent it from acting as a fifth-column for the invaders. Members of the minority groups began to flee to the line for their very lives; even in their flight they were cut down. Trains arrived at Delhi and at Lahore filled with nothing but corpses: maddened men had mounted them and murdered all aboard before the train reached the line. At Delhi station, those trying to escape to Pakistan were turned into heaps of corpses: one towering Sikh, raising his sword over an old Muslim woman, was asked, 'Why are you killing her?' and answered, 'I don't know, but I must,' as he brought his sword down and cleaved her skull.

There was much heroism as Nationalist Hindus risked their lives to protect Muslim families and even whole villages, especially in the Ganges plain; doubtless there was like heroism in Pakistan. Congress leaders tirelessly toured Delhi trying to stop the killing. As it subsided, Gândhî insisted that India accept its burden of guilt without waiting for Pakistan to do likewise; possible war between the new states was averted and confidence began to return in most of India. (Later Gândhî was murdered by an extreme communalist Hindu group largely in revenge for his pro-Muslim intervention at this time.)

There were vast numbers of refugees in Bengal, but the face of the Panjâb was changed. In a matter of days, many hundreds of thousands were dead and millions were penniless refugees on each side. The big cities of West Pakistan and northern India, already poor enough, were swamped with the homeless and broken newcomers. In west Panjâb, indeed in all West Pakistan (as the remnant of Hindus, largely businessmen in all-Muslim Sindh and Baluchistan, withdrew), almost no Hindu or Sikh families remained. In east Panjâb almost no Muslim families remained. The unplanned transfer of population was complete. A few years after the extermination camps and incendiary and atomic bombs of the Second World War seemed to have confirmed the worst condemnations Indians had levelled against the materialistic Modern West, Modern India, Muslim and Hindu, confronted horrors of its own making.

When Pakistan had thus become a reality, the Muslims who had created it had to rethink their positions. In Pakistan, the Muslim League had to discover how to make viable the fragments of provinces it had received, territories among the poorest in the Indian region, whose natural economic relationships had been disrupted by partition. But perhaps even more important, in the long run, it had to face the fact that the emotional response it had evoked among the Muslims was no mere political manœuvre but a true religious passion which would not readily be assuaged by the conventional arrangements of politicians. In India, the forty million Muslims who remained had to learn how to make terms with Indian nationalism from a far less advantageous position than they had had before; being now a much weaker minority and universally suspected to be agents of a hostile and ruthless foreign power. So far as their Islam had amounted to a political communalism, they had to rediscover a spiritual meaning in Islam or sink, as many educated Muslims seemed to do, into hopeless disillusionment.

VII

The Drive for Independence: The Twentieth Century

With the weakening of European world hegemony after the War of 1914, the various Muslim peoples began to assume a more independent responsibility for their destiny. As this responsibility has increased, in the course of the twentieth century, Muslims have been faced with their share in the problems with which Modernity has confronted the world as a whole. The terms on which independence and international responsibility came to the non-Western lands were posed by the contradictory processes through which independence was achieved. It came more suddenly than anyone at the end of the nineteenth century imagined it could; more suddenly, indeed, than it probably would have, were it not for circumstances that undermined European power internally at the height of that power. As a result, the new independence was not based on equal participation in technicalistic society but on a precarious world situation, within which the newly independent states were forced to strive to achieve substantive equality in order to maintain their independence. Such efforts led to the desperate human pressures of a forced pace of technicalization under overwhelming handicaps; but they also led to unexpected opportunities for national dignity and spiritual self-reliance.[1]

A. THE COLLAPSE OF THE EUROPEAN WORLD ORDER

Colonialism in the first half of the century (1905–49)

In 1904, when the rival British and French governments came to an understanding, the European powers had completed assigning the Muslim lands of sub-Saharan Africa to their several imperial masters (though it took several years, and in some corners decades, for the Muslim states to be fully subdued). But in the same year began the Russo-Japanese war, in which a major European power was defeated by an 'Oriental', an 'Asiatic' one, and in 1905 all the citied peoples on the wrong side of the development gap took heart that such a thing was possible.

[1] In this last chapter and in the Epilogue I shall doubtless be all things to all men, though not in a comfortable way. To Americans I shall seem a communist and to Russians a neo-imperialist; to Muslims I shall seem a Christian missionary and to Christians an apologist for Islam. Doubtless they are all partly right. But I shall be satisfied if they agree anyway that my presentation is coherent, and consistent with what I have developed in the rest of the work.

Japan's internal social development had paralleled that of northwest Europe in the preceding millennium more closely than any other extra-European society. Perhaps more important, by a combination of circumstances in the seventeenth and eighteenth centuries Japan had been able, in a policy designed to keep its own mercantile elements from enriching themselves in trade abroad, to keep foreigners from enriching themselves in Japan and indeed from having any serious effect on the course of Japanese evolution—that is, it had rather accidentally forestalled most of the disruptive effects of the Western Transmutation and had kept its economy and institutions intact. When it finally accepted intercourse with the world, it had become fully conscious of what had happened, and it used all its intact resources to adopt the more nuclear aspects of technicalism, and successfully avoided slipping into an economy of complementary dependence on the West; it was after strenuous independent development, and in a carefully chosen field of action, that at length it was able to match the West itself. The Japanese initiative, therefore, was not something that could be imitated overnight by less fortunate peoples, already dependent on the West. But in the face of the Western tendency to ascribe 'Oriental' backwardness to racial inferiority, the Japanese success had a psychological as well as a symbolic value. The younger generation of Modern-educated intelligentsia everywhere, recognizing that their own consciousness of the national cause was greater than that of their elders, and also of having a fuller knowledge of the West and its works, saw their own nationalist mission heralded in the Japanese victory.

We have seen how the several revolutionary movements of that time, in the Ottoman empire and in Egypt, in the Iranian lands and in India, came to an unsatisfactory issue by the time of the War of 1914. The Japanese example was as yet unmatchable. Indeed, direct European rule seemed to spread steadily. By 1896 the British had imposed their control on some inland portions of the Malay peninsula; in 1910 and 1914 they extended their control to all of the peninsula which they did not concede to Thailand. In 1907, on the other side of the water, the Dutch finally subdued the historic sultanate of Acheh. The French added to their empire not only the last Sudanic sultanate (Wadai, 1911), but Sharîfian Morocco.

Typical was the fate of Morocco, which could be anticipated by the few remaining independent states. By the end of the century, the Moroccan dynasty, alone left independent in the Maghrib when first Algeria and then Tunisia had been occupied by the French, proved unable to maintain the control of its states which the Europeans demanded of it; the sultan was impotent in the face of rival European interests and tribal unrest. But no potential successor dynasty was in a position to gain the European support that would have been required for it to rule. The French, accordingly, offered the sultan assistance in reorganizing his government so as to maintain his throne. The Germans, who had thought of occupying the land themselves, interposed for a while; but after a conference of several European powers, the

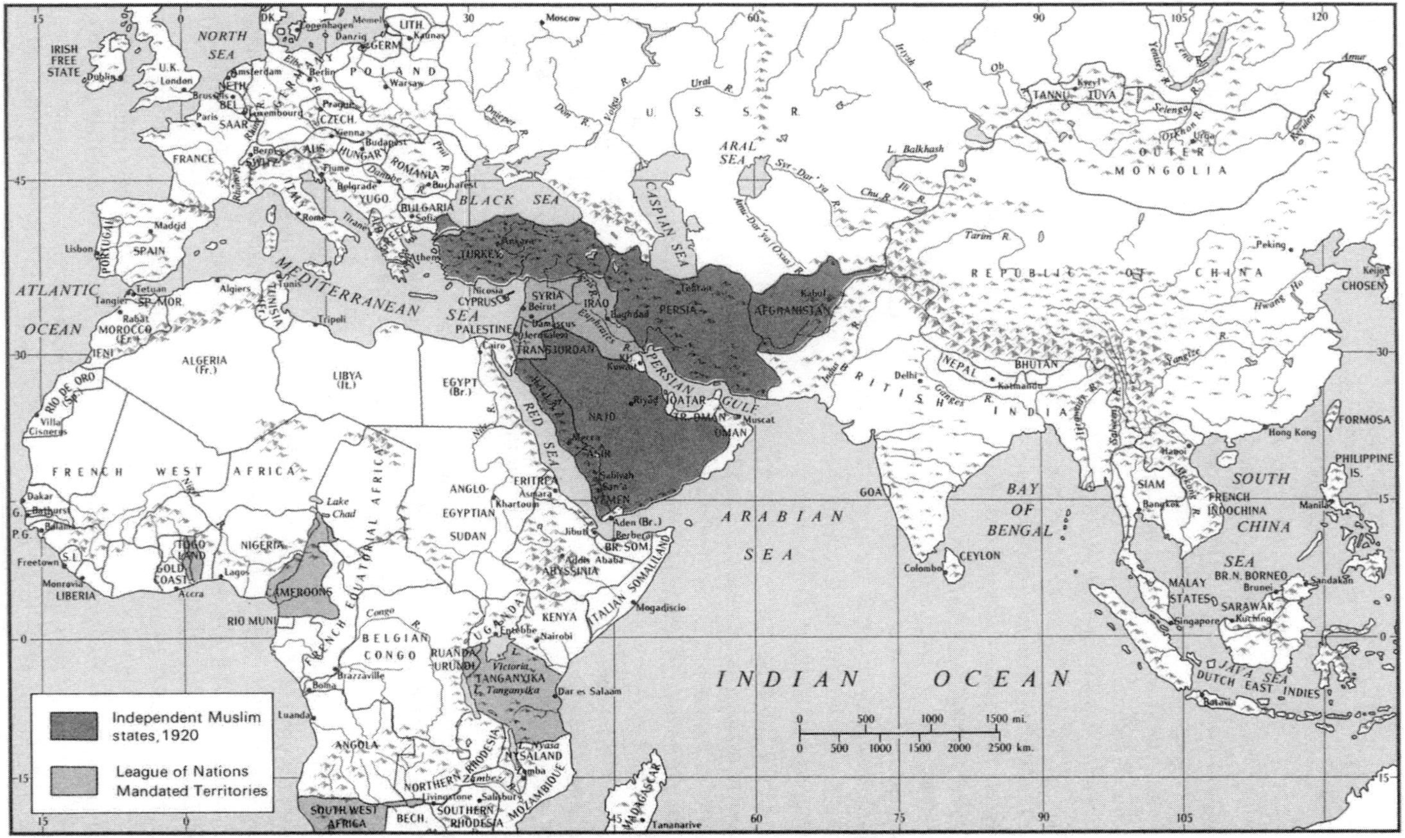

The Muslim world after the Versailles Conference

French were approved by Europe and the sultan accepted them as advisers. By 1912, the French had occupied Morocco outright (save for a zone in the north allowed to Spain). They proceeded in the next decade or so to erect a model of benevolent colonial rule in the sultan's name, establishing large prosperous farms under European ownership, erecting well-planned modern cities (and also taking measures to preserve the picturesque old city of Fez as a living museum), and suppressing what was called tribal disorder.

But the War of 1914 changed the European position and gave the Modernizing Muslims more substantial ground for hope than had the Japanese victory. The falling-out which had long threatened among the European powers led to a full-scale holocaust among them, in which (as we have noted) their overseas dependencies were also involved in various degrees, and out of which they emerged weakened. The Germans being knocked out of the contest by defeat and the Russians by revolution, at the end of the war the British and French governments proceeded to reorganize the European hegemony in their own interests as far as they could; but their resources were limited and their populations were anyway being swept by the idealism of the 1920s, which frowned on colonial wars. They were unable fully to maintain the pre-war European supremacy.

In the most of the more central lands of Islamdom, the Muslims had had relatively long experience of involvement in the technicalistic world and a large proportion of them were relatively Modernized in outlook; most of them had also, hitherto, avoided direct Western rule. From Turkey and Egypt to Afghanistan, most of the Muslim areas managed to exact a more or less complete recognition of sovereign governments from the Europeans. Elsewhere, Muslims had less good fortune. In the Syr–Oxus basin in the name of communist revolution, in the Maghrib in the name of bourgeois law and order, European rule was maintained: attempts at independence were unsupported by the more conservative elements among the Muslims and collapsed. Indonesia saw only the first breaths of a stirring of new Modernizing elements against Dutch rule, while the older resistance had been crushed. In sub-Saharan Africa the colonizing process was carried forward on the pre-war basis. But the new status of the central Muslim lands carried implications for all Muslims: though the 'colonial' areas were still represented in the League of Nations only by the 'metropolitan' Western rulers, the 'independent' Muslim lands had their own representatives, who sat as equals in the League and disputed, among Western colleagues, points of what had grown up as Western international law.

By 1922, then, in most of the central Muslim lands, the Modernizing nationalist elements had succeeded in some measure, at least superficially. In many states was established at least a minimum of recognized self-government, normally with some element of responsible representative institutions. In the following decades, in Turkey, the west Iranian kingdom, and Turkistan the Modernizers had things largely their way and old social patterns seemed on the surface almost to disappear; even in Afghanistan (but not in Sa'udi Arabia) such an attempt was launched, though it was partially frustrated for a time. In other relatively Modernizing countries the next two decades were punctuated by periodic unavailing efforts to throw off the Western yoke and that of its local collaborators, and marked time politically. Yet the life of the cities of the major central Muslim lands, even those not independent and reformist like Turkey, was more and more reshaped in imitation of what was happening in the West: buses and typewriters, toothpaste ads and aeroplanes, unveiled women hurrying to their jobs and grey-suited businessmen consulting their watches, gradually appeared or even became routine in all these cities, though the squalid poverty of the ordinary people was not relieved. Even power-mechanized factories and labour unions had been introduced at key points in most of these countries. The nuclear elements of the Western Transmutation were making their way into central Muslim territory.

The same sort of Modernization was beginning, at least, among Muslims in most other lands. There, however, even more than in the central lands, Modernization took the form of direct cultural assimilation to Europe. The Modernization and world-rule of the independent central Muslim peoples had not yet established a focus for Muslim cultural (let alone political) forces alternative to the West. The independence, or relative independence, of a few central states only partially diluted a process which was moulding the growing numbers of Modernized élites of almost all other Muslim lands: assimilation to the cultural system of the imperial power which controlled a given land.

In the more independent lands, the language of Western culture was determined largely by the region. In the east Mediterranean, an originally Italian lingua franca had gradually given way to French as French commercial interests rose, and as the all-European prestige of French affected the educated classes. In the Southern Seas, it was English that was the international language. Even so, in independent lands the language of administration was local, and Western culture was often filtered through translation at least. But in most other areas the élite learned the language of the ruling power, partly for the sake of advancement in the government machinery and partly for commercial reasons. They knew the West more intimately in some ways than those whose careers depended more on some Islamicate language, but they received their notions of the Modern West exclusively through the one language. Rarely did even scholars learn a second Western language such as their Western models commonly controlled. Hence there was growing up a large bloc of Muslims who were culture-Frenchmen, living in northern Syria, in the Maghrib, and in western and central Sudan; another block who were culture-Britishers, living in Palestine and Iraq, in India, in Malaya, in East Africa, in the Nile Sudan, in Nigeria and elsewhere; another bloc who were culture-Russians, living in the centre and south of the Soviet Union; while other smaller groups of Muslims were culture-Dutchmen (in most of the Malay archipelago) or culture-Italians (Tripoli, Somalia, etc.). The pattern was broken only sporadically by missionaries from America or from non-imperial European states who offered an independent schooling for those who could afford to exclude themselves from official channels of advancement.

Culture-French Muslims could understand each other, even if from distant regions, much more easily than they could understand culture-British Muslims from a neighbouring territory. This was not merely because of the common language, but because of common presuppositions about life and society. Culture-Frenchmen read the French novelists and philosophers, culture-Britishers the British ones. For culture-Frenchmen, Paris was the hub of civilization, even when they hated French power and boasted of the Muslim past; their notion of just government was made concrete in the centralized French bureaucracy. For culture-Britishers, Oxford and Cambridge were the only true source of gentlemanliness, even when they hated British snobbery and boasted of their Muslim past; their notion of just government was coloured by the ideal of the local gentleman-magistrate. The culture-Russians, whatever they thought of the presence of European settlers in their lands and of imperious directives from Moscow, quickly not only became good Marxists but measured literary excellence by Pushkin and Gorky, and good administration by the all-foreseeing Russian bureaucracy.

The colonial orientation made a difference not only in the Modernizers' sense of life and society but in their sense of the development gap itself—in their sense of relations between the West and other peoples. Each imperial power had its own theory of empire. The French measured their success by a vision of the ancient Roman empire as universal civilizing force: carrying to barbarians the Latin tongue and Latin institutions and assimilating the barbarians into its own superior culture. Hence the French were socially receptive to culture-French Muslims but tended to be scornful of local traditions and institutions; they liked to establish direct French rule in their territories. The British measured their success by a vision of the ancient Roman empire as universal arbiter among peoples, each of which could pursue its own destiny within the overall framework of law and order imposed by a superior people. Hence the British were socially more reserved toward culture-British Muslims, who could not in any case really belong to the superior people, but were more open to local traditions and institutions; they preferred indirect rule through indigenous authorities whenever possible. Hence even in their expectations from and resentments against the West, the Muslims were not at one—some might hate it as a racialist insult to their manhood, others as a denationalizing threat to their Islamic identity.

The new Westernizing dignity of Muslims as participants in a world in which Westerners no longer had a complete monopoly on technicalistic forms was symbolically consummated when an Indian Muslim, the Agha Khân (head of the Nizârî Ismâ'îlîs), representative of the British Indian government to the League of Nations, was elected to preside over that world body. But his elevation symbolized at the same time the degree to which the dependent societies were admitted to world affairs strictly on Western terms. He was eminently a culture-Britisher and a convinced upholder of the status quo.

In the 1930s came a further stage in the collapse of European hegemony: the world depression. This was perhaps a greater blow than the Great War of 1914. Again it undermined the financial resources of Western governments attempting to maintain control of far-flung empires. More, it undermined the prestige of the West: the Western economic superiority, on which all else was built, seemed to flounder. Even so, the embarrassments of the West did not seriously weaken its relative political power, if only because the depression hit the dependent economies at least as severely. But it was this last fact which in the long run was most dangerous to the European hegemony. In the world at large (except, of course, for the Soviet Union), the depression meant a partial collapse of the mechanism of the international capital market, which was the economic core of the hegemony; it meant ruin or at least serious insecurity for those middle-class members of the dependent societies who profited by collaborating with the world market; and it meant disastrous poverty for many of the lower-class elements, urban labourers and peasantry, who were integrated into the market. The capital market as such righted itself before long, but the economic disorganization of the general world market did not seem to end. Outside the Soviet Union, where open discussion was not allowed anyway, those of the middle classes who were inclined to be conservative and accept the Western status quo began to lose confidence; while the ground was laid for a more active political participation by the lower-class elements which had been forced as never before to see the consequences of their situation. It took the War of 1939, however, to precipitate these vague awarenesses.

The War of 1939 did not involve the central Muslim lands more directly than had the War of 1914, but it did produce widespread suffering and perhaps even greater dislocation of some populations; it also brought hitherto relatively isolated areas into the midst of world ideological quarrels. In any case, it determined the life, for the time being, of every Muslim people. As we have seen, even the Muslims of the Soviet Union were mobilized for the war effort—and inundated with Russians and Ukrainians to run the new industries, though any political expression of dissent was rigidly suppressed. Turkey was neutral, but the pressures of neutrality were the dominant fact in its life. The west Iranian kingdom saw the toppling of its proud modernizing independence and joint occupation by its old enemies. The eastern Arabs witnessed helplessly but at close range a contest between British and Germans, during which only pro-British governments were permitted by the British to exist. At the end, as we have seen, those governments could not halt a flood of Jewish refugees from Europe into the midst of them, refugees who, in 1948, established a Zionist state despite the Arabs' combined efforts.

Often enough wartime events brought independence nearer; but only at great cost. In India it was the pressures of wartime that created Muslim zeal for partition and a separate Muslim state. This was achieved in 1947, but only at the expense of vast massacres, millions of refugees and radical disruption of a society. Further afield, the Maghrib became the scene of an American invasion and a contest between those Frenchmen who were willing to rouse hopes of equal dignity and even eventual self-rule in order to defeat the Nazis, and those who preferred a guaranteed status quo even if the guarantors must be German. In Indonesia, the Japanese occupiers made a point of humiliating the Dutch, who represented the West, and tried to persuade the Indonesian Muslims that the Japanese, as 'fellow-Orientals', would enable them to reach equality with the West if only they would accept Japanese guidance—and control. They established throughout the population, notably among the 'ulamâ' scholars, propagandistic organizations of a modern technicalistic type and accustomed the populace to the idea that a new life had arrived. In the end they actually facilitated the erection of an independent Indonesian government led by the Muslim Modernizers. That government had to fight off the Dutch, who came back in the wake of the victorious American forces, and at great sacrifice succeeded in doing so and winning a genuine independence of its own in 1949.

But in many areas (though not all) the most pressing consequence of the war and of its aftermath was a bloating of the cities (doubling and tripling their size) with rootless, poverty-stricken new urban groups. The several lands had become more dependent than before on machine-manufactured goods and, with normal commercial channels disrupted, the war offered a great stimulus to local industrial production. But it was not only this but the accentuation by the war of the cumulative disruption of the depression years which filled the cities, during and after the war, with peasants who could no longer be supported on the land. After the war, the displaced peasants were joined by other displaced persons—by refugees from the partition of Palestine and from the partition of India; but even where there were no refugees (for instance, in the Maghrib) the displaced peasants were transforming the cities—and also the attitudes of their relatives in the countryside. They had no real means of support in the cities, for the new industries were not that strong. They lived, if not by outright begging, then partly from relatives, partly from odd jobs here and there—most visibly from a desperate sidewalk retail trade, in which a young man would offer a handful of undershirts or other cheap machine-made goods for sale at the smallest possible mark-up. When the old slum sections of the cities became even more helplessly overcrowded, they spread out into vast makeshift suburbs, shanty towns in which the houses were thrown together using old oil cans or junk lumber, and no sanitary facilities were provided. A bureaucratic government might be minded to protect health standards by ruling that new houses must meet the city code, or be torn down. But rather than tear down everything that was built, concessions had to be made: once the house was completed, it could stand. Desperate families would join together to get the walls up and the new roof on all in the course of one night, and next day could present the authorities with a *fait accompli*.

The new poverty has sometimes been misunderstood as a mere continuation of the 'age-old' poverty of 'the East'. It has sometimes been supposed that all that was new, was a new level of expectations of hitherto undreamt-of better things, the possibility of which was brought home by the presence of Westerners living in their accustomed manner and by such stimuli as Western films. It is true, indeed, that the masses in all agrarianistic societies (not just 'the East') had lived on a level which, by technicalized Western standards, was poverty-stricken; and people were indeed learning that this poverty could be remedied, and hence demanded improvement. But a more potent and immediate political force was a more material fact: that in important ways people were getting poorer than they had ever been. One factor in this was the rise in population with the end of the great scourges, so that there was less land to go round and less food per mouth. But at least as important, in many places, was what may be called 'functional' poverty.

We recognize that within a given city or nation poverty is a function of the general level of consumption; that, for instance, once telephones have become common in most homes, it can become a hardship to do without them. This is not, of course, because of envy or desire to keep up with 'the Joneses', but because the formerly prevalent less expensive alternatives cease to be available. Thus the neighbourly grapevine of yore no longer functions well for a scattered minority without telephones. In a society without private automobiles, working men did not need them, not because they did not know their lack but because the pattern of factory location and job choice presupposed the use of less rapid or more public forms of transportation, and the man who used such transportation was not at the competitive disadvantage that the American worker without an automobile is now likely to be. Something comparable happens also on the international scene. The 'revolution of expectations' is only partly the result of a new awareness of what life might offer. More important is that once the local balance has been upset, what once was a tolerable level of subsistence can no longer be achieved. When trucks and buses become cheaper (for overall competitive purposes) than camels and donkeys, the camels and donkeys tend to disappear. But with the camels and donkeys, disappears a whole range of related opportunities and facilities that could formerly be counted on: by-products, manure, short-range roadless mobility, etc. As the whole economy is transformed in such ways, a certain level of cash and even of foreign exchange becomes crucial even to very humble levels of society. It becomes poverty, for instance, not to be able to buy imported goods. A poor competitive position in the world market threatens not just luxuries but necessities. Quite apart from population pressure on the land, the poorer elements are often no longer able to live on a 'subsistence level' with the same satisfactions they could once derive from that level: they are not only attracted to a higher scale of consumption by a wider exposure to travel and the films, they are driven to demand it by the disappearance of the old substitutes for it.

Among these new and disorganized lower classes (where they became important), economic demands rapidly turned to political demands. The Modernizers had long complained of the inertia of the mass of the population, ignorant and afraid to move. This was no longer so: acquainted with such aspects of technicalized life as bus travel and films and modern clinics, the poorest classes knew things could be better. They might be cautious but they were no longer indifferent.

If the War of 1939 had produced an explosive situation in many Muslim lands, it had drastically weakened the major European states. Germany and Italy had been crushed in the settlement, but France had first been crushed by the Germans and was slow to recover an equal position; even the British were having to recognize that, considering the expensive methods of war to which the steady process of technicalization had led, and the vast scale on which it could be waged, they were a match for neither the Russians nor the Americans. The British made little resistance to demands for independence in India. When independence was recognized after this war—in India, Pakistan, Indonesia, Syria, and Lebanon, even Iraq and Egypt—it was a much more substantial independence than it had sometimes been after the War of 1914. The European world hegemony, as such, was over.

But the weakness of the old west European powers was compensated by the new prominence of two other Western powers: the United States and the Soviet Union. For a time (despite the enormous destruction which the Soviet Union had endured), these two vast states seemed to control all the power in the world between them. But they were radically at odds, the one representing the capitalist world market as traditionally organized by the West, the other being the leading force in a revolt against it. The Muslims were expected to play a crucial role in the contest. For with the addition of China to the communist bloc in 1949, the bulk of the less technicalized yet long-citied regions of the Eastern Hemisphere still within the capitalist world market almost coincided with the old domains of Islamdom and its various semi-enclaves. The Americans expected the independent Muslim states to line up on the American side in a world-wide Western-bloc alliance to prevent extension of Soviet power, while the Russians did their best to encourage the Muslim peoples to rebel against governments which tolerated a dependent role in the capitalist world market.

Since the two powers soon both possessed atomic bombs, regarded as 'ultimate weapons' capable of total destruction and hence to be used against an atomic opponent only if one's own destruction was preferable to surrender, the contest soon took on the air of a stalemate—at least on the level of direct confrontation between the two powers. But both powers became all the more active in attempting more indirect moves, aimed at maintaining or advancing their position in the less technicalized parts of the world, and notably in

Islamdom. These lands were recognized as belonging to a single world society: they were not set off on the basis of religious or cultural allegiance—not even that they were not Western—but rather on the basis of a neutral point, the level of technicalistic investment. The lands of low investment were called 'underdeveloped' or, more optimistically, 'developing'. On this basis, with the understanding that the form in which they would ultimately be developed, that is technicalized, was not yet settled, they were thought of as 'uncommitted': when they were fully developed, as it was assumed they must be, it was supposed they would have come down in one Western camp or the other. On the outcome of the contest for their allegiance would seem to depend what would take the place of the old European world hegemony. Neither capitalists nor communists expected the Muslim peoples to be able to work out for themselves a destiny independent of the terms posed by the deadlocked heirs to Western power.

The end of colonialism (1949–62)

The independence of the non-Western states was premature in the sense that it resulted more from internal crises in the West than from the actual strength of the dependent peoples. Almost necessarily, therefore, these peoples found themselves taken up with a continuing conflict with the Western bloc powers, even after independence. This conflict in turn gave urgency and direction to their drive for Modernization.

But the conflict did not mean that they must substitute a Western communist world hegemony for a Western capitalist one. In the contest between the capitalist world market and the communist powers led by the Soviet Union, most Modernizing Muslims outside the Soviet Union itself were reluctant to take sides. They identified culturally with the values of the several Occidental societies in whose traditions they had been trained, and the more alert recognized there the special values associated in practice with capitalist democracy: broad freedom of information and inquiry, personal freedom to dissent, and freedom for multiple and independent social initiative, which seemed to be the institutional presupposition of the other freedoms. All these seemed to be excluded by the drastically centralized communist method of Modernization. Many of the Modernizers would not care personally, in any case, for the regimentive equalizing which would have to be expected in a communist solution, if only because precisely the more educated, as representing the old exploitive classes, would be eliminated or at least severely restricted so as to prevent their conscious or unconscious sabotaging of the new order. Yet most Muslims did not want to line up with the Western bloc against the communist bloc.

They were not apprehensive of the imposition of communism from outside (not the normal procedure for a communist revolution) and saw no reason to look to a Western alliance to prevent it. Moreover, they continued to distrust the west European powers far more than they did the Soviet Union, which in practice had proved relatively innocuous along its sourthern borders ever since the revolution. Turkey formed the great exception: the Turks were historically fearful of Russian covetousness of the Thracian straits, and the Soviet Union at the end of the war had in fact made some attempt to intimidate the Turks so as to gain a privileged position there, and were frustrated only by the support of Britain and the United States for Turkey. The Soviet Union made an attempt to encourage Azerî Turkish (and even Kurdish) separatism from the west Iranian kingdom before it withdrew its occupation troops at the end of the war. Yet finally it was persuaded to withdraw entirely behind the old boundaries in return for concessions in oil prospecting, concessions which (upon the objection of the west Iranian Majles) were never even put into effect. The Afghanistan government felt very little threat at all, though after Soviet economic progress became obvious it limited its subjects' direct contacts with Soviet Muslim subjects.

Even after the majority of the lands of the old citied Oikoumene had, by 1949, gained an effective independence, their chief tensions continued to be with Occidental powers. Even more important than the Soviet withdrawal from the direct military side of the European world hegemony (except always within the pre-1914 Russian boundaries) was the Soviet withdrawal, since the revolution, from the economic side of that hegemony. If foreign private capital was no longer allowed in Russia, a corollary was that Russian private capital no longer entered the world market; if there was trade between the Soviet Union and other states, it was arranged primarily between the two governments involved, and thus was readily subject to control. But in the Occident a private capital market still prevailed. In less technicalized lands which did not rigorously control their internal economy, the competition of uncontrolled Western products and the presence of the Western capital market still posed much the same problems as they had throughout the nineteenth century. Even if a certain amount of economic control were imposed by a nationalist-minded government, the dependent economies which had been developed were still subject to decisions made at the centres of the capitalist world market in Occidental lands. Moreover, inevitably the Western governments, officially or more subtly, brought pressures to bear in support of Western economic interests and therefore against any of the more obvious ways of attempting to alter the dependent character of the local economies.

All too often, a Western power intervened directly, if unobtrusively, to maintain governments in power which could be expected to avoid upsetting the status quo. For the Westerners, the most important political consideration was 'stability', for unforeseeable changes in government, especially changes that could lead to unexpected new economic regulations or even confiscations in the supposed national interest, could make investment insecure or unprofitable. As they saw it, the greatest need of the less technicalized societies was 'development', and development required even more investment;

which would come most efficiently from Westerners and from their indigenous allies. If such investment were made unprofitable by 'instability', it would turn elsewhere (the international capital market being open to it) and local development would be hindered. Hence Westerners felt it was not only in their own interest but in that of the land concerned to do what they could to encourage stable government—that is, government that would continue to represent the established interests and would resist any pressure to make glamorous moves which would seem to relieve the immediate pressure of mass poverty but would make things worse in the long run. With their superior economic and political bargaining power, the Western powers were in a position to have great influence through means which, according to the Western international law, were entirely legal, even without making use (at the request, say, of a local government threatened by popular pressures) of the military force represented in Western military bases still scattered throughout Islamdom. But from the viewpoint of the less technicalized lands, such exercise of influence was simply interference, legal or not, and was outrageous.

Accordingly, most of the independent Muslim lands quite as much as those still under direct west European rule still felt the strong pressures of west European power while corresponding Russian pressures seemed to have ceased. Whereas the more privileged elements, profiting from the dependent economy, might be at ease with such pressures (and in states such as Sa'udi Arabia, where other elements were for a while still inarticulate, the pressures aroused little resentment), the more serious of the Modernizers, bound on escaping the limitations of a dependent economy, resented them bitterly. Hence 'imperialism' was identified strictly with overseas imperialism by the non-communist Western powers, and expansionist tendencies by other states into contiguous areas (frequent enough!) were not put under the same rubric.

The conflict with the non-communist West was heightened by the entry of lower-class elements as potential participants in the political scene in the less technicalized lands. Such people were distrustful primarily of the local privileged classes, but readily identified them with their Western allies. The newly conscious lower classes found sympathizers in an increasing sector of the educated Modernizers. For these now increasingly called themselves 'socialists'.

Whereas after the War of 1914 the watchword of progress had become 'democracy', after the War of 1939 it was often, in western Europe, 'socialism'. In Britain itself a 'socialist' party came to power. Whatever else 'socialism' meant, it called attention to the economic and social handicaps of the masses and to the impossibility of 'democracy' being greatly effective among them till these handicaps were removed. More especially in the case of the less technicalized lands, it called attention to the difficulty of establishing a full-scale technicalized society, which demanded mass participation on all levels, as long as the masses remained in desperate poverty. And it suggested that the effect of the capitalist world market, if allowed free play, would be to perpetuate a dependent economy and the accompanying contrasts between privilege for the possessing classes and poverty for the rest. This could be avoided only by planning and controlling the investment of capital in such a way as to escape the domination of world capitalism, and of its local allies—that is, by socialism—and by the massive industrialization which would then become possible and make a country economically self-sufficient as well as providing jobs for its poor.

Accordingly, Western idealism (now in socialist form) combined, again, with local pressures to provide the more zealous of the Modernizers with their platform: formal independence was not enough—it still meant subservience to the West; it must be reinforced by economic independence; and this economic independence must take the form of raising the economic level of the masses, who could no longer be denied, and doing so by way of industrialization and some sort of socialism. Most of these Modernizers did not want to become communist; but they were at least as concerned to escape non-communist Western control. With the ever-threatening support of the masses behind them, they rejected vehemently alignment with the Western bloc and with its American leaders; to the extent that they could influence a Muslim government, it refused the proffered American world alliance system.

The new anti-Western struggle sometimes turned upon an economic relationship that had become newly important during the war: the supply of petroleum by Muslim lands to the lands of the Western bloc. Oil production was different from most production of raw materials in three ways. First, it was essential to the West itself, not merely a useful commodity: during the War of 1939 and after, both military and civilian use had multiplied, while in the same period the Muslim lands in the mid-Arid Zone, specifically in the Persian Gulf and the Caspian regions, became far the most important producers in the Eastern Hemisphere. The oil field at Baku, north of the Soviet border, served chiefly the Soviet market; but those in the Iranî and Iraqî states and in Arabia were rivalled only by various fields in the Americas and, as the chief source of oil for western Europe, possessed as a group a potentially semi-monopolistic position. Second, the sale even of crude oil was extraordinarily lucrative, and a government which could claim, as royalty on oil production in its territory, even a fraction of the profits had a major source of income. Competition among various companies for rights to oil exploration was keen and, during the war and especially after it, independent governments could exact a high rate: Sa‘udi Arabia, where exploration got under way in the 1930s and major production only during the war and after, exacted fifty per cent of the profits from a group of American companies, and this became the standard rate. Hence, in addition to being an object of special Western concern, oil was an object of special hopes for the producing lands. Finally, those hopes were accentuated by the technicalistic character of oil production: many oil workers almost necessarily received a highly technicalistic training, and, especially to the extent that refining as well as extracting could be done in the producing land, oil seemed to form a ready-made occasion for developing an important technicalized industry. So far as that industry could be integrated positively into the national economy (which did not necessarily happen), it could contribute to technicalizing the whole economy.

It gradually became clear that a government's income from oil, in the producing lands, ought to be used (so far as it could be spared from the ever-needy current government budget) for technicalistic investment so as to raise the general economic level. But the idea arose almost equally soon that it should be possible to do more than just use the royalties which the foreigners could be persuaded to pay: a government might transform the oil industry itself from a foreign investment draining away irreplaceable natural resources from the country on foreign terms, to a national investment managed outright as a means of Modernizing the country. It was established in Western international law that an independent state had the right by eminent domain to seize in the national interest even foreign property within its borders, provided it paid proper compensation, to be determined in its own courts. (This last point was later confirmed by the World Court.) If a producing land was really independent, it could seize and 'nationalize' the oil wells as state property, and the governments of the Western oil interests would have no grounds on which to object. Oil was so essential to the West that it was hoped the West would then have to buy it on terms set by the producing land.

This theory was first put to the test in the west Iranian kingdom. After the British and Russians had deposed and exiled Reżà Shâh, they installed his son Muḥammad Reżà, but the government was left in the hands of the Majles, provided that assembly would work through an anti-German cabinet. When the British and Russians left, the Majles was supreme. The Majles was dominated by wealthy businessmen and especially landowners, who could control the votes of their dependent peasants, and was not eager for the more far-reaching reforms which the Modernizers were advocating; but on the nationalization of oil, the Modernizers and the Majles seemed able to agree. Under the leadership of a popular advocate of Modernization, Dr Muḥammad Muṣaddeq, who had already led the resistance to going through with the oil concession promised to the Soviet Union—and despite the contrary wishes of the young shâh, who was hoping for Western financial aid—the Majles in 1951 agreed to nationalize the British-held oil field and refinery in the south. It was hoped that the British would not interfere with troops, partly because such overt interference would jeopardize their relations with all other independent but poorly technicalized states, and the British could no longer afford to ignore such sentiment; but also because British interference could lead to Soviet counter-interference, which no Western-bloc power desired, as Soviet expansion would mean curtailment of the sphere open to the capitalist world market.

The British did not send troops; but neither did they accept the nationalization. They believed that to turn over the oil operation to the unprepared Iranian government would lead to disruption of the operation and perhaps its ruin, as well as setting a dangerous precedent, and was not in the best interests of the Iranians themselves. They found what they regarded as a legal and peaceable means of imposing good sense and stability. They used their superior economic resources to impose boycott. The British oil company was able to persuade practically all Western consumers of oil that the seizure of the company property, which was done contrary to the terms of the concession, was illegal and that the oil belonged not to the west Iranian government but to the company. Purchasers of oil dared not touch it, lest they have to pay both the Iranians and the British company for the same oil; indeed oil tankers, controlled by the oil companies, would not carry it; and even if the oil could be transported and sold, it was proving hard to produce and especially to refine, as the British technicians would not work on the Iranian government's terms. Oil income, on which the government was increasingly dependent, ceased. But while the pressure on the west Iranian state was severe, the pressure on the West proved slight. It proved possible for oil production in neighbouring Muslim lands, in the Iraqi kingdom and in the Arabian states, to be increased rapidly, so that very soon the Western market felt no loss from the stoppage of Iranian oil. The West expected the west Iranian government to concede defeat and accept the company's terms for renewal of production.

Popular feeling in Iran was fervent, despite the considerable economic difficulties which were felt especially by the lower classes, many of whom found themselves jobless. Sentiment was already strong against the Americans, as leading power in the Western bloc, but a visiting American could feel fortunate, even among the uneducated out in smaller towns, that he was not an Englishman: the British were hated. Both communists, who had built a considerable following in the west Iranian state since the Soviet occupation of the north, and radically Sharî'ah-minded exponents of Islam, who had likewise built a movement since the deposition of the secularizing Reżà, in reaction against his reforms, joined in supporting Muṣaddeq or at least his nationalization. In other Muslim lands, sentiment was strong for Muṣaddeq; passing through Egypt, he received a rousing welcome. But no governments of oil-producing states would take measures to support the west Iranian position (for Iran's loss was at the moment their gain). Supported by mass sentiment, the Modernizers wanted to hold out despite the Western boycott and despite lack of support from other Muslim governments. They felt that, even if it meant a sacrifice of the oil money, at issue was Iranian independence.

But the privileged elements represented in the Majles became restive and ceased to support Muṣaddeq; by 1953 he was having to act by direct popular mandate, without the Majles and against the shâh—as well as having to face increasing rivalry from the communists. Despite active popular demonstrations in his favour in the streets of Tehran, Muṣaddeq's position became weaker and at last the army intervened, in the name of the shâh, and deposed and arrested him. With the backing of the army, popular feeling was suppressed and the shâh and the Majles worked out an arrangement with Western oil interests whereby, without indeed bringing back the hated British company in the old form, the oil and the royalties from it started flowing again. At about the same time, the shâh entered into a military alliance with the Western bloc (along with the governments of Iraq, Turkey, and Pakistan). This was to guarantee him support from the British, especially in case of any conflict with the Russians; it also brought large amounts of aid for his army from the United States, as well as a certain amount of financial aid to supplement the oil revenues in developing the west Iranian economy. Muṣaddeq's attempt to use the peculiar situation of oil production to hasten economic independence had failed, and had yielded instead to an outright alignment with the Western bloc, both economic and political.

But most people in the Muslim lands did not accept the decision as final. In the midst of Muṣaddeq's period as premier, another attempt had been launched, in Egypt, to achieve the more ambitious ends of the Modernizers. Like the other east Arabs, the Egyptians were smarting from the Palestine defeat. It was blamed on the pettiness of the Arab governments in power; on their subservience to the West, but still more on their catering to the interests of the established privileged classes, landlords and others, allied to the West; and on the general corruption which subordination to the interests of a small group carried with it. Sad tales were told of how funds and material destined for the Palestine war had been mismanaged. The younger army officers felt such failings doubly. Themselves technicalistically trained, they were readily inspired by reforming ideals. Moreover, personally, and often by family origin, they had little stake in the privileges of the established classes, which might be threatened by reform. The senior ranks in the army, as elsewhere, were aligned with established government and with the king; but the younger officers felt, for that very reason, alienated from them. In 1952 the populace of Cairo, largely unemployed and hopeless, was showing its anger: one day a vast riot resulted in the burning of the chief luxury hotel in which Europeans commonly stayed and in the murder of Europeans on the streets, as well as much other and sometimes rather random destruction. A group of younger officers found the time opportune for a *coup*: some months after the great riot, they arrested the top command at Cairo. In due time they declared a republic and set about building the national base for their own struggle with British interests.

They had come to power in a revolution and they made a point of comparing their revolution with the French and the Russian revolutions: it was to be gentler, entailing little bloodshed (for, they said, Egyptians were a humane people), but it was to be equally decisive. In contrast to Moṣaddeq, ruling through a Majles assembly that represented the privileged interests, from the very beginning they did away with the Egyptian Parliament and its parties, who represented much the same sort of interests for the same sort of reasons, and they took firm measures to ensure that the most privileged interests would not be in a position to work against them. After a period of jockeying, one of the officers most responsible for engineering the *coup*, Jamâl 'Abd-al-Nâṣir, emerged as the dominant figure, though his committee of officers continued to rule the country as such. At first supported (as Muṣaddeq had been) both by the communists and by the more radical representatives of Sharî'ah-minded Islam, he quickly excluded both groups, and especially the latter, from power. By measures for distributing the great landed estates among the poorer peasants, by espousing actively—and above all without corruption—the more immediate measures of reform which had already been more or less ineffectively attempted, and by an aspiring nationalist rhetoric aimed against the West, he won the support of a section of the villagers and most of the Modernizing educated class, and the vigorous enthusiasm of the city lower classes.

Meanwhile the British looked on, disquieted. After the war they had withdrawn their garrisons from most of Egypt to the Suez Canal, which they felt it necessary to Western-bloc interests to keep open to the international market. Now, to ensure himself against the possibility of intervention, 'Abd-al-Nâṣir made his chief campaign that to eliminate British garrisons from any part of Egypt, that is, from the Canal. After a long period of harassment, he persuaded the British that if they were to have stable relations with Egypt, and yet were not prepared to garrison the whole country outright, they must yield; finding an alternative military base in Cyprus, they did.

Meanwhile, 'Abd-al-Nâṣir had selected building a new high dam at Aswan in the south as the next major objective for the economic development of Egypt. The high dam would allow more efficient water storage and therefore permit a larger area to be irrigated, reclaimed from the desert; but scarcely enough to make up for more than a few years' worth of the rapid increase in Egypt's population. Perhaps more important, it would generate a substantial amount of hydroelectric power, making possible new industrial projects. And it was not overlooked that the very building of it would take many of the unemployed off the streets of Cairo. The American government had offered to finance it at low interest rates, in the hope of adding to the 'stability' of the Egyptian polity. The populace tended to pin exaggerated hopes on the high dam. Then, however, 'Abd-al-Nâṣir (like other east Arab rulers, still at odds with the Zionists in Israel), unable to get the military aid he wanted from Western-bloc powers unless he entered an alliance with them, which he refused, arranged to get arms from the Communist bloc, and pledged a good part of Egypt's cotton crop for them. The Americans were shocked at his willingness to accept such ties with the Communist bloc and especially to burden his economy for the purpose, and abruptly cancelled the agreement to support the high dam in 1956. The Cairo papers headlined the American move as an American attack on Egypt.

Egypt had next to no oil, but it had another resource almost as important to the non-communist West—the Suez Canal, through which, indeed, much of the oil was shipped. The Canal too was owned and run by a European company on a concession agreement. With the British troops gone, the Canal was in Egyptian power. Basing himself on the same point in international law as Muṣaddeq had used, 'Abd-al-Nâṣir retaliated by nationalizing the Canal. In all the east Arab lands, and further afield also, people were thrilled at his daring and speculated whether he would get away with it. As in Iran, the company tried to halt the operation of the Canal by removing its experts; but Egypt was able to find freelance experts from elsewhere, and above all was able to train its own men, drawing on a pool of technicalistically skilled labour larger than could be found in the Iranian lands; the Canal kept on operating with no accidents. The company tried to get ships to pay tolls to the company elsewhere rather than to Egypt, or to go round the Cape of Good Hope, but such measures proved impractical; the Canal was irreplaceable. 'Abd-al-Nâṣir seemed to be getting away with it.

By the end of 1956, the British government, no longer a socialist government inclined to be tolerant of colonial independence anyway, was desperate: if the Canal, a great international artery of trade, could be nationalized, the whole structure of the capitalist world market would prove to be at the mercy of the rising new nationalisms everywhere, which were known to be hostile to Western-bloc interests. Their concern was shared by the French, who also had a stake in the Canal and were annoyed at Egyptian support for the Muslim rebellion then going on in Algeria. The two powers decided that international law and order could be maintained only if the West asserted its strength and resorted to force. From their bases in Mediterranean islands (and in conjunction with a land attack from Israel), the British and French launched an attack on Egypt, attempting to seize the Canal and hoping to topple 'Abd-al-Nâṣir's régime. 'Abd-al-Nâṣir's position was far more solid than Muṣaddeq's and in the emergency his régime received the support not only of the populace but of the whole organized society. Marginal support came even from some other Arab states. The Israelis swept all before them, but the British and French had not planned adequately and met more resistance than they expected. The Americans, in a fit of moralism, and the Russians, unwilling to let the capitalist West win the day, both intervened diplomatically, the Russians with a near threat of war. The United Nations organization ordered a cease-fire; and the French and British found themselves in no position to refuse. A withdrawal was painfully agreed on and 'Abd-al-Nâṣir finally emerged triumphant.

All, including the Western bloc, accepted the lesson of Suez: though the Western powers still admittedly had a preponderance of military strength (and retained world-wide bases), yet under the conditions posed by the atomic bomb, they could no longer intervene overseas with gunboats (or airplanes) to support specific Western interests against a hostile local government. This was a corollary of the end of the European world hegemony. A further corollary was that overseas territories could no longer be maintained in subjection, as a rule, anywhere: not only in the formerly citied territories, so many of which had already gained their independence by 1949, but even in what had been the most undeveloped territories. Already during 1956, the French had been forced to grant independence to Morocco and Tunisia (and the British had granted it to the Nile Sudan). In 1958, the French began a programme of allowing autonomy to their colonies within close ties to France, which was to lead to independence in 1960 for practically all their sub-Saharan territories, though in most cases some ties to France were retained. In a less systematic way, the British sub-Saharan territories with Muslim populations were becoming independent at the same time, notably Nigeria in 1960. All around the Southern Seas, likewise, some form of independence was being established almost everywhere, notably Malaya in 1957, Somalia in 1960, and Zanzibar in 1961, though some chieftains along the southern and eastern Arabian coasts clung to British protection for some years longer.

The only major overseas Muslim territory which a Western-bloc power tried to cling to was Algeria. As we have noted, French settlement there had been heavy and of long standing and, though the Arab and Berber Muslims outnumbered the French nine to one, the French felt that Algeria was (as it was legally proclaimed) an integral part of France. When Tunisia and Morocco, technically only protectorates, were given independence after violence there had risen, it did not occur to most Frenchmen that Algeria might be in the same case. The Muslims of Algeria, increasingly bitter at French intransigence, had to wage a frightfully costly guerilla war from 1954 to 1961 to force the French to recognize that they were not Frenchmen; then the majority of the million French settlers, on whose direction and skills the economy largely depended, and who had insisted bitterly on French rule even after the Paris government had faltered, fled; in 1962 an Algerian national government, at last independent, set about picking up the pieces.

Independence and interdependence

Though the new states,[1] once the mass of the population had been aroused to insist on a new order based on independence from Western control, could win that independence, the dilemmas which a technicalistic world presented to any relatively less technicalized society persisted. The various states could not really be independent—unless they could seal themselves off rigidly from

[1] In American usage, because of American political accidents, the word 'state' has come to mean 'province', and for 'state' the term 'nation' is made to serve. Hence the new states are rather misleadingly called 'new nations' as if political fiat could create a nation; and too often American writers (though most of them really know better) write as if in fact they really were nations, if only embryonically, and as if divisions among them were merely 'sectional' disputes within a people whom nature had definitively marked out.

world trade: and for most of them, such an isolation, even if it would be permitted to subsist, would have meant an end to any possible technical development. Ways had to be discovered of keeping up helpful relations with the world at large and yet not allowing those relations to vitiate and undermine the precious independence. What was required was forms of interstate association which could effectively take the place of the European hegemony. Solutions were sought on several levels. Cumulatively, these began to amount to at least a provisional outcome of the dilemma posed by the deadlocked contest between the Western bloc and the Communist bloc, and certainly expressed the response of most Muslim peoples to that contest.

The problem was accentuated by the artificiality of the units which were now setting themselves up as independent 'national' states. We have noted how the Europeans delighted to settle permanent boundaries, during the nineteenth century, even where they did not occupy a land militarily; and how the boundaries so settled were often arbitrary and accidental, little reflecting natural ethnic or other geographical actualities. Often the lines split ethnic groupings between rival states—thus the Kurds were split three ways, between the west Iranian state, Turkey, and the Iraqî state; the Pashtô-speakers (Pathans or Afghans, according to the level at which one made ethnic distinctions) were split between Afghanistan and Pakistan; the Malay-speakers on the two sides of the Malacca Straits were split between Indonesia and Malaya. In almost all such cases, either rebellions (potential or actual) or interstate disputes drained the energies of the states involved. Or the lines united in single units highly diverse peoples: most especially they united Muslim and pagan peoples in the various states among which the Sûdânic territories were divided. Thus, because the British had penetrated inland from the sea till blocked by the French, Nigeria included a northern (that is, Sûdânic) section which was Muslim and, incidentally, conservatively privilege-minded in politics, tied to a southern section (that is, the part of the state located in the Guinea coast rain forests) which was pagan or Christian, Modernizing in tendency, and resentful of domination by the weight of the 'backward' northern population. Because the British had penetrated along Arab slave-trade routes up the Nile, the Nile Sudan republic united a northern Sûdânic (and Arabic-speaking) Muslim majority, which was relatively Modernized, with a southern pagan and Christian population, more typical of the Negro sub-Saharan region, and which had till recently been pre-literate and still counted as 'backward' and resented domination by the advantaged (and formerly slaving) Muslims. In such cases, the new states were bound to be torn by internal oppositions.

Often what held a new state together was chiefly the fact that all its educated élites spoke the same formerly imperial language—French, say, or English—and thought in terms of the corresponding cultural pattern. In such a case, it was only by accentuating the cultural dependence symbolized in the imperial language that the state could tone down the internal conflicts that would undermine its political independence. But it would be very dangerous for the new states to attempt a general reshuffling of boundary lines. Only in the Indian Union, where the British empire had left behind a legacy of political unity among diverse peoples which had yet a degree of cultural homogeneity, was it relatively easy to draw new ethnic boundaries for political purposes; even there the reshuffling was long resisted by the administration as uneconomical and dangerous to Indian unity. In other, smaller new states, uneconomic revisions could be ill afforded and the ethnic disputes that an attempt at redrawing boundaries would let loose could not be kept in hand by a deep-rooted larger loyalty such as existed in India. Such considerations confirmed the several new state apparatuses in their determination to hold on to such power as they had, and to change boundaries only if this meant expanding their own jurisdiction. But the ambiguous position of each state internally and in relation to its neighbours added to the need for finding a tolerable pattern of interstate relations.

The most convenient arrangement, and perhaps the most fortunate if it were really adequate, was a voluntary association with a Western power on a new basis—with guarantees that the less technicalized and initially more dependent state should receive help toward technicalization and general economic strength so as to rise as quickly as possible to an economic level where a genuine 'interdependence' could come into being. The 'culture-British' of the former British empire were glad to see the former empire being transformed into the Commonwealth of Nations, within which special preferences were established in such matters as trade tariffs, agreed on as mutually beneficial, and within which extensive plans were set on foot for direct technical aid. Such arrangements came even more naturally to the 'culture-French'. The French president, de Gaulle, who saw the need for independence of the 'colonies' and acted to give it them as smoothly as possible, at the same time persuaded the élites of the new states to join in what was at first a fairly formal 'French Union' but soon became a more informal association with France, and yet more intimate than the British Commonwealth. These arrangements paralleled the situation of the culture-Russian élites within the Soviet Union, except that, not having gone through the process of achieving independence, the Soviet Muslim republics remained far more closely dependent on the lead given by the Russian republic than did the Commonwealth states or those associated with France or their former colonizers, even in the time of liberalization that followed the death of Stalin in 1953.

Such arrangements presupposed the notion of technical aid and, generally, of assistance given a less technicalized state by a more technicalized state. This had been increasingly becoming a standard expectation in the world since the War of 1939. The ultimate advantage, to the assisting power, of giving such assistance at the expense of its own taxpayers was to make the world at large more livable for its citizens. Ever since technicalization had got under way, and increasingly in the twentieth century, people did not actually live within the boundaries of any one state: the condition of the whole world affected their lives intimately. With the collapse of the European hegemony, it was at least as important to the Western powers, especially those participating in the capitalist world market, as to the formerly dependent states that some substitute pattern be found which would make for endurable conditions in all lands.

Former imperial powers recognized that their colonial offices had long been spending considerable sums to make the colonies a fit environment for their businessmen and other citizens who felt called to go there—not only by way of military expenditure, but in supplementary grants for schools and other needful projects which the colonial economy was found unable to support from the funds directly available to it. After independence, it seemed appropriate to continue such expenditures, since it was still necessary to live with the new state. It was hoped that to maintain the level of government services and, if possible, to increase the level of consumption among the people at large through economic development would help ensure the 'stability' of the new state. The United States, though without many colonies, was drawn in by a convergent development. During the War of 1939, the less exhausted powers, notably the United States, gave aid to their more hard-pressed allies; after the war, the United States realized the advantage to itself of giving help in rebuilding western Europe; it seemed appropriate for the United States to extend similar aid, military and economic, to the less technicalized states to help them, also, become viable neighbours.

At the same time, just as the pattern of technical aid meant continuity with the patterns of enlightened imperialism as it had been evolving, so it also meant continuity with the patterns of the more private missionary endeavours as they had been evolving: already in the inter-war period, Western missionary work had stressed increasingly such service as hospitals and schools, and less a direct attempt at conversion; and many of the more idealistic youth had turned from missionary work to freewill 'work-camping' in less privileged lands to express solidarity with them through manual labour and at the same time bring them the advantage of the skills they had gained in a more advantaged society. Eventually, even governments took up the idea of work camps.

As the European societies gained back their strength after the war, many private bodies, religious, philanthropic, and even industrial, in both Europe and the United States, turned to the effort to help the less technicalized peoples to 'develop' by sending technical aid. Most European governments did the same, those without former colonies sometimes seeking out smaller new states (Sweden, for instance, Tunisia) where their aid would have the largest proportionate effect. Technical aid became the object of what sometimes was a frank competition both for prestige and for psychological and technical footholds. Thus if new equipment came from a given Western state, new parts had to be ordered there, and the basis for trade was laid. It came to be that every economically developed country had its programme for assisting others; not only the Western-bloc lands but most of the Communist countries as well as Japan, Israel, and even the Indian Union. In all this it was the states of Islamdom and its former near-enclaves which benefited the most.

Based on an industrial plant as large as the rest of the world combined, United States assistance (both military and economic) was on a relatively large scale. It tended to be sent wherever it seemed most important to attach a poorly technicalized state to the capitalist world market as a whole, lest the state enter the Communist bloc in despair of achieving adequate development otherwise. But apart from American aid, the largest amount of aid tended to come through the special association of a new state with a former imperial state in Europe. Such an arrangement had important advantages. As contrasted with dependence on American aid, for instance, it made for a more comprehensive and predictable pattern of 'interdependence': sales of basic 'colonial' products would be guaranteed in the European country, for instance, even while the new state was being helped to diversify its production for the future. But the arrangements of special association with a Western power had drawbacks also. It was necessarily hard to keep in view the long-range goal of building an independent economy, when short-run decisions were made in an already established and pervasive context of immediate interests growing out of a past dependent relationship. The immediate interests to be considered were not only those of the dominant elements in the European country, but also those of their local allies, still dominant in the new state; and these interests were tied to perpetuation of the dependent relationship, whatever might be government policy in the hands of the Modernizers. And the Europeans concerned had ample leverage to prevent any radical change.

It was hard to envisage a social revolution in such circumstances, and hence any great realignment of the balance of interests within the new state. Yet without such a realignment, serious moves toward basic equality would be hindered if not made impossible. Hence the relatively covert domination of the European state in such arrangements—and even elsewhere, wherever technical aid tended to produce a like situation—came to be called 'neo-imperialism' and to be feared among the Modernizers almost as much as the old imperialism had been.

A less dangerous form of voluntary association with the West was to be found in international organizations such as the United Nations, successor to the League of Nations. New states with special associations with a Western power turned to the United Nations as a counterbalance; other poorly technicalized states were at least as much interested. At first the United Nations, as befitted the heir of the Concert of Europe and the League of Nations, was an essentially Western body. Each state had one vote, and numerically most independent states were of Occidental background: almost every little sovereignty in Europe and Latin America had a vote, while all of China and all of the Indian Union had but one vote each. But gradually, with the proliferation of small independent states in the Arab lands, in the Far Southeast, and especially in sub-Saharan Africa the balance was redressed so that, though not with any exact representativeness, the former 'colonial' states came to have at least equal weight—in general voting, that is—with the West. The Western-bloc powers meanwhile were creating special 'European' organizations for their own affairs. Hence the United Nations became largely an organ to handle relations between the West and others more or less on a basis of equality. The United Nations and its specialized agencies, such as UNESCO, provided a channel for multilateral political initiative and even for some technical assistance free of political or cultural ties, but the organization was structurally limited by a practical requirement of unanimity among all major blocs and could not adequately overcome the isolation required by independence.

Turkey found a more direct way of associating with the West without tying itself to any one power. In line with its policy of Westernization, it sought entry into the specifically west European organizations which were serving the old Occidental states themselves as a means of escaping their own relatively small scale as compared with the United States and the Soviet Union. At the same time it took advantage of United States aid on the basis of its anti-Soviet posture. But such a course was open neither psychologically nor geographically to most states. Most of the poorly technicalized non-Western states welcomed the possibility of a solidarity among all states on the wrong side of the development gap which would give them better bargaining power vis-à-vis the Western-bloc powers. 'Abd-al-Nâṣir of Egypt, Nehru of India, and Sukarno of Indonesia took the lead, Muslim and non-Muslim together, in gathering a conference of representatives from such states in Indonesia at Bandung in 1955. The conference generated much enthusiasm, and led to attempts at common action both within and without the United Nations by what was at first called the 'Arab-Asian' and then, as more sub-Saharan states became independent, the 'Afro-Asian' bloc. Sometimes this sort of grouping was conceived as grouping neutral ('non-aligned') states over against both the Western and the Communist blocs, and then it might include even some neutral European powers. More often it was conceived as grouping those states which had had to struggle for their independence against the Occident, and then it might include Communist powers like China or even the Soviet Union (the inclusion of which in an 'Afro-Asian' bloc could be technically justified on the ground that its territory was partly 'Asian', by the accidental decree of European geographers). But in any case attempts at such non-Western solidarity could not achieve major importance, for the less technicalized states could not give each other very much practical help except for a certain amount of rethinking of possible trade patterns.

A further way offered for building strength among the less technicalized states. In part because of the fragmentation which had resulted from colonial administration, they were mostly relatively small, even in population. But often if states similarly situated could form regional federations, these would be much larger. Such federations would reduce the weakness that isolation produced—if the Muslim oil-producing states had been federated in the time of Moṣaddeq, they could have met the Western boycott with an effective counter-boycott; and incidentally federations might help solve the problems raised by the presence of arbitrary boundary lines dividing cultural groups. Several such regional federations were envisaged in sub-Saharan Africa, but proved hard to implement. For a moment, the predominantly Muslim states of Indonesia and Malaya wanted to unite together with the chiefly Christian Philippines in a union of the whole Malaysian archipelago.

The most important attempt at a regional federation was that of the eastern Arabs, in which the western Arabs joined to a lesser degree. Pan-Turkism was out of the question with most Turkic lands firmly under Soviet control and Turkey a part of Europe. Pan-Iranianism never had much chance. But pan-Arabism remained much alive, and dominated Arab history after 'Abd-al-Nâṣir's triumph at Suez. The Arabs felt themselves increasingly one nation, with a single destiny, and were irritated at the divisions among them left over by imperialism. United, they could have a large and strategically placed area; they could distribute the oil royalties to the common advantage of all the Arabs; and presumably would finally be able to defeat Israel.

Emotionally, the presence of Israel provided the most vivid motive for seeking Arab unity. Israel still posed a European settler threat in the midst of the east Arab lands. It would be especially dangerous in any possible conflict with the West, as in 1956, when it effectively supported the British and the French invasion of Egypt. Moreover, as Israel brought in more and more Jewish immigration from various parts of the world, the internal pressures on Israel's narrow resources became more and more obvious; even if the Israeli leaders were sincere in not intending to use Israel's Western support in capital and influence to expand Israel's frontiers, the Arabs could not know when popular pressure might force those leaders, or find new ones, to carry out such an expansion if any weakness appeared on the Arab side, and to drive yet more Arab populations into exile. Israeli patriots could not but inwardly wish that the state could include all of the ancient territory of Israel, as had been originally planned. Even if guarantees could be found against Israeli expansion at the expense of accepting the presence of Israel in its present form, the potential commercial and industrial resources of Israel, with its Western capital backing, were such as to frighten all the business classes of the neighbouring Arab lands with a threat of competition which could not be matched. Accordingly, continuing concrete interests combined to keep alive the bitter hatred of Israel among the Arabs, who had lost so much psychologically and often personally as a result of Zionism. It would have been foolhardy for any Arab politician to suggest even the slightest accommodation with Israel. But divided, the Arabs showed no signs of being able to overcome Israel either.

Most eastern Arabs made almost as much a point of desiring Arab unity as they did of desiring the elimination of Israel. But there were innumerable obstacles. Apart from the tendency of each state apparatus to perpetuate itself, the very motives for unity helped block the way: the presence of oil royalties in some states and not others made the people in those states want to retain it for local development, and the presence of Israel blocked overland contact between the most powerful Arab state, Egypt, and the heart of eastern Arabism, the Fertile Crescent. Even the strong sense of Arabism made for cultural rivalries among Egypt, the Syrian lands and the Iraq for leadership, and the tendency of many Muslim Arabs to identify Arabism with a specifically Islamic heritage made the Christians of Lebanon resist closer union. But the presence of the British seemed at first to constitute the greatest obstacle of all: they were felt to be behind the scenes still wherever they had ruled, encouraging, in the name of 'stability' in the several states, just those local interests which would have to yield most if there was to be unity; and particularly the monarchies in Iraq and Jordan (over against the monarchy in Sa'udi Arabia, which anyway had increasingly American ties by way of oil). After the revolution in Egypt in 1952, the British influence against change was eliminated there, but it remained strong in Iraq.

The prestige of 'Abd-al-Nâṣir of Egypt became so high after his victory in 1956 that he was able to take the lead in pressing for immediate unity. In the republic of Syria, political life had been very uncertain ever since the French had left. Now a socialist party there, the Ba'th party, found the rising hopes for Arab unity to coincide with its particular fear of a communist *coup*; in 1958 it led the Syrians in turning to 'Abd-al-Nâṣir, who proclaimed that Egypt and the Syrian state were united in the United Arab Republic. He brought a firm hand into Syria, suppressing the communists there as he had in Egypt and also suppressing the parliament and its representation of privileged interests; and he called for the other Arab states to join the new union. This proved enough to generate the enthusiasm against British interference and privileged corruption in Iraq required for a group of younger army officers, parallel to those of Egypt in 1952, to overthrow the king. Iraq knew its moment of revolutionary morality: building on a new palace was stopped, whores disappeared from the streets, and everyone believed that a new just and responsible life was to begin.

But the new Iraqî régime proved hesitant about accepting 'Abd-al-Nâṣir's firm hand as the price of Arab unity and tried to continue the sound plans of its predecessor in using the oil royalties for development within Iraq. The British were finally gone, but the Arabs remained disunited. By 1961, the Syrians were ready to break their special ties with Egypt and were led out of the United Arab Republic by the Ba'th party again. In consequence, the fractional Arab states continued to leave the loyalties of the Arabs confused.

Political and even economic plans tended always to be ambivalent and even on the level of cultural self-identification, as to the use of language or the role of religion, the eastern Arabs remained torn between an ideal Arab unity and a present congeries of largely arbitrarily defined states. Without a satisfactory definition of their place in the larger world, the individual states were unable fully to enjoy their independence.

B. PROGRAMMES FOR NATIONAL RECONSTRUCTION

Whatever relations the various Muslim states might have with the outside world, internally it became increasingly obvious in the decades after the War of 1939 that some sort of bold programme would be needed to transform the social order more drastically than most Muslims had seriously contemplated between the wars. Technicalization in its nuclear sense was rapidly advancing, in some form or other, almost everywhere. The resulting dislocations—social, economic, even intellectual and spiritual—were increasingly the primary object of political concern. Mere independence as a state was far from sufficient, even if independence brought with it effective control of international economic ties. Some way must be found to assimilate and tame the explosive results of the technicalization of key sectors of national life. Very often a few persons in top positions of power made fortunes out of new economic and social situations, while the new poverty made such fortunes seem less innocuous than wealth had seemed in the past.

Moreover, even independence remained precarious so long as a way was not found for a sudden and drastic reshaping of the local social and economic order. The ever-accelerating pace of technical change which technicalism has meant poses the heart-breaking problem of 'catching up': for whatever advance a low-investment land may make, necessarily the lands of high investment have been able to make a greater one meanwhile, and the actual economic gap in productivity can get steadily greater. One particular facet of this situation has become still more pressing after independence than under imperial rule: the 'terms of trade' as between a country producing raw material and one producing finished manufacture may become steadily worse for the former; that is, it gets steadily less for what it produces and hence has less for other investment. Though this may not be theoretically necessary, yet the dynamic of the development gap does impose this sort of outcome time and again. In general, 'underdevelopment' and 'imperialism' remain two sides of the same coin; without special measures, it seems impossible for an 'underdeveloped' land to avoid 'imperialistic' domination.

The lands of low investment have had one potential advantage. They have relatively little investment in obsolete equipment, so that what investment they do make can be quite up to date. Some have seen this as a major advantage: in both science and technology the countries newly building up their research and plant might even spring ahead of some older countries burdened by commitment to outmoded forms and equipment. Unfortunately, this could happen only under very favourable circumstances, when a large amount of simultaneous investment is possible unhampered by countervailing handicaps. Such circumstances are unlikely to be reproduced in most of Islamdom.

On a superficial level, a fairly well definable overall course has seemed called for, whatever one's general social outlook. To meet the many dislocations produced by the Technical Age—to meet most especially the massive fact of the new poverty—radically rapid economic development of the most positive technicalistic sort was called for. And this meant that each state must gain control of its own economic and social life in some measure, so as to escape the mercy of the international market. Moreover, at the same time, so far as possible, a world order must be developed within which it can safely and fruitfully develop whatever resources it has.

The development of a sound world order is inevitably delayed (at best) by the jockeying for power among the major world blocs and even among individual states, each of which hopes to be in a position, as the imagined final settlement is worked out, to enforce what will be most advantageous to itself. But meanwhile each independent state can at least try to order its internal affairs in such a way as will enable it actually to do a maximum of independent planning. Hence the meaning of those popular twentieth-century terms, *nationalism, industrialism, democracy, socialism,* takes on an urgent tone. 'Nationalism' is not just patriotism, but insistence on the full autonomy of the nation and the unhampered power of its government, free if possible even from the ambiguous role of uncontrolled foreign investment. 'Industrialism' is not just a form of economic productivity, but a means of giving the nation the most essential attributes of an independent Modern society. 'Democracy' is felt to be not so much recognition of the free rights of all individuals to personal inviolability and a political voice, but rather chiefly the participation of all classes in Modern technicalistic life, including (in whatever form) participation in the political process. 'Socialism' means not, as in the classical analysis, specifically the assumption of collective social authority over economic activities that are already becoming collective in practice under private authority; rather it comes to mean more generally the recognition of social responsibility for the national economy, in whatever institutions this may be expressed.

Toward winning the requisite national self-direction, two sorts of programmes have had special appeal in independent Muslim states since the War of 1939. One sort has grown from the hope that the specifically Islamic religious and legal heritage would prove not only adequate to modern needs but able to provide the moral stability which the Modern West seems unable to find. Because of their emphasis on the role of reformed Shari'ah law in this task, we may call these programmes 'neo-Shar'î'. The other sort of programme has grown from an acceptance of Modern Western social forms as generally normative, and a relegation of Islam to such a role as Christianity or Judaism play in the West, yet with the hope that special forms of development may be found which will enable other lands to avoid the more obvious mistakes that Westerners have made. Such programmes have tended to share a number of elements in common, which at their most complete may be summed up under terms like 'directed democracy' or 'nationalist socialism'. A few Muslim peoples have tried to solve their problems by adopting directly the forms of Western society—either those of the old Western bloc (especially Turkey) or those of the Communist bloc (the Muslims of the Soviet Union). But where Muslims have insisted on an independent development, programmes set forth to achieve this can generally be described as taking one of these two forms. For the most part, such programmes have as yet more effectively informed future hopes and plans than the actual achievement of the present; yet in some countries they have played a key role, and almost everywhere the possibility of some such programme is the most seminal fact of political life.

Islamic resurgence: neo-Shar'ism as a practical programme

The neo-Sharʿî programmes have undertaken, in effect, to produce deliberately that society which might conceivably have evolved out of the old Islamicate society if a technicalistic mutation had taken place within Islamdom before it did in the Occident. But they do so almost necessarily not in terms of the resources and orientations of Islamicate culture generally but in terms of the Islamic religion in particular, and indeed in terms of one particular interpretation thereof. This is a latter-day form of the Sharîʿah-minded approach to Islam.

Several circumstances converged to give twentieth-century Islam a strong bias toward the sort of concerns which had earlier been represented by Sharîʿah-mindedness. We have noted that in the nineteenth century the more alert of the Muslims had commonly rejected the immediate past of the Islamicate heritage, as the corrupt occasion for the weakness they found in Islamdom about them; and how this led to a rejection not only of the Persianate tradition in favour of an idealized earlier Arabism, but also to a rejection of Ṣûfism in favour of the more politically and socially conscious tradition represented by the more Sharîʿah-minded. This tendency was reinforced in the twentieth century. In areas under Western rule, the Sharîʿah law was commonly enforced by the Western authorities at the expense of local customary law, in the name of 'law and order'. This was done partly out of a desire to govern according to the best indigenous norms and partly in the hope of achieving common legal standards throughout a given territory, for the sake of administrative efficiency and so that corruption could be more readily detected and controlled. The Sharîʿah, so extended in jurisdiction, was not exactly the old Sharîʿah. Its scope was very precisely limited to family law and related matters, of course, but even within that sphere its spirit was changed. In British territories, it was treated as a case law (in imitation of the Common Law) and the consequent admission of judicial precedent, together with other procedural arrangements, materially altered its spirit and effect. In French territories it was not only altered in procedure but was sometimes shifted from a universal to a national basis: in the Maghrib, for instance, some of the French wanted to believe that Islam was a national Arab religion (scholars wrote books to show this) and that the Berbers should and could be weaned away from it as a 'foreign' intrusion (and be made French instead)—hence even while the Sharî'ah was being generalized among the Arabs, customary law among the Berbers was being systematized and upheld against Sharî'ah jurisdiction even in cosmopolitan circumstances where the Sharî'ah might normally have applied. Nevertheless, the net effect was to draw attention to the Sharî'ah as the most evident expression of the presence of Islam. As younger generations increasingly lost touch with any wider Islamicate heritage, the Sharî'ah and the associated legal and societal outlook could become the one point at which they could clearly identify themselves as Muslims and dissociate themselves from the West.

But the new and almost accidental emphasis on Sharî'ah-mindedness was appropriate to the persistent social pressures that the Muslims felt most anyway. The over-riding concern of Modernizers was, in fact, political. If anything specifically Muslim was to become the driving force of social resistance and transformation, it had to be an Islam which was political and social in orientation. It had been the Sharî'ah-minded who had traditionally expressed concern with history and with social order as such, if only by way of their legalism. Indeed, the most ḥadîth-minded of the 'ulamâ' scholars had been the most consistent critics of the status quo—as reformers, like the Ḥanbalîs, or even as rebels. Moreover, that side of Islam which seemed most consistent with a Modern social order—that is, which most reflected a mercantile cosmopolitanism, individualistic and pragmatic, in contrast to the aristocratic norms of the pre-Modern agrarian order—had been carried by the Shar'î 'ulamâ'. In contrast, the Ṣûfîs, with their emphasis on the inner dimensions of faith, had been concerned above all with interpersonal relations, had ministered to the needs that arose within the actual social institutions of pre-Modern times, and now tended to be politically conservative.

In particular, the political orientation brought by Sharî'ah-mindedness turned out often to meet the needs of new ethnic groups and new classes in revolt against the more privileged elements that tended to co-operate with the West. In Indonesia, the force of Sharî'ah-mindedness was directed at once against the old aristocratic order and the relatively more recent pre-eminence of the Javanese in the archipelago.

In Indonesia, as elsewhere, the nineteenth century had brought a reaction against the Ṣûfî dominance and an interest in a purer enforcement of the Sharîʿah law; this was reinforced by more active contact with south Arabian merchants, by much more frequent pilgrimage to Mecca (made possible by steamships), where new ideas found a world audience, and even by contact with Sharîʿah-minded reformers in Cairo. Like the French among the Berbers, the Dutch inclined to hope that the new and potentially revolutionary vigour in Islam could be reduced to an Arabism which the Indonesians would find foreign and ultimately disregard; as Islam came to be identified with the Sharîʿah law, the Dutch discouraged the mounting drive to replace local customary law (ʿâdah) with Sharîʿah. But in fact it was the Dutch administrative and even legal activities which had done most to foster respect for the Sharîʿah law, and the drive persisted. The Ṣûfî ṭarîqah orders lost strength and prestige.

But as ever, the drive for a new Sharîʿah-mindedness was complicated by other conflicts. Under Dutch rule, the Javanese of the old inland rice kingdoms (who came to be involved most extensively in production of raw materials for the world market) multiplied greatly and threatened to dominate the Dutch part of the archipelago. The Inner-Javanese society, commonly loyal to its agrarian aristocracy, tried to cling to older ways. Their literary language was Javanese, which enjoyed a rich pre-Islamic past. Over against the Inner-Javanese, the cities of the coasts (as well of Java as of the other islands) tended more readily to welcome the new Sharîʿah-minded tendencies; perhaps (with their mercantile ways) they never had been so fully committed to Ṣûfism as the inlanders. Their literary language tended to be Malay, more strictly associated with the Islamicate heritage, even in its Ṣûfism. Hence the Malay language and the cultural traits associated with the coastal areas came to be thought of as more properly Sharʿî and Islamic than the ways of the Inner-Javanese and especially of their aristocracy. A sort of wrestling dance that was popular in the coastlands came to be regarded as properly Muslim; the shadow puppet shows of Inner Java, in which old Sanskritic heroes and their legends were given a Ṣûfî interpretation, were frowned on as pagan survivals. At the same time, in Inner Java itself an ardently Sharîʿah-minded element developed to lead resistance in the name of Islam to the continued cultural leadership of the Ṣûfî-minded old aristocrats—though, as often elsewhere, the new element was at first organized in the form of new ṭarîqahs. Even away from Inner Java, in such areas as Sumatra, the conflict between the new Sharîʿah-mindedness and the older local traditions often became the expression of local ethnic and even class conflicts. The Sharîʿah law became the symbol on several levels and in several contexts of the dynamic new as against the deadening old.

No simple revival of the older Sharîʿah law, nor of the general orientation that went with it, would serve the Modern Muslim needs, however. In the main centres of Muslim thinking, Islam itself was reconceived, and with it the nature and role of the Sharîʿah. Increasingly in the twentieth century,

Muslims referred to Islam as a 'system'. Rather than as a personal posture of faith or as loyalty to an historical community, it now was thought of as a complete pattern of ideal life, subsisting in itself apart from the community which might embody it, a pattern that communities (even more, perhaps, than individuals) ought to adopt. The 'system' of Islam was partly based on that developed by the Sharî'ah-minded after the High Caliphal Period, when the notion of an overall Shar'î polity was being developed and the details of a 'Shar'î' political life were being worked out as a guide to the local rulers who were replacing the caliphs. But whereas even in that period the Shar'î norms were thought of as a series of particular commands incumbent upon individuals who happened to be in responsible positions, whose islâm still consisted primarily in their personal devotion whether this led them to respect the commands or not, now Islam was commonly felt to consist in almost a blueprint for a social order which could be set off against capitalism or communism as rival social systems.

The contrast stemmed partly from modern notions of social and intellectual analysis, in which almost any sort of activity could be treated as forming an autonomous system. It probably owed something also to the tradition of Falsafah studies, in which a religious teaching was considered as a primarily political phenomenon. For centuries, philosophically-minded Muslims had stressed the disciplinary uses of the ṣalât worship, for instance, as a means of encouraging social good order. Men like Afghânî had kept a political approach of this general sort circulating. Now among some Muslims this approach was made central to Islamic loyalty, yet that loyalty was not subordinated to the personal independence which had been primary to the Faylasûf thinkers. In extreme cases ṣalât, for instance, could be felt to be almost exclusively a social discipline, to which any personal spiritual benefits would be incidental; yet its adoption was recommended as a transcendent duty, not merely a rational historical judgment. Many Muslims seemed to express their submission to God less by way of a direct personal act of Islâm to Him, than in the form of a submission and loyalty to Islam itself, at once the ideal 'system' and the historical manifestation, in which acceptance of God was but one element among many. An observer has noted that it can seem less dangerous now, in some Muslim lands, to say something slighting about God or even to be an atheist than to imply anything that might seem disrespectful about Islam or its Prophet.

It came to be very generally felt that Islam, as the ideal social system, offered the 'true' democracy, because it established equality among its adherents and required the ruler to 'take counsel' in state affairs; that it offered the 'true' socialism, because in the zakât tax on capital it imposed the principle of social responsibility on the wealthy. These general notions were elaborated and justified in detail in numerous works in most parts of Islamdom. The writers quoted Qur'ân and ḥadîth reports at length and invoked such rules of the traditional fiqh jurisprudence as seemed relevant.

But they discarded almost entirely the older discipline of Qur'ân interpretation, in which the meaning of a passage was carefully elucidated by documented reference to linguistic usage at the time and to reports from the Prophet's generation, and alternative interpretations were taken note of. They discarded the old isnâd criticism of ḥadîth reports as well; appealing to the results of modern Western criticism of the validity of the isnâds, they felt free to reject any reports that did not suit them even while they cited those that did. As to fiqh, the Modernizers soon reclaimed the right, even in Jamâ'î-Sunnî circles, to revise it by way of ijtihâd inquiry; but they did not feel bound by the rules of evidence which had governed ijtihâd inquiry since al-Shâfi'î's time. Very commonly such works were apologetic and anything seemed justified which would tend to support the honour of Islam.

But within this overall atmosphere of Modernizing Islam, a more disciplined movement took form after the War of 1939, to which the term 'neo-Shar'î' may more particularly apply. It took form almost simultaneously in a number of different areas, offering a substitute at once for the secular nationalism of the particular area and for the various sorts of international ties, such as those of the United Nations, within which the nationalism found essential support. These neo-Shar'î movements could in principle hope to unite all the scattered states of Islamdom on a new basis: each Muslim nation would be bound together internally on essentially Shar'î legal principles; but this would mean that there would be nothing in the basis of the national unity to divide one nation from the next—hence all Muslim peoples ought to be able to be bound together in a wider all-Muslim whole on the same basis. (For these Muslims, the truest basis for international co-operation of the poorly technicalized states was neither their situation as low-investment lands in contrast to the West, nor their opposition to the Western bloc, but a positive pan-Islamic ideal.) But more significant was the neo-Shar'î internal programme, in which nationalism itself would be recast on an Islamic basis.

If the technicalistic mutation had taken place not in the Occident but somewhere within Islamdom, one can guess at some of the lines it might have progressed along. On the basis of a particularist corporativism, for instance, in the Occident, Modern technicalism has, in fact, presupposed the structure of a strong territorial state. On the basis of a Shar'î contractualism, universally extensible, technicalism might have developed in a more directly international form. A contract-based capitalism might have built up a new and more flexible international code for its operations which would have overridden the jurisdiction of any local establishments and been maintained, perhaps, by a decentralized complex of recognized foci of world authority. Such a pattern might, indeed, have been more suited to world technicalism than the actual pattern which originated in the Occident; it might even have obviated some of the problems of a development gap. But it can obviously not be established by Muslims at this date; the European-type state seems inescapable. Hence neo-Shar'ism has had to work out its pattern on bases set by the Occident. In particular, this has meant a recognition of the state as a legal institution, a notion unprecedented in Shar'î history. The Sharî'ah is to be not an autonomous set of rulings which are incidentally binding on the ruler as a Muslim, but rather the 'constitution' of the state itself, which is responsible as a legal entity not only for enforcing but even for developing the Sharî'ah further as needed.

The most developed neo-Shar'î theory has been that of the Jamâ'at-e Islâmî movement in India and Pakistan, led by Abu-l-Alâ Maudûdî. Maudûdî was developing his doctrines already before the War of 1939, and opposed the creation of Pakistan, presumably as much because a Pakistan state would bring secular Modernists to power as because it would abandon definitively so many Indian Muslims to non-Muslim rule. But when Pakistan was set up, the centre of the movement was transported to Pakistani territory and Maudûdî initiated a campaign to make Pakistan truly an Islamic state, despite its founders' intentions; a campaign which received widespread support among the 'ulamâ' scholars. The movement was also very popular among college students, both in India and in Pakistan. Maudûdî and his collaborators worked out theoretical solutions to at least the most obvious points at which Modern institutions had to be recast in Shar'î terms. They were not content simply to justify Western practices by a reinterpretation of the Shar'î provisions, but tried to find a new form. Thus they were concerned to show how Modern large-scale finance, which seemed to call for banking and for the interest on which banking has been based, could be adequately (and more justly) carried out on the basis of co-operative banking without payment of interest, and hence without building up private fortunes not founded on personal productive activity. They were morally shocked likewise at a legal system which—even in the name of the Sharî'ah, treated in India as if it were case law—presupposed antagonistic advocates, each presenting only such facts as happened to further his case and professionally unconcerned with the truth as such. They were concerned to show that a legal pattern using not interested advocates but the neutral muftî, whose professional role was to help the judge come to impartial justice, could develop the technical competence to handle Modern legal traffic.

Their programme still struck most outside observers as naïve; it had little influence among the specialists charged with making modern institutions work effectively in Pakistan. Unfortunately, it was a different side of their activity that had the most concrete results. If Islam was to be the basis of the state, it must be clear what Islam actually meant as well as who was to be accounted a Muslim, with voting power in Muslim councils. They turned their attention to dissident Muslims, and in particular to the Aḥmadiyyah sect, which (founded late in the nineteenth century by Ghulâm-

Ahmad, who claimed to be the Mahdî and used peaceful methods) had succeeded in building an effective social organization, with economic co-operatives and other exemplary establishments, but on the basis of strict allegiance to its own particular body, to which other Muslims were expected to be converted. The Aḥmadiyyah represented a community within the community and their very successes accentuated the threat of schism which they posed. The claims to special divine guidance, and even a sort of prophethood which they made on behalf of their founder, struck the 'ulamâ' scholars as heretical, and the energies of the Jamâ'at-e Islâmî were diverted into attacks on the sect, attacks which degenerated into riots. The neo-Shar'î movement thus became caught in a renewed communalism, and itself was found guilty (by the secular government) of the divisiveness of which it accused the sectarians. In a society ordered on technicalistic principles, illegal violence was less in repute than ever. Such communalism was discredited and the power of the Jamâ'at-e Islâmî was reduced for the time being.

Among the eastern Arabs, the most important neo-Shar'î movement was that of the Muslim Brotherhood (al-Ikhwân al-Muslimûn) founded by Ḥasan al-Bannâ' in Egypt. He hoped to turn sentiment for Arab unity into a force for general Muslim unity—in which non-Muslim Arab minorities, such as the Christians in Egypt, would play a tolerated but not an equal role, and in which eventually other Muslim peoples would join (but with a certain deference to the Arabs as natural leaders of Islam). But in practice he started out not with remote political programmes but with concrete social action: setting up schools and other practical social services in the towns of Egypt. For a time after the Egyptian revolution of 1952, 'Abd-al-Nâṣir had to work with the Muslim Brethren, for they had a more effective grass-roots following than any other comprehensive social movement, even than the communists. But they proved dangerous allies: they were not unwilling to use assassination to eliminate obstacles to their power. Here too neo-Shar'ism was implicated in political violence and discredited. The Muslim Brotherhood was suppressed in Egypt, but it has continued active, at least in presenting its theories, elsewhere among the Arabs.

In Indonesia, after the War of 1939 and the advent of independence, the new nationalist demand for ways of giving the society complete self-determination found expression, as elsewhere, not only in general demands for 'Islamic socialism' but also in a neo-Shar'î movement (Darul-Islâm) which wished to set up a government on strictly Shar'î principles. It led a series of sufficiently destructive revolts, but (like the new Sharî'ah-mindedness generally) it found its main strength away from Inner Java, in the coastal lands of the other islands. It could not win Java, where, on the contrary, an explicitly anti-Islamic communist movement gained far more popular following than in any other independent Muslim land.

The neo-Shar'î movements, wherever they occurred, represented the most dramatic intervention of the Islamic vision into technicalistic society. But Ṣûfism, though it declined in organization and material resources, did not die out even among the educated classes. Many a young educated Muslim still had his pîr whom he consulted privately about the state of his conscience, though publicly there was little indication of a Ṣûfî interest. Such a Ṣûfism, usually deprived of any major institutional function in the newer and more decisive sectors of social organization, was reduced again almost to a personal affair. The Ṣûfîs in the nineteenth century had tended to play a defensive, conservative role, and in the twentieth century they played little political role at all except in special cases, as where a reforming ṭarîqah had become the political mouthpiece of an ethnic group. But at least in the personal sphere, Ṣûfism could continue to express the deeper implications of the Islamic vision in a form not uncongenial to the technicalistic situation in which people found themselves. Indeed, in the twentieth century Ṣûfism experienced a certain revival, sometimes in noticeably new forms.

In Indonesia, it was especially among the traditional aristocratic classes that a revived Ṣûfism became popular. But it was not simply the Ṣûfism of a century before, stripped of its social ramifications. Among many, at least, it was a more personal and intellectualized Ṣûfism, strongly influenced from Europe. It was by way of European scholarship that Javanese Muslims came to realize that the old Sanskritic figures which entered into not only the shadow-plays but into much of the Javanese Ṣûfî lore represented a vast heritage of mystical experience and speculation in Sanskritic India. Many Javanese intellectuals proved willing to look explicitly to Sanskritic traditions, as popularized by Western scholarship, for new light on their Ṣûfism; a number of new mystical movements arose of frankly Sanskritic inspiration. In the Maghrib a popular new Ṣûfî movement, systematically intellectual, universal in its claims, and explicitly willing to come to terms with modern science and notably with some elements of modern psychology and philosophy, won a number of French and other European adherents. From India, more than one Modernized and popularized version of Ṣûfism, disseminated in English, also found Western adherents.

All these movements carried essentially conservative political implications: their preoccupation with the inner life of the relatively well-to-do, among whom they spread, placed them, so far as they had political effects at all, on the side of the status quo. The active social implications which ṭarîqah Ṣûfism had once carried were lost. Yet they did carry latent political implications of a potentially significant sort. They stood for a universalism and an openness to new cosmological and historical awareness that suggested the possibility of the Islamic heritage playing a new and positive role in coming to terms with the problems posed by Modernization if ever the most immediately pressing dilemmas could be solved.

In the Shîʿî parts of Iran, despite great pressures for outright rejection of Islam among the intelligentsia, heirs to the old freethinking tradition, the decades after the fall of Reżà Shâh saw an Islamic revival probably more vital than anywhere else. In political life, the most prominent expression of this revival was the revived Sharî'ah-mindedness associated with the mujtahid Kâshânî, who looked, ideally, to building Iranian independence along neo-Shar'î lines. Kâshânî gave protection to an actionist group opposed to any who compromised with Westerners; they called themselves the 'Devotees of Islam' (Fidâ'îyân-e Islâm), and initiated a series of assassinations with the murder in 1946 of Kasravî, who had led the secularist nationalist attack on conventional Islam under Reżà Shâh.

But perhaps more significant, spiritually, was a remarkable growth in the Ṣûfî ṭarîqah orders. Already early in the nineteenth century, the persecution of Ṣûfîs (even explicitly Shî'î ones) by the Shî'î 'ulamâ'—so vigorous since later Ṣafavî times—had weakened; executions became rare and finally ceased. Reżà Shâh had suppressed the public activity of the Qalandar-type darvîshes, whose begging was a nuisance and whose outlandish costume offended Modernized taste; but he had not troubled those Ṣûfîs who stayed in their khânagâhs. (This fact led to a reform to the Qalandars, who settled into khânagâhs and became relatively conventional.) After the war, the several more conventional Ṣûfî orders added both numbers and wealth. Some were administered in novel ways: one retained its central authority, which normally would have been in the hands of a supreme pîr (in Shî'î Iran called a quṭb) in a board of ten members. Other movements which reflected a Ṣûfî consciousness without recognizing ṭarîqah Ṣûfism also flourished, notably the Shaykhîs. In this latter environment Ṣûfî thought received a special impetus when selected Shî'î mystical speculation of Ṣafavî times was creatively reinterpreted in the light of Western existentialist thought by the French scholar Henry Corbin. Corbin's work was widely welcomed, though the only sort of independence it could foster would be that spiritual and intellectual independence which could result from building an undeniably Modern speculative tradition on genuinely Islamicate bases.

Secularistic revolution: 'directed democracy' as a mediating alternative

The most knowledgeable of the alert younger generation rejected a neo-Shar'î solution as impractical and also dangerously communalistic. Most of them scarcely considered a radical departure on Gândhist lines, which would have seemed too daring or too sacrificial. They inclined toward attempting to match, or (at most) modestly improve on, what had been accomplished in the West, aiming either at the sort of society found in the Modernized Occident, or at its Soviet counterpart.

As we have noted, the attempt to be integrated directly into the Western bloc was generally felt to be humiliating if not impractical. The example of the western Turks in their Westernizing republic was inspiring but not fully convincing. They emerged from the tutelage of Atatürk's party in 1950 with a genuinely free election in which the increasingly active business classes and the still sceptical peasants combined to elect to power a party as Modernizing and Western-orientated as the old, but less committed to state controls and to repression of religious expressions. In time, the new party succumbed to the temptation of harassing its opposition, and it took a military *coup* to enforce free elections again; but on the whole, parliamentary institutions of an Occidental type, though they produced no revolution, proved capable of protecting the more evident interests of most classes. The peasants, notably, won both the right to revive many of the Islamic religious practices that had been frowned on and an economic support which made tractors and other amenities increasingly available in the countryside. City slums and rural poverty remained problems even in Turkey, however.

In other lands, many who admired the Soviet solution became outright communists, hoping to link their forces to other communist groups around the world and produce drastic immediate results at whatever cost. But the communist solution implied not merely (as we have already noted) personal regimentation but also a breach with loyalties to the national heritage and its autonomous dignity: not only would it bring a certain degree of subservience to established communist states; beyond that, the party discipline, which included the comprehensive Marxist dogma, would have to be substituted for any other cultural patterns even in relatively indifferent spheres (such as art or letters) including, of course, most especially anything expressly Islamic. Many Muslims who were not ready for a neo-Sharʿî plan were still not ready for a total break with the Islamicate past; moreover, they respected the leading Occidental societies and shared largely in their contemporary culture. Hence most of those who expected to follow Western examples preferred to think in terms of the Western-bloc lands, despite their quarrels with them.

Yet it was generally acknowledged that the model could not be simply imitated. Among many who inclined to Occidental models and even among some who inclined to Soviet models, the hope rose that the more enlightened sector of the population, under strong leadership, could take power and force the pace of change without recourse to Communist-bloc ties or communist regimentation but without waiting to go through the long stages of evolution which the Occident had gone through. 'Democracy' was a key slogan in both Occidental and communist societies, referring ideally to the participation of all citizens on an equal basis in the duties and benefits of technicalistic society. But if democracy meant waiting for popular initiative to over-rule the old vested interests, it would be long coming and might be needlessly destructive when it came. What passed for constitutional democracy (i.e., majority voting among candidates presented by parties) was almost everywhere, as in the west Iranian state or Egypt before the revolution, simply a means to continue the existing distribution of power, in which those economically strong enough to control the media of popular opinion and to command the votes were interested above all in preserving their own strength—and hence in blocking any major change. The slogan invented in one Muslim land suits the hopes of many others: what was wanted was a 'guided democracy' in which as many of the virtues of 'democratic' society as possible would be maintained or built, but under strong and unquestionable guidance powerful enough to sweep away the strong social forces standing in the way of progress. (It will be more convenient for us to substitute the explicit term 'directed' for the vaguer 'guided'.)

We may abstract from several instances a fairly identifiable pattern, not exactly fitting any one case, though exemplified reasonably closely in the first successful effort toward such a directed democracy, 'Abd-al-Nâṣir's Egypt. Under the name, in this case, of 'Egyptian socialism', concern centred on several large and immediate practical problems which became pressing as the nuclear aspects of technicalism came to characterize the most determinant sectors of society and as the new poverty enforced a mood of crisis. The most important problems were three. Control of agricultural land by large private owners who carried off to the towns whatever was produced above the barest needs of the peasants, became intolerable: not only were the peasants increasingly badly hit by such a process and increasingly aware that it was unnecessary; in addition, the consequent discouragement of any productive investment in the land (for the rich did not need it and the peasants would reap no advantage from it) made it very difficult to bring more technicalistic methods into the agricultural sector, on which the society was dependent for its food supply. 'Land reform' became a prime symbol of social progress. But almost as great a preoccupation as land reform was effective industrialization. The presence of a certain number of Modern factories might decisively upset the old social balance, but it need not mean industrialization of the economy as a whole. For this purpose, industry must be internally balanced so that one industry supported another; this called for national planning rather than uncontrolled private initiative; but too often even such national planning and state investment as had occurred was directed (under governments controlled by the old vested interests) toward confirming the old imbalance.

The third problem, along with land reform and industrialization, resulted in part from the first two. In a society where the positive action every serious person believed was necessary seemed frustrated by the very institutions which should have furthered it, people became cynical and accepted corruption in government as normal. Where under direct European supervision high standards of honesty had been maintained, after independence every sort of irregularity was condoned. Corruption made use of forms which had been common enough in agrarianistic times—various sorts of bribery and nepotism—but it was not simply a continuation of the old patterns. The component in it of ancient usage was probably less and that of personal opportunism greater. But more important, it played a rather different role. What is called corruption had once openly served, often enough, to allow for leeway in which what was sometimes very positive local activity could escape too rigorous a bureaucratic control; now it often served to frustrate the efforts of the healthiest elements, even on the local level. Corruption now reinforced the difficulty of meeting the other problems, for private interests could win their way illegally if they could not do so legally; and the more corruption prevailed, the less possible it was to take measures (such as paying government servants decent salaries, a measure no private interest was concerned to push) which might have lessened the corruption itself. Corruption became the bottleneck through which even the best plans for land reform and for industrialization could not pass.

The classes which were most frustrated by such problems were not the very poor, who could hardly realize what was the trouble, but those classes most dedicated to technicalistic society. Among these were the professionals and technicians of various sorts, who unlike businessmen, landlords, or even peasants, had no way to come to terms with an irregular situation: technical progress was to them the only alternative to hopeless frustration. Among these were also the students whose studies introduced them to the possibilities of a technicalized society, who wanted to rise above the level of their parents, and whose only chance of doing this was to see to it that society at large was changed. Among these were finally also the army officers, or rather the lower ranks of army officers (for the top generals were commonly integrated into the existent society at its upper levels). The army officers formed, in effect, the largest single body of technically trained experts in the society. When (as happened in the Palestine war, for instance) corruption prevented effective action, they had at least as little recourse as any group in the country, and suffered the consequences.

When a military *coup* has been carried out by the top command of the army itself, it has commonly served the interests of one or another of the competing interest groups within the status quo, or has even served to defend the status quo against innovation from below (as when Muṣaddeq's nationalist experiments in Iran were put an end to by the army, and the monarch restored). But when, as in Egypt in 1952, it has been the lower ranks of officers who have taken the lead and the top command has been set aside, such a military *coup* has commonly served the interests of the sort of programme we are calling 'directed democracy'. Such a military *coup* can bring a new technicalistic class to power at the expense of the old upper classes, just as surely (if normally less ruthlessly) as can a communist revolution in the streets or the countryside. But it can bring that class to power with a minimum of dislocation in the society as a whole, for it need not fear serious resistance. In Egypt, the old landed aristocrats (who were felt to represent an alien Turkish tradition anyway) were steadily eased aside after the revolution; the new army officers who had power did not trust the representatives of the old régime and preferred to have men of humbler origins about them, with whom they could talk on an equal level. But the aristocrats were not killed nor even completely dispossessed. Gradually they lost their lands; their business advantages were restricted; they lost access to new posts; but, though in reduced circumstances, they were mostly allowed to vegetate quietly in their clubs.

The first task of a revolutionary government after a *coup* was to attack corruption. This was launched first by a wave of 'revolutionary morality'. At such a time, everyone is inspired by the new hopes, to suppose that henceforth all will be different so that he, too, will be ashamed not to be honest (or is afraid he may get caught when so many others are honest). If the government is at all successful, it can maintain this mood. But the mood is reinforced by appointing new men pledged to a new order, and by taking care that officials are paid so regularly that they have no pressing reason to take bribes; and finally by drastic imposition of penalties on those who stand out by being corrupt.

Then the government must launch land reform. This means confiscating, for a reasonably low sum, the great estates of the aristocrats, who now have no means to resist this. But it also means ensuring that control of the land is not simply reconcentrated into the hands of a new wealthy class, by way of moneylenders and others exploiting the ignorance of the peasants. It also means that productivity must be kept up or increased—whereas if land is simply divided into small individual plots for each peasant who formerly worked it as a tenant, the individual plots are likely to be uneconomic and so less productive than the larger estates. The best-known answer to this problem in a peasant country is some sort of co-operative among the peasants of a village, so that tenure can be assured to the members, technical activities (such as the use of a tractor or even of fertilizers) can be undertaken jointly, and marketing done on a sufficiently wide base to make possible effective financing and bargaining. All this requires a competent administration from the centre—for left to themselves, the peasants will not immediately trust each other well enough to allow one of themselves to run the co-operative affairs honourably, but may instead (out of habitual expectations of the worst) simply hand the co-operative over to the local moneylender or the ex-landlord to run it in his own interest. In Egypt, the requisite new funds were hard to get at first. But drastic action by the revolutionary officers commandeered them, at the expense of endless delays in compensation due to ex-landlords. Serious mistakes were made, and bureaucracy had a way of bogging the whole programme down, but gradually the face of the land was changed. And the per capita consumption of wheat did increase.

Finally, the government must see to the industrial economy. This means not only planning new investment without regard to local or private special interests, but controlling the available capital in the country. This requires what is called a 'directed' economy. This, in turn, may well seem to mean, as it did in Egypt, confiscation of the capital investment not only of foreign firms but of resident alien businessmen, such as the Greek- and Italian-speaking petty bourgeoisie of the Egyptian cities, against whom measures were popular among the Arab populace. Such ethnically inspired measures may have carried great immediate political advantages, and may have increased the government's freedom for long-term economic manœuvre. But they had doubtful immediate economic results. And their immediate human results were despicable.

But the revolutionary government must also work out political institutions through which to express its new 'democracy'. In the Occident, 'democracy' as a political order is expected to provide an arena in parliamentary institutions where representatives of the most important interest groups can bargain with each other; if all classes of citizens find themselves more or less represented in one or another of the recognized interest groups, such a system can be reasonably effective. But the term 'democracy' can have quite different implications. Ideally, at least, the communist version of democracy (which assumes that all citizens have or ought to have the same essential interests) calls for a single directive policy-forming organization (the party), in which problems are worked through not so much by the representatives of the several interests concerned, as by a body of persons selected for their broad outlook and disciplined in a context where no one interest group can prevail, so that they will speak for the public interest generally. Then popular participation would be largely by way of plebiscite: the people would vote not for individuals who would represent their particular interests, but *en bloc* for the programme of the party, showing their satisfaction or, in theory, their possible discontent with it.

In the low-investment countries, the great problems seemed sufficiently pressing, and the consensus of the more alert of the educated classes about them sufficiently strong, for it to seem appropriate for all the citizens to be looked on as having an over-riding common interest in the independence of the nation and its technical development. Hence, even when communism as such was rejected, not only did Marxism remain a popular doctrine, but the communist conception of democracy seemed more attractive than the Occidental. Accordingly, it was a preoccupation of several governments, embarked on a programme of 'directed democracy', to try to create a national 'party', carefully protected from infiltration by the old vested interests, which should bring a national voice to bear on issues. This was not easy to create from the top after a military *coup*, however, especially when it was felt that the soldiers would decide everything anyway. (Atatürk had succeeded in creating a dynamic national party, but in an era when a much less comprehensive programme was expected, and less widespread participation.) 'Abd-al-Nâṣir made successive attempts at it without success.

But in addition to a national forum for policy formation, it was important to get the less educated classes involved in the reforms, for, as in any technicalistic institutions, their conscious co-operation was indispensable. This might in part be arranged through a national party: this was attempted in

Egypt, where, indeed, discussions of high-level reform policies became vigorous even in the villages just after the revolution. Generally, the steady growth (beginning long before the revolution) of governmental technicalistic intervention in the villages accelerated the involvement of the peasants. The spread of agricultural co-operatives, even though they were at first imposed from above, brought home to the peasants the sort of social patterns that were wanted. The new government concentrated the effort to bring modern social and medical services to the villages into larger units in the larger villages. In the first instance, this need not make much concrete improvement in the services given, and the smaller villages perhaps suffered; but it opened the way to a greater variety of hospital care, schooling, club activities, and the like in each area, and so to a more rapid broadening of rural horizons. But village participation in the new order tended to remain perfunctory and politically almost inert.

A crucial issue in any reform project in the low-investment lands has been family planning, socially indispensable if rising population is not to wipe out all economic gains as fast as they can be made. Here excellent techniques may be available, but people are not easily persuaded to use them. Any given couple has no direct interest in limiting the national population growth in their own persons. Precisely the more alert persons can be those for whom added children may prove a boon, under favourable agrarian circumstances, since they will best be able to use them economically; and it is the example of the more alert that the others will follow. Generations of experience, indeed, have taught people that the more children, the more hands to support the parents in the end; and moral standards have been moulded to encourage begetting children both for personal and for social reasons in an age of a high infant death rate. It cannot become immediately clear to all, that the past experience has become permanently invalid, in that the old minimal agrarian prosperity is permanently gone and now each individual's training will mean more economically than the numbers in his family; or that the moral standards which confirmed experience are to be scuttled on the basis of current inconveniences. Couples facing obvious destitution might be induced to take some measures, once the lapse of time has made the idea familiar. But only as the population genuinely enters into the mood of technicalistic society in some measure, learning to evaluate their future not simply according to family solidarity but also according to prospects of technical competence, can a programme in family planning be fully successful. It has been only very gradually that family planning has begun to show even incipient results in the Egyptian villages.

The pattern of social reform which we have called 'directed democracy' was not based on any prepared ideology. Rather it emerged in each case from the situation in which a given country found itself. What it had in common in different lands depended on the common situation of the times. We may group together roughly under this rubric the various régimes which were assimilated neither into the parliamentary pattern of western Europe nor into communism, but attempted, on the basis of military intervention, of support by the technicalistic classes, and of participation by a well-policed mass base, to eliminate corruption; to dispossess not only Western influences but also more local privileged elements, especially those felt as alien; and to carry out central planning toward co-operative land reform, as needed, and a balanced industrialization. Leaders in one country consulted with leaders in others with similar aims, but even within some such common pattern, the reforms in the several countries were very diverse, as were their degrees of intensity and success. We may take as examples, each contrasting in certain ways to the Egyptian case, yet all expressing in some degree a common spirit and willing to recognize each other as engaged in more or less analogous efforts, Indonesia, Pakistan, and Algeria.

The Indonesian economy after the war was relatively unstrained, at least in the sense that there was little prospect of imminent mass starvation; for agriculture still provided—even in heavily populated Java—enough food at least for the rural population. Nonetheless, even there the demand arose for a rapid transformation. We have noted how both a neo-Shar'î and a communist movement became strong. Basing himself on military support, Sukarno emerged as unquestioned leader, with a programme intended to force the pace of national development. The programme was very radically conceived. Sukarno referred to 'Indonesian socialism'. But it failed to produce the full results intended.

Sukarno concentrated by choice on a problem that had doubtless to be solved first—and which proved a stumbling-block elsewhere too: that of creating a sense of nationhood on which to build. The Javanese aristocracy and the ardently Sharî'ah-minded 'ulamâ' from the outer coastlands, the locally oriented peasantry and the world-orientated merchants, had to believe they were one people. But in creating a sense of nationhood, he made the economic and social problems worse than they had been. His plan for development required that the Malaysian Muslim society be cleared of the power of alien elements and then that its economy be made independent. But this must be done on the basis of a consensus that would allow internal peace among all the indigenous population. Sukarno tried to hold together, as elements all of which would have to be satisfied if Indonesia's development were to be genuine, those who stressed the Sharî'ah, the communists, and the technically-minded army: each element was to keep the others within bounds. Presiding over all was to be the guiding genius of Sukarno himself, inspired by a rather neutral Islamic spirituality and legitimized directly by mandate from the masses. All were to pledge loyalty to him in the name of their common national purposes. This formula was more successful in the direction of liberation from foreign elements than of economic development. Sukarno drove out most of the resident Dutch and even the families of mixed Dutch-Indonesian background, as representing a foreign privileged stratum. Then he largely ruined the Chinese retail merchant class, to whom the peasants were not friendly.

The result was to throw those elements identified exclusively with the Indonesian nation onto their own resources. But whatever ultimate social advantages this might have, it effectively limited any general economic development by getting rid of those most likely to have the personal and financial resources to carry it on. It also necessitated internal accommodation among the Malaysian population itself, to make up for the economic inconveniences the policy carried with it. This made rigorous financial policies impossible, and consequently effective industrial or even agricultural reform. It also required the postponement of effective land reform—the land-reform law was not really implemented, lest it upset national unity. (But this fact in turn drove the Javanese peasants most affected still closer into the hands of the communists, who encouraged land reform by direct action, against Sukarno's wishes.) And without real social reform or sound financial policies, a scarcely controlled inflation forced government servants into a pattern of corruption. In these circumstances, Sukarno was unable to impose his conception of internal unity.

Moreover, the corollary of such militantly nationalist policies internationally, was intervention against British 'neo-imperialism' in the rest of the Malaysian archipelago, within which the Indonesians could not easily recognize boundary lines as anything but artificial alien impositions. (Indeed, the Indonesians extended their reach outside the archipelago proper and took over, by threats of violence, the Dutch portion of the neighbouring island of Papua, despite the fact that the Papuan population was radically different from the Indonesian and had far more to fear and far less to gain from the Indonesians than from their innocuous Dutch masters.) The resultant military efforts consumed even the resources provided by foreign aid, and made not only reform but even gross economic development on any basis impossible for the time. Nevertheless, Indonesia emerged as unmistakably master in its own house.

In Pakistan a much less radical programme (unlike that of Egypt and Indonesia, it was not even called 'socialist') produced somewhat clearer results than in Indonesia. A pattern of government by electioneering political parties was inherited from British India and was given a reasonably long chance to prove itself. But Pakistan faced severe problems arising out of the very act of its creation, in addition to the already desperate problems of poverty and dissension shared by all the Indic lands. It could sometimes appear that the idea of founding a state on an Islamic allegiance alone was an irretrievable mistake.

Partly because of the religious basis of its origin, party politics did not prove so relatively successful as in the Indian Union. Pakistan was born, as much as any state, out of the will of a handful of men who were exploiting sharply conflicting illusions in masses caught up in the stress of a very exceptional moment of crisis. The demand for an Islamic Pakistan arose only in the frightened cross-currents of the War of 1939, and apart from the special circumstances of the moment of its birth, it almost certainly would not have existed. But of that handful of men who forced its creation, the only ones of any great moral stature (and in particular Jinnâḥ) died almost immediately after the state came into being. Their party, the Muslim League, had been built on a crisis loyalty and when once it had achieved its aim, discipline relaxed. Most of its representatives proved susceptible to the temptations of corruption and there was no one at the top to check them. They rapidly lost popular respect and fell from power, leaving no single national party but only disparate local parties to meet the necessarily desperate national needs, and, in particular, to meet the other problems with which the circumstances of Pakistan's creation had confronted it. Only in the Pathan district, where Gândhî's disciple 'Abdulghaffâr Khân had built up a new spirit of co-operation (though 'Abdulghaffâr himself was imprisoned by the Pakistanî régime), did it seem possible to build without being bogged down in corruption.

The violence of the nation's origin combined with its arbitrary composition to make things worse. The problems of the refugees from partition—far more massive in proportion to the nation's size than in India—simply compounded the inevitable jealousies of the peoples brought together in Pakistan. The educated immigrants from the Gangetic plain (who tended to take the place of the leading elements who had fled Pakistanî Panjâb and Bengal as Hindus) were often mistrusted by their Panjâbî hosts; but together with the Panjâbîs they formed a potent bloc which gained positions of power everywhere and against which the rest of the new nation was even more bitter. Symbolically, the bloc tried to impose Urdu (the language of the Gangetic plain and also widely used in the Panjâb), as the 'Muslim' language, upon the Sindhîs and even the Bengalîs, who were trying to assert their cultural identity through their own languages. At moments the nation seemed ready to break up.

The only creative basis for working out these problems would have to be a sense of national spirit to which all would contribute; but the nationalities of Pakistan had in common only their Muslim allegiance and their Indic past. The latter point was negative, but emotionlly it loomed large and Pakistanî governments found it politically necessary to maintain hostility to the Indian Union, which they chose to regard as representing Hinduism. As in Indonesia, the need for a sense of nationality dictated an aggressive foreign policy. The majority-Muslim territory of Kashmîr had remained in India after partition largely because the Muslim leadership there believed (at the time) that the secular Indian government would be more conducive to social progress; the Pakistanîs insisted that it should go to Pakistan, launched a local rising and tribal invasion on its borders, and landed themselves in a stalemate with an India that proved stronger than they had expected. The alternative basis for a Pakistanî national spirit, Islam, was pre-empted by the neo-Shar'ism of Maudûdî's Jamâ'at-e Islâmî, which issued, as we have seen, in communal riots. The inability of Pakistan to come to terms with itself (despite the elimination of many of the Hindu and Sikh 'alien' elements) was epitomized in its failure to adopt a national constitution for nine years after independence.

Perhaps because its problems were more desperate, and because its people were allowed to flounder in them together under party rule for a longer time (because of the inheritance of British parliamentarism), Pakistan found (at least temporarily) a reasonably durable solution. In 1956 (when, indeed, a constitution had finally been voted, but the substantive problems remained unsolved), the army dispossessed the politicians and suppressed the political parties. Its chief, Ayyûb Khân, tried to build a new and sounder democracy on the basis of mass participation (and popular plebiscite).

Islam as such played no more evident a role in solving major problems than in Indonesia. Ayyûb was influenced by many sorts of ideals. He studied the examples of 'Abd-al-Nâṣir in Egypt and Tito in Yugoslavia; the latter had shown that even a movement which chose communism could remain national. Ayyûb Khân did not nationalize industries, but he instituted a careful economic plan and new industries were launched by the state. As a Pathan from the Afghan highlands where 'Abdulghaffâr had worked, he respected some aspects of Gândhî's work, and it was consistent with this that he stressed the importance of creating what he called 'basic democracy', responsible self-rule on the local level which would then form a basis for regional and national self-rule as the population matured politically. Land reform (of not too drastic an extent) was effectively carried out, and landed capital was encouraged to shift to urban investment. But perhaps most fundamentally, Ayyûb remained representative of a culture-British orientation and even when gathering power into his own hands, he allowed a relative liberty of discussion and eventually even of balloting in the country at large. It was in this culture-British spirit that he respected the national cultural heritage: in the hope of finding a positive role for Islam less disastrous (and more gentlemanly) than that of neo-Shar'ism, he founded and gave high priority to an institute which was to study the Islamic heritage in a Modern scientific spirit and re-think its implications. The problems of Pakistan were slow to yield under his tolerant guidance, but the Pakistanîs were able to eliminate much outright corruption and begin moving ahead in education and industry.

In Pakistan, not only was the theory mild but in fact the old privileged classes (among the Muslims, that is) were little disturbed by Ayyûb's remoulding of the political structure. In contrast, Algeria (when it finally won its independence) found itself radically revolutionary both in theory and in fact. The French settlers had composed the greater part of the privileged classes, and when their intransigent opposition to independence had left them little alternative but flight, most of the economic establishments of the country were left at the disposal of the ordinary Muslim inhabitants. Many of the great settler farms, on which laboured numerous Muslim employees, were spontaneously turned into producers' co-operatives when their settler-managers left. The long bloody struggle of the revolution had done the work of eliminating alien elements and breaking down the power of the privileged classes that had co-operated with the West; the task of the new government (necessarily based upon the army) was to bring order into the dangerously fluid new economic adventures. Whereas in Egypt the problem was to teach the long-cowed peasants how to run a co-operative without letting the old landlord or moneylender take it over, in Algeria the problem was often to teach a self-liberated peasantry how to gear their local activities in with national plans so that their labour might attain the most success. As in Egypt or in Indonesia or in Pakistan, however, what seemed required was a central direction from the top, embodying the goals of the technicalistic classes and based on popular plebiscite (and if possible on a single policy-forming mass party created from the top), which would undertake national planning and guide the less technicalized elements of the population to the point in development at which, it was hoped, the military would be able to step aside from its directive role.

Despite the relative mildness of most revolutions of 'directed democracy', the social patterns they have set up have been plagued by some of the same problems that have presented themselves in the communist countries. The struggle against the notoriously heavy hand of governmental bureaucratic red tape has preoccupied the concerned reformers in and out of government: where nothing else but government bureaus is available to carry out central planning, a cautious refusal by employees to take responsible initiative may be as disastrous as a willingness to accept bribes, and yet it is precisely in the spirit of centralized direction to discourage independent initiatives. Perhaps more insidious has been the danger of social regimentation. Where all efforts are to be bent toward the supremely urgent national cause, dissident voices can readily be silenced and few will care. In 'Abd-al-Nâṣir's Egypt the Bahâ'î sect, whose few members gave proof in Egypt as did their more numerous fellow-believers in Iran, of a high level of personal integrity and of creative social initiative, was suppressed; that the Bahâ'î world headquarters happened to be at a town which had been included in the state of Israel might serve as pretext, but the communalist prejudice of Muslims who hated to see the descendants of Muslims choose another faith was surely the real cause for the stifling of one of the few groups which might have offered channels for non-governmental and non-bureaucratic thinking and experiment.

Those countries where an old agrarianistic ruling class managed to maintain its position past the first decade after 1945, when so many old régimes were overthrown by the technicalizing Modernizers, were forced to emulate in some measure the nations which had embarked on a directed democracy. In the west Iranian kingdom, after the shâh had succeeded in suppressing the militant nationalism of Muṣaddeq by the aid of the army, he consolidated his personal power and finally began himself to defy the landed classes and their organ, the Majles parliament. He learned to by-pass the Majles by direct appeals to a well-policed popular plebiscite. His purpose was a reform from above which would carry out the most essential objectives of eliminating corruption, reforming land tenure, and efficient industrialization yet without a serious breach with the old social privileges. For instance, the landlords were to be expropriated in favour of peasant co-operatives. But they were to be compensated in a form which would encourage them to move their capital into industry, thus keeping their aristocratic family traditions but making use of them more appropriately in the national interest. The hope was that some of the dangers of bureaucratization would be eliminated if numerous private firms undertook industrialization in a context of national planning. But the shâh was unable to win the confidence of the more active of the technicalistic classes. The corruption born of cynicism persisted, and served to prove its own predictions of failure in the projects for reform. Even more than elsewhere, the endemic problem of low-investment countries, that their best young men, after an education abroad, refused to come home, afflicted the Iranians. (The shâh's best hope was, perhaps, his attempt to win the very young by enlisting them in concrete work for reform, such as literacy campaigns in the villages.)

Other royal governments attempted less ambitious reforms from above. Even the Sa'ûdî dynasty in Arabia realized how necessary was some sort of reform if it was to survive. Like the shâh of Iran, the Sa'ûdîs tried to clear away corruption; and they encouraged multiple small-scale private economic development in co-operation with the American oil company from whose revenues the government lived. But here again the growing international community of governments dedicated to reform independent of the West did not recognize such a reform from above as truly independent, and the loyalty of the more alert educated youth remained questionable.

In most areas neither a neo-Shar'ism nor a reform from within the old leading classes of Islamicate culture seemed likely to win out. Despite the failings of particular attempts at directed democracy, some such pattern seemed called for, and with it a steady rejection of any major role for Islam in society.

Islamic cosmopolitanism as a force in the world

The Islamicate society which endured down through the eighteenth century has been broken up. The Muslim peoples, each for itself, form members of a larger world-wide society. At best, what remains of the Islamicate high tradition finds itself a marginal element in the practical culture of the more active classes: it enters insofar as it colours the popular mores of a nation, or as a privileged ingredient in a new high culture which is primarily Modern technicalistic in tone and hence in large part formed by Western antecedents. In some countries, and not only those under communist rule, the very classes which have been the prime carriers of Islamicate high culture are being excluded from political and social power. Yet Islam as an explicitly religious tradition continues vital almost everywhere. It is on this level that the heritage remains potent. Many aspects of the wider culture of which it was the nucleus cannot be disengaged from the religion; they remain resources potentially accessible to all Muslims, embedded in the languages of the great religious texts which serious Muslims must read, and likely to become influential under the right circumstances. But it is in religious life itself, with all this can mean for human life generally, that Islam is a great force for the immediate future.

Conditions of the later nineteenth and the twentieth centuries have helped to increase both the range and the depth of Islamic penetration in most parts of the world. Some of these conditions have been accidental and have applied almost equally to any other religious or cultural group. With a great increase in population in the older citied lands and with the opening up of the remotest areas to commercial exploitation by steamship, railroad, automobile and aeroplane, Muslims, like Europeans and Hindus and Chinese, have migrated in large numbers. From Dutch-ruled Indonesia they migrated to Dutch settlements elsewhere, from British-ruled India they migrated to other parts of the British empire. In such ways they have increased notably in eastern Africa, in some islands of the South Pacific, in some Caribbean lands. From the Maghrib, Arab and Berber workmen settled by the hundred thousands in the cities of France and Belgium, some of them permanently. In smaller numbers they have settled in the towns of West Africa and of North and South America.

More significant than further distribution by migration has been conversion. This has taken place at an accelerated pace where pockets of pagans remained in predominantly Muslim regions. Toward the end of the nineteenth century the ruler of Afghanistan, using relatively up-to-date weapons, was able at last to subdue the pagans of Kafiristan in the sub-Pamir mountains, forcing them to become outwardly Muslim. In Siberia, despite severe tsarist pressure, some new tribes chose to embrace Islam. In Malaysia various groups in the interior of the islands found the appeal of their neighbours' Islam attractive despite the efforts of Dutch Christian missionaries. Above all, in sub-Saharan Africa pagan individuals and tribes have been adopting Islam in a steady flow. With the suppression of the slave trade at the end of the nineteenth century, hostility to the Muslim slaver lessened; with the opening up of more regular routes of trade, contact with Muslims increased. Though Christians have poured large sums into missionary work and Muslims have expended very little in such organized work, it seems that Muslim success in conversion has been at least as great as or even greater than that of Christians in a wide belt of African territory where the two allegiances appear as rivals.

Christian missionaries have tried to account for Muslim success by explaining that Islam makes fewer demands morally on a convert, especially since it tolerates at least a degree of the polygamy which wealthy African pagans indulge in; or even by suggesting that the simplicity of its doctrine makes it easier for untutored minds to understand: in short, that Islam stands on a lower level than Christianity, less removed from 'primitive' people. But no real case can be made in this direction. In simplicity, certainly in the abstract and rather stark simplicity of the Muslim doctrine of God, lies no ease of access for people used to the intimately involved cults and myths of most pagan tribes. The Christian mysteries bear a closer analogy to the pagan ones.

So far as there is a difference in the obvious requirements made by the two allegiances, it is not an inherent difference but a difference in the current expectations of those who invite to the new allegiance. Monogamy is no more required, of ordinary believers, in the Bible than in the Qur'ân (and some Christian groups have allowed polygamy, as have even prominent Occidental theologians). Hard drink is even more popular than polygamy; and though some sorts of Christians ban it despite Biblical tolerance of it, it is notoriously rejected by all Islam. It is only if, in fact, a Christian missionary chooses to demand that a convert give up plurality of mates and hard drink, and if the representatives of Islam choose to overlook the more stringent requirements of the Sharîʻah, that Islam will seem less morally demanding. In fact, the degree to which adoption of one or the other allegiance has been disruptive of tribal patterns has depended largely upon the area of Africa concerned; that is, partly upon the conditions under which Islam or Christianity happened to be offered locally. Nevertheless, it remains true that in many areas Christianity has been offered in a more prohibitive form than has Islam.

This fact reflects a deeper difference between the role of the two religious traditions in the Modern world. The appeal of either Islam or Christianity over paganism has been largely the appeal of a cosmopolitan outreach—of an outlook situating one in the world at large, over a parochial outlook which has no validity or meaning beyond the tribal lines. In many areas, tribal men who are purely pagan at home reckon themselves Muslims when they travel; in this way they acquire a status in the outer world where the local gods bear no sway. But travel and the sort of contacts that travel brings shape people's lives more and more. The need for some sort of universal orientation daily becomes more urgent. Here Islam and Christianity have their opportunity: they are both universal. But the quality of their universality differs.

Christian missionaries offer the best in modern science: hospitals, government-recognized schools, foreign scholarships. But they make their offer, for the most part, with strings attached. They have represented the alien ruling class (already a point against them) and they demand a certain degree of assimilation to the whole cultural pattern of those aliens. (It is, in fact, often just such cultural demands that pass, in the missionary's mind, for the higher moral standards of Christianity.) Yet even so the converted group has had to pass through a long apprenticeship under the daily guidance and even tutelage of foreign representatives of the faith, final decisions being reserved for a governing body in Europe or America. That is, Christianity has had the strength and the weakness of representing Western world rule on its most intimate level. As representative of the West, it could not easily afford to compromise certain cultural positions which have been integral to the Western world pattern; if missionaries in the field were inclined to make such compromises, they were caught up by the church boards at home. It has not been easy to change this pattern in the new mood of independence.

Islam has offered an equal universalism on other terms. Of all the religious allegiances it has been, after Christianity, the most accessible geographically and the most active in looking for converts. Yet it has represented nothing but itself—it is recommended simply by the personal enthusiasm of its devotees, who can make any allowances that seem suitable in the local context. Moreover, so soon as the convert has taken the crucial step of recognizing the One God and the prophethood of Muḥammad, he is welcomed into full and personal membership in the Muslim world-wide fellowship—a fact often symbolized by members of newly converted groups making the ḥajj pilgrimage to Mecca and returning as recognized and independent authorities in the faith. Perhaps it might even be added that Islam carries more obviously the intellectual and moral traits of cosmopolitan civilization than does the complex dogma and ritual of Christians: it gives the satisfaction, sometimes, of a cleaner mental and spiritual break with the past.

Still more important, no doubt, than the spread of Islam into new areas has been its deepening in areas already at least nominally won. Even among the educated in urban areas, outside the Soviet Union, parallel with the weakening of traditional social patterns identified with Islam has gone an intensification of awareness of the Muslim allegiance and even a revival, in the mid-twentieth century, of Muslim ritual observances and respect for secondary tokens of Islam, such as the wearing of beards. In rural areas, especially those converted only during fairly recent centuries, where the Sharîʿah has been as yet little observed, the age-long pressure for closer conformity to international Muslim usage has been stepped up and pushed with revivalist rapidity. This movement has been associated in part with the reaction against Ṣûfism and the exaltation of Sharîʿah-mindedness. But it reflects also the rising sense of the importance precisely of the universal, the international aspects of Islam among peoples hitherto content to remain marginal. The cosmopolitanism of Islam has become of enormous import. It is ultimately in its cosmopolitanism that it presents a positive and powerful response to the challenge of Modernity.

Epilogue

The Islamic Heritage and the Modern Conscience

When the Islamic tradition was launched, the Muslims were promised that they should be 'the best community ever raised up for mankind'. The impulse issuing from the acceptance of such Qur'ânic interventions by committed men and women proved extraordinarily fruitful. Partly, the Qur'ân was powerful in itself; partly, it proved appropriate to the social and spiritual situation in its time in the region from Nile to Oxus, a region which had a central role to play in the expanding agrarianistic Oikoumene. The community that was committed to the Qur'ânic event, and the cultural dialogue it carried on, thus came to form by the sixteenth century the most widespread and influential civilization in the world. But in the seventeenth and especially the eighteenth centuries, the high power and prosperity of the Islamicate society were brought to an end by the transformations then going on in the Occident, changes that deprived the Nile-to-Oxus region of its special position in the hemisphere and that throughout Islamdom undermined the social and economic structure. By the twentieth century, though the Islamic allegiance continues strong in most regions where Islam had once come to prevail, these Muslim regions no longer form a single society with a common ongoing cultural tradition, but rather are severally articulated into a wider world society, the institutions of which have largely been evolved in the Occident. Moreover, in that new world society, no longer agrarianistic in its dominant sectors, all the cultural heritages from agrarianistic times, including even the Occidental heritage itself, have been put in question; still more so, then, that associated with Islam.

What meaning can the Islamicate heritage at large, and the Islamic religious heritage in particular, still have for modern human beings? Even for the immediate heirs, those who are still committed at least to Islam as a faith, the answer is not clear. Still less is it clear what meaning the heritage can have more generally 'for mankind', as the Qur'ân promised, for people of the Modern world society as such, among whom Muslims form an integral part, and from whose destinies the destinies of the Muslims can no longer be disengaged. Is the Islamicate culture to be relegated to the history books and the museums? Is the Islamic faith to merge (after whatever loyalistic but parochial resistance) insensibly into some general ecumenical religiosity, or perhaps to disappear altogether in the face of technicalistic enlightenment? Or will it somehow remain a peculiar possession of those among Modern mankind who happen to be Muslims, but be so circumscribed in effect (unless in the form of communal fanaticism) that to others it need be at most an object of curiosity? Or might it prove, by virtue of its inherent vitality, to be of potential significance for all of Modern technicalized mankind, whether they accept an explicitly Islamic allegiance or not?

We find ourselves almost instinctively allowing a certain sacredness to anything great that is potentially enduring, but irreplaceable if once lost. One rock is much like another, but an engineering project which, for mere convenience, would destroy the special contours of a mighty mountain is felt as in some measure a desecration. To destroy a single bird may be wanton, but to kill off a whole species, so that such a bird will never be seen again, is sacrilege. Even a single human being we know must die and to shorten his life is perhaps worse in the intention than in the act; it is not mere perversity that we may become more aroused over a war's destruction of great works of art, like the Parthenon, than over its destruction of the human beings who happened to be at the Parthenon when it was exploded, but who anyway could have lived only a few years longer. A human culture shares something of this sacredness. The spectacle of the fall of a mighty civilization, however cruel were its rulers and however bigoted its mentors, arouses in us awe and pity. We may find ourselves wanting to see the Islamicate heritage preserved in some form more out of romantic zeal than out of genuine human respect for its carriers past and present.

But in fact, of course, a civilization—and a given society carrying a given complex of cultural traditions—is rarely so well definable an entity that it can be said to have 'fallen' in the same sense in which a temple may collapse or a human being die. The civilization of the Sâsânians died a slow death at the hands of the Muslims, but at the same time may be said to have been transmuted, re-invigorated, and extended at precisely the same hands. Even without a change in language and religious allegiance, we may as well say that the civilization of the High Caliphate had perished by the time of Saladin, or that it had matured. The civilization of the Islamic Middle Periods was being at once fulfilled and replaced in the sixteenth and seventeenth centuries. What we must deal with is the heritage which the living traditions have brought to our generation. What will be its relevance in turn for our time? We will find such a question neither simply academic, nor even merely a parochial question for those who happen to be Muslims, but an inseparable part of the wider question of what all our cultural heritages mean to all of us together.

The most significant element of the Islamic heritage now is religion and the religious conscience. Religion is again now, as in the first generation of Muslims, the core of the community heritage—so far as that does actively survive; it is the effective residue of the centuries of Islamicate evolution. For some, it shows its force in neo-Shar'î communalist revival; for others, in a precious spiritual retirement—while a person's daily life may be fragmented and traditionless, secretly at home he becomes a Ṣûfî. In whatever form it appears, it is unquestionably still vital. We must consider at least, then, whether Islam may have anything to say to the Modern conscience.

The monotheistic conscience developed in an agrarianistic social context and had to deal—whether by way of prophetic social vision or personal deepening or chiliastic militancy—with the injustices and falsehoods, and the possibilities for justice and for growth in truth, that were then offered. The Modern conscience must face, correspondingly, the dilemmas and the opportunities presented by the Technical Age. These are world problems not only in the sense that they appear everywhere but in the sense that any attack on them in one place conditions and is conditioned by the way they are being dealt with everywhere else.

This indivisibility of the Modern world problems results in part from the political evolution of our century. By the mid-twentieth century, the various Muslim peoples were having to face internally, as were the Westerners, the profound long-term effects of the nuclear aspects of the Great Transmutation, of technicalistic society and all the opportunities and dangers it opened up. But the Muslims' independent responsibility has been at the same time increasingly limited by the same conditions that limit that of the most technicalized nations: their new responsibility is increasingly a joint responsibility with the rest of mankind for common human problems. In the League of Nations and still more in its successor organization, the United Nations and its several specialized agencies, their representatives have been expected to share with those of non-Muslim peoples in working through the most pressing of those problems which cross national boundaries —an ever larger proportion of all problems. Apart from official international organizations, they have had at least the moral obligation to share in facing the still wider range of problems confronting mankind in common which seem postponable and to which no urgent committee is assigned, but whose human significance is commonly deeper than that of the immediate urgent tasks.

The indivisibility of the world problems arises not only from recent political evolution: it is built into the nature of technicalism itself. This will become clearer as we define those problems in a Muslim perspective, and especially as we compare the forms they take on the two sides of the development gap which so overwhelmingly determines the Muslim perspective. Then we shall be in a better position to consider what must happen to Islam if it is to rise to their challenge; and then to consider, if we will, the more intimate question: What has Islam, what has a Muslim conscience to say to the problems of the Technical Age, not only on a local scale but also on the level of mankind as a whole?

The moral unity of Modern mankind

It can be argued that the crises modern Europe has passed through, and which made possible Muslim independence, were at least as much a consequence of the historical dynamics of the full development of technicalization as was the unprecedented social power that the Europeans had acquired. The business classes whom the earlier stages of the Transmutation had brought to social dominance did not have the same temptations as had had agrarian or military rulers in agrarianistic times, but they had their own dilemmas, as has often been pointed out. Dedicated to multiple private initiative, and riding waves of innovation which made every established position insecure, they found it difficult to operate in concert and maintain the levels of social responsibility required for control of the technicalistic order. For instance, the new all-powerful states could be manipulated by given interested businessmen toward special ends abroad, while the business community as a whole could not hold within due limits the international rivalries thus overstimulated: hence the universally disastrous War of 1914 which no one had expected. Worse, the 'business cycle', in which investment periodically got out of adjustment with the possibilities of the market (so that mobilized capital and labour found themselves disastrously unemployed), could not be controlled within the original presuppositions of a universal, but unco-ordinated, planning for continuous expansion: hence the depression of the 1930s.

Perhaps even more radically revealing was the moral breakdown displayed in the War of 1939. Under technicalistic conditions, not only the ruling classes but even large elements of the lower classes identified themselves unprecedentedly with the national state which so intimately bounded their lives, and they could lose the sense of moral commitment to any standards other than those set by the demand for national prosperity and pride. In the 1930s, in the defeated but potentially still powerful Germany, this led to the rise of the immoralist authoritarian nationalism of the Nazis, determined to reverse and compensate for the defeat of 1918 by any means available—including the techniques of war and *Schrecklichkeit* terror; and in the course of the war that resulted, they further indulged the national pride, without regard to traditional human moral standards, by systematically murdering en masse the members of disliked minorities (notably Jews and Gypsies). By the end of the war, the moral irresponsibility was spreading. The Americans had long shown an unusual degree of moral sensitivity on the international scene. But to enforce on Japan their prideful demand for unconditional surrender without face-saving reservations, even the Americans, who were shocked by Nazi German brutality, were not ashamed to demonstrate their mass-murdering atomic bomb not on open areas but on major cities, not once but twice within a few days: *Schrecklichkeit* on a new mechanized level, dispensing with the sentimental limitations imposed even among Chingiz Khân's Mongols by personal involvement.

In the face of these outrages, few other Westerners had a right to be complacent. Too many Frenchmen, for instance, gave their assent to the

Nazi murdering of Jews; and even though (or just because) in the Soviet Union the old privileged classes had been eliminated and businessmen were kept under direct social control, there too the technicalistic state proved as capable of over-riding all humane moral considerations as in Nazi Germany, and its master, Stalin, supported his rule with terror. But many Muslims congratulated themselves that they were not subject to the moral depravities of the 'materialistic' West. No Muslim people had, in fact, possessed sufficient power as yet to be tested on the scale that Westerners were tested. Yet even in the excesses of the West, Muslims were not without complicity; we may cite an ominous instance.

In most of the independent Muslim lands between the wars, the Germans were looked on as special friends, since they were the opponents of the imperial powers; and this special attachment continued at least as strong after the advent of Nazism, which seemed to offer a more effective alternative power. It became easy, then, for Muslims to go further: in Turkey, in the Arab lands, in the Iranian lands, even in the Muslim lands of the Soviet Union and in India, numerous and sometimes influential Muslims were found who could sympathize with or give actual support to Nazi Germany and its immoralism, rejecting such degree of 'democratic' idealism as was, despite everything, embodied in the British, French, and Russian cause. Some argued that the Nazi type of totalitarian nationalist state was the answer to Muslim needs both for an effective nationalism and in all the dilemmas of Modern society. In some cases, at least, admiration for Nazis was explicitly joined to anti-Jewish fanaticism. Though, especially in the Soviet Union, most Muslims did not respond, yet there was a moment when it could appear that the Nazi bid for general Muslim support would have a good chance of success if only German arms could advance far enough into the Muslim areas to make such support realistic.

The support for Nazism among Muslims was for the most part, indeed, not a support for the full range of Nazi doctrine and practice, even when it included a certain degree of support for Nazi racism. Yet it was not purely a political accident. Many Muslims who were not friendly to the Western imperial powers did refuse support to Nazism because they rejected what it stood for. Decisions such as that for or against the Nazis, indeed, could be among the most important which socially active Muslims could make. For increasingly, in the interdependent world society, a genuinely world-wide pattern of public opinion was growing. Especially in the decades following the War of 1939, this common world public opinion has come to be formed almost as much in the poorly technicalized non-Western areas as in the older centres of the West.

As the United Nations has ceased to be simply a vehicle of Western policy, it has become the most important forum for this growing world public opinion; and this not only in political questions but in a more general way. For a very broad field of human concerns has been at least vaguely being articulated, most notably in UNESCO, where a certain degree of common cultural outlook and even of social ethic is being expressed across all the cultural and political divisions of mankind. On this level (not only in UNESCO but in the many other channels of international activity), alignments associated with such movements as communism, fascism, or liberal capitalism have been more significant, in most disputes, than differences among Christianity, Islam, and Hinduism; and agreements on human aims among representatives of the communist and the capitalist blocs have been more immediately noteworthy, when achieved, than the mutual understandings worked out from time to time between representatives of the several pre-Modern traditions. Simultaneously with winning political independence, Muslims have found themselves enmeshed in all the international moral issues that have sprung from the technicalistic world order. Even on an immediately practical level, they can no longer honestly look at the moral problems of the technicalized West as alien to themselves; the problems and temptations of the West now are their problems and temptations too.

The new Muslim political responsibility has coincided with a growing mood of chastened optimism concerning the fundamental Modern problems in all the world. In discussing the background of Gândhî's ideals, we have noticed how the idealistic ferment of the first decades of the twentieth century inspired hopes that a new freer, truer life was about to open up for all. In the 1920s, 'democracy' became a standard everywhere to which even the most privilege-minded had to give at least grudging honour; governments were recast better to reflect the popular will and needs; and in the most advanced circles highly experimental movements toward emancipation and self-expression blossomed, their exponents regarding the 'Victorian' nineteenth century as having offered at most only a piecemeal beginning toward the anticipated progress. To some degree, many Muslim intellectuals shared in this mood, and not only those Muslims who were attracted to Gândhî. But in the 1930s with the Great Depression and in the 1940s with the Second War and its moral monstrosities, the optimism of the twenties was damped down. Even while, at the end of the war, various Muslim peoples were gaining their independence, disastrous events like the Palestine war and the partition of India were forcing Muslims also, like Westerners, to take a cautious view of what progress might be possible, at least without destructive upheaval. There were many to despair both of Modernity and of Islam.

Only gradually has confidence in an immediately practical future been reviving. By the mid-sixties the outlook seemed less bleak. The hopes of the twenties are being taken up again all over the world, even within the most rigidly established of churches and parties, and under the cautious patronage of many governments, new and even old. At the moment one may see a more responsible yet opening idealism breaking through everywhere; and in this atmosphere of cautious optimism Muslims too have their share.

Modern problems across the development gap

The form which Modern problems have taken has varied drastically from Muslim land to Muslim land. Indeed, to some extent Islamdom, as already in the eighteenth century, has been a microcosm of the Modern world. The different cultural evolutions already foreshadowed in the eighteenth century have carried the several Muslim peoples to highly contrasting points. The Bulghâr Tatars of the Volga seem to have merged socially and culturally into the industrialized Russian life, retaining little more than a difference of language and historical memories. At the other extreme, relatively uninvolved in technicalistic society, the Muslims of the Niger and Chad Sudan find themselves among the peoples least agitated by demands for international contacts and technicalized facilities. To the irritation of some of their non-Muslim southern neighbours, they form a bulwark of agrarianistic social and political expectations as well as of the Sharî'ah law. Other Muslim lands stand somewhere between, varying according to their specific experiences in the nineteenth century and the responses thereto of Modernizers in the twentieth century: diverse even in their visions of the Islamicate heritage, as in the Western powers whose culture their leaders have assimilated. Nevertheless, one can state in very general terms the deeper problems which each of these societies must face in some measure, and which are increasingly acute for most of them; and we will find that the most basic of these are problems that not only all Muslim societies, but all Modern societies of whatever background, must face.

Central to Modernity has been the development of large-scale technical specialization and of a consequent world interdependence on the mass level. It is from this central phenomenon that derive the specifically Modern problems, the temptations and opportunities, that face any people in the Modern world. We may summarize these problems somewhat arbitrarily under five headings: Two sorts of problem flow directly from the very nature of technicalization:

(1) It produces disruption of cultural traditions, which means at best, even in the West, the uprooting of individuals and the atomizing of society. For non-Western lands, such things are complicated further by the inconsistencies between the requirements of the Modern environment and a background of family life rooted in a culture quite alien thereto.
(2) It produces pressure on natural resources, which means at best human crowding and the loss of much that has been prized in the natural landscape; for the non-Western lands, it means poverty and even mass famine.

Then these problems in the cultural and natural spheres lead to a range of needs which themselves turn out to produce further problems; needs which again can be indicated under two heads:

(3) We find a need for social planning, at best to maintain the growth of the economy and avoid chaos; but in the non-Western lands, to escape the new mass poverty and achieve even a minimum of dignity for their people vis-à-vis the outside world. But comprehensive social planning, especially when it is desperately urgent, implies the possibility of arbitrary human manipulation on an unprecedented scale.

(4) We find a need for lettered mass culture; but this leads at best to such seeming contradictions as trying, at the same time, to make education accessible to all, and to educate for the creativity which technicalism also requires. In non-Western lands, any education for creativity seems almost ruled out by overwhelming day-to-day pressures, which can yet be solved only with creativity.

(5) Finally, deeper than any of these problems, since any ultimately true solution to the other problems requires some resolution of it: we confront a radical unsettling of moral allegiances, and the need to find adequate human vision to give people a new sense of what life can mean to them. Even at best, in the West, the old heritages seem to offer less and less of the sort of vision now required; a non-Western heritage such as the Islamicate may seem not merely irrelevant but drastically at odds with all the possibility of creative moral growth.

All these sets of problems have consequences for what role is required of the pre-Modern heritages, and notably that of Islamdom, if they are to play a significant role at all. In particular, all carry moral implications which the individual conscience must face.

Most immediately, all Modern societies must face a dislocation in people's relation to continuing social patterns: a *disruption of cultural traditions*. All patterns of life become subject to change without notice, as technical improvement becomes an overriding norm; and a substantial proportion of patterns are in fact shifted in every generation, often indeed again and again within an individual's span of maturity. Not only can one generation not pass on to the next generation adequate rules for handling everyday situations; each generation must be constantly revising its own expectations. Cultural traditions must evolve at a forced pace—with opportunity only for rapid dialogue among their carriers before the most extensive adjustments must be made. Such exchange and dialogue are facilitated by new technical methods, but even so, established points of reference tend to become irrelevant long before new points of departure, new inventions, new techniques new discoveries have been tested and their incidental by-products or side-effects in the whole cultural pattern can have been more than guessed at. People tend to have to plan their personal life patterns in partial blindness, relying less and less on ancestral or even personal experience to know what will be possible in the near future; they must be ready to shift pace unexpectedly, in conditions where they can hope for little but to follow the current pattern set for the crowds, impromptu or by industrial planners. At the very moment when the individual conscience is called on increasingly often to make increasingly far-reaching decisions, that conscience finds itself lacking the accustomed guidance from the past.

In the West, this disruption of traditions can be relatively easily absorbed. At the least, the new features of technicalized life have developed within the older traditions of the region. There has been a direct continuity from the ox-cart to the horse-drawn wagon to the rapid stagecoach to the railroad to the automobile to the airplane; each shift was relatively moderate, and the tradition was never broken. Similarly, from the Scholastics to Descartes to Hume to Kant to Hegel to Hüsserl to the Existentialists, the philosophical dialogue has been continuous. By and large, the old books continue to be read, and some of the same terms continue to be used, even if in transformed contexts. It has seemed feasible to integrate Modern technicalistic elements with the various elements of the older heritage. At the very least, the specialists are working, each in his own specialty, within the full flow of their own special traditions, and the dialogue among themselves is direct and continuous. In other lands, the specialists are too often attempting to keep up with a tradition which they do not fully share, in which they are excluded by a relative backwardness from up-to-date and creative participation in the ongoing dialogue.

Yet even in the West, with the development of specialism to the point where even a 'universal' genius can no longer control directly all the conditions of what he undertakes, the socially concerned are full of complaints about the fragmentation of life into mutually ignorant circles, the members of none of which are capable of seeing the total social picture; and about personal loss of roots and alienation in the mass.

In Islamdom, the disruption of traditions is more problematic. Where the transition has been directly from the ox-cart to the automobile (bus or truck) or even to the airplane, a much more severe break in tradition has occurred. To be sure, human culture is wondrously resilient. The folkways of Persian buses have rapidly developed their own roots. When the bus breaks down between scheduled stops, the passengers know just how to make themselves at home along the road, making good use of the opportune break in the discomfort of a cramped ride. If the bus driver is more skilled and has his own vehicle in good repair, no one is surprised if he stops along the way to help other drivers in distress; nor do they begrudge it if he collects an extra fare when passengers remount after a stop when all visit a local shrine. Nonetheless, the transformation in relations between village and urban centre that results from bus travel is not to be absorbed by adapting all the other relevant Western social patterns in the way that Western bus travel has been adapted. And even the day-to-day resources to meet the challenge are fewer: they can less afford the battery of service clubs, parish churches, neighbourhood settlements, political parties, social workers, legal aid bureaus and the like, which in much of the West serve to guide even the least fortunate citizens through the maze of Modernity.

When Sartre's existentialism is expounded in an Arabic newspaper, it has been superimposed much more directly on Aristotle than it was in France; and no one expects many Arab philosophers to be in a position to make a major contribution to the rapidly evolving philosophical tradition which the Arabs yet do share in now. Even in fields relatively easy to master with little traditional background and little stimulus and co-operation from the environment, such as mathematics or the exact sciences, most Muslim scholars are too preoccupied with keeping up, to be at the forefront of developments. A chemist in Cairo who has had to study at first from textbooks translated from the French or English is already behind to the extent that translations come necessarily from last year's or even last decade's publications; and his most important scientific task, if he is not employed in the desperately urgent task of building new industries, may not be fresh research but keeping up with and translating the latest that is going on in the West. Thus the same basic problem of disruption in traditions, common to all Modern societies, takes a different and more acute form on the wrong side of the development gap.

The same holds for the second specifically Modern problem. We face unprecedented dislocation not only in people's relation to continuing social patterns, but in the relation of social processes to nature: a dislocation which is expressed in *pressure on natural resources*. This is the direct result of uncontrolled technicalization, in that possible forms of technical exploitation multiply indefinitely while the physical resources of the planet do not. The rapid rate at which we are using up irreplaceable mineral and fossil resources, especially in the West but everywhere else too in some cases, is notorious. Even ground water is receding in some well-watered but industralized Western lands. But the most obviously limited and indispensable resource is space, that is, the surface, especially the land surface, of our globe. In many places there seem already to be too many people for the land area that is to support them.

This pressure on the land takes two forms. Most obviously, the land is used for producing most of our food; a large expanse of arable land is needed to support a given number of people, and if the people multiply faster than the arable land increases, a crisis must occur sometime. But this pressure can be relieved: people can give up eating flesh, especially wasteful of land, and turn to such things as soybeans, which will provide protein nourishment quite as well; or even to concentrated chemical production of vegetation or to the vast resources of the sea. But a second form of pressure on the land is more intractable. Sheer space is needed for the leisure and privacy of human beings: if all people were to make as full use of the possibilities offered by technicalization as some now do in American suburbs, our cities would require, even for home living space, many times the space they now do, though already they are devouring the countryside. But people also need space to get away in: wilderness. And other creatures too, with which we share this planet, have a right to space unhampered by humans: space is needed for chimpanzees, zebras, and gazelles.

It is pressures of the second sort, the destruction of wilderness (like the immediately more alarming tendency of technicalistic life to poison the land and the atmosphere with waste products and even with intentional poisons), which are most prominent in Western lands. Elsewhere, it is the first, more elementary sort of pressure that threatens most: the notorious 'population explosion' means pressure of food production, which the local technical plant has not enough investment capital to increase rapidly enough; it means an increasingly unmanageable problem of mass poverty, and increasingly frequent threats of famine if anything goes wrong. But on both sides of the development gap, the root problem is the same and, indeed, both forms of the problem are present in different proportions. On both sides, the new pressures threaten to undermine any inherited image of the human relation to the natural world which might have offered a basis for dealing with them, unless it can make effective sense of them.

In the West, the most prominent vehicles for the disruption of traditions and the pressure on resources are the growth and evolution of technicalized industry and its products, and the development of social homogeneity and industrial and political centralization in national states. So also in Islamdom, the vehicles of dislocation are industrialization and nationalism. But, for the problems which these pose either in the West or in Islamdom, the only solution seems to be more of the same—more and ever more industrial technicalization, more and ever more national centralization seem to be needed as the earlier doses thereof take effect. Even apart from the inherent tendency of technicalization to proliferate, the tensions that arise between technicalized patterns and both social and natural resources call urgently for resolution through further technicalization—thus a problem of over-population calls for yet further use of medical and industrial techniques. One does not face the problem simply, but rather compounded by the effects of the problem itself.

We may push the dilemma yet further. Any attempt at solving the primary problems that technicalization gives rise to, on either side of the development gap, produces a range of what might be called secondary problems, almost equally far-reaching in effect. In the political sphere, we discover an increasingly pressing *need for social planning;* the interdependence produced by technicalization imposes co-ordination and integrated organization on whole societies. But in what form and under what auspices is the social planning to be? The United States makes use of a multiplicity of autonomous and theoretically voluntary bodies—ranging from single great 'private' corporations to industrial or educational or commercial associations and councils—and, at the top, a minimum of government regulative authority. But this pattern presents problems of its own: sometimes the price of liberty seems to be social irresponsibility, and American politics commonly centre on the control of social planning. In any case, the pattern could not be imitated overnight in other lands. The communist countries have been at the opposite pole, depending on intense centralization, but control of social planning is at least equally problematic there, where many have been insisting that most economic and perhaps even social difficulties that have arisen have resulted from the overcentralizing of social planning, which has shown even stronger tendencies to arbitrary manipulation of human beings than in the Occident. The fundamental demand for justice requires everywhere social planning, but even at best the planning threatens to undermine in turn that personal liberty which is the chief boon justice can bring to anyone.

On the low-investment side of the development gap, social planning is at least as pressing a need as in the high-investment lands, and poses as many dangers. But again the need for it takes a different form, and it poses dangers of its own. It is not called for so much to deal with the anarchy which, without it, would in the West soon bring to a standstill technicalistic progression toward ever more wealth; but rather to deal with the drastic poverty which results from the by-products of technicalism. It is called for to deal with absolute poverty—the sheer want of enough food when fixed land resources cannot feed a growing population; it is called for increasingly even more to deal with relative, or functional, poverty—the want of facilities which, once they become common in some areas or on some levels of society, become increasingly necessities for others as well.

As we have noted, even where population pressure is relatively light, the new poverty sets up demands for sudden forced technicalistic development which can be met only through a high degree of social planning. And social planning in such a setting—whether it be envisaged in a neo-Shar'î mould, or in the form of 'directed democracy', or of communism—presents ramifying problems touching on all spheres; even spheres of life which in the West might seem sufficiently settled not to be touched by any planners. It becomes an even more far-reaching question than in the West: Who shall control the planners? Not only individual liberty at the moment but the whole course of future social evolution seems at the mercy of whoever can hold on to power long enough. Yet at the same time, the need for some sort of planning is so urgent that to press such more remote considerations may seem a luxury that society cannot afford.

Corresponding to the need for social planning in the political sphere arises, in the sphere of society at large, a *need for rapid mass culture on a lettered level*. As technicalization proceeds, with its proliferating demands for specialists (in whom at least literacy is desirable even when they are only the *ad hoc* unskilled 'specialists' at one spot on an assembly line) and its presupposition of a constantly expanding mass market, the masses are integrated into citied, lettered society. Gradually what was the 'folk' level of agrarianistic culture disappears as such, and tends to merge with elements of what had been the élite learnèd culture into what may now be called 'popular' culture. But this process can lead to a mass culture lacking in such harmony and personal fulfillment as the old folk culture did bring, and yet absurdly inadequate to the creativity which technicalism at its best can make possible. The uprooting of the masses makes for a certain decay of old cultural patterns, in any case. Their rapid increase in numbers, then, makes it hard for new patterns to be introduced systematically to replace the old ways except so far as a pattern is spontaneous and reflects the disorganized conditions themselves. But in the very act of making those conditions livable, it often helps to confirm and perpetuate them. Slum life, whether in inner Chicago or in the makeshift shanty suburbs of Algiers, tends to become ingrown and develop its own pressures upon its inmates which sometimes prevent even the more gifted of them from venturing to take advantage of such opportunities for self-improvement as may be offered. The ties to what little one has become so intense that one may not dare to break ranks and invest desperate, if unfulfilled, time in what seems futile social organization or technical training.

This situation accentuates the problem of developing productivity on sound lines or—on the wrong side of the development gap—of overcoming the new poverty as well as meeting the new expectations. The problems presented by the need for rapid lettered mass culture stand out most evidently, however, in the sphere of formal education and of the mass consumption of such popular culture as comes with at least a minimum of such education. The demand for education for everyone raises the well-known problem of how to uphold sophisticated intellectual standards and yet meet the needs of those not prepared to come up to such standards. In particular how can one avoid the temptation to provide merely for a lowest common denominator?—that is, to produce education or cultural works that would indeed appeal to all, at some level, but would not meet the best possibilities of even the least intelligent individuals, insofar as every individual, in his own area of greatest sensitivity, rises above the common minimum.

As we know, even in the West it is hard to know (if one is indeed trying to educate all, and to an increasingly high level) how to give an education which is at once 'democratic' and effective. It must be appropriate to an ever-changing technical and even cultural situation in which no rule stays fixed, it must keep the student open to a world-wide context, and withal it must remain accessible to ordinary people; yet at the same time as it fulfills these technicalistic requirements, it must retain serious intellectual and aesthetic standards, it must offer, if not a fixed common content, then anyway some common basis for serious intellectual communication, and it must not allow the cultural roots of the student—necessarily regional or even parochial—to wither. It must stress resources for meeting change and also provide common grounds of continuing dialogue, it must be both cosmopolitan and national.

But the West has at least prosperity and moreover a basic continuity of tradition between the old folk culture and the Modern 'popular' culture. Parents are at least literate. For the lands on the wrong side of the development gap, the same problem presented by Modernity to all takes on special colours. Thus in the West the writer or artist can always distinguish two audiences, two settings for his work: that provided by popular culture, where the drive to the lowest common denominator presses hard, can be continuously leavened by the existence of a more restricted audience, the serious élite. The artist may even speak in one setting in earning his bread and butter, while his best hours are reserved for the less certain but yet potentially important rewards of the other setting. In Cairo or Delhi, it is hard to get a book published if it will have a restricted audience. There tends to be a single, 'popular' audience; the most sophisticated novel is likely to be published serially in a mass-circulation newspaper; musical experimenting is likely to take place in the sound-track of popular films—and within the limits imposed by a very unsophisticated box-office.

The advantages of universal literacy, as against merely family or even bâzâr-level literacy, have been very notable only in technicalistic times. Universal literacy makes not merely for communication of thoughts by way of writing, but for immediate technical flexibility on the job and in the home: the literate can read signs for himself in the factory, which is faster than having them read aloud; and above all, he can be more readily retrained as jobs change, and trained to ever higher levels as work becomes more technical—for literacy is the key to all further education. The demand for literacy, then, is a function of the demand for general technicalization, and if universal literacy is attempted where the local technical context does not require it, it remains pointless. The ordinary peasant who has duly gone to school for years is likely to forget how to read within months of returning to normal life.

In the rest of education, the sort of schooling demanded is still more tied to technicalistic conditions for both its strengths and weaknesses. We have noted the stultifying effect of education in the Agrarian Age and the close relation of this effect to the purposes for which the education was undertaken: to ensure social stability, the individual must be narrowed in, and the student as much as any other. In technicalistic society there is less pressure against creativity, for with less isolation and a wider margin for survival there can be greater tolerance of risk, and with a rising level of investment there is more room for experiment; indeed, the need for flexibility in response to ever-new situations puts a premium on creativity. But there are contrary pressures which tend to mute the desired creativity and to have a stultifying effect of their own such as an agrarianistic society could more readily avoid.

One problem can be met by changing the very conception of education as acquisition of knowledge. As we know, when the rapid increase in essential knowledge makes it impossible to establish a minimum corpus that everyone should learn if he is to understand the environment he must deal with, then the student must learn not so much facts as how to find facts at need—and how to judge the authorities on whom he must depend. But a second problem is more resistant. The first noticeable spiritual casualty of the Great Transmutation was the ability of even the greatest men to see their work whole, in all its ramifications. As is repeatedly noticed and deplored, pressures arise for ever narrower specialization, requiring ever earlier concentration if mastery is to be acquired in the prime years, and ever more exclusive preoccupation later if a constantly developing field is to be kept up with. The very openness and creativity which everyone knows the Technical Age requires threaten to be stopped at the source by the specialization which is inseparable from it.

Such dilemmas in Modern education appear on both sides of the development gap, but on the Muslim side they are given a knotty twist by the new poverty, as well as by the presence of an overwhelming Western rival. When both physical and cultural survival seem to be at stake, it is hard to encourage education for creativity. In such fields as still seem amenable to an older Islamicate approach, something like the old methods of inculcation may seem not only easier and more congenial, but actually better calculated to produce what seems to be the required conformity. Even in 'Modern' fields, the individual pressure for success at examinations and the social pressure for quick production of specialists combine to inhibit an open education. Education for creativity may seem as useless to a forced-pace engineer as sheer literacy to an old-line peasant.

The need for vision, and the insufficiency of the heritages

Perhaps more far-reaching, at last, as a pervasive Modern problem than either the need for social planning or that for a lettered mass culture will be the *unsettling of moral allegiances* which Modern technicalism tends to bring. The pressure on natural resources and the disruption of cultural traditions lead not only to strains in the political and the social spheres but also to strains within the individual.

The strains are twofold. Negatively, as everyone has heard, we face a steady erosion of old norms and loyalties. In some lands even a sense of family solidarity has been undermined by the repeated contrasts between the generations and by the increasing sphere of personal life which is regulated or fulfilled, even in youth, outside the home. All kinds of traditional notions, including most especially those of religion, are constantly threatened by the penetration of experimental and cosmopolitan science and scholarship through the schools and the mass media of communication. The old ideas of the universe and the nation, of morality and propriety, may not be explicitly replaced, if they were the object of explicit loyalty; but they tend to be attenuated and made innocuous as the substantive details which had gone to make them up have to be dropped. But even when a family solidarity can be maintained and a religious outlook reinterpreted to be less vulnerable to facts, a positive new moral outlook is called for in addition. This demand may be explicit on the part of a ruling party in some lands, but it is anyway implicit in the whole structure of technicalistic society. This new moral outlook absorbs more and more of a person's attention and, indeed, time.

Ideally the Modern individual should be a paragon of 'democratic' virtues which were never called for before: he must not only adapt to the clock and to precision tooling and be ready to be retrained as his old skills are superseded; he must develop a whole psychology of egalitarian co-operativeness. He must be able to work as member of a 'team'. Even in marriage, a man is asked to renounce dominating over his wife (who may get an independent job, and can divorce him) and must instead work to make the marriage a 'success'; and he can less and less pre-ordain his children's careers, but must raise them to be ready for whatever an unknown future may demand of them, accepting the likelihood that they will inevitably regard him as old-fashioned and irrelevant once they are grown. On the job, he must adjust himself to committee work or joint projects where command and obedience and individual glory are replaced in principle by something like 'collective leadership, and an *ad hoc* company loyalty. To the educator and the physician and psychiatrist falls the duty of eliminating everything that may block his full and open responsiveness and prevent his becoming the intelligent and responsible citizen required; and he must be prepared to follow their technically expert guidance at every step, from the clinic for pre-natal care to the centre for maintaining an active old age. If the ideal has not been fully achieved in the West, it is adumbrated equally in such diverse lands as the United States and the Soviet Union, though under different names. In Islamdom many elements of this picture are already appearing.

But the new moral outlook presents us with pervasive problems of its own. It may make for human greatness or for the reverse. In itself, technicalization calls for a certain number of moral qualities in a population—openness to new ways, industriousness, a sense of precision, a certain level of public honesty and dependability; and at least at its creative centres, inventiveness and intellectual courage. In its origin, at least and perhaps for its perpetuation, it has called also for a general appreciativeness of diverse human potentialities, especially for knowledge, and for a certain level of humanness, of respect for the inviolability of the individual and his liberty, and even of egalitarian social consciousness. Yet at best the range of required qualities is not inclusive of all the qualities some humans have found of highest significance; and it seems possible sometimes to maintain or even develop an effective degree of technicalistic life, once the Technical Age has been launched with a minimum of the higher human qualities. The greatest moral significance of the Great Transmutation is probably not what it requires but what it merely makes possible: that by clearing away old limitations it opens the way to a fuller unfolding of the diverse potentialities of the individual in all spheres of living, and not merely those spheres whose possibilities have been specially tapped by multiple specialization. But such an opportunity may or may not be fulfilled. And in fact precisely the technicalistic specialization and disruption of tradition threaten to frustrate this. It is readily possible to imagine technicalism leading to the inane pursuit of meaningless comfort portrayed in Huxley's *Brave New World*, with any one individual impotent to change the vastly complex social patterns in which he is reduced to helpless conformity along with four billion others all watching identical television sets round a world undifferentiatedly up-to-date in its technical efficiency.

We may suppose that the outcome can hinge on the quality of moral vision available to people. Thus it has been pointed out that the widespread problem of juvenile delinquency and of youthful rebelliousness in general, which troubles most Western lands, capitalist or communist, might be solved in two ways. It might be in the manner of *Brave New World*, by teams of teachers and social workers and psychiatrists and city planners who learned how to persuade each youth to identify with the established order and find his greatest pleasure in conforming to it; or it might be solved by inspiring enough youths with a vision of something great to do with their lives that they would set new and creative fashions among their peers. But greatness of vision is problematic. The structure of technicalistic society stresses identification with the national social body and encourages a viewpoint limited by specialist training, at the expense of either breadth of loyalty or the sort of trans-rational, non-utilitarian outlook which, as religion, was so formative of the great pre-Modern heritages. Yet the nations are incomplete units, incapable within their limited boundaries of providing fit horizons for youthful vision in an age when men are going to the moon; indeed, even the several pre-Modern heritages, such as the Islamicate, can seem parochial. Great vision now must be world-wide. Moreover, it is unclear how greatness of vision—unlike utilitarian practicality—can be rooted simply in that ever-changing pattern of technical expertise which goes to make up technical Modernity as such: our poets suggest that on that level life remains simply absurd. Vision must transcend mere technicalistic goals. The deepest problem of the Modern world is to find a vision at once challenging and genuine.

But whereas Westerners, in their relative ease, possess the intellectual and spiritual leisure to hope to confront such a problem, in Islamdom, by and large, there hardly seems time for this. If anything, the Islamicate heritage (so far as it might serve as resource to this end) is put more in doubt than the Occidental. The need to solve immediate problems, in any case, is so overwhelming that few of the more realistic take the trouble to think through, with any detachment, the broader moral questions of long-range purpose and ultimate vision. Such people may cling ardently to Islam as a spiritual foothold, yet they do not work through more than superficially what it can really mean to them; hence it remains a loyalistic slogan, or a façade for received Modern values, without showing the way to genuinely new solutions.

All the major problems of technicalistic Modernity, then, confront all the peoples together; but they take a thornier form on the low-investment side of the development gap. And they are at their thorniest in the sphere of norms and ideals—where the Islamicate heritage might be crucial. The most immediate problems of cultural dislocation merge with the seemingly most abstract problems of ultimate allegiance and vision. At the heart of the development gap is a contrast in a society's relation to cultural tradition. Modernity has necessarily created a breach with all the cultural traditions of the pre-Modern past. But as we have seen, in the West that breach with tradition is relatively mild: the West is relatively traditional in that there, all the major aspects of Modern society grow from traditions relatively continuous with an indefinite past. Generally speaking, the non-Western lands and especially the Muslim lands are mostly—on the level of historical action, that is, in the realm of technicalistic life where decisive decisions must be made—relatively non-traditional: the new, the Modern, has no older roots: it is purely modern. For them the breach in tradition, which is real enough in the West also, is harsh and drastic. To make a turn upon a common usage, it may be said that the heart of Modern world problems is that a *traditional* West, benefiting from the moderating effects of continuity, contrasts painfully to the rest of the world, which is untraditional where it matters most and, instead, starkly, unrelievedly *modern*.

Hence the differences in Modern problems as between West and elsewhere often loom larger than the similarities. The Muslim peoples in particular must build, as Modernity proceeds ever further, not from economic and social advantages based on yet earlier advantages, but rather from disadvantages based on yet earlier disadvantages. For Westerners, all Modern problems may be envisaged, on the basis of the Western experience, as secondary difficulties to be solved in time, or perhaps as exhilarating challenges. The drawbacks of the received Western social patterns may seem to be but the necessary costs of progress, eminently worth the trouble, and some Westerners of a sterner cast insist that it would be folly for any people to try to avoid or escape the difficulties which have arisen under the Western hegemony, on the grounds that they are inseparable from Modernity. Certain Western economists, devoted to the sovereign virtues of the market mechanism, tend to advise the peoples of the low-investment lands to suffer in patience and hope that eventually they will win through to Western affluence by a path essentially like that of the West itself: that is, in practice, to accept a complementary dependence upon the capital market of the Western bloc for an indefinite future. Nevertheless, the other peoples know that, in fact, their case is different from that of the West—though they may not have the technical scientific ability to prove it. They have often tended to grasp at theoretical straws, at any sort of theory which Westerners may have thrown up, to account for their difficulties and to justify the most desperate efforts to overcome them; for they hope that once they have achieved independence, they will be able to reach the Western level of prosperity without suffering further bad effects associated with Western patterns. Whatever their theoretical inadequacies, they are right, up to a point, to look for a pattern different from that offered by the Occident.

On a more fundamental level, however, much of this more extreme thinking is not merely naïve but as crucially unrealistic as that of the Western market mechanists. Too often it overlooks the degree to which high-investment lands and low-investment lands are not only inseparably part of the same historical complex but share fundamentally the same Modern problems, though in different forms. For, finally, the problems are not merely alike; they can probably not be fully solved in one place till they are solved everywhere else too. Hence it cannot be said that even the special problems facing Islamdom are the Muslims' concern alone. For one of the greatest of Modern problems which all share is the development gap itself. It is the very existence of the development gap which puts the lands on the unfavourable side of it into such stress, whether they are ruled from the West or not. But for Western lands, also, the development gap looms large as a problem—and tends to be the most decisive single fact in the political life of several major states. Until Algeria won independence, the gap was an internal problem for France and toppled the governments that could not deal with it; but elsewhere also, most notably in the United States, military commitments and foreign policy at large (which is largely a function of the development gap) tend to be decisive not only in shaping the national budget but more subtly in the psychological life of the nation, from the ramifying institution of military conscription down to the popular legendry of anti-communism. The Great Transmutation has posed a common set of problems to the whole world and they will probably be truly solved only in common, even while each people must face them as best it can for itself within the conditions set by its own situation.

We can imagine that eventually the development gap will be closed not by an old-style direct industrialization of those lands at present suffering from low levels of investment, but by a more comprehensive process which is already reshaping the whole technicalistic economy everywhere. Even for the near future, many inquirers foresee the day when automation and computer use, along with nuclear or solar energy and the use of 'plastic' chemical compounds for basic industrial functions, may make industrialization in a new area relatively inexpensive, so that achievement of an elementary level of technicalistic prosperity can come almost suddenly, once sufficient education has been introduced. We can go further: as ever fewer man-hours are required for automated factory production, the number of persons required to devote much attention to that may well be reduced to a fraction of the population; and just as agriculture has become but one economic activity among many (so that one can speak of a 'diversified' basic economy even where agriculture plays little part), so manufacturing may likewise be reduced in status. To the extent that activities entering into a process of economic exchange continue to structure society at all, we may find that the demand for economic activity will be so apportioned that agriculture or manufacturing will loom no more crucial to an area's having a strong basic economy than will tourism or education (increasingly life-long), or the entertainment arts or sports, or even religion. Though technicalization in the wider sense will be fundamental everywhere, industrialization as such may prove a transient affair in some countries. Though such a day seems especially remote in the low-investment lands, yet it is precisely in the more active sectors of even those populations that social concerns geared to such an ultimate situation will first appear. Certainly, adequate human vision must prove relevant to some such future anywhere.

The heritages in Modernity

Iqbâl rather hoped that the Muslims could wait for the West to destroy itself and then take the West's place in world leadership, thus fulfilling the mission which already the Qur'ân had indicated to them. Such a notion has lost any plausibility since 1945. If the West destroys itself, either physically or morally, it will hardly perish alone. But the hope seems equally implausible that the pre-Modern antecedents of modern populations—the difference between Occident and Islamdom—may be disregarded, essentially, in plotting our future course. At the very least, the distinction between heritages Western and non-Western is an element in the contrast between the forms world problems take on the two sides of the development gap. But so far as it is the quality of human vision that is crucial to how we solve all our world problems, the heritages may make all the difference. But what sorts of role can they actually play?

Superficially, a cultural tradition can appear, to Modern eyes, as a bloc of patterns given from the past, irrelevant to rational calculations except as it happens to include functionally useful procedures or (more commonly) to get in the way of adopting better procedures. Perhaps such traditions can be reduced to the status of museum pieces and local colour for attracting tourists; or to eclectic sources of 'inspiration' for professional designers. Where the official doctrine is that all pre-Modern culture was class-bound, this is almost official policy. But everywhere else, also, the values to be found within technicalized society, changing from generation to generation, can seem to be self-sufficient within each generation. Even in universities or art museums, the achievements of the remoter past can seem to have only antiquarian interest except so far as they give rise to pernicious nationalisms or religious communalisms. If this assessment is valid, then however desirable it might be for the heritages to help provide vision, the hope is futile.

But when we recognize that in fact a cultural tradition is not essentially a set pattern of behaviour but rather a living dialogue grounded in common reference to particular creative events, such an assessment becomes more dubious. Certainly we cannot escape or set aside tradition as such: all cultural action takes place within a setting of tradition, even when in sharpest revolt against particular creative events of the past. As we have seen, tradition is not the contrary of progress but the vehicle of it, and one of the problems of Muslims is that on the level of historical action their ties with relevant traditions are so tenuous. It is out of the hopes and dreams carried in a tradition that the exceptional individual can forge new creative possibilities at those interstitial points in historical action when currently established ways no longer suffice and a new vision has its chance. At the very least, some sort of tradition will play this moral role—even if only traditions of very recent origin, rooted (for all practical purposes) only within strictly Modern times, such as the Marxist.

However, on the deepest level it is the traditions forming the great pre-Modern heritages which even now continue to provide, among most thoughtful Modern persons, the widest resources for new vision. It cannot even be ruled out, yet, that in fact technicalistic culture as such, with its atomizing specialism, might be incapable of providing (out of a strictly technicalistic perspective) the integral visions of what life can mean that have been offered in earlier traditions. We do need experiment in art and science and philosophy and ethics and education and law and religion. But also, by our very human nature, which (as they say) demands definition through irreversible particular choices, we seem to need historical commitment in all these fields: the commitment to a given tradition and its norms which allows a deep exploration of its implications; and such a commitment is not to generalizations discoverable anew for each generation, but to the irreplaceable, biographical engagements in which we find ourselves almost involuntarily as members of particular groups lasting beyond our own lifetimes. The historical, traditional mode of human involvement cannot be reduced to psychological or social regularities, in which one commitment can be replaced by an equivalent at will. But to such irreducible commitments, technicalism has been uncongenial. It is possible, then, that if our moral vision is in fact to transcend technicalistic goals, we cannot dispense with the challenges to which the older traditions of vision still give rise. At any rate, in the immediate practical situation and perhaps even more ultimately than there, the quality of our lives (at least outside of the Marxist traditions) seems to be bound up with the quality of our pre-Modern traditional heritages— and that means not so much with what they have amounted to in the past as with the quality of the current cultural dialogue which expresses them in our time.

This applies especially, of course, in the field of our ultimate sense of orientation in the cosmos, where creative vision can be most far-reaching:

the traditional realm of religion. The individual's spiritual orientation to life as a whole need not be formed by an explicitly religious tradition; but more often than not it has been so formed, whether directly or through such intermediaries as a national literary tradition, through which even assured atheists may innocently participate in the religious dialogue. The spiritual core of the religious tradition can be crucial in forming expectations and ideals precisely where the larger purposes of social decision come to be put in question and where a strictly technical answer, based on a specialist's expertise, will not suffice. Whether, indeed, religion will continue to play such a role cannot be foretold; but it is such a role that can give any religious tradition historic meaning in Modern times, if it is to have any.

As in other sorts of tradition, of course, it is not so much the past moments of the tradition as the present interaction among its heirs that matters here. And as in other sorts of tradition, a given religious tradition is no longer so nearly autonomous as in agrarianistic times. Increasingly, like all other aspects of culture—literary, artistic, scientific, philosophical—a religious tradition forms only a special milieu within a world-wide network of religious culture, in which the boundaries between religious allegiances are no longer decisive and religious ideas that develop in one milieu rapidly find their way into the dialogue of another milieu.

In the West, despite the exclusivity of the Christian and Jewish traditions as prophetic monotheisms, ordinary persons, at least in their religious conceptions, are increasingly becoming heirs to all the major religious traditions. On the scholarly level, the nineteenth century saw a significant wave of Sanskritic influence in the West; more recently other traditions have been felt: it is not uncommon for writers to have recourse to classical Chinese terms like *Tao* or *Yin* and *Yang* to express their thoughts, even though the original concept may not be properly grasped. Perhaps more important than this level of formal literature is the level of sectarian cult: in the big cities of the West have proliferated new religious bodies founded in one degree or another on religious notions stemming from other societies, and notably from India. The ease with which such bodies gain followers illustrates a third level on which alien religious notions have come to prevail: in the popular expectations of what religion may amount to, among the vast public not seriously committed to a Christian or Jewish doctrine. As late as the mid-nineteenth century, if a woman began to utter phrases, without conscious control, which seemed more appropriate to given individuals among her ancestors, it was debated whether this was evidence for the old Occidental notion of possession by spirits, i.e., ghosts. In the mid-twentieth century, such a phenomenon gave rise in the American newspapers to a debate not about possession by spirits but about the notion (formerly essentially alien to the Occident) of reincarnation; for meanwhile reincarnation had become a more living religious issue than possession by spirits.

Among peoples of non-Western heritage such a process has not gone so far yet. But there are many indications among Muslims that it is beginning to take place. It has been shown that modern Muslim usage of the word *islâm* has been deeply coloured by the necessarily external approach to their faith which outsiders—notably Westerners—have used, making the word refer not to an act of submission to God nor even to an ideal religious system but to the observable historical Islamicate society.[1] That is, the sheer fact of confrontation with alternative religious traditions has apparently brought Muslims to define themselves and their faith in outward terms which outsiders can recognize. But not merely the form in which they conceive their faith but also the substance of their expectations has been influenced from the wider world. Serious Muslim writers are full of reflections of Christian conceptions, not least when their intention is polemic against Christianity, and even Sanskritic references occur. One finds a modern Ṣûfî who has read and appreciated Western mystical writings, including current minor items. Even on the level of popular preconceptions, at least in that growing section of the population where there is no serious commitment to Islamic doctrine, one can find suggestions of alien notions. A widely read Egyptian popular journal, not unwilling to make light of religion, has found it appropriate to show cartoons of figures in a heavenly afterlife sitting on clouds and wearing disk halos—a notion of the afterlife taken from the Christian imagination rather than from the Muslim, but which is clearly intended to hit at Muslims also. Conceptions of many provenances have always mingled among Muslims, of course; but now there is a more conscious confrontation with other traditions than perhaps at any time since the life of Muḥammad.

As the religious traditions lose their assured independence, the meaning of such things as ummah and Sharî'ah must be reassessed. On the level of basic spiritual insight, an interpretation of community and law will be increasingly inadequate to actual experience until it can confront creatively the presence of contrasting spiritual traditions of equal status in a single world-wide society. This must take place on at least two planes: the community as such must overcome its exclusivity without sacrificing its formative discipline, and the heritage it carries must be in dialogue with contemporary culture common to all communities, yet without sacrificing its integrity.

The basis of community allegiance needs to be reformulated in a society where the religious community is but one of several, none serving as foundation for their common culture. There are probably many possibilities; I shall suggest one: in such a world, religious communities may play a crucial role, that of communities intermediate between the individual and the global

[1] Wilfred C. Smith, 'The Historical Development in Islam of the Concept of Islam as an Historical Development', in School of Oriental and African Studies, *Historical Writings on the Peoples of Asia*, 1958, brings out the degree to which this latter external usage originates in the works either of non-Muslims or of those responding to non-Muslim criticism. But it might be helpful to complement a study of such terms as *islâm* and *îmân* with a study of the usage of older terms for the historical reality, such as *ummah*.

mass of four billions, all potentially watching the same television programmes and buying the same products. In such a mass, a single voice can seem almost meaningless; at best, the various organs of society, whether governed by electoral vote or by market selection, can hardly be expected to reflect more than a dead-level lowest common denominator. Yet increasingly the individual's fate depends on the course of society at large. In a society of technicalistic specialization, the concerns of an individual may be expected to affect the course of society at large through his functional specialization; through his labour union or his business firm or his professional association, he can initiate moves relevant to the interests or competence of that specialty. But it seems hard to express more general concern for historic decisions through such channels. An intermediate group in which people share common basic expectations and may be seized with a common creative vision can form a fuller channel for integral personal expression: a party, a religious sect, even a small nation with a strong common heritage. Such a group can be small enough so that each individual may, if he has a sufficiently compelling vision, play a role in forming its attitudes and policies; yet large enough so that the community, in turn, may share in shaping the course of mankind as a whole (I have in mind, for instance, the tiny Quaker society, from whose work camps or co-operative houses or educational programmes significant, if modest, historic consequences have flowed). Islamic groups may have an irreplaceable calling in such a role.

But for such an intermediate community to play a genuinely creative role in the technicalistic world, it must be capable of some sort of interplay with those who do not accept the basis of its own discipline. This necessity brings into a new focus the standing tension between universalism and communalism. Every community formed in a common tradition (and hence every effective community of any sort) must face this tension in some degree, for openness in the dialogue, which keeps a tradition alive, is inseparable from that commitment to central points of departure which keeps a tradition in being at all. The tension has strongly characterized all the monotheistic communities; it has formed an especially crucial problem for the Muslim conscience almost from the beginning, when Muḥammad saw that what humans needed was to escape loyalism to this or that community and come to the God of Abraham who was beyond all communities—yet at the same time found that those who responded to his summons to this needed themselves to be guided and disciplined by a strong community loyalty, if their moral life were to be brought to fruition. In the tension between the universal responsiveness of the Ṣûfîs and the loyalistic discipline of the Sharîʿah-minded of all ages, in such crises as those of Akbar's India, and of Iqbâl's, Muslims have found that they cannot neglect with impunity the responsible discipline embodied historically in the Sharîʿah law, with its demands for communal conformity and exclusivity.

Those Muslims of the past who acknowledged this responsibility and yet responded to the human demand for a more universalistic outlook commonly cast their wider response into esoteric form, thus leaving the exoteric communalism untouched—but deprived of much of its power. But we have noted that during the nineteenth century most Muslims came to reject the conventional esoteric approaches to the problem, believing that the Muslim heritage could not be effectively defended without a more rigorous common discipline than esotericism encouraged; nor is esotericism congenial to the temper of a technicalistic world in which every idea and every standpoint is subject to repeated public investigation without respect for authority. A more dynamic way must be found for resolving the tension between universalism and communalism if Islamic communities—or, indeed, any other such intermediate communities—are to play the creative role in the world which they might.

The required reformulation of the basis for community discipline will be more feasible if, at the same time, the community's heritage is brought into living interaction with world-wide cultural currents. It has always been true, among human beings, that a person cannot ultimately respect himself unless he can respect others; and that a person cannot respect others without coming to terms somehow with what is most precious to them. The maxim has applied as truly to groups as to individuals. It is especially relevant, however, in the common world society produced by Modern technicalization, where the basic problems posed to any section of mankind are essentially common to all mankind together and are unlikely to be solved by any peoples in isolation. We can no longer dismiss adherents of a rival outlook as being either knaves or fools. We must learn to respect each his own tradition by way of learning respect for other traditions.

What may be called for is already partly in the making: a grand dialogue among the heritages. There is little point in trying to distill abstractions from the several pre-Modern heritages, which then all Moderns can learn to share; such abstractions tend to be vacuous, needing no support from a tradition anyway. (If they did, then probably all the great abstract values are to be found already, in some form, within each of the great cultural heritages.) Nor do most who have considered the problem hope for a syncretistic or eclectic reduction of the several heritages to mere sources of traditional legitimation for arbitrary new schemes of thought. But without abandoning the more intimate dialogue within itself, moving from its own creative points of departure, each tradition can enlarge the range of its dialogue, in some less intensive degree, to include dialogue with representatives of other traditions: interchange of viewpoints and mutual response from what are yet recognized as contrasting and even mutually exclusive positions, however mutually respected. It was a pregnant gesture of the papal Catholics in their second Vatican council, to invite representatives of other traditions in to watch them struggling with their own internal dialogue; and then to pay attention to their comments. If such dialogue be genuine, it must have the virtue that it will be as effective in maintaining the vitality of the several traditions themselves as in relating the traditions to a wider human context, for the common questions which must be raised in the dialogue among dialogues are just those that must be raised frankly within each dialogue if the dialogue is to remain abreast of realities.

Islam in Modernity

We have seen that finding a moral vision that will make up for the undermining of parochial allegiances can be a key to the other major Modern world problems, all of which can be seen in part as matters of conscience: a key not only to the disruption of cultural traditions, where a new vision may provide guiding lines to a new sort of continuity, but even to the pressure on natural resources, where also an assertion of moral norms and hence practical priorities is required, whatever else may also be required; a key not only to the need for mass culture without repression of creativity, where an adequate vision may keep temporary expedients from being frozen into permanent dilemmas, but even to the need for social planning without arbitrary manipulation, where again a moral vision may effectively intervene if it is comprehensive and open enough. And we have seen that it is the sort of vision offered by the great pre-Modern religious heritages, with their challenges to an ultimate orientation, that may possibly offer bases for such vision in a technicalistic age. We cannot say that the religious heritages are in fact able to offer such vision: it may be that they are too drastically handicapped by the element of wishful thinking that has been so rooted in their whole history. But if they are to prove worthy of future devotion, they must do no less; offering high vision, if anything, is their calling. Otherwise, they must prove ineffective even as bases for intermediate communities, and even the most creative dialogue among them must prove at last futile.

We cannot discuss here the quality of Islam as a source of vision; but we can discuss in what ways such vision as it may indeed be able to offer may become effectively accessible to Modern human beings. Current vitality in religion is not likely to prove sufficient. Religion must be capable of providing the vision required.

It is possible that in the West there is more moral and intellectual leisure than elsewhere for experiments in creatively reformulating community discipline or reinterpreting community heritages. Something of the leadership in this direction for all mankind is likely to come from the West. But moral vision cannot be left to the West alone. Muslims must face their share of the tasks. There is much in their heritage itself that should help them find the relevance of that heritage to Modern mankind.

The Islamic heritage was built in a relatively cosmopolitan milieu and its traditionally world-wide outlook should make it possible for Muslims to come to terms with Modern cosmopolitanism, for (unlike so many more parochial religious traditions) they need not find ways to validate or transcend the sacrality of local and transient cultural forms. Moreover, the relative sophistication of pre-Modern Islam carried with it a tendency to look to the whole of a person and of his society—with relatively little distinction between sacral and natural spheres, between a person's soul and his bodily life, between religious norms and social norms generally. In a society not tied to agrarianistic routine, such an integral vision may still, as before, be difficult to maintain, but it alone may be adequate to give continuing meaning to the kaleidoscopic scene in which no aspect of life is safe from re-evaluation and reinterpretation. Muslims should find that their vision will be equally relevant in the most diverse possible circumstances, and even where the very notion of a spiritual sphere apart from the rest of life has been rejected as inconsistent with Modern experience.

But perhaps the greatest potential asset of Islam is the frank sense of history that from the beginning has had so large a place in its dialogue. For a willingness to admit seriously that the religious tradition was formed in time and has always had a historical dimension makes it possible to assimilate whatever new insights, into the reality of the heritage and of its creative point of origin, may come through either scholarly research or new spiritual experience. Al-Shâfi'î was carrying forward a tendency already latent in Muḥammad's own work when he insisted on understanding the Qur'ân quite concretely in its historical interaction with the life of Muḥammad and his community. He did this at the expense of historical accuracy, indeed, but this was not his intention; and though later Muslims went still further in substituting a stereotyped irenic image of the Islamic past for a candid study of the actuality, yet they never denied the principle that historical accuracy was the foundation of all religious knowledge.

Modernizing Muslims as yet have generally failed to take historical fact even so seriously as did the generations immediately before them, whose intellectual qualifications they despise.[2] This failure is surely the result of the intense pressures for self-identification and self-assurance under which Modern Muslims have laboured; they dare not admit anything that would detract from their glorious image of an earlier age, an image which has served to show that the Modern European dominance is not inherent (as Europeans used to think) in the nature of peoples; more profoundly, they dare not admit that the historical Islam which they have placed at the focus of their loyalties is any less perfect than the God with whom, in practice, they tend to identify it. But if there are Muslims whose confidence in God Himself is strong enough so that they dare risk everything, even community prestige

[2] H. A. R. Gibb, in the last chapter of his *Modern Trends in Islam* (University of Chicago Press, 1947) has documented in some detail the romantic disregard of historical fact which has characterized Modernizing Muslims in the twentieth century, and has also shown how disastrous this wilful ignorance has been for sound intellectual or spiritual growth in Islam.

or solidarity, for the sake of truth, then for such Muslims, facing historical realities and coming to terms with even the most painful of them is encouraged by the Islamic tradition itself.

More deep-rooted (and probably harder to overcome) than Modern apologetic are the inadequacies of the historical image which was built into Islamic dogma beginning at latest in Marwânî times. Sharî'ah-minded Muslims, like most Christians till recent times, have been tied down by a timid literalism, which paradoxically has frustrated their hopes for historical accuracy; for the literalism has been applied less insistently to the detailed evidence on which they have built than to the more general propositions which they have assumed were essential to their faith. Hence, despite the painstaking efforts of al-Shâfi'î, the Islamic tradition has failed as yet to recognize fully the many ways in which Muḥammad's life and the Qur'ân itself were geared to the mental horizons which bounded the Arabs of Muḥammad's time. It has correspondingly left obscure the ways in which the whole earlier Irano-Semitic prophetic tradition to which the Qur'ân bears explicit witness, did in fact contribute to building Islam: to illuminating the Qur'ân itself, that is, to showing what it could mean in various contexts; as well as to producing the Sharî'ah law—and even to forming the revered figure of Muḥammad himself as it appears in the ḥadîth reports.

What given words of the Qur'ân meant to Muḥammad and his generation must be understood not merely with close reference to linguistic usage and to local customs, as al-Shâfi'î understood them, but also with reference to the range of moral and spiritual possibilities historically open to the Arabs at the time, on which points al-Shâfi'î could not have sufficient perspective. But this new understanding must not be simply negative. It will not do (as some Muslims suggest), to suppose that whatever seems to have been conditioned by time and place and hence transitory is to be written off and only absolutely general eternal verities are to be abstracted out as giving the true message. Instances and principles alike are to be seen as presupposing a human response to events found to be revelatory; alike they must stand open to new insight growing out of wider human experience—if not out of further revelatory experience such as first produced them. And alike they must retain their full force in the Qur'ânic text. In practice, a particular instance or prescription may be more revelatory, may come to an individual with fuller force, than a general statement of principle by its side; then, it may be, the general statement must be understood or even transcended in the light of the particular prescription, rather than the reverse (and this might be true, even if the particular prescription were not taken literally at all).

When the Qur'ân prescribes chopping off the hands of a thief, such a prescription stands permanently as a judgment upon the human condition—both on the act of a thief and on the passions of those who resent or pity him; it may warn us in our most exalted and in our most sentimental moments alike. In the day of the 'democratic virtues', Modern Muslims must set it aside in practice. This can be justified spiritually so far as they think they have found a better way of responding to the same divine challenge than was open to the original community. Yet even so it must be set aside with trepidation: never with a smug assurance that we Moderns have a more advanced culture; still less with a legalistic (and historically false) assurance that the 'rule' is merely in abeyance (as some Muslims have it) and will still hold when social conditions are perfected, so that thieves have no longer any good reason for stealing. Either of these rationalizations eviscerates the demand posed by the Qur'ân. Moderns may well be taught to bear in mind that however polished and civilized we may seem to be, there is raw, mean passion at the threshold of our minds (as Hitler has shown us) and we are not ultimately so very different from even the seemingly crudest of past generations; we must stand continuously ready to reassess our practice in the light of the Qur'ânic judgment.

Just as the role of the Qur'ân in Muḥammad's generation must be seen in full historical perspective, so also the dependence of Islam on its Irano-Semitic heritage must be seen frankly and creatively: in particular, its dependence on the Jewish tradition. Surely one of the spiritual tragedies of both Christianity and Islam, and perhaps especially of Islam, has been the failure to maintain an active and vital confrontation with the Jews. Both Christianity and Islam may be seen as presenting specialized developments out from the Hebrew prophetic tradition. Oversimplifying, we may describe Christianity as a venture, inspired by the prophets' promise of God's repeated forgiveness, in transforming lives through the resources of redemptive, creative love. (How successful the venture has been is another question.) Similarly, we may describe Islam as a venture, inspired by the prophets' demand for uncompromising justice, in transforming the world's social order through the resources of prophetic vision. Each venture, each special development of the older Hebrew tradition, was of profound importance, but each was in some sense incomplete as compared with the full range of insight to be found in the Hebrew prophets.

Christians had at least the good fortune to retain the Hebrew Bible, though they rather badly misread it in the process (as many of them now acknowledge). But even more important, the presence of Jews has time and again afforded a reminder, among Christians of sensibility, that serious persons exist who revere the Hebrew prophets but understand them quite differently. And because the Jews could read the original Hebrew, they could not quite be ignored. For the rare Christian willing to stretch his mind so far, they have represented a testimony to values which Christians may have sacrified. In the earlier periods of Islam, the presence of Jews (at least in the form of converts) had very creative effects among Muslims. To an outsider it must seem a calamity that the Muslims rejected the Hebrew Bible (including its profoundly human narrative of the struggles of David and the prophets with their God) and failed to respect the study of Hebrew. From this point of view, it would be perhaps the greatest calamity of all that has come with Zionism, when (mistaking their calling, as some suppose) so many Jews chose (or had forced upon them) a path that, while it obscured the relevance of their presence in Christendom, has even more drastically distorted it among many Muslims.

Finally, Muslims must face frankly the ambivalent relations of the several forms of spirituality in the later, mature Islam to the Qur'ân itself and to each other; especially the spirituality of the Sharî'ah-minded and that of the Ṣûfîs. Such thinkers as Junayd and Ghazâlî and Ibn-al-'Arabî have opened these questions up, but Muslim theologians of the future must go a great deal further. They must find ways of understanding and renewing Muslims' experience of the Qur'ân as a vehicle of the inward life at the same time as they renew their response to the Qur'ân as a guide to social relations.

If the realities of the Islamic heritage can be frankly faced—its historical actuality good and bad, the problems which it presents as well as the spiritual opportunities it offers—then Islam as a heritage might conceivably prove able to serve flexibly in the Modern crises. Facing up to their history in this way might help Muslims—and possibly others as well—to overcome the cultural dislocations of our time and provide a basis for creativity in the midst of lettered mass culture, a basis consistent with, but able to transcend, the 'democratic virtues'. More generally, it might show that Islam was able to fill the modern need for moral vision, for a creative illumination of the human conscience in a technicalistic world.

One would like to suppose that Muslims placed in a situation like that of the Muslims of the Indian Union might take the lead in such an endeavour. Since partition, the Muslims there—though more numerous than the Muslims in either part of Pakistan—have formed a scattered minority of only ten or eleven per cent; a minority whose traditionally urban and privileged status, in many parts, is being inevitably undermined as egalitarian principles open up opportunities for advancement to all alike. The Muslims of the Indian Union find themselves, within the bounds of one national state, in a position which all Muslims occupy in reality (if less visibly) in the world at large—for the Muslims of the world likewise form a scattered minority in a world society they cannot control. Many Muslims in the Indian Union have been resentful and unwilling to accept what has happened. Thus in the former Haidarabad state in the Deccan, a tiny minority of Muslims had ruled, till independence, a vast majority of Hindus; these Muslims feel discriminated against by the Hindu-dominated elected governments now in power. Sometimes, indeed, an official does favour members of his own caste, and a minority such as the Muslim suffers; but Muslim complaints too often reflect, in effect, the Muslim mentality which—after Indian independence—was willing to accept 'equality', but only in the sense that the Muslim and Hindu communities should have equal representation in the government, whatever their relative numbers in the population. Such residual communalism must make difficult any creative response to the new opportunities for exploring the relevance of Islam in a multi-religious society. On the other hand, some Muslims in the Indian Union have been so accommodating that their Islam has become little more than a veneer of traditionality decorating vague civic sentiments. But there are some Muslims in the Indian Union who are seriously attempting to face the challenges on the highest possible level. They have a great opportunity.

It cannot be assumed that, in fact, the sort of valorization of the Islamic heritage that I anticipate here can be achieved. But if it can be achieved—if Islam can be shown to be capable of providing fruitful vision to illuminate the Modern conscience—then all mankind, and not only Muslims, have a stake in the outcome; even those who explicitly or even militantly reject any religious tradition. This is not merely because they must find a way of co-existing with Muslims, but because the ultimate spiritual commitments of any sector of mankind must be taken account of by every other sector in evaluating its own ultimate commitments. Even if the jihâd holy war were interpreted away, for instance, into sweetness and light, this might ultimately be worse for all concerned than a fuller facing of its implications. For if in fact it stands as close as it seems to the heart of the Qur'ânic challenge, to which so many generations of Muslims have responded at their best, then none who care for truth about the human condition will dare take it lightly, even if the Muslims themselves are remiss in their duty to explore its meaning.

But even if the Muslims of the near future succeed unimaginably well in working through the deepest implications of their heritage, Islam as an identifiable institutional tradition may not last indefinitely. It is a question, for Muslims as for all other heirs of a religious heritage, how far any creative vision for the future—whether or no the vision is based on renewal of commitment to transcendent truth—will depend on preserving and developing the heritage; and how far it will depend on escaping the inhibiting effects of the wishful thinking and even the grand (but partial) formulations of truth which the heritage seems to impose. It is possible that eventually Islam (like Christianity already in some circles) will prove to have its most creative thrust by way of the great 'secular' literature in which its challenge has been embedded, and will move among its heirs like a secret leaven long after they have forgotten they were once Muslims. Persian poetry will not die so soon as the disquisitions of fiqh or kalâm. And Persian poetry may eventually prove to be as potent everywhere as among those who use language touched by the Persianate spirit, and so by Islam.

A Selective Bibliography for Further Reading

NOTE: General works are listed in the Bibliography of volume 1.

On Iran since 1500:

(Much important work is in Russian.)

Bertold Spuler, ed., *Geschichte der Islamischen Länder*, Vol. III, *Neuzeit* (E. J. Brill, Leiden, 1959). Brief compendium of political developments.

Ann K. S. Lambton, *Landlord and Peasant in Persia* (see above). Chiefly on this period.

Tadhkirat al-Mulûk, translated by Vladimir Minorsky (E. J. W. Gibb Memorial, London, 1943). An edition and commentary of a revealing handbook of Ṣafavî administration; Minorsky has done several important monographic studies in the Ṣafavî and immediately pre-Ṣafavî periods.

Roger Savory has studied developments in the early Ṣafavî period; his journal articles may be traced through the *Index Islamicus*.

Peter Avery, *Modern Iran* (Ernest Benn, London, 1965). A political narrative.

Edward G. Browne, *The Persian Revolution of* 1905–9 (Cambridge University Press, 1910) is a careful attempt to persuade Britishers to see the events through Persian eyes and remains the chief study in a Western language; it is partly continued by Wm. Morgan Shuster, *The Strangling of Persia* (Century, New York, 1912), angrily describing his own experience as American treasurer-general of Persia in 1911.

Amin Banani, *The Modernization of Iran*, 1921–41 (Stanford University Press, 1961).

Leonard Binder, *Iran: Political Development in a Changing Society* (University of California Press, 1962). A penetrating study of political institutions especially since Reżà Shâh, building on a basic political-science analysis of certain alternatives open to low-investment countries in the Technical Age.

On India since 1500:

The Cambridge History of India [1922–53]. Monumental but old and done from a British imperial point of view. A shorter general survey is *The Oxford History of India*, 3rd ed., ed. T. G. Percival Spear (Oxford University Press, 1958); the modern part is rewritten from Vincent Smith's earlier version.

S. M. Ikram, *History of Muslim Civilization in India and Pakistan* (Star Book Depot, Lahore, 1962). An intelligent study from a responsible Muslim viewpoint; to be complemented by the stimulating brief study by K. M. Panikkar, *A Survey of Indian History* (Asia Publishing House, Bombay, 1947), stressing Indian unity.

Ram P. Tripathi, *The Rise and Fall of the Mughal Empire* (Central Book Depot, Allahabad, 1956). A good survey of Indo-Timuri history. It is more satisfactory in interpretation than S. M. Edwardes and H. L. O. Garrett, *Mughal Rule in India* (Oxford University Press, 1930), which is comprehensive (not merely political) but pedestrian and dependent on old misconceptions.

Irfan Habib, *The Agrarian System of Mughal India* 1556–1707 (Asia Publishing House, Bombay, 1963). A revisionist study. May be compared with William H. Moreland, *The Agrarian System of Moslem India* (W. Heffer, Cambridge, 1929).

Bâbur, *Bâbur-Nâmah* (*Memoirs*), translated by Annette S. Beveridge (Luzac, London, 1922) or by John Leyden and William Erskine, revised by Lucas King (Oxford University Press, 1921): The famous autobiography, monument of Turkî letters and of Muslim attitudes to India.

Abulfażl, *Akbar-Nâmah*: historical portions (Akbar and his ancestors) translated by H. Beveridge in three vols. (Asiatic Society of Bengal, Calcutta, 1907, 1912, 1939); and description of state and society (*Â'în-e Akbar*) translated by H. Blochmann and H. Jarrett (Asiatic Society of Bengal, Calcutta, 1873–94), Vol. I revised by D. C. Philott, Vols. II–III by J. Sarkâr (Asiatic Society of Bengal, Calcutta, 1939–49). (The older translations are wanting in technical precision.) Best introduction to the more secular aspects of Indo-Timurî life.

Murray T. Titus, *Islam in India and Pakistan* (Y.M.C.A. Publishing House, Calcutta, 1959; revised from *Indian Islam*, 1929). A useful compendium of historical, social, and religious facts; marred by misspellings and other errors.

Wilfred Cantwell Smith, *Modern Islâm in India, a Social Analysis*, 2nd ed. (Gollancz, London, 1946). At once a history of religious movements, and a study in sociology of religion from a Marxist viewpoint by a Christian; Smith has repudiated much of his viewpoint but the facts are sound and the work is not yet replaced.

Akshayakumar R. Desai, *The Social Background of Indian Nationalism* (Oxford University Press, 1948). Comprehensive and perceptive, covering both Hindu and Muslim history from a more general viewpoint.

On the Ottoman Empire since 1500, *and the earlier Turkish republic:*

Edward S. Creasy, *History of the Ottoman Turks* [1854], rev. ed. (Richard Bentley, London, 1878; repr. Khayat's, Beirut, 1961). The most usable one-volume chronicle of political events from about 1400 to about 1800; it is based on J. von Hammer-Purgstal, *Geschichte des Osmanischen Reiches* [1827–35], a monumental compendium from the Turkish chroniclers; the French translation is not dependable.

Leften S. Stavrianos, *The Balkans since 1453* (Rinehart, New York, 1958). Includes a clear and concise account of Ottoman history.

H. A. R. Gibb and Harold Bowen, *Islamic Society and the West: A Study of the Impact of Western Civilization on Moslem Culture in the Near East*, Vol. I, *Islamic Society in the Eighteenth Century*, Parts 1 and 2 (Oxford University Press, 1950 and 1957). The fundamental study of Ottoman institutions and society before the end of the eighteenth century; mainly supersedes Albert Howe Lybyer, *The Government of the Ottoman Empire in the Time of Suleiman the Magnificent* (Harvard University Press, 1913), which remains the best presentation of the institutions of the sixteenth century as such. With the knowledge of newer sources of information, some of the basic assumptions of the Gibb and Bowen work are being reassessed.

Fernand Braudel, *La Méditerranée et le monde méditerranéan à l'époque de Philippe II* [1949], 2nd ed. (A. Colin, Paris, 1966). Of central importance for understanding the European environment of the Ottomans in the sixteenth century.

E. J. W. Gibb, *A History of Ottoman Poetry*, 6 vols. (Luzac, London, 1900–9). A multi-volume survey which gives insight into the whole cultural life.

Alessio Bombaci, *Storia della Letteratura Turca* (Nuova Accademia, Milano, 1956); French translation by I. Mélikoff (C. Klincksieck, Paris, 1968). An excellent one-volume study.

Bernard Lewis, *The Emergence of Modern Turkey* (Oxford University Press, 1961). Excellent historical study of the intellectual and social dimensions of (west) Turkish life in the nineteenth and twentieth centuries.

Şerif Mardin, *The Genesis of Young Ottoman Thought: A Study in the Modernization of Turkish Political Ideas* (Princeton University Press, 1962). The best introduction to nineteenth-century intellectual currents.

Ziya Gök-Alp [Selected Writings], translated by Niyazi Berkes as *Turkish Nationalism and Western Civilization* (George Allen and Unwin, London, 1959). Outlines the thought of this important Turkish Modernist.

Mustafa Kemal (Atatürk), *Speech delivered by Ghazi Mustapha Kemal* (Koehler, Leipzig, 1929). A poor (and censored) official translation of Atatürk's long speech to his party, recounting his part in the national struggle from 1919.

On the northern Muslims since 1500:

(The basic materials on the Muslims of the Syr-Oxus and Volga basins and eastward are mostly in Russian and are not listed here.)

Emanuel Sarkisyanz, *Geschichte der orientalischen Völker Russlands bis* 1517 (Oldenbourg, Munich, 1961). Encyclopedic, chiefly political, survey.

V. V. Barthold and Zeki Velidi Togan have each done several valuable studies of pre-twentieth century history available in Turkish and Western languages. Owen Lattimore has studied the more easterly Muslims.

Mary Holdsworth, *Turkestan in the Nineteenth Century* (Central Asian Research Centre, London, 1959). A brief but useful introduction.

Serge A. Zenkovsky, *Pan-Turkism and Islam in Russia* (Harvard University Press, 1960). Comprehensive historical study of the social and intellectual development of Muslims of the empire from the time of Russian domination through the Revolution, with emphasis on the early twentieth century; distorted by nineteenth-century stereotypes, by ignorance of things Islamic, and by a tendency to Russian nationalist apologetic; to be corrected by

Alexandre Bennigsen and Chantal Lemercier-Quelquejay, *Les mouvements nationaux chez les musulmans de Russie: I: le 'Sultangaliévisme' au Tatarstan* (Mouton, the Hague, 1960). A scholarly study of the Volga Tatars in the Revolution, with considerable pre-1917 background, more scholarly and perceptive than Zenkovsky. Other studies by Bennigsen are also important, including

Alexandre Bennigsen and Chantal Lemercier-Quelquejay, *Islam in the Soviet Union* (F. A. Praeger, New York, 1967). A recent survey.

Vincent Montel, *Les musulmans soviétiques* (Editions du Seuil, Paris, 1957). A knowledgeable study sympathetic to the Muslims as such.

Baymirza Hayit, *Turkestan in XX. Jahrhundert* (Leske, Darmstadt, 1956). Detailed historical study of the Syr-Oxus basin and the Steppe, especially of Russification; puts whatever the Russians do in the worst possible light;—to be corrected for the earlier period by the thorough and fair-minded Alexander G. Park, *Bolshevism and Turkestan* 1917–27 (Columbia University Press, New York, 1957).

Edward Allworth, ed., *Central Asia: A Century of Russian Rule* (Columbia University Press, 1967). A collection of essays surveying changes under Russian influences.

On the Arab lands since 1500:

(For pre-twentieth century history, the references on the Ottoman empire are relevant.)

Peter M. Holt, *Egypt and the Fertile Crescent* 1516–1922*: A Political History* (Cornell University Press, 1966). A survey of some political events without deep insight.

Nevill Barbour, ed., *A Survey of North West Africa* (*The Maghrib*), 2nd ed.

(Oxford University Press, 1962). A general introduction to the contemporary period.

Royal Institute of International Affairs, *The Middle East: A Political and Economic Survey*, 3rd ed. (Oxford University Press, 1958). Still a useful general introduction.

Hisham B. Sharabi, *A Handbook on the Contemporary Middle East: Sectional Introductions with Annotated Bibliographies* (Georgetown University, Washington, 1956). A still useful bibliography on politics, society, and economics, chiefly on the eastern Arabs, also Turkey and Persia.

Edward Atiyah, *The Arabs: The Origins, Present Conditions, and Prospects of the Arab World* (Penguin Books, 1955). The central portion of this brief book presents nineteenth and especially twentieth-century Arab history succinctly from a moderate Arab viewpoint; the last chapter is badly out of date.

Charles Issawi, ed., *The Economic History of the Middle East* 1800–1914 (University of Chicago Press, 1966). By Middle East he means Anatolia and the eastern Arab lands. A collection of abridged sources indicating the influences of European expansion.

William R. Polk, *The Opening of South Lebanon* 1788–1840: *A Study of the Impact of the West on the Middle East* (Harvard University Press, 1963). Surveys the effects on a village.

Gabriel Baer, *Egyptian Guilds in Modern Times* (Israel Oriental Society, Jerusalem, 1964). Studies the effects on the guilds.

Jacques Berque, *Les Arabes d'hier à demain* (Editions du Seuil, Paris, 1960); translated by Jean Steward as *The Arabs: Their History and Future* (Faber and Faber, London, 1964). A long, beautiful essay interpreting sensitively and subtly the present moral position of the Arabs, between their heritage and their aspirations. (Some of the illustrations in the French edition have nothing to do with Arabs.)

Morroe Berger, *The Arab World Today* (Doubleday, New York, 1962). Fair-minded and substantial study of social patterns in Egypt and the Fertile Crescent, from family life to economics and politics.

Taha Hussein [Ḥusayn], *The Future of Culture in Egypt* [1938], translated by Sidney Glazer (Amer. Council of Learned Societies, Washington, 1954). Far-sighted analysis, by a premier littérateur and future minister of education of Egypt, of educational problems in 1938.

William R. Polk, David M. Stamler, and Edmund Asfour, *Backdrop to Tragedy: The Struggle for Palestine* (Beacon Press, Boston, 1957). A composite treatment of the conflict between Zionists and Arabs; its conclusions seem still valid.

On Muslim thought in modern times:

Hamilton A. R. Gibb, *Modern Trends in Islam* (University of Chicago Press, 1947). A brief and masterly analysis of the several lines along which modern Muslims have tried to solve intellectually their religious dilemmas, especially up to the war of 1939.

Wilfred C. Smith, *Islam in Modern History* (Princeton University Press, 1957). A concerned and penetrating commentary on what modern Muslims have been doing with Islam as religion, especially the Arabs, Turks, Pakistanis, and Indians in their several post-World War II political and social contexts.

C. A. O. van Nieuwenhuijze, *Aspects of Islam in Post-Colonial Indonesia: Five Essays* (van Hoeve, the Hague, 1958). Reports and commentary on Muslim religious situations and thoughts; ably supplements Smith for Indonesia.

Gustave E. von Grunebaum, *Modern Islam: The Search for Cultural Identity* (University of California Press, 1962). In the perspective of classical Arab Islam and Islamicate culture, studies modern Arabs' self-images in their attempts to cope with the various cultural, political, and social challenges presented by the Modern West.

Albert Hourani, *Arabic Thought in the Liberal Age*, 1798–1939 (Oxford University Press, 1962). A solid, perceptive, and detailed analysis of several generations of religious and social reformers, Muslim and Christian.

Leonard Binder, *The Ideological Revolution in the Middle East* (Wiley, New York, 1964). From a sophisticated political sociology viewpoint, analyses the transition from Islam as an ideological base to nationalism; and the post-war political thinking among the eastern Arabs.

Muhammad Iqbal, *The Reconstruction of Religious Thought in Islam* (Oxford University Press, 1934; repr. Muhammad Ashraf, Lahore, 1962). The best starting point for understanding Iqbal's thought.

Isma'il R. A. al-Faruqi, *Christian Ethics: A Historical and Systematic Analysis of Its Dominant Ideas* (McGill University Press, 1967). A provocative analysis by a Modernist Arab Muslim.

Seyyed Hossein Nasr, *Ideals and Realities of Islam* (George Allen and Unwin, London, 1966). An interpretation of Islam today by a Modernist Ṣûfî-oriented Persian Muslim.

Fazlur Rahman, *Islam* (Holt, Rinehart and Winston, New York, 1966). Though a historical survey of the development of Islam bearing comparison with Hamilton A. R. Gibb's *Mohammedanism*, the work is confessedly interpretive; the author is a Modernist Pakistani Muslim.

Glossary of Selected Terms and Names

Listings in the Glossary are technical terms frequently appearing in the text. Definitions and explanations given in the text of other terms, including geographical designations, may be located by consulting the Index.

'âdah (also *âdet*): 'customary' law used among Muslims in addition to or instead of the *Sharî'ah* (q.v.). Terms vary. *'Âdah* is often contradictory to, and *'urf* is usually regarded as supplementary to, the *Sharî'ah*.

akhbâr (sing. *khabar*): reports; often used like *ḥadîth* (q.v.).

'Alid: a descendant of 'Alî, cousin and son-in-law of the Prophet; the Shî'îs believed certain 'Alids should be *imâms* (q.v.). 'Alî's first wife was Fâṭimah, the Prophet's daughter, 'Alî's descendants by her (the only descendants of the Prophet) were in particular called Fâṭimids. Descendants of her son Ḥasan are often called *sharîfs*: those of her son Ḥusayn are often called *sayyids*.

'âlim (p. *'ulamâ'*): a learnèd man, in particular one learnèd in Islamic legal and religious studies.

Allâh: an Arabic (both Muslim and Christian) name for the One God.

amîr (also *emir*): a general or other military commander; after classical 'Abbâsî times, many independent rulers held this title; sometimes assigned to members of the ruler's family. *Amîr al-mu'minîn*, commander of the faithful, was the proper title of the caliph; *amîr al-umarâ'* meant supreme commander, generalissimo: used especially of the military ruler in the decline of the High Caliphate.

'aql: 'reason', 'reasoning'; in Islamic law systematic reasoning not limited to *qiyâs*.

'askerî: in the Ottoman empire a member of the military ruling class, including wives and children of that class.

awqâf: see *waqf*.

a'yân (sing. *'ayn*): notable persons, in the Middle and Late Periods, town notables with prestige and influence; in the later Ottoman times, they were holders of a recognized political power.

bâb: gate, especially in a city wall; also, a short treatise, a chapter; also, the representative of the Twelver Shî'îs' Hidden Imâm.

bâshâ: see *pâshâ*.

bâṭin: the inner, hidden, or esoteric meaning of a text; hence Bâṭinîs, Bâṭiniyyah, the groups associated with such ideas. Most of these groups were Shî'îs, particularly Ismâ'îlîs.

beg (bey): a high Turkish military title which became more generalized and in its modern form *bey* is used as an equivalent for 'mister'.

capitulations: provisions of legal grants by Muslim powers giving limited privileges to resident aliens.

Dâr al-Islâm: lands under Muslim rule; later, any lands in which Muslim institutions are maintained, whether or not under Muslim rule. It is converse of *Dâr al-Ḥarb* the 'lands of war'.

derebey: 'lord of the valley'; used especially to refer to local chieftains in eighteenth-century Anatolia practically independent of the Ottoman sultan.

dervish: *see* Ṣûfî.

dhikr (also *ẕikr*): Ṣûfî (q.v.) practices designed to foster the remembering of God; usually phrases to repeat, often more elaborate devotional services.

dhimmî (also *ẕimmî*): a 'protected subject', follower of a religion tolerated by Islam, within Muslim-ruled territory. The protection is called *dhimmah.*

dîwân (also *dîvân*): a public financial register; or a government bureau, or council; or its chief officer; also, the collected works of a poet.

emir: see *amîr.*

fakir: *see* Ṣûfî.

fallâḥ (pl. *fallâḥîn*): Arabic word for peasant.

Falsafah: philosophy, including natural and moral science, as expounded, on the basis of the Greek tradition, in the Islamicate society. A *Faylasûf* (pl. *Falâsifah*) is an exponent of *Falsafah.*

faqîh: see *fiqh.*

faqîr: *see* Ṣûfî.

fatwà: the decision of a *muftî* (q.v.).

fez: a red felt cap which became symbolic of nineteenth-century Ottoman modernism in contrast to the turban of the *'ulamâ'*, called in Arabic *ṭarbûsh.*

fiqh: jurisprudence; the discipline of elucidating the *Sharî'ah* (q.v.); also the resultant body of rules. A *faqîh* (pl. *fuqahâ'*) is an exponent of *fiqh.*

ghâzî: a warrior for the faith carrying out *jihâd* (q.v.); sometimes applied to organized bands of frontier raiders.

ḥabûs: see *waqf.*

ḥadîth (also *ḥadîs*; pl. *aḥâdîth*): a report of a saying or action of the Prophet, or such reports collectively. Sometimes this is translated 'tradition', as having been transmitted from reporter to reporter; it has nothing to do with traditions in the ordinary sense of anonymously inherited group lore.

ḥajj: the annual pilgrimage to Mecca in the mouth of Dhû-l-Ḥijjah, the last month of the Muslim calendar; required of every Muslim once in his life if possible.

Ḥanafî: referring to the Sunnî legal *madhhab* (q.v.) ascribed to Abû-Ḥanîfah (699–767 CE).

Ḥanbalî: referring to the Sunnî legal *madhhab* (q.v.) ascribed to Aḥmad ibn-Ḥanbal (780–855 CE).

ijtihâd: individual inquiry to establish the ruling of the *Sharî'ah* (q.v.) upon a given point, by a *mujtahid*, a person qualified for the inquiry. The Jamâ'î-Sunnîs long considered *ijtihâd* permissible only on points not already decided by recognized authorities; on points already so decided they required *taqlîd*, adherence to the usual view of one's *madhhab* (q.v.). The Shî'îs have mostly permitted full *ijtihâd* to their great scholars.

'ilm: learnèd lore; particularly, religious knowledge, of *ḥadîth* (q.v.) reports, of *fiqh* (q.v.), etc. In modern Arabic the word is used to render 'science'. Among many Shî'îs it was supposed the *imâm* (q.v.) had a special secret knowledge, *'ilm*.

imâm: leader of the *ṣalât* worship; or the leader of the Muslim community. Among Shî'îs 'Alî and his descendants as proper leaders of the Islamic community, even when rejected by it, are held to have a spiritual function as successors to Muḥammad. Among Jamâ'î-Sunnîs, any great *'âlim* (q.v.), especially the founder of a legal *madhhab* (q.v.), was called an *imâm*.

iqṭâ': an assignment or grant of land or of its revenues by a government to an individual; sometimes granted as payment for military service. Sometimes misleadingly translated 'fief'.

Jamâ'î-Sunnîs: *see* Sunnîs.

jâmi': *see* mosque.

Janissary (*yeñi-cheri*): member of an Ottoman infantry corps formed at one time from captured or conscripted young Christians converted to Islam.

jihâd: war in accordance with the *Sharî'ah* (q.v.) against unbelievers; there are different opinions as to the circumstances under which such war becomes necessary. Also applied to a person's own struggle against his baser impulses.

kalâm: discussion, on the basis of Muslim assumptions, of questions of theology and cosmology; sometimes called 'scholastic theology'.

ḳâẓî: see *qâḍî*.

khân: a Turkish title, originally the ruler of a state; also, a hostel for travelling merchants (caravansary).

khâniqâh (also *khângâh*): a building for Ṣûfî (q.v.) activities, where *dhikr* (q.v.) was observed and where one or more *shaykhs* (q.v.) lived, entertained travelling Ṣûfîs, and taught their disciples. This form is originally Persian; synonyms are *tekke* (from *takyah*), largely Turkish in use; *zâwiyah* (Arabic); and *ribâṭ* (Arabic), also used for a frontier fortress.

madhhab (pl. *madhâhib*): a system of *fiqh* (q.v.), or generally the system followed by any given religious group; particularly, four *madhâhib* were ultimately accepted as legitimate by the Jamâ'î-Sunnîs while Shî'îs and Khârijîs had other *madhâhib*. Sometimes rendered 'sect', 'school', or 'rite'.

madrasah: a school for *'ulamâ'*, especially for *fiqh* (q.v.), generally built in the form of a specially endowed mosque (q.v.), often with dormitories.

majlis (also *majles*): an assembly, now used for 'parliament'.

Mâlikî: referring to the Sunnî legal *madhhab* (q.v.) ascribed to Mâlik b. Anas (715–95 CE).

masjid: *see mosque.*

mas̄navî (Arabic, *mathnawî*): a long poem in Persian and related literatures, on almost any subject, with rhyme *aa bb cc dd ee* etc.; sometimes called 'epic'.

millet: in Ottoman empire, one of the recognized autonomous religious communities.

mosque (arabic, *masjid*): any place of worship for Muslims where the *ṣalât* worship is performed in a group; a major one, where official Friday services are held, is called *jâmi'*.

muftî: an expert in the *Sharî'ah* (q.v.) who gives public decisions in cases of law and conscience.

mujtahid: see *ijtihâd*.

murîd: disciple of a Ṣûfî *pîr* (qq.v.).

pâdshâh: a Persian title, roughly, 'emperor'.

pâshâ (Arabic, *bâshâ*): a Turkish title, often amounts to 'governor'.

pîr: a Ṣûfî (q.v.) master, able to lead disciples on the mystical way.

qâḍî (also *ḳâẓî*): a judge administering *Sharî'ah* (q.v.) law.

qânûn: laws apart from the *Sharî'ah* (q.v.), sometimes as promulgated by the government.

sayyid: *see* 'Alid.

sepoy: see *sipâhî*.

Shâfi'î: referring to the Sunnî legal *madhhab* (q.v.) ascribed to al-Shâfi'î (767–820 CE).

shâh: an Iranian royal title; also used for subordinate personages; when used before the name, it often implies a Ṣûfî (q.v.) saint. *Shâhanshâh* means 'king of kings'.

shaikh: see *shaykh*.

Sharî'ah (or *Shar'*): the whole body of rules guiding the life of a Muslim, in law, ethics, and etiquette; sometimes called *Sacred Law* (or *Canon Law*). The provisions of the *Sharî'ah* are worked out through the discipline of *fiqh* (q.v.) on the basis of *uṣûl al-fiqh* (basic sources of legal authority), which Sunnîs commonly list as Qur'ân, *ḥadîth* (q.v.), *ijmâ'* (consensus of the community), and *qiyâs* (legal analogical reasoning). Shî'îs commonly substitute *'aql* (q.v.) for *qiyâs* and interpret *ijmâ'* as consensus of the *imâms* (q.v.).

sharîf: *see* 'Alid.

shaykh: literally 'old man'; the chief of a tribe (and, by extension, head of certain petty states); any religious leader; in particular, an independent Ṣûfî (q.v.), in a position to lead aspirants on the Ṣûfî way; in this sense called, in Persian, *pîr* (q.v.); his disciple is a *murîd* (q.v.).

Shî'ah ('party [of 'Alî']): general name for that part of the Muslims that held to the rights of 'Alî and his descendants to leadership in the community whether recognized by the majority or not; or any particular sect holding this position. Shî'î is the adjective, or refers as a noun to an adherent of the Shî'ah. Shî'ism (*tashayyu'*) denotes the attitude or doctrines of the Shî'ah. The most well known Shî'î groups are the Zaydîs, the Ismâ'îlîs or the Seveners, and the Twelvers.

sipâhî: a soldier; used of various troops, especially cavalry in the Ottoman empire; in India often spelled *sepoy*.

Ṣûfî: an exponent of Ṣûfism (*taṣawwuf*), the commonest term for that aspect of Islam which is based on the mystical way. The Arabic *faqîr* (fakir) and the Perskan *darvîsh* (dervish), both meaning 'poor', are applied to Ṣûfîs in reference to their poor or wandering life.

sulṭân: the reigning sources of authority; in the Earlier Middle Period, applied to the actual, often military holder of power in contrast to the caliph; later became the normal Muslim term for sovereign.

sunnah: received custom, particularly that associated with Muḥammad; it is embodied in *ḥadîth* (q.v.).

Sunnîs: properly *Ahl al-sunnah wa-l-jamâ'ah* ('people of the custom and the community'), in this work often Jamâ'î-Sunnîs: that majority of Muslims which accept the authority of the whole first generation of Muslims and the validity of the historical community, in contrast to the Khârijîs and the Shî'îs; Sunnî as adjective refers to the doctrinal position, as noun it refers to an adherent of the position. Sunnism is sometimes referred to as 'Orthodoxy'. The term 'Sunnî' is often restricted to particular positions within the Jamâ'î-Sunnî camp; e.g., often it excluded Mu'tazilîs, Karrâmîs, and other groups which did not survive to command recognition. In older Muslim works it sometimes included only the particular faction of the writer.

Tanẓîmât: reforms, in particular those of the nineteenth-century Ottoman government.

taqlîd: see *ijtihâd*.

ṭarbûsh: *see* fez.

ṭarîqah: the mystical way; specifically, any one of the Ṣûfî (q.v.) 'brotherhoods' or 'orders'; groupings of Ṣûfîs with a common *silsilah* (sequence of *shaykhs*) and a common *dhikr* (q.v.).

tekke: see *khâniqâh*.

'ulamâ': see *'âlim*.

Ummah: any people as followers of a particular prophet, in particular Muslims as forming a community following Muḥammad.

'urf: see *'âdah*.

uṣûl al-fiqh: see *Sharî'ah*.

vizier: Anglicized form of *wazîr* (q.v.).

waqf (pl. *awqâf*): a pious endowment (or 'foundation') of certain incomes, commonly rents or land revenues, for the upkeep of a mosque, a hospital, etc.; in the Maghrib called *ḥabûs*. Sometimes the main purpose of such an endowment was to provide entailed and unconfiscatable income for one's descendants.

wazîr (Anglicized, *vizier*): an officer to whom a ruler delegated (as 'minister') the administration of his realm; often there were several who divided the job among them.

zâwiyah: see *khâniqâh*.

ẕikr: see *dhikr*.

ẕimmî: see *dhimmî*.

Index

NOTE: Names and terms beginning with the Arabic definite article (al-) are indexed under the letter following the article.